# Indigenous Visions

**The Henry Roe Cloud Series on American Indians and Modernity**

*Series Editors*

Ned Blackhawk, Professor of History and American Studies, Yale University

Kate W. Shanley, Native American Studies, University of Montana

Named in honor of the pioneering Winnebago educational reformer and first known American Indian graduate of Yale College, Henry Roe Cloud (Class of 1910), this series showcases emergent and leading scholarship in the field of American Indian Studies. The series draws upon multiple disciplinary perspectives and organizes them around the place of Native Americans within the development of American and European modernity, emphasizing the shared, relational ties between Indigenous and Euro-American societies. It seeks to broaden current historic, literary, and cultural approaches to American Studies by foregrounding the fraught but generative sites of inquiry provided by the study of Indigenous communities.

# Indigenous Visions

## Rediscovering the World of Franz Boas

Edited by Ned Blackhawk
and Isaiah Lorado Wilner

155.82 Indigenous
Indigenous visions
$35.00 30519009940357

Yale UNIVERSITY PRESS | NEW HAVEN AND LONDON

PROPERTY OF
HIGH POINT PUBLIC LIBRARY
HIGH POINT, NORTH CAROLINA

Published with assistance from the income of the Frederick John Kingsbury Memorial Fund.

Parts of Chapter 11 originally appeared in Benjamin Balthaser, "'Travels of an American Indian into the Hinterlands of Soviet Russia': Rethinking Indigenous Modernity and the Popular Front in the Work of Archie Phinney and D'Arcy McNickle," *American Quarterly* 66, no. 2 (2014): 385–416, and Benjamin Balthaser, *Anti-Imperialist Modernism: Race and Transnational Radical Culture from the Great Depression to the Cold War* (Ann Arbor: University of Michigan Press, 2016).

Copyright © 2018 by Yale University.
All rights reserved.
This book may not be reproduced, in whole or in part, including illustrations, in any form (beyond that copying permitted by Sections 107 and 108 of the U.S. Copyright Law and except by reviewers for the public press), without written permission from the publishers.

Yale University Press books may be purchased in quantity for educational, business, or promotional use. For information, please e-mail sales.press@yale.edu (U.S. office) or sales@yaleup.co.uk (U.K. office).

Set in Adobe Garamond type by IDS Infotech, Ltd.
Printed in the United States of America.

Library of Congress Control Number: 2017944783
ISBN 978-0-300-19651-1 (paperback : alk. paper)

A catalogue record for this book is available from the British Library.

This paper meets the requirements of ANSI/NISO Z39.48-1992 (Permanence of Paper).

10 9 8 7 6 5 4 3 2 1

# Contents

# Acknowledgments

This book began with an interdisciplinary conference held at Yale on September 15–17, 2011, in commemoration of the centennial of Franz Boas's treatise on the dynamism and diversity of modern belonging, *The Mind of Primitive Man.* We wish to thank our sponsors at the Howard R. Lamar Center for the Study of Frontiers and Borders, John Mack Faragher, Jay Gitlin, and Edith Rotkopf, and our cosponsors at the Gilder Lehrman Center for the Study of Slavery, Resistance, and Abolition, David Blight, Dana Schaffer, and Thomas Thurston. Two members of Yale's faculty, Glenda Gilmore and William W. Kelly, played instrumental roles in planning the meeting.

Stephen Pitti and Alicia Schmidt Camacho hosted the memorable dinner at Ezra Stiles College where much of the conversation that inspired this book began. We also benefited from the involvement of the Beinecke Rare Book and Manuscript Library, particularly that of the curator of Western Americana, George Miles, and the special interest taken by Harvey Goldblatt of Pierson College and Mary Miller, the dean of Yale College at the time.

Several of Yale's interdisciplinary centers and programs provided much-needed support. We thank the program in Ethnicity, Race, and Migration; the MacMillan Center for International and Area Studies; the Committee on

Canadian Studies; the European Studies Council; the Council on Latin American and Iberian Studies; and the Center for Comparative Research. We thank the departments of History, English, Anthropology, and African American Studies for their financial and intellectual involvement. The Edward J. and Dorothy Clarke Kempf Memorial Fund and the Stanley T. Woodward Lectureship made it possible for us to invite international speakers, and for these investments we would like to thank the Office of the Provost and the Office of the Secretary.

A few scholars have played critical roles in the conversation that created this book. We thank Elizabeth Alexander, Taiaiake Alfred, Elijah Anderson, Seyla Benhabib, Jonathan Holloway, Matthew Jacobson, J. Kēhaulani Kauanui, Kerwin Lee Klein, Joshua L. Reid, and Michael Warner for discussions of race, indigeneity, migration, and modernity that contributed directly to the development of the project. Our thinking about the global circulation of knowledge benefited from exchanges with Sebastian Conrad, Joanna Radin, and James C. Scott. Finally, our editors at Yale University Press, Christopher Rogers, Adina Popescu Berk, and Erica Hanson, helped bring the book to fruition.

# Introduction

Few Western thinkers have engaged with Indigenous people more closely or reaped greater rewards from that engagement than Franz Boas, the founder of modern anthropology. In the early twentieth century, as the world's self-declared advanced nations competed to colonize the globe and exploit its natural resources, Boas drew upon what he had learned among Native peoples to present an alternative approach to modernity. Questioning the assumption that the West could claim the prerogative to rule "the rest" by right of natural endowment, Boas critiqued the idea of race, the master concept of colonialism. He shaped the modern notion of culture as an interactive process to which each of the world's peoples has contributed its portion of knowledge. And he framed the idea of grammar as a universal characteristic of human cognition, the borderless ability to structure linguistic meaning. These interrelated concepts interrogated the standards by which the world measured progress, ultimately projecting visions of a shared global community.[1]

Today Boas is beginning to undergo a reevaluation.[2] This is partly because of his unmistakable importance to contemporary discussions of race, inequality, empire, and migration—conversations emergent from the peoples he worked with and the places he worked in, which coalesce around the vulnerability of the biosphere and the problem of human survival. Unlike Karl Marx, Max Weber, or Sigmund Freud, who similarly drew upon the intellectual heritage of the European Enlightenment to construct the social sciences, Boas opened modern inquiry to a multitude of viewpoints, diversifying the subject of scientific observation and who would conduct it.[3] As he institutionalized his methods across a nascent discipline, helping to establish America's first university departments of anthropology, Boas trained a diverse group of women and men—including Margaret Mead, Ruth Benedict, Zora Neale Hurston, Melville Herskovits, Ella Deloria, and Edward Sapir—many of whom, like Boas, faced ethnic, religious, or sexual discrimination. These scholars contributed to a global reconfiguration of the politics of culture. The Boasian tradition, which began among Indigenous peoples from Baffin Island to imperial Siberia, increasingly produced insights about the diversity of human experience while steadily building status for its practitioners. Indeed, inheritors of one or another strand of this tradition came to be regarded as the founding figures of national schools of their own, including Gilberto Freyre in Brazil, Manuel Gamio in Mexico, Marius Barbeau in Canada, and Claude Lévi-Strauss in France, who always cherished his close contact with "the last of those intellectual giants produced by the nineteenth century, the likes of whom will probably never be seen again."[4]

Yet, in comparison to Boas's wide reception, little attention has been paid to the vast network of Indigenous collaborators upon whom he relied. This anthology considers their influence, revealing the underrecognized centrality of Native peoples and other peoples treated as subjects of scientific study in the making of the Boasian tradition. Through their interactive relationships established with Boas and other anthropologists, Indigenous peoples transmitted insights that have extended beyond national communities, germinating developments from history to linguistics, literary studies, philosophy, and social theory. To take just one of many possible examples, after the Second World War Kwakwa̱ka̱'wakw concepts of reciprocity, first expressed to Boas decades earlier in British Columbia, contributed to a new rhetoric of decolonization and anticapitalist critique. Ranging from the work of Marcel Mauss to that of Guy Debord, ideas about gift economies and communal redistribution became centrally lodged in Continental philosophical debates about the meanings of value and language as well as expression. These ideas became so ubiquitous that Parisian activists in the events of 1968 looked to a journal named *Potlatch,* a nod to Northwest Coast Native cultural and ceremonial practices. The idea of the gift was only one of many ways in which Indigenous peoples helped to redirect the currents of Western metaphysics, drawing upon their own cultural values and their experiences under colonial rule.[5]

A little more than a century has passed since 1911, when Franz Boas introduced his modernist ideas in a burst of landmark publications: *The Mind of Primitive Man,* "Changes in Bodily Form of Descendants of Immigrants," and the *Handbook of American Indian Languages.* Each of these works disproved the dominant ideology of his time through careful reconsideration of then-operative assumptions about human difference and the supposed inferiority of Indigenous, immigrant, and racialized peoples.[6] The centerpiece of this trifecta was *The Mind of Primitive Man,* a book of essays drawn in large part from Boas's study of Native societies. The book takes the form of a thought experiment that attempts to disassemble the confining features of Western thought and read the diversity beyond it. While the very colonizing outlook that the book attempts to critique stands today in its title, its contents helped to inaugurate a century of cultural inquiry. More than any of Boas's works, this title encapsulates the opportunities as well as the limitations inherent in the transcultural study of diversity, identity, and belonging.

To commemorate the centennial of Boas's watershed publication, a group of scholars representing many of the disciplines and several of the communities impacted by Boasian research met in New Haven to discuss this complex legacy.[7] The discussion was spirited and at times difficult. Eventually a common understanding emerged, one that views Boas as a formulator, in both theory and practice, of what might be termed global cultural studies. Even when anthropologists think they are studying the local, they are engaged in a global practice. Moreover, the Indigenous peoples who form the subject of classic anthropology turn out, on second look, to be agents of their own forms of globalization.[8] Boas cast a sharp light on globalization, considering it not as a mere economic or political system but as a total social and cultural phenomenon that interconnects plants and animals as well as humans. As Europe's empires networked the earth and humankind realized the industrial power to radically alter it, Boas studied the intermixture of cultures and peoples in an age of media connectivity preceding the rupture of the First World War. He also put in place, in the form of academic anthropology, a new network that disseminated ideas across borders.

Owing to his role as a global connector, Boas can provide an unusually acute lens for a historical investigation of the social networks that shaped him. These networks are often studied within their respective silos—as European history, anthropology, Native American studies, African American studies, and so on. We wanted to get to the interactions *between* these subjects. After the conference, we assembled a group of scholars to deepen the investigation. Drawing upon a range of methodologies from history, anthropology, ethnic studies, philosophy, political theory, and linguistics, we made use of Boas's knowledge network to examine the diversity of discourses in which he participated. This approach decenters Boas and recenters those, such as the Kwakwaka̱ʼwakw, who similarly helped to build global cultural studies but whose contributions have remained erased and elided. The result is a collective experiment in the global history of knowledge that attempts to trace the circulation of some key modern concepts. This anthology reveals the vast intellectual and cultural influence of Indigenous and colonized communities upon the modern world.

Our focus is the *world* of Boas: the assemblage of individuals and communities who influenced the production and dissemination of modern concepts of diversity, identity, and belonging. We call this network of communities, cutting across binaries of race and boundaries of empire, the Boasian Circle. Previous definitions of this circle emphasize Boas's students; we spotlight Indigenous intellectuals, African American and pan-African scholars, German and Jewish scientists, and Latino writers and thinkers, all of whom contributed to the making of global cultural studies.[9] Represented by these individuals, and foremost in Boasian research, are three kinds of communities—Natives, descendants of slaves, and immigrants—whose experiences of state violence, dislocation, and diaspora contributed to the politics of modernity across the Western hemisphere and beyond. The Boasian Circle recorded and disseminated the knowledge of these largely non-Anglophone communities, yet no historical account has grappled with their collective impact. It is time to peel away the racial and colonial assumptions that have obscured our view of these seminal thinkers, disclosing a network of knowledge that globalized the world of thought.

The diversity of communities linked by Boasian anthropology testifies to the non-Western origins of some significant modern knowledge. As the fourteen essays herein suggest, the classically defined attributes of Boasian anthropology—from its rejection of the evolutionism and racial typologies inherited from the nineteenth century to its methodological imperatives for thick description—were constituted across sets of ethnographic landscapes not only by professional ethnographers but also by Indigenous intellectuals. Relevant actors who must be studied if we are to understand the making of modernity include Native speakers and translators (often called "informants"), hosts, village guides, and political leaders of nonstate communities facing colonization. The interrelations of these actors with Western science yielded a redefinition of the concept of culture, remaking it from a static social status—imposed by the colonizer to justify the permanent subordination of the colonized—into a dynamic social process in which anyone may participate, connecting the expertise of all the world's peoples.

Visions of cultural transformation and coexistence articulated by Indigenous thinkers, while never universally accepted—and even partially rejected by midcentury anthropologists such as Julian Steward—wielded an increasing influence over the course of the twentieth century.[10] In politics, academia, and the arts, nonhierarchical understandings of ethnicity and belonging became identifiable attributes of cultural inquiry and expression, producing a methodological spirit of relativism and a humanist spirit of universalism that paralleled and animated many of the century's movements for justice and equality. The impact of such ideas has only increased in recent decades as the challenges of resource depletion, rising inequality, state violence, and transnational migration have pointed to the multispecies contexts of culture.[11] Though it came to be assimilated by the thermonuclear nation-state, "culture" remains, in the hands of those who create it, a tool for accomplishing a nonviolent form of fusion: the attempt by humans to connect with one another within and across a world injured by the ongoing injustices of the past.

As dynamic concepts of culture disseminated across the Boasian Circle, they propagated the insights of decolonizing philosophies that long have catalyzed movements for freedom, sovereignty, and self-determination within colonial and imperial spheres. Several essays in this volume indeed suggest that Indigenous, pan-African, Latino, mestizo, and other multiracial communities, which all produced autochthonous accounts of modernity, enabled Boas and other ethnographers to understand the meanings of what came to be called diversity. By authorizing, researching, and even writing the ethnographies published within the Boasian Circle, these unacknowledged authors contributed to the transformation of Western thought, destabilizing and at times transcending the Self / Other binary.[12] Their views established a conceptual vernacular for envisioning shared forms of belonging, based not on fixed hierarchies of race or culture but on fluid understandings of reciprocity and entanglement. Such mutually constituted visions we term Indigenous visions because they draw their energy from the nonstate communities who served as anthropology's core research subjects—and who often flipped the script. Native people in particular have continually attempted to transmit through the communications medium of anthropology their visions of what modernity can be: of what it means to belong, to possess roots, to survive in a ruptured world.[13]

While projections of indigeneity make convenient myths for nation-states that seek to appropriate the sovereignty of those they claim to rule, there is a flip side to that colonizing coin.[14] *Indigenous Visions* reconsiders the directional flows of influence, beginning with an origin moment of the Boasian Circle: the day in 1886 when the budding German ethnologist met a group of Nuxalk performers from Bella Coola, a spectacular river valley in the shadow of the Coast Mountains on the western edge of British Columbia. The Bella Coola dances Boas witnessed in Berlin introduced him to the arresting performance of culture on the Northwest Coast.[15] Wearing giant masks of supernatural beings, the Nuxalk tantalized Boas with the mystery of another way of life. He yearned to know the meanings behind the masks, and so he traveled to Canada to go, as he later put it, "behind the veil" that obscured understanding of America's Native peoples.[16] By choosing the image of a veil to describe his work—the basis of the notion of double consciousness coined by his interlocutor W. E. B. Du Bois in *The Souls of Black Folk*—Boas positioned himself as an intellectual discoverer of Indigenous people.[17] But who else was seeing in this moment, and what were their visions?

If, from a Western standpoint, the masks blocked sight, from an Indigenous standpoint they were second faces that advanced the visions of those who wore them. On the Northwest Coast, masks are thought of not as camouflage but as hosts that convey to the guests who step inside them the power to cross into and participate in new realms.[18] In Berlin the Nuxalk made use of their masks—metonyms for culture—to transmit their concepts to a potentially willing recipient of their visions.[19] The Nuxalk demonstrated a process to Boas that he would continue for a half century to come, leading to the realization that knowledge production is not a one-way street. Ideas, like dances, can travel in multiple directions, and the imperial appropriation of a culture does not prevent its owners from exercising their own influence.

We have organized this book to trace the globalization of modern knowledge in multiple directions, showing how ideas from many continents propagated themselves across the Boasian network. We begin by embedding the key concepts within their originating locations. We then analyze the intermixture and recombination of these ideas within the mind of Franz Boas, pinpointing moments of epistemic shift as well as ironies and shortcomings within the Boasian canon. Next we turn to the dissemination of the knowledge across the racial and imperial landscapes of the twentieth century through the practice of anthropology and the art of ethnography. Last, we survey the circulation, transmission, and transmogrification of the modern concept of culture.

Part I reveals the Boasian Circle as a global crossroads. We examine a group of Indigenous, Africana, and European concepts of enlightenment—transformation, freedom, expression, and evolution—that all proved crucial to Boas's intellectual development. These ideas are examined within their formative contexts: the transformation narratives of the Northwest Coast; the philosophy of freedom invented by the African diaspora; the philosophy of language initiated by Johann Gottfried von Herder and Wilhelm von Humboldt; and the psychological tradition of global music studies that arose within the German Empire. To understand modernity, these four essays assert, we must take into account many sources of thought, ranging from the Kwakwa̱ka̱'wakw intellectual George Hunt, whose family history is explored by Isaiah Lorado Wilner; to the Haitian anthropologist Anténor Firmin, whose struggle against dehumanization is reconstructed in Lewis R. Gordon's exegesis of Africana philosophy; to Indigenous activists like Carlos Montezuma, a cofounder of the Society of American Indians, whose rhetoric of worldmaking leads Ryan Carr on a transatlantic venture into the affect of modernity; and finally to the psychologist Carl Stumpf, whose investigations into the "beginnings" of music, ranging from birdcalls to harmonies to Bella Coola rhythms, open for Harry Liebersohn a window into Boas's mental evolution.

The influence exercised upon Stumpf by Nuskilusta, one of the performers from Bella Coola, highlights another unrecognized yet recoverable moment of Indigenous agency and authority in the creation of modern knowledge. Though treated as an object (or Other), Nuskilusta imposed his subjectivity (or Self) upon Stumpf, correcting his views of Indigenous culture and expression. Subsequently, Stumpf's student Edmund Husserl would deploy such psychological encounters to question the Self / Other binary, creating the idea that consciousness is intersubjective.[20] Similarly, Gordon defines the African diaspora's great idea as the reversal of its rejection, which created the idea of freedom-with rather than freedom-from—freedom as *belonging*.[21] Boas, who had faced anti-Semitism in Germany, understood exclusion well enough to grasp the picture. As Carr illuminates, whereas the racial theorist Daniel Garrison Brinton defined modernity as "man's" separation from the world (Self / Other), for Boas modernity imposed a duty to immerse oneself in the world, exchanging ideas with its peoples (Self–Self). But Boas approached this relation only because of the influence of Hunt, who made use of masks as teaching tools to convert Boas from the study of signs, which may be divorced from their referents, to the study of messages, which retain the meanings of their speakers, thus producing an anthropology of selves.

Part 2 tracks this mode of thinking from its origins to penetrate the mind of Boas, the central node of the network. Boas's ideas arose from the German Enlightenment and also from Indigenous visions of enlightenment, such as the transformation philosophy of the Northwest Coast. These concepts merged in Boas's linguistic approach to ideology, a conceptual blade that he used to cut away the language of conquest, exposing the idea of "the primitive" as a modernist mythology that Western empires used to justify their rule. Here, the essence of Boasian thought comes into focus in a rediscovery of *The Mind of Primitive Man* by James Tully, who traces the development of Boas's ethos amid the destruction of the twentieth century. Reading Boas's treatise alongside his writings on war and democracy, Tully identifies the book as the start of a lifelong attempt, only partially achieved, to move beyond the violence of imperialism and generate a nonviolent relationship with the world and its peoples—precisely the purpose of the Raven stories that Northwest Coast elders use to transmit lessons to their children. Tully likens the Boasian thought process to a Raven dance: "Beginning to take the slow, difficult, courageous, and unpredictable steps . . . against the dominant currents of his and our time."[22]

Boas's transcultural discourse of enlightenment produced significant, albeit gradual, transformations of racial ideology, but it also perpetuated aspects of colonial modernity. Analyzing Boas's critically new insights under the lens of philology, Michael Silverstein redefines Boasian linguistics as a globalizing mode of mutual enlightenment through the exchange of grammatical concepts between selves across borders of sound and sense—a process he calls "comparative calibrationism," the asymptotic pursuit of the always-inaccessible yet ever-closer universal truth. This vision of exchange, as Audra Simpson demonstrates through a comparison of Boas and Lewis Henry Morgan, may have helped the United States rethink racial prejudice, but it produced an erasure of the Indigenous sovereignty at its basis. For all the labor they performed and the insights they provided, Native peoples possess no political future in Boas's picture of modern society. The civilized / primitive binary lives on in Boasian anthropology, replicating the Subject / Object syntax of settler colonialism.

The second half of the book moves from language to the global circulation of Boas's other two preoccupations: race and culture. Part 3 explores the differential experience of race by members of the Boasian Circle, beginning with Boas's failed attempts at the World's Columbian Exposition of 1893 to categorize Indigenous skin color—race in a nutshell. To overcome the silences in Boas's writings about race, Martha Hodes turns to a yet more silent sort of evidence, anthropometric field data, discovering in their combination the signs of Boas's personal struggle to overcome the illogic of anthropometric measurement. Such ironies deepen in Kiara M. Vigil's investigation of the tragic killing of William Jones, the first American Indian to earn a doctorate in anthropology, who died after finding few professional opportunities in America among the Ilongot of Luzon, where the Field Museum had sent him to collect artifacts shortly after America's seizure of the Philippines. Vigil's research offers a mordant commentary on the contradictions of imperialist rule. Similarly, in a tense exploration at the intersections of race, class, gender, sexuality, and empire, Eve Dunbar examines Zora Neale Hurston's creative deployment of Haitian zombie discourse to resist the white gaze of Ruth Benedict's Boasian relativism. Race was consistently imposed on Boasian intellectuals, but they also reappropriated race and put it to use, as Benjamin Balthaser shows through the Russian passage of Archie Phinney, the Niimíipu anthropologist who cofounded the National Congress of American Indians. Finding in Soviet Siberia forms of oppression and hopes of liberation that illuminated the situation at home, Phinney converted them dialectically into a new, pan-Indian political vision of sovereignty and solidarity. Anthropology and indigeneity fused in Phinney's hands, creating a modern race consciousness.

Part 4 turns to culture, globalizing the genealogy of knowledge by investigating the concept's dissemination across sites of intellectual production. We begin in West Africa, a locus of antislavery, imperialism, and interreligious translation explored by Sean Hanretta. Juxtaposing the lives of Edward Wilmot Blyden, the father of Pan-Africanism, and the Ghanaian doctor and poet Raphael Armattoe, one of the first Africans nominated for the Nobel Peace Prize, Hanretta illuminates the diverse networks and shifting political valences that shaped the rise, redemption, and circumscription of the culture concept in Africa from colonialism to neoliberalism. We then turn to Brazil, where the culture concept continued to thrive, producing a modernist logos of vibrant intermixture, even as the German origins of such theories of hybridity were erased. Maria Lúcia Pallares-Burke uncovers Gilberto Freyre's loving theft of Boas disciple Rüdiger Bilden's ideas about Brazil, a metonym for contact that itself leads in two directions: both to the globalization of American knowledge brought about by the Columbia historian William Shepherd's promulgation of Latin American perspectives and to the "tropicalization" of European social thought. The final essay is set in the Andes, an icon of Indigenous civilization and the source of a civilizing mission pursued by Julio Tello, the Indigenous "Boas of Peru." In the skeletal remains of Huarochirí, which Tello dug up and read anew to restore his people's place in history, Christopher Heaney locates a tale of scientific patrimony that asks who owns human knowledge.

Our investigation into this multitude of culture concepts points to the tense relationship between disclosure, the revelation of new knowledge, and enclosure, which is about who colonizes the new knowledge, claiming the credit.[23] Ideas, like lands, are often considered to be sovereign possessions: as with land, the one who cultivates is not always the one who profits. We find that the concept of culture, though fenced and claimed as its domain by the discipline of anthropology, was in fact generated within a diversity of contact zones by a multiracial set of actors whose travels ranged from Africa to Latin America and

Europe.[24] Exploring the roots of "culture" illuminates the multiplicity of intellectual production, embedding concepts in the social conditions—such as the intimate relations of humans and their intellectual ecosystems—that the abstraction of ideas often screens out. The result discloses the global sources of modern thought, bringing focus to the dissemination of knowledge from those supposedly under study to those who supposedly carry the study out—a binary that imposes false assumptions about who is acting and who reacting, and that therefore requires rethinking and revision.

Together, these fourteen essays reframe our understanding not merely of race and culture and language, of indigeneity and diversity, but of the basic relationship between Self and Other that lies at the heart of modernity. Who gets to be called a Self and who is labeled Other? Who makes the labels, and who reproduces them? Is it necessary to continue replicating this static way of thinking, or might there exist within our past the sources of a different outlook?

The roots of globalization are more like the roots of a banyan tree than the typical genealogy of knowledge. Complex structures of invention and tradition interweave with one another, casting seeds to foreign hosts, which yield epiphytic groves of thought, producing unpredictable universes of knowledge creation and exchange.[25] These are often sites of violence and trauma, but also of hope and coexistence. Bringing these complex networks of knowledge into the light of sustained study will, we hope, invite fresh consideration of our received categories of analysis, yielding the creation of more enabling methodologies for the study of race, culture, science, modernity, migration, and empire. Disclosing the global sources of modern knowledge can also call into question the ongoing erasure of Indigenous people and other peoples of color within an ever more fragile, interdependent, and cultured biosphere. If so, we may yet locate and approach the global vistas imagined by Franz Boas and by his diverse circle more than a century ago, fulfilling some hopes that all too often remain a distant vision.

## Notes

1. The classic statement of these views is Franz Boas, *The Mind of Primitive Man* (New York: Macmillan, 1911). On the universality of dynamic cultural and linguistic processes, see esp. 105–14, 122, 140–48, 211, 218, 225–26, 242.
2. See Regna Darnell et al., eds., *The Franz Boas Papers*, vol. 1, *Franz Boas as Public Intellectual—Theory, Ethnography, Activism* (Lincoln: University of Nebraska Press, 2015), the first of a projected twenty-five volumes of scholarship connected to the digitization of Boas's correspondence at the American Philosophical Society.
3. For the social influence of Boasian anthropology, see John S. Gilkeson, *Anthropologists and the Rediscovery of America, 1886–1965* (New York: Cambridge University Press, 2010);

Vernon J. Williams Jr., *Rethinking Race: Franz Boas and His Contemporaries* (Lexington: University Press of Kentucky, 1996); Lee D. Baker, *From Savage to Negro: Anthropology and the Construction of Race, 1896–1954* (Berkeley: University of California Press, 1998).

4. Claude Lévi-Strauss, foreword to Franz Boas, *Indian Myths and Legends from the North Pacific Coast of America,* ed. Randy Bouchard and Dorothy Kennedy (Vancouver: Talonbooks, 2002), 13. Indeed, Lévi-Strauss's oft-told narrative of Boas's death, which occurred in his presence, served him as a succession myth, a passing of the baton.
5. See Greil Marcus, *Lipstick Traces: A Secret History of the Twentieth Century* (Cambridge: Harvard University Press, 1989), 390–405, and Christopher Bracken, *The Potlatch Papers: A Colonial Case History* (Chicago: University of Chicago Press, 1997), 38, 45–46, 100–107, 140–41, 152–65. Other thinkers influenced by the potlatch include Georges Bataille and Jacques Derrida.
6. Boas, *The Mind of Primitive Man;* Franz Boas, "Introduction," *Handbook of American Indian Languages, Part I* (Washington, DC: Government Printing Office, 1911), 5–83; Franz Boas, "Changes in Bodily Form of Descendants of Immigrants," *Reports of the Immigration Commission,* vol. 38, 61st Cong., 2d sess., document no. 208 (Washington, DC: Government Printing Office, 1911).
7. For a description of the conference, see "Yale to Host Conference for Centennial of Franz Boas's *The Mind of Primitive Man,*" Aug. 24, 2011, accessed May 23, 2017, http://historynewsnetwork.org/article/141409. The focus of our discussion was *The Mind of Primitive Man,* Boas's keystone text, which grew from a set of lectures he delivered in Spanish to students in Mexico City, where he had founded a transnational school of archaeology and ethnology, and in English at the Lowell Institute in Boston, which gave him a rostrum following the shocking announcement of his scientific findings—they had emerged from extensive measurements of southern and eastern European immigrants—that human crania conform to no racial categories. See Franz Boas, *Curso de Antropología General,* Publicaciones de la Escuela de Altos Estudios, Sección de Ciencias Sociales, Políticas y Jurídicas (Mexico City: Universidad Nacional de México, 1911); A. Lawrence Lowell, Cambridge, MA, to Franz Boas, New York, June 8, 1910, and Franz Boas, New York, to José López Portillo y Rojas, Mexico City, Aug. 29, 1911, Franz Boas Papers, ser. 1, Correspondence, American Philosophical Society.
8. On anthropology and indigeneity as global contact zones, see James Clifford's dialogical trilogy, *The Predicament of Culture: Twentieth-Century Ethnography, Literature, and Art* (Cambridge: Harvard University Press, 1988), *Routes: Travel and Translation in the Late Twentieth Century* (Cambridge: Harvard University Press, 1997), and *Returns: Becoming Indigenous in the Twenty-First Century* (Cambridge: Harvard University Press, 2013).
9. For a narrow delimitation of the circle, including only Boas and his students, see Adam Kuper, "The Boasians and the Critique of Evolutionism," in *The Reinvention of Primitive Society: Transformations of a Myth* (1988; repr. New York: Routledge 2005), esp. 125–32.
10. For the critique of Boas's relativist approach to history and cognition and the postwar renascence of ideas about cultural evolution and ranked difference, see Ned Blackhawk, "Julian Steward and the Politics of Representation: A Critique of Anthropologist Julian Steward's Ethnographic Portrayals of the American Indians of the Great Basin," *American Indian Culture and Research Journal* 21, no. 2 (1997): 61–81, and Marc Pinkoski, "Back to Boas," *Histories of Anthropology Annual* 7 (2011): 127–69. Leslie A. White

summarized the midcentury critique of Boas in "The Ethnography and Ethnology of Franz Boas," *Bulletin of the Texas Memorial Museum* 6 (April 1963): 1–76. This debate corresponds to a wider conflict over authenticity in the human sciences and who gets to determine it. See Joel Isaac, *Working Knowledge: Making the Human Sciences from Parsons to Kuhn* (Cambridge: Harvard University Press, 2012), and Lorraine Daston and Peter Galison, *Objectivity* (New York: Zone, 2010).

11. See S. Eben Kirksey and Stefan Helmreich, "The Emergence of Multispecies Ethnography," *Cultural Anthropology* 25, no. 4 (2010): 545–76.
12. See Edward Said's canonical commentary on the Self / Other binary in Western Orientalist discourse, where he quotes Friedrich Nietzsche's insight that "truths are illusions about which one has forgotten that this is what they are." Edward Said, "Latent and Manifest Orientalism," in *Orientalism* (1978; repr. New York: Vintage Books, 1979), 202–3. For the role of the Self / Other binary in creating subjects of colonial rule, "sealed into that crushing objecthood," see Frantz Fanon, "The Fact of Blackness," in *Black Skin, White Masks,* trans. Charles Lam Markmann (Paris: Editions de Seuil, 1952; New York: Grove Press, 1967), 109. On the historical burdens assumed by second-class citizens of the United States, who find they must emancipate the minds of those who oppress them in order to emancipate themselves, see James Baldwin's "My Dungeon Shook: Letter to My Nephew on the One Hundredth Anniversary of Emancipation," in *The Fire Next Time* (1963; repr. New York: Vintage International, 1993), 8–10. "The really terrible thing, old buddy," Baldwin tells his nephew James, "is that *you* must accept *them.*" Ibid., 8.
13. On the relationship between American Indians and anthropology, see Thomas Biolsi and Larry J. Zimmerman, eds., *Indians and Anthropologists: Vine Deloria Jr. and the Critique of Anthropology* (Tucson: University of Arizona Press, 1997), and Beatrice Medicine, *Learning to Be an Anthropologist and Remaining "Native": Selected Writings* (Urbana: University of Illinois Press, 2001). Two classic products of intellectual exchanges between a North American scholar and an Indigenous community are Mountain Wolf Woman's *Mountain Wolf Woman, Sister of Crashing Thunder: The Autobiography of a Winnebago Indian,* ed. Nancy Oestreich Lurie (Ann Arbor: University of Michigan Press, 1961), and Peter J. Powell, *Sweet Medicine: The Continuing Role of the Sacred Arrows, the Sun Dance, and the Sacred Buffalo Hat in Northern Cheyenne History* (Norman: University of Oklahoma Press, 1969).
14. On the appropriation of Indigenous ontologies for settler colonialism, see Patrick Wolfe, "On Being Woken Up: The Dreamtime in Anthropology and in Australian Settler Culture," *Comparative Studies in Society and History* 33, no. 2 (1991): 197–224.
15. Douglas Cole, "Franz Boas and the Bella Coola in Berlin," *Northwest Anthropological Research Notes* 16, no. 2 (1982): 115–22.
16. Franz Boas, *The Kwakiutl of Vancouver Island,* Memoirs of the American Museum of Natural History, vol. 8, pt. 2 (Leiden: E. J. Brill, 1909; New York: G. E. Stechert, 1909), 307. For Du Bois's use of the veil image to describe the "double consciousness" of African Americans, see W. E. B. Du Bois, "Of Our Spiritual Strivings," in *The Souls of Black Folk* (1903; repr. New Haven: Yale University Press, 2015), 3–11. Interestingly, Du Bois's image—the basis of his idea of an African American mode of "second-sight," in which the veiled black viewer sees himself as he seems to himself and also as he is seen by the white world—draws on the transatlantic tradition of African American folklore

concerning those born with a caul who are gifted with visionary powers. See Robert Gooding-Williams, *In the Shadow of Du Bois: Afro-Modern Political Thought in America* (Cambridge: Harvard University Press, 2009), 77–78, and Jonathan Scott Holloway, introduction to *The Souls of Black Folk,* xi.

17. For the mutual influence of and resonances between the two men, see Lewis R. Gordon's essay in this book. See also Julia E. Liss's discussion of Boas and Du Bois in "Diasporic Identities: The Science and Politics of Race in the Work of Franz Boas and W. E. B. Du Bois, 1894–1919," *Cultural Anthropology* 13, no. 2 (1998): 127–66.
18. On masks in Western thought, see Susan Gubar, *Racechanges: White Skin, Black Face in American Culture* (New York: Oxford University Press, 1997), 38–40; Oscar Wilde, "The Truth of Masks," in *Intentions* (New York: Brentano's, 1905), 219–63; and James H. Johnson, *Venice Incognito: Masks in the Serene Republic* (Berkeley: University of California Press, 2011), 47–140. On masks in Indigenous thought, see Irving Goldman, *The Mouth of Heaven: An Introduction to Kwakiutl Religious Thought* (New York: John Wiley and Sons, 1975), 63, 124–25, 183–84; and Robert Joseph, "Behind the Mask," in Peter Macnair, Robert Joseph, and Bruce Grenville, *Down from the Shimmering Sky: Masks of the Northwest Coast* (Vancouver: Douglas and McIntyre, 1998), 18–35. See especially Joseph's description of his thought process while dancing in a mask: "My universe is the mold of the mask over my face. I am the mask. I am the bird. I am the animal. I am the fish. I am the spirit. I visualize my dance. I ponder every move. I transcend into the being of the mask." Ibid., 24.
19. On the agency of Indigenous performers at the ethnographic shows and world's fairs of the late nineteenth century, see Andrew Zimmerman, *Anthropology and Antihumanism in Imperial Germany* (Chicago: University of Chicago Press, 2001), 15–33; Paige Raibmon, *Authentic Indians: Episodes of Encounter from the Late-Nineteenth-Century Northwest Coast* (Durham: Duke University Press, 2005), 15–73; Mae Ngai, "Transnationalism and the Transformation of the 'Other': Response to the Presidential Address," *American Quarterly* 57, no. 1 (2005): 59–65.
20. All consciousness is consciousness *of something,* which makes thinking intersubjective. The Self / Other binary results from this intersubjectivity, thus it may be changed. See Alessandro Duranti, "Husserl, Intersubjectivity and Anthropology," *Anthropological Theory* 10, nos. 1–2 (2010): 16–35; Michael Jackson, *Minima Ethnographica: Intersubjectivity and the Anthropological Project* (Chicago: University of Chicago Press, 1998), 11; and Maurice Natanson, *Edmund Husserl: Philosopher of Infinite Tasks* (Evanston: Northwestern University Press, 1973), 71–72. "Objects on their own have intersubjective implications," Natanson writes. "Seeing the stone is seeing it *as* seeable by others." Thus, at the basis of intersubjectivity, we find the ecological outlook so basic to Indigenous philosophy.
21. This "portrait of belonging," as Gordon puts it, challenged the natal alienation imposed upon slaves by masters. See Orlando Patterson, *Slavery and Social Death: A Comparative Study* (Cambridge: Harvard University Press, 1982), 5–8.
22. See James Tully's chapter in this book, "Rediscovering the World of Franz Boas: Anthropology, Equality / Diversity, and World Peace."
23. For a different view of enclosure, see Paul Kockelman, "Information Is the Enclosure of Meaning: Cybernetics, Semiotics, and Alternative Theories of Information," *Language*

*and Communication* 33 (2012): 115–27, and "Enclosure and Disclosure," *Public Culture* 19, no. 2 (2007): 303–5.

24. Here we extend Mary Louise Pratt's nomenclature, seeing contact zones as "social spaces where disparate cultures meet, clash, and grapple with each other, often in highly asymmetrical relations of domination and subordination." Mary Louise Pratt, *Imperial Eyes: Travel Writing and Transculturation* (New York: Routledge, 1992), 4.
25. For this metaphor we are indebted to the late Hal Conklin. Isaiah Lorado Wilner, conversation with Harold C. Conklin, New Haven, CT, July 18, 2012. For another view of the banyan, see Eben Kirksey, *Freedom in Entangled Worlds: West Papua and the Architecture of Global Power* (Durham: Duke University Press, 2012), 55–57.

# Part One **Origins and Erasures: The Emergence of a Boasian Circle**

# Chapter 1 Transformation Masks: Recollecting the Indigenous Origins of Global Consciousness

*Isaiah Lorado Wilner*

Indigenous people are no longer seen as a "people without history," but all too often their history remains unheard. The basic premise of global history is this: the West is the agent of change; after all, the modernizing Western state made the world what it is. Chocolate, tomatoes, the rise of a corn economy, and the potency of certain Indigenous empires may be itemized as sideshows to the main program of imperial power. But when it comes to agency, we are taught to privilege the people who ride roughshod upon history over those who bite the dust, and there is no narrative in which the guns of the West do not drive the show.

This essay proposes a new narrative. It argues that Indigenous people were no mere recipients of history, showing up in bit roles to accommodate others' inventions or stage a forlorn act of resistance. They were inventors of modernity, innovators on a global stage who transformed the lives of people beyond their communities. In order to understand this history of Indigenous influence, we need to move beyond the theme of brute power to grasp the theme of idea power: the agency to reinvent thoughts and perceptions. Through their idea power—their agency as makers, shapers, and long-distance communicators of worlds of thought—Indigenous people contributed to the formation of global consciousness: the modern perception that the world is one and that all people belong equally to it.[1]

We can investigate the Indigenous origins of global consciousness if we make use of new methods to study an untapped archive: the corpus of thought and action collected by anthropologists. Between the abolition of slavery and the start of the Second World War, anthropologists traveled to virtually every corner of the globe, recording the words and ways of colonized people. They were the tape recorder of an emerging global society. Arriving amid the maelstrom of colonialism, alongside epidemic diseases, settlers seeking land, and corporations in pursuit of proteins and minerals, anthropologists, who sought to extract skulls, bones, and artifacts, presented an ironic opportunity to Indigenous communities locked in a desperate struggle for survival. Thrown back on their inalienable resource—their minds—a generation of Indigenous intellectuals converted the people who had come to categorize them into mediums of Indigenous thought. They sent these human vessels back to the worlds they had come from, bearing messages from colonized society.[2]

The anthropologists brought home with them a rich transcript that records the attempts of Indigenous people to transmit their ideas to the West.[3] This transcript, made up of words but also of objects, has been catalogued by social science, but it has yet to be granted the status of history: interpreted holistically through reading and reflection. In the following pages, I hope to share a method of reading this transcript, which I have developed through my research into the life of George Hunt, an Indigenous intellectual from Vancouver Island, in British Columbia. Hunt's achievements influenced the anthropologist Franz Boas in ways he hardly knew—and in ways he knew well and tried to obscure.[4]

At the moment of its emergence on America's Northwest Coast, Boasian anthropology relied on the erasure of its Indigenous origins. The first effacement was that of Hunt, who created the template for a new mode of global interaction. Before he met Hunt, Boas viewed himself as a bearer of modernity, a "civilized" scientist who created knowledge of "primitive" life by collecting its signs—in the form of masks—in order to assemble a Western replica of a vanishing Indigenous lifeworld. After he met Hunt, Boas changed. He turned from the sign-based project of classification toward a new mode of communication in which the anthropologist recorded Indigenous messages and transmitted them to the West. In this new project, conducted not upon a dead Indigenous society but by a living one, Hunt positioned himself as an agent of modernity civilizing the Western scientist.

The communicative mode Hunt developed with Boas grew into his guiding principle. Stimulated by Hunt, Boas extended beyond his heritage to infuse the

Western tradition with the energies and insights of foreign worlds of thought. He became a spokesman for the exchange of values and concepts in a global society, one that he hoped would abolish the discourse of civilization and the inequities it has justified.[5] That Boas announced these ideas in a book titled, of all things, *The Mind of Primitive Man*—a product of his education by someone he came to learn was no "primitive"—epitomizes the ironies of the Boasian legacy, part of a long and ongoing struggle to face the heritage of empire.

What follows is a story about how we begin to remember this global history of interconnection and exchange. To develop a global history of ideas, we will need to overcome the legacy of categorization that segments and thereby renders silent Indigenous forms of knowledge. Here, my approach embraces two areas of study that are usually treated separately: material culture and mythology. On the Northwest Coast, masks and "myths" are parts of a whole.[6] The mask, once worn, allows a dancer to inhabit a history and share it with others. The story expressed through the mask is an enacted idea, bringing thought into being through performance. Masks and stories unite to create a *narrative,* a packet of messages, embedded in expression, that convey a worldview, which individuals transmit to the world.[7]

As mnemonic devices, masks serve as cues to ideas, affording access to silenced narratives. Through an effort to recover the narratives embodied in masks yet masked by the Western archive, scholars may draw upon this stream of agency, reuniting objects and stories to read the messages Indigenous performers and intellectuals have communicated.[8] Such study can begin a process of mental transformation, converting the imperial legacy of collection into the quite different project of recollection, an effort to remember our shared global history.[9]

## BELLA COOLA *BILDUNG*

At Lansstraße 8, in a leafy suburb of Berlin, there sits a piece of history that encodes the story of how Franz Boas came to change. It is nearly three feet long, made out of cedar, and the name of its owner was Spouter of the House.[10] In 1885, at the age of twenty-seven, Boas received the assignment of cataloguing this mask, which the explorer Johan Adrian Jacobsen had purchased on northern Vancouver Island and sent back to the Royal Museum of Ethnology. During the previous year, the museum had seized upon the German Empire's expansion to assemble the world's largest collection of bones and curios from "vanishing" cultures.[11] But this mask was no artifact of the past. It was in use until the moment its owner removed it from her box of treasures, and even in Berlin it remained alive with power.[12]

The mask belonged to Lucy Homiskanis, the wife of George Hunt.[13] Lucy had contributed to her husband's ascent among the Kwakiutl of Fort Rupert by displaying her dances—property rights that Hunt, the son of an English trader and his highborn Tlingit wife, mixed with wealth, rhetoric, and political genius to join the Kwakiutl nobility.[14] As a teenager Lucy had disappeared while digging for clams, leaving only a pile of clothes on the beach. For a month she was thought to be gone—until the winter ceremonies, when the dance leaders of Fort Rupert called the people to their secret spot in the woods to compose two songs for the supposedly vanished girl. That night a Killer Whale dancer appeared in the house, spouting water from his blowhole. Suddenly he pulled a hidden string, splitting his face in two and revealing the form of a supernatural Monster Fish said to have taken the girl away. Following this transformation, and shocking those who thought her gone, Lucy emerged to dance, enacting her role as a bearer of wealth for her family.[15]

Boas, who printed a picture of this mask in 1897, would not learn the identity of its owner, much less the dramatic story of Lucy's disappearance and reappearance, until the early 1920s, when Lucy had been dead for more than a decade and Hunt, approaching his seventies, sent Boas a list of corrections to their monumental, coauthored ethnography. Almost as if posing a counterpoint to the classifying outlook Boas expressed in his title for the book, *The Social Organization and the Secret Societies of the Kwakiutl Indians,* Hunt titled his latest work "name of the masks on the Book and who there Belong to." In each sentence Hunt contradicted Boas's pursuit of the typical and tribal with an account of the personal and particular—beginning with his own family. "This mask," Hunt wrote Boas, "was my wife killer whale mask."[16]

It was Hunt, it turns out, who had sent the mask to Germany. In 1881 Hunt had served as Jacobsen's guide, aiding in his collection of the more than five hundred Kwakwa̱ka̱'wakw ceremonial objects now in Berlin that stirred in Boas visions of a foreign world. "My fancy was first struck," Boas recalled, "by the flight of imagination exhibited in the works of art of the British Columbians as compared to the severe sobriety of the eastern Eskimo." Sea monsters, fantastical birds of prey, tangle-haired hags assaulted his senses, striking him as strange, "grotesque." But as he held the masks in hand, noting mouths, eyes, snapping mandibles, faces that divided by the pull of a string to reveal a second face within, Boas realized "what a wealth of thought" lay hidden behind the designs.[17]

Boas's newfound interest in masks, a layer interposed between the self and the world, was more than a metaphor for his interest in culture. Boas lived behind a kind of mask, assuming the status of a white man even though a look at his face revealed cracks in the facade: three scars over the eye, one across the nose, and a long, cruel slash from cheek to ear.[18] Boas had earned his *Schmisse* while fencing at university between 1877 and 1881, when a revived version of the *Judenfrage,* or Jewish question, posed by the distinguished historian Heinrich von Treitschke gripped the country, and students rallied to "emancipate the German people from a kind of foreign domination."[19] Boas, a secular Jew, fought several duels to defend his honor against attacks from anti-Semites, but his attempt to escape his outsider's identity, living by the code of his German secret society, marked him as the outsider he did not wish to be.[20] Few frontal portraits of Boas survive today because he tended to present his profile to the camera, leaving the scarred side in shadow.[21]

The violence inscribed on Boas's face signified a deeper conflict between his self-image as a romantic explorer and the flesh-and-blood reality of a scientist measuring humans in an age of empire.[22] Inspired by the globetrotting humanism of Alexander von Humboldt, whose magnum opus, *Cosmos,* offered Europeans a vision of New World grandeur, Boas had set off in 1883 to live with the Inuit of Baffin Island, there awakening to the radical variety of human practice, the universality of human experience, and the sordid power performances involved in extracting information about both.[23] He returned in 1885 to an altered Germany, which had acquired an empire in his absence and now possessed colonies in Africa and the Pacific. The merging of imperial politics and romantic science provoked a profound crisis for Boas, now defined at home as the ethnic outsider he had traveled so far to see.[24]

As his mentors Rudolf Virchow and Adolf Bastian received packets of salted skin, hair, and severed hands from German collectors around the globe, Boas groped for a new self-understanding. He came to the conclusion that science must change. Though categorizing experience and generalizing data to form laws of nature could be one way of seeing the world, one must not lose one's sense of feeling. The "affective" search for the inner nature of the thing itself, rather than the way one might define it from the outside, could reveal a different form of truth.[25] Just as he came to this insight, the Northwest Coast artwork arrived, opening a door to affective perception. Lucy's transformation mask, representing two faces, linked three states of being, those of the human (Dancer), animal (Killer Whale), and supernatural (Monster Fish) realms. It was an image of interconnection, portraying the relationships of humans with the nonhuman members of an animate cosmos. Even as Boas classified the mask, categorizing it by region and tribe, the object escaped his grasp, permeating the borders of being that locked Boas ("the Jew") in place. This global consciousness remained dead to Boas so long as the mask remained severed from the message. But a potential existed. If the mask and the message could be reunited, they would transmit to Boas an Indigenous narrative.

Through this opening, this crack in thought, danced "die Bella Coola." In 1885 the Hamburg animal merchant Carl Hagenbeck, who would later contribute to the invention of the modern zoo, toured Germany with an exhibition of humans.[26] Nine Nuxalk dancers from Bella Coola, a village north of Hunt's home in Kwak'wala land, spent a year performing in zoos, hotels, and theaters across Germany.[27] The ethnographer Aurel Krause, who had recently returned from a stay with the Tlingit of Alaska, invited Boas to join him on a visit to the performers at Krolls Etablissement, the amusement center where they lived and danced.[28] The following days proceeded for Boas like a dream or a vision as the dancers took the artifacts he had been struggling to lock into place and spun them, for a moment, into splendid motion.

Donning the masks collected by Hunt, cocking their beaks to the beat, the Nuxalk posed as supernatural cranes and ravens. They rolled up their sleeves to display their scars, explained to Boas that the masks were tied to the secret societies of the Northwest Coast, and described the arduous initiation rituals—an experience to which Boas, a secret society initiate himself, could relate. A conversation began. The Nuxalk taught Boas their local trade jargon. They sang of love, and of loss, in the Puget Sound hop fields ("Ya, that is good! Ya, that is good! That worthless woman does not like me").[29] One man, a skilled storyteller named Nuskilusta, taught Boas the rudiments of the Nuxalk language.[30] After four days Boas wrote to his fiancée, Marie Krackowizer, that he felt "wie in Himmel," as if he were in heaven. By the time the group left for Breslau he had recorded four songs, sent a report to the *Berliner Tageblatt,* described the Nuxalk language, and written a sketch for the American magazine *Science.* Boas had found his affective inspiration, a message for his developing medium.[31]

The performers offered Boas an Indigenous education, a Bella Coola *Bildung.* Making use of another people's masks as found objects, they code-switched Boas to their mnemonic logic, transmitting their messages to him. The embodied materialism of this meeting, in which ideas moved through masks, blankets, and even scars, accommodated Boas's German ideas about culture, for the ornate carvings of the Northwest Coast showed that this so-called "primitive" people in fact possessed a richly developed civilization.[32] When the Nuxalk danced, Boas wrote, "we saw ourselves transported into a foreign world whose outlook, whose customs, have taken a quite different course from ours, but which we must acknowledge as a high cultural state."[33] Yet even by altering his judgment, Boas retained the authority to be the judge. A more powerful transformation was under way, one concerning the question of agency.

As he studied the artwork displayed by the Nuxalk, Boas noted an aesthetic feature of the Northwest Coast: the eye design.[34] This "repeated motif" decorated nearly every spoon, blanket, and mask that he saw. Boas did not yet know that sight—vision—was a central idea on the Northwest Coast. Visions of encounters with animals and spirits were a form of social currency. By performing visions, elites claimed their ancestral privileges and responsibilities. By experiencing visions, shamans received their healing powers. Stories were visions shared by a teller, pictures painted in words.[35] Through visions, through the metaphor of vision, the people of the coast depicted themselves as Eyes, not Others: vision seekers, vision speakers. Ultimately it is the person with vision, the person who glimpses a potential that others have missed, who is capable of altering a situation, thus bringing about a transformation.

At the heart of this transformation was the idea of a mask. In the European outlook familiar to Boas, a mask concealed: it hid the wearer's true identity, superimposing a false front. For the Nuxalk and for the Kwakwa̱ka̱'wakw, masks were not merely coverings but skins, part and parcel of the substance beneath. A mask enabled its wearer to alter states, to don a second face. It provided a new way of being and of seeing.[36] Rather than hiding behind the mask, the people of the Northwest Coast took on the mask's identity. When they put on their masks, they positioned themselves not as objects of anthropology but as subjects of history. Agents of change, they possessed the power to transform.

There is no evidence to suggest that Boas felt tempted to wear one of these masks, thus donning the skin of the Nuxalk and their neighbors, seeing the world through their eyes. If he did so, quietly and out of view, we have no record of it.[37] We do know that Boas sought the meanings behind the masks. He asked what each design depicted, but the performers from Bella Coola could not tell him. The masks collected by Jacobsen were not their masks, they said. They did not know the stories behind them.[38] Once intrigued, Boas now found himself confronted by a mystery, and with this mystery the door opened wider. To find out more, it would be necessary to visit the place where the masks were made.

Twenty-five years later Boas would look back upon this moment, the moment of his Bella Coola *Bildung*, as the beginning of his own transformation. The performers from Bella Coola, Boas wrote, offered him a chance to "cast a brief glimpse behind the veil that covered the life of these people."[39] Had it not been for the Nuxalk performers, Boas might very easily have remained at home, where he would have become a professor of geography in Germany and, had he lived long enough, a stumbling stone on the streets of present-day Berlin.[40] It was due to the influence of Indigenous performers that his life veered in a new direction and began to take consequential shape. In

1886 Boas took leave of the museum to travel to the Northwest Coast. "The attraction," he later wrote, "was irresistible."[41]

## DRIFTED ASHORE HOUSE

Boas arrived on Vancouver Island like a parody of a detective, clutching sketches of the masks as his clues. The only drawback to these clues was that they lacked any connection to a case. Boas envisioned the masks as signs that Natives could connect to referents, lifting the veil that obscured their world of thought. But the masks were not signs. They were property that related the histories of their owners, and knowledge of the designs was limited to the circle whose history they discussed. No one else had a right to talk. After a week of sodden searching in the labor camps of Victoria, poking his head into tents, sharing pictures, requesting information in the shards of Chinook trade jargon he had learned from the Nuxalk, Boas had come no closer to the meanings that had eluded him in Berlin. He gave up his hunt in order to buy new masks, thus creating a clean set of signs and referents.[42]

As he headed north on an old steamer toward Kwakwa̱ka̱'wakw country, a case of tobacco and a bolt of cotton by his side, Boas formed the perfect caricature of the white man's globalization. Money for masks, tobacco for tales, was Europe's colonial calculus. Boas, no exception, needed masks to fund his trip. His pursuit of "handsome" objects to sell to Bastian in Berlin formed the subtext of his dealings at Newitti, a remote island town off the northern tip of Vancouver Island, twice razed by British gunboats yet still a bastion of the potlatch, the outlawed form of Indigenous governance that took place through a reciprocal exchange of feasts, dances, and most important to Boas, the display of masks.[43]

The potlatch was an answer and an ode to the experience of modernity. It had taken a new form after the smallpox epidemic of 1862, when more than 50 percent of the people died within a year, some villages vanished, and Northwest Coast peoples faced the possibility of imminent destruction. The potlatch was their survival strategy, a gift-giving system that soldered bonds between peoples, redistributed wealth—often in the form of fabricated metal plates known as coppers that were worth thousands of trade blankets—and spread stories across a thousand-mile coastline from the salmon-fishing grounds of the Columbia River to the eulachon harvesting spots by the Nass. Through this system of material and intellectual exchange, thousands of people responded to the existential threat that Western networks of power and pathogens posed to their homes, families, and communities. They fashioned a new Indigenous lifeworld, drawing one another into an ongoing conversation that constructed a peaceful, pancoastal community. Because the potlatch system perpetuated Indigenous independence, Canada's government had banned it in 1884. But this did not stop the Kwakwa̱ka̱'wakw, who determined to live—as one chief now put it to Boas—by "the strict law that bids us dance."[44]

The people of Newitti greeted Boas quizzically. Why would a white visitor ask to see the same dances that the white government had only just banned? Boas, compelled to communicate, clarified that he was not a missionary or a government agent but a traveler who had come to learn. "I do not wish to interfere with your celebration," he promised the head chief, who had called a town meeting, asking the foreigner to explain his purposes. "My people live far away," Boas said, "and would like to know what people in distant lands do. . . . And so I went and I came here and I saw you eat and drink, sing and dance. And I shall go back and say: 'See, that is how the people there live. They were good to me and asked me to live with them.' "[45] In response to the stimulus provided by the people of Newitti, Boas had begun to reconsider his research methods. He talked about himself as the people wanted to see him, not as a collector but as a transmitter of information.

During the next week, as Boas put together his collection, the people took time out from their dances to chat with the visitor. "Everyone," Boas wrote, "is most anxious to tell me something."[46] By revealing what they valued—their stories—those assembled at Newitti turned Boas from the material products that possessed Western value to the narratives that the objects encoded, which held greater wealth in the Indigenous world. Boas saw the masks in the context of their makers, who expressed their social history in carvings—masks and also poles, posts, family benches, and feasting dishes—all of which related the narratives of their owners.[47] At night, the head chief of Newitti gathered his people around the fire, where he related legends that Boas scribbled down with the help of a young translator. Sitting on the chief's settee, carved with the heraldry of his lineage, Boas realized that the designs surrounding him told the history of the house. The people of Newitti lived within their narratives, enfolded by their stories. Although Boas styled himself as the intellectual, it was the Kwakwa̱ka̱'wakw who turned him from objects to ideas.[48]

Boas continued to collect, and he would succeed in paying for his trip by selling his collection (the "best masks available," he reported home, including "all the ornaments that belong to one dance").[49] But the object of his interest shifted from the masks that brought him there to the storytelling style of the Northwest Coast. So eager was Boas to hear more stories, and to see stories play out in dances, that he placed his masks at risk to do so, traveling through a severe storm to reach some potlatches at the town of Alert Bay. When his guide, blown ashore, refused to venture out again, Boas hired a Native boatman, stowed the masks in his craft, and pushed off into a ferocious wind. They might have died, and were once pushed into a rocky peninsula, but somehow Boas and his new pilot managed to catch a friendly gust and steer for the totem poles of Alert Bay. A crowd rushed to bring the boat in, Boas springing out so eagerly that his guide burst into laughter. "You were just like a deer," he said, "so quickly you jumped ashore!" Relieved, Boas walked to the dock to find George Hunt's white brother-in-law Stephen Allen Spencer, the owner of the local salmon cannery, whose attention immediately gravitated toward the masks, the constant object of imperial interest. "The first thing he told me," Boas wrote, "was that my belongings would be locked up."[50]

Despite all the effort Boas had expended on masks—first to determine the meanings of the masks he had seen in Berlin, then to collect a second group of masks at Newitti, and finally to transport and secure them—his attempt to "cast a glimpse behind the veil" was a failure. The masks were not signs that could be lifted out of the Northwest Coast to generate principles. They were mediums, which their owners used to transmit messages. Even as Boas attempted to collect, and by collecting to categorize a culture, the people of the Northwest Coast attempted to communicate, and by communicating to transmit a history that defied categorization. As a result, Boas's interest began to shift from masks to the mnemonic knowledge they encoded.

It was in this context—the play between categorization and communication—that he met the Hunt family and, without realizing it, learned their family story. On his first night in Alert Bay, after dinner with Stephen Allen Spencer and his two brothers-in-law—each, like Spencer, was married to a sister of Hunt—Boas spent some hours in conversation with Annie Spencer, Hunt's younger sister, who regaled him with Indian tales. "Mrs. Spencer was very gracious and told me many stories," Boas wrote to Krackowizer, "which I recorded later in the evening."[51] Four days later, Boas mentioned in a new note to his fiancée that he had visited Annie Spencer again and asked her to tell more tales. "She relates well and is very gracious," he emphasized. "Unfortunately she is not well or I should really bother her."[52] Nevertheless, Boas trod back to the Spencers' home the same day. There he found Hunt's sister either improved or doubly gracious, for she was "kind enough to tell me all I wanted to know. . . . The information I obtained from her was the most valuable I received in Alert Bay."[53]

The stories of Annie Spencer opened a vista on a narrative legacy linking all the peoples from Yakutat Bay to the Columbia River, who, though divided by physical and linguistic differences and by histories of conflict, held in common a heritage of thought. A centerpiece of this heritage was the Raven Cycle, one of the oldest and largest bodies of oral literature in the Americas. In 1886 the bards who performed the Raven tales, and who daily altered them, were members not of a single school but of a living tradition whose members had innovated a stance toward the world in response to cycles of change from the Ice Age to the smallpox apocalypse. They had created a body of thought about people's relationships to one another and to the cosmos, the beings within it, and the capacity of humans to right those relationships.[54]

The star of the drama was Raven, scheming, ravenous, bumbling in his arrogance toward ever greater disgrace, yet always surviving, evolving, and through his accidents and exploits establishing the present state of affairs.[55] Born before the earth had acquired its form, it was Raven—Old One, Great Inventor, Chief of the Ancients, Heaven Maker, Giving to the End, Going Around—who established the tools and forms of existence.[56] With the world veiled in darkness, Raven stole the box that held the sun and opened it, lighting the world by his ingenuity. He made man from grass and elderberry bushes, brought salmon to the people, fed the rivers with eulachon. He established the shapes and traits of his fellow animals and gave them their present powers and appearances. And though affairs could hardly change as radically in contemporary times as in the days of beginning, by his actions and infractions Raven pointed toward a way of being human. "So many stories are told about him," Boas remarked during his first visit to the coast, "that they have a saying that human life is not long enough to tell all of them."[57]

Every Native of the Northwest Coast was woven into the fabric of the Raven Cycle through the warp and weft of a storytelling practice that linked speakers and listeners—messengers and mediums—within a pattern of call and response. There were no galleries around the fire, no lines dictating who paid and who performed. There were no observers, no outsiders, no Others. People did not merely listen to the Raven Cycle; they took part, asking questions, repeating refrains, goading the storyteller toward feats of ingenuity.[58] There was saltiness and sport in the Raven tales, sex and waste, greed and hate. The bards were like Raven: they begged, borrowed, stole, and in doing so created. They were origin poets who fostered possibilities by defying the rules of the system they had made.[59]

The stories they told, often ending in just-so pronouncements—explaining, say, how wolves had come to behave so diffidently around humans ("they really became wolves after this," one storyteller put it)—wove a fabric of thought that embraced every notable rock, tree, and stream in the neighborhood, encompassing the human community within an animate cosmos.[60] "I remember with the greatest pleasure many trips in colorful canoes with Indian guides who did not stop telling tales," Boas wrote in one account of this storytelling culture for a German audience. "It was that mountain peak which alone reached above the waters during the great flood, and from this peak the earth was populated again. Here, the battle took place in which the stone giants were outwitted and killed by the brave Indians. A dangerous rapid, formed in prehistoric times in a narrow strait, reminds us of the Son of God, who killed and sank a dangerous sea monster into the ocean at that place. Each strange place is woven into a legend."[61]

Yet, while the storytelling tradition of the Northwest Coast had survived long enough to envelop the landscape, the Raven Cycle had emerged from only a portion of it. As Boas's first conversation with an elderly storyteller in Victoria revealed, only the northern peoples, including George Hunt's mother's people, related the origins of the world through the exploits of Raven.[62] Other peoples credited competing narratives, starring different figures.[63] Among the Kwakiutl people of Fort Rupert, the hero associated with light was not Raven but Mink, the son of the supernatural man who carried the sun across the sky. Much like Raven, Mink possessed an insatiable appetite, but not for food. A priapic scavenger after advantageous marriages, Mink lusted after women.[64] It was said of the mischievous Mink that he had sliced off a girl's clitoris and attached it to a branch, wearing it on his forehead as a ludicrous headpiece. On another occasion he convinced a flock of female ducks to enter the forest and there sit upon a rare type of elongated mushroom, which turned out to be Mink's penis.[65] If Raven was Ego, Mink was Id. He pointed toward the urge within, the presocialized desire. The Kwakiutl went so far as to envision Mink as a child, given to daydreams and pranks. When performing the role of Mink, they reveled in his youth by making the grammatical mistakes of a child.[66] But there was more than comedy in the Kwakiutl depiction of Mink's youth, for the child had attained a precious status in a society that now possessed precious few children.

Among the Kwakwa̱ka̱'wakw, Mink—T̓łisa̱lagi'lakw, or "Born to Be the Sun"—was the most sympathetic of figures, the fatherless child. The rights of the Kwakwa̱ka̱'wakw passed from father to son, meaning that Mink had to make his own way in the world.[67] The Kwakwa̱ka̱'wakw traced the origins of modern times to Mink's response to his fate. Teased by the other children because he had no father, Mink came home depressed, whereupon his mother related a wondrous tale. Mink did have a father, his mother assured him, and he was not just any father. He was the man who lit up the world by carrying the sun across the sky. Hoping to meet his father, Mink shot an arrow into the sky, then a second arrow into the back of the first, and a third into the second, constructing a ladder of arrows that he ascended to the Upper World. Warmly greeted by his father, he was invited to try out his future occupation. Mink began well enough, walking calmly across the sky with the sun in his arms, but soon he grew impatient. He began to run, scorching the earth and bringing about a deluge. Disgraced, Mink was thrown to the earth by his father, fated to spend his life among men.[68]

In the Kwakwa̱ka̱'wakw version of history, the origin of modern life was a great mistake, an ecological disaster that unleashed a scourge upon humankind.[69] The hero was a fallen child. His actions warned of the dangers of hubris, a trait ever present in the avaricious fur trade. But the Kwakwa̱ka̱'wakw storytellers who related the narrative were careful to show that the disaster did not befall an individual only; it impacted everybody. Mink tales epitomized the black humor of the Northwest Coast, a tone infused with portentous irony. They had bravado, an acute awareness of human foibles, and epic warnings about the transitory nature of greatness—a style that had risen to prominence in a period of existential horror inhabited by many human Minks, many fatherless children struggling for survival on a broken coast scorched by smallpox.

Transformation—making change—not only created the world, it was what enabled people to make their way in it, negotiating a path through the currents of destruction. Mink's essence as a transformer, as a hero, consisted not in his creation of the apocalypse but in his response to the apocalypse of everyday life. Smaller and weaker than the others, bearing no special talents, Mink survived by his wits—and it was his terrible wit, his deadeye for the jugular, that especially pleased the Kwakiutl of Fort Rupert. Mink, they said, had lived at nearby Turnour Island, where the sons of the Wolf chief had terrorized him, stealing his salmon from his trap. Threatened with starvation, Mink grabbed his spear, lay in wait for Wolf's sons, and slaughtered them. But this was only the beginning of his revenge, for it was the insult, not the injury, that offended Mink—and which he aimed, in turn, to deliver.[70]

By decapitating the eldest son of the Wolf and converting his head into a mask, Mink managed to impersonate his persecutor. In this blood-drenched costume he arrived at the Wolf chief's winter ceremonies to perform the dances of his heir. Three times Mink circled the fire, displaying the Wolf's winter dances. On the fourth circuit he revealed his true form, throwing off his mask to mock his host: "Yahai, yahai, Mink wears as his cap the face of the son of the Wolf!" This was genocide: Mink had assassinated the Wolf's heirs, taken their dances, and arrived at the crucial moment to deliver the coup de grâce. When he raised the head of his enemy, Mink announced a new future for his descendants, the Kwakiutl. This, it was said, was the origin of the winter dances that Boas had come to see.[71]

At the center of the dances was a single mask: a mask that allowed Mink to assume the form and take the name of a Wolf. Only by wearing this mask could

Mink cross a boundary, enter the realm of the Wolves, and claim his prize. Mink transformed not because he was born to do so, but because he possessed vision. He saw and seized his chance to act, writing for himself a new history.

Although the Mink stories emerged from an ancient tradition, that tradition had altered as Indigenous people reshaped it into something new. Mink's actions were an outgrowth of and an answer to the experience of modernity. The tales Boas studied as generalities, looking for ideas that defined social groups, were the product of personal genealogies, formulated by storytellers whose innovations shaped the intellectual material of the coast to their purposes. This was especially true of the Hunt family, possessed of numerous storytellers, including Annie Spencer. Among the tales she shared with Boas was one about Raven and Mink, which would come to be of such importance to Boas that the story is worth recounting in full.[72]

The first part of the story relates an adventure of Raven and Mink, who met at the Nass River, made friends, and decided to wander the earth together. Because they had no means of getting across the ocean, they were forced to rely on their wits. Coming upon Whale, they mentioned their desire to cross the water. "Won't you take us across?" they asked. Whale opened his mouth and Raven and Mink stepped in. They had not been inside the Whale for long when Raven pinched Mink, who let out a scream. "Why does the little one cry?" Whale asked. When Raven replied that Mink was hungry, Whale generously offered a piece of himself. "I have lots of meat," he said. "Cut him off a piece." Raven and Mink soon finished their meal, whereupon Raven pinched Mink again. "What's happening now?" Whale asked. "The little one is hungry," Raven said. "Take as much as you want," Whale consented, "only don't cut my throat, because that would kill me"—whereupon Raven cut Whale's throat.[73]

In the second part of the story, the Whale went into convulsions and died. Raven and Mink ate heartily, but they could not get out of the Whale. After some time the corpse drifted ashore on a foreign beach, where a group of boys came to play. Raven called out as loud as he could, urging the boys to slice apart the Whale. The boys ran back to their village, found their friends, and together they cut into the corpse. When they saw its insides they marveled, for meat had been removed. At last the boys opened the Whale's stomach, and Raven and Mink sprang out. Several days later the villagers took the Whale ashore to cook the blubber. Then the insatiable Raven, always hungry, hatched a plan to eat some more. Transforming himself into a one-eyed crone, he relieved himself on the ground. "I'll go into the village," he instructed his feces. "You shout *hoo, hoo* in a moment!" Raven appeared at the edge of town in his woman's guise. "Enemies are coming!" he cried. "Enemies! They will kill us all!" Next the feces called out, "hoo, hoo," as if warriors were storming the camp. The villagers scrambled off, leaving no one but Raven, who gobbled up the rest of the Whale.[74]

The violent end of the Whale that had drifted ashore meant something different to those who owned the story than to those who claimed other stories as their own. To most of the people who told the story, its associations with theft, with the stranger coming upon an unsuspecting village intending to do the people harm, and its core Raven theme, the danger of an insatiable appetite, imposed a warning. Among the Tlingit, for example, the drifted ashore narrative—that is, the narrative of Raven and Whale, since the Tlingit did not include Mink—was often interpreted as a morality play. In Wrangell, Alaska, where the anthropologist John Swanton collected a version of the story, the chief of the Kaasx̱'agweidí Tlingit told him, "In our days when a person is making a living dishonestly by lying and stealing he is not told so directly, but this story is brought up to him and everyone knows what it means."[75]

But the phrase "in our days" implies that there may be other readings, from other mouths, in other days. In the absence of a record of Annie Spencer's intentions, it is difficult to know in our day precisely why she told the story to Boas. She may simply have wished to share an enjoyable tale that she knew well. But Boas had drifted ashore much in the manner of Raven, looking to gather the masks of Natives, feast upon their stories, collect and catalogue their thoughts. He had revealed a ravenous appetite, coming around, like Raven, for a second bite at the Whale. One interpretation of the story Annie Spencer told Boas is this: Do not take what is not yours. Do not use deceit to get what you want. Beneath her polite exterior, Spencer may have been making use of the story to deliver a message sharp as a knife.[76]

Yet there was more to the story for Annie Spencer, who in the process of relating the do-not-steal narrative offered Boas something more valuable. Boas did not realize it, but through Raven and Mink Spencer communicated some important facts, not about "the Kwakiutl" but about herself. She was telling the story of her family.

The Hunts claimed a portion of the Raven Cycle as their family history and had made use of that story as a meaning-making narrative that defined their position in their homeland and far beyond. Annie Spencer's mother—George Hunt's mother—was Mary Ebbets, or Anisa̱laga̱, the daughter of a Tlingit chief. Ebbets had grown up on and nearby Tongass Island, the southernmost part of Tlingit territory, as a descendant of wealthy traders dating back to Chief Shakes, who had personally greeted Captain Cook upon his arrival.[77] She belonged to the Raven clan, or G̱aanax̱.ádi, of the Taant'a Kwáan, or Sea Lion people, of the Tlingit. Within that clan, near the Nass River, her family belonged to the chiefly lineage of Yan Wulihashi Hít, or "Drifted Ashore House." This high-ranking and historically wealthy house had gained a key position in the coastal sea otter trade, forging alliances with Russian, English, and American traders and with the British and American militaries. Its chiefs had also forged alliances with Natives by marrying their daughters to the chiefs of nearby peoples, and to other chiefs not so nearby.[78]

Yan Wulihashi Hít owned the rights to the Raven crest. More important, those who belonged to the house owned the right to tell a single Raven story, the episode of Raven and Whale. Drifted Ashore House was not merely their name; it was their narrative. For the members of Yan Wulihashi Hít, especially the high-ranking women, the story of Drifted Ashore House served as a lifelong leitmotif, bringing meaning to the experience of traveling far from home, drifting upon the waters as Raven had done, to establish new lives and seek new opportunities among foreign peoples, where they accommodated their personalities to foreign ways.[79] Throughout their lives, the women of Drifted Ashore House would be members of other houses, but they always remained members of Yan Wulihashi Hít. As a collector and researcher among the Tlingit, George Thornton Emmons, observed in 1910, "A name once given survived the mere structure."[80]

These members of Drifted Ashore House embraced the narrative not as a cautionary tale but as an example of what may be gained through travel, creativity, and a willingness to form new bonds. They converted a warning into a heroic narrative. This was especially true of Mary Ebbets and her sisters, who spread the story of Drifted Ashore House to their neighbors, carrying the armature of their past—a name—where social structure could no longer protect them, and transmitting its meanings to other members of the Haida, Tsimshian, and Tlingit. Among the Haida, where one of Mary's female relations married among the Masset people, the Drifted Ashore House story spread, linking the Tlingit and Haida through the families of two chiefly clans, the Ebbets and the Edenshaws, which would grow into two of the dominant families in the perpetuation and expression of Northwest Coast tradition.[81]

Mary Ebbets, for her part, brought the story south after she met Robert Hunt, a trader for the Hudson's Bay Company at Fort Rupert, a new post where her family stopped to trade shortly after his arrival in 1850. They sealed their bond in Indigenous law, distributing blankets at a Nass River wedding that established trading relations between the company and the powerful chiefs of the southern Tlingit.[82] When Ebbets traveled south with her husband, the move represented a diplomatic mission for her family. It is now said that she arrived with slaves, attendants who were instructed to take care of her needs, perform labor for her, and ensure that she was treated properly in her new home. The attendants remained, living in the fort with the company consort, preparing her headdresses, rattles, bowls, utensils, and other noble accoutrements, all of which maintained her in comfort and symbolized her towering rank to anyone who might dare attempt a challenge.[83]

In Fort Rupert, while Robert Hunt ascended the company ladder, the story of Drifted Ashore House provided a homing identity for Ebbets as she fused the prerogatives of a Tlingit princess, an English trader and rent-holder, and a participant in the Kwakwa̱ka̱'wakw potlatch. The Drifted Ashore House story was not her sole link to her past. Ebbets brought her feasting dishes south.[84] She brought her abilities as a weaver of Chilkat blankets, heraldic dancing robes made of mountain goat wool, fashioned on great wooden looms according to a method that the Tlingit credited to the Tsimshian of which Ebbets proved to be a skilled practitioner.[85] She brought her gold-coin and silver bracelets, including some made by the noble carver Charles Edenshaw, which maintained a physical connection to her family in Haida Gwaii.[86] But above all she brought the power to tell a story.

For it is clear that, once relocated at Fort Rupert, Ebbets began to acquire knowledge of the local narratives. And when she related her stories to her growing children, she wove together, as a skilled weaver would do, the warp of her northern inheritance and the woof of her southern existence. The version of the Drifted Ashore House narrative told on Vancouver Island—the version related by Anisa̱laga—is the only one to bring together Raven and Mink.[87]

Over the next few decades Boas and several other researchers would continue to collect versions of the Raven Cycle. Boas would also continue to collect the Mink stories of Vancouver Island among the Kwakwa̱ka̱'wakw, Nuu-chah-nulth, and Comox. Boas ultimately collected thirteen versions of the Raven-Whale or Mink-Whale episode. Every one of these variants except for one deals with Raven or it deals with Mink. There is only one version that brings together Raven and Mink within the Whale: the one that Boas learned from Annie Spencer.[88]

Storytelling is always conscious. When Anisa̱laga shared her family story with her children, she meant to give them their family story, carrying the name of Drifted Ashore House beyond its familiar social structure. When she gave her children their story, she made a choice—a decision—to unite in one narrative the hero figures of the north and south, fashioning for her children a pan-Indigenous identity.

Every family has its origin story, the narrative that makes sense of its members as a unit, telling of where and to whom they belong, how they reside in the world. The Hunt family story, the narrative that Anisa̱laga spread to Fort Rupert, emphasized the identity of the wanderer. But by carrying on this story, and by reconstructing it, the Hunts also rewove their narrative, combining the traditions of two communities. By moving beyond their former Raven identity, the role of the wealth swallower, to embrace the identity of Mink, the seeker of adventageous marriages, the Hunts positioned themselves as double transformers who could create new realities by crossing a border.

Boas, in short, learned the Hunt family story even before he met George Hunt. Before he knew what the man looked like, he held in his hands—among thousands of other stories—the organizing narrative of his life. But because Boas attempted to categorize "Kwakiutl culture" rather than understand the stories of Kwakwa̱ka̱'wakw individuals, the personal meanings of the Drifted Ashore House story would remain obscure to him for decades. In fact, it wasn't until 1921, when Hunt was sixty-seven years old, that he at last explained to Boas the importance of the Drifted Ashore House narrative to his family, writing down his own account of Raven, Mink, and Whale.[89] Crucially, Hunt located the tale at the Nass River, in the homeland where his Tlingit family had risen to prominence. But in Hunt's version the story had altered further, so that Raven, the hero of the north, starred in a distinctly Mink-ish drama. Raven no longer wished to consume the Whale, for his focus had turned toward another form of wealth. "Hā ᵋhā ᵋhā ᵋhā," Raven sang in Hunt's version, telling the people to cut open the Whale. "I am He who Brought the Daylight in this world. . . . I come to marry your Doughter so as will Have Each other name all in one."[90] Which was the story of Hunt himself, who had married into the Kwakwa̱ka̱'wakw.

There was a third message within this tale, a message implicit in all the variants, which a Haida from Masset made explicit when he related his version to John Swanton. This version paid particular attention to Raven's speech to the Whale:

> He came out opposite to where a whale was blowing about. And when he stood opposite it, he said to the whale, "Hahai'ya, whale, swallow me." He said this to it because he wanted to eat it. And it swallowed him.[91]

Within the Drifted Ashore House story there consisted a riddle about influence. In order to swallow the Whale, the Raven first had to be swallowed by the Whale. In order to eat, he had first to be eaten. In this transformer tale, this Hunt family tale, it was the person who seemed at first to be consumed, to be collected, who ultimately emerged triumphant. The family could drift ashore, making marriages with faraway people, and seem to be lost and swallowed. But soon it became clear that Drifted Ashore House had made use of its host body to extend itself.

If the Hunts positioned themselves as Raven and as Mink, then Boas was the Whale. And when Annie Spencer shared with him the story of Drifted Ashore

House, she was not so much warning Boas about the ethics of his actions as making use of him to carry a Hunt family story to a new and more distant shore.

## TS'Ā'ĒQAUNAKULIS

*Ts'ā'ēqaunakulis,* "bringing all people together," was the Kwak'wala word for the World's Columbian Exposition of Chicago, where George Hunt arrived to meet Franz Boas in the summer of 1893. Not all people, however, were brought together that summer on the same terms or in the same way. The world's Indigenous people arrived as exhibits. On the Midway, a sideshow of "primitive" wonders in the shadow of the steel Ferris wheel, "dancing girls" and "pretty peasant[s]" of the world's invaded spaces—Ireland, Tunisia, the South Seas—induced President Grover Cleveland to slow his carriage and bow in recognition just as he considered whether to condone an American coup that had deposed the queen of Hawaii, hardly imagining that the dance troupe from Dahomey consisted of survivors weathering the similar incursions of France. The American Indian house—it was said to be Sitting Bull's last cabin—commemorated, by contrast, a mission accomplished. Reporters noted that it was riddled with bullet holes.[92]

These "living exhibits" were justified by the fair's organizers as a two-way object lesson. "Primitives" provided animate testimony to civilization's progress. They embodied the darkness of the recent human past—a lesson made literal by the electric lights bathing the fair in white, which often failed to work on the Midway.[93] But the "primitives" would also serve as carriers of civilization. Arriving unschooled, illiterate, they would be altered by the West, returning to their homelands to spread the news of law, order, and accomplishment. "What does it all mean, this stirring-up of the man from Senegambia?" asked the fair's driving force and chief architect, Daniel Hudson Burnham. He answered, "If you can shake the lowest barbarian—the brute man—loose from the most debasing fetishes of the human race, you have . . . 'washed the feet,' that the whole body may be clean."[94]

But the whitewashing did not proceed as he hoped. Burnham himself visited the Indigenous spaces of the Midway, there meeting up with the ethnologist Frank Hamilton Cushing, who for his part marveled over the Javanese theater and *sekaha,* a royal court orchestra whose virtuosic gamelan players would influence the impressionist chords of Claude Debussy, even as the percussionists of the Dahomeyan dance troupe impressed Haiti's delegate to the fair, none other than Frederick Douglass, the *New York Tribune* music critic Henry Krehbiel, and the songwriter Will Marion Cook, who soon infused popular culture with

African rhythms when he cowrote the first musical to star a black cast, the smash hit *In Dahomey.*[95] The Midway, wrote Stewart Culin, an ethnologist who spent a good deal of his time there conversing with a Bishareen family from Aswan, taking in the dances of the Tunisian village, and scrutinizing the efforts of a Fon goldsmith, was "a field for wide and important investigations."[96] But these investigations were carried out as much by the exhibits as by the anthropologists. In a moment of riotous intermixture, Native people from around the world discovered in their display the sources of a strategy of performance politics. Living beside the trained animals of Carl Hagenbeck's circus, Indigenous performers reached out from within the confines of prejudice to stake a claim to kinship in the human family.[97]

It was in the context of this cultural shift that George Hunt and Franz Boas began to work together in a way that neither expected. If anthropology, the science of man, had begun as a science of dehumanization, it now grew, in the hands of these two men, into a form of exchange, one that could lead to a rehumanization.

Like the performers of the Midway, Boas and Hunt came to the fair in the roles that were available to them. Playing a role was like buying a ticket: once you paid the price, you were inside the gates, free to take the ride. For Hunt, the price of civilization—the ticket price for his entry—involved collecting the material possessions of his people and staging their performance. In 1891, on a trip to the Northwest Coast, Boas had met with Hunt in Victoria and offered him the chance to bring Kwakw̱a̱ka̱'wakw performers to the fair. Had Hunt turned down the offer, he could not have come: this was the path available to him.[98]

Boas, too, was compelled by a power beyond his reach—in the form of his American mentor, Frederic Ward Putnam—to play a less than congenial role. Putnam hired Boas to introduce the public to the field of "Anthropology," a nascent term introduced at the fair to describe a burgeoning scientific discipline. Only Boas, who had trained with the eminent Rudolf Virchow in the measurement of racial features, could position anthropology at the cutting edge of international science. Putnam placed Boas in charge of his department's most scientific wing, physical anthropology, and Boas therefore spent his time at the fair designing exhibits on the typology of race.[99]

It was as if Hunt and Boas came to the fair wearing masks, one playing the role of a "primitive," the other a "racist" who would study him. But these would turn out to be transformation masks, affording both men an opportunity to cross a boundary. The transformations that were now possible, inside the gates, immediately became visible during Hunt's Kwakw̱a̱ka̱'wakw dance performances, given to crowds ranging from curious tourists to ethnologists and the Infanta Eulalia of Spain. Hunt, onstage, indulged in a Ravenesque reversal. As a photograph and newspaper articles reveal, he did not wear the blanket and cedar bark that he would have worn during such performances at home. His outfit was a pair of sturdy trousers, a button-down shirt framed by a generously cut sportcoat, and a high-crowned hat befitting a gentleman. These were, in fact, Hunt's ordinary clothes, now transformed, by being worn on stage, into the costume of a white man.[100]

The accepted history of Hunt at the world's fair is limited to the account of this trickster figure. It is based on newspaper reports of a man in costume, performing onstage.[101] There has been no account of Hunt the transformer, the man offstage. In the narrative terms of Kwak'wala that Hunt offered Boas, the secondhand history that we now possess is called *ᵋëtâlā*, or rumor, "telling again what the People are talking about." We have yet to discover the *q!āᵋyâlā*, the firsthand account, or "telling about what he have seen and what he Heard."[102] Because the newspapers did not cover such firsthand history, it has been harder to document.

But there is one way into the q!āᵋyâlā, the firsthand history. In Philadelphia, among a vast collection of manuscripts documenting the languages of Native North America from *A* ("Achumawi") to *Z* ("Zuni"), there sits a leather-bound notebook that records what Boas saw and heard in Chicago. Filled with Boas's scrawl, and with details of Hunt's life, the book records the origins of their lifelong collaboration. It documents the emergence of a new experiment in interactive thinking, which Boas registered in the scientific language of linguistics. By reading the texts Boas recorded in this book, we can piece together his conversations with Hunt.[103]

It had been ten years and more since Hunt, without knowing it, inspired Boas to travel to the Northwest Coast. Now Boas found himself face to face with the one man who could resolve the questions he had set out from Berlin to answer. Pulling out his sketches, Boas began to show Hunt and his dance troupe pictures of the masks in Berlin, the masks he had been unable to identify for the better part of the last decade. Hunt, who remembered the masks, offered Boas a series of object lessons: a primer on Indigenous life, drawing upon the collections he had made. As masks and stories came together again, the fair designed to be the crowning achievement of four hundred years of Western conquest transformed, in Hunt's hands, into an opportunity for Indigenous people to reverse the power flow.[104]

What we see in Boas's notebook is the emergence of a method. Boas would show Hunt a drawing of a mask. Hunt would explain to Boas its meaning and use. If one of the performers in the dance troupe owned a mask, he could tell the story connected with it and how it came to be the property of the person who wore it. Johnny Wanuk, for example, who possessed the right to play the role of Mink in Fort Rupert's winter ceremonies, explained to Boas the meaning of the headpiece that the Mink dancer wore, commemorating his victory over the Wolves, and sang the song of Mink.[105] Through this headpiece Boas learned the origin story of Fort Rupert's winter dances. Instead of categorizing the object according to a prearranged system, Boas elevated to primary importance the narrative communicated to him by Wanuk.

The conversation that emerged was between two ways of learning, the way of signs and the way of messages. As Boas jotted the stories down, translating unfamiliar words in collaboration with Hunt, he compiled terms and made use of each in a sentence. He saved the new vocabulary for index cards, assembling key words related to gifting and feasting, dances and ceremonies, rivalry and oratory, story cycles, origin heroes, and so on.[106] Word by word, name by name, Boas attempted to assemble the signs of a Native lifeworld. But even as he did so, the storytellers who lived within that lifeworld offered Boas something more personal and more particular. They explained their names, taking him from signs to messages.

When Boas learned the word for a chiefly giveaway, *maxwa,* he did so by learning Hunt's name in the Se'nL!Em *nemima,* or descent group, of the Fort Rupert Kwakiutl: Maxwalagalis, "Giving Potlatches Around the World."[107] When Boas learned the word *heiltsaqoala,* "speaking in the right way," he learned another of Hunt's names, Heiltsaqoalis, which means "the one who speaks in the right way."[108] These names communicated a message. The Kwakwa̱ka̱'wakw, Boas learned, considered the name of a person his "head." A chief, for instance, was thought of as the "name" of his people, who, in turn, formed the body of the chief. Every individual within the nemima also possessed a name of his own, which he wore on his head. Like a mask, the name transformed the person who wore it. Putting on a name meant changing identities: by assuming a new name, one suddenly took on the identity of the ancestor who first had borne it. By explaining this Kwakwa̱ka̱'wakw view of names, Hunt shared with Boas the conceptual basis of transformation: people inhabited new identities as they ascended the social structure, playing new roles within their communities.

At first, Boas could not grasp the idea that a name, like a mask, allows an individual to don a new identity, the concept at the core of the transformation narrative. But the dance troupe attempted to drive the concept home through an object lesson. When Boas showed one performer, GweyołEelas, a sketch of a post he had drawn at Newitti in 1886, GweyołEelas, who came from that town, explained to Boas that the carving depicted the story of a man who had obtained the mask of the Thunderbird. The descendant of this man was a Thunderbird dancer. He owned the unique privilege to take part in both major dance series of Newitti, the Nō'NLEm and the Ts'ē'ts'aēqa. The people of Newitti held these dances in opposition, barring participants in one from joining the other. But for the Thunderbird dancer, and only for the Thunderbird dancer, this rule did not apply. While wearing his Thunderbird mask, one man could transcend the division between dances. He could move between realms.[109]

Though GweyołElas carefully explained this lesson, emphasizing the point that the Thunderbird dancer could dance in both houses—not only belonging to two ceremonial communities but also switching between one and the other—Boas missed the message. In his notebook he wrote that the Thunderbird dancer could participate in both dances, but by the time he came to draft his book the story had escaped him. He therefore upheld the division between the Nō'NLEm and the Ts'ē'ts'aēqa, obscuring the crucial detail that one man was able to dance in both series if he wore the appropriate mask.[110] Eliminating the dynamic theme of transformation, of crossing realms by donning a mask, Boas printed a static generalization of a structure. Yet the concept of transformation emerged in many more discussions that subtly influenced Boas's thinking, not only about the Kwakwa̱ka̱'wakw but about the world. It especially emerged when the Kwakwa̱ka̱'wakw discussed the theme that was so visibly present at the fair, globalization.

Narratives of transformation—messages sent by people who had drifted ashore—were encoded in many of the masks Boas had seen in Berlin. Now he began to understand their meanings. One set of eight masks from Newitti depicted eight human faces. A chief at Newitti had told Boas that the masks represented Raven's slaves. By the time he sold them a year later to Bastian's museum, Boas thought at least two portrayed an "Eichkätzchen," or squirrel.[111] At Chicago a member of the dance troupe, likely Hunt, told Boas that the same masks belonged to the Tongass Tlingit, who had inherited the dance from their Tsimshian neighbors. The masks then came to Vancouver Island in an unexpected manner after some paddlers set off from Newitti, becoming lost in a storm and drifting off course. When the canoe came within sight of land, in foreign territory, the paddlers proved unexpectedly fortunate. The Tsimshian people welcomed them, took them in, gave them the Ādixanē'sElas dance (as the Tongass called it), and sent them home with songs.[112]

During the Ādixanē'sElas dance, a Tsimshian dance named by the Tongass and offered in friendship to the Newitti, eight masks appeared on the floor at the same time, worn by eight dancers who worked together.[113] Their song, sung in unison, provided a stirring testament to the idea of a global community, which must be reinvented through individual acts—a mask, a song, a welcoming—often including gifts from abroad:

I am the one making the clouds.
I am the one making red sky in the morning.

I come to you from the real good copper maker.
I come to you from the north end of our world.[114]

The song relates the binding power of the stranger who drifts ashore, bringing news, bringing hope, later returning with treasures. This narrative of the visitor from abroad arrived in Chicago with Hunt, who sang the song for Boas and lived its lyrics every day.

It is now possible to understand the fundamental nature of the exchange between Boas and the Kwakwa̱ka̱'wakw that began with Hunt's arrival at the fair. Boas offered the Kwakwa̱ka̱'wakw the language of signs he had invented, a method of stabilizing the mental productions of a way of life and thereby defining a group, "the Kwakiutl." The Kwakwa̱ka̱'wakw performers made use of this recording capacity to offer Boas messages: meanings embedded in individual experience and expressed through performance. These messages slipped the boundaries of definition that Boas sought to impose with his signs. A semiotic or structural study of the signs alone reimposes Boas's outlook, missing the dynamic process of exchange that was at the heart of his work and misreading the messages the Kwakwa̱ka̱'wakw transmitted—messages that the dance troupe used to *narrate,* to fill with meaning, their place in the world.

For Hunt, this mode of collaboration was familiar. Showing a mask, singing a song, giving a dance, then explaining how the narrative came into one's possession, was precisely what people did during the potlatch. For Boas, it was new. For a decade Boas had used masks as signs: clues to a vanishing past that he believed Indigenous people could not know.[115] Now, for the first time, he asked Indigenous people for their thoughts. He looked to masks not as signs of the history of a people to be categorized by an outsider but as messages to communicate from within. The masks, he learned, were sources of insight into Indigenous knowledge not because they defined a cultural type but because they expressed individual lives and standpoints.

As a result of his work with Hunt at the fair, Boas began to see anthropology not as a form of categorization but as a form of communication. Ideas would be like gifts, circulating between communities and, in the process, transforming them. Anthropology could become a kind of potlatch—a circulation of ideas as gifts—affording people from different places and traditions a chance to assert their identities, exchange views, and link lives. Boas's vision of mental exchange transcended the dehumanization of science to imagine the possibility of a ground-up global philosophy: an interactive process of communication that would draw on the local knowledge of all the peoples of the world to globalize the Western mind.

By modeling this potlatch process of narrative transformation, Hunt and Boas freed the object of study from the fixity of Enlightenment classification, yielding a global humanism in which each place and time, valuable in its own right, could yield insights for the here and now.[116] They recapitulated and crystallized a long human history of contact and exchange. Yet they also brought about the mode of existential exchange—the deep listening—that lies at the heart of all social transformation, yet which history so often fails to achieve. Through this self-questioning via another self, Hunt shifted Boas from dehumanization to rehumanization, the concrete process of thinking through the position of someone to whom one has been blind and drawing upon the experience of seeing that person for the first time to become more deeply aware of one's own being.[117]

The story of Drifted Ashore House is an archetype for this experience of modernity: two lonely souls on an empty beach forge a friendship, find a way forward, catch a ride, and make use of their guile to extract sustenance from a dangerous world—leaving wreckage in their wake. There is a bitter moral in the story, for who among us would fail to identify, as Lucy had done, with the awesome generosity of the Whale, spouting its wealth upon the world? But those who survive are the Ravens and Minks: animated, in motion, eyes open for the next chance, motivated to move, to learn, at times forced to twist the knife, reinventing themselves and others as they forge new narratives. The story of Drifted Ashore House is a story about what it means to *belong* to that state of brokenness and searching: to fashion from the whirl of events a place, a *home*, within the global world. To know that narrative from the inside is one way to be modern. It is to know what it means to survive a holocaust.

Colonialism does not come with a consolation prize for the people who lose their lands, resources, and 90 percent of their relatives.[118] The influence of Drifted Ashore House has not yet altered the balance of global power that its members know well. Yet the story of Drifted Ashore House offers a lesson about power. It shows us that power is rooted in perception: our sense of what is real and what is possible. Indigenous people have made use of their inheritance of stories to open a vista of narrative perception, a door that history may yet follow them through. If any outlook can be called primitive, in the sense of being parochial, it is the Western preference for concealment that has prevented us from attaining this wider field of vision. The Western mask creates the "conquered," including those who have never surrendered an inch of territory, by spreading the mythology that they have contributed nothing to modernity but their accommodation or resistance. But the Western habit of collecting betrays its erasure instinct. The archive shows us that colonized people were modern before the "moderns" were modern, and the mythology of modernity is built on the denial of their history. Yet it is still possible to learn from the world of ideas long denied us—if we work with the past the way Hunt worked with masks: one story at a time.

Over the course of nearly a decade on the Northwest Coast, Boas had moved from classification to communication, from quantifying and comparing things from the outside to observing and understanding them from within. Before he met Hunt, Boas may have been moving away from a study of culture as a bounded totality toward a study of culture as a dynamic process, made and remade through the interactions of individuals. Nonetheless, Boas always reserved for himself the responsibility to serve as the collector and categorizer of objective truth. In Boas's model it was always Boas, the observer, who possessed the supreme authority. In 1893 Boas realized that if he wanted to get the story right, he could not be the master of the narrative, collecting and categorizing another people's signs from the outside. Now he hoped to attain an inner understanding of Indigenous messages that would inevitably contradict the surface of signs on which he had relied, destabilizing his familiar boundaries of meaning by presenting singular, irreducible truths.

The change agent was George Hunt, who sent the masks that began the journey, interpreted them twelve years later, and now invited Boas back to the Northwest Coast—where Boas soon took part in Fort Rupert's winter dances, witnessing the concept of transformation in action. As this exchange deepened, Boas would set aside his claims to superiority and embrace the modest aim of coming to understand someone else through immersion in that person's point of view. How significant was this point of transition in Boas's career? It was so significant that in later years Boas would discredit the research he had published on the Kwakwa̱ka̱'wakw before 1893 because he believed he had collected it under faulty premises. The work he did after he met Hunt, the work he did with Hunt, Boas stood behind.[119] Yet Boas never realized his own role in the global process of diffusion and dissemination that he otherwise studied so closely. He never recognized Hunt's impact on his methods.

Even as he thought of himself as guiding and directing Hunt, Boas came to envision culture—another person's way of life—in the same way that the transformation philosophers of the Northwest Coast envisioned a mask. Culture was no mere veil, no shell or covering, but an ontological skin, a layer of perception that was part of one's being, influencing and interacting with one's lifeworld. By slipping into the skin of someone else's life, the anthropologist could undergo an alteration, much like a dancer donning a mask. Wearing the mask of another way of life, the anthropologist could come to know what seemed strange from within it—opening, like Raven, a "box of light" to see the world anew.[120]

According to Western thought, the masks were inanimate relics. According to Indigenous thought, they were animate, alive with power. Whose perspective turned out to be true? If Boas remained ignorant of the Indigenous influences upon him—a history enacted and encoded in the message-bearing masks that he so long persisted in seeing as signs—there were others who recognized 1893 as a moment of change. A year later, when Boas returned to the Northwest Coast, having been invited by Hunt to witness the winter ceremonies at Fort Rupert, he spent the afternoon of November 24 in the company of Johnny Wanuk, his friend from the fair, who played the role of Mink in the winter ceremonies.[121]

That day Wanuk hosted a feast, pressing wealth upon his guests, including Boas, who shared a platter with two Indians, proudly wearing a Native blanket. As Wanuk's retainers ladled eulachon oil upon the berries, they sang Wanuk's feasting song, a genre recognizable by the refrain *hamamai,* which stands for the act of eating. Now, at last, it was Mink's turn to be eaten—to give freely of his wealth—and therein lay his claim to power. For in this version of the song there were some lyrics that would appear to be new, noting Wanuk's most recent activities and alluding to his influence abroad:

> I went to the far end of our world.
> I am liked by all as far as the edge of our world.
> All try to imitate me, *hamamai.*[122]

## ANISA̱LAGA̱'S POLE (JULY 2013)

In Fort Rupert one summer, at the northern end of Vancouver Island, two canoes appeared on the horizon. A team of paddlers aged five to fifty stroked toward a shell-strewn beach, where a crowd of chiefs and elders, cloaked in Chilkat blankets, ermine frontlets, fleeces, jeans, sandals, sunglasses, sat silently on the rim of an embracing shore. A dozen mobile phones rose, ringers silenced, capturing the moment.[123]

On the beach were descendants of the Hunt family who had experienced the horror of residential schools. There were sons, elders now, whose mothers had made sandwiches for boys and girls who were not their own, hidden meals passed hand-to-hand to hungry children away from home, forbidden from speaking their language.[124] One of those sons was George David Hunt

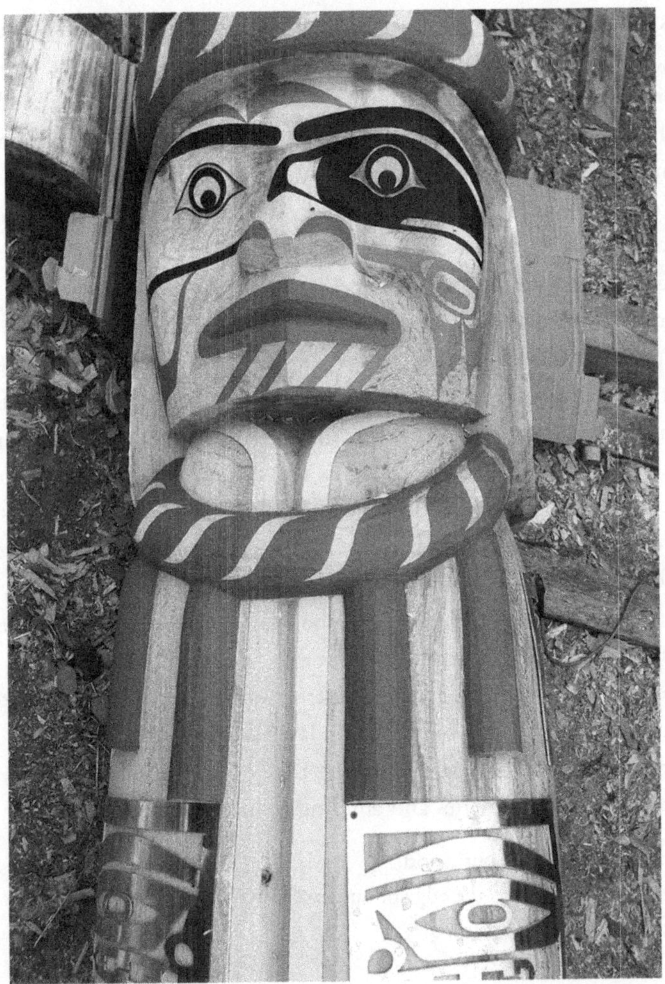

Anisa̱laga's pole outside the workshop of its carver and designer, Calvin Hunt. Anisa̱lag̱a wears the red cedar bark rings of the winter dance, symbols of survival. Below, two copper designs by Corrine Hunt, part of a Chilkat blanket Anisa̱lag̱a is wearing, represent the treasures from the north that she brought south for her descendants. Courtesy of Marina Dodis Photography.

Sr., the great-grandson of George Hunt. At the age of five, disciplined by a teacher because he did not understand English, young "Georgie Pie," as he is known, had stood up with what dignity he had, by rising from his seat, spreading his arms out, and releasing the wild call of an elite Hamatsa dancer, causing the other children to break into laughter.[125] Now eighty-one, he would host a feast the next winter, sponsoring the passage of dance rights to the next generation.[126]

In the canoe were more descendants of the Hunt family, including some who had known little Kwak'wala two decades earlier, yet who now, amid the public revival of Native tradition on the Northwest Coast, in which members of the Hunt family have played a central role for half a century, were struggling to learn their language and to teach the next generation the stories and songs—including some old lyrics and also many new ones, expressive of new ideas, new activities, new demands voiced by a living community conscious of its past.[127]

They had come to mark a moment: the unveiling of a pole for Anisa̲laga̱, the teller of the Drifted Ashore House story, who was buried without a stone upon her death nearly a century before.[128] On the pole were the Raven, the Sun (father of the Mink), and, joining them at the center, a carved likeness of Anisa̲laga̱ herself, now the hero of her own narrative. She was enfolded in her heritage, a Chilkat blanket made of copper representing the wealth she had brought into the world.[129] As the paddlers stroked in unison no song or call was heard, only the wind and the cut of blades striking water. But as the canoes reached the beach a drumbeat rose up and those waiting to greet them broke into "K̓wila'yalas Iwanukwdzi," a song of celebration reserved for great and exciting things.[130] It was a joyous yet contemplative occasion. In the slow motions of the participants, there was a consciousness of connection, depth. There was a feeling about home—what it meant, in this place, to be drifting ashore.

## Notes

The research for this essay was supported by a Ruth Landes Memorial Research Fund grant from the Reed Foundation. Earlier versions of the essay were shared in a research colloquium at the Berlin Program for Advanced German and European Studies at the Freie Universität Berlin and in the Andrew W. Mellon Foundation Seminar on Violence and Non-Violence of the Mahindra Humanities Center at Harvard University. I thank my friends and colleagues for their generous readings.

1. If we are to see global history in the round, we must begin by understanding all people as full-fledged historical actors rather than mental figments of or resisters to other people. Numerous fields of study impacted by postcolonialism, including subaltern studies, settler colonial studies, American studies, Latin American and Caribbean studies, transnational history, and imperial and colonial history, have mounted convincing critiques of Western representations of Indigenous peoples. Less successful have been attempts to think through the ideas of Indigenous people themselves, much less trace their broader influence. Keywords like *subaltern* and *the Other* and discussions of resistance, modernity, and empire frame Indigenous people in foreign terms, defining those who have faced colonization only

in relation to their colonizers. What I propose here is a turn toward the study of Indigenous ideas on their own terms—the first step toward a study of all ideas in global interaction.

2. Native people had many reasons for telling stories. Anthropology did not often top the list of priorities, nor was it the only outlet. Yet storytellers did recognize the power of Western visitors to publish information, thus helping societies keep their traditions alive. If we set aside this question of intent, recognizing that motives are always complex and often unknowable, we can focus better on what is knowable: actions. Anytime someone tells a story, that person communicates a message. The question is whether the speaker influences the listener.
3. On the use of oral narratives as historical transcripts, see James C. Scott, *Domination and the Arts of Resistance: Hidden Transcripts* (New Haven: Yale University Press, 1990), 18–19, 160–66.
4. Isaiah Lorado Wilner, "A Global Potlatch: Identifying the Indigenous Influence on Western Thought," *American Indian Culture and Research Journal* 37, no. 2 (2013): 101.
5. Franz Boas, *The Mind of Primitive Man* (New York: Macmillan, 1911), 1–17, 155–73, 251–78.
6. The word "myth" is problematic in that it labels Native stories as falsehoods while implying that Western stories ought to masquerade as truth. Boas perceived this difficulty as early as 1901, writing, "Mythology, theology, and philosophy are different terms for the same influences which shape the current of human thought." Franz Boas, "The Mind of Primitive Man," *Journal of American Folk-Lore* 14, no. 52 (1901): 7.
7. The narrative approach to the history of thought taken here begins with the principle that peoples' narratives encode their ideas. Such ideas are best witnessed not through their relationships to other ideas within a lattice designed by an outsider but through the lived history of the social participants who make, own, and carry on the stories. Individuals in the act of creation, relating to one another and to their surroundings, communicate the meanings of a society to those within and beyond the community. These meanings are revealed and remade in storytelling moments through which people reshape the burden of the past, fashioning new understandings.
8. On the agency in human–object networks, see Jane Bennett, *Vibrant Matter: A Political Ecology of Things* (Durham: Duke University Press, 2010), viii–x, chaps. 1–2, and Bruno Latour, *Reassembling the Social: An Introduction to Actor-Network Theory* (Oxford: Clarendon Press, 2005), 63–87.
9. For another view of the collection-recollection relation, see Giuliana Bruno, "Collection and Recollection: On Film Itineraries and Museum Walks," in *Camera Obscura, Camera Lucida: Essays in Honor of Annette Michelson,* ed. Richard Allen and Malcolm Turvey (Amsterdam: Amsterdam University Press, 2003), 231–60.
10. Object IV A 1025, Standort 55 Li, F: 2 Wand, Amerikanische Ethnologie Studiensammlung, Ethnologisches Museum, Staatliche Museen zu Berlin (hereafter EM); George Hunt, untitled corrections to "The Social Organization and the Secret Societies of the Kwakiutl Indians," 5613, ser. W1a.3, Kwakiutl Materials, pt. 5 [1 of 2], American Council of Learned Societies Committee on Native American Languages (hereafter ACLS), American Philosophical Society; Franz Boas, "The Social Organization and the Secret Societies of the Kwakiutl Indians," *Report of the United States National Museum for the Year Ending June 30, 1895* (Washington, DC: Government Printing Office, 1897), 628 fig. 195.

11. Andrew Zimmerman, *Anthropology and Antihumanism in Imperial Germany* (Chicago: University of Chicago Press, 2001), 189–97.
12. Franz Boas, "Material of the Kwakiutl Language. Summer 1893," 214, ser. W1a.9, Kwakiutl Texts, American Council of Learned Societies Committee on Native American Languages (ACLS).
13. George Hunt, "name of the masks on the Book and who there Belong to," 1938, ser. W1a.3, Kwakiutl Materials, pt. 3 [1 of 3], ACLS.
14. George Hunt, "the Begenning of the marreage Rules of all the Indians," *Manuscript in the Language of the Kwakiutl Indians of Vancouver Island, with Interlinear Translation* 14:2238–90, Columbia University Rare Book and Manuscript Library (hereafter CU); George Hunt, untitled corrections to "The Social Organization and the Secret Societies of the Kwakiutl Indians," 5613, ser. W1a.3, Kwakiutl Materials, pt. 6 [2 of 2], ACLS.
15. George Hunt, untitled corrections to "The Social Organization and the Secret Societies of the Kwakiutl Indians," 5613, ser. W1a.3, Kwakiutl Materials, pt. 5 [1 of 2], ACLS.
16. George Hunt, "name of the masks on the Book and who there Belong to," 1938, ser. W1a.3, Kwakiutl Materials, pt. 3 [1 of 3], ACLS.
17. Franz Boas, *The Kwakiutl of Vancouver Island,* Memoirs of the American Museum of Natural History, vol. 8, pt. 2 (New York: G. E. Stechert; Leiden: E. J. Brill, 1909), 307; Objects IV A 550, 555, 883, 892–93, 1286; Franz Boas, notes on the catalog card for Object IV A 892 [n.d.], Standort 55 Li, F: 2 Wand, Amerikanische Ethnologie Studiensammlung, EM.
18. See the *Worcester Sunday Telegram,* "Dogs Vivisected, Scientific Torture at Clark University," Mar. 9, 1890, 8, and "If He Be a Cur Cut Him Up," Mar. 16, 1890, 7, quoted in Lee D. Baker, *Anthropology and the Racial Politics of Culture* (Durham: Duke University Press, 2010), 141–46.
19. Shelley Baranowski, *Nazi Empire: German Colonialism and Imperialism from Bismarck to Hitler* (New York: Cambridge University Press, 2011), 24–28.
20. On Boas's "bloody comradeship," see Julia E. Liss, "Patterns of Strangeness: Franz Boas, Modernism, and the Origins of Anthropology," in *Prehistories of the Future: The Primitivist Project and the Culture of Modernism,* ed. Elazar Barkan and Ronald Bush (Stanford: Stanford University Press, 1995), 118–19, 122, 399 n. 15; see also A. L. Kroeber, "Franz Boas: The Man," in *Franz Boas: 1858–1942,* Memoir 61 of the American Anthropological Association, *American Anthropologist* 45, no. 3, pt. 2 (1943): 7–8.
21. Becker and Maass, Franz Boas Portrait, ca. 1920, F8.1.18, and "Franz Boas, at desk in Grantwood, N.J.," ca. 1942, F8.1.22, ser. 2, Graphics, Franz Boas Papers (hereafter BP), American Philosophical Society.
22. On this contradiction in German anthropology, see Glenn Penny, *Objects of Culture: Ethnography and Ethnographic Museums in Imperial Germany* (Chapel Hill: University of North Carolina Press, 2002), esp. 90–96, 100–101, 115–23; H. Glenn Penny and Matti Bunzl, "Introduction: Rethinking German Anthropology, Colonialism, and Race," in *Worldly Provincialism: German Anthropology in an Age of Empire,* ed. H. Glenn Penny and Matti Bunzl (Ann Arbor: University of Michigan Press, 2003), 14–19; Zimmerman, *Anthropology and Antihumanism in Imperial Germany,* 1–11, chaps. 2, 6, 7.
23. For the journals of Boas and his traveling companion, see Ludger Müller-Wille, ed., *Franz Boas Among the Inuit of Baffin Island, 1883–1884: Journals and Letters,* trans. William Barr (Toronto: University of Toronto Press, 1998), and Wilhelm Weike, *Bei Inuit und*

*Walfängern auf Baffin-Land (1883/1884): das arktische Tagebuch des Wilhelm Weike,* ed. Ludger Müller-Wille and Bernd Gieseking (Minden: Mindener Geschichtsverein, 2008).

24. See Rainer Baehre, "Early Anthropological Discourse on the Inuit and the Influence of Virchow on Boas," *Études/Inuit/Studies* 32, no. 2 (2008): 19–25.
25. Franz Boas, "The Study of Geography," *Science* 9, no. 210 (1887): 137–41.
26. Eric Ames, *Carl Hagenbeck's Empire of Entertainments* (Seattle: University of Washington Press, 2008), 45–46, 53, 56–57, 107–10. On Hagenbeck's enterprise as a forerunner of the theme park, see chap. 2, "The Living Habitat."
27. Douglas Cole, "Franz Boas and the Bella Coola in Berlin," *Northwest Anthropological Research Notes* 16, no. 2 (1982): 115–24.
28. Ibid. Aurel Krause's brother Arthur also regaled Boas with tales of his research in Alaska in 1883 and 1884. Franz Boas, *The Kwakiutl of Vancouver Island,* Memoirs of the American Museum of Natural History, vol. 5, pt. 2 (New York: G. E. Stechert; Leiden: E. J. Brill, 1909), 307.
29. Franz Boas, "Chinook Songs," *Journal of American Folk-Lore* 1, no. 3 (1888): 222.
30. Franz Boas, "Letter-Diary to Parents," Oct. 2, 1886, in *The Ethnography of Franz Boas: Letters and Diaries Written on the Northwest Coast from 1886 to 1931,* ed. Ronald P. Rohner (Chicago: University of Chicago Press, 1969), 30; Franz Boas, *Indian Myths and Legends from the North Pacific Coast,* ed. Randy Bouchard and Dorothy Kennedy (Vancouver: Talonbooks, 2002), 497.
31. Cole, "Franz Boas and the Bella Coola in Berlin," 118; see also Boas, *Indian Myths and Legends,* 497.
32. Franz Boas, "Captain Jacobsen's Bella Coola Indians," *Berliner Tageblatt,* Jan. 25, 1886, quoted in Cole, "Franz Boas and the Bella Coola in Berlin," 119.
33. Ibid., 120.
34. Ibid., 122; Bill Holm, *Northwest Coast Indian Art: An Analysis of Form* (1965; repr. Seattle: University of Washington Press, 1988), 37–41, 45–49, 61.
35. See, e.g., Allen Wardwell, *Tangible Visions: Northwest Coast Indian Shamanism and Its Art* (New York: Monacelli Press with The Corvus Press, 1996), esp. chap. 3.
36. Compare masks and masking in Oscar Wilde, "The Truth of Masks," in *Intentions* (New York: Brentano's, 1905), 219–63, and James H. Johnson, *Venice Incognito: Masks in the Serene Republic* (Berkeley: University of California Press, 2011), 47–140, with Robert Joseph, "Behind the Mask," in Peter Macnair, Robert Joseph, and Bruce Grenville, *Down from the Shimmering Sky: Masks of the Northwest Coast* (Vancouver: Douglas and McIntyre, 1998), 18–35, and Irving Goldman, *The Mouth of Heaven: An Introduction to Kwakiutl Religious Thought* (New York: John Wiley and Sons, 1975), 63, 124–25, 183–84.
37. Erwerbungen dürch Dr. Boas, Pars I B. 1, 1885–1890, Museum für Völkerkunde Acta, EM.
38. Boas, "The Mythology of the Bella Coola Indians," *Memoirs of the American Museum of Natural History,* vol. 2, pt. 2 (New York: American Museum of Natural History, 1898), 27.
39. Boas, *The Kwakiutl of Vancouver Island,* 307.
40. I refer to Gunter Demnig's *Stolpersteine,* stone-sized memorial plaques for victims of the Holocaust placed in the sidewalks before their former residences, which provide their names and dates of birth, deportment, and extermination. See Kirsten Harjes, "Stumbling Stones: Holocaust Memorials, National Identity, and Democratic Inclusion in Berlin," *German Politics and Society* 23, no. 1 (2005): 138–51.

41. Boas, *The Kwakiutl of Vancouver Island,* 307; Douglas Cole, *Franz Boas: The Early Years, 1858–1906* (Seattle: University of Washington Press, 1999), 100.
42. Boas, "Letter-Diary," Sept. 18–30, in Rohner, *The Ethnography of Franz Boas,* 19–29; Boas, *The Kwakiutl of Vancouver Island,* 307; Boas, "The Indians of British Columbia," *Popular Science Monthly* 32 (March 1888): 628.
43. Boas, "Letter-Diary," Oct. 5, 7, 10–12, 1886, in Rohner, *The Ethnography of Franz Boas,* 30, 32, 34, 38–39. On Newitti, see George M. Dawson, *Notes and Observations on the Kwakiool People of the Northern Part of Vancouver Island* (Montreal: Dawson Brothers, 1888), 8–10.
44. On the potlatch as a modern survival strategy, see Wilner, "A Global Potlatch," 87–114. On the potlatch as a political system, see also Helen Codere, *Fighting with Property: A Study of Kwakiutl Potlatching and Warfare, 1792–1930* (Seattle: University of Washington Press, 1950), and Philip Drucker and Robert F. Heizer, *To Make My Name Good: A Reexamination of the Southern Kwakiutl Potlatch* (Berkeley: University of California Press, 1967), 106.
45. Boas, "Letter-Diary," Oct. 7, 1886, in Rohner, ed., *The Ethnography of Franz Boas,* 34; Franz Boas, "The Indians of British Columbia," *Popular Science Monthly* 32 (March 1888): 631.
46. Boas, "Letter-Diary," Oct. 13, 1886, in Rohner, ed., *The Ethnography of Franz Boas,* 39.
47. Boas, "The Use of Masks and Head-Ornaments on the North-West Coast of America," offprint, *Internationales Archiv für Ethnographie* 3 (1890): 8.
48. Boas, "Letter-Diary," Oct. 13, 1886, in Rohner, ed., *The Ethnography of Franz Boas,* 40.
49. Boas, "Letter-Diary," Oct. 12, 1886, and Oct. 15, 1886, ibid., 38, 40.
50. Boas, "Letter-Diary," Oct. 19, 1886, ibid., 41–43.
51. Boas, "Letter-Diary," Oct. 19, 1886, ibid., 44.
52. Boas, "Letter-Diary," Oct. 23, 1886, ibid., 46.
53. Boas, "Letter-Diary," Oct. 26, 1886, ibid., 47.
54. See, e.g., Robert Bringhurst, *A Story as Sharp as a Knife: The Classical Haida Mythtellers and Their World* (Vancouver: Douglas and McIntyre, 1999), and Colin Browne, *Entering Time: The Fungus Man Platters of Charles Edenshaw* (Vancouver: Talonbooks, 2016).
55. Franz Boas, "The Indians of British Columbia," *Transactions of the Royal Society of Canada* 6, sec. 2 (1889): 53.
56. For Raven's many names, see Boas, "Material of the Kwakiutl Language. Summer 1893," 133, ser. W1a.9, Kwakiutl Texts, ACLS; Boas, *Indian Myths and Legends,* 444; Franz Boas, *Tsimshian Mythology,* Thirty-First Annual Report of the Bureau of American Ethnology to the Secretary of the Smithsonian Institution, 1909–1910 (Washington, DC: Government Printing Office, 1916), 584.
57. Boas, "The Indians of British Columbia," *Popular Science Monthly,* 53. For Boas's masterful treatment of the Raven tales as a "well-organized cycle" (582), see Boas, *Tsimshian Mythology,* 567–84, 618–722. Had Raven succeeded in carving people out of wood, the story goes, then human beings would have been able to live forever. Because he could not do so, we are all destined to face death. Ibid., 663–64.
58. Melville Jacobs, *The Content and Style of an Oral Literature: Clackamas Chinook Myths and Tales* (Chicago: University of Chicago Press, 1959), 1; Melville Jacobs, "Unstructured Stimuli and Literary Creativity," draft manuscript, "Christmas Paper," American Anthropological Association, Detroit, Michigan, Dec. 3, 1954, Box 20, Folder 15, Melville Jacobs Collection, University of Washington Special Collections; Dell Hymes, "Folklore's Nature and the Sun's Myth," *Journal of American Folklore* 88, no. 350 (1975): 352–53, 359.

59. See Lewis Hyde, *Trickster Makes This World: Mischief, Myth, and Art* (New York: Farrar, Straus and Giroux, 1998), 6–10, 13–14, 20–27, 42–47, 51–54, 62–63, 70–79, 89–91, 189, 268, 283, 288, 293–300, 311–12; Gerald Vizenor, "Trickster Discourse," *Wicazo Sa Review* 5, no. 1 (1989): 2–7; and Barbara Babcock-Abrahams, "'A Tolerated Margin of Mess': The Trickster and His Tales Reconsidered," *Journal of the Folklore Institute* 11, no. 3 (1975): 147–86.
60. Franz Boas, *The Religion of the Kwakiutl Indians*, Columbia University Contributions to Anthropology, vol. 10 (New York: Columbia University Press, 1930), 2:81; George Hunt, "live all the History or nox̣ᵋnē'mēs at qalogwes," in *Manuscript in the Language of the Kwakiutl Indians of Vancouver Island*, 11:3398, CU. Many of these narrative sites are mapped in Franz Boas, *Geographical Place Names of the Kwakiutl Indians*, Columbia University Contributions to Anthropology, vol. 20 (New York: Columbia University Press, 1934). On narrative maps of the world, "place-worlds," and "place-making," see Keith H. Basso, *Wisdom Sits in Places: Landscape and Language Among the Western Apache* (Albuquerque: University of New Mexico Press, 1996), 5–8, 32–33, 86–92.
61. Franz Boas, "Herr Dr. F. Boas: Über seine Reisen in Britisch-Columbien," *Verhandlungen der Gesellschaft für Erdkunde zu Berlin* 16 (1889): 257–68.
62. Boas, "Letter-Diary," Sept. 30, 1886, in Rohner, ed., *The Ethnography of Franz Boas*, 29; Franz Boas, "Einige Mythen der Tlingit," *Zeitschrift der Gesellschaft für Erdkunde zu Berlin* 23 (1888): 159–72; Boas, *Indian Myths and Legends*, 613–23; Boas, *Tsimshian Mythology*, 620.
63. Boas, *Tsimshian Mythology*, 584–620.
64. Ibid., 640–41, 876–77.
65. Boas, *Indian Myths and Legends*, 260–61, 353–57, 379–82, 454–55.
66. Boas, untitled writings on the winter ceremonies of the Kwakiutl of Fort Rupert, MSS 100, 106, p. 7, ser. 14, Kwakiutl Folklore and Ethnography, ACLS; George Hunt to Franz Boas, [ca. 1918], ser. W1a.3, Kwakiutl Materials, pt. 1 [2 of 2], ACLS; Franz Boas, [Bolton Landing, NY], to George Hunt, Beaver Harbor, BC, June 27, 1918, and George Hunt, Beaver Harbor, BC, to Franz Boas, Bolton Landing, NY, Aug. 5, 1918, ser. 1, Correspondence, BP.
67. Rights could also move and, as heirs died, did move through marriage. This adds resonance to Mink's comical attempts to marry women such as Kelp and Diorite-Woman, who prove painfully wrong for him. See Franz Boas and George Hunt, *Kwakiutl Texts—Second Series*, Memoirs of the American Museum of Natural History, vol. 10, pt. 1 (New York: G. E. Stechert; Leiden: E. J. Brill, 1908), 117–18, 122–23.
68. Annie Spencer's lively Kwakiutl version exemplifies Fort Rupert's comic touch. It ends on an "up note" as Mink, having lost consciousness during the holocaust he brought about, wakes up in the sea to remark laconically, "Oh, I believe I have been asleep for a long time." Boas, *Indian Myths and Legends*, 353–54.
69. Boas, "The Indians of British Columbia," *Transactions of the Royal Society of Canada*, 54.
70. Boas and Hunt, *Kwakiutl Texts—Second Series*, 103–5; Boas, "The Social Organization and the Secret Societies of the Kwakiutl Indians," 538–39; Boas, *The Religion of the Kwakiutl Indians*, 2:58–59, 62, 64–65, 74–77.
71. Boas, "Material of the Kwakiutl Language. Summer 1893," 49, 59–65, ser. W1a.9, Kwakiutl Texts, ACLS; Boas, "The Social Organization and the Secret Societies of the Kwakiutl Indians," 478–79, 538–39; Boas and Hunt, *Kwakiutl Texts*, 108–10; Boas, *The Religion of the Kwakiutl Indians*, 2:65, 80–82, 86–87, 90–92.

72. Annie Spencer's version appears in Boas, *Indian Myths and Legends,* 379–80.
73. Ibid., 379–80. This is Annie Spencer's version.
74. Ibid., 380. For the children, see John Swanton, *Tlingit Myths and Texts,* Bureau of American Ethnology Bulletin 39 (Washington, DC: Government Printing Office, 1909), 13.
75. Swanton, *Tlingit Myths and Texts,* 92. For the identification of the speaker, Katishan, see Swanton's introduction.
76. See Donald N. Abbott, ed., *The World Is as Sharp as a Knife: An Anthology in Honour of Wilson Duff* (Victoria: British Columbia Provincial Museum, 1981), esp. 209–24.
77. Elizabeth Wilson, interview with Marius Barbeau, Fort Rupert, 1947, B-F-270.14, Northwest Coast Files, Collection Marius Barbeau, Canadian Museum of History, Gatineau, Quebec (hereafter CMB); Marius Barbeau, *Totem Poles* (Ottawa: King's Printer, 1950), 2:651, 654; Franz Boas, "The Girl Who Was Taken Away by a Bear," ser. 14, Kwakiutl Folklore and Ethnography, ACLS.
78. On the Tlingit Drifted Ashore House in Alaska, see R. L. Olson, *Social Structure and Social Life of the Tlingit in Alaska,* Anthropological Records 26 (Berkeley: University of California Press, 1967), 10–11, 56–57, 87, and Judith Berman, "Raven and Sunbeam, Pencil and Paper: George Hunt of Fort Rupert, British Columbia," unpublished manuscript on file with the author, 5–9.
79. On the Drifted Ashore House narrative and its Raven crest in British Columbia, see George Hunt, "Raven or yäł story of the łen'get or gedᴇ'xᴇᵋnēts[.] the Painting on the copper," [ca. June 18, 1922], ser. w1a.3, Kwakiutl Materials, pt. 6 [1 of 2], ACLS; Tony Hunt, interview with the author, Victoria, BC, Feb. 4, 2014; Mervyn Child, interview with the author, Fort Rupert, BC, Jan. 25, 2014; Elizabeth Wilson, interview with Marius Barbeau, Fort Rupert, 1947, B-F–270.14, Northwest Coast Files, CMB; Barbeau, *Totem Poles,* 2:651, 654–57, 660.
80. George Thornton Emmons, *The Tlingit Indians,* ed. Frederica de Laguna, Anthropological Papers of the American Museum of Natural History 70 (Seattle: University of Washington Press, 1991), 66.
81. Beau Dick, interview with the author, Fort Rupert, BC, Jan. 25, 2014; George Alfred, interview with the author, Alert Bay, BC, Jan. 29, 2014. In Hunt's rendition of this narrative the connector was a male: Raven himself, who "took off his Raven suit" after jumping out of the Whale, revealing himself in human form as Sāʟän, or Great Mountain, the chief of the G̱aanax̱.ádi. He married the daughter of chief Edᴇnsu of Yaku. Sāʟän's son Kāᵋo, half Haida on his mother's side, returned to Tongass to assume the chieftaincy of the G̱aanax̱.ádi, carrying the Edᴇnsu name. "This is why the gᴇdᴇ'xāᵋnets People and the yäkwen Haida tribes got mixed togather," Hunt concluded his account, "and they can use Each other names." George Hunt, "Raven or yäł story of the łen'get or gedᴇ'xᴇᵋnēts[.] the Painting on the copper," [ca. June 18, 1922], ser. w1a.3, Kwakiutl Materials, pt. 6 [1 of 2], ACLS.
82. Elizabeth Wilson, interview with Marius Barbeau, Fort Rupert, 1947, B-F–270.14, Northwest Coast Files, CMB; Barbeau, *Totem Poles,* 2:651; Mona Jean Horn, "The Kwakiutl Version of the Chilkat Blanket on Vancouver Island, British Columbia" (MA thesis, Oregon State University, 1972), 16, 18.
83. Tony Hunt, interview with the author, Victoria, BC, Feb. 4, 2014. In family memory the attendants are described as slaves, which they must have been in Alaska. On

Hudson's Bay Company ground they would have continued the same work, perhaps euphemistically redefined as servants or laborers working off a period of indenture.

84. For some of these dishes, featuring Bear, Sea Lion, Killer Whale, and Wolf, which David Hunt inherited at a potlatch in 1894, see Boas, "The Social Organization and the Secret Societies of the Kwakiutl Indians," 552–53.

85. Anisa̱lag̱a is thought to have made at least thirteen Chilkat blankets still in existence, including one for each of her children. Horn, "The Kwakiutl Version of the Chilkat Blanket," 3, 22–24, 34–60, 85–86; Susan C. Douglass, "Kwakiutl Chilkat Blankets" (MA thesis, University of Victoria, 1972); Donna Cranmer, interview with the author, Alert Bay, BC, Jan. 28, 2014; Trevor Isaac, interview with the author, Alert Bay, BC, Jan. 27, 2014; Jack Knox, "Lost for Generations, a Blanket Returns Home," *Times Colonist* [Victoria, BC], Apr. 12, 2014, A3; Barbeau, *Totem Poles*, 2:654.

86. Leonora McMahon, interview with the author, Fort Rupert, BC, July 5, 2013, and correspondence with the author, June 24, 2016. "All I know is she bought a lot of jewelry from him," says her great-granddaughter McMahon, who inherited several of Anisa̱laga's Edenshaw bracelets, "and I heard the elders say, 'Oh yes, they were related.'"

87. The Raven and Whale pole at Klawak park, featuring Tlingit carvings from Tuxekan, depicted Raven and Whale but not Mink. The pole at Tongass erected in memory of "Ebbits, Head Chief of Tongass, January 11, 1892," likewise did not feature Mink. Viola E. Garfield and Linn A. Forrest, *The Wolf and the Raven: Totem Poles of Southeastern Alaska* (Seattle: University of Washington Press, 1948; rev. ed. 1961), 50, 51 fig. 24, 102 figs. 41–42, 103, 105. However, Mink appears on the Hunt family pole in Seattle. The Seattle Pole, author's notes and photographs, Pioneer Square, Seattle, Mar. 1, 2013. And George Hunt specifically cited Mink's role in the voyage inside the Whale "after the Raven stold the sun Box" in a letter to Boas describing his family histories. George Hunt, Beaver Harbor, BC, to Franz Boas, New York, Dec. 4, 1921, ser. 1, Correspondence, BP.

88. For Boas's index of the thirteen versions that he knew, see Boas, *Tsimshian Mythology*, 687–89. The only accounts containing the entire two-part narrative—the journey overseas followed by Raven's theft of the Whale from the village—are Haida, Tlingit, and Kwakwa̱ka̱'wakw, the three groups linked by the marriages of Drifted Ashore House. For the versions collected by John Swanton, see *Haida Texts—Masset Dialect,* Memoir of the American Museum of Natural History, vol. 10, pt. 2 (New York: G. E. Stechert; Leiden: E. J. Brill, 1908), 294; John Swanton, *Haida Texts and Myths,* Skidegate Dialect, Bureau of American Ethnology Bulletin 29 (Washington, DC: Government Printing Office, 1905), 131; Swanton, *Tlingit Myths and Texts,* 12, 91–92.

89. George Hunt, "Raven or yätl story of the tlen'get or gedᴇ'xᴇ$^{\varepsilon}$nēts[.] The Painting on the copper," [ca. June 18, 1922], ser. W1a.3, Kwakiutl Materials, pt. 6 [1 of 2], ACLS.

90. Ibid., 4.

91. Swanton, *Haida Texts—Masset Dialect,* 294.

92. "Viewing the Parade," *Chicago Daily Tribune,* May 2, 1893, 4; Gertrude M. Scott, "Village Performance: Villages at the Chicago World's Columbian Exposition, 1893 (PhD diss., New York University, June 1991), 289–300, 340; "Incidents of the Dahomey War," *Chicago Daily Tribune,* Dec. 18, 1892, 41; "Sitting Bull's Cabin Open," *Chicago Daily Tribune,* July 9, 1893, 2.

93. "Lights on Midway," *Chicago Daily Tribune,* May 16, 1893, 2; "Darkness Reigns in the Palaces," *Chicago Daily Tribune,* May 28, 1893, 3.

94. Daniel Hudson Burnham, "Uses of Expositions" (1895), lecture to the Chicago Literary Club, Daniel Hudson Burnham Papers, Ryerson and Burnham Archives, Art Institute of Chicago.
95. Frank Hamilton Cushing, Aug. 10–12, 1893, in "Journal, Aug. 3–12, 1893," Frank Hamilton Cushing Journals, MS 1997-28, National Anthropological Archives (NAA), Smithsonian Institution; David R. Wilcox, "Anthropology in a Changing America: Interpreting the Chicago 'Triumph' of Frank Hamilton Cushing," in *Coming of Age in Chicago: The 1893 World's Fair and the Coalescence of American Anthropology,* ed. Curtis M. Hinsley and David R. Wilcox (Lincoln: University of Nebraska Press, 2016), 153–211; Sue Carter-De Vale, "The Gamelan," *Field Museum of Natural History Bulletin* 49, no. 1 (1978): 3–7; Vincent McDermott, "Gamelans and New Music," *Musical Quarterly* 72, no. 1 (1986): 16 n. 2; Scott, "Village Performance," 302–3; Christopher Robert Reed, *All the World Is Here! The Black Presence at White City* (Bloomington: Indiana University Press, 2000), 135, 159–60, 164, 168, 223 n. 51.
96. Johnson, *A History of the World's Columbian Exposition,* 2:335–37.
97. See, e.g., Mae Ngai, "Transnationalism and the Transformation of the 'Other': Response to the Presidential Address," *American Quarterly* 57, no. 1 (2005): 61–64; Scott, "Village Performance," 253–54, 267, 302, 308–9, 327, 331, 340–45, 347–54, 357, 360–69; Melissa Rinehart, "'To Hell with the Wigs!' Native American Representation and Resistance at the World's Columbian Exposition," *American Indian Quarterly* 36, no. 4 (2012): 403–42; Rossiter Johnson, *A History of the World's Columbian Exposition,* vol. 1, *Narrative* (New York: D. Appleton, 1897), 79, and vol. 2, *Departments* (New York: D. Appleton, 1897), 335–41, 444.
98. Rohner, *The Ethnography of Franz Boas,* 82; Ira Jacknis, "George Hunt, Collector of Indian Specimens," in *Chiefly Feasts: The Enduring Kwakiutl Potlatch,* ed. Aldona Jonaitis (Seattle: University of Washington Press; New York: American Museum of Natural History, 1991), 181–83.
99. See the *Official Catalogue of Exhibits and Descriptive Catalogue, World's Columbian Exposition Department M., Anthropological Building, Midway Plaisance, and Isolated Exhibits,* rev. ed. (Chicago: W. B. Conkey, 1893), 40–46, Frederic Ward Putnam Papers, Peabody Museum Archives, Harvard University (hereafter PM); Frederic Ward Putnam to George R. Davis, June 4, 1892, Sept. 9, 1892, Oct. 26, 1892, and Dec. 10, 1892, World's Columbian Exposition Correspondence: D, Box 32, Frederic Ward Putnam Papers, Harvard University Archives; Lee. D. Baker, *From Savage to Negro: Anthropology and the Construction of Race* (Berkeley: University of California Press, 1998), 49–50; Franz Boas, "Report on the Section of Physical Anthropology," 159–93, World's Columbian Exposition Reports, Peabody Museum Director Records, PM.
100. "Alaskan Indians" [*sic*], Midway People [*sic*], World's Columbian Exposition, Prints and Photographs Collection, Chicago History Museum. See also "Fun for the Infanta," *Chicago Daily Tribune,* June 13, 1893, 1; "Ghost Dance Beaten," *Sunday Inter Ocean,* May 7, 1893, 6.
101. "Horrible Scene at the Fair," *London Sunday Times,* Aug. 20, 1893, 3; "A Brutal Exhibition," *New York Times,* Aug. 19, 1893, 5; "Race Types at the World's Fair," *Chicago Daily Tribune,* July 30, 1893, 25. See also Paige Raibmon, *Authentic Indians: Episodes of Encounter from the Late-Nineteenth-Century Northwest Coast* (Durham: Duke University Press, 2006), 15–16, 50–73.

102. George Hunt, "this is to show the Defferent way of talking," MS 4624, ser. W1a.3, Kwakiutl materials, pt. 3 [3 of 3], ACLS.
103. Franz Boas, "Material of the Kwakiutl Language. Summer 1893," ser. W1a.9, Kwakiutl Texts, ACLS.
104. Ibid., 3, 30, 31, 41, 44–50, 91, 132, 135–36, 193–94.
105. Ibid., 49, 59–72. See also Boas, "The Social Organization and the Secret Societies of the Kwakiutl Indians," 478–79, 725–28.
106. Boas, "Material of the Kwakiutl Language. Summer 1893," 3, 28–29, 47, 55–56, 133, 186–91, 200, 204, 207, ser. W1a.9, Kwakiutl Texts, ACLS.
107. Ibid., 187–89.
108. Ibid., 3, 212.
109. Ibid., 195–97; see also Edward S. Curtis, *The North American Indian,* vol. 10, *The Kwakiutl* (Norwood, MA: Plimpton Press, 1915), 244. I have used Hunt's spelling. Boas spelled the man's name "GoayōLElas."
110. Boas, "The Social Organization and the Secret Societies of the Kwakiutl Indians," 416, 685–86. The theme of transformation ("going from one house to the other") appears in an appendix providing a transcript of the Kwak'wala story but not in Boas's ethnological gloss.
111. Objects IV A 6882–89, Standort 55 Li, F: 2 Wand, Amerikanische Ethnologie Studiensammlung, EM; Objects IV A 6884–85, IV A 2 Abschrift, Amerika Naturvölker Abschrift, EM; Franz Boas, "Material of the Kwakiutl Language. Summer 1893," 45, ser. W1a.9, Kwakiutl Texts, ACLS.
112. Boas, "Material of the Kwakiutl Language. Summer 1893," 45–46, ser. W1a.9, Kwakiutl Texts, ACLS; Franz Boas, notes on the catalog card for Object IV A 6882 [n.d.], Standort 55 Li, F: 2 Wand, Amerikanische Ethnologie Studiensammlung, EM.
113. Boas, "The Social Organization and the Secret Societies of the Kwakiutl Indians," 631.
114. Boas, "Material of the Kwakiutl Language. Summer 1893," 45, ser. W1a.9, Kwakiutl Texts, ACLS. See also Boas, "The Social Organization and the Secret Societies of the Kwakiutl Indians," 631, 730. I have used the unpublished translation in Boas's notebook. For the choreography of this dance, see George Hunt, "name of the masks on the Book and who there Belong to," 1937, ser. W1a.3, Kwakiutl Materials, pt. 3 [1 of 3], ACLS.
115. See, for example, Franz Boas, "The Aims of Ethnology," in *Race, Language and Culture,* 629–32, "The Indians of British Columbia," *Transactions of the Royal Society of Canada,* 47–57, "On Certain Songs and Dances of the Kwakiutl of British Columbia," *Journal of American Folk-Lore* 1, no. 1 (1888): 49–64, and "The Development of the Culture of Northwest America," *Science* 12, no. 299 (1888): 194–96.
116. Some parallel approaches to potlatch anthropology may be seen in forms of transcultural enlightenment ranging from Clifford Geertz's symbolic anthropology to Lawrence W. Levine's cultural history, Edward Said's postcolonial humanism, Jürgen Habermas's theory of communicative action, and Charles Taylor's critique of liberal modernity.
117. For Boas's translation of transformation dialogue, see Franz Boas, "Some Traits of Primitive Culture," *Journal of American Folk-Lore* 17, no. 67 (1904): 243–54, and "Psychological Problems in Anthropology," *American Journal of Psychology* 21, no. 3 (1910): 371–84.

118. This is the issue at the core of the so-called politics of recognition—including land claims negotiations, reconciliation efforts, and Native campaigns for sovereignty—which exposes a conflict between the goal of consolation and the goal of changing the political, economic, and environmental relationships instituted by colonialism.
119. See David R. Michaelson, "From Ethnography to Ethnology: A Study of the Conflict of Interpretations of the Southern Kwakiutl Potlatch" (PhD diss., New School for Social Research, Nov. 1979), 19–38.
120. On the parallels between Indigenous and Western romantic concepts of enlightenment, see James Tully, "Rediscovering the World of Franz Boas: Anthropology, Equality / Diversity, and World Peace," this volume.
121. Boas, "The Social Organization and the Secret Societies of the Kwakiutl Indians," 585–88.
122. Ibid., 588.
123. Author's notes, Fort Rupert, BC, July 6, 2013.
124. Alfred "Hutch" Hunt, interview with the author, Fort Rupert, BC, Jan. 26, 2014.
125. Gloria Roze, interview with the author, Fort Rupert, BC, July 6, 2013; Mildred Child, telephone interview with the author, Sept. 4, 2017.
126. At this memorial feast for the late John Hunt-Humchitt, Pat Hunt displayed his Thunderbird dance in honor of his departed relative, whose Nunłtsistalał dance will later be given to a new baby in the family, Eli. Author's notes, Jan. 25, 2014, and author's correspondence with Ema Child Sheena, Mar. 12, 2016.
127. On the Hunt family's global legacy, see Ross Hunt, "Recognizing and Honoring Relatives: The Hunt Family's Trip to West Germany to Attend the Bundesgarten Show," *Anthropology News* 48, no. 2 (2007): 20–21. The transmission of Kwakwa̱ka̱'wakw culture never ceased, but we may date the resurgence of the public potlatch to Mungo Martin's legal, state-sanctioned potlatch in 1953. Phil Nuytten, *The Totem Carvers: Charlie James, Ellen Neel, and Mungo Martin* (Vancouver: Panorama, 1982), 94–100.
128. Scott Sedgemore, interview with the author, Fort Rupert, BC, July 6, 2013.
129. In the words of the pole's carver and designer, Calvin Hunt, Anisa̱laga is depicted "bringing her treasures to us." Calvin Hunt, remarks upon the unveiling of the Anisa̱laga pole, Fort Rupert, BC, July 6, 2013.
130. This *'Walasila'yu*, or "song for great occasions," belonged to Iwanukwdzi, an ancestor of Hunt's grandson Thomas Hunt, a chief of the Fort Rupert Kwakiutl who once sang it to celebrate the bestowal of a dowry upon a nephew. This was a *walas* (big or great) occasion because culture reproduces itself through marriage, and the stories in that dowry transmitted to its future inheritors a Native family history. Alan Hunt, correspondence with the author, Aug. 26, 2017; William Wasden Jr., correspondence with the author, Aug. 28, 2017; Tom Child, correspondence with the author, Aug. 30, 2017. By singing this song at this time, Anisa̱laga's children sent a message about the survival of their culture.

# Chapter 2 Franz Boas in Africana Philosophy

*Lewis R. Gordon*

To appreciate the importance of Franz Uri Boas in Africana philosophy requires an introduction to that area of thought. "Africana philosophy" is a term for African diasporic philosophy.[1] It is a contemporary area of philosophy born from Euromodern philosophy but ironically transcending its progenitor. To understand this, one must first realize that even the term "African" is not African.[2] Thus, even "Africanness" is actually imposed on the people who became known as "African."[3] There was no reason for the people who were kidnapped and brought to the shores of distant lands in North America, the Caribbean, South America, Western Asia, and even East Asia to consider themselves anything other than the variety of ethnic groups to whom they belonged and whose names were the mark of their upbringing, such as Asante, Bamileke, Bamum, Fante, Igbo, Tallensi, Xhosa, Yoruba, Zulu, etc. Yet the imposition of "African" has become, as we know, metonymic, in which case its referents exceed its emergence. Thus Africans paradoxically preceded their birth. In similar kind, the ideas and people who became part of Africana philosophy preceded even the West for the obvious reason of origins: the African continent is the birthplace of our species.

The African diaspora, people from the continent of Africa spread, mostly by force, across the globe, thus carry along with them the mark of what psychoanalysts call melancholia, that is, the condition of loss or bereavement without having the previous condition by which belonging could have been secured.[4] This is because the correlative conditions with Africanness, namely, blackness and the pejoratives "Negroeness" and "niggerness," were born from the impositions of a world that rejected what it created. Blacks, and especially "negroes" and "niggers," are indigenous to the world to which they do not belong; they are, in a word, "bastards" of Euromodernity.[5]

The existence of Africana peoples poses a variety of philosophical problems. First is the consideration of "existence."[6] To exist is to appear. From *ex sistere*, it means to stand out. The problem, however, is that as not belonging, the appearance of such people would be illicit. It would mean the appearance of that which should not appear, to stand out as illegitimate, which means the standing out would be something wrong. In effect, then, the legitimacy of the system that produces illicit appearance requires an erasure of such emergence, a suppression of being, *non*-existence, or what Frantz Fanon has called relegation to "the zone of non-being."[7]

Nonexistence is a consequence of a philosophical anthropology that posited Africans, black people, "Negroes," and "niggers," although not identical, to categories of property, subhumanity, or below-human status. They are not identical categories because there are Africans who are not black, not "Negroes," and certainly not "niggers," which is one of the follies of race-evasive discourses: nonblack Africans are, after all, Africans. There are blacks who are not Africans, not "Negroes," and although not often "niggers," certainly often treated as such, as the experience of Australian Aboriginals and varieties of East Indians and Polynesians attest.[8] Yet the logic is at an impasse with "Negroes," since it was sub-Saharan Africans who were made into such, which means there are no "Negroes" who are not of African descent. "Niggerizing" is, however, an even more complicated matter, as it pushes all of these categories into a lower level beyond which even they consider themselves alien while paradoxically adopting the term: There is no group of designated "niggers" that does not refer to those beneath them or even themselves as such.[9]

This exercise into racial designations spells out an important consideration. It reveals the plasticity of the racial concepts, and it also brings to the fore another element. What, we may ask, do these terms mean except for the challenge to the humanity of the people so designated? And this being so, we are left compelled to meditate on the notion of humanity presumed in such challenges.

The philosophical anthropological question, especially because of its plasticity, raises the question of the extent to which human beings can transcend such impositions. It raises the question of freedom. We come, then, to the second major concern of Africana philosophy. As a modern philosophy, it addresses the problem of freedom, but it does so through also acknowledging the contradictions of its avowed practice. Modern white philosophers nearly all extol its value but come to a halt with regard to its extension to Africana people.[10] The relationship between the philosophical anthropological and the freedom questions then comes to the fore, and an additional and now third element surfaces: Is the reasoning across these relationships legitimate? And more: are they justified? And even further: what, ultimately, are conditions of justification—is justification justified?[11]

Africana philosophers address these questions, and as our discussion thus far has already delinked the racial logic of the categories of African, black, "Negroes," and "niggers," the question of the *Africana philosopher* should then take on a metaphilosophical reality of transcending those categories. Simply put: the Africana philosopher needn't be black or African. Thus understood, we could now ask, Should Franz Boas's contributions to Africana thought make him also an Africana thinker? As I hope the rest of this chapter will show, the answer is resoundingly yes.

Franz Boas began his career with a dissertation in physics in 1881 at the University of Kiel.[12] His topic was, given his subsequent research, prophetic: an effort to understand the color of water. Reflecting on his inaugural work, Boas admitted, "There are domains of our experiences in which the concept of quantity . . . with which I was accustomed to operate are not applicable."[13] This admission at first brought him into Kantian territory, where the role of the active mind in the organization of knowledge needed to be taken into account.[14] Sometimes, however, one walks great distances in search of what one has already begun. Color, after all, was to become the theme for the rest of his life. Mediated by detours as he attempted a career as a physicist in an anti-Semitic environment, he found his way to Arctic shores, where he began the next stage of his career studying the Inuit people of Baffin Island. Though trained in the quantitative world of positivist science, he reached out to the human domain, where experience offered continued resistance. His journey eventually took him to the United States, where, after overcoming considerable obstacles, he emerged as a premier force in American anthropology through the critical power of his scientific expertise.[15] The primary subject of American scientific efforts for the study of the human being was, however, wedded to two concepts, to the critique of which Boas made enormous contributions: race and primitivism. Both were crystallized under the rubric of the so-called Negro problem.

A major tenet of Africana philosophy is the critique of this supposed problem. Across the Atlantic, the Haitian jurist and anthropologist Anténor Firmin had already outlined a monumental study of the fallacies governing this circular formulation where the question itself presumes the consequence, for already presumed in the equation was the legitimacy of the category *Negro* as a designation for people of African ancestry.[16] Further, the problem already had a hidden additional problem in its avowal—namely, the problem of problem people. In these formulations, the elimination of the humanity of the designated Negro already collapsed him or her into the problem at hand. Thus, instead of people who face problems, they became the problems themselves. This is an observation articulated by W. E. B. Du Bois in his famous "Study of the Negro Problems" and in his more elegant formulation in *The Souls of Black Folk*.[17] Both Du Bois and Firmin saw these problems as a feature of the impact of prejudice on scientific inquiry, which enabled them to ask the obvious though often denied question: Why does so much bad science emerge, especially by white scholars, in the study of race?

Du Bois and Firmin were, however, men of African descent, black men, men located in the category of the Negro. They were thus ignored while the objects of their criticism, from Paul Broca and Arthur de Gobineau to Herbert Spencer, held sway by virtue of the same fallacy turned upside down: the whiteness of their skin. Truth, supposedly proper critique, unfortunately required a white face from which to make its case. Boas, however, wasn't so simple a protagonist. After all, he found himself in the American context because of the limits science offered in his defense as a Jew in the European one.[18] The American one offered him a metonym for his own condition, a step removed, as it were, through the Negro. Thus Boas could speak scientifically about race through the absence of self-reference, even though, to some extent, there was such subtextual reference.[19] As Frantz Fanon, building on Jean-Paul Sartre, who had ironically done the same through Richard Wright, pointed out three-quarters of a century later, anti-Semitism and antiblack racism had a symbiotic relationship.[20]

While unaware of the complex etymology of race, Fanon and Sartre were right in pointing to an intimate relationship between anti-Semitism and antiblack racism. The term itself evolved from the medieval Spanish word *raza,* which referred to breeds of dogs, horses, Jews, and Moors.[21] An expression of Christian hatred during eight hundred years of Afro-Arabic colonization of the Mediterranean (as far north as southern France), this expression first had theo-naturalistic significance, where Christians were also natural because properly human in the eyes of Christendom. As deviations, Jews and Moors were marked, and the history that unfolded after the Reconquista, the defeat in

1492 of the Moors in Spain, was one in which theo-naturalism shifted into secular naturalism in an anthropological quandary over the New World and the new science that followed. The grammar of *raza* remained, however, in the transformation to "race," which meant that along with naturalistic differentiation there were also theodicean expectations. A philosophical anthropology of the human being as normatively Christian and white meant that its contradictions were relegated to the "outside." Thus the Jew and the world of color, whose darkest region was the black, became primary targets of race.[22]

Racial normativity, however, raised some peculiar problems when also wedded to notions of modernity, progress, and, eventually, evolution. Christian eschatology took root in the new science, in spite of its effort to shake off its scholastic foundations, which led to the inevitable verdict on the present as a time in which deviant races did not belong and the future as a time in which they would eventually disappear.[23] Primitivism thereby emerged as a feature of race discourse, where some groups are marked as properly belonging to the past. This development, however, required important shifts. After all, the previous model of white normativity was premised on an original whiteness tainted by the emergence (through sin) of color.[24] Africana thinkers such as Anton Wilhelm Amo and Ottobah Cougano offered responses to these positions, including, in the case of the latter, one premised on a theodicy of language in which enslavement and racism were articulated as actual sin; but their plea fell on deaf ears.[25] The Darwinian turn led, however, to a shifted telos in which the question of overcoming past weaknesses began to dominate. This led to the thesis that while whites have supposedly progressed, other groups remained stuck in an early human condition. Thus groups such as Native Americans and (black) Africans became analogues of an earlier period of development—in short, primitives.

The unfolding racist logic took on a subversion of the relationship between exception and rule. While contradictions to the primitivism thesis were many, they were all treated as minor exceptions. This logic continues into contemporary times, when, for example, whites who fail are considered exceptions to the thesis of white superiority, whereas blacks who succeed are considered exceptions to that of black inferiority. Principles of verification are, in other words, thwarted.

Boas took on the project of demystifying this false logic.[26] The first stage was to break the hold physical science had on the study of human beings. Anthropology, in other words, had to expand itself beyond physical anthropology into what is known today as cultural anthropology. As a researcher trained in physical science, Boas was well equipped for this task. But the problem required more than training as a physicist, for the question at hand was whether scientific methodology was, in a word, complete. Boas himself found this difficult to overcome since, as Vernon Williams Jr. has shown, he remained committed to scientific models of essential difference. Williams called this "the paradox" of Boas's thought.[27] The difficulty, however, was that Boas also faced scientific inquiry as a *political* struggle. He needed, in other words, to be persuasive, but this required, constantly, his credibility *as a scientist.* He faced, in other words, what I call disciplinary decadence, a phenomenon in which methodological fetishism pushes reality to the wayside and ontologizes either a discipline or a specific disciplinary perspective.[28] The task, then, was to point out the fallacy of certain disciplinary perspectives on the study of human beings. Anthropology, in other words, while including insights from biology, organic chemistry, and physics, was not reducible to them.[29] This was a view supported earlier by Firmin.

Although arguing against a racist wilderness, his ideas for the most part falling on proverbial deaf ears primarily because of the prejudices of the white social scientific community in Europe, which had a low regard for thought that emanated from black researchers, Firmin brought potentiated double consciousness to bear on anthropology as a science through posing two important challenges. The first concerned the gap between how a science presents itself and how it actually is, which requires recognition of the need for it to transcend itself; the second raised the important question beneath the question of racial study—namely, the problem of human study. But that problem, he understood, is weighed down by a metaphysics premised on a conception of the human being as capable of living and being outside of human relations. In other words, the understanding of a proper *human relation* leads to a philosophy of relationality, which, in the end, amounts to the understanding of the complexity of meaning by which a human world is constituted, and that is, in today's parlance, a philosophy of culture.[30] The language Firmin used for the first critique, of the scientificity of scientific inquiry into "man" and races, into anthropo*logy,* is, building on Auguste Comte, *positivism.*[31]

Firmin's conception of a positivist approach to anthropology raises a problem subsequently formulated by Du Bois—namely, the problem of studying people *as a problem.*[32] This is at the forefront of much of Firmin's critique, wherein the problem of black people becomes the problem itself. From an antiblack approach to the study of blacks, for instance, blacks are queer (out-of-line or unaligned), pathological (nonnormative), stubborn (overdetermined) objects of study.[33] Anticipating the thought of Fanon, for instance, Firmin argued, in his discussion of the education of blacks, that problems become stark where questions of sexual maturation and social responsibility come to the fore because of the lack of coherent conceptions (and perhaps also fear) of black adulthood; blacks, in other words, are expected to be, at best, girls and boys.[34] A misguided disciplinary approach attempts to squeeze people into the norms of the discipline. "Particularly in the field of anthropology," Firmin writes, "one must be wary of exclusive specialization, for it narrows the mind's horizons and renders the intellect incapable of considering every facet of a given reality."[35]

Firmin's approach—and, as we shall see, Boas's—is what I would call *a teleological suspension of disciplinarity* or *transdisciplinarity.*[36] In effect, he argues that the human being exceeds the dictates of a singularly disciplinary approach because the methodological resources for the discipline emerged out of the specificity of its object of study, which is often one dimension of human reality instead of the entire human being. The *entire human being* is, however, metaphorical, since wholeness and completeness for human beings would require closed subjects that do not comport well with the human capacity for self-reflection as possibility. Firmin's philosophical anthropology is nonreductive; it raises the question of the human being as a multidimensional reality, where each dimension emerges as a vital relationship with the others.[37]

Firmin thus issues against his contemporaries the charge of subordinating inquiry into humanity to subfields of disciplines that in effect ontologized themselves in an assertion of supposed completeness and hence reach over all of reality against the variety of sciences making claim to rigor in human study. Even ethnography and ethnology, for instance, fall prey to this fallacy. Firmin's criticism is that such an approach to the study of human beings in effect puts anthropology in the background.[38] Citing Clémence Royer, known, among other things, for her French translation of Charles Darwin's *On the Origin of Species,* in support of his position, Firmin argues that ethnography confuses a part of the human being with the whole.[39] He also argues that ethnography is more properly cosmological and pertains to the study of peoples, whereas ethnology sets the basis for the distinctions on the basis of race. Anthropology, Firmin contends, goes beyond ethnography and ethnology by problematizing both.

The language he uses for the second kind of critique is more complicated, however. For although he is critical of philosophical idealism, he is indebted to that kind of critical philosophy precisely because the anthropological question is, to some extent, a self-reflective critique of man by man, or, as Sylvia Wynter and others have put it recently, the question of the human being beyond the discourse of man.[40] This is a condition-of-possibility kind of argument, and Firmin achieves it through a two-pronged negotiation of the empirical and the conditions by which it is possible.

These ideas, like those of Boas, are inspired by Kant's transcendental idealism or critical philosophy, which involves thinking through the conditions for the emergence of forms of knowledge. In philosophy, these conditions ranged from experience to history to materiality to language to signs and symbols to culture.[41]

On Kant, Firmin writes,

> Not only does [Kant] give the word anthropology a meaning and a definition different from those subscribed to by scientists, but he also contests the appropriateness of the term applied to the natural studies of Man. . . . Ignoring the great philosopher's opinions, scientists continued to work in their various fields and persisted . . . in considering the word anthropology as synonymous with the natural history of Man. . . . However, on closer examination one undisputable fact emerges: the method used in natural history to study minerals, plants, and animals inferior to Man, is not always fruitful when it comes to the study of the last addition to creation. Whereas the inferior beings are programmed essentially for vegetative and animal life, Man is programmed for social life, which he ultimately always achieves by making his own history.[42]

Firmin later reminds us that "man is the only creature who cannot stand alone. The pride of depressive misanthropy which occasionally inspires such a desire for isolation is nothing but a pathological case triggered by some lesion in the organism. The fact is, Man needs Man in order to develop or even to know his individual personality."[43]

A rigorous anthropology requires understanding the human being on human terrain, and, in similar kind, race on its own terms. Boas thus, much like Firmin, took on a variety of physical anthropological idols such as phrenology and brain size. That "men of high genius," as he put it, existed among whites without meeting phrenological and brain-size criteria suggests that in cases of group underachievement other factors must be at work.[44]

Boas then came upon an argument that recurs in Africana thought: the fallacy of excluding important variables in the human sciences. Racist scientists presented black underachievement as evidence of black inferiority as though there were pristine laboratory conditions in which to assess capabilities of various groups. The presumption of such arguments was that black people lived in a nonracist environment with ample opportunities for human flourishing. How could the so-called Negro ascend when he or she was blocked from doing so? In other words, is it right to call a group a problem when a society places its members in unequal and problematic situations? The series of papers in which Boas issued this critique made him an immediate ally of the cause of African diasporic thought.

Boas, however, offered an additional argument. Darwin's work fueled a variety of white supremacists and antiblack racist doctrines of the time. I separate white supremacy from antiblack racism since it is possible to reject the former while maintaining the latter: Even if whites aren't superior, it doesn't follow that blacks are equal to everyone else. Nevertheless, in an age of Manifest Destiny, the idea that the human species was perfecting itself through whiteness was unavoidable. Evidence was thus sought for this doctrine everywhere, including, as is well known, in two primary products of human activity: civilization and culture. The first was by definition out of the reach of primitive humanity, and the second, even where accepted as a feature of all human beings, was placed on a hierarchical system leading to white civilization as its telos. One could think of the famous series of depictions of human evolution from ape to burly, bearded man, to white urban man.[45] Oddly enough, there are no ellipses or question marks after the portrait of contemporary or modern man, and these images rarely have a woman representing its culmination. What is clear about this portrait is that neither a black man or black woman nor a Native American nor an East Asian emerges in the culminating narrative. They, too, are presumed elsewhere, or more accurately *else-when,* in an earlier or primordial time.

Much of this comes from a fundamental misreading of Darwin's argument (an error also sadly made by Darwin) exemplified in the work of social Darwinists and sociobiological theorists such as Herbert Spencer and many late nineteenth-century social scientists.[46] What they missed was that the theory of natural selection did not support the thesis that human beings evolved out of chimpanzees but instead that modern human beings, chimpanzees, and other forms of coexisting primates were equally evolved. Every living thing is nothing short of a survival of certain traits adapted to their environment. Where conditions conducive to their survival disappear, so, too, do many species. Thus, it doesn't follow that there is an *internal* or *inherent* progress where there is natural selection. Evolving versus devolving are concepts introduced through the human world of meaning to reflect human experience and interpretation. The error of the social Darwinists was to presume an isomorphic relationship between culture and biology, but Boas (and many others such as Firmin and Du Bois) showed that culture was an independent variable.[47] Human beings are simply not like Tarzan (the Great White Man), who could be plopped into any setting and emerge, willy-nilly, as superior to everything in his environment.

The traits held dear by the social Darwinists required at bottom human participation in language, the communicative practice through which culture is possible. Boas argued the obvious: every human being (barring individual defect such as genetic anomalies or injury such as brain damage) has the capacity to learn or embody the culture in which he or she is either born or in which he or she is nurtured. At each moment, any set of human beings is hardwired (because belonging to the same time or stage of species development) for such acquisition.[48] Thus, in principle, what makes the so-called Negro's condition a miserable one is a cultural context that militates against him or her: the social options available through which to live her or his potential are intentionally restricted.[49] And if the rejection of biological racial difference is taken seriously, what also makes the so-called Negro is culture as well.

The logical implication of Boas's argument is that the potential of people from sub-Saharan Africa isn't any more or less than that of any other group. Yet Boas himself adhered to positions that contradicted this claim: he argued, for instance, that whites had a greater propensity to produce "men of high genius" than any other group, especially blacks.[50] This is a familiar problem in race discourse with regard to evidence: a circular logic required looking at the outcome instead of a priori considerations on what could be otherwise. Yet even there one finds a serious problem. Even if one concedes such a claim, the question must be asked: Is this empirically so? Most people, including many (if not most) blacks, don't actually know African history, and even in cases of black achievement in North America, South America, and Europe, the tendency is to presume a white agent when in fact there was a black one. A priori assertions of an absence of black achievement abound, even as modern society makes use of technologies, ranging from brakes to filament and stoplights, doorknobs, plasma, and many more, invented by black individuals.[51] The history of black protest alone contradicts such a thesis on its own terms (that is, writing). Boas understood that he needed to respond to this consideration, and he launched a campaign of doing so through his own study of African history.

Human beings have been making innovations on our environment ever since we emerged in sub-Saharan Africa two hundred thousand years ago, and so have other kinds of hominids that preceded us and even, as research on Neanderthals and Denisovans shows, those who were for a time our contemporaries.[52] The cultivation of fire required intelligence, and so, too, did the smelting of iron and the accompanying technologies in the course of human survival across Africa into other continents. Archaeological work revealed multitudes of civilizations whose achievements over the past ten thousand years yielded innovations that have resulted in human flourishing. That different communities of human beings developed varying technologies to adapt to their environments (for example, extreme cold versus heat, limited access to food versus abundance, and the cultivation of land) is akin to the point about confusing survival with superiority: There was no point in developing innovations where circumstances didn't make them necessary.

This aspect of Boas's thought had influence beyond his expectations. When Du Bois invited him to speak on the fallacies of racialism and racism in a commencement address at Atlanta University in 1906, Boas chose instead to give an oration on why blacks should not be ashamed of their past.[53] He lamented the prevailing ignorance of African history and outlined the many achievements of Africans. The talk didn't fall on deaf ears. It had a profound impact on Du Bois and many others, who then took up the task of reconstructing that history, as evidenced in Du Bois's *The World and Africa*.[54] In Du Bois's words, "I did not myself begin actively to study Africa until 1908 or 1910. Franz Boas really influenced me to begin studying this subject and I began really to get into it only after 1915."[55]

An important dimension of this turn is that it addressed the damage wrought by historical misrepresentation. In effect, the question of decolonizing historiography came to the fore. While anti-Semitism attacks Jews as being inferior to Christians, knowledge of the important role of the Israelites even in the Christian texts offered an important counternarrative. Judaism and Jewish history could bolster Jewish self-esteem and self-respect. These psychic elements are crucial to the health of any group of people. That blacks were living under the presumption of being without a history and without an understanding of the importance of that history for world history (contra Hegel) had a profound effect even on those who sought to combat racism. Ironically, given the attacks on Africologists such as Maulana Karenga and Molefi Asante by some white Jewish scholars at the end of the twentieth century, it was Boas who formulated an important tenet compatible with, if not also of, Afrocentricity and Africology—namely, the importance of each group of people understanding itself as an agent of history.[56]

Boas's path thus took a turn into what in Africana philosophy has been characterized as classic movements of double consciousness. The first stage of double consciousness, classically formulated by Du Bois in 1903, was to see oneself or the group in question through the eyes of those who dominate them.[57] Thus the construction of people of African descent as "Negro" and even "black" was, as Fanon later observed, an imposition of whiteness.[58] This is what we earlier saw as *being a problem*. The next stage emerges from realizing

W. E. B. Du Bois at Atlanta University in 1909, the year he cofounded the National Association for the Advancement of Colored People. Boas was a charter member. W. E. B. Du Bois Papers (MS 312), Department of Special Collections and University Archives, W. E. B. Du Bois Library, University of Massachusetts Amherst.

the distinction between being such and facing problems. This requires recognizing the contradictions of a society premised upon imposing such onto some of its members and organizing others to do such. The critique that results from this realization is called *potentiated double consciousness.*[59] This dialectical movement affords an advance in knowledge, although it is not concluded as a final moment or universal. It is a *universalizing practice,* by which is meant that it moves knowledge forward without presumed closure. Boas's engagements with the plight of the so-called Negro stimulated self-reflection and critique not only of his location in American society but also at the epistemological levels of science. Human science was also brought under the lens of critical reflection, and its potential is realized through paradoxically transcending itself in what I earlier called a teleological suspension of disciplinarity. Although in love with science and anthropology, Boas ultimately faced their transcendence for nothing short of reality.

## MOVING ON WITH CONTINUED RELEVANCE

We return, then, to a set of important themes to consider about Boas's relation to Africana philosophy. First, there is his obvious contribution to philosophical anthropology. Boas's arguments ultimately showed the error in making whites the standard for all other groups. While European societies produced their standards of how to live as a human being, the error is to conclude that theirs were and continue to be *the standards* or, worse, the *only* ones. While some critics may think this would lead to a relativism of standards, to do so would be to miss the point. The theoretical issue at hand is an interrogation into standards themselves—indeed, the very notion of *a standard of being human*. The human being, after all, has the capacity to create and defy standards, to accept or build alternative ones. This means, then, that human experience, as Boas had reflected on early in his career, while exceeding, through the lived reality of the human world, many of the dictates of positivist science also demands theoretical reflection on where human beings would like to go, what human beings would like to be. In "Sociology Hesitant," Du Bois said it well when he wrote of such an effort as nothing short of creating a "Science that seeks the limits of Chance in human conduct."[60] We are thus here on the terrain of freedom, one of the primary concerns of Africana philosophy. Freedom, however, extends beyond liberty. It pertains as well to the sense of responsibility experienced by human agents. That there used to be challenges to the thesis that black people experience this boggles the mind, but such it is. The question of moral responsibility and ethical life, while important for understanding the condition of freedom, is, however, insufficient for addressing the lived reality of limits posed on human flourishing. Whether as Negroes or black people or African diasporic people, such people are, after all, rendered homeless in the world that created them.[61] What Boas, in stream with many Africana thinkers, was addressing in his articulation of African history was the question of whether such people "belong," so to speak, to the story of humankind. Although they were rejected by European modernity, there was no legitimate reason for them to be denied their membership in the human community. Boas's historicism was, in other words, a form of redemptive history, one linked to a conception of freedom as also a portrait of belonging.

The final element, which I hope is evident from the argument of this chapter, is the importance of critical assessments of justificatory practices. Boas unsettled notions of complete science through identifying the fallacy of forcing people into disciplinary scientific methodology instead of adjusting the methods to human reality, to women and men of flesh and blood, speech and deed. He, in effect, initiated a teleological suspension of the science of his day for the sake of reality.

These three features of Africana philosophy suggest that Boas should be read, as indeed he has been, as an important contributor to Africana philosophy. While his presence has been directly established through his students, such as Melville Herskovits, Zora Neale Hurston, Ashley Montagu, and many others, especially through critical work on race in Africana philosophy, I hope this discussion has shown his reach beyond those confines. The expansiveness of Africana philosophy, which reaches through analytical philosophy, critical theory, existentialism, feminist philosophy, hermeneutics, phenomenology, poststructuralism (archaeological, genealogical, and textual), pragmatism, transcendental idealism, sage philosophy, and more, brings these elements of philosophical anthropology, discourses of freedom, and critique of method to the fore in ways that suggest a portrait not only of what Africana philosophers (of all racial backgrounds) learned from foundations set by Boas but also, as the intellectual history is reconsidered, what Boas learned from his productive engagement with such an intellectual struggle. It is perhaps fitting, then, to conclude with a reflection of an Africana thinker whom he knew and who, like him, demonstrated admiration for science, truth, freedom, and human dignity: "You are not and yet you are; your thoughts, your deeds, above all your dreams still live. . . . Let then the Dreams of the Dead rebuke the Blind who think that what is will be forever and teach them that what was worth living for must live again and that which merited death must stay dead. Teach us, Forever Dead, there is no Dream but Deed, there is no Deed but Memory."[62]

## Notes

1. See Lucius T. Outlaw, *On Race and Philosophy* (New York: Routledge, 1996), chap. 4; Lewis R. Gordon, *Existentia Africana: Understanding Africana Existential Thought* (New York: Routledge, 2000), chap. 1; and Lewis R. Gordon, *An Introduction to Africana Philosophy* (Cambridge, UK: Cambridge University Press, 2008), introd.
2. For discussion of the etymology of the term, see Gordon, *An Introduction to Africana Philosophy*, 14–18.
3. V. Y. Mudimbe, *The Invention of Africa: Gnosis, Philosophy, and the Order of Knowledge* (Bloomington: Indiana University Press, 1988).
4. See, e.g., Sigmund Freud, "Mourning and Melancholia," trans. James Strachey, in *The Standard Edition of the Complete Works of Sigmund Freud*, vol. 14 (New York: Vintage, 2001), 243–58. Cf. also Judith Butler, "Thresholds of Melancholy," in *Prism of the Self: Philosophical Essays in Honor of Maurice Natanson*, ed. Steven Galt Crowell (Dordrecht: Kluwer Academic Publishers, 1995), 3–12. And for discussions specifically in the context of Africana philosophy, see Lewis R. Gordon, "Theory in Black: Teleological Suspensions

in Philosophy of Culture," *Qui Parle: Critical Humanities and Social Sciences* 18, no. 2 (2010): 193–214.

5. This is a familiar motif in Africana philosophy, but for more discussion, see Paget Henry, "Race, Ethnicity and Philosophical Entrapment," *Journal of Speculative Philosophy* 18, 2 (2004): 129–48. See also Gordon, "Theory in Black."
6. See Lewis R. Gordon, *Bad Faith and Antiblack Racism* (Atlantic Highlands, NJ: Humanities International Press, 1995), and *Existentia Africana.*
7. Frantz Fanon, introduction to *Peau noire, masques blancs* (Paris: Éditions du Seuil, 1952), available in English as *Black Skin, White Masks,* trans. Charles Lamm Markmann (New York: Grove Press, 1967). Fanon's, to some infamous, discussion of violence also addresses this problem of illicit appearance, where for the black simply to appear is treated as a violation of decent social space; see his *Les damnés de la terre* (Paris: La Découverte, 2002 [originally published in 1961]); available in English as *The Wretched of the Earth,* trans. Constance Farrington (New York: Grove Press, 1963).
8. See, e.g., Michelle Harris, Martin Nakata, and Bronwyn Carlson, eds., *The Politics of Identity: Emerging Indigineity* (Sydney, Australia: UTS ePress, 2013).
9. See Gordon, *Bad Faith and Antiblack Racism,* chap. 15, "Black Antiblack Racism."
10. This is another well-known aspect of so-called mainstream philosophy from the perspective of Africana philosophy. See Cornel West, "A Genealogy of Modern Racism," chap. 2 in *Prophesy, Deliverance! An Afro-American Revolutionary Christianity* (Philadelphia: Westminster, 1982); Emmanuel Chukwudi Eze, ed., *Race and the Enlightenment: A Reader* (Oxford: Blackwell, 1997); Robert Bernasconi and Tommy Lee Lott, eds., *The Idea of Race* (Indianapolis: Hackett, 2000).
11. See Gordon, "Theory in Black." Cf. also Lewis R. Gordon, "Essentialist Anti-Essentialism, with Considerations from Other Sides of Modernity," *Quaderna: A Multilingual and Transdisciplinary Journal,* no. 1 (2012), http://quaderna.org/wp-content/uploads/2012/09/Gordon-essentialist-antiessentialism.pdf.
12. Franz Boas, *Beiträge zur Erkenntnis der Farbe des Wassers* (Kiel: Schmidt und Klaunig, 1881).
13. Quoted in George W. Stocking Jr., *Race, Culture, and Evolution: Essays in the History of Anthropology* (New York: Free Press, 1968), 143.
14. Kantianism is metonymic for transcendental idealism (sometimes called critical philosophy), where the conditions of concepts, perceptions, and experience are taken into account. For discussion of Boas as a neo-Kantian, see Greg Urban, "Neo-Kantianism," in *Theory in Social and Cultural Anthropology: An Encyclopedia* (Los Angeles: Sage, 2013), 592.
15. See Vernon J. Williams Jr., *Rethinking Race: Franz Boas and His Contemporaries* (Lexington: University of Kentucky Press, 1996).
16. Anténor Firmin, *De l'égalité des races humaines: anthropologie positive* (Paris: Librairie Cotillon, 1885), available in English as *The Equality of the Human Races: A Nineteenth-Century Haitian Scholar's Response to European Racialism,* trans. Asselin Charles (New York: Garland, 1999).
17. W. E. B. Du Bois, "The Study of Negro Problems," *Annals of the American Academy of Political and Social Science* 11 (1898), 1–23, repr. in *Annals of the American Academy of Political and Social Science* 56 (2000), 13–27, and *The Souls of Black Folk: Essays and*

*Sketches* (Chicago: A. C. McClurg, 1903). For discussion, see Gordon, *Existentia Africana,* chap. 4.

18. See Williams, *Rethinking Race,* chap. 2.
19. This is a path also taken by Freud, who was fearful of psychoanalysis being labeled a Jewish science and thus addressed such concerns through discussion of the mulatto. See Jean-Paul Rocchi, "Dying Metaphors and Deadly Fantasies: Freud, Baldwin and Race as Intimacy," *Human Architecture* 7, no. 2 (2009): 159–78. According to Vernon Williams (chap. 2), Boas, unlike Freud, moved beyond the conceptual to ongoing relationships with blacks, which suggests that the metonymic significance of blacks, if present, was secondary in Boas's case. His, in other words, may have been a genuine case of identification against injustice. For anxieties and fears of anthropology as a Jewish science, see Jeffrey D. Feldman, "The Jewish Roots and Routes of Anthropology," *Anthropological Quarterly* 77, no. 1 (2004): 107–25.
20. Fanon, *Black Skin, White Masks,* chap. 5. For Wright's influence on Sartre, especially with regard to the correlation between "the Negro problem" and "the Jewish problem," the result of which is "the anti-Semite's problem," see Ronald Hayman, *Sartre: A Biography* (New York: Carroll and Graff, 1987), 220.
21. See, e.g., Sebastián de Covarrubias Orozco, *Tesoro de la lengua* (1611), quoted, translated, and discussed in David Nirenberg, "Race and the Middle Ages: The Case of Spain and the Jews," in *Rereading the Black Legend: The Discourses of Religious and Racial Difference in the Renaissance Empires,* ed. Margaret R. Greer, Walter D. Mignolo, and Maureen Quilligan (Chicago: University of Chicago Press, 2007), 71–87.
22. See Lewis R. Gordon, "Race, Theodicy, and the Normative Emancipatory Challenges of Blackness," *South Atlantic Quarterly* 112, no. 4 (2013): 725–36.
23. See Gordon, *Existentia Africana,* chap. 8.
24. See, e.g., Kant's philosophical anthropology in Eze, *Race and the Enlightenment.*
25. See Gordon, *An Introduction to Africana Philosophy,* chap. 2.
26. For his critique, see Franz Boas, *The Mind of Primitive Man* (New York: Macmillan, 1911).
27. Williams, *Rethinking Race,* chap. 1.
28. Lewis R. Gordon, *Disciplinary Decadence: Living Thought in Trying Times* (Boulder: Paradigm, 2006).
29. Cf. also Firmin, *The Equality of the Human Races,* 4.
30. This portrait of these structuralist themes as being rooted in a philosophy of culture emerges from the thought of Ernst Cassirer and his philosophy of symbolic forms. See his famous multivolume work bearing that name. Drucilla Cornell and Kenneth Panfilio recently made explicit how Cassirer's and similar accounts come to bear on the study of human phenomena, especially race. See their *Symbolic Forms for a New Humanity: Cultural and Racial Reconfigurations of Critical Theory* (New York: Fordham University Press, 2011). Cassirer's text is *Philosophy of Symbolic Forms,* 3 vols., trans. Ralph Manheim (New Haven: Yale University Press, 1953–55). For a discussion of its relation to structuralism, see Peter Caws, *Structuralism: The Art of the Intelligible* (Atlantic Highlands, NJ: Humanities International Press, 1988).
31. See Paul Gilroy, *Against Race: Imagining Political Culture Beyond the Colorline* (Cambridge: Belknap Press, 2002).

32. Du Bois introduced this question in his article "The Study of Negro Problems." For discussion, see Gordon, *Existentia Africana,* chap. 4, and Jane Anna Gordon, "Challenges Posed to Social-Scientific Method by the Study of Race," in *A Companion to African-American Studies,* ed. Lewis R. Gordon and Jane Anna Gordon (Malden, MA: Blackwell, 2006), 279–304.
33. See Lewis R. Gordon, *Existentia Africana,* chap. 4, and "Theory in Black"; Jane Anna Gordon, "Challenges Posed"; Sara Ahmed, *Queer Phenomenology: Orientations, Objects, Others* (Durham: Duke University Press, 2006); David Ross Fryer, "African-American Queer Studies," in *A Companion to African-American Studies,* ed. Gordon and Gordon, 305–29, and *Thinking Queerly: Post-Humanist Essays on Ethics and Identity* (Boulder: Paradigm, 2008).
34. See Fanon, *Black Skin, White Masks,* chap. 6. On this matter of being treated as children, see also Gordon, *Bad Faith and Antiblack Racism,* and Charles Wm. Ephraim, *The Pathology of Eurocentrism: The Burdens and Responsibilities of Being Black* (Trenton, NJ: Africa World Press, 2003).
35. Firmin, *The Equality of the Human Races,* 4.
36. See Gordon, *Disciplinary Decadence.* A teleological suspension of disciplinarity involves a practitioner of a discipline going beyond her or his discipline for the sake of reality. See also Gordon, "Theory in Black."
37. Gordon, *Disciplinary Decadence,* 10–11.
38. Ibid., 12.
39. Royer, by the way, took liberties with Darwin's text by adding a sixty-page introduction and many notes defending claims for which Darwin was tentative. See Joy Harvey, *Almost a Man of Genius: Clémence Royer, Feminism, and Nineteenth-Century Science* (New Brunswick: Rutgers University Press, 1997).
40. Firmin, *The Equality of the Human Races,* 5. Cf. Sylvia Wynter, "On How We Mistook the Map for the Territory, and Re-Imprisoned Ourselves in Our Unbearable Wrongness of Being, of *Désêtre:* Black Studies Toward the Human Project," in *Not Only the Master's Tools: African-American Studies in Theory and Practice,* ed. Lewis R. Gordon and Jane Anna Gordon (Boulder: Paradigm, 2006), 107–72, and B. Anthony Bogues, ed., *After Man, Towards the Human: Critical Essays on Sylvia Wynter* (Kingston, Jamaica: Ian Randle, 2006).
41. Discussions of this kind of argument abound. See, e.g., Quassim Cassam, "Transcendental Arguments, Transcendental Synthesis, and Transcendental Idealism," *Philosophical Quarterly* 37, no. 149 (1987): 355–78.
42. Firmin, *The Equality of the Human Races,* 6.
43. Ibid., 7.
44. It took some time, however, for Boas to reach this point, as his problematic article "Human Faculty as Determined by Race," premised on comparative brain size, attests. See Williams's discussion in *Rethinking Race,* chap. 1. For Boas's article, see George W. Stocking Jr., *A Franz Boas Reader* (Chicago: University of Chicago Press, 1974), 221–42. For his full-frontal assault on brain-size arguments, see, e.g., Boas, "The Problem of the American Negro," *Yale Quarterly Review* 10 (Jan. 1921): 384–95.
45. Of which there are many—but for a familiar portrait, see, e.g., http://www.dailymail.co.uk/sciencetech/article-1070671/Evolution-stops-Future-Man-look-says-scientist.html.

46. See Benjamin Farrington, *What Darwin Really Said* (New York: Schocken Books, 1996). For discussion of the impact of social Darwinism on late nineteenth-century and early twentieth-century social science, especially with regard to the constellation of researchers at the University of Pennsylvania, see Williams, *Rethinking Race,* chaps. 1, 2.
47. See Firmin, *The Equality of the Human Races,* and for Boas, see, e.g., *The Measurement of Differences Between Variable Quantities* (New York: Science Press, 1906).
48. This argument has been updated in Africana philosophy on questions of cross-cultural communication in the work of Kwasi Wiredu. See, e.g., his *Cultural Universals and Particulars* (Bloomington: Indiana University Press, 1996).
49. In other words, the limited options offer little room for meaningful choice. I elaborate on this issue in *Existentia Africana,* chap. 4. Cf. also Lewis R. Gordon, *Fanon and the Crisis of European Man: An Essay on Philosophy and the Human Sciences* (New York: Routledge, 1995), chap. 3.
50. A position, as pointed out earlier, which he eventually repudiated. See Williams, *Rethinking Race,* chaps. 1, 2.
51. The many books written on this subject seem to have had little impact on the general perception of black underachievement. For an example of such books, see Keith C. Holmes, *Black Inventors, Crafting Over 200 Years of Success* (New York: Global Black Inventor Research Projects, 2008).
52. There is debate among paleoanthropologists on various aspects of this portrait, but there are certain constants or points of agreement, such as the period of Neanderthal and then Homo sapiens' evolution. See, e.g., Ian Tattersall and Jeffrey H. Schwartz, "Hominids and Hybrids: The Place of Neanderthals in Human Evolution," *Proceedings of the National Academy of Sciences* 96, no. 13 (1999): 7117–19, and more recent discussion for general audiences such as Sarah Zielinski, "Neanderthals . . . They're Just Like Us?" *National Geographic News,* Oct. 13, 2012, http://news.nationalgeographic.com/news/2012/10/121012-neanderthals-science-paabo-dna-sex-breeding-humans/.
53. Franz Boas, "Commencement Address at Atlanta University, May 31, 1906," *Atlanta University Leaflet,* no. 19: http://www.webdubois.org/BoasAtlantaCommencement.html.
54. W. E. B. Du Bois, *The World and Africa* (New York: International Publishers, 1979). This is not to say that Boas was the sole source of this kind of argument in the African diasporic world. Firmin's impact, for example, has genealogical influence in the Afro-Francophone world, as seen, e.g., in Cheikh Anta Diop, *Nations nègres et culture: de l'antiquité nègre-égyptienne aux problèmes culturels de l'Afrique noire d'aujourd'hui* (Paris: Éditions Africaines, 1955). Cf. also Diop, *Civilisation ou Barbarie: Anthropologie Sans Complaisance* (Paris: Présence Africaine, 1981), available in English as *Civilization or Barbarism: An Authentic Anthropology,* trans. Yaa-Lengi Meema Ngemi (Chicago: Chicago Review Press, 1991).
55. Quoted in Harold R. Isaacs, *The New World of Negro Americans* (New York: Viking Press, 1964), 207. Cf. also Williams, *Rethinking Race,* 74–78.
56. See Molefi Asante, *The Afrocentric Idea,* rev. ed. (Philadelphia: Temple University Press, 1998). Cf. also Asante, "Sustaining Africology: On the Creation and Development of a Discipline," in *A Companion to African-American Studies,* ed. Lewis R. Gordon and Jane Anna Gordon (Malden, MA: Blackwell, 2006), 21–32. An example of attacks on Afrocentricity and Africology is Mary Lefkowitz, *Not Out of Africa: How Afrocentrism*

*Became an Excuse to Teach Myth as History* (New York: Basic Books, 1996). Lefkowitz's previous work was, by the way, on Greek poetry and women in Greece. One could imagine what Boas might have said to Lefkowitz, given his knowledge of Africa and issues of race versus her a priori assertions on a side of the debate (Africa) of which she was ignorant. What is striking about the conflict of the 1990s was how much it mirrored the white vitriol against which Boas fought.

57. While he examined twoness (belonging to two worlds) in his earlier *The Conservation of the Races* (Washington, DC: American Negro Academy, 1898), Du Bois's classic, phenomenological formulation emerged in *The Souls of Black Folk.*
58. Fanon, introduction to *Black Skin, White Masks.*
59. For elaboration, see Paget Henry, "Africana Phenomenology: Its Philosophical Implications," *C. L. R. James Journal* 11, no. 1 (2005): 79–112.
60. W. E. B. Du Bois, "Sociology Hesitant," *boundary 2* 27, no. 3 (2000): 44.
61. See Gordon, *Existentia Africana,* chap. 2, and Gordon, "Theory in Black."
62. W. E. B. Du Bois, *The Autobiography of W. E. B. Du Bois: A Soliloquy on Viewing My Life from the Last Decade of Its First Century* (New York: International Publishers, 1968), 422–23.

# Chapter 3 Expressive Enlightenment: Subjectivity and Solidarity in Daniel Garrison Brinton, Franz Boas, and Carlos Montezuma

*Ryan Carr*

In September 1899, a German journal of geography called *Globus* published an obituary for the American ethnologist Daniel Garrison Brinton. It was one of a handful of signed obituaries that its author, Franz Boas, would write in his long career. Boas concluded his words on Brinton with the following evaluation: "The importance of his example for the development of American anthropology cannot be overstated. For many years, his voice was the only one that called us back from the excessive specialization that had begun to pose a threat to the general scientific point of view in itself. If anthropology is to find a firm footing in America, it is thanks in no small part to the labors of the deceased."[1] Boas's memorial to Brinton is a statement of devotion, an homage to a colleague who inspired and defended a collective scholarly enterprise (an "us") with which Boas clearly identified. Yet his devotion has gone entirely unremarked in histories of American anthropology, and this is not just a matter of archival oversight. Although Brinton has long been dismissed by historians as a racist, he also began a momentous new movement in American anthropology, a movement that Boas himself would bring to fruition. Yet to understand the affiliation that linked Boas to Brinton, it will be necessary to think in new ways about anthropology at the turn of the twentieth century and

# GLOBUS.

ILLUSTRIERTE ZEITSCHRIFT FÜR LÄNDER- UND VÖLKERKUNDE.

**VEREINIGT MIT DEN ZEITSCHRIFTEN: „DAS AUSLAND“ UND „AUS ALLEN WELTTEILEN“.**

HERAUSGEBER: DR. RICHARD ANDREE. VERLAG VON FRIEDR. VIEWEG & SOHN.

Bd. LXXVI. Nr. 11. **BRAUNSCHWEIG.** 16. September 1899.


Nachdruck nur nach Übereinkunft mit der Verlagshandlung gestattet.

## Daniel Garrison Brinton †.

Von Franz Boas. New-York.

Am 31. Juli d. J. verschied nach langer Krankheit Daniel Garrison Brinton. In ihm hat die Ethnologie, speciell die amerikanische Forschung, einen ihrer bedeutendsten Vertreter verloren.

Brinton wurde am 13. Mai 1837 zu Thornbury in Chester County in Pennsylvanien geboren. Im Jahre 1858 graduierte er am Yale College, New-Haven, und studierte dann am Jefferson Medical College Medizin. Im Jahre 1861, nach bestandenem Examen, begab er sich nach Europa (Paris, Heidelberg), um seine Studien fortzusetzen. Nach seiner Rückkehr, im August 1862, trat er als Militärarzt in die Armee der Vereinigten Staaten ein und machte in dieser Stellung den Bürgerkrieg mit. Im Jahre 1863 war er bis zum Generalarzt des 11. Armeecorps befördert. Infolge eines Sonnenstiches mufste er den Dienst in der Linie aufgeben und fungierte bis zum Ende des Krieges als Hospitaldirektor. Hierauf liefs er sich in Philadelphia nieder, wo er noch längere Zeit als Mediziner praktisch und schriftstellerisch thätig war. Mit seinem wachsenden Interesse an der Ethnologie, das schon im Jahre 1856 bei einem Besuche in Florida erwacht war, beschränkt sich seine medizinische Thätigkeit mehr und mehr. Seit Ende der achtziger Jahre widmete er sich gänzlich seinen ethnologischen Studien und einer vielseitigen litterarischen Thätigkeit. Im Jahre 1884 wurde er zum Professor der Ethnologie und Archäologie an der Academy of Natural Sciences in Philadelphia ernannt, und bekleidete aufserdem viele Jahre als Ehrenstelle eine Professur der amerikanischen Sprachen an der Universität von Pennsylvanien.

Daniel Garrison Brinton.

Der Einflufs des Verstorbenen auf die Entwickelung der amerikanischen Ethnologie war aufserordentlich grofs. Seine vielseitige Kenntnis, scharfe Beobachtung und treffliche Combinationsgabe, vereint mit bedeutender litterarischer Begabung und Beredsamkeit, haben es ihm ermöglicht, mit Wort und Schrift einerseits das Interesse an der Ethnologie zu wecken, anderseits durch Stellung neuer Probleme und durch lebhafte Teilnahme an der Diskussion der Tagesfragen die Richtung wissenschaftlicher Arbeit zu beeinflussen, wie vielleicht kein anderer. Während J. W. Powell durch seine administrative Thätigkeit die Forschung unter den Indianerstämmen organisierte; während F. W. Putnam der archäologischen Forschung Bahnen wies, war es Brintons Verdienst, die theoretische Ausbeutung der gewonnenen Ergebnisse nach allen Richtungen zu fördern. Die drei Namen Brinton, Powell, Putnam werden mit Recht als die der Begründer moderner amerikanischer Ethnologie genannt werden.

Brinton vertrat in der Ethnologie den extremen psychologischen Standpunkt. Er wies durchaus die Frage der allmählichen Verbreitung ethnologischer Erscheinungen von der Hand und erkannte in ihrer Gleichartigkeit nur das gesetzmäfsige Wirken des menschlichen Geistes. Er war einer der ersten Vertreter dieser Richtung und viele der Ideen, welche er in seinem Werke „The Myths of the New World“, New-York 1868, ausgesprochen hat, sind für die mythologische Forschung grundlegend geworden. Hierher gehört seine Erklärung der Vierzahl und des Kreuzes als der Symbole der vier Winde. Durch seine Stellungnahme hat er wesentlich dazu beigetragen, den unwissenschaftlichen Versuchen ein Ende zu bereiten, die darauf hinstrebten, eine historische Beziehung zwischen Indianern und den verschiedensten Völkern der Alten Welt nachzuweisen. Seine



Franz Boas's obituary for Daniel Garrison Brinton, who died in 1899.

the social, moral, and discursive world within which this nascent discipline found itself.

For a long time now, scholars have agreed that Boas's relationship to Brinton was one of deliberate and successful supersession. Boas, the story goes, displaced Brinton and his methods on the way to becoming the preeminent anthropologist of his time.[2] Little evidence exists to suggest that Boas and Brinton understood their relationship in this way, but this has rarely bothered historians of anthropology. They relate the narrative of Boas's supersession of Brinton as part of a larger and more profoundly moralized story about how the American anthropological establishment learned to stop using race as an explanation for human difference and human behavior and to rely instead on the "modern, relativistic, pluralistic anthropological approach to culture."[3] These two narratives have become so thoroughly conflated, with Brinton playing the racialist foil to the rise of the Boasian culture concept, that it has become all but impossible to understand why Boas would want to single out Brinton as the "lone voice" who put American anthropology on a "firm footing."

The difficulty facing us can be traced back to Boas himself. Recent research by Lee Baker has shown that by the turn of the twentieth century Boas had come to see the fight against racism as the decisive struggle of his age. That struggle required that he deal with Brinton, a powerful, indeed founding, figure in the profession who was also a vocal segregationist and antimiscegenationist, extremely gingerly.[4] In the context of the struggle against racism, a public affiliation with Brinton would have introduced an unneeded twist into the moral narrative of racial inclusiveness that Boas was striving to construct. Yet Boas's calculated effort to dodge any close connection with Brinton in the North American press might also be seen, in light of his far-flung obituary, as an effort to protect his predecessor's reputation by keeping him out of a fight that Boas knew he was doomed to lose. Boas recognized that history had drawn him into a global fight against racism, and he embraced the challenge; but his homage to Brinton can be read as an acknowledgment that their conflict over race had made it impossible to actualize other scholarly possibilities, affiliations, and struggles. Boas's memorial demands that these possibilities be brought to light. It compels us to ask, What intellectual projects had to be displaced or silenced in order for the culturalist critique of race to become the basis of American anthropology?

In this essay I want to recover one of these set-aside projects, the one that Boas saw Brinton as having fostered, thereby providing the "firm footing" he stood on throughout his career. This project, which Brinton referred to as "the philosophy of expression," he first conceived as an intervention in the field of comparative philology inspired by Wilhelm von Humboldt's axiom on the fundamental nature of language. "In itself," Humboldt had proclaimed, language "is no product *(Ergon)*, but an activity *(Energeia)*."[5] Language, Brinton learned from Humboldt, was not a ready-made object that could be looked upon from the detached perspective favored by natural scientists, for it was only by virtue of linguistic practice—people using words—that different forms of human experience (including the experience of scientific knowledge) were constituted.

On the basis of this understanding, which came to be known as the "expressive-constitutive" dimension of language, Brinton departed from his American contemporaries. He elaborated in the 1880s a methodological critique of the ascendant naturalistic school of linguistic anthropology, a critique he would soon apply to all those scientists who had fallen under the sway of "the positive philosophers, who insisted that events and institutions must be explained solely from the . . . objective world."[6] It was owing to Brinton's attempt to conduct the human sciences from a first-personal perspective—an intervention that began with his Humboldtian reconceptualization of language as expression—that Boas credited him with putting their common discipline on a "firm footing," notwithstanding the fact, which Boas also saw, that Brinton never ceased to defend a theory of "psychic unity" that contradicted, even fettered, his most promising insights.

Boas took over Brinton's philosophy of expression and reformed it by abandoning its naturalistic ontology of the human psyche. One outcome of this work of rectification was a thesis that might be read as a leitmotif of Boas's entire career. "To the ethnologist," Boas wrote, "the most trifling features of social life are important because they are expressions of historical happenings," and not, as Brinton had thought, because those facts are "expressions of the general consciousness of Humanity."[7] What is the difference between "history" and "the consciousness of Humanity," and why did it matter to Franz Boas? And why, at the same time, was it important to him to retain the concept of expression? If we can come to some understanding of the stakes of this highly abstract disagreement—which is also a moment of concurrence and continuation—we can begin to make sense of Boas's *Globus* memorial and, more important, reconstruct how Boas built upon Brinton's "firm footing" a viable discipline, universal in scope and possessed of a moral vision of knowledge as a collective practice of symbolic self-becoming.

The mode of expressive enlightenment in which Boas and Brinton both took part, far from being limited to the pages of journals, was an ethical attitude distributed far and wide across turn-of-the-century American culture.

Anthropologists participated in it, but they were not its inventors. What we risk failing to see, if we consider Boas's understanding of human language solely from the perspective of Euro-American intellectual history, is that circulating media like the Yavapai physician Carlos Montezuma's activist newspaper *Wassaja* and the NAACP's *Crisis,* edited by W. E. B. Du Bois, also drew upon and fulfilled a "philosophy of expression" that bore a family resemblance to, but was not wholly descended from, the kind of disciplinary knowledge put into practice by Boas himself.[8] Instead of positioning Brinton and Boas as adversarial stand-ins for race and culture, we can understand both better when we recognize their mutual imbrication in this wider discursive field—a rhetoric of expression that charged the cultural politics of race with philosophical urgency, inspiring a social project to understand the symbolic activities of humans and make use of them to bring into being new transcultural futures.

## "SPEAK!"

Although the term "expression" has a long Euro-American history, it took on a new significance following the emergence in Europe of a self-consciously modern form of subjectivity that the philosopher Charles Taylor has referred to as the "disembedded" or "buffered" self. This new kind of self found itself possessed of new "powers of moral ordering" that enabled and encouraged an attitude of holding oneself apart from the natural world and the extrahuman influences that, in a previous era, had penetrated the "porous" self as part of that world.[9]

The newness of this situation manifested in a kind of philosophical inquiry into the history of the human faculties, an inquiry whose classic question—How did human language originate and develop from prehistory to the present?—inspired a richly variegated genre of speculative history. This genre of philosophy was about more than language considered objectively. By inquiring into the origins of language, the philosophes of the eighteenth century were engaged in a process of self-interpretation, a coming-to-terms with the mysterious sources of their own peculiar form of experience. How one answered the question of language's origin carried high stakes because variant answers entailed different attitudes about how one ought to live one's life in the present day.

This was the ethically charged context in which an expressive theory of language emerged in the modern West, most decisively in the writings of Johann Gottfried von Herder. Herder's impact on American anthropology has been discussed in many ways, but what I want to trace here, following Taylor, is the way Herder took it upon himself to theorize and model a whole style of modern self-comportment.[10] Like other philosophers of his time, Herder celebrated the buffered self's new powers of self-definition. Yet he worried that the people of his age were morally lost, set adrift from one another in a vast and increasingly confusing world from which older forms of belonging and certainty had vanished. Herder exhorted would-be philosophers of his day to consider the demands placed upon reason by their historical predicament. "You can no longer have effect like Socrates—for you lack the small, narrow, active, compressed *stage!*" he exhorted in his 1774 essay *This Too a Philosophy of History for the Formation of Humanity.* "*A citizen of the earth,* and no longer a citizen at *Athens,* you naturally also lack the *perception* of what you should do in Athens, the *certain feeling* of what you do, the *sensation of joy* at what you have accomplished."[11] Herder's preeminent concern, given the eclipse of this older moral universe, was to discern how modern experience might give rise, in a fundamentally new way, to "a perception of what you should do . . . the certain feeling of what you do."

The trouble with modernity, as Herder saw it, was that its ways of organizing social space could no longer provide an obvious path to older feelings of moral certainty. The flip side of the buffered self's new powers of moral ordering was that such feelings could no longer be seen as immanent in predefined roles and relationships, as they had been in ancient Athens. "The . . . feeling of what you do," if you are Socrates (or, more precisely, Herder's imaginary Socrates), is bound up with the fact that it's a common practice to talk about metaphysics over a six-hour dinner or to cajole one's neighbors on their way home from the marketplace. Herder saw that he inhabited a much larger and more impersonal world, one increasingly mediated not by face-to-face interaction but by infrastructures of communication like newspapers, scholarly institutions, and the state. These media abstracted speech from its scenes of utterance and reproduced discourse as an objective social fact, what would later be called information.

This state of affairs could not simply be rejected. Herder's powerful new idea was to associate the "feeling of what you do" in modernity with the very practice that modern life seemed to have rendered obsolete or at least invisible, namely, the act of speech itself, undertaken against all odds and even with no interlocutors present at hand. As he urged his modern Socrates,

> The *scope* of your sphere perhaps compensates for the *less determinate* quality and *lacking* quality of your beginning! A hundred people will read you and not understand you, a hundred read and yawn, a hundred read and despise, a hundred read and slander, a hundred read and prefer to have the dragon-chains

> of habit and remain who they are. But keep in mind that perhaps a *hundred* still remain left over with whom you bear fruit—when you are long since decayed, still a *world of posterity* which reads you and applies you better. *World* and *world of posterity* is your Athens! *Speak!*[12]

What's remarkable about this passage is the way it enacts what it's trying to describe. Herder communicates to his readers with a kind of speech capable of demonstrating how speech itself can be experienced as answering to a moral imperative. He thinks speech can be made intelligible to his readers in this way because they are buffered selves living in a social world that has closed down certain "feelings of what to do" but opened other ones up—above all, the feeling that, by being brave enough to "*Speak!*" to a world of strangers, one might give rise to a kind of enunciation that circulates with an unprecedented range, beyond this "*world*" and into a "*world of posterity.*" Herder's text is a foundational elaboration of the constitutive picture of language that would soon become associated with the term "expression."

Herder's early formulation of the expressive-constitutive dimension of language would have profound ramifications in Germany and beyond. Kurt Müller-Vollmer and others have shown, for instance, that Wilhelm von Humboldt's picture of language as an Energeia rather than an Ergon was indebted to Herder's notion of speech as a medium of worldmaking.[13] Herder's understanding of what Sean Kelly has called "perceptual normativity"—his sense that the "feeling of what you do" is given not by some impersonal moral law but by one's embodied experience of a specific situation—might also be seen as a source of Humboldt's insistence that the historian has a moral obligation to "enliven and refine our sense of acting on reality" and to shun "metaphysical" forms of inquiry that require an "abstracting from all experience."[14] Herder and Humboldt too thus developed one way of coming to terms with the historicity of the buffered self and its powers. But it was not the only way.

Today, the best-known account of the origins of humans' linguistic powers is Étienne Bonnot de Condillac's *Essay on the Origin of Human Knowledge* (1746). Like Herder, Condillac had both a theoretical story about language's relation to modern experience and a moral vision of how that story pertained to the scientist's task. Whereas Herder argued that forms of subjective experience vary throughout history, Condillac insisted that human experience is the trans-historical process through which we take in sensory data and organize them into thoughts. We do this by means of the "operations of the mind," chiefly language, since "ideas connect with signs."[15] Condillac's idea of language can be understood as a naturalistic philosophy of experience, since the fact that "ideas connect with signs" is in the first instance a fact about nature, not about human beings.[16] According to Condillac, our cognitive faculties never fundamentally change, even though we learn over time based on trial and error. History, in this view, is the story of our coming to a better understanding of the limits we've been placed under by nature. And since we already have a good sense of how nature works from mechanical sciences like physics, we can get more certain about who we are by trusting the same methods.

While claiming to avoid the "confusion which now prevails in metaphysics and moral philosophy," Condillac conferred an implicit moral duty upon the buffered self. He insisted upon humans' obligation to live within nature-determined limitations on what it is permissible to think about oneself and one's place in the world—a view that would later be called the "ethics of belief."[17] What distinguishes this ethical project of the buffered self from Herder's is that it understands our "feeling of what to do" as the result of objective laws, not as a historically emergent activity arising from the contexts of particular forms of life. It is a scheme of moral improvement designed for the buffered self, and only the buffered self, to excel at.

While Herder's philosophy of language, through the mediation of Humboldt, found its way into the learned institutions of Prussia, Condillac's found fertile ground in the young United States, where it would captivate the imagination of American linguists until well after the Civil War.[18] In the generation leading up to Brinton's entrance onto the scene, its most up-to-date articulation was William Dwight Whitney's theory of languages as institutions. For Whitney, to say a language was an institution meant that it was collectively invented or instituted, not discovered. This was a significant departure from Condillac's conception of language as a naturally endowed faculty, but it reproduced his view that language had a purely instrumental role in human betterment. Whitney saw language, like "steam-engines," "tubular-bridges," and "Brussels carpets," as an "instrument of thought, the machinery with which the mind works; an instrument by which its capacity to achieve valuable results is indefinitely increased, but which, far from being identical with it, is one of its own products; with and by which it works with freedom."[19]

Central to this understanding of language is the supposition that the human mind can abstract itself from the flow of experience, bringing the freedom of a third-personal perspective to bear upon itself. It is only from this detached standpoint that human freedom can be imagined to exist in a purely negative relation to its products—indeed, so much so that it would seem to diminish human freedom to argue, as Herder had, that language is in some way constitutive of our "feeling of what to do." Whitney called linguistics a historical discipline because its object of study was a human invention; yet by construing language as an invention—a product, an Ergon—he did what Humboldt said the historian should never do. He considered historical phenomena in abstraction from experience. "The facts of language," Whitney famously remarked, "are almost as little the work of man as is the form of his skull."[20] One can understand why the founder of semiology, Ferdinand de Saussure, whose linguistics course was premised on the regimentation of the diachronic and experiential by the synchronic and systematic, spoke of Whitney as "l'Américan Whitney que je révère."[21]

Shortly after his return from graduate school in Europe, Brinton dedicated himself to articulating a Humboldtian "philosophy of expression" capable of standing up to the naturalistic school that predominated in the human sciences of his time. He did everything he could to play Herder to Whitney's Condillac. Whereas Whitney insisted that language was an internally coherent formal system that obeyed natural laws, Brinton saw each language as a "thought world in tones" shaping our experience such that it couldn't be analyzed in a purely objective fashion.[22] Whereas Whitney cautioned his readers against metaphysical theories of language coming out of Germany, theories that could only constrain human freedom by misidentifying it as one of its institutional creations, Brinton insisted that language, "which will perish only when intelligence itself, in its highest sense, is extinguished," was indistinguishable from human cognition and thus from freedom itself.[23]

Brinton made his neo-Humboldtian project relevant to late nineteenth-century Americans by emphasizing dimensions of language that could be characterized only from the first-personal point of view of a historical subject. These dimensions had been utterly effaced by naturalistic linguistic methods, which approached language as an Ergon—not as a creation of God, necessarily, but as something that existed in nature as a complete, coherent system. To say language is complete and coherent is to assume that there exist clear boundaries that separate it from other entities in the order of Nature. It was owing to Brinton's sense of the inadequacy of this parceling out of the precincts of Nature that Boas would later remember him as having "called us back from the excessive specialization that had begun to pose a threat to the general scientific point of view in itself."

And yet, despite Brinton's avowed allegiance to the Humboldtian way of looking at language, in key respects he departed from the Humboldtian historian's task of refining "our sense of acting on reality." Boas put his finger on this problem in his obituary, where he wrote that "Brinton's strengths and weaknesses were conditioned by his intellectual disposition, which saw in all particularities above all the verification of the universal law. . . . Hence the richness of his stimulating thought and the lack of penetrating analysis of individual phenomena."[24]

Boas's identification of Brinton's shortcoming as an inattentiveness to "particularities" is more than just a question of scale, of Brinton being interested in big things and Boas being interested in small things. What's at stake here is Brinton's oscillation between the two styles of being a buffered self that I identified earlier with Condillac and Herder. Thus the unresolved conceptual tension—reflected in Brinton's famous slogan, "Man is everywhere different, and everywhere the same"—between the constitutive power of human language on the one hand and, on the other, what Brinton called the "psychic unity of man."[25] The question that repeatedly arises in Brinton's work is whether this "psychic unity" does not itself possess the character of an Ergon, something coherent and complete that we step into when we are born—in which case the "sense of what you do" that manifests itself to particular people in particular situations would have little relevance to a general characterization of human experience. A similar question can ultimately be raised about the way Brinton understood the term "expression," as for instance in the slogan I cited earlier, that "the facts of ethnology must ever be regarded as the expressions of the general consciousness of Humanity."[26] Are the members of humanity giving rise to these facts to be understood as constituting historically variable forms of life, or does "expression" refer merely to the mechanical process through which behavioral tokens are reproduced from a fixed psychic type?

Boas's worries concerning Brinton's ideas about language were borne out in the way Brinton imagined the anthropologist to engage with the world he studied. Unlike Herder and Humboldt, Brinton's study of subjectivity entailed a radical decontextualization of the self. He held that everything important about our experience is reducible to the contents of our consciousness. "Men," Brinton wrote, "do not live in material things, but in mental states; and solely as they affect these are the material things valuable or valueless."[27] Neither our unconscious bodies nor the world beyond the buffered self can provide us with any moral guidance about the kinds of beings people essentially are. For Brinton, the most successful strategy for coping with the "milieu" beyond the mind was to withdraw from it entirely. "The progress of man," he declared, "is his progress of gaining independence from nature, of making her forces his slaves and not leaving them his masters."[28] The metaphor of mastery here is not unrelated to Brinton's investment in scientific racism. The downfall of the nonwhite races, Brinton proposed, was that they remained too embedded in environments that, over time, corrupted their bodies and minds: "The peculiar traits of races can with entire propriety be considered pathological; for the more completely they adapt a group to one environment, the more do they unfit it for any other."[29] Brinton's inclination to blame the environments that nonwhites inhabited for their racial "pathologies" thus worked hand in hand with his investment in a certain picture of what it is to be a buffered self, a sum of "mental states" utterly cut off from one's environment, and the more cut off, the better.

The longer one spends with Brinton, the more difficult it becomes to determine whether the ethics of belief he deployed to police his theory of "psychic unity" is best interpreted as an inconsistency in a fundamentally Humboldtian way of looking at the world, or whether Brinton's entire "philosophy of expression" was just a way of sugarcoating the deflationary pessimism that followed from his erection of an unbridgeable psychic barrier between the world and the self's experience of it. Ultimately, the best way to make sense of Brinton is to see him as attempting to rise to the challenge of self-interpretation that Taylor associates with modern selfhood, a project that is as much about coping as it is about coherence. Undoubtedly, Brinton was attuned to something unsatisfying about the intellectual world of his day. He saw in the Humboldtian tradition a theoretical solution to some of the problems posed by that world; but as a matter of practice, the third-personal, policing attitude gave him a clearer sense of moral purpose.

Boas, in "The Limitations of the Comparative Method of Anthropology," recognized this attitude in Brinton when he interpreted his predecessor's notion of psychic unity as a consequence of having adopted the position that "anthropological studies *must be confined* to researches on the laws that govern the growth of society."[30] By maintaining that stance, Brinton left open a possibility—a way out of his confinement—that he himself was not able to realize. The question left open for Boas was, What else could anthropology be?

## EXPRESSIONS OF HISTORICAL HAPPENINGS

The epochal insight that Boas brought to American anthropology—the insight that, as we shall shortly see, made him a great if sometimes unwitting affiliate of the many projects of collective self-determination taking shape at the outset of the twentieth century—was that knowledge could be a means of affiliating oneself with the world and its people. In formulating this insight, Boas drew on many intellectual sources, including experiences with Indigenous collaborators.[31] His first major statement of it was "The Study of Geography" (1887), written shortly after his return from Baffin Island. In this essay Boas concluded, of the "effort to delineate the earth's surface," that "every step that brings us nearer the end gives ampler satisfaction to the impulse which induces us to devote our time and work to this study, gratifying the love for the country we inhabit, and the nature that surrounds us."[32] As Matti Bunzl has argued, Boas showed himself in this essay to be engaged in a scholarly project closely aligned with that of Humboldt and Herder.[33]

If Herder and Humboldt worked out a certain style of being a buffered self, one that seeks "to enliven and refine our sense of acting on reality" (Humboldt) and that also seeks the "feeling of what you do" (Herder) by turning outward and confronting one's particular historical predicament, it was Boas who advanced this modern mode of self-interpretation by showing how the "feeling of what you do" derives from the affective solicitation presented by the objects one studies. Boas advanced a new form of science that paid homage to the ideas of Alexander von Humboldt's *Cosmos* and that Boas named "cosmography": science that "has its source in the personal feeling of man towards the world, towards the phenomena surrounding him."[34] Whereas the physicist or naturalist seeks to gratify an "aesthetic impulse" driving him to systematize the chaos of experience, the force of the "affective impulse" drives the research of the cosmographer. Whereas Brinton thought that humans refine their psychic faculties by insulating themselves from their environment, Boas reimagined anthropological knowledge as a process of directing oneself outward, into the world.

We are now in a position to understand the difference between Boas's interest in historical happenings and Brinton's interest in the "consciousness of Humanity." "The Study of Geography" might profitably be read as a theorization of the historian's responsibility, as imagined by Wilhelm von Humboldt and his followers, to "enliven and refine our sense of acting on reality." Boas viewed cosmography (and, later, anthropology) as a "historical science," not merely, as Brinton had assumed, an effort to discover causal laws that history may bear out but never change.[35] At this early phase of his career, Boas was concerned to expand dramatically the scope of whom and what an intellectual might care about—hence his statement that "the most trifling features of social life are important because they are expressions of historical happenings."[36] What makes these happenings expressive is not their emanation from humanity's "universal consciousness" but their existence as part of an affective exchange between the world "we inhabit" and the inquiring self.

Boas's continuation of Herder's project raises two questions. First, how could a vision of anthropology's task that is so focused on the particularities of experience aspire to the universality and progressiveness of modern science? Second, in what way is Boas's affective account of anthropological knowledge not—as the "philosophy of expression" might ultimately have been for Brinton—a just-so story told to render the alienation of the modern subject more bearable? Answering these questions in the right way can forestall a common misinterpretation of Boas's project that holds he was engaged in a project of Counter-Enlightenment.[37] This view sees Boas as part of a long intellectual movement traceable to Herder's teacher Johann Georg Hamann, who abandoned the imperious claims of modern reason in favor of a relativistic celebration of the primal attachments of the "Volk." Such an abandonment would amount to a reenchantment, or unbuffering, of the modern buffered self: it would solve the predicaments of modern truth telling by demystifying modernity itself.

But this isn't at all what Boas wanted, for himself or anyone else. Boas shared in the characteristically modern aspiration to advance science, an endeavor he believed "helps free us from the errors of the past."[38] Boas's understanding of scientific progress was somewhat unusual since he did not think the correction of scientific error developed from the replacement of bad explanations with better ones. Instead he followed Goethe in holding that "a single action or event is interesting, not because it is explainable, but because it is true."[39] If one approaches a phenomenon with an idea that it is a piece of data to be explained, one has already ceased to act as a world-oriented scholar and become something else: a naturalist governed by an internal "aesthetic impulse."[40] Unlike Brinton, Boas wanted to get back in touch with the phenomena of the world. He sought not only explanations but a heightened feeling of connectedness.

As in the case of Brinton, Boas's idea of the scholar's proper relation to the world connected to his understanding of language. In his "Introduction" to the *Handbook of American Indian Languages*, Boas grounded his career-long inquiry into human symbolic activity in a theory of what he called "secondary explanations."[41] Secondary explanations are reflexive linguistic phenomena: they comprise our explicit self-understanding of our experience in all its dimensions. And yet, despite our modern aspiration to cognitively master our experience, Boas argued that these understandings are subject to contingencies of unconscious experience that are largely beyond our control. "Even our scientific views, which are apparently based entirely on conscious reasoning," Boas explained, are formed "under the influence of strong emotions." To square the "Introduction" with "The Study of Geography," our views are responsive to the "affective impulse" governing our experience, according to which the self finds itself ineluctably drawn into the world without knowing why ahead of time.[42] In order for one's secondary understandings to become better attuned to one's environment, one has to get into the right relation not just with the world but also with oneself. One has to recognize oneself as the kind of being whose picture of the world is changeable.

Boas's theory of secondary understandings showed the attitudes of scientific experts to be subject to the very same impulses as the people whom they typically studied. This motivated his departure from Brinton on the question of how to respond to modernity and of who could take part in that response. In "The Aims of Ethnology," Boas wrote that "the same kind of struggle that the genius has to undergo among ourselves in his battle against dominant ideas or dominant prejudice occurs among primitives and it is of particular interest to see in how far the strong individual is able to free himself from the fetters of convention."[43] Moments like these, which recur throughout Boas's writings, reveal their author's enthusiasm for a certain project of enlightenment, a freeing of humanity from superstition. But in order to understand the modes of relation to the people Boas persisted in calling primitive—that is, colonized people—that his version of that project made possible, it is important to grasp the term "enlightenment" in its full dimensionality.

One understanding of the Enlightenment, Enlightenment with a capital E, holds that it was a period of intellectual and cultural history. Those who see Boas as part of the Counter-Enlightenment tend to assume that he looked back upon the Enlightenment as a discrete period of history that was already complete or that had proven itself incapable of completing itself, such that a new kind of inquiry, the Counter-Enlightenment, had to be initiated. It's true that Boas, in his 1904 essay on "The History of Anthropology," traced the origins of modern anthropology back to the classic Counter-Enlightenment figures: to Jean-Jacques Rousseau's voicing of "the deep-seated feeling that political and social development was the result of a faulty development of civilization" and to Herder's *Ideen zur Geschichte der Menschheit* (Ideas on the History of Mankind), in which, "perhaps for the first time, the fundamental thought of the development of the culture of mankind as a whole is clearly expressed."[44] There is a real sense in which everything Boas accomplished, his whole updating of the Humboldtian philosophy of expression, can be seen as the unfolding of a possibility emergent in this late eighteenth-century moment. This raises the question of whether Boas did not take up a project that was anachronistic—or, worse, intellectually imperialistic—from its very origin: what right did Boas have to recreate "primitive man" in the image of a Galileo or Spinoza, engaged in a "battle against dominant ideas or dominant prejudice"?

If we take Boas seriously, such a question, which casts colonized peoples as an object (or Ergon) of scientific inquiry, examination, and explanation, misconstrues anthropology's significance as a modernizing practice of enlightenment. For Boas, as for Herder, modernity named a moral crisis that required a new receptivity to the constraints and possibilities emergent within a given form of life. Over time, Boas came to study colonized peoples not to understand modernity's prehistory but to explore the variety of ways in which human beings attune themselves to the crises of the present. As he wrote in his preface to *Race, Language and Culture,* "Growing up in our own civilization we know how we ourselves are conditioned by it, how our bodies, our language, our modes of thinking and acting are determined by limits imposed on us by our environment. Knowledge of the life processes and behavior of man under conditions of life fundamentally different from our own can help us to obtain a freer view of our own lives and of our life problems."[45] In turning back to Herder and Rousseau, Boas's purpose was not to locate himself within a grand narrative of intellectual history, but to specify a problem that emerged in his own experience. Boas saw in these eighteenth-century figures the germ of an account of "our life problems" as historical in the particular sense with which he used that term, the sense of being solicited by a world toward which the self has to get in the right relation.

Enlightenment, then, can also be understood in the lowercase, not as a closed moment but as a continuing process, a coming-to-terms with history through the cultivation of a certain style of being a buffered self. We find a cognate understanding expressed in Michel Foucault's later formulation of enlightenment as an "ethical attitude": a mode of relating to the present times and to oneself as a modern subject. "To be modern," Foucault writes, "is not to accept oneself as one is in the flux of the passing moments; it is to take oneself as object of a complex and difficult elaboration. . . . This modernity does not 'liberate man in his own being'; it compels him to face the task of producing himself."[46] It is this style of being a buffered self, this reckoning with today that culminates in the discursive constitution of a self with "a freer view," that I want to understand as expressive enlightenment.

This form of expressive enlightenment—self-enlightenment through affective exchange with the world surrounding the buffered self—could be achieved only through an interaction with a world that was always already social, a world comprised of other selves possessed of other secondary explanations, all, Boas hoped, striving to get themselves attuned to the world in a way that gratified their "affective impulse" toward it. For Boas, expressive enlightenment was a mode of discursive affiliation that would connect the members of the human community with time. Toward the end of his life, he wrote, "It is my conviction that the fundamental ethical point of view to be taken is that of the in-group which must be expanded over the whole of humanity. This leads naturally to the conclusion that the individual must be valued according to his own worth and not the worth of a class to which we assign him."[47] To recognize individuals according to their "own worth" is to presuppose in those individuals themselves a capacity for self-production. Boas did not hesitate to say that this was the way he looked at the world and the way he sought to empower others. "My whole outlook upon social life is determined by the question: how can we recognize the shackles that tradition has laid upon us?" he wrote. "I consider it the duty of those who are devoted to the study of social problems to become clear in regard to these questions and to see to it that through their influence the intellectual chains in which tradition holds us are gradually broken."[48]

Boas looked for allies in this project of enlightenment wherever he could find them, in other societies (where he found "primitives" engaged in the "same kind of struggle that genius has to undergo among ourselves") as well as in his own. To Boas, an enlightened attitude toward oneself seemed the only condition of modern belonging worth endorsing at a time when secondary understandings were creating new barriers between people. Boas, like Herder, saw that the modern creation of "the whole of humanity" followed from the unavailability of older forms of attachment. "On the whole in the history of mankind as the size of groups has increased, their solidarity has been weakened," he wrote, "and with that the rights of the outsider have been recognized."[49] What makes up for the weakening solidarity of these expanding groups is a mode of belonging facilitated through discourse circulating among those outsiders, those who never subscribed to the in-group's traditions or who expressively defined themselves in opposition to them.

A solidarity constituted through the circulation of discourse requires peculiar protocols of mutual recognition through which members of expanding in-groups can manifest themselves to one another across time and space. One such protocol of mutual manifestation, for those committed to expressive enlightenment, was the term "expression" itself. As Foucault observes, Kant understood the Enlightenment slogan *Sapere Aude!* (Dare to know!) as a *Wahlspruch,* or "a heraldic device, that is, a distinctive feature by which one can be recognized, and . . . also a motto, an instruction that one gives oneself and proposes to others."[50] Near the end of the nineteenth century, expression became the Wahlspruch of a new mode of enlightenment. Brinton and Boas both had a role to play in bringing this to pass; whatever their theoretical differences, they used the term to convey a shared intention to deal with the world, and one's ethical relation to oneself as a knower of that world, in a new and more receptive way. From

Brinton's slogan that the facts of ethnology are "expressions of the general consciousness of humanity" through Boas's maxim that "the most trifling events are significant because they are expressions of historical happenings," we can witness the gradual refinement of a specific style of being a buffered self, one designed to cope with and contest a rival style of knowledge making that looked upon the world as Ergon.

## BECKONING

Expressive enlightenment was not merely a form of scholarly knowledge, a Boasian strategy to build upon Brinton's "firm footing" a viable scientific discipline. It was a relational form of becoming that gratified the "affective impulse" directing the inquirer outward, into affiliation with the world and its people. This activity of imagining new cross-cultural understandings made a difference in twentieth-century America, but to appreciate its significance we need to look past the precinct of anthropology. Beyond the human sciences, the mode of expressive enlightenment was also discovered—simultaneously, as it were—by poets, philosophers, politicians, and social activists, who developed it in a diversity of inflections. Across American society the Wahlspruch of expression, and the modern attitude of self-production it signaled, facilitated the affiliation of disparate individuals who resolved to become themselves by speaking out in public.

We can begin to appreciate the breadth of this collective manifestation by briefly considering the field of philology, a field that, like ethnology, underwent a momentous transformation in the last decades of the nineteenth century. One can trace this shift, closely connected to the emergence of the modern discipline of literary studies, precisely by following the etymology of "expression" in the published works of critics and rhetoricians around the beginning of the twentieth century. Prior to the rise of the English department in America, "expression" was a synonym for enunciation. It was part of a scholarly discipline through which teachers taught students to speak according to established rules of conduct. As late as 1887, J. H. Gilmore, a professor of rhetoric at the University of Rochester, could hope to find an audience for his *Outlines of the Art of Expression*, a "little book," as described in its introduction, that "has grown, in the author's class-room, out of an attempt to supplement the defective early training of his pupils . . . [with] a knowledge of those particular elements of Grammar which are distinctively characteristic of the English tongue." Gilmore's vision for the progress of his students' knowledge had nothing to do with the process of self-becoming I've been calling expressive enlightenment. Speech was always to be governed according to elocutionary protocols written by experts who had foretold all possible scenarios of decorous utterance.[51]

By the 1880s, the days of Gilmore's brand of prescriptive rhetoric were numbered. According to an influential cadre of ambitious young professors who taught English, not Latin, and who counted themselves as proponents of modern philology, the study of a literary text was to be imagined precisely as a mode of enlightenment. When the Columbia professor Joel Spingarn, a leader of this new movement, insisted that great works of literature ought to be seen as exemplifying an "art of expression," he explained at length that this phrase meant not that works of literature conformed better than other texts to certain prescribed rules but that the meaning of literature depended on its exemplary effect on the life of a reader. Like Brinton and Boas, Spingarn traced this understanding of expression across the Atlantic and backward in time to thinkers like Goethe, Herder, and Hegel. It was with them in mind that he wrote, in his lecture "The New Criticism" (1910), that the basic objects and aims of literary inquiry were fundamentally expressive: "What has the poet tried to do, and how has he fulfilled his intention? What is he striving to express and how has he expressed it? What impression does his work make on me, and how can I best express this impression?"[52] In modern philology as in Boasian anthropology, as witnessed later by Ludwig Lewisohn's *Expression in America* (1930) and F. O. Matthiessen's *American Renaissance: Art and Expression in the Age of Emerson and Whitman* (1943), the Wahlspruch of expression came to serve as a watchword for those who saw literature as Energeia rather than Ergon.[53]

Now, one could argue that this realignment of literature as a project of expressive enlightenment was not, in relation to anthropology, a simultaneous discovery so much as a parallel development derived from a common tradition, a separate branch of the same Romantic family tree. But this is not the path I want to pursue here, for two reasons: first, expressive enlightenment flourished even among peoples avowedly hostile to Euro-American intellectual traditions; and, second, even among the scholarly elites we've been examining it was experienced not primarily as a set of theoretical propositions but as a way of reimagining the social world in which they lived. The really important question raised by the ascendancy of expression in ethnology and philology is not how an idea traveled, in ways we might not have recognized, between one intellectual and another, but how, at this particular moment in time, expression became a discursive basis for a new kind of collectivity. This gives us a way of coming back to the historiographical question about collective identity with which we started, the question of why the cultural politics of race can be thought about as unfolding within, traveling alongside, or even surrounding the history of expression.

One figure who can help us measure the scope of expressive enlightenment and its relation to the politics of cultural belonging is Carlos Montezuma, the Yavapai doctor, pamphleteer, and founding member of the Society of American Indians. Montezuma was a self-declared "abolitionist." Throughout his career he advocated the immediate dissolution of the United States Bureau of Indian Affairs (BIA), known then as the Indian Bureau or Office, which he saw as the latest in a line of Euro-American institutions designed to keep Indian people in a state of political and moral dependency. The result of these institutions' influence, Montezuma said, was the stifling of a people's self-expression:

> The aborigines of America have never been in a position to express themselves. The game of "the survival of the fittest," competition of life in God's appointed way, "by the sweat of the brow," have been too one-sided. It has been an awful unfair play to speculate and weaken, to satisfy your aesthetic propensities.
>
> To judge a race relative to their standard we must put ourselves in their place; better still, be one of them.[54]

One could be forgiven for mistaking this for a rumination of Franz Boas, yet no evidence exists to suggest that Montezuma ever read a word Boas wrote. Montezuma's opposition between expression and enlightened self-interpretation on the one hand ("to judge a race relative to their standard we must put ourselves in their place") and, on the other, an aesthetic picture of an orderly universe subject to natural laws ("'the survival of the fittest' . . . in God's appointed way") shows that he had found his own way to distinguish between affective and aesthetic speech, Energeia and Ergon. Throughout his career, Montezuma consciously modeled for his audience this expressive attitude—an attitude he thought could help his people come to terms with the predicament from which, as he put it in another speech, "we Indians are struggling in the dark to find a way out."[55]

We can begin to understand how Montezuma imagined Indian expression as a response to his people's historical predicament by looking at his self-published newspaper, *Wassaja: Freedom's Signal for the Indian. Wassaja* arose as a counterpublication to the official organ of the Society of American Indians, the *Quarterly Journal of the Society of American Indians* (later, the *American Indian Magazine*), which *Wassaja* frequently upbraided for its conciliatory attitude toward the Indian Bureau. Despite this political disagreement, though, the papers shared a commitment to fostering a new pan-Indian public by adopting a deliberately ecumenical attitude toward Indian speech. In the first issue of the society's *Quarterly Journal*, its editors announced their intention to print "any expression on any Indian subject."[56]

What sets *Wassaja* apart for our purposes is the way it envisions the thematic open-endedness of Indian speech as an ethical attitude adopted at the level of the self. It wasn't enough for Montezuma to publish "any expression on any Indian subject"; those expressions had to be loudly announced as historical events because Montezuma thought it was always politically significant when an individual Indian came into his or her public voice. "AN INDIAN EXPRESSING HIMSELF," reads the headline over one letter to the editor, a letter that Montezuma framed in order to convey his understanding that expression was not merely a way of transmitting information about Indian affairs but was itself the best kind of news. *Wassaja* modeled the attitude of expressive enlightenment that Montezuma wanted his readers to adopt. Not unlike Herder enjoining the modern Socrates of his imagination to speak, Montezuma set out to enact and solicit the same kind of speech he purported to describe.

Montezuma signaled to his readers his intention to use print discourse differently from journals like the *Quarterly Journal* by undertaking formal experimentation in his prose and, as Robert Dale Parker has argued, in his poetry. Consider, for instance, the long poem "I Have Stood Up for You."[57] Thematically, the message of the poem seems relatively straightforward: the speaker wants his readers to know that they have a friend in *Wassaja.* "I have stood up for you," he says, through all "your" struggles against the Indian Bureau and against what "the palefaces said." But even as *Wassaja* gives his "you" the credit for surviving the antagonisms of civilization while offering encouragement by asserting his loyalty, a strange sense emerges at the end of the poem that *Wassaja* also wants to say the opposite. "You have proven yourselves to be / Whatever I have stood up for you to be," he avers—as if Indians ought to see themselves as having been constituted as a collective subject by virtue of what *Wassaja* has said on their behalf. Here *Wassaja* presents itself as unconditionally committed to Indian people and responsible for Indians' being what they are.[58] But how does this work? How can a paper stand behind—that is, follow—what it also claims to lead? More fundamentally, who stands behind, or leads, *Wassaja?*

Wassaja, it turns out, is the name Montezuma was given as a child by his Yavapai grandmother. The word can be translated into English as "signaling" or "beckoning," which captures Montezuma's sense of himself as a speaker to his people and, as such, the creator of a new community. Montezuma gave his newspaper his name because he observed no distinction between his subjectivity and its discursive manifestation. He was committed to an ethical attitude

Edited by Wassaja (Dr. Montezuma's Indian name, meaning "Signaling") an Apache Indian.

Vol. 2, No. 10 ISSUED MONTHLY January, 1918

## OUR APPEAL FOR FINANCIAL AID

WASSAJA wishes to say that we do not expect anything from those who have given us their aid already, but we do from those who have not responded and still feel that they want to help the Indians in their freedom. WASSAJA realizes that appeals are many at this hour in behalf of our soldiers, but we Indians want the country to know we are also pushing forward in the cause of liberty. If the Indians can be emancipated, see how much more we can help in the cause of national liberty. If we are not free how can we free others? WASSAJA, in the broadest sense, is trying to untangle the web that keeps the Indians from freedom. We again ask aid from those who have the Indian at heart, to help financially in the publication of WASSAJA.

### WASSAJA'S PLEA TO THE INDIANS

We must be united; there must be harmony; we must stand together. We must be of one accord. We must get together and walk in the same trail. We must bring all of our forces and all pull together in one direction—namely free ourselves from the Indian Office and become American citizens, entitled to the rights and privileges thereof. You reservation Indians are given the idea that the Indian Office will free all the Indians bye-and-bye. The Indian Office will never free the Indians. They would be foolish to free us when they are making their bread and butter just as long as we are wards. You may ask how can you go at it to help this high and noble object of freedom and citizenship for yourself and our people? Sit right down and write a few lines to your Congressman or Senator from your state that you are in favor of abolishing the Indian Office and for them to use their influence in the matter. The women of our country have gained their plea by going at it in the same way.

It is high time that we Indians stand out and act as men for our rights as aboriginal Americans. We do not deserve freedom and citizenship if we stand back and wait until it is handed out to us. What is worth having, is worth working for. The opportunity is right here now for every Indian in the country to war whoop for what other races enjoy and are blessed with. It is gratifying to know many of our young men are in the war to fight for their country. But the country does not know that we Indians are not free and have not equal rights as we should have. Let us be just as loyal in our racial rights as we are to our country. If we have faith in our country let us have faith in the people, that when the people know that we Indians are in bondage they will come forth as they did with the negroes and they will make us free. But they will not know unless each one of us Indians TELLS THE PEOPLE THAT WE ARE NOT FREE AND THAT WE WANT TO BE FREE. This is the plea from WASSAJA to the Indians throughout the country.

### A NATION "MISINFORMING A RACE"

It is a well known fact that the Indian side has never been presented to the public. Interest of the Indian has only been fostered by the reports of the Indian Office. For years and years the wrong side has been hammered out to feed the

The January 1918 issue of Carlos Montezuma's *Wassaja,* the newspaper he described as "freedom's signal for the Indian." *Wassaja* 2, no. 10 (1918), Carlos Montezuma Collection, Arizona Collection, Arizona State University Libraries.

of expressive enlightenment that required him to continually reconstitute himself in response to the exigencies of the present.

The verse form of "I Have Stood Up for You" communicated this. Wassaja wanted to be a poet but, like Walt Whitman, he wrote most of his poetry in such a way that it sounded like prose when read aloud. Even today we recognize "I Have Stood Up for You" as a poem not because of its rhyme or meter but because when we look at the page we can see white space between the line breaks and capital letters at the beginning of each line. *Wassaja*'s identity was bound up with the look and feel of print discourse, with speech spread over great distances into the hands and minds not only of associates but also of strangers. This is one way in which Montezuma modeled, in the content and form of his discourse, an ethical attitude committed to an ongoing project of self-production.

In the pages of *Wassaja* we can begin to see what it means to say that the mode of solidarity engendered by expressive enlightenment is fundamentally *discursive*. It is made for a world in which the voices of individuals circulate among strangers: "The wrong concept of us Indians which the public entertains, is a phantom which can be cleared away only by education and by our personal contact with the masses of the country," Montezuma wrote in *Wassaja* in 1916. "It therefore behooves us to stand together and to teach the public differently."[59] The implication is clear: if Indians don't start speaking for themselves in view of a broader public, then they can't be free. Like Boas, Montezuma understood freedom to consist in the revision of secondary understandings—the "phantom" caricature of Indianness that "[must] be cleared away"—through a kind of proleptic speech that constitutes the people to which it repeatedly refers.[60]

Montezuma's advocacy of expressive enlightenment in *Wassaja* has discomfited commentators of all persuasions because it served as the engine of an emancipatory project, the abolishment of the Indian Bureau and its colonial infrastructure. At the center of this project was Montezuma's animus for the Indian reservation. "The reservation," he declared, "is a demoralizing prison, a barrier to enlightenment, a promoter of idleness, gamblers, paupers, and ruin."[61] Montezuma thought that Indians faced with the choice between the reservation and enlightenment should opt for enlightenment and leave the reservation behind. As reservations became sites of political and cultural mobilization and ultimately homes and communities, many scholars came to see Montezuma as an assimilationist. After all, he seemed to advocate the abandonment of a distinctively Indian identity for a form of life imposed by a foreign power.[62] This view has its merits, but it effaces Montezuma's keenest insights into the mutual imbrication, in modern society, of power and discursivity.

Montezuma attacked reservations because the government made use of them to squelch opposition. "There is a good reason why you do not hear from the Reservation Indians on freedom," he wrote. "THEY ARE AFRAID to open their mouths."[63] Notwithstanding his antireservationism, this was a powerful new way of soliciting a reconstituted, mass-mediated pan-Indian subject into being.

Montezuma's insistence on the need to speak was based on his notion of enlightenment as an expressive process of self-transformation. The reservation system, he insisted, produced a caricature of Indians that served as propaganda for the colonial state. As he put it in a 1905 commentary on a newspaper interview given by the commissioner of Indian Affairs, Francis Leupp, "The reservation system has been a monument to the want of knowledge of human nature on the part of those who have been instrumental in perpetuating it. The failure to recognize the brotherhood of man in the Indian, that he was a multiple being, however ignorant he might be, and not more unified in his natural endowments and faculties than other men subject to similar conditions and environments, has been his greatest handicap."[64] Indian identity, Montezuma insists here, must be seen as an instantiation of human nature as a whole. It is in human nature to be a "multiple being," not the cigar store "phantom" (Montezuma's coinage) that stood in for Indians in the public eye. I understand Montezuma's idea of a "multiple being" to mean that Indians cannot, and must not, conform to the reductive and unilinear understanding of human development advanced by the Bureau of Indian Affairs.

Far from seeking to abandon a distinctively Indian identity in favor of a scripted vision of civilizationist progress, Montezuma saw expressive enlightenment as a way for Indians to fulfill their multiple and protean selves, embedded in families, communities, tribes, and broader regional networks that government-imposed identities obscured. Montezuma's misrecognition of the reservation as the source of his people's troubles was a consequence—though not a necessary one—of his prescient search for a broader, self-determining Indian identity. But how could this more diffuse form of discursive solidarity be relevant or useful to American Indians living under a specific kind of settler-colonial repression?

Montezuma's answer to the challenge of living Indian life globally paralleled Boas's idea of affective solicitation through the exchange of secondary understandings. Speaking in a genre of persuasion that parallels Herder's *This Too a Philosophy of History*, Montezuma enjoined his Indian public to constitute itself in dialogue with those whose just-so stories about Indians threatened to flatten them into caricature: bureaucrats, politicians, and anthropologists too. In practice, the boundaries of *Wassaja*'s emergent public were necessarily porous. Montezuma wanted it that way. After all, he wrote, it was only "by our personal contact with the masses of the country" that Indian people could hope to correct the "phantom" image generated by the Indian Bureau.

Montezuma's motivating responsibility as an agent of expressive enlightenment came from his Indian public, just as Boas's came from anthropologists and Springarn's from readers and writers of English. *Wassaja* listened to what the wider world—for instance, anthropologists—had to say, too. From time to time, when a sympathetic non-Indian wrote him a letter, Montezuma would publish it in *Wassaja*. But it counted as *news* only when a new Indian correspondent emerged or, better yet, when word came to him of a new Indian newspaper getting off the ground. "More Indian papers by the Indians the better," he wrote in 1918. "It shows the Indians are coming out to express themselves."[65] By showing Indian and multiracial publics how one could "Speak!" from a position of phantom-like unfreedom, Montezuma, like Boas, fulfilled his own project of ethical self-fashioning.

In his effort to make expressive enlightenment the basis of a pan-Indian social movement, Montezuma adopted an ethical attitude toward history and language that faces in the same direction as that of Boas. As far as we know, the two never came into contact, but Montezuma's expressive opposition to the "aesthetic propensities" of the Indian Bureau parallels the disciplinary critique of "excessive specialization" and "positive knowledge" that Boas developed on the "firm footing" provided by Brinton's philosophy of expression. It was through his own commitment to this scientific project that Boas was able to imagine anthropology as a collective emergence from the thralldom of tradition—not the thralldom to nature Brinton feared—and thereby imagine into being a global community comprised of those who would make it their personal responsibility to think and speak for themselves.

For both Boas and Montezuma, the main obstacle facing the global community they envisioned—the secondary understanding to be overcome—was the widespread conception of human history as an unending race war. This was the understanding to which Montezuma referred when he spoke of "the game of 'the survival of the fittest,' competition of life in God's appointed way, 'by the sweat of the brow.'" In place of this prevailing understanding Boas and Montezuma elected to put forward not a new master theory of human history—"WASSAJA is not writing a thesis," Montezuma wrote in 1916—but a practice: a new form of expressive solidarity mediated by circulating discourse.[66]

To observe Boas's unknowing affiliation with Montezuma is to see Boas from the global perspective for which he so often searched and thereby, perhaps, to discover a broader set of communities in which he moved. This pairing may run against Boas's own sense of his intellectual-historical singularity, but in another way it confirms his intuition that exemplary forms of subjectivity, even of "genius," can be recognized across the parochial boundaries between disciplines and endeavors. I want, in closing, to draw attention to two insights that this perspective brings into view.

The first is that expressive enlightenment cannot be accounted for by tracing the transmission of knowledge among Euro-American elites. We must look backward from Boas to Brinton, Humboldt, and Herder, but we must also look sideways to figures like Spingarn and Montezuma—that is, to Boas's contemporaries—in our effort to understand the pressures motivating Boas's reformation of anthropological practice and the ideas those pressures generated. The second is that this sideways perspective on Boas can decenter the telos of the expanding in-group that emerged as his hope for modern cross-cultural solidarity. As Montezuma and the Society of American Indians demonstrate, expressive enlightenment constitutes a subject who is a "multiple being," a being who makes manifest his responses to local concerns within a particular discourse that addresses itself to a universal audience.

This tenuous relation between the local and the global is encapsulated in the first number of the newspaper Montezuma competed with, the *Quarterly Journal of the Society of American Indians.* It occurs in an article by the editors advocating the study of ethnology in Indian boarding schools: "And a new and still nobler and more important work awaits us: to demonstrate that there is a higher and more significant bond; the relationship of created things, one with another, and their inseverable kinship and relation with that Sovereign Power and Intelligence, whom some men reverence as God, and whom other men call the Unknowable, the Unseen, but whom Philosophy regards as the Totality of all things. And the American Indian race should be found in advance in this important labor."[67] There is something undeniably paradoxical about the way this universalistic effusion culminates in a statement of ethnic pride. Then again, there is something paradoxical about the situation of the Boasian knower, whether modern or "primitive," who can create an enlightened global in-group only by wrestling with the misunderstandings furnished by his local discourse community. In both situations the enlightened subject is expressed as a multiple self whose location lies at the center of plural solidarities of very different scales. Montezuma and the social movement he helped bring into being can thus help us see something Boas himself might not have realized: that the mediation of local concerns in the public discourse fostered by expressive enlightenment reproduces the same tension between in-group and out-group to which it claims to offer a solution.

Today, there exist a number of scholarly vocabularies for discussing phenomena like expressive enlightenment that exist in both local and translocal, or "glocal," social space.[68] The history of expressive enlightenment from Herder to Montezuma reminds us of the anxiety such glocal discursive phenomena produce in individuals. Much like Herder's warning to his would-be Socrates that he set out from "weak and indeterminate beginnings," Montezuma's assertion that the modern American Indian could never be "reconciled to his situation" must be read as an expression of the modern self writ large. The phenomenon of expressive enlightenment reveals the extraordinary motivation such irreconcilable situations provide for the constitution of discourse, and of subjects themselves.

## Notes

Research for this essay was supported by grants from the Newberry Library's D'Arcy McNickle Center for American Indian and Indigenous Studies, the American Antiquarian Society, and the American Philosophical Society. I am deeply grateful to these institutions for their support, to the editors of this book for their passion about its topic, and especially to Isaiah Wilner for his encouragement and incomparable editorial feedback.

1. Franz Boas, "Daniel Garrison Brinton," *Globus: Illustrierte Zeitschrift für Länder-und Völkerkunde* 76, no. 11 (1899): 166.
2. On the displacement of Brinton by the Boasian revolution in Americanist anthropology, see Regna Darnell, *And Along Came Boas: Continuity and Revolution in Americanist Anthropology* (Amsterdam: John Benjamins, 1998). George Stocking has been the most influential exponent of the view that modern anthropology came into being with Boas's pluralization of the culture concept. See George W. Stocking Jr., "Franz Boas and the Culture Concept in Historical Perspective," *American Anthropologist* 68 (1966): 867–82.
3. George W. Stocking Jr., *Delimiting Anthropology: Occasional Inquiries and Reflections* (Madison: University of Wisconsin Press, 2001), 23, cited in Lee Baker, *Anthropology and the Racial Politics of Culture* (Durham: Duke University Press, 2010), 8.
4. Ibid., chap. 1, p. 3. On Brinton's racism, see, e.g., George W. Stocking Jr., "Lamarckianism in American Social Science, 1890–1915," in *Race, Culture, and Evolution: Essays in the History of Anthropology* (New York: Free Press, 1968), 234–70.
5. Brinton ascribed the neglect of linguistics by anthropologists to "a strong aversion which I have noticed in many distinguished teachers of physical science to the study of language and the philosophy of expression." Daniel Garrison Brinton, *Essays of an Americanist* (Philadelphia: Porter and Coates, 1890), 193. Brinton's most sustained discussion of Humboldt and the Ergon–Energeia distinction is "The Philosophic Grammar of American Languages, as Set Forth by Wilhelm von Humboldt," *Proceedings of the American Philosophical Society* 22, no. 120 (1885): 306–31.
6. On the "expressive-constitutive" view of language, see Charles Taylor, *Philosophical Arguments* (Cambridge: Harvard University Press, 1995), 109–12; Daniel Garrison

Brinton, *An Ethnologist's View of History: An Address Before the Annual Meeting of the New Jersey Historical Society* (Philadelphia, 1896), 13.

7. Franz Boas, "The Aims of Ethnology," in *Race, Language and Culture* (New York: Macmillan, 1940), 632; Brinton, citing Albert Hermann Post, in *An Ethnologist's View of History*, 13.
8. See Robert Gooding-Williams, *In the Shadow of Du Bois: Afro-Modern Political Thought in America* (Cambridge: Harvard University Press, 2009), 1–65.
9. Charles Taylor, *A Secular Age* (Cambridge: Harvard University Press, 2007), 27.
10. For a different view of Herder's influence on American anthropology, see Gerald Broce, "Relativism and Discontent: Herder and Boasian Anthropology," *Annals of Scholarship* 2 (1891): 1–13, and Stocking, *Race, Culture, and Evolution*, 214. For Taylor's reading of Herder, which I'm largely following here, see "Language and Human Nature," in Charles Taylor, *Human Agency and Language*, Philosophical Papers 1 (Cambridge: Cambridge University Press, 1985), 215–47, and "The Importance of Herder," in *Isaiah Berlin: A Celebration*, ed. Edna Margalit and Avishai Margalit (London: Hogarth Press, 1991), 40–63.
11. In Johann Gottfried von Herder, *Philosophical Writings*, ed. Michael Forster (New York: Cambridge University Press, 2002), 342–43 (emphasis in original).
12. Ibid., 343.
13. Kurt Mueller-Vollmer, "Thinking and Speaking: Herder, Humboldt and Saussurean Semiotics: A Translation and Commentary on Wilhelm von Humboldt's 'Thinking and Speaking: Sixteen Theses on Language,'" *Comparative Criticism* 11 (1989): 159–214; Taylor, "Language and Human Nature," 232.
14. Sean Kelly, "Perceptual Normativity and Human Freedom," accessed at http://philpapers.org/rec/KELPNA; Humboldt, "On the Historian's Task," translated in *History and Theory* 6, no. 1 (1967): 61, 60.
15. Étienne Bonnot de Condillac, *Essay on the Origin of Human Knowledge*, ed. and trans. Hans Aarsleff (New York: Cambridge University Press, 2001), 4, 5.
16. In Eden, Condillac tells us, Adam and Eve lived human life to its fullest without ever having recourse to language (see *Essay*, 113). But when humankind was cast out into the fallen world, language was there, waiting to be discovered. God didn't have to invent it at the moment of the fall; it was already part of the plan.
17. Condillac, *Essay*, 80. For the "ethics of belief," see W. K. Clifford, "Ethics of Belief," *Contemporary Review* 29 (1877): 289–309. Like Condillac, Clifford aligns our improvement as moral beings with our aptitude at coming to terms with the cognitive limitations nature has put us under.
18. The best accounts of the influence of Condillac on early American philologists in the first half of the nineteenth century are Hans Aarsleff's introduction to Wilhelm von Humboldt, *On Language* (New York: Cambridge University Press, 2001), xi–xxxix, and Sean Harvey, "'Must Not Their Languages Be Savage and Barbarous Like Them?': Philology, Indian Removal, and Race Science," *Journal of the Early Republic* 30, no. 4 (2010): 505–32.
19. William Dwight Whitney, *Language and the Study of Language* (New York: C. Scribner, 1867), 420.
20. William Dwight Whitney, "Are Languages Institutions?" *Popular Science Monthly* 7 (June 1875): 142–60, 154.

21. Cited in John Joseph, *From Whitney to Chomsky: Essays in the History of American Linguistics* (Amsterdam: John Benjamins, 2002), 19.
22. Brinton, "Philosophic Grammar," 311.
23. Whitney, "Are Languages Institutions?" 144; Brinton, *An Ethnologist's View of History*, 10.
24. Boas, "Daniel Garrison Brinton," 166.
25. Daniel Garrison Brinton, *Notes on the Floridian Peninsula* (Philadelphia: J. Sabin, 1859), 26. For a discussion of Brinton on "psychic unity," see Regna Darnell, *Daniel Garrison Brinton: The "Fearless Critic" of Philadelphia* (Philadelphia: Department of Anthropology, University of Pennsylvania, 1988), 87–92.
26. Brinton, "An Ethnologist's View of History," 13.
27. Ibid., 14.
28. Brinton, "The Factors of Heredity and Environment in Man," *American Anthropologist* 11, no. 9 (1898): 271–77, 276.
29. Ibid., 275.
30. Boas, "The Limitations of the Comparative Method of Anthropology," *Science*, n.s., 4, no. 103: 901–8, repr. in *Race, Language and Culture*, 270 (emphasis added).
31. See Isaiah Lorado Wilner, "A Global Potlatch: Identifying the Indigenous Influence on Western Thought," *American Indian Culture and Research Journal* 37, no. 2 (2013): 87–114.
32. Originally published in *Science* 9, no. 210 (1887): 137–41; repr. in *Race, Language and Culture*, 647.
33. Matti Bunzl, "Franz Boas and the Humboldtian Tradition," in *Volksgeist as Method and Ethic: Essays on Boasian Ethnography and the German Anthropological Tradition*, ed. George W. Stocking Jr. (Madison: University of Wisconsin Press, 1996), 17–78.
34. Boas, *Race, Language and Culture*, 644.
35. Bunzl explores the likelihood of Boas having encountered Humboldtian texts in "Franz Boas and the Humboldtian Tradition," 24. Douglas Cole has argued that Boas initially pursued universal causal laws in his historical investigations but that over time he lost interest in this goal; see Douglas Cole, *Franz Boas: The Early Years* (Seattle: University of Washington Press, 1999), 261–75.
36. Boas, "The Aims of Ethnology," in *Race, Language and Culture* (New York: Macmillan, 1940), 632.
37. On the influence on Boas of "Counter-Enlightenment skepticism," see Bunzl, "Franz Boas and the Humboldtian Tradition," e.g., 56. This view is implicit in George Stocking's influential formulation of the Boasian culture concept; he writes in *Race, Culture, and Evolution* that "Boas's thinking on ethnic diversity was rooted in the same soil" as Herder's "organic diversitarianism" (214).
38. Boas, "An Anthropologist's Credo," in *I Believe*, ed. Clifton Fadimon (New York: Simon and Schuster, 1939), 23.
39. Boas, *Race, Language and Culture*, 644.
40. Ibid.
41. Boas, "Introduction," *Handbook of American Indian Languages* (Washington: Government Printing Office, 1911), 67, 70. My reading of this text is indebted to Michael Silverstein, "Language Structure and Linguistic Ideology," in *The Elements: A Parasession on Linguistic Units and Levels*, ed. Paul R. Clyne, William F. Hanks, and Carol L. Hofbaue (Chicago: Chicago Linguistic Society, 1979), 193–247.

42. Boas, "Introduction," 70; Boas, *Race, Language and Culture,* 642.
43. Boas, *Race, Language and Culture,* 638.
44. Franz Boas, "The History of Anthropology," *Science* 20, no. 512 (1904): 513–24, 514.
45. Boas, *Race, Language and Culture,* v.
46. Michel Foucault, "What Is Enlightenment?" in *The Foucault Reader,* ed. Paul Rabinow (New York: Vintage, 1984), 32–50, 38, 42.
47. Boas, "An Anthropologist's Credo," 24.
48. Ibid., 21.
49. Ibid.
50. Foucault, "What Is Enlightenment?" 35.
51. J. H. Gilmore, *Outlines of the Art of Expression* (Boston: Ginn, 1887), 3.
52. J. E. Spingarn, *The New Criticism: A Lecture Delivered at Columbia University, March 9, 1910* (New York: Columbia University Press, 1911), 20, 18.
53. I have traced this development in "Toward a Genealogy of Americanist Expressionism," *J19: The Journal of Nineteenth-Century Americanists* 3, no. 1 (2015): 89–117.
54. "Reminiscences of Self and In[dian] Characteristics," n.d. [ca. 1902], *The Papers of Carlos Montezuma, M.D., Including the Papers of Maria Keller Montezuma and the Papers of Joseph W. Latimer, 1871–1952,* ed. John W. Larner Jr., microform (Wilmington, DE: Scholarly Resources, 1983), reel 5.
55. Carlos Montezuma, *The Indian Problem from an Indian's Standpoint: An Address Delivered before Fortnightly Club of Chicago, Feb. 10, 1898* (Chicago, 1898), 1.
56. Anonymous (Arthur Parker [?]), "Think Upon These Things," *Quarterly Journal of the Society of American Indians* 1, no. 1 (1913): 7–8.
57. *Wassaja* 4, no. 3 (1919): 3. This poem has been anthologized in Robert Dale Parker, ed., *Changing Is Not Vanishing: A Collection of Early American Poetry to 1930* (Philadelphia: University of Pennsylvania Press, 2011), 292–93.
58. Julianne Newmark has observed a similar ambiguity in the way Montezuma deploys the persona of the doctor: "Montezuma established himself as simultaneously a member of the 'race' group suffering from a potentially fatal ailment and as a person who might potentially bring to this group a remedy . . . in each issue of *Wassaja.*" Julianne Newmark, "A Prescription for Freedom: Carlos Montezuma, *Wassaja,* and the Society of American Indians," *American Indian Quarterly* 37, no. 3 (2013): 139–58, 146.
59. *Wassaja* 1, no. 6 (1916): 2.
60. Scott Richard Lyons has argued that Indian intellectuals of the Society of American Indians generation "started a trajectory of Indian public formation" without which later groups like the American Indian Movement would have been hard to imagine. Scott Richard Lyons, "The Incorporation of the Indian Body: Peyotism and the Pan-Indian Public, 1911–23," in *Rhetoric, the Polis, and the Global Village,* ed. C. Jan Swearingen and David Pruett (Mahwah, NJ: Lawrence Erlbaum, 1998), 147–53, 153.
61. Carlos Montezuma, quoted in *Proceedings of the Tenth Annual Meeting of the Lake Mohonk Conference of Friends of the Indian, 1892,* ed. Martha D. Adams (Lake Mohonk, NY: Lake Mohonk Conference, 1892), in Larner, ed., *The Papers of Carlos Montezuma,* reel 2.
62. Lucy Maddox, notwithstanding her dislike of the term "assimilationist," has referred to a "willingness and ability" on the part of Indian intellectuals like Montezuma to

"perform their public roles on a universal stage according to a script they did not write themselves." Lucy Maddox, *Citizen Indians: Native American Intellectuals, Race, and Reform* (Ithaca: Cornell University Press, 2005), 11, 14.

63. *Wassaja* 1, no. 11 (2017): 2.
64. Carlos Montezuma,"A Review of Commissioner Leupp's Interview in the *New York Daily Tribune,* Sunday, April 9, 1905, on the Future of Our Indians," in Larner, ed., *The Papers of Carlos Montezuma,* reel 3.
65. *Wassaja* 3, no. 2 (1918): 1.
66. *Wassaja* 1, no. 6 (1916): 2.
67. J. N. B. Hewitt, "The Teaching of Ethnology in Indian Schools," *Quarterly Journal of the Society of American Indians* 1, no. 1 (April 1913): 30–35.
68. On glocalization, see, e.g., James Tully, *Public Philosophy in a New Key* (New York: Cambridge University Press, 2008), 2:243–310.

# Chapter 4 "Culture" Crosses the Atlantic: The German Sources of *The Mind of Primitive Man*

*Harry Liebersohn*

Anyone who wishes to write on Franz Boas and his German sources faces two recent traditions of writing about German anthropology. One tradition places Boas in the German humanist tradition that goes back to thinkers from the late eighteenth and early nineteenth century like Johann Gottfried von Herder and Wilhelm von Humboldt. According to Roger Langham Brown and, more recently, Matti Bunzl, a continuous German preoccupation with the understanding of foreign cultures runs from these thinkers in the age of Goethe to Boas and his students, in particular Edward Sapir. This tradition from the beginning envisioned a global humanity that made distinctive contributions to a global culture.[1] Taking the long view of this school of interpretation, one might say that it is a corrective to the post-1945 condemnation of the German educated elite for xenophobic and nationalist habits that contributed to Germany's twentieth-century political and moral catastrophe. While the interpretive tradition foundered and fell apart in Germany itself during the Nazi years, Boas performed what one might call an elegant act of salvage anthropology by carrying it to the United States, where it continues today in cultural anthropology.

The countertradition argues that so-called German humanism was from the start a Eurocentric enterprise, saturated with a racialized conception of non-European cultures. The late Suzanne Zantop made the case against German cosmopolitanism before 1870 as a strategy for a weak and disunited cultural region to identify with Europe as a whole as the world's normative civilization, versus the non-European rest, who were graded in a descending hierarchy from competing world civilizations to so-called savage peoples. Andrew Zimmerman's deeply researched history of early twentieth-century German anthropology shows how the nascent discipline was intertwined in its organization and views with Germany's belated scramble to put together a global empire.[2] By the logic of this approach, Boas would be an anomaly. It is not hard to imagine the factors that set him apart from his forbears and contemporaries: his family's loyalty to the ideals of the abortive revolutions of 1848; the upper-class anti-Semitism that only grew after the late 1870s and pervaded German universities; his move to the democratic, immigrant society of the United States. With these influences in mind, one can interpret Boas's work as a break from the culture of his German education, not a continuation of it.

I have some sympathy with each of these schools of interpretation. I have made my own contributions to the case for the cosmopolitanism of German culture in the so-called *Sattelzeit,* or transitional moment, from the late eighteenth to the early nineteenth century in travelers and writers like Georg Forster, Wilhelm von Humboldt, and Adelbert von Chamisso. On the other hand, I have tried to show how the intoxication with overseas empire distorted academics' judgment by the early twentieth century. No one, no matter how sympathetic to German traditions of interpretation, can read deeply in the primary sources of the latter period—and in particular the sources relating to travel and early anthropology—without encountering the era's nationalism and offhand arrogance toward the peoples beyond northern Europe.[3]

We need to think beyond this antithesis, however, in order to come to an adequate understanding of Boas's culture concept. Tracing out long lines of continuity across a century or situating Boas unmediated in the high age of European imperialism means operating at a high level of abstraction and disconnection from what Boas wrote. To do this would be rather anti-Boasian, in the sense that it would be a way of working from a schema external to the particular cultural phenomenon at hand and categorizing it according to externally imposed criteria instead of working from its specific context and history. One doesn't need to be uncritically loyal to Boas in order to look beyond the generalizations of pro- and antihumanism for a different approach.

One way to do so is to turn to the text of *The Mind of Primitive Man,* in which Boas presented his culture concept to a broad reading public for the first time, and ask which German sources Boas uses and how he uses them.[4] A quick way to get an overview of Boas's sources is to go to the footnotes. They are not particularly indebted to any one language or nationality; rather they ground the book in several scholarly literatures, German to be sure but also English-language and French. By 1911 the scholarly world *was* international, with a busy back and forth between Western scholars of different languages and nationalities.[5] On a topic like skull and brain measurement, Boas could—indeed had to, in order to survey the field—roam from American to Australian, French, and British authorities.[6] Even this list from a single note suggests how widely across languages and countries Boas had to read in order to assemble the state of the scholarly literature. At this basic level of tallying up Boas's sources, German authors were one collection of contributors among others. The same is true if we move from the notes to the text, where Boas is responding to the ideas of individual authors, not rooting for national teams.

If we look more closely at the text, then more specifically German controversies and causes start to take shape. Boas was, after all, entirely educated in the German university system. And the German university system was not just any educated establishment, but the hegemonic power in late nineteenth- and early twentieth-century research. Germany had pioneered the creation of the modern university, above all with the founding of the University of Berlin in 1810; it later led the way to the creation of the modern large-scale research university, eminently represented in German-speaking Europe at the end of the nineteenth century by Leipzig, Munich, Vienna, and Berlin. According to Douglas Cole, Boas planned to write his dissertation under Hermann von Helmholtz at the University of Berlin, but family considerations led him instead to the provincial University of Kiel. However, he ended up going to Berlin for his second academic qualifying work, his habilitation on Baffin Island, and lectured in April 1885 to a faculty colloquium that included Helmholtz and Wilhelm Dilthey.[7] For his trip to Baffin Island, his first field experience, he depended on the geographers and polar experts of Berlin, who clearly recognized a gifted and enterprising young researcher and generously aided him with their knowledge, contacts, and equipment.[8] Finally, one should not underestimate the importance of Boas's early employment in Berlin at the Royal Ethnological Museum (Königliches Museum für Völkerkunde), a bold and burgeoning enterprise that gave him a conception of how to build a research institution. It was in the ethnological museum that he first encountered Pacific Northwest Indian artifacts of a kind that were central to his later research.[9] All of these factors situate Boas in the German and, more specifically, the Berlin scientific community of the late nineteenth century.

What, then, does *The Mind of Primitive Man* take away from German sources? There is empirical fieldwork: Boas scatters through his discussions references to travelers like the famous mid-nineteenth-century Africa explorer Heinrich Barth and the Brazil explorer Karl von den Steinen, to name only two of the best known.[10] But there is nothing significantly "German" about these sources, which do not shape the significance of his book in any way different from non-German travel sources. One could almost say the same for the medical and anthropological literature propagating racial ideas; while there was a specifically German discourse of skull science from the late eighteenth to the twentieth century, for the purposes of Boas's book it did not differ significantly from French or British writings on the same subject. Under the conditions of European industrialization and the creation of modern nation-states, Europeans and their counterparts in North America and beyond brought back home mountains of artifacts and information, on a scale different from anything seen before, and Boas could choose abundant sources from any one of the imperial powers.

When we go up a methodological level, Boas's relationship to the Germans gets more interesting. There was his estimation of the researchers in his own field of geography; his own anthropology had slowly emerged from geography, as one can see clearly in the case of his Baffin Island research. That began as a geographic survey of one strip of this Arctic site and only slowly and incompletely concentrated on the region's inhabitants. But Boas does not, in fact, pay more than passing attention to geography in a passage near the beginning of *The Mind of Primitive Man.* For example, he cites Friedrich Ratzel, one of the most famous so-called anthropogeographers of the day, as an authority on the high state of development of pre-Columbian civilizations of the Americas but does not take up Ratzel's own geographic theories.[11] When the book does turn in a more systematic way to geographic theories of culture, it is in order to set limits to the causal claims of his former discipline. Nineteenth-century anthropological observers were fascinated by the appearance of seemingly similar institutions and artifacts in widely separated parts of the globe and were tempted to offer different kinds of explanations that would link them. One of these was geographic determinism, the assertion that like geographic conditions would always lead to like cultures. Not so, replies Boas, drawing on his own experience among the Baffin Islanders as well as others' field experiences. Empirical evidence, he writes, shows great differences between "the mode of life of the hunting and fishing Eskimo and the reindeer-breeding Chukchee." The persistence of custom and the interests of status groups tripped up any direct correlation between environment and culture. More important was what one might call the psychological turn in Boas: "We must remember," he states, "that, no matter how great an influence we may ascribe to environment, that influence can become active only by being exerted upon the mind; so that the characteristics of the mind must enter into the resultant forms of social activity."[12] Whatever he learned from his native discipline, he clearly broke away from it as he formed his own concept of culture.

*The Mind of Primitive Man* provides a stronger link to German academic discussions near the end of chapter 7, his critique of evolutionary social theories. After criticizing the evidence and assumptions of evolutionary social theory, Boas turns to the work of Carl Stumpf, a professor of psychology at the University of Berlin and longtime researcher into the psychology of music, for a refutation of the evolutionists' assumption that human society has progressed in all its endeavors from primitive simplicity to civilized complexity. Stumpf was an important thinker, one who enjoyed professional success in the German university system and whose work, mediating between philosophy and empirical psychology, influenced the founders of Gestalt theory as well as Edmund Husserl, the founder of phenomenology.[13] He gave a series of popular lectures on the origins of music and published them as *Die Anfänge der Musik* (The Beginnings of Music) in 1911, the same year *The Mind of Primitive Man* was published.[14] The musical example merits special attention, for, as we shall see, the analysis of music and its cultural and psychological significance attracted some of the leading scientists and German scholars of the second half of the nineteenth century. Though narrow in scope, music and the particular preoccupations of pre-1914 researchers permit us to specify from one well-defined point of view what exactly Boas meant by "culture." Starting from the musical example, we can link Boas more widely to German discussions of the interpretation of culture that still belong to our understanding of the term today.

Stumpf's book provides a neat parallel to Boas's: like Boas, Stumpf was usually an uncompromising scientist who wrote for his fellow scientists but tried with this publication to reach a wider audience. Boas referred to Stumpf's lectures in order to challenge the validity of evolutionary schemas for the arts. Turning near the end of the chapter from language to "the art of primitive man," he wrote,

> In music as well as in decorative design we find a complexity of rhythmic structure which is unequalled in the popular art of our day. In music, particularly, this complexity is so great, that the art of a skilled virtuoso is taxed in the attempt to imitate it (Stumpf). If once it is recognized that simplicity is not always a proof of antiquity, it will readily be seen that the theory of the evolution of civilization rests to a certain extent on a logical error. The classification of the data of

Carl Stumpf, right, recording a Tatar musician on a wax cylinder, 1915. The singer was a soldier in a German prisoner of war camp where captives were requested to perform folksongs for the Royal Prussian Phonographic Commission, a critical yet long-unacknowledged point of origin for the discipline of ethnomusicology. Seized by the Red Army in 1945, Stumpf's wax cylinders were returned in 1991 to the Ethnological Museum of Berlin, where they were reunited with the records preserved in East Berlin, resuscitating a trove of long-inaccessible knowledge. © Berlin Phonogramm-Archiv, Ethnologisches Museum, Staatliche Museen zu Berlin.

> anthropology in accordance with their simplicity has been reinterpreted as an historical sequence, without an adequate attempt to prove that the simpler antedates the more complex.[15]

We are dealing here with Boas at his best, the penetrating critic of evolutionary theory who uses empirical research to counter lazy generalizations about the difference between primitive and civilized peoples. Evolutionary theory presumes a growth over time from the simple and primitive to the complex and civilized. But the arts reveal just the opposite: the so-called primitive arts have a complexity that European virtuosos can hardly reproduce. You have to distort the data to make them work as an historical sequence. Boas, in his scientistic-distanced language here, with its use of the past tense and impersonal voice, speaks of data "reinterpreted as an historical sequence" and a lack of "adequate" proof for the assumption of growing historical complexity. The implication of Boas's argument is that just the opposite of the evolutionary assumption may be true: so-called primitive music may have elements more complex than historically later musical forms.

This musical example is the culmination of the chapter in which Boas first sketches the evolutionary social theories of the nineteenth century and then points out their factual and methodological shortcomings. The evolutionary theories come in several waves. The first mentioned by Boas consists of the racial theories of Arthur de Gobineau and others. These are revived in modern nationalism "with its exaggerated self-admiration of the Teutonic race" and similar ideologies like pan-Slavism, but, he drily notes, "these views are not supported by the results of unbiased research." Although Boas does not use the phrase, these are political ideologies: for Gobineau, a right-wing defense of social privilege against the claims of modern democracy, and for nationalists, the myth of Germanic and Slavic racial types that belong in a single nation-state with claims to superiority over the peoples who are not part of the master race. Boas then turns to the social theorists who argue that there is a growing complexity of culture which can be linked to racial type. He cites Edward Burnett Tylor, Johann Jakob Bachofen, Lewis Henry Morgan, and Herbert Spencer as proponents of this evolutionary theory.[16] George Stocking has persuasively pieced together the paradigmatic assumptions of these thinkers' mid- to late-nineteenth-century anthropology: in their various ways they tended to believe in a unity of human Mind that went through the same stages of development in different times and places. Within this paradigm one could argue about whether there was one creation or multiple creations, whether diverse races were doomed to limited development or could ascend to the full height of northern European civilization, and where different peoples fit on the scale from savagery to civilization.[17] Finally, Boas mentions a third cluster of evolutionary theorists, Charles Darwin and his successors, whose "fundamental ideas can be understood only as an application of the theory of biological evolution to mental phenomena." This Darwinian school, too, proposes that history evolves as a movement from simple to more complex types of modern civilization.[18]

Boas uses two methods to refute this racial evolutionary theory. The first is that its facts are wrong. The best evidence for evolutionary theory comes from archaeology, but archaeology does not support the idea of a steady, uniform growth of Mind and its works around the world. "The facts, so far as known at the present time," writes Boas, "are entirely contrary to this view." So, for example, Boas notes that "the well-advanced tribes of Northwest America have no pottery" even though these tribes are highly differentiated in other areas of life. The same is true of other areas of technical skill: when it comes to metallurgy and agriculture, people with some skills lack these arts. In other words, the so-called stages of civilization are just a generalization of supposed European stages of development that do not, in fact, hold for other parts of the world.[19]

Boas's second method of refuting the evolutionary theorists is to point out a fundamental flaw in their thinking, namely, their assumption that similar-looking outcomes must result from similar causes. The different meanings of masks serve as an example: They may be worn "to deceive spirits," to commemorate a deceased friend, to illustrate mythical figures in a theatrical performance. Masks have no single origin; they do not mean a single thing; to put masks from different cultures in a single museum room and assert that they represent a single stage of historical development is to impose a retrospective and falsified historical unity on them. The significance of artifacts like masks must be established by reconstructing their context and history: this is one of the fundamental insights that Boas arrived at in the late 1880s. It fatally undermined the structure of sociocultural evolutionary theory even as it served as one starting point for his own contextual and historical anthropology.

Later in the chapter Boas comes to a decisive point, the lack of any uniform development from simplicity to complexity in *any* society. He calls this "an important theoretical consideration" that "has also shaken our faith in the correctness of the evolutionary theory as a whole." Over time, technology tends to grow from simple to complex, writes Boas, while other areas do the reverse and go from complex to simple. He points to historical changes in language as one such area: "The grammatical categories of Latin, and still more so those of modern English, seem crude when compared to the complexity of psychological or logical forms which primitive languages recognize." Boas turns soon after this to the arts, with a brief mention of ornament and then his longer comment (cited above) on "primitive" music that baffles civilized observers with its complexity.[20] Stumpf is Boas's source and witness for this observation.

If we look beyond the passage in *The Mind of Primitive Man* and turn to Stumpf's own writings, what does he have to offer that makes Boas single him out as an authority? Or to put it in the terms of Boas's own essay: What does Stumpf provide in the way of empirical evidence and methodology to prove the complexity of music from traditional, non-European societies? Where does he turn to non-European societies in a way that refutes the racial theorists?

And does he have a level of psychological insight that satisfies Boas's demand for an actor-oriented social science grounded in historical and contextual understanding?

The answers take us beyond Stumpf's lectures in *Die Anfänge der Musik* to his larger project of an experimental psychology of music. In 1886, recalls Stumpf, Rudolf Virchow complained at the Berlin Anthropological Society (Anthropologische Gesellschaft) about the lack of any integration of music into the study of primitive peoples (*Urgeschichte*); by 1903, according to Stumpf, a speaker at the same organization could praise the opening up of music as an area of previously unimaginable breadth and significance. The technological advance that had transformed music from a deficient to an established field was the phonograph.[21] Stumpf himself was one of the earliest and most persistent gatherers of music from different places around the world, and he took immediate advantage of the new possibilities offered by phonographic recordings. Beginning in 1900 he established an archive for musical recordings, the Phonogramm Archiv. Its director from 1905 to 1933, Erich von Hornbostel, was a formidable talent in his own right: born into a wealthy, cultivated Viennese family, Hornbostel was one of those independent scholars whose uninhibited dedication to the arts and sciences enriched pre-1914 European culture. Hornbostel had a doctorate in chemistry in addition to being an accomplished musicologist, and, like Boas and Stumpf, he crossed back and forth easily and expertly between science and culture. The archive was quickly recognized as a central repository for music from around the world. Three-minute recordings came into the archive as wax cylinders. Hornbostel, putting his scientific skills to work, took copper castings of the wax cylinders, a process that destroyed the fragile, damage-prone originals but preserved them in copies that do not deteriorate with age and have lasted down to the present day. Stumpf composed his lectures on the beginnings of music in collaboration with Hornbostel, to whom he dedicated the book, and who, he wrote, went through every line, melody, and note. Stumpf and Hornbostel brought to their analysis of music the combined resources of the philosopher and the natural scientist.[22]

Boas and the Phonogramm Archiv organizers were aware of one another's work at an early date and kept up their friendly mutual interest. A chance to hear non-Western music in Berlin linked Boas's and Stumpf's careers from the beginning when Captain Johan Adrian Jacobsen brought nine Nuxalk from Bella Coola in coastal British Columbia to Germany. In his work at the ethnological museum Boas was responsible for organizing artifacts from the Pacific Northwest that Jacobsen had brought back from a previous voyage. Now he actually had the chance to meet with some representatives of the region that would become the site of his lifelong fieldwork and research (most often associated in scholarly memory with the Kwakwa̱ka̱'wakw and the potlatch). Stumpf met the Nuxalk in November 1885 while teaching in Halle and saw them perform at a meeting of the local geographic society. At first he was overwhelmed by their performance and could barely make out individual notes amid this *Teufelsmusik* (devil's music). But he took aside one performer, Nuskilusta, and worked with him repeatedly until he could decipher a musical system that included non-Western tone intervals. After the group's departure he found himself enjoying the songs that were still echoing in his mind. As Stumpf describes it, the experience was a rebuke to travelers' superficial accounts of Indigenous music and a decisive advance in his own understanding of mediating between musical cultures. The resulting article became a founding document of ethnomusicology.[23] The Nuxalks' tour led to a collaboration between Boas and Stumpf: Stumpf thanked Boas in his article for sending him transcriptions of two songs he heard in Berlin and translating one of them.[24] Boas sent recordings of Kwakwa̱ka̱'wakw music to the Phonogramm Archiv in 1893 and 1897, and Hornbostel and his colleague Otto Abraham elegantly reciprocated when they contributed an analysis of some of the recordings to a 1906 Festschrift published in Boas's honor.[25] Boas's reference to Stumpf in *The Mind of Primitive Man* was one of a series of friendly scholarly exchanges. The exchanges went in the other direction, too: in *Die Anfänge der Musik* Stumpf singles out Boas's work for praise, beginning with his prephonographic transcriptions in *The Central Eskimo* (1888), his English-language monograph on the Baffin Islanders.[26]

The appeal of Stumpf's *Die Anfänge der Musik* to Boas is not hard to understand. Stumpf begins his lectures with a critique of Darwin's evolutionary explanation of the origins of music: that music is the male means of sexually attracting females. Stumpf notes factual objections to this, for example, that birds sing at other times, and many "primitive" human songs don't have to do with love. But he then goes on to a more theoretical objection: What is music? Not just the production of tones but the setting of tones in a specific order. Specific to human music, according to Stumpf, is that the order is independent of absolute pitch (*absolute Tonhöhe*). That is, human beings can recognize a series of tones even when it is transposed to a higher or lower key, an ability that has no counterpart among birds or animals. Human beings may prefer a certain pitch and ascribe specific expressive effects to it; for example, to expand on Stumpf's discussion, a song may be normally assigned to a bass voice and would sound different or even ridiculous if taken up to a soprano register. But regardless of the aesthetic effect, the recognition of relative pitch is a feature of

A cabinet card of the Nuxalk troupe from Bella Coola. The picture was taken in 1886 by Carl Günther, a photographer in Berlin. Courtesy of Cowan's Auctions, Cincinnati, Ohio.

human musical intelligence: "The piece remains just as understandable and is as such recognizable without difficulty. It would not occur to anyone to deny the possibility of the transposition; only the expression and the effect seem to us to be less than independent of the absolute pitch." Darwin and the zoologists never notice this defining and distinctive feature of human music.[27]

Stumpf's critique of this Darwinian explanation of the origins of music leads to a more general revaluation of "primitive" culture: the supposed higher expressive and intellectual capacities that nineteenth-century racial theories associated with civilization were already present in so-called *Naturvölker,* or primitive peoples, for their music was already a demonstration of their fully developed capacity for pattern recognition: "This capacity for abstraction is already highly developed in primitive peoples, and we have to take it as a given in man in his original state, unless we want to dispense entirely with a comprehension of development." Together with the formation of concepts, this capacity for abstraction is the foundation of the human spirit (*Grund des geistigen Lebens*).[28] Against all theories, earlier or later, of a specifically primitive intelligence or way of ordering things, Stumpf argues here for an identical intelligence. Gone from Stumpf's discussion at this point were racial distinctions between peoples who had an intellectual capacity and people who lacked it.

Stumpf brought scientific method to another subject of great interest to Boas, the ability of ethnographers to hear and correctly reproduce oral expressions in foreign cultures. Boas's essay "On Alternating Sounds" (1889) addressed this issue for speech: Western observers "heard" more than one word for the same thing in foreign cultures because they were educated in their own culture to perceive only a limited set of sounds accurately. Confronted with foreign languages, they heard the same word differently on different occasions.[29] The essay was an incisive rebuke to all observers who thought they brought an adequately informed intelligence to the task of recording a foreign culture; Boas instead insisted on the culturally defined limitations of any listener's ability to perceive an unfamiliar language. Boas's essay on alternating sounds was a brilliant aperçu rather than a developed argument and relied on anecdotal evidence to call into question the scientific objectivity of late nineteenth-century ethnographies. Stumpf buttressed the analogous musical case with exhaustive research. He and his assistants were also able to provide detailed documentation and controlled experiments to make the point for music by going beyond "the numerous unverifiable [*unkontrollierbaren*] transcriptions in travel writings." Setting himself against the skeptics who thought that "savages" just sloshed around in their music making anyway and that the phonograph was superfluous, he insisted on the indispensability of recordings as the material for exact notation and quantitative analysis of rhythmic intervals and pitch. In his instructions to travelers Stumpf asked them to make multiple recordings of the same song so that the range of variation in music making could be determined. He also had his assistants record and note the same range of variation in Western musical performance. The pitch irregularity among Western performers, both classical and folk, was rather wide. Among Indigenous peoples, he noted, some tones and intervals varied while others were reproduced with considerable precision. Only with the aid of the phonograph could one carry out an investigation of this kind. It definitively put to rest the imaginary differences between the capacity of Western and Indigenous performers to control musical pitch.[30] This piece of myth busting extended the insight of "On Alternating Sounds" through a Boasian reliance on scientific investigation.

Both Stumpf's critique of evolutionary views on music and his painstaking analysis of musical sound production could appeal to Boas and merited the inclusion of *Die Anfänge der Musik* as a witness against the evolutionary theorists' notion of a uniform progression from simplicity to complexity in human societies. However, one should not assimilate Stumpf too completely to the program of Boasian anthropology. Boas turns to Stumpf to validate the argument that rhythm in Indigenous performance can surpass the virtuosity of Western musicians, but *Die Anfänge der Music* specifically excludes the production of rhythm from its definition of music, which is present only when there is a system of tones, not just sounds.[31] And in the end Stumpf defends the complexity of modern Western music as historically distinct. His argument, a familiar one to musicologists, is that the full development of harmony is a Western achievement that surpasses the complexity of all other music making. According to Stumpf, while Asian musical forms occasionally take pleasure in the production of simultaneous intervals, and one can from time to time observe an impulse toward harmony in Indigenous music, there is nothing comparable to the development of simultaneous, consonant tones in the diatonic scale; this is a musical system that begins in thirteenth-century Europe and develops over time to its fully articulated modern form.[32] Stumpf's project turns into a historical one of discovering what he calls "the *main forms of primitive creation of melody* and its gradual perfection" (die *Hauptformen primitiver Melodiebildung* und ihre allmähliche Vervollkommnung).[33] Stumpf and Hornbostel believed that Western harmony had brought music to a new, historically unprecedented stage of development. By this standard, all other forms of music were inferior and could be graded on a hierarchy leading up to it.

Despite its obvious limitations, this conception of the historical development of music was not the same as the racial evolutionary schemas of nineteenth-century theorists. It did not contain any hint of attributing different abilities to different peoples, and it left Stumpf's work open to an appreciation of the complexity of other, nonmelodic aspects of non-Western music. Stumpf, Hornbostel, and their professional community did an astonishing job in a short amount of time of creating a world archive of musical cultures and opening up scientific perspectives on music that made it possible as never before to get beyond notions of the naturalness or superiority of Western music. Whatever the tensions between his work and theirs, Boas was fully conversant with their project and was correct to use Stumpf as a witness for the complexity of non-European arts.

The comparison of Stumpf and Boas leads to a larger perspective on Boas's place in nineteenth- and twentieth-century intellectual history. Their reflections on music belong to a broader panorama of scientists and humanists engaged in discussions of harmony, which in turn was a focal point for arguments about the role of natural scientific versus psychological and interpretive methods. As Sebastian Klotz has noted, Stumpf's analyses drew on a rich legacy: Western thinkers have pondered the appeal of music since classical antiquity, and early modern scientists were drawn again and again to the subject in attempts to understand and systematize the logic of music and the nature of its effects on the human psyche. The starting point for subsequent nineteenth-century German debates was Hermann Helmholtz's work *On the Sensations of Tone* (1862).[34] Stumpf offered his own work on the psychology of tone as a corrective to Helmholtz, putting it forth in the form of an aggressive critique as well as a scientific alternative. Helmholtz asserted that sensations of harmony and disharmony had their physical basis in the overtones of individual notes and their mathematical relationship to each other, which could easily be measured. The inner ear was a mechanism capable of reproducing and comparing those overtones, leading in varying degrees to the pleasant or unpleasant sensations of harmony or discord. Stumpf shifted the weight of the analysis to a dimension neglected by Helmholtz: the psychological reception of sound. Even if one could understand the physiological basis of the sensation of tone more completely than nineteenth-century scientists could, declared Stumpf, it still would not explain the immediate pleasure or displeasure created by a combination of notes. Rather, one had to make the experience of music the subject of inquiry. Stumpf began with introspection, his own experiences of consonance and dissonance, and moved from there to psychological experiments. Among other inquiries, he polled listeners, both musical professionals and nonprofessionals, for their perception of consonance and dissonance in chords, and discovered a wide range of judgments. This was in keeping with historical evidence that perceptions of consonance and dissonance had in fact changed again and again over time. According to Stumpf, even an interval as natural to nineteenth-century European ears as the fifth had lesser importance to earlier eras or was perceived even as dissonant. Musical perceptions derived from culture, not nature. Stumpf exaggerated the contrast between his work and that of Helmholtz, who had made similar observations about the historicity of pitch. Nonetheless, his insistence on the psychological dimension of pitch placed his work in distinct proximity to Boas's conception of culture.[35]

What Boas owed to German sources is a vast subject, and with our turn to Stumpf, Hornbostel, and comparative musicology we have perused only one small part of it. At the same time, even our brief sketch of this relationship allows us to suggest some conclusions about what Boas did and did not take from his own native culture. *The Mind of Primitive Man* is not a manifesto for an intellectual program derived from Herder and the age of Goethe. To be sure, at a high level of generalization one can argue plausibly that the idea of a world culture adumbrated in late eighteenth- and early nineteenth-century Germany continues in Boas's conception of a historical and contextual science of humanity. When one examines the book, however, there is no mention of early nineteenth-century neohumanism, and acknowledgment of the broad similarity is not a substitute for trying to understand the meaning of the text. On the other hand, *The Mind of Primitive Man* complicates any notion of a thoroughgoing antihumanism in early German anthropology. The comparative music project was a starting point for one of the great adventures in cross-cultural understanding, modern ethnomusicology. Boas was sympathetic to its founders and made use of Stumpf's writings for his critique of evolutionary social theories.

The debate about the humanism or antihumanism of Boas's German contemporaries does little to illuminate *The Mind of Primitive Man,* since those are not the categories of Boas's own thought. It is more fruitful to note the specific affinities that emerge from Boas's references to his German counterparts. Boas was a proud graduate of the German research university, and after his move to the United States he continued to practice its virtues, above all its emphasis on detailed empirical research and methodological self-consciousness. The dense empiricism is not evident on the surface of *The Mind of Primitive Man* as a popularization of Boas's work; but its generalizations are supported by his habits of skepticism and careful accumulation of evidence from the time of his earliest research on the Baffin Islanders. His methodological criticisms, such as his dissent from evolutionary schemas of cultural development, distilled decades of research and reflection, often recorded in short pieces like his essay on alternating sounds. The hard discipline of his scientific education in the German university underlies the broad sweep and straightforward style of *The Mind of Primitive Man.* His intellectual friendship with Stumpf, a prewar Berlin professor par excellence, underlines the intellectual style of a time and place. Both Boas and Stumpf had training in the natural sciences and brought its rigor to the understanding of culture; both worked in the German professorial style, famously associated with Berlin, as entrepreneurs and institution builders; both combined a deep grasp of a large body of evidence with a search for valid methodology that led to critiques of their competitors and assertiveness about the correctness of one's own approach. One can point to other researchers in other places who more or less shared these qualities. But Boas was educated, began his career, maintained his patriotism, and kept up his collaboration in 1911 and long after with his German colleagues.

The comparison with Stumpf also evokes a crucial contrast. To be sure, Stumpf's historical and psychological inquiries seem to place his research firmly on a path to the local and specific patterns of meaning making that we associate with culture. The affinity between their approaches was great enough, as we have seen, that their mutual appreciation lasted over decades. At the same time, Stumpf thought of musical systems as self-enclosed totalities. The same applied more broadly to his conception of culture: In keeping with the general understanding of nineteenth-century educated Germans, Stumpf viewed a culture worthy of the name as a unified whole. This is why the rich legacy of German scientific and humanistic culture could serve as an education but never as an adequate set of assumptions about the shaping and reshaping of culture in a democratic society.

By moving to the United States, Boas left behind the rich humanistic and scientific culture of imperial Germany. The move also, however, permitted him to grapple with what we would today call a multicultural society. Boas's transatlantic passage gradually fractured the European conception of culture as a unified totality and replaced it with a different conception that was better able to account for diversity and change in an immigrant society. In Boas's anthropology, culture became a fluid, historical concept, relatively autonomous but open to new elements and reconfiguration. In the end it was Boas, not the ingenious Stumpf and not his colleagues in the superbly knowledgeable and cultivated universities of prewar Germany, who was the founder of the modern study of culture.

## Notes

1. Roger Langham Brown, *Wilhelm von Humboldt's Conception of Linguistic Relativity* (Paris: Mouton, 1967); Matti Bunzl, "Franz Boas and the Humboldtian Tradition: From *Volksgeist* and *Nationalcharakter* to an Anthropological Concept of Culture," in *Volksgeist as Method and Ethic: Essays on Boasian Ethnography and the German Anthropological Tradition*, ed. George W. Stocking Jr. (Madison: University of Wisconsin Press, 1996), 17–78.
2. Susanne Zantop, *Colonial Fantasies: Conquest, Family, and Nation in Precolonial Germany, 1770–1870* (Durham: Duke University Press, 1997); Andrew Zimmerman, *Anthropology and Antihumanism in Imperial Germany* (Chicago: University of Chicago Press, 2001).
3. Harry Liebersohn, *The Travelers' World: Europe to the Pacific* (Cambridge: Harvard University Press, 2006); idem, "Coming of Age in the Pacific: German Ethnography from Chamisso to Krämer," in *Worldly Provincialism: German Anthropology in the Age of Empire*, ed. H. Glenn Penny and Matti Bunzl (Ann Arbor: University of Michigan Press, 2003), 31–46; idem, *The Return of the Gift: European History of a Global Idea* (Cambridge: Cambridge University Press, 2011).
4. Franz Boas, *The Mind of Primitive Man* (1911; repr. New York: Macmillan, 1924).
5. Andrew Zimmerman, *Alabama in Africa: Booker T. Washington, the German Empire, and the Globalization of the New South* (Princeton: Princeton University Press, 2010), is a study of this turn-of-the-century internationalism.

6. Boas, *The Mind of Primitive Man,* 280–81.
7. Douglas Cole, *Franz Boas: The Early Years, 1858–1906* (Seattle: University of Washington Press, 1999), 54–55, 57, 89–93. I have greatly benefited from Cole's biography, an indispensable work for anyone wishing to understand Boas.
8. On this expedition, see Douglas Cole and Ludger Müller-Wille, "Franz Boas's Expedition to Baffin Island, 1883–1884," in *Études/Inuit/Studies* 8 (1984): 37–63, and Cole's description in *Franz Boas,* 65–68.
9. Cole, *Franz Boas,* 96–97.
10. Boas, *The Mind of Primitive Man,* 279, 291, 293.
11. Ibid., 7–8, 279.
12. Ibid., 161, 163.
13. For a biographical overview, see Helga Sprung and Lothar Sprung, "Carl Stumpf: Experimenter, Theoretician, Musicologist, and Promoter," in *Portraits of Pioneers in Psychology,* ed. Gregory A. Kimble and Michael Wertheimer (Washington, DC: American Psychological Association, 2000), 4:50–69. On Stumpf and the Gestalt theorists, see Mitchell G. Ash, *Gestalt Psychology in German Culture, 1890–1967: Holism and the Quest for Objectivity* (Cambridge: Cambridge University Press, 1995), chap. 2.
14. Carl Stumpf, *Die Anfänge der Musik* (Leipzig: Barth, 1911). An English translation, Carl Stumpf, *The Origins of Music,* ed. and trans. David Trippet (Oxford: Oxford University Press, 2012), came to my attention too late for me to cite from it.
15. Boas, *The Mind of Primitive Man,* 194–95. Boas does not cite the passage he has in mind, but it seems to have been Stumpf's discussion of rhythm in *Die Anfänge der Musik,* 47–48.
16. Boas, *The Mind of Primitive Man,* 174–75.
17. George Stocking Jr., *Victorian Anthropology* (New York: Free Press, 1987).
18. Boas, *The Mind of Primitive Man,* 175.
19. Ibid., 182–84.
20. Ibid., 193–94.
21. Stumpf, *Die Anfänge der Musik,* 8.
22. Ibid., 5. I have briefly discussed Stumpf and the Phonogramm Archiv in "Race at the Fin de Siècle: Skulls, Pictures, Sounds," presented at the conference "Race, Gender, Cultures: Creating Identities Within Cross-Cultural, Historical Contexts," Groningen, Netherlands, June 16–17, 2011, and at a second workshop in Groningen held on June 14–15, 2012. For an introduction to the Phonogramm Archiv, see Susanne Ziegler, *Die Wachszylinder des Berliner Phonogramm-Archivs* (Berlin: Ethnologisches Museum—Staatliche Museen zu Berlin, 2006), and Artur Simon, ed., *The Berlin Phonogramm-Archiv, 1900–2000: Collections of Traditional Music of the World* (Berlin: Verlag für Wissenschaft und Bildung, 2000). Philip V. Bohlman assesses the place of Hornbostel's work in the history of world music in *World Music: A Very Short Introduction* (Oxford: Oxford University Press, 2002), 26–32.
23. Cole, *Franz Boas,* 96–97. On Jacobsen and the German tour of the Nuxalk troupe, see Eric Ames, *Carl Hagenbeck's Empire of Entertainments* (Seattle: University of Washington Press, 2008), 56–57, 107–9. On Jacobsen and Boas, cf. H. Glenn Penny, *Objects of Culture: Ethnology and Ethnographic Museums in Imperial Germany* (Chapel Hill: University of North Carolina Press, 2002), 61, 84–85. For the location of the Nuxalk,

see Carl Waldman, *Atlas of the North American Indian* (New York: Facts on File, 1985), 37–38. Stumpf describes his experience with the Nuxalk in "Lieder der Bellakula-Indianer," *Vierteljahrsschrift für Musikwissenschaft* 2 (1886): 405–26. Bruno Nettl assesses the article's place in the history of ethnomusicology in *Nettl's Elephant: On the History of Ethnomusicology* (Urbana: University of Illinois Press, 2010), 18–19.

24. Stumpf, "Lieder der Bellakula-Indianer," 408, 420.
25. See the list of Boas's recordings in Ziegler, *Die Wachszylinder,* 108–9. Otto Abraham and Erich Hornbostel, "Phonographierte Indianermelodien aus British Columbia," in *Boas Anniversary Volume: Anthropological Papers Written in Honor of Franz Boas,* ed. Berthold Laufer and H. A. Andrews (New York: Stechert, 1906), 447–74.
26. Stumpf, *Die Anfänge der Musik,* 64–65, seems to criticize Boas's documentation of music in *The Central Eskimo* (1888) for paying less attention to intonation than to rhythm and structure. In historical retrospect this documents a limitation of Stumpf's own conception of music, which was fixated on pitch intervals.
27. Stumpf, *Die Anfänge der Musik,* 8–13. "Aber das Stück bleibt uns doch immer ebenso verständlich und wird als dasselbe ohne weiteres wiedererkannt. Die Möglichkeit der Übertragung zu bestreiten, wird niemand einfallen; nur der Ausdruck und die Wirkung scheinen uns nicht unabhängig von der absoluten Höhe" (13).
28. Ibid., 25. "Bei den Naturvölkern ist diese Fähigkeit der Abstraktion schon in hohem Maße entwickelt, und beim Urmenschen müssen wir sie in gewissem Grade voraussetzen, wenn wir nicht vollständig auf ein Begreifen der Entwicklung verzichten wollen."
29. Franz Boas, "On Alternating Sounds," in *A Franz Boas Reader: The Shaping of American Anthropology, 1883–1911,* ed. George W. Stocking Jr. (Chicago: University of Chicago Press, 1982), 72–77.
30. Stumpf, *Die Anfänge der Musik,* 69, 73.
31. Ibid., 22.
32. Ibid., 43–45, 100.
33. Ibid., 55.
34. Hermann L. F. Helmholtz, *On the Sensations of Tone as a Physiological Basis for the Theory of Music,* trans. Alexander J. Ellis (1885; repr. New York: Dover, 1954); Sebastian Klotz, "Tonpsychologie und Musikforschung als Katalysatoren wissenschaftlich-experimenteller Praxis und der Methodenlehre im Kreis von Carl Stumpf," *Berichte zur Wissenschaftsgeschichte* 31 (2008): 195–210; Julia Kursell, "Hermann von Helmholtz und Carl Stumpf über Konsonanz und Dissonanz," *Berichte zur Wissenschaftsgeschichte* 31 (2008): 130–43.
35. Helmholtz discusses at length the historicity of pitch and harmony; he also recognizes that the Western preference for harmony is an aesthetic choice, not an absolute given in nature. See Helmholtz, *Sensations of Tone,* 235–49.

# Part Two **Worlds of Enlightenment: Boasian Thought as Process and Practice**

# Chapter 5 Rediscovering the World of Franz Boas: Anthropology, Equality / Diversity, and World Peace

*James Tully*

## INTRODUCTION

This essay is an attempt to rediscover the world of Franz Boas by examining his work on two general (non-Indigenous) world visions. The first is the world-view or picture (*Weltanschauung* or *Weltbild*) of civilized and primitive peoples and cultures that became dominant in the nineteenth and twentieth century: the civilized / primitive vision (CPV). Boas argued critically that this world-view misrepresents the world of cultures and serves to legitimate the racism, imperialism, genocide, and militarism of the civilized nations. The second, marginal vision, Boas argued constructively, is a more accurate representation of a world of diverse cultures: the equality / diversity vision (EDV). If his anthropological critique of the former and evidence for the latter were widely taught and accepted, he argued prospectively, this world-historical cultural transformation would lead away from racism, imperialism, and war toward world peace.

Boas argued that this transformation of Western civilization from the antagonistic civilized / primitive vision to a peaceful equality / diversity vision could be brought about by the gradual diffusion of the revolutionary method he set out in the 1911 and 1938 editions of *The Mind of Primitive Man.* It enables Westerners to see that they do not stand above a world of unequal and antagonistic cultures and states, as the CPV discloses the world to them. Rather, as they free themselves from this worldview, they come to realize that all humans are deeply embedded participants in diverse, interdependent, and interacting cultures with equal capacities to respect, communicate, and cooperate across their differences. In his writings on nationalism, democracy, war, and world peace, Boas went on to suggest that this method thus provides the basis for an ethics that can cultivate toleration and fellow-feeling across cultures, in place of the intolerance and war-generating antagonism of the modern world system, and, in so doing, lay the groundwork for world peace. Since the antagonistic CPV continues to prevail today, cloaked in the postdecolonization language of modernization, democratization, and globalization, and armed with even more destructive weapons, Boas's radical argument remains as important now as before.[1]

The first and revised final editions of *The Mind of Primitive Man* begin with Boas's portrayal of the dominant worldview.[2] He argues that this CPV ensemble comprises both the background cluster of habitual judgments *and* the practices in which these judgments are grounded, and these govern the more reflective forms of thought and action of most "civilized" people, including most scholars in the humanities and social sciences.[3] CPV is both world disclosing and action guiding.[4] Moreover, it misrepresents and rationalizes the history, operation, and effects of the practices, institutions, and cultures it describes. It is a "secondary explanation."[5]

In this vision, European scientific institutions and political, economic, legal, military, and educational forms of knowledge and modes of subjectivity are definitive of civilization.[6] They are recognized by the civilized states as the standard of civilization in international law. Only peoples or races that possess these civilized institutions are recognized as sovereign states under international law. These civilizing and civilized institutions are seen as the product and highest stage of universal processes of world-historical development and progress.

All other peoples or races and their cultures are recognized, classified, ranked, studied, and colonized as if they belong to lower, inferior, and simpler stages of historical development relative to the European and Euro-American nation-states at the top. Africans, African Americans, Indigenous peoples, and peoples lacking written language and European institutions are placed at the lowest stage of development; as primitive. They are seen as either incapable of development toward civilization or potentially capable of development through universal stages under the tutelage or guardianship of civilized peoples. By 1911, 80 percent of the world's so-called uncivilized peoples were subject to the imperial control of the competing civilized state-empires by various means.[7] The civilized imperial states gave themselves the mission and duty to civilize the uncivilized peoples under their control. This duty consists in the exploitation of the resources and labor of the colonized peoples, since these violent processes and institutions of private property, slave and wage labor, authoritarian rule, and residential schools spread the foundations of civilization throughout the world. The duty also includes governing the subject peoples, if possible, through the developmental stages so they may become civilized and self-governing peoples in replication of civilized states, or, in the case of Indigenous peoples, assimilated into the civilized states imposed over them, or marginalized on reservations, or exterminated due to their incapacity to cope with modernizing conditions. The justificatory orientation and faith of these developmental processes is toward an eventual just world order of civilized states and world peace.[8]

Thus, civilized states present themselves as oriented toward ending imperialism and war in the long run, even though their Faustian project consists in making the world over in the image and replication of one particular civilization. This remarkably successful sleight of hand within the vision is concealed by the civilization / primitive binary and its developmental or evolutionary language of "civilizing" processes.[9]

This picture became dominant in statecraft, international law, and academic research by the middle of the nineteenth century. The horrors of the "scramble for Africa" after 1885 and the First World War called it into question, but it was reformulated in response. The League of Nations established the mandate system to classify the uncivilized peoples into categories and to monitor the corresponding types of civilizing colonial rule. Primitive peoples and races—Indigenous and most African peoples—were classified as incapable of self-government and thus as wards of the nations to which they were subject. After decolonization and the right of self-determination of peoples (1960), the former colonies demanded that the language of civilization be removed from the United Nations and international law because of its role in legitimating colonialism and neocolonialism. Nevertheless, critical scholars argue that it has been replaced by the language of modernization and democratization that plays the same misrepresenting and legitimating role for the contemporary informal imperialism of the great powers and institutions of global governance over the former colonies—the developing world.[10] The refusal of the United Nations Commission on Human Rights to recognize the petitions of African Americans is seen by its critics as an analogous form of subordination and assimilation.[11] Although 350 million Indigenous peoples won the United Nations Declaration on the Rights of Indigenous Peoples in

2007, many argue they are constrained to exercise it within a continuing civilizing worldview and structure of internal colonization imposed over them by the new civilized states (former colonies).[12]

As Boas advanced his revolutionary criticisms of CPV he also worked on his alternative, EDV. In this worldview, the world of humans, plants, and animals is a multiplicity of roughly seven thousand diverse, overlapping, interacting, and changing cultures.[13] Individual and collective members of human cultures interact and negotiate within and over their own cultures and with members of other cultures, borrow from each other, cooperate and compete, exhibit cultural similarities and dissimilarities, and thus coevolve in unpredictable ways. The diversity of cultures is the *manifestation* of the underlying equality of basic capabilities of individuals and peoples to create cultures. These equally distributed culture-creating capacities are not independent, causal antecedents of cultures but always embedded and enacted in—and in modification of—the diverse cultural relationships in which humans live and interact. Cultures disclose the world in distinctive yet overlapping ways, and critical cross-cultural understanding is possible through participation and comparison, whereas the universalization of the classification and standards of any one human culture, as with CPV, is the error of parochialism and speciesism. The equality of culture-creating capabilities and the overlapping diversity of their manifestations give rise to complex webs of cultural relationships that unify all members of humankind in their ever-changing diversity. Boas inherited this general EDV from Johann Gottfried von Herder, Alexander von Humboldt, and Adolf Bastian, but he criticized aspects of their formulations, advanced his own substantive changes, went far beyond them in providing ethnographic, empirical, historical, and comparative evidence for it, and always treated it as a working hypothesis open to review and revision.[14]

The concept of culture is not a rigid designator with necessary and sufficient conditions for its application in every case. It is used in a family of related senses that have some but not all features in common.[15] In general, it refers to the multiplicity of formal and informal ways of life—living patterns of organization and interaction—that comprise four main types: (1) the activities of a single community, society, or people; (2) the interactive relationships among neighboring communities and peoples; (3) the interactive relationships among human communities and peoples on the one hand and nonhuman beings and their shared natural (biological and geological) cultures (ecosystems) on the other; and (4) the culturally diverse ways in which humans participate in these three types of cultural relationships (practices of self-formation, or *Bildungstrieb*).[16] The aim of anthropology is to give a survey-able representation

(*Ubersichtlichen Darstellung*) or ethnographic redescription of the living experience that animates forms of life.[17]

As we will see, Boas uses his unique anthropological method to undermine CPV by falsifying the scientific theories of race and stages of development used to justify it. He exposes it as a particular cultural outlook masquerading as universal that misrepresents and legitimates the subjection and exploitation of colonized peoples. Once he frees himself and his readers from this false worldview, he brings to light the world of equality and diversity it conceals. He explores this world and points out the new ways and values of equality-diversity awareness it makes possible: mutual toleration, fellow-feeling, peace, and the new idea of progress they entail. And, he claims, if people then turn, look back, and reevaluate CPV from this perspective, they will see clearly and come to abhor the imperious way of life it embodies and exalts: "Then we shall find, if we were to select the best of mankind, that all races and all nationalities would be represented. Then we shall treasure and cultivate the variety of forms that human thought and activity has taken, and abhor, as leading to complete stagnation, all attempts to impress one pattern of thought upon whole nations or even upon the whole world."[18]

## THE CRITICAL ANTHROPOLOGICAL METHOD

The anthropological method Boas uses to criticize CPV and advance EDV is set out in *Anthropology* in 1907, and it developed further as his research progressed.[19] Anthropology is the most general of the human sciences in that it studies "the multifarious forms of human life."[20] The feeling of "solidarity of mankind," but much more of antagonistic group solidarity, which today finds its "strongest expression in the strife of the nations," brings about an interest in "minute differences" between "different races, types and social groups." Anthropology responds to this interest by addressing two fundamental questions: "Why are the tribes and nations of the world different, and how have the present differences developed?"[21] To answer these, it should investigate "human types and human activities and thought the world over." However, other human sciences, such as biology, psychology, history, economics, philology, and sociology, have taken over anthropological problems from their specialized perspectives, and no one could master all of these fields. So anthropology is assigned the specific investigation of "the primitive tribes of the world that have no written history, that of pre-historic remains, and of the types of man inhabiting the world at present and in past times."[22] However, anthropology cannot ignore research in other disciplines since it endeavors "to investigate the history of mankind" as a whole.[23] Anthropology can do this by becoming a method of posing "problems from an anthropological standpoint" in many disciplines. As specialization increases, he concludes, anthropology "will become more and more *a method* that may be applied by a great number of sciences, rather than a science by itself."[24]

This unique anthropological method of posing problems is necessary because it is critical in a reflexive way that other human sciences and anthropological approaches are not. Boas argues that the majority and most basic practices of any culture are nonreflective and customary. Some practices and institutions are created by explicit, rational design, but these are embedded in a broader background field of shared, habitual patterns of thought and action. Participants acquire the know-how to think and act within practices but speculate on and generate second-order explanations of them only when these customary ways of acting together rise into consciousness. These explicit representations of cultural practices are "secondary explanations" relative to the primary nonreflective understandings of practitioners. "The importance of the constant occurrence of such secondary explanations cannot be overrated," Boas writes. "They are ever present."[25]

Secondary explanations are of crucial importance for several reasons. First, investigators "will always receive explanations based on secondary explanations," but these "do not represent the history of the custom or belief in question, but only the results of speculation with regard to it."[26] Second, the secondary explanations that gain widespread support and become customary in turn draw on the conventional descriptive-evaluative language of acceptability of the culture and they, in return, reinforce this background language. Accordingly, secondary explanations, while allowing for a constrained range of differing views within their cluster of assumptions, generally serve to rationalize and legitimate the cultural practices they misrepresent.[27] Third, as secondary explanations become the customary representations of cultural practices, they extend and intensify the powerful visceral "emotional attachments" members already have to their basic practices into the secondary explanations themselves, and the corresponding emotion of hostility toward challenges to them. Thus, through both reason and emotion members become deeply attached to their familiar secondary explanations.[28] Finally, customary practices and their secondary explanations exist in all cultures, civilized and primitive.[29] Boas's primary example of a secondary explanation and its corresponding practices is CPV.[30]

Boas's critical anthropological method takes this complex secondary relationship between thought and action into account, whereas other approaches in the social sciences do not. Almost all social sciences except anthropology study civilized societies from within civilized societies. As a result, researchers who live and work within them are critical *within* the prevailing forms of civilized / primitive secondary explanations within their discipline, yet uncritical of the civilized / primitive background because they do not come up against an alternative that would throw it into question.[31] Even the most critical Western philosophers such as Nietzsche work within this framework.[32] Only anthropologists study noncivilized societies. Yet, since most anthropologists are members of civilized societies, they also take for granted the general form of secondary explanations of civilized and primitive practices for granted and work within it (CPV).

Moreover, social scientists and anthropologists do not question their own presuppositions because they believe that human activities are based on and follow from reasoning (primitive or civilized) and that their rational form of secondary explanations represents the general laws of evolution of cultural practices as humans become civilized and rational, and which anthropological data are presumed to illustrate.[33] But the relation of thought to action tends to be the other way round. They fail to see that, as with all humans, the reasons they give tend to be rationalizations of the ways of acting and patterns of thought to which they are accustomed and emotionally attached. They are not the reasons by which they arrive at their conclusions but the explanations they give for their conclusions.[34] For Boas, as for Goethe, "in the beginning was the deed."[35]

Accordingly, a critical anthropological method takes this feature of the human condition into account; enables practitioners to free themselves from the general form of secondary explanations of civilized and primitive practices and to expose the roles it plays; and makes possible more accurate ethnographies of cultural practices: "It enables us to free ourselves from the prejudices of our civilization, and to apply standards in measuring our achievements that have a greater absolute truth than those derived from a study of our civilization alone."[36]

The way to do this is to cultivate a distance from civilized thought and practice by preparation and sustained, intensive participation and dialogue with members of primitive cultures in their daily activities. This participatory practice is a radical mode of self-transformation:

> Activities of the human mind exhibit an infinite variety of forms among the peoples of the world. In order to understand these clearly, the student must endeavor to divest himself entirely of opinions and emotions based upon the peculiar social environment into which he is born. He must adapt his own mind, so far as feasible, to that of the people whom he is studying. The more successful he is in freeing himself from the bias based on the group of ideas that constitute

> the civilization in which he lives, the more successful he will be in interpreting the beliefs and actions of man. He must follow lines of thought that are new to him. He must participate in new emotions, and understand how, under unwonted conditions, both lead to actions.[37]

This radical method frees practitioners from their civilized self-understanding and enables them to acquire primary understanding of the practices and secondary stories, myths, folktales, ceremonies, and dances they participate in and discuss with members, as Boas did with the Kwakwa̱ka̱'wakw and George Hunt. This participatory understanding is the basis of thick ethnographies that are closer to the "absolute truth" than the superficial and untrustworthy comparative descriptions of the evolutionary ethnographers and their imposed schemes.[38] The lived experience of being in this cultural world and worldview then enables practitioners to problematize and take a genuinely critical and comparative stance to what remains unquestioned from studies undertaken *within* civilized practices and their secondary explanations (CPV), as Boas would do throughout his career.[39] It enables practiced-based investigators to use their understanding of primitive science to "shatter the illusions" of civilized social science.[40]

Such a method "teaches better than any other science the relativity of the values of civilization."[41] By the "relativity of values" Boas means the complex internal relationship of values to cultural practices outlined above. Yet, this is not an incommensurable or "negative" relativity precisely because it enables practitioners to move around and critically compare and reevaluate both cultures, "civilized" and "primitive," from reciprocal perspectives and even to advance, as Boas does, new values commensurate with the equality and diversity this approach discloses. Indeed, "this broader outlook" makes possible a whole new way of thinking about progress, one that is different from the "dominant [evolutionary] ideas of our times."[42] There is nothing contrived about this critical, comparative, and often analogical mode of cross-cultural reasoning. It is grounded in the commonplace ethical practice humans engage in whenever they try to put themselves in the shoes of others.[43] Boas's method thus overcomes what he sees as the constitutive mistake of civilized social science and anthropology—that of presupposing the universality of their values. On his view of critical comparative rationality, it is the civilized scientist who is the unwitting cultural relativist in the negative sense by preemptively universalizing their own values and prejudging the values of other cultures relative to them, thereby closing off the possibility of understanding and learning from others.[44]

This radical method and transformative ethos brings to consciousness a new way not only of thinking of progress and *being* progressive but also of enlightenment and *being* enlightened. In the dominant view, enlightenment is brought about as the civilizing processes of development are spread around the world by the most enlightened nations until the darker races are enlightened by assimilation or exterminated. From Boas's critical perspective, the civilizing processes and their secondary theories do the opposite. They keep civilized peoples in the dark regarding the falsehoods of their legitimating theories and the global destructiveness of their civilizing practices. In contrast, his method enlightens. It brings to light the falsehoods and destruction of CPV on the critical hand, and it brings to light the unifying equality and diversity of humankind and the corresponding new values (EDV) on the constructive hand, and it does this by cultivating an enlightening ethos or attitude. In concluding, Boas writes that he hopes his lecture may have "engendered the feeling that we are striving for a goal that is bound to enlighten mankind, and which will be helpful in gaining a right attitude in the solution of the problems of life."[45]

This enlightening critical method and ethos can be seen as the innovative continuation of the view of enlightenment put forward by the Humboldtian-romantic tradition from Herder to today and beyond in opposition to the civilizing tradition and its modernizing successor.[46] Yet it can also be seen as drawing on the transformative Raven stories Boas learned from the Kwakwa̱ka̱'wakw, Nuu-chah-nulth, Tsimshian, Haida, Tlingit, and other Northwest Coast peoples. Raven stories, masks, and dances are about the practices through which Raven and humans can transform themselves so as to see and experience the world from the multiple perspectives of not only culturally different human beings but also animals, plants, rocks, rivers, mountains, sun, moon, and Mother Earth herself. The aim of Raven stories and performances is to teach by examples to their young listeners the transformative ethics and right attitude of "bringing light (truth) to the world"; of helping to enlighten fellow human beings who are in the dark about the solution to the problems of life.[47]

## CPV CONCEALS EQUALITY / DIVERSITY

Boas opens *The Mind of Primitive Man* with his synopsis of the contrastive features of CPV:

> Proud of his wonderful achievements, civilized man looks down upon the humbler members of mankind. He has conquered the forces of nature and compelled them to serve him. He has transformed inhospitable forests into fertile fields. The mountain fastnesses are yielding their treasures to his demands. The fierce animals which are obstructing his progress are being exterminated,

A Haida Raven dancer "brings the light" to two young minds. This dance took place upon the 2013 raising of the Gwai Haanas Legacy Pole, carved by Jaalen Edenshaw with his brother Gwaai Edenshaw and Tyler York for the twentieth anniversary of a Haida land stewardship agreement with Canada. Courtesy of Jason Shafto/Full Moon Photo.

> while others which are useful to him are made to increase a thousand-fold. The waves of the ocean carry him from land to land, and towering mountain-ranges set him no bounds. His genius has moulded inert matter into powerful machines which await a touch of his hand to serve his manifold demands.
>
> With pity he looks down upon those members of the human race who have not succeeded in subduing nature; who labor to eke a meagre existence out of the products of the wilderness; who hear with trembling the roar of the wild animals, and see the products of their toils destroyed by them; who remain restricted by ocean, river or mountains; who strive to obtain the necessities of life with the help of few and simple instruments.
>
> Such is the contrast that presents itself to the observer. What wonder if civilized man considers himself a being of higher order as compared to primitive man, if he claims that the white race represents a type higher than all others![48]

This contrastive representation of civilized and primitive ways of life and the emotions it mobilizes matches exactly his account of secondary explanations. Civilized people see their achievements in global expansion, conquering and subduing nature, and bringing nature under their knowledge, control, and exploitation. These representations of their achievements are then used as standards by which the achievements of primitive peoples are represented, evaluated, and explained. Because primitive peoples have not brought nature under their control they must be under the control of nature and thus inferior mentally and lower developmentally. "All other civilizations," Boas comments, "appear [in contrast] as feeble beginnings cut short in early childhood, or arrested and petrified at an early stage of development."[49] This set of binary contrasts induces an emotional sense of superiority over and pity toward the lower peoples. If they fail to conform to European ideals of physical beauty, an additional emotion of " 'instinctive' aversion" arises.[50]

Once this picture is taken for granted, civilized people "like to support [their] emotional attitude towards the so-called inferior races by reasoning": secondary explanations support the worldview–emotions nexus already in place.[51] Boas argues that the various secondary explanations of civilized social scientists and anthropologists are based primarily on two theses and conclusions: (1) since Western civilization is higher than any other culture, the innate aptitudes for cultural development must be higher in the European or white race that produced the achievements (scientific racism); and (2) since European civilization represents the highest stage of development of the human mind and culture, all other cultures must be on lower stages (evolutionary theory).[52] He then takes up each in turn.

Before "accepting this [first] conclusion," Boas begins, "which places the stamp of eternal inferiority upon whole races of man, we may well pause, and subject the basis of our opinions regarding the aptitude of different peoples and races to a searching analysis."[53] He examines the claims that aptitudes are relative to race and concludes: "Our brief consideration of some of the mental activities in civilized and primitive society has led us to the conclusion that the functions of the human mind are common to the whole of humanity."[54] He then examines the second thesis of Charles Darwin, Herbert Spencer, Lewis Henry Morgan, and others that cultures can be ranked in stages with primitive culture as simple and civilization as complex. These are shown to be unfounded and untenable.[55] Customs, he argues, do not develop in a definite sequence; cultural features do not develop from the same causes; many cases lack comparability and cannot be measured objectively; several features of primitive societies are actually more complex than those of civilized societies; and so on. In conclusion, "the question with which we began our consideration—namely, whether the representatives of different races can be proved to have developed independently, in such a way that the representatives of some races stand on low levels of culture, while others stand on high levels of culture—may be answered in the negative."[56] In general, Boas shows that the two theses, which are presented as if they are propositions to be tested, actually function as unquestioned premises or presumptions that determine the way the data are described, classified, and explained. Following his critical, participatory method, he converts them into hypotheses to be tested by the evidence as it is gathered and set out by an investigator "freeing himself from the bias based on the group of ideas that constitute the civilization in which he lives" and following "the lines of thought that are new to him."[57]

I would like to mention two of Boas's arguments that he took to be important and decisive and which illustrate his method. One of the central arguments for the racial and developmental inferiority of primitive people was that they are incapable (or not yet capable) of the mental processes of abstraction, inhibition, originality, logical thought, and concentration presumptively characteristic of civilized people. This conclusion was advanced and generalized by Gilbert Sproat after interviewing Nuu-chah-nulth on Vancouver Island and then cited by Spencer.[58] Boas interviewed Nuu-chah-nulth people a few decades later. He discovered that they possessed and exercised all the mental capacities Sproat claimed they lacked. They carried on lengthy, abstract discussions of various kinds, Boas often growing weary and inattentive before they did. They simply lost interest in Sproat's questions, which "seem mostly trifling to the Indian," who "tires of a conversation carried on in a foreign language, and one in which he finds nothing to interest him."[59] Sproat, under the spell of CPV, misunderstood and misrepresented what he heard and saw. Boas's methodological revolution is profound yet simple (once you see it): the "proper way to compare the fickleness [or "self-control" and other capacities] of the savage and that of the white man is to compare their behavior in undertakings which are equally important to each."[60] Once anthropology is carried out in this new way, "the view cannot be maintained that the present races of man stand on different stages of the evolutionary series and that civilized man has attained a higher place in mental organization than primitive man."[61]

The second argument is Boas's transmission or diffusion thesis. Bastian introduced the thesis that there is a similarity of processes of thought and fundamental ideas across all cultures, thereby challenging a key premise of the stages view. He argued that the similarities he observed are explained by an innate stock of ideas common to humanity. Boas agrees with the similarity in capacities, processes, and some general ideas. However, he argues that they are explained by the actual diffusion of ideas, practices, institutions, and technologies among human groups throughout history. Peoples interact, negotiate, trade, exchange, and borrow ideas from other cultures, and then they reinterpret, modify, and transform them as they integrate them into their home culture. Consequently, the actual meanings and uses of transmitted (similar) elements can be understood only by studying them in their diffuse cultural contexts.[62]

The transmission, diffusion, reinterpretation, and innovative usage of ideas and practices clearly would be impossible under both the race-based and stages theses. Further, it is an important correction to a convention inherited from Herder. In opposition to the stages thesis Herder argued that there is a plurality of world cultures, each with its own unique features (genius), and thus it is the error of Eurocentrism to rank them according to the history and standards of one particular culture. He explained cultural plurality as a result of "varied external [environmental] conditions acting upon general human characteristics."[63] However, he also assumed that cultures develop more or less independently. For Boas, diffusion is as important as, and inseparably intertwined with, the exercise of culture-creating capacities.[64] Thus, cultural "diversity" fits Boas's worldview better than cultural pluralism. Owing to diffusion, the elements of different cultures crisscross and overlap in complex ways. Cultures are interactive, interdependent, and entangled forms of life that coevolve in indeterminate ways. Accordingly, anthropologists should study the unique "inner growth" and their interactive and interdependent relations with their environment, as Herder argued, but also their "relations to neighbors" to understand diffusion and its complex effects.[65]

## CPV RATIONALIZES IMPERIALISM

Next, Boas argues that once we (civilized peoples) "free ourselves from the prejudices of our civilization" we see that CPV and its secondary explanations misrepresent and rationalize the unjust imperial practices of the civilized nations. Boas confronted two main explanations of European imperialism. The first explanation, as we have seen, was that it is a grand exercise in civilizing primitive peoples. The second, "struggle for existence" explanation, which emerged in the 1860s and was associated with Darwin, Spencer, and T. H. Huxley, sought to explain why the civilizing mission was failing in practice, that is, why millions of primitive people were dying off after coming into contact with European colonizers.[66]

In *On the Origin of Species* (1859) Darwin argued that there is a natural struggle for existence among all living species in which the fitter exterminate the less fit.[67] In *The Descent of Man* (1871), chapter 7, he applies this evolutionary theory to "the races of man, viewing him in the same spirit as a naturalist would any other animal."[68] In the section "On the Extinction of the Races of Man" he explains how struggles for existence lead to the "partial or complete extinction of many races and sub-races of man" through history and, in particular, in the contemporary context of European colonization.[69] "When civilized nations come into contact with barbarians," he writes, "the struggle is short." Of the various "causes that lead to the victory of civilized nations," the major one is the inability or unwillingness of primitive peoples to "change their habits" and adapt to the changed conditions that civilized people introduce, such as agriculture, European diseases, and alcohol. In general, the "most potent of all the causes of extinction appears in many cases to be lessened fertility and ill-health . . . arising from changed conditions of life, *notwithstanding that the new conditions may not be injurious in themselves.*"[70] As they are "induced to change their habits of life, they become more or less sterile, and their young offspring suffer in health," just like elephants and hunting-leopards.[71] Thus, primitive peoples are unable to adapt to "changed conditions or habits of life," whereas the "civilized races" alone can "resist with impunity great diversities of climate and other changes."[72] Moreover, there is no point in trying to protect and civilize primitive people, for the evidence shows that "death followed the attempts to civilize the natives."[73] Extinction due to inadaptability to civilizing processes is as natural and inevitable as the extermination of the native rat of New Zealand "by the European rat." Although comprehending this massive extermination is difficult for the imagination, reason explains it by the general theory of the struggle for existence, which leads to decrease and later to extinction, "the end, in most cases, being promptly determined by the inroads of conquering tribes."[74]

Darwin concludes *The Descent of Man* with a portrayal, as he saw it, of the extreme contrast and unbridgeable inequality between progressive-civilized and disappearing-primitive man. Civilized man may be excused for "feeling some pride" for reaching "the summit of the organic scale" with his "god-like intellect." Yet, he should feel a "noble sympathy" for the "most debased" primitive man, "who delights to torture his enemies, offers up bloody sacrifices, practices infanticide without remorse, treats his wives like slaves, knows no decency, and is haunted by the grossest superstitions," for he is the "lowly origin" from which civilized man descends.[75]

Boas challenges this quasi-scientific rationalization of Western imperialism and genocide.[76] He also may have had Darwin's prejudiced portrayal of civilized and primitive man in mind when he composed his own picture of CPV.[77] He was equally critical of the civilizing mission explanation and rationalization. He presents a critical account of ongoing Western imperial expansion that exposes the falsehoods of both. First, European diseases destroy Native people, their economic life and social structure: "The suffering and devastation wrought by epidemics which followed the discovery are too well known to be described in full." Those who survive are then "swamped" by massive immigration and forced removal and given no time to adjust. Their Indigenous forms of life are overwhelmed, destroyed, and exterminated by European machine production and the life-destroying conditions of capitalist exploitation. Finally, European colonizers, with their sense of superiority, remain apart from the Native people and destroy them, whereas Arab colonizers in Africa intermarry and either assimilate or amalgamate, to which Africans have time to adjust and accommodate.[78] Consequently, the arrested development and devastation of non-European peoples has nothing to do with an inability to adapt their habits to "changed conditions" or to develop further. When Europeans "swept across the world" there was a diversity of cultures developing in their distinctive and interactive ways. The destructiveness of European imperialism is the reason these so-called primitive cultures were cut short: "Our conclusion drawn from the foregoing considerations is the following: . . . The rapid dissemination of Europeans over the whole world destroyed all promising beginnings which had arisen in various regions. Thus no race except that of eastern Asia was given a chance to develop independently. The spread of the European race cut short the growth of the existing germs without regard to the mental aptitude of the people among whom it was developing."[79]

Boas immediately concludes that the whole mythology of higher and lower aptitudes and stages is designed to cover up this imperial genocide, the only truly significant reason for the different growth of world cultures: thus, "historical events appear to have been much more potent in leading races to civilization than their innate faculty, and it follows that achievements of races do not without further proof warrant the assumption that one race is more highly gifted than another."[80] Why would social scientists and theorists construct such false and destructive theories? "All such views," Boas goes on, giving five reasons, "are generalizations which either do not sufficiently take into account the social conditions of races, and thus confound cause and effect, or were dictated by scientific or humanitarian bias, by the desire to justify the institution of slavery, or to give the greatest freedom to the most gifted."[81]

In a letter to the *New York Times* in 1916 Boas explains that when he moved to the United States he thought that it would provide an exception to the destructive imperialism of the old European powers. As an anti-imperialist, he thought the United States would exercise his ideal of self-restraint: it would "refrain from active interference in the affairs of others, and would never become guilty of the oppression of unwilling subjects." He initially "maintained that the control of colonies was opposed to the fundamental ideas of right held by the American people." He also thought that rapid expansion westward over Indian country and the invasion of Mexico would prove to be digressions from an ideal of nonexpansion. Then, the Spanish-American War and the colonization of the Philippines came as a "rude awakening." These anti-imperial "ideals lay shattered."[82] In their place "stood a young giant, eager to grow at the expense of others and dominated by the same desire of aggrandizement that sways the narrowly confined European states." Boas then expresses his admiration for Carl Schurz, the outspoken German American anti-imperialist. He and others now "took the view that the control of alien peoples is destructive to the principles on which our nation is founded; that we have a higher duty to ourselves [of anti-imperial self-restraint] than to those whom, flattering ourselves, we like to call the wards of the nation."[83]

## FROM STANDING OVER TO PARTICIPATING IN THE WORLD

At the center of CPV is the presupposition that humanity progresses from simple primitive tribes to complex civilized nations by investigating the causes of natural and social phenomena, discovering the "mechanism" (or "single cause") that brings them about and uncovering and confirming the laws of its operation. This scientific knowledge frees humans from their primitive embeddedness in and subjection to nature and from the corresponding irrational—mythical, religious, and traditional—explanations of it, and it empowers them to stand apart from and over the world (autonomy) and to bring nature under their control and to make society over in accord with applied social scientific rationality. This modern philosophical and scientific worldview developed in the seventeenth century, and then Enlightenment philosophers and scientists introduced a new way of thinking of the underlying causal and explanatory mechanism. Adam Smith's hidden hand that guides market competition toward economic growth; Immanuel Kant's natural antagonism and war that lead humanity from savagery to civilization and, eventually, to civilized states, perpetual peace, and morality; Thomas Malthus's conflicts between population growth and food scarcity; Karl Marx's class wars and gravedigger's dialectic that lead from barbarism to communism; and Darwin's struggle for existence that naturally selects the fitter, leading to the spread of civilization and the extermination of primitive peoples and, eventually, to morality—all these are examples of this mechanism and of the modern natural and social sciences founded on them.[84]

So far we have seen Boas criticize the ethnographies and explanations based on this background picture of scientific knowledge and progress. In this section we see him criticize this dominant background picture itself and then re-embed (or reintegrate) humans back into the world and describe the alternative participatory science appropriate to this worldview (EDV). This is the project of the entire Goethe–Herder–Humboldt tradition, but Boas's contribution is deeper and unique for the methodological reason he gives: he was able to free himself from this background picture more than his predecessors and see it from an engaged perspective within non-European cultures.[85]

Boas's specific criticisms so far, the discovery of the equality of capabilities and diversity of manifestation and the legitimations of genocide and slavery, serve to call into question not only this or that evolutionary theory, but also this general modern form of scientific explanation (causal and covering law) and its methods of empirical testing as well as its background picture. These criticisms strongly suggest that the laws of human evolution that are supposed to be caused by the mechanism posited by the theories are not confirmed by research but are presupposed, and the data are redescribed to accord with them.

This more radical critique is confirmed for Boas when he tests the universally accepted evolutionary law that societies develop from simple forms (primitive) to complex forms (civilized). This law is falsified by careful research in "late years." Recent research suggests diversity: "Two tendencies intercross—one from complex to simple, the other from simple to the complex."[86] He gives examples of language, art, and music, which tend to be more complex in many primitive societies.[87] It "will readily be seen," he concludes, "that the theory of the evolution of civilization rests to a certain extent on a *logical error.* The classification of the data of anthropology in accordance with their simplicity has been reinterpreted as a historical sequence, without an adequate attempt to prove that the simpler antedates the more complex."[88] This has "shaken our faith in the correctness of the evolutionary theory as a whole."[89]

In 1932 Boas presented his radical critique of this general form of scientific explanation and its modern philosophical assumptions.[90] He argues that the "interrelations" among humans, plants, animals, and the enveloping social and environmental cultures are far too complex and interrelated to be understood in terms of cause and effect and general laws. Hence, "every attempt to deduce cultural forms from a single cause is doomed to failure."[91] Multicausal accounts also fail because causes are also effects: everything is interdependent on everything else. Human and biological cultures are not atomistic but "integrated."[92] While "some valid interrelations between general aspects of cultural life" may hold for a time in some contexts, yet "cultural phenomena are of such complexity that it seems to me doubtful whether valid cultural laws can be found."[93] "A critical investigation rather shows that forms of thought and action which we are inclined to consider as based on human nature are not generally valid, but characteristic of our specific culture."[94] Most important, human beings are free and indeterminate interactive agents within their complex cultural relationships, and thus "the causal conditions of cultural happenings lie always in the interaction between individuals and society, and no classificatory study of societies will solve this problem."[95] He roundly concludes, "These brief remarks may be sufficient to indicate the complexity of the phenomena we are studying, and it seems justifiable to question whether any generalized conclusions may be expected that will be applicable everywhere and that will reduce the data of anthropology to a formula that may be applied to every case, explaining the past and predicting the future."[96] Accordingly, we should abandon this discredited model of science and adopt his Humboldtian scientific method: "For each individual case we can arrive at an understanding of its determination by inner and outer forces, but we cannot explain its individuality in the form of laws."[97]

The result of this "critical investigation" is that humans are seen to be always embedded in noncausal and non-lawlike cultural relationships of diverse kinds. They are integrated into the cultural and ecological world. Human capabilities are always embedded and exercised in cultural relationships. They do not stand over the world as a whole and comprehend, command, and control it but rather participate in and engage with it.[98] Thus, there will always be "traditional elements" (cultural practices, forms of knowledge, and linguistic "classifications of experience") that are taken for granted and form the intersubjective background picture in which rational faculties are exercised.[99] Consequently, the fundamental assumption of modern philosophy and science that there is an evolutionary process of societal rationalization from nonrational, primitive societies based on myth and tradition to modern societies based on science and reason is false.[100] Boas acknowledges the differentiation of value spheres and the separation of instrumental reason in modern societies, in contrast to their integration in primitive societies. However, he does not see this as progress, and he refers to the minority of Europeans who seek to reintegrate value spheres under a comprehensive aesthetic sensibility.[101] There also may be more institutions in modern societies than in primitive societies based on instrumental rationality.[102] However, as he has just shown (in 1932), these institutionalized sciences are themselves based on background, traditional presuppositions and practices that are not examined by the members of them, and when they are examined by Boas they are shown to be culturally relative. Thus, the habitual way his contemporaries work within and continuously reinforce their unexamined modern philosophical and scientific worldview provides "performative" proof of his basic point about the participatory relation of humans in the world in any culture.[103] Civilized and primitive thinkers are thus no different in this regard. They tend not to carry critical analysis "to completion"; they develop strong emotional attachments to the forms of explanation; and they both take their background traditional elements for the "absolute truth."[104]

It follows from this remarkable critique that one must always employ the critical methodology manifested in it: "It would be vain to try to understand the development of modern science without an intelligent understanding of modern philosophy; it would be vain to try to understand the history of medieval science without a knowledge of medieval theology; and so it is vain to try to understand primitive science without an intelligent knowledge of primitive mythology. 'Mythology,' 'theology,' and 'philosophy' are different terms for the same influences which shape the current of human thought, and which determine the character of the attempts of man to explain the phenomena of nature."[105] In arguably his most radical criticism of CPV, Boas turns and employs his method to understand primitive science and mythology and their representation in evolutionary theories. As we have seen, primitive people are portrayed by civilized scientists as ignorant and fearful of nature; they explain nature's all-powerful forces in the animistic stories of their mythologies, which, from the civilized viewpoint, are anthropomorphic and irrational.[106]

In contrast, Boas argues that the linguistic expressions of animism in primitive societies are "not merely a form of speaking," as they are in civilized societies, but rather the "linguistic expression [of animism] is alive among primitive people and finds expression in many ways in their beliefs and actions." The "anthropomorphic interpretation of nature prevalent among primitives may also be conceived as a type of classification of experience."[107] By a "classification of experience" he means the basic form of classification through which any culture brings experience to language in its everyday practices; the vocabulary through which it discloses and brings forth the world. Primitive science takes place within it. Such a basic classification is the ground of reasoning, a way of disclosing the world that makes sense of the experience of the world. Whereas civilized classifications divide experience into animate and inanimate, "it seems probable," Boas conjectures, "that the analogy between the ability to move of men and animals as well as of some inanimate objects, and their conflicts with the activities of men which could be interpreted as an expression of their will power led to it that all these phenomena were combined under one category [i.e., animate]."[108] The disclosure of the world as alive is thus as basic to primitive societies and their sciences as the causal, animate / inanimate, causal and covering law disclosure is to civilized societies:

> To primitive man—who has been taught to consider the heavenly orbs as animate beings; who sees in every animal a being more powerful than man; to whom the mountains, trees and stones are endowed with life or with specific virtues—explanations of phenomena will suggest themselves entirely different from those to which we are accustomed, since we still base our conclusions upon the existence of matter and force as bringing about the observed results. The confusion of the popular mind by the modern theories of relativity, of matter, of causality shows how profoundly we are influenced by ill understood theories.[109]

Once primitive man, science, and mythology are seen from this comparative perspective, the civilized representation of them can be seen to be as flawed as the Faustian portrayal of civilized man, science, and philosophy. Through his participation in and experience of Indigenous ways of being in the world Boas came to realize that most primitive peoples see themselves as active agents embedded in living (animate) relationships of mutual reciprocity with nonhuman living agents (plants, animals, mountains, streams, stones, the sun and moon, and so on).[110] To understand this complex animate world and to live within it, they describe their interactive relationships to nonhuman agents in the terms of family or kinship relations. All living beings are kin or relatives and compose an immensely complex family of families. Boas saw this as a reasonable way of making sense of their experience.[111]

As he explains in remarks on totemism, primitive people are perfectly capable of distinguishing between kinship groups (the field of totemism) and their relationships to nature. However, they use the complex language of kinship relations to make sense of and interact with the living world.[112] The great advantage of this language is that it reminds the users that they are always *in* relationships with human and nonhuman beings, and each specific relationship has its reciprocal responsibilities.[113] The complex potlatch system of self-government of the Indigenous peoples of the Northwest Coast, which Boas publicly defended as a reasonable form of government equal in status to civilized forms, is part of and modeled on the life-sustaining relationships of gift-gratitude-reciprocity-gift that comprise the living earth (Mother Earth).[114]

It seems to me that Boas could understand and appreciate animism, disclosed in the language of kinship, not only because of his participation in Indigenous cultures and dialogues with George Hunt, as crucial as this experience was in freeing him from civilized prejudices and emotions. He could do so also because this animistic way of thinking about cultural relationships among humans, nonhumans, and the environment is akin to his own participatory and relational view of cultures (including nature) and akin also to the integrated and embedded view of cultures of the Humboldtian tradition.[115]

Boas's defense of an animistic worldview had little influence at the time. However, in the 1960s one of the world's leading earth scientists, Sir James Lovelock, introduced the Gaia hypothesis: the idea that the earth is a complex living system of diverse and interrelated living ecological systems that interact in such a way as to sustain life over vast expanses of geological time, and humans are participants within it.[116] By the 1980s it was recognized as the Gaia theory and endorsed by many leading climate scientists. Moreover, they argue that the scientific view Boas criticized is a major cause of climate change and the ecological crisis. Lovelock's students have gone on to relate the Gaia theory to the animistic view of nature in the Goethe and Humboldt tradition and to the animistic myths and sciences of Indigenous peoples of the world.[117] So, perhaps Boas's work should be seen in this positive light, as an important step in the effort to reintegrate culturally diverse humans into a living world, showing how Indigenous science and ecological science can join hands and work together on our common problems.[118]

## ANTHROPOLOGY AS THE WAY TO WORLD PEACE

Throughout his career Boas was deeply concerned with the wars and economic rivalry among the civilized states and over Indigenous peoples. He saw war as the greatest problem of the twentieth century.[119] He came to see his anthropological ethos (as I will call it)—consisting in his method, its critical attitude, and the ethics it involves—as a response to the problem. If this anthropological ethos were widely taught and practiced, he argued, people would gradually move from CPV to EDV, and this transformation would lead toward world peace.[120]

Boas sets out the problem and hints at the solution in 1912: "If we understand that the feeling of opposition to the stranger which accompanies the feeling of solidarity of the nation, is the survival of the primitive feeling of specific differences, we are brought clearly face to face with those forces that will ultimately abolish warfare as well as legislative conflicts between nations; that will put an end not only to the wholesale slaughter of those representing a distinct ideal, but also prevent the passage of laws that favor the members of one nation at the expense of all members of mankind."[121] The problem of war in the modern state system is that the feeling of national solidarity comes along with the feeling of opposition and antagonism to other nations. This combination of solidarity and antagonism is not unique to civilized nations but is the survival and intensification of a primitive feeling of specific differences common to all societies.[122] The feeling of group solidarity is grounded in habituation to a set of "specific differences" that are said to give the group a unique and superior identity in opposition to the specific differences of other groups.[123] This oppositional stance generates mutual distrust, antagonism, competition, war preparation, war, war preparation in time of peace, and so on.[124]

This solidarity–opposition nexus is more destructive in civilized states and under CPV.[125] It leads to the extermination of Indigenous peoples, as we have seen, and to wars between modern states by highlighting their allegedly opposed specific differences.[126] In particular, democratic states such as the United States see their specific and far from perfect form of democracy as the universal form of democracy for all people. They see its standards as "absolute standards," and the "more idealistic" members set themselves up as the "arbiter of the world" and wish to "raise everyone up" to their standard by extending it "over other countries."[127] The logic of the civilized / primitive picture and the civilizing mission is thus carried on under the rubric of democratization. Thus, he concludes, "a league of imperialistic nations will never lead to lasting peace."[128]

How does Boas's anthropological ethos dissolve this problem that continues to plague the world system down to today? I set out the relevant features of his ethos in the previous sections so we can understand how he saw it as a possible way toward peace. The four main steps are as follows.

First, Boas's method and the EDV hypothesis enable practitioners to see that the specific differences that unite each nation in opposition to others are inculcated fictions, underpinned by the false secondary explanations of social and anthropological theory that he exposes in *The Mind of Primitive Man* and held in place by manufactured emotional attachments.[129] The characteristics of any nation are more diverse and changing than the "homogenizing" official narrative due to diffusion and interaction, and many of the same characteristics can be found in other nations. The family of nations is composed of overlapping similarities and dissimilarities, and these are continually negotiated. These identities, as he calls them, unlike specific differences, are not fixed, tied to a race, arranged in stages, or constitutive of a particular form of civilization or democracy. As humans become aware of the falseness of conventional differences and the diversity of overlapping identities, by means of the anthropological ethos, a higher tolerance becomes possible:

> It is difficult for us to recognize that the value which we attribute to our own civilization is due to the fact that we participate in it, and that it has been controlling all our action since the time of our birth, but it is certainly conceivable that there may be many other civilizations, based perhaps on different traditions and on a different equilibrium of emotion and reason, which are of no less value than ours, although it may be impossible for us to appreciate their values

> without having grown up under their influence. The general theory of valuation of human activities, as developed by anthropological research, teaches us a higher tolerance than the one we now possess.[130]

Second, the ethos enables its practitioners to see and experience a feeling that is overlooked in the Darwinian model of feelings of solidarity within the group and of opposition to those without. This is a third "feeling of fellowship" toward neighboring groups with which groups interact.[131] Although it is not as strong as the feeling of opposition, intensified by oppositional specific differences, it also is historically related to the feeling of group solidarity. Boas's anthropological method discloses this crucial peacemaking feeling because it focuses not only on societies but also on their relations to and interactions with their neighbors. The feeling of fellowship and its ethic of "mutual toleration," as he calls it, develops as societies grow, interact with their neighbors, become interdependent, and diversify through diffusion, and these factors call into question oppositional specific differences.[132]

Fellow-feeling and cooperation beyond (porous) cultural borders arise as families and tribes interact, borrow from each other through diffusion, become more internally diverse, enter into treaty relationships, and invent a new form of political organization: the confederation. "Thus the feeling of specific difference gradually 'wore off,' and although the attitude to the stranger retained a background of hostility, a certain amount of mutual toleration developed."[133] The exemplar is the Iroquois Confederacy and the Great Law of Peace.[134] While destructive antagonism and conflict with nations outside the confederacy and treaty partners remain, the feeling of fellowship, the ethos of mutual toleration of differences, and the practice of negotiated federalism as the alternative to antagonism and war with one's neighbors provide the historical foundations of world federalism and peace.[135]

Third, the transformation from antagonism to world fellowship requires another element. Federations and leagues that lack this element tend to increase the scale and destructiveness of war, as Boas argues with respect to civilized leagues of "imperialistic nations."[136] The crucial element of transformation from antagonism to fellow-feeling is cultural: participatory education in the equality and diversity of tribes and nations. Since humans' mode of being in the world with others is shaped so powerfully by the lived experience of their different cultures, it is necessary to experience other cultures in order to undergo self-transformation.

There are two ways this radical self-transformation can be achieved. The primary way is to participate in and engage with the lived experience of other cultures, as Boas's ethos requires.[137] The secondary way is to participate in an educational experience that critically elucidates the cultural experience and values of one's own and other cultures and their interrelations. Boas claims that he had this second kind of schooling. He was taught "not only to love the soul of my own country but also to seek to understand and respect the individualities of other nations."[138] This teaches a new kind of ethical–cultural nationalism and solidarity that transcends the feeling of antagonism toward the Other, the ground of war. One loves one's own culture, he explains, because one sees it as the "medium in which every individual can unfold freely his activities," and one respects other cultures because they are the media in which individuals within them develop freely in their culturally diverse ways.[139]

Boas refers to J. G. Fichte when he outlines this kind of self-transformative education, but it is shared by the whole Humboldtian tradition.[140] It is a "substitute" for the lived experience of actual participation in different cultures that is meant to cultivate a mode of self-awareness and self-formation referred to as an aesthetic sensibility: a mode of being in which humans are integrated into the diverse world of overlapping cultures and into the living earth (anima mundi).[141] Here is how Alexander von Humboldt articulates it:

> The [animate] earth reveals to them [Indigenous peoples] all at once its manifold formations, just as the starry firmament conceals from them none of its shining worlds. In the wealth and culture of languages, in the lively imagination of poets and painters, we [Europeans] find a satisfying substitute [*Ersatz*]. The magic of the representational arts transports [*versetzt*] us to the farthest reaches of the earth. . . . Through [languages and arts] we live at once in past and present centuries. Gathering around us what human effort has discovered in the most distant parts of the globe, we remain equally near to all.[142]

Humboldt, like Boas, means that through Indigenous peoples' animistic ways of being in the world, living nature is disclosed to them in a way that is concealed to modern Europeans under their causal and covering law world-view. This gives primacy to learning from the practices of Indigenous peoples. However, the "gathering around us" refers to the imperial appropriation of cultural artifacts for European and American museums and universities. Boas was involved in this destructive imperial practice. The only way such a substitute education would work is if all cultural artifacts are returned to Indigenous nations; they become thriving and self-determining cultures once again (neither "cut short" nor pillaged); and then, and only then, reciprocal and lengthy student exchange programs take place among students from diverse cultures. Only then would the experience be "equally near to all." It would be as close as possible to Boas's primary way of self-transformation. Such a practice-based education in equal and reciprocal learning across cultures would have as one exemplar the way Hunt and Boas moved back and forth between cultures and educated each other.[143]

The fourth and final step is that primary or substitute practice-based education discloses and brings forth the world of equality, diversity, and fellow-feeling, and the corresponding ethics follows. For, as we have seen throughout, ways of knowing are grounded in ways of being, not the other way around.[144] Boas states that this new ethics is radically different from the ethics taught in national education systems: "It is obvious that the standards of ethical conduct must be quite distinct as between those who have grasped this ideal and those who would still believe in the preservation of isolated nationality in opposition to all others. In all countries the standard of national ethics, as cultivated by means of national education, are opposed to this wider view."[145] From his practice-based education, Boas sketches some features of such a future ethics in his public writings. In addition to the respect for other cultures and the ideal of individual self-development discussed above, the foreigner will be seen as a fellow "member of mankind," a world family, and this will become the basis of respecting "international human rights" in practice.[146] The freedom of self-determination of peoples, that is, the "fundamental importance of freedom for all societies to develop their own ideals," will be recognized.[147] Furthermore, the "rights of citizens of each nation to free existence according to their mode of life must be recognized."[148] As education and fellow-feeling spread, government officials will also grow into these ethical practices. They will gradually replace self-assertion and self-aggrandizement with self-restraint; preparation for war with nonpreparation (disarmament); manipulation of international law to suit their interests with obedience to international law in the general interest; and war with international institutions of negotiation.[149] The growing world culture of EDV will be the ground of expanding peaceful federal relationships, eventually uniting the whole world—a condition that is "destined to come."[150]

At the core of this political ethics is the respect for the global diversity of forms of democratic government and the recognition of the particularity of each. As we saw at the beginning, the basic form of antagonism in the system of civilized states that fuels war after war is the "abhorrent" rationalized and emotional attachment to a "particular form [of democracy] in which we have grown up and which we desire to extend over other countries."[151] It is precisely this intolerant and war-reproducing attitude that the anthropological ethos is designed to make us see as abhorrent and want to abolish:

Franz Boas, top right, with George Hunt, top, second from left, and his family during a field trip to Fort Rupert, British Columbia, ca. 1894. Graphics no. 5390, American Philosophical Society.

> Our intolerant attitude is most pronounced in regard to what we like to call "our free institutions." Modern democracy was undoubtedly the most wholesome and needed reaction against the abuses of absolutism. . . . That the wishes and thoughts of the people should find expression, and that the form of government should conform to these wishes is an axiom that has pervaded the whole Western world, and that is taking root even in the Far East. It is a quite different question, however, in how far the particular machinery of democratic government that we have developed is identical with democratic institutions [in general]. . . . To claim, as we often do, that our solution is the only democratic and the ideal one, is a one-sided exaggeration of Americanism. I see no reason why we should not allow other nations to solve their problems in their own ways, instead of demanding that they bestow upon themselves the benefactions of our regime. The very standpoint that we are right and they are wrong is opposed to the fundamental idea that nations have distinctive individualities, which are expressed in their modes of life, thought and feeling.[152]

However, for Boas, people can appreciate and begin to enact respect for diverse forms of government only through the transformative experience of participating in them, as he did, not by studying ethics in the classrooms of the warring civilized states and learning the scientific and philosophical justifications for their presupposed superiority. If he is correct about the primacy of being to knowing, then he must have come around to his radical views of mutual respect for democratic diversity and self-determination by his participation in different Indigenous practices of government, such as the potlatch system of government of the Kwakwa̱ka̱'wakw, which he publicly defended prior to his broader public writing on ethics.[153]

Boas realized that this anthropological ethos that I have briefly summarized was marginal, and he compared himself to Tacitus, the Roman historian who alerted his fellow citizens to the destructiveness and self-destructiveness of imperialism.[154] Notwithstanding, in the final edition of *The Mind of Primitive Man* he added a sketch of a new way of thinking about progress, and "at the same time the slowness of this progress."[155] He rehearses the steps by which his ethos could lead to world peace, yet with full weight given the dominant antagonistic ethos, and ends by mentioning that his ethics teaches a "higher tolerance." Perhaps this higher tolerance refers to the tolerance required for the new way of thinking about progress that EDV brings into view.[156] Ethical progress is not an evolutionary process guaranteed by an antagonistic mechanism, but, like a Raven dance, beginning to take the slow, difficult, courageous, and unpredictable steps he outlined and took himself against the dominant currents of his and our time.

## Notes

For their most helpful comments I would like to thank Michael Asch, Ned Blackhawk, Johnny Mack, Robert Nichols, David Owen, Mark W. Rowe, Quentin Skinner, and Isaiah Wilner.

1. I focus on what I consider to be important and valuable aspects of Boas's work. For problematic aspects, see Audra Simpson, this volume.
2. Franz Boas, *The Mind of Primitive Man* (1911; repr. New York: Macmillan, 1922), 1–2; Franz Boas, *The Mind of Primitive Man* (New York: Macmillan, 1938), 4–5.
3. Boas inherited the two general world visions, as well as several other features of his thought, from the Humboldtian tradition in which he was educated. This anthropological and philosophical tradition includes Johann Gottfried von Herder (1744–1803), Johann Wolfgang von Goethe (1749–1832), Johann Georg Adam Forster (1754–94), Alexander von Humboldt (1769–1859), Henry David Thoreau (1817–62), Adolf Bastian (1826–1905), Franz Boas (1858–1942), Oswald Spengler (1880–1936), and Ludwig Wittgenstein (1889–1951), among others. He went on to test, substantiate, modify, reject, extend, transform, and add to these inherited features, but the influence is unmistakable. For an introduction, see George W. Stocking Jr., ed., *Volksgeist as Method and Ethic: Essays on Boasian Ethnography and the German Anthropological Tradition* (Madison: University of Wisconsin Press, 1996). Boas singles out Herder as the most important influence in the areas of his work that this chapter discusses (see the references below).
4. For a characterization of a worldview in this broad sense, see Ludwig Wittgenstein, *On Certainty,* trans. Denis Paul and G. E. M. Anscombe (Oxford: Blackwell, 1974), ss. 93–97.
5. See the discussion that follows in "The Critical Anthropological Method" for secondary explanations.
6. My synopsis of CPV is based on Anthony Anghie, *Imperialism, Sovereignty and the Making of International Law* (Cambridge: Cambridge University Press, 2003); Brett Bowden, *The Empire of Civilization* (Chicago: University of Chicago Press, 2009); James Tully, *Imperialism and Civic Freedom* (Cambridge: Cambridge University Press, 2008).
7. The means included formal colonies, indirect rule, free-trade imperialism, dominions, protectorates, garrisons, the Monroe Doctrine of the United States, and the internal colonization of Indigenous peoples within the European colony-states implanted on their traditional territories in the Americas, Australia, New Zealand, India, and elsewhere.
8. The classic presentations are Immanuel Kant, *Perpetual Peace: A Philosophical Sketch,* in *Kant: Political Writings,* ed. Hans Reiss (Cambridge: Cambridge University Press, 2001), 93–130, and Karl Marx and Friedrich Engels, *The Communist Manifesto,* ed. David McLellan (Oxford: Oxford University Press, 1992). For a survey of the vast variations on this theme, even among critics of its racism and genocide, see Gregory Claeys, *Imperial Sceptics: British Critics of Empire, 1850–1920* (Cambridge: Cambridge University Press, 2010) and Bowden, *The Empire of Civilization.*
9. This discursive formation is now called modernity / coloniality among postcolonial scholars. See Walter D. Mignolo, *Local Histories / Global Designs* (Princeton: Princeton University Press, 2000). For the blind faith in it, see Gilbert Rist, *The History of Development: From Western Origins to Global Faith,* trans. Patrick Camiller (London: Zed Books, 1997).

10. Balakrishnan Rajagopal, *International Law from Below: Development, Social Movements and Third World Resistance* (Cambridge: Cambridge University Press, 2004).
11. Roger Normand and Sarah Zaidi, *Human Rights at the UN* (Bloomington: Indiana University Press, 2008), 162–66.
12. For example, Anthony J. Hall, *Earth into Property* (Montreal: McGill-Queens University Press, 2007), Taiaiake Alfred, *Wasase: Indigenous Pathways of Action and Freedom* (Peterborough, ON, and Orchard Park, NY: Broadview Press, 2005), and James Tully, "The Struggle of Indigenous Peoples for and of Freedom," in *Democracy and Civic Freedom* (Cambridge: Cambridge University Press, 2008), 257–88.
13. For the suggestion that there are at least seven thousand cultures today, see Wade Davis, *Wayfinders: Why Ancient Wisdom Matters in the Modern World* (Toronto: House of Anansi Press, 2009).
14. For Herder, see Vicki A. Spencer, *Herder's Political Thought: A Study of Language, Culture and Community* (Toronto: University of Toronto Press, 2012); for Humboldt, see Matti Bunzl, "Franz Boas and the Humboldtian Tradition: From *Volksgeist* and *Nationalcharakter* to an Anthropological Concept of Culture," in *Volksgeist,* ed. Stocking, 17–78; for Bastian, see Klaus-Peter Kopping, *Adolf Bastian and the Psychic Unity of Mankind: Foundations of Anthropology in Nineteenth Century Germany* (Piscataway, NJ: Transaction Publications, Rutgers University, 2005).
15. This unique way of thinking about concepts and meaning is a core feature of the Humboldtian tradition. For the classic presentation, see Ludwig Wittgenstein, *Philosophical Investigations,* trans. G. E. M. Anscombe, P. M. S. Hacker, and Joachim Schulte (Oxford: Basil Blackwell, 2009), ss. 65–69.
16. Boas, *The Mind of Primitive Man* (1938), 159: "Culture may be defined as the totality of the mental and physical reactions and activities that characterize the behavior of individuals composing a social group collectively and individually in relation to their natural environment, to other groups, to members of the group itself and to each individual to himself. It also includes the products of these activities and their role in the life of the groups."
17. Ibid., 175–95. See also Judith Berman, "'The Culture as It Appears to the Indian Himself': Boas, George Hunt, and the Methods of Anthropology," in *Volksgeist,* ed. Stocking, 215–56. The members of the Humboldtian tradition contrast this interpretative approach with the mechanistic or causal and covering law form of explanation characteristic of scholars working within the CPV tradition.
18. Boas, *The Mind of Primitive Man* (1938), 272.
19. Franz Boas, *Anthropology* (New York: Columbia University Press, 1908), a lecture delivered at Columbia University, Dec. 18, 1907. Sections of *Anthropology* are included in the 1911 and 1938 editions of *The Mind of Primitive Man* and his other publications on method, which are collected in Franz Boas, *Race, Language and Culture* (New York: Macmillan, 1940), 243–311.
20. Boas, *Anthropology,* 5.
21. Ibid., 7.
22. Ibid., 7–8.
23. Ibid., 9.
24. Ibid., 9–10.

25. Ibid., 24; Boas, *The Mind of Primitive Man* (1911), 225–27, Boas, *The Mind of Primitive Man* (1938), 238–51.
26. Boas, *Anthropology*, 23.
27. Boas, *The Mind of Primitive Man* (1911), 113.
28. Boas, *Anthropology*, 25; Boas, *The Mind of Primitive Man* (1911), 194.
29. Boas, *Anthropology*, 25–26. This is a constant theme in his work.
30. Boas, *The Mind of Primitive Man* (1911), 1–4; Boas, *The Mind of Primitive Man* (1938), 1–5.
31. Boas, *Anthropology*, 9.
32. Boas, *The Mind of Primitive Man* (1922), 100.
33. Boas, *Anthropology*, 15–16. For his later, more systematic criticism of this whole approach, see the discussion that follows in "From Standing Over to Participating in the World."
34. Ibid., 26–27. "We pride ourselves on following the dictates of reason and carrying out our careful weighed convictions. The fact which is taught by anthropology,—that man the world over *believes* that he follows the dictates of reason, no matter how unreasonably he may act—and the knowledge of the existence of the tendency of the human mind to arrive at a conclusion first and to give the reasons afterwards, will help us to open our eyes; so that we recognize that our philosophical views and our political convictions are to a great extent determined by our emotional inclinations, and that the reasons which we give are not the reasons by which we arrive at our conclusions, but the explanations which we give for our conclusions."
35. In the 1938 edition of *The Mind of Primitive Man,* Boas criticizes Sir James Frazer in particular for failing to "open his eyes" to this rationalizing tendency, but he claims that it is shared by most social scientists and anthropologists (238). For a similar criticism of Frazer and defense of Goethe's thesis, see Ludwig Wittgenstein, *Remarks on Frazer's Golden Bough,* ed. Rush Rhees (1931; repr. Doncaster, UK: Brynmill Press, 1987).
36. Boas, *Anthropology*, 26.
37. Boas, *The Mind of Primitive Man* (1911), 98.
38. Boas, *Anthropology*, 15–20.
39. See Berman, "'The Culture as It Appears to the Indian Himself,'" and Isaiah Lorado Wilner, "A Global Potlatch: Identifying the Indigenous Influence on Western Thought," *American Indian Culture and Research Journal* 37, no. 2 (2013): 87–114.
40. Boas, *Anthropology*, 14. Boas uses the example of the discovery of the "proof" of cultural transmission (diffusion) in "folklore" as the refutation of the theory that the development of humankind follows universal laws of evolution. He concludes that this kind of "investigation has developed an entirely new view regarding the relation of different races" (20).
41. Ibid., 26.
42. Boas, *Anthropology*, 26.
43. This comparative rationality is similar to Wittgenstein's alternative to Frazer in *Remarks* and *Philosophical Investigations.* For a defense of this nontranscendental, comparative mode of reasoning of the Humboldtian tradition, see Douglas Hofstadter and Emmanuel Sanders, *Surfaces and Essences: Analogy as the Fuel and Fire of Thinking* (New York: Basic Books, 2013).

44. On Boas's critical relativity, see Wilner, "A Global Potlatch," 87–114.
45. Boas, *Anthropology*, 28.
46. For the philosophical tradition of romanticism, of which the Humboldtian anthropology tradition is a part, see Nikolas Kompridis, ed., *Philosophical Romanticism* (London: Routledge, 2006).
47. See, for example, Roy Henry Vickers and Robert Budd, *Raven Brings the Light* (Madeira Park, BC: Harbour Publishing, 2013). For the influence of Kwakwa̱ka̱'wakw storytelling and performances on Boas, see Wilner, "A Global Potlatch."
48. Boas, *The Mind of Primitive Man* (1911), 1–2; Boas, *The Mind of Primitive Man* (1938), 3–6.
49. Boas, *The Mind of Primitive Man* (1938), 6. Note the subversive (equality / diversity) use of "civilizations" to describe non-European peoples.
50. Ibid., 4.
51. Ibid. Compare Wittgenstein, *On Certainty*, remark 105.
52. Boas, *The Mind of Primitive Man* (1911), 1–4; Boas, *The Mind of Primitive Man* (1938), 1–6.
53. Boas, *The Mind of Primitive Man* (1911), 4.
54. Boas, *The Mind of Primitive Man* (1938), "Preface," 143. In addition, the diverse manifestations of common mental capacities in different cultures cannot be ranked as superior / inferior or higher / lower.
55. For his refutation of the simple / complex ranking, see the discussion that follows in "From Standing Over to Participating in the World."
56. Boas, *The Mind of Primitive Man* (1911), 195; Boas, *The Mind of Primitive Man* (1938), 130. His criticism of the stages thesis is expanded in his revised and final edition (1938).
57. Boas, *The Mind of Primitive Man* (1911), 98.
58. Ibid., 107–13. See Gilbert Malcolm Sproat, *Scenes and Studies of Savage Life* (London: Smith, Elder, 1868).
59. Boas, *The Mind of Primitive Man* (1911), 110–11; Boas, *The Mind of Primitive Man* (1938), 130–38.
60. Boas, *The Mind of Primitive Man* (1911), 107.
61. Boas, *The Mind of Primitive Man* (1938), 130.
62. The diffusion thesis and its relation to Bastian is introduced in *Anthropology*, 22; substantiated in Boas, *The Mind of Primitive Man* (1911), 155–95, and Boas, *The Mind of Primitive Man* (1938), 159–95; and summarized in Boas, "Evolution or Diffusion" (1924), in *Race, Language and Culture*, 290–94.
63. Boas, *The Mind of Primitive Man* (1938), 32. Herder's argument is directed at Kant's Eurocentric stages thesis in *Idea for a Universal History with a Cosmopolitan Purpose*, in *Political Writings*, 41–53. See Johann Gottfried von Herder, *J. G. Herder on Social and Political Culture*, ed. F. H. Barnard (Cambridge: Cambridge University Press, 1960). Herder's outspoken anti-imperialism influenced the whole Humboldtian tradition.
64. See Wilner, "A Global Potlatch."
65. Boas, *The Mind of Primitive Man* (1938), 33, 169.
66. For this genocide or holocaust, as it is now called, see Mike Davis, *Late Victorian Holocausts: El Niño Famines in the Making of the Third World* (London: Verso, 2002). For the spread and later criticism of both justifications of imperialism, see Prasenjit Duara,

ed., *Decolonization: Perspectives from Now and Then* (Chicago: University of Chicago Press, 2004).

67. Charles Darwin, *On the Origin of Species by Means of Natural Selection, or the Preservation of Favoured Races in the Struggle for Life*, 1859, ed. Joseph Carroll (Peterborough, ON: Broadview Press, 2003). The struggle for existence among human races is mentioned in the subtitle and included, but he does not discuss it in detail until *The Descent of Man*.
68. Charles Darwin, *The Descent of Man, and Selection in Relation to Sex*, introd. James Moore and Adrian Desmond (London: Penguin, 2008), 194–240, at 195.
69. Darwin, *Descent*, 211–22. For the context and spread of Darwin's views, see Patrick Brantlinger, *Dark Vanishings: Discourse on the Extinction of Primitive Races, 1800–1903* (Ithaca: Cornell University Press, 2003).
70. Darwin, *Descent*, 212–13 (emphasis added).
71. Ibid., 220, 221.
72. Ibid., 218.
73. Ibid., 214.
74. Ibid., 222.
75. Ibid., 689.
76. He criticizes Darwin's application of his evolutionary theory to human history from *Anthropology* onward as well as the kind of general theory Darwin advances.
77. Boas criticizes "Darwin's Fuegian" at *The Mind of Primitive Man* (1911), 120, and *The Mind of Primitive Man* (1938), 142.
78. Boas, *The Mind of Primitive Man* (1911), 11–12, 16–17; Boas, *The Mind of Primitive Man* (1938), 11–16.
79. Boas, *The Mind of Primitive Man* (1938), 15. For the extermination of Indigenous peoples in what is now called British Columbia two decades prior to Boas's arrival, see Tom Swanky, *The True Story of Canada's "War" of Extermination on the Pacific* (Burnaby, BC: Dragon Heart Enterprises, 2012). For Boas's arrival when Indigenous peoples were rebuilding after this holocaust, see Wilner, "A Global Potlatch."
80. Boas, *The Mind of Primitive Man* (1938), 16.
81. Ibid., 16–17. These explanations are consistent with his methodological theses outlined earlier in "The Critical Anthropological Method." They are very similar to the explanations Martti Koskenniemi gives for the use of both civilizing and exterminating justifications of imperialism by sociologists and international lawyers between 1850 and 1914 in *The Gentle Civilizer of Nations: The Rise and Fall of International Law, 1870–1960* (Cambridge: Cambridge University Press, 2001), 98–228.
82. Franz Boas, "American Nationalism and World War One," in *The Shaping of American Anthropology, 1883–1911: A Franz Boas Reader*, ed. George W. Stocking Jr. (New York: Basic Books, 1974), 331–35.
83. Ibid., 332. "Wards of the nation" refers to the internal colonization of Native Americans and the colonization of the Philippines.
84. See James Tully, "Progress and Scepticism," in *An Approach to Political Philosophy* (Cambridge: Cambridge University Press, 1992), 262–80. The main sources of Darwin's mechanism are known to be in Malthus, but T. H. Huxley also mentions the influence of Kant for seeing a mechanism of competitive antagonism in nature.

85. For the history of these two views of science, see Richard Tarnas, *The Passion of the Western Mind* (New York: Ballantine Books, 1991), 223–414.
86. Boas, *The Mind of Primitive Man* (1911), 193.
87. Ibid., 193–95. See especially Franz Boas, "Literature, Music, and Dance," *General Anthropology*, ed. Franz Boas (Boston: D. C. Heath, 1938), 589–608.
88. Boas, *The Mind of Primitive Man* (1911), 195.
89. Ibid., 193. These deeper criticisms of the picture underlying all evolutionary theories are collected and expanded into a separate chapter in Boas, *The Mind of Primitive Man*, (1938), chap. 10.
90. Boas, "The Aims of Anthropological Research," in *Race, Language, and Culture*, 243–80. Remarkably, he presented this radical lecture to the American Association for the Advancement of Science when he was president.
91. Ibid., 256.
92. Ibid.
93. Ibid.
94. Ibid., 258.
95. Ibid., 257.
96. Ibid.
97. Ibid. This interpretive or Humboldtian view of science derives from Goethe's *Metamorphosis of Plants*. For a philosophical defense, see Henri Bortoft, *The Wholeness of Nature: Goethe's Way Toward a Science of Conscious Participation in Nature* (Hudson, NY: Lindisfarnee Press, 1996).
98. That is, there is no such thing as the autonomy of theoretical and practical reason in Kant's sense.
99. Compare Wittgenstein, *Philosophical Investigations*, 115.
100. Boas, *The Mind of Primitive Man* (1911), 193–96. He describes the rationalization thesis as an essential claim of evolutionary theory (along with simple to complex) that "extended fields of human culture have developed under more or less rationalistic impulses" (193).
101. Ibid., 210. This is the objective of the romantic and Humboldtian tradition. Boas studies the value dimensions of human activities as "interrelated" in his method.
102. Ibid., 206.
103. Ibid., 204; Boas, *The Mind of Primitive Man* (1938), 22. It is a performative contradiction of what they say.
104. Boas, *The Mind of Primitive Man* (1911), 204; Boas, *The Mind of Primitive Man* (1938), 22; Boas, *The Mind of Primitive Man* (1922), 205. "It seems to my mind," Boas roundly concludes, "that the mental attitude of individuals who thus develop the beliefs of a tribe is exactly that of a civilized philosopher"; that is, the thinker develops ideas out of the accepted background. Boas, *The Mind of Primitive Man* (1911), 113.
105. Boas, *The Mind of Primitive Man* (1911), 204.
106. The defenders of modern science since the seventeenth century called the description of nature as animate the anthropomorphic fallacy.
107. Boas, *The Mind of Primitive Man* (1938), 212. Recall, also, the discussion of this kind of classification of experience in terms of *Weltanschauung* in the introduction to this essay and in its first section, "The Critical Anthropological Method."

108. Ibid. Note that Boas sees a basic form of human reasoning at play, analogical reasoning.
109. Ibid., 222.
110. His many volumes of ethnology are full of animistic myths and folklore, and this provides the data for his more general remarks here.
111. Boas, *The Mind of Primitive Man* (1938), 212, 222.
112. Boas, "The Origin of Totemism," 323. He refers to Wilhelm Wundt and Emile Durkheim as thinkers who misunderstand the use of kinship.
113. For example, Basil Johnston, *Ojibway Heritage* (1996; repr. Toronto: McClelland and Stewart, 2005). See also Franz Boas and Truman Michelson, eds., *Ojibwa Texts Collected by William Jones,* Publications of the American Ethnological Society, vol. 7, pt. 1 (Leyden: E. J. Brill; New York: G. E. Stechert, 1917).
114. Franz Boas, "Letter to the Editor," *Vancouver Province,* Mar. 6, 1897. See Marc Pinkoski, "Back to Boas," *Histories of Anthropology Annual* 7 (2011): 127–69. I am indebted to this fine study of Boas's defense of the potlatch in relation to his critique of evolutionary theory and on Boas's method in general.
115. For a philosophical defense of the holistic view of science advanced by Goethe and the Humboldtian tradition, see Bortoft, *The Wholeness of Nature.*
116. James Lovelock, *The Ages of Gaia: A Biography of Our Living Earth* (New York: Norton, 1988). Gaia is the Greek term for Mother Earth.
117. Stephan Harding, *Animate Earth: Science, Intuition and Gaia* (White River Junction, VT: Chelsea Green, 2013).
118. See, for example, Zoltan Grossman and Alan Parker, eds., *Asserting Native Resilience: Pacific Rim Indigenous Nations Face the Climate Change* (Corvallis: Oregon State University Press, 2012).
119. Boas, "American Nationalism" (1916), 332.
120. Franz Boas, "Solidarity" (1917), in Franz Boas, *Race and Democratic Society* (1945; New York: Biblo and Tannen, 1969), 125–32; Franz Boas, "Nationalism" (1919), in *Race and Democratic Society,* 113–24.
121. Franz Boas, "An Anthropologist's View of War," *Conciliation: The American Association of International Conciliation* 52 (1912): 103.
122. See also Boas, "Nationalism," 115.
123. For the habitual basis of oppositional specific differences, see Boas, "Solidarity," 131. It is analogous to the herd instinct in animals, and "it is not difficult to see that the same instinct continues to sway us." Boas, "Nationalism," 114–15.
124. Franz Boas, "Units of Man" (1912), in *Race and Democratic Society,* 97–103. This is called the security dilemma at the basis of the modern state system in international relations theory. Boas's example of a specific difference is the Aryan race ideology. For this ideology and war, see James Bradley, *The Imperial Cruise: The Secret History of Empire and War* (New York: Little, Brown, 2009).
125. For a recent restatement of this internal relation between CPV and war, see Brett Bowden, *Civilization and War* (Cheltenham, UK: Edward Elgar, 2013), and Tully, *Imperialism and Civic Freedom,* 243–350.
126. Boas, "An Anthropologist's View of War," 100; Boas, "Nationalism," 113–24.
127. Franz Boas, "The International State" (1919), in *Race and Democratic Society,* 141–52; Boas, "Social Justice—Individuals" (1916), in *Race and Democratic Society,* 168–71.

128. Boas, "The International State," 152, and compare "Nationalism," 124. It appears to be a clear reference to Wilsonian imperialism and the League of Nations. See James Tully, "Lineages of Contemporary Imperialism," *Lineages of Empire: The Historical Roots of British Imperial Thought,* ed. Duncan Kelly (Oxford: Oxford University Press, 2009), 3–30.
129. As he summarizes in "Units of Man," 101–92, and "Solidarity," 132.
130. Boas, *The Mind of Primitive Man* (1938), 225; Boas, "Solidarity," 132.
131. Boas, *The Mind of Primitive Man* (1922), 223. Boas himself ignored this third feeling in "An Anthropologist's View of War." A more robust assertion of the feeling of fellowship was developed in opposition to Darwin by Peter Kropotkin in *Mutual Aid* (1898). For other responses to Darwin along these lines, see Ashley Montagu, *Darwin: Competition and Cooperation* (1952; repr. Westport, CT: Greenwood Press, 1973).
132. Boas, "Nationalism," 113–14.
133. Ibid.
134. Ibid., 129–30.
135. Ibid. For a powerful development of the view that the practices of treaty making on Great Turtle Island between Natives and newcomers are the means to peace among diverse nations, see Robert Williams Jr., *Linking Arms Together: American Indian Treaty Visions of Law and Peace* (New York: Oxford University Press, 1997).
136. As we have seen in Boas, "American Nationalism." See also Boas, "Nationalism," Boas, "The International State," and Boas, *The Mind of Primitive Man* (1938), 223.
137. See the preceding discussion in "The Critical Anthropological Method" and "From Standing Over to Participating in the World" for the reasons why this kind of cross-cultural participation is necessary.
138. Boas, "Social Justice—Individuals," 169.
139. Boas, "National Groupings" (1919), in *Race and Democratic Society,* 111–12.
140. See Kompridis, ed., *Philosophical Romanticism.*
141. It is formulated in North America by Henry David Thoreau and Aldo Leopold. See Donald Worster, *Nature's Economy: A History of Ecological Ideas* (Cambridge: Cambridge University Press, 1995).
142. Alexander von Humboldt, *Cosmos: A Sketch of a Physical Description of the Universe,* 5 vols. (Stark, KS: De Young Press, 1997), 1:40. See also Michael Dettelbach, "Global Physics and the Aesthetic Empire," in *Visions of Empire: Voyages, Botany, and Representations of Nature,* ed. David Philip Miller and Pere Hans Reill (Cambridge: Cambridge University Press, 1996), 258–92.
143. For this interpretation of the Hunt–Boas relationship, see Wilner, "A Global Potlatch." For two examples of such an education operated by Indigenous educators, see the Indigenous Governance Programs (www.uvic.ca/igov) and the Indigenous Law Research Unit (www.uvic.ca/law/about/indigenous/indigenouslawresearchunit) at the University of Victoria.
144. For a brilliant defense of this basic thesis, see Evan Thompson, *Mind in Life: Biology, Phenomenology, and the Sciences of Mind* (Cambridge: Harvard University Press, 2007).
145. Boas, "National Groupings," 112.
146. Boas, "National Groupings," 111.

147. Boas, "Social Justice—Individuals," 168. This ideal has been partially recognized by the 1960 UN Resolution of Decolonization (Resolution 1512) and the 2007 UN Declaration on the Rights of Indigenous Peoples (endorsed by Canada and the United States in 2010).
148. Boas, "The International State," 152.
149. Boas, "An Anthropologist's View of War"; Boas, "The International State."
150. Boas, "National Groupings," 112.
151. Boas, "The International State" 147. For the quotation on the abhorrence of universalizing and imposing a particular form of democracy on others, see Boas, *The Mind of Primitive Man* (1938), 272.
152. Boas, "Social Justice—Individuals," 170–71.
153. See Pinkoski, "Back to Boas," Wilner, "A Global Potlatch," and the preceding discussion in "From Standing Over to Participating in the World." For an extension of Boas's argument for governmental diversity, see Julius E. Lips, "Government," in *General Anthropology*, ed. Boas, 487–534. Stocking also notes that Boas did not begin his career as a public intellectual until after his defense of the potlatch ("Introduction," *Boas Reader*, 7).
154. Boas, *The Mind of Primitive Man*, (1911), 6.
155. Boas, *The Mind of Primitive Man* (1938), 223–25.
156. The new line of progress that his method discloses is first mentioned in Boas, *Anthropology*, 26.

# Chapter 6 Of Two Minds About Minding Language in Culture

*Michael Silverstein*

At the Columbia University Men's Faculty Club luncheon that he hosted for Paul Rivet on December 21, 1942, Franz Boas's final words before he fell back, dead, were to the effect that "we must fight ceaselessly against the racism that trammels the mind of man."[1] An Enlightenment hero to the very end, he had been carrying on this particular battle since his youth, in the spirit of his '48er parents and of his maternal uncle, the pediatrician Abraham Jacobi.

A particularly culminative moment along the way had been the simultaneous publication, in 1911, of *The Mind of Primitive Man* from Macmillan, a popular presentation of his multifaceted work, and the first volume of the *Handbook of American Indian Languages,* published as Bulletin 40 of the Smithsonian Institution's Bureau of American Ethnology, consisting of a technical compilation of grammatical sketches by Boas and several younger men, for which he wrote a synthesizing introductory essay.[2] Large sections of that introductory essay, which must date in relatively final form to 1908 or so, are also printed in the general work as chapter 5, "Race and Language."[3] In this context they contributed to the book's sustained anti-social-evolutionary argument directed at the central pillar of educated though still visceral racism in the America of the day, a perspective that in the political sphere both accepted Jim Crow and advocated restricting or excluding further immigration to the United States from anywhere but northwest Europe.

The intellectual pillar of such racism was the belief that each so-called race of humanity can be seriated along a single cline of biological and thus, concurrently, of moral—we now say sociocultural—and mental—we now say cognitive—development or "progress" relative to the others. It was generally argued as well that approaching the matter through a comparison of sociocultural and linguistic realms, the realms of belief and custom and of language as a group's communicative medium, reveals parallel, mutually reinforcing evidence of the biological, "racial" facts of different stages of advancement of one or another group of humans.

Early in his American career, while a docent at Clark University, Boas had begun his empirical demonstrations of the environmentally correlated dynamic plasticity of the characteristics of human organismal morphology, such as cephalic indices, that supposedly differentiated one race definitively from another.[4] In matters of culture and language he also carried on his antiracist work, approaching the argument in two ways: first, he showed that there is no "purity" of descent of belief and custom or of language relative to any discernible social grouping of humanity, cross-group diffusion and subsequent integration of elements being the rule; and second, he showed that the typologies invoked in conceptions of the stagelike "evolution" of customs and beliefs or of linguistic structures were themselves based on ignorance of the facts as well as on incoherence that resulted from perspectivally biased evaluation of such purported facts they comprehended—in short, such views could not form part of a modern, dispassionate, and ultimately disinterested anthropological science of culture and language.

There is a certain irony in the fact that the *Handbook of American Indian Languages* and, with it, its introduction by Boas appeared as a publication of the Bureau of American Ethnology, since the empirical investigations by Boas and his students on the Indigenous languages of North America called into question all the taken-for-granted generalizations about these languages held by figures central to the ethnology and linguistics of Indigenous North America, such as John Wesley Powell (1834–1902), the bureau's founder, and by scholars such as Daniel Garrison Brinton (1837–99) of Philadelphia. Each man was essentially an autodidact in matters of ethnology and linguistics (as was Boas himself!). Powell was an army man noted for his geological surveys of the greater West, mapping the Colorado River for the first time in 1869 and taking note of the varied Native American populations of the region yet to be properly documented for Euro-American science.[5] Brinton, a physician by training—he was a medic at the Battle of Gettysburg, for example—developed a learned gentleman's avocational devotion to library research on Indigenous languages and literatures of the peoples of the Western Hemisphere, and he was appointed in 1886 to a nonremunerated and apparently nonteaching professorship in these subjects at the University of Pennsylvania's University Museum.[6]

During the first three-quarters of the nineteenth century, though there was continued interest in the nature of the languages of Native American peoples, there was precious little documentation beyond the compilation of word lists, except that by missionaries long resident among communities in order to convert them to Christianity. Actual grammatically focused fieldwork, even such as the brief systematic samplings of Horatio Hale, the ethnographer and philologist of the United States Exploring Expedition (1838–42) of the Pacific and later research projects, was rare. The dominant view of these languages had, in fact, been established, principally from manuscript and other library sources, early in the century in an Enlightenment "natural philosophy" mode, by gentleman scholars such as Peter Stephen Du Ponceau of Philadelphia, John Pickering of Boston, and certainly the Prussian statesman Wilhelm von Humboldt. Du Ponceau published a prize-winning monograph in 1838 on the structure of American languages that reprinted his coinage from 1819 of the term "polysynthesis" for what he saw as the common type of grammatical formation in all North American languages, where the semantic purport of a whole proposition is coded in a single predicating word built around a verb root.[7]

The nineteenth century, to be sure, was a time of great progress in the detailed reconstruction of features of the Indo-European parent language, based on careful comparison of the later forms attested in all the branches of the family. By the late 1870s, in fact, the principle was well established that the regularity of autonomous "sound change" from earlier states was what underlay the systematicity of relatedness of forms that scholars had been discovering in all the descendent languages of their unique familial ancestor. Methodologically, working from these documented forms, scholars of Indo-European or Semitic or Finno-Ugric were able to use the principle to reconstruct hypothetical prehistoric forms that seemed to some to parallel the putative biological ancestors of living and paleontological species to which Darwin's systematization of the evolution of life forms pointed. Even as a twenty-year-old university student in 1878 the eminent Ferdinand de Saussure was thus able to reconstruct certain "coefficients sonantiques"—we now term them laryngeal consonants—in the Indo-European parent language that were confirmed by the forms of a newly deciphered descendent language, Hittite, only in 1927!

Other than by professional philologists such as the Sanskritist William Dwight Whitney at Yale, such progress in Indo-European was not, however, well understood on the American side of the Atlantic, particularly by the gentleman scholars cum natural philosophers. Indeed, the heady successes of European comparative-historical linguistics, and in particular its suggestive, somewhat misleading parallelism to biological prehistory or "evolution," encouraged the view that the languages of the Americas needed, in some sense, to be located with respect to the languages of the great Old World civilizations in some of the fanciful schemes of the evolution of human mentality for which, it was hypothesized, the very forms of American Native languages—their sound systems, their grammars, their styles of lexicalization—would serve as evidence for typologically "earlier" or "more primitive" stages of humanity.

So, for example, Brinton, elaborating the importance of the views of Wilhelm von Humboldt, noted that "the science of language misses its purpose unless it seeks its chief end in explaining the intellectual growth of the race."[8] He saw in the structures of the languages of Indigenous America atavisms in respect of humankind's mental evolution. Their "holophrastic" character, through word-building techniques of "polysynthesis" and "incorporation" on the morpho-syntactic plane "points unmistakably to . . . that primordial period of human utterance when men had not yet learned to connect words into sentences, when their utmost efforts at articulate speech did not go beyond single words, which, aided by gestures and signs, served to convey their limited intellectual converse. . . . [T]he aborigines of this continent . . . continued the tradition of this mode of expression in the structure of their tongues long after the union of thought and sound in audible speech had been brought to a high degree of perfection."[9]

Brinton averred that such "distinctions"—distinctions of morpho-syntactic type—have "great ethnographic interest. They almost deserve to be called racial traits."[10] His universal schema of mental evolution tracked by and revealed in grammar is a racialized one, evidenced in such passages as the following:

> The *mental aptitude* of a nation is closely dependent on the type of its idiom. The mind is profoundly influenced by its current modes of vocal expression. When the form of the phrase is such that each idea is kept clear and apart, as it is in nature, and yet its relations to other ideas in the phrase and the sentence are properly indicated by the grammatical construction, the intellect is stimulated by wider variety in images and a nicer precision in their outlines and relations. This is the case in the highest degree with the languages of inflection, and it is no mere coincidence that those peoples who have ever borne the banner in the van of civilization have always spoken inflected tongues. The world will be better off when all others are extinguished, and it is only in deep ignorance of linguistic

A posthumous portrait of Daniel Garrison Brinton by Thomas Eakins, commissioned around 1900. Friends of the scholar felt the painting captured how he "appeared to us when full of that vigorous life which took such hold upon his friends." Cat. no. 58.P.39, American Philosophical Society.

> ethnography that such a language as *Volapük*—agglutinative in type—could have been offered for adoption as a world-language.[11]

In the new era of applying the analytic techniques of philological science to the textual materials gathered in new fieldwork on otherwise unwritten American languages, Boas indeed subverted the validity of such syntheses by revealing them to be simply incorrect or, worse, incoherent or ill-defined. Boas had a penchant for this kind of science, especially when erroneous notions ill-informed public discourse and policy: basing the argument on observations amassed in some area crucial to a misguided inference, he demonstrates that the data either reveal its incoherence or show something other than what the misguided generalization—if even coherent—predicts ought to be the case. Hence, he would show, the social-evolutionary inference, such as of the so-called mental inferiority of a "race" speaking a particular type of language, is uninformed by the complexity of the facts to be brought to bear and at best too hasty and inadequate a generalization from a narrowly biased point of view rather than from a dispassionately scientific approach. In point after cumulative point, the scientific rhetoric of the "Introduction" in the *Handbook of American Indian Languages* that presented ten actual grammatical sketches of Indigenous languages served to dismantle the oft-repeated common wisdom about American languages that, for example, the bureau and its network of collaborators promoted or that the educated public took as scientific truth based on the prestige of writers like Brinton.

For example, consider the sounds of a language, what we now term its phonemic or phonological system at the plane of expressible (hence, utterable) form.[12] What we term sounds are really norms of language-users' conceptual categorizations of "sameness" versus "difference" of produced or perceived segments of signal form that allow the users of a language to recognize—to categorize and interpret—the infinite number of actually articulated phonetic stimuli impinging on their auditory cognition as they perform rapid signal-processing. The finite stock of sound categories in any language is dimensionally organized by abstract principles, habitual in operation, implicitly shared by members of a language community, while the corresponding phonetic stimuli processed in the actualities of pronunciation and audition, if individuated by appropriate physical measures, would yield a highly variable cloud of data points clustering around mean values and potentially infinite in number.

Now the conventional wisdom about such "exotic" languages as those of the Indigenous Americans was that sounds used in communication were frequently not properly categorical, that is, of no determinate and fixed characteristics, while other sound categories of these languages were "compound" in the sense of overlapping the characteristics of what ought to be—note the ought, not the is!—actually two or more distinct sounds. How "primitive" not to have sounds in the same way "we" do, easily reducible to the Latin alphabet, in which, ideally, one distinct sound is represented by one distinct letter![13]

Thus, Powell in the second edition of his *Introduction to the Study of Indian Languages* (1880) warns would-be transcribers of American Native languages that "in the study of the sounds of a savage or barbaric language the simplest elements into which each can be resolved are oftentimes even more complex than the elementary sounds of the English language" and "there are perhaps sounds in each of such a character, or made with so much uncertainty that the ear primarily trained to distinguish English speech is unable to clearly determine what these sounds are, even after many years of effort."[14] Such "more complex" sounds were generally termed synthetic, Powell cautioning would-be Euro-American transcribers of American Native languages that

> they are made by the organs of speech in positions and with movements comprehending in part at least the positions and movements used in making the several sounds to which they seem to be allied. Such a synthetic sound will be heard by the student now as one, now as another sound, even from the same speaker. Such sounds are very common in Indian tongues and occasion no little difficulty to collectors, but much trouble can be avoided by a proper understanding of their nature. The student . . ., as hearer, will suppose [the speaker] to be constantly changing the sound from that represented by one, two or more letters to another of the same group, and when he himself attempts to pronounce the word the Indian is equally satisfied whichever of the sounds is employed.[15]

Brinton, too, differentiated the manifestation of sounds in "barbaric tongues" from those in "languages of civilization" such as English. Not only did he point out the fluctuating and indefinite character of sounds in American Native languages—"In spite of the significance attached to the phonetic elements, they are, in many American languages, singularly vague and fluctuating. If in English we were to pronounce three words, *loll, nor, roll,* indifferently as one or the other, you see what violence we should do to the theory of our alphabet. Yet analogous examples are constant in many American languages. Their consonants are 'alternating,' in large groups, their vowels 'permutable' "[16]—he thought as well that these languages violated what has come to be termed the principle of duality of patterning or double articulation, differentiating the phonological plane of structure from the morpho-syntactic (or narrowly grammatical) one:

> In all European tongues, the mere letters of the alphabet, by themselves, have no meaning and convey no idea; furthermore, their value in a word is fixed; and, thirdly, arranged in a word, they are sufficient to convey its sound and sense to one acquainted with their values.
>
> Judged by certain American examples, all three of these seemingly fundamental characteristics of the phonetic elements were absent in primitive speech, and have become stable only by a long process of growth. We find tongues in which the primary sounds are themselves significant, and yet at the same time are highly variable; and we find many examples in which they are inadequate to convey the sense of the articulate sound.[17]

Under the influence of Benno Erdmann, a Kant-*und*-Leibniz philosopher at Kiel, Boas came eventually to anthropology as a science of culture-framed epistemologies from studying physics and psychophysics. And, after a productive

John Wesley Powell, right, with Taugu, a chief of the Paiute, in southern Utah, ca. 1870. Denver Library Photographic Collection, US Geological Survey.

year, 1885–86, immersed as an apprentice in a milieu of his philologically trained contemporaries Felix von Luschan, Wilhelm Grube, and Albert Grünwedel in Berlin's new ethnological museum, he set out for his own fieldwork in British Columbia in September 1886, beginning his empirical data-gathering career in earnest. As early as 1889, a mere eight years after earning his doctorate on the psychophysics of the visual perception of seawater, he published a marvelous short epistemological paper on the apperception of speech sounds in "exotic" languages such as he had been documenting.[18] He concluded that, absent special training in phonetics, a person will perceive the physical stimuli of speech of a radically distinct phonological system through the distorting filter of the perceiver's own phonological system. This constitutes a so-called apperceptional grid of norms to which an individual's categorical perception is trained and relative to which foreign sounds will seem sometimes to fluctuate or alternate between two or more native-perceiver's categories and sometimes even to have the properties of two or more of the native-perceiver's categories seemingly compounded, as it were, in the consciousness projected upon the foreign perceiver.

All languages, whether "barbarous" or "civilized," Boas asserts in the *Handbook of American Indian Languages* and in *The Mind of Primitive Man,* have determinate phonological systems of a limited number of sound categories—phonemic segment-types, we now term them—in terms of which production and perception of the linguistic signal takes place. The category boundaries and apperceptional norms of American languages are demonstrably different from those widely known in Europe and America, but have otherwise precisely the same functional properties requiring the scientific observer to overcome his or her limiting apperceptional grid to discover the system of categories immanent in the signals of a new language. So the assertion of "primitive" pre- or conflated categoriality of Indigenous language phonetics is wrong; it thus can hardly be evidence for the mental inferiority of the speakers of such languages.

With one exception every topic Boas covered about American languages is structured as a comparably sane, complexifying refutation of simplistic and prematurely or hastily formulated views that ill fit the known data.[19] Evolutionists such as Powell and Brinton cited the phenomenon of primitive "holophrasis"—"expressing a complex idea [like a whole proposition] by a single term"—as an index of the conceptual capacities of speakers of such languages who, by under-differentiating the expected Latinate "parts of speech" syntactically arranged in phrases and clauses to code equivalent senses, revealed a tendency to under-analyze reality. Brinton characterized holophrasis as due to "the psychologic impulse which lies at the root of polysynthesis and incorporation . . . the effort to express the whole proposition in one word . . . instigated by the stronger stimulus which the imagination receives from an idea conveyed in one word rather than in many."[20] Such holophrasis he sees as coordinate with what various writers incorrectly perceived as the incapacity of speakers of holophrastic languages for making logically connected discourse: "It is evident that the primitive man did not connect his sentences. One followed the other disjointedly, unconnectedly. This is so plainly marked in American tongues that the machinery for connecting sentences is absent. This machinery consists properly of the relative pronoun and the conjunction. You will be surprised to hear that there is no American language, none that I know, which possesses either of these parts of speech."[21]

In his refutation Boas derived the relativistic result that "every language may be holophrastic from the point of view of another language."[22] That is to say, the very perception of holophrastic characteristics is itself filtered through the morpho-syntactic apperceptions of those expecting Latinate part-of-speech lexico-grammatical categories and the particular phrase-, clause-, and sentence-syntax of the modern Indo-European languages. And languages present "incorporative" and "(poly)synthetic" construction types as well as their opposites simultaneously: English has genericizing compound predicates like the "incorporating" [to] window-wash-, [to] steam-clean- (as in the derived gerunds or nominals, window-wash+ing/-er and steam-clean+ing/-er); English as well codes an indication of a "third person" grammatical subject in [John] walk+s [the dog]; but English expresses the possessive or genitive relationship in a more "civilized" way with the suffixed clitic–s as in John#'s [dog].

Again, so-called primitive languages such as those of Native America were said to over-differentiate in their lexicons, revealing a lack of generalizing conceptual thought, among other faults of "barbaric" mental capacity. All the while getting in a dismissive criticism of Powell, Brinton, for example, observes,

> As the effort to speak in sentences rather than in words entails constant variation in these ["holophrastic"] word-sentences, there arise both an enormous increase in verbal forms and a multiplication of expressions for ideas closely allied. This is the cause of the apparently endless conjugations of many such tongues, and also of the exuberance of their vocabularies in words of closely similar signification. It is an ancient error—which, however, I find repeated in the official "Introduction to the Study of Indian Languages," issued by our Bureau of Ethnology—that the primitive condition of languages is one "where few ideas are expressed by few words." On the contrary, languages structurally at the bottom of the scale have an enormous and useless excess of words. The savage tribes of the plains will call a color by three or four different words as it appears on different objects. The Eskimo has about twenty words for fishing, depending on the nature of the fish pursued. All this arises from the "holophrastic" plan of thought.[23]

Because, for example, the Inuit have four distinct word-stems for denoting different presenting states or aspects of what we denote with the single noun form snow, which needs modification with adjectival phrases like crusted on the ground, thickly falling, etc., to yield the precise Inuit senses, the latter people are said to lack the acuity to conceptualize all of these as "snow" phenomena. Note how a conceptual ontology is being read from lexical versus phrasal forms. In like manner Boas shows that we, by Dakota language standards, over-differentiate with predicates *kick, bundle together, bite, be proximal to,* and *pound,* verbs all based on the generalizing root-√*xtaka* "grip" in Dakota.[24]

Where evolutionists found non-European languages to represent a stage in conceptual expression where what should be, to their view, single words were thus needlessly cluttered with the conceptual content of whole phrases and sentences in the languages of civilization—"polysynthesis," as we have seen, it had been termed since Du Ponceau's analysis of 1819—Boas shows that such an analysis errs by taking the modern European languages' radically perspectival division between facts of lexicon and facts of grammar as a natural and neutral measure (it is neither, to be sure) of correspondence to some "reality" denoted in linguistic form. Looking at a more inclusive range of American languages without such bias reveals that there are attested many degrees of so-called polysynthesis—as of noun-incorporation and any other generalizations based on too little data and arbitrary, language-centric criteria for comparing languages in the first place.

Point by point the "Introduction" to the *Handbook of American Indian Languages* (tracked in the "Language and Race" chapter of *The Mind of Primitive Man*) dismantled every plank in the language-focused platform on which inferences of evolutionary primitivism stand. Boas even went after the very applicability to American languages of the comparative method of historical linguistics, from which inferences of so-called linguistic families descended from single—hence, pure-pedigree-conferring—proto-languages emerged in the nineteenth century, which was to be a continuingly irksome index of his limitations for Edward Sapir and for A. L. Kroeber, who among his students were classifiers par excellence. But in pushing his skeptical refutations, Boas established, in passing, two exceedingly important more general principles about the anthropological analysis of cultural forms, language included.

First, if the ethnocentric and language-centric standards of comparison are abandoned, what, if anything, can replace them? Ethnology and linguistics in the Boasian idiom seek, with constant empirical testing against new exemplars, to create and to critique an appropriate framework for comparison of systems. It is neutral by intent, so that in its terms the conceptual categorizations—the implicit ontological primes—of any specific culture or language can be revealed only through the universals-sensitive analysis of many specific linguistic and cultural forms relationally considered.[25] The Boasian epistemological bedrock of empirical ethnology and linguistics is not so much a doctrine of "relativism," then, as is commonly misunderstood from his "but-if-we-take-the-other's point-of-view" rhetoric; it is what we should term *comparative calibrationism* as a scientific approach. It essentially and inherently involves a dialectic triangulating across the general covering law, the aggregated cross-cultural data already covered, and the new specific instance to hand, much like Charles Sanders Peirce's "abduction" as the centerpiece of scientific creativity.[26] So: an abductive, hermeneutic methodology dictated by the comparative enterprise of studying of "culture"-in-"history."

Second, there is a kind of population-biological naturalism about Boas's understanding of linguistics no less than of ethnology, "the science dealing with the mental phenomena of the life of the peoples of the world." In linguistics I have long termed it a *psychophysical conception of language,* as though language were an implicit response observable in denotational behavior to the universe of stimuli in perceptual experience and cognitive imagination.[27] Phenomena of cultural practice, too, imply categorizations and classifications immanent in the way in which people's behavior differentiates one entity, one situation, from another; categories of kinship and similarly relational status differentiations are, for example, clear universals showing how such diacritic behavioral forms function in society. And for all of these ethnological phenomena, language included, Boas differentiates between what we might term the categories of the collective *un*conscious—note the difference from Durkheim's "conscience collective"—of normative custom implied by behavior and affect, that exists at a plane different from an individual and even aggregate psychology of conscious association (analogy) and rational (logical) inferencing. In the space between the unconscious and the conscious all ethnological phenomena live, grammatical structure at the first pole, in Boas's view, phenomena like religious doctrine at the second.

Language, in the sense of what Saussure was, in 1911, coevally terming *langue* in his lectures on general linguistics, is, for Boas, at one pole as a phenomenon of culture. It is the most perfect example of an ethnological phenomenon because "the laws of language [= grammatical structure] remain entirely unknown to the speakers . . . never ris[ing] into . . . consciousness."[28] This theme of the reflexively unconscious but luxuriant subtlety of categorial distinctions in the grammatical structure of "primitive" languages—the unwritten languages of small-scale, local language communities—would become a leitmotif of Sapir's more romantic relativism, culminating in the popular writings of Benjamin Lee Whorf.[29] By contrast, for Boas, "all other ethnological phenomena" are to varying degrees constituted by "the misleading and disturbing factors of secondary explanations," whereby unconscious classifications "often rise into consciousness and thus give rise to secondary reasoning and to re-interpretations."[30] That is to say, institutional areas of social life such as religion, economy, and identities like gender, "race," ethnicity, etc. consist to a considerable degree, if not almost totally, of systems of explicit conceptualization reflexively interacting with and in a very real sense performatively biasing and even *constituting* category-inducing social practices ("social action" in Max Weber's sense, based on reflexive *Verstehen*). And, to be sure, the reflexive interaction that does so much to distort or re-functionalize people's consciousness of the systematic basis of their normative social practice is most often manifested in . . . *discourse*—communication.

It would seem that Boas has reinvented Marx's particularly negative reading of ideology, the means by which an oppressive system of capital emerging in the fetishism of exchange value in money and price—David Ricardo's economics—deflects workers from realizing their enchainment by capitalists who are themselves deflected from seeing their own folly of extractive accumulation. But while Marx is a descendent of Sadi Carnot and the "thermodynamic"-like limitations of the capitalist engine, Boas is a more direct descendent of John Locke. All the while answering the evolutionists, remember, on the so-called primitive mentality of Native Americans, he himself is reflexively caught in his own intellectual dilemma—the intellectual dilemma, in a sense, of all "relativists."

Are we—as a Claude Lévi-Strauss or Marshall Sahlins would say—all simply creatures driven by the unconscious structures of categories in language and culture, perhaps "misrecognizing" or "fetishizing" these unconscious social systems through "misleading and disturbing factors of secondary explanations," a.k.a. positioned ideology? Where is the progress of universal human consciousness through generalizing empirical science, for Boas a force of liberation, of untrammeling the human mind and freeing it—his, for example—from the shackles of collective cultural tradition? Boas seems, in a sense, to be of two minds. But let us look more closely.

"When we try to think at all clearly," he notes, "we think, on the whole, in words; and it is well known that, even in the advancement of science, inaccuracy of vocabulary has often been a stumbling-block which has made it difficult to reach accurate conclusions."[31] Are the evolutionists, who impugn the so-called inferior languages as not having words bespeaking conceptual abstraction and generalization, right after all? But Boas wishes to maintain at the same time that

> it seems very questionable in how far the restriction of the use of certain grammatical forms can be conceived as a hindrance to the formation of generalized ideas. It seems much more likely that the lack of these forms is due to the lack of their need. Primitive man, when conversing with his fellow man, is not in the habit of discussing abstract ideas. . . .

> It is . . . perfectly conceivable that an Indian trained in philosophic thought would proceed to free the underlying [inalienably possessed] nominal forms from the possessive elements, and thus reach abstract forms strictly corresponding to the abstract forms of our modern languages.[32]

And:

> The fact that generalized terms of expression are not used, does not prove inability to form them, but it merely proves that the mode of life of the people is such that they are not required; that they would, however, develop just as soon as needed.[33]

So the critical distinction is indeed between language-as-unconscious-normative-lexico-grammatical-structure and the words and expressions of discourse consciously focused on the tasks of ratiocination, the "needs" of discourse, Saussure's *parole.* While words and expressions, the phenomenal material we experience of language, are in a sense at once the individual's tools of rational discourse, yet constructed, as denotational form, out of the categorial elements of grammar, the critical question is the degree to which one's cultural expression at the plane of discourse (and hence conscious thought) is constrained by grammar or by other factors. Boas clearly seems to think by other factors, as viz., he argues negatively about grammar's effect on culture:

> It does not seem likely . . . that there is any direct relation between the culture of a tribe and the language they speak, except in so far as the form of the language will be molded by the state of culture, but not in so far as a certain state of culture is conditioned by morphological traits of the language.[34]

And:

> Language alone would not prevent a people from advancing to more generalized forms of thinking, if the general state of their culture should require expression of such thought; that under these conditions, the language would be moulded rather by the cultural state.[35]

So it is a group's "state of culture" that has differential impact upon the untrammeling of the human mind, where institutional "culture" in all matters other than language consists to a significant degree of the dialectic of praxis and ideologically driven rationalization. Indeed, thus Boas claims on the one hand that

> while in the logical processes of the mind we find a decided tendency, with the development of civilization, to eliminate traditional elements, no such marked decrease in the force of traditional elements can be found in our activities. These

> are controlled by custom almost as much among ourselves as they are among primitive man. We have seen why this must be the case. The mental processes which enter into the development of judgments are based largely upon associations with previous judgments. This process of association is the same among primitive men as among civilized men, and the difference consists largely in the modification of the traditional material with which our new perceptions amalgamate.[36]

And, on the other hand, how do such "modification[s] of the traditional material" come about upon which systematizing rationalization focuses? Boas cites here "the gradual elimination of what might be called the social associations of sense-impressions and of activities, for which intellectual associations are gradually substituted."[37] That is, so-called civilization grows in the ever-widening internal connectivity of systematic explanatory—rationalizing—concepts in reflexive discursive relation to praxis, and the ever-narrowing scope of analogistic cognitive associations derived from the suggestivity of social custom driven by the collective unconscious.

The mind of even us "civilized" primitive humans thus *talks itself* toward an asymptote of freedom as systems of empirically grounded but systematized knowledge realized in discursive form become increasingly internally anchored one to another rather than to habits of social praxis. Enlightenment, indeed.

*Crescat scientia vita excolatur*—may knowledge grow, may life be enhanced—proclaims my university's motto. It's such a painful retrospective irony for me that the University of Chicago's founding president, the former Yale professor William Rainey Harper, explicitly declined to hire the young Franz Boas, whose Enlightenment antiracism proclaimed precisely the same thing.

## Notes

1. There are multiple accounts of Boas's death, differing in detail. There are even two by Rivet himself, one in the émigré journal *Renaissance,* published shortly after the event in early 1943, and a variant account included in a tribute written for an issue of the *International Journal of American Linguistics* for its Boas centennial series in 1958 (Boas, born in 1858, had founded the journal in 1917). See Paul Rivet, "Franz Boas," *Renaissance* 1, no. 2 (1943): 313–14, and Paul Rivet, "Tribute to Franz Boas," *International Journal of American Linguistics* 24, no. 4 (1958): 251–52. Claude Lévi-Strauss is quoted on the matter in his conversation with Didier Eribon, *De près et de loin* (Paris: O. Jacob, 1988). And Gene Weltfish, a Boas student and later a colleague at Barnard, gives an account with a different quotation in a 1980 reminiscence, though probably relayed from someone actually present at the time, since her presence is not noted in any of the eyewitness accounts. Gene Weltfish, "Franz Boas: The Academic Response," in *Anthropology: Ancestors and Heirs,* ed. Stanley Diamond (The Hague: Mouton, 1980), 123–48.

2. The second part of Bulletin 40 appeared in 1922. Franz Boas, *Handbook of American Indian Languages,* pt. 2, Bureau of American Ethnology Bulletin 40 (Washington: Government Printing Office, 1922).
3. Franz Boas, *The Mind of Primitive Man* (New York: Macmillan, 1911), 124–54. On the fashioning of the paradigm-shifting *Handbook of American Indian Languages,* see George Stocking's essay "The Boas Plan for the Study of American Indian Languages," in *Studies in the History of Linguistics: Traditions and Paradigms,* ed. Dell Hymes (Bloomington: Indiana University Press, 1974), 454–84, written partly in response to an earlier one by Carl Voegelin, "The Boas Plan for the Presentation of American Indian Languages," *Proceedings of the American Philosophical Society* 96, no. 4 (1952): 439–51, that discerned the realization of a distinctive "Boas plan" for the grammatical sketches in the *Handbook of American Indian Languages.*
4. See the admirable account of Boas's foray into anthropometric measuring of schoolchildren in Worcester, Massachusetts, in 1891 and the suspicions whipped up by xenophobic press coverage of his activities in Lee D. Baker, *Anthropology and the Racial Politics of Culture* (Durham: Duke University Press, 2010), 137–46. Boas's cumulative results of this and other such studies were published in his 1911 report to the US Senate sponsored by the US Immigration Commission, to which reference is made in *The Mind of Primitive Man* in the note (p. 283) to 53ff. in chap. 2, "Influence of Environment upon Human Types." By 1925 Boas was targeting the developmental plasticity of human psychodynamic functions, gaining funding for Margaret Mead's field trip to American Samoa. See Michael Silverstein, "Boasian Cosmographic Anthropology and the Sociocentric Component of Mind," in *Significant Others: Interpersonal and Professional Commitments in Anthropology,* ed. Richard Handler (Madison: University of Wisconsin Press, 2004), 131–57.
5. See Wallace Stegner, *Beyond the Hundredth Meridian: John Wesley Powell and the Second Opening of the West* (Lincoln: University of Nebraska Press, 1954), and Donald Worster, *A River Running West: The Life of John Wesley Powell* (Oxford: Oxford University Press, 2001).
6. See Regna Darnell, *Daniel Garrison Brinton: The "Fearless Critic" of Philadelphia,* University of Pennsylvania Publications in Anthropology 3 (Philadelphia: Department of Anthropology, University of Pennsylvania, 1988), and Baker, *Anthropology and the Racial Politics of Culture,* chap. 3, esp. 126ff.
7. Pierre-Étienne [=Peter Stephen] Du Ponceau (1760–1844), *Mémoire sur le système grammatical des langues de quelques nations indiennes de l'Amerique du Nord* (Paris: A. Pihan de La Forest, 1838). The "Rapport sur le caractère général et les formes grammaticales des langues américaines, fait au Comité d'histoire et de littérature de la société philosophique américaine, par son secrétaire correspondant," of 1819, is reprinted at 415ff; the term *polysynthétique* occurs at p. 22, and at p. 425 of the reprinted "Rapport."
8. Daniel G. Brinton, "Wilhelm von Humboldt's Researches in American Languages," in *Essays of an Americanist* (Philadelphia: Porter and Coates, 1890), 328–48; see esp. 333.
9. Daniel G. Brinton, "American Languages, and Why We Should Study Them" [repr. from *Pennsylvania Magazine of History and Biography,* 1885], in *Essays,* 308–27; see 322–23.
10. Daniel G. Brinton, *Races and Peoples: Lectures on the Science of Ethnography* (New York: N. D. C. Hodges, 1890), 63.

11. Brinton, *Races and Peoples,* 66–67. Volapük is a proposed universal language created in 1879–80 by Johann Martin Schleyer, a Roman Catholic priest in Baden, Germany. Schleyer felt that God had told him in a dream to create an international language. Its success was severely eclipsed by another constructed—and agglutinative!—language, Esperanto, promulgated by Ludwik Lazarus Zamenhof in 1887.
12. The concept of a phonological system underlying or immanent in the production of articulate speech was, in fact, just emerging clearly as a theoretical and methodological breakthrough in the early decades of the twentieth century, in large part stimulated by the field study of the "exotic" languages of America at the center of the Boasian program. A crystallizing moment can be seen in Edward Sapir, "Sound Patterns in Language," *Language* 1, no. 2 (1925): 37–51. See also Michael Silverstein, "The Diachrony of Sapir's Synchronic Linguistic Description; or, Sapir's 'Cosmographical' Linguistics," in W. Cowan, M. K. Foster, and K. Koerner, eds., *New Perspectives in Language, Culture, and Personality: Proceedings of the Sapir Centenary Conference . . .* (Amsterdam: John Benjamins, 1986), 67–110.
13. One might note with an ironic eye how many of the Indo-European languages and other languages of Europe need massive digraph and diacritic marking of the basic Latin alphabet to capture their phonemic inventories in writing. Thus English /θ/ is written as the initial digraph of <<think>>—and, oddly enough, English /ð/ is written as the same initial digraph in <<this>>. Similarly, Spanish, Portuguese, and French /s/ can be found to be sometimes written as the diacritic-laden <<ç>> in certain words before graphic <<a, o, u>>: thus, for example, French <<commencer>> /komɑ$^{n}$se/"to begin" but <<commençons>> /komɑ$^{n}$so$^{n}$/"we/let us begin."
14. J. W. Powell, *Introduction to the Study of Indian Languages,* 2d ed. (Washington, DC: Government Printing Office, 1880), 1–2. Here Powell followed the pattern established by William Dwight Whitney (1827–94), who in setting out transcription guidelines in the edition of 1877 warned collectors of "the indefinite or undecided character of some of the sounds of a language." See W. D. Whitney, "On the Alphabet," in J. W. Powell, *Introduction to the Study of Indian Languages* (Washington, DC: Government Printing Office, 1877), 6. This doctrine was entirely Anglo- (or Euro-) centric, notwithstanding Whitney's experience with Sanskrit and other "exotic" languages.
15. Powell, *Introduction,* 2d ed., 12–13. In his last observation Powell has clearly characterized the later-understood fact that so-called allophones, phonetically close but distinct sounds, occur conditioned by their surrounding sounds but do not contrast as two distinct phonological categories. And if a speaker uses one or another of the allophones of a phonemic segment in a nonnative context, it still counts for the native as an accented but acceptable instance of the phoneme. Voiceless stop consonants like /p,t,k/ in English are aspirated—followed by a puff of breath—at the beginning of stressed syllables (thus: [p$^{h}$, t$^{h}$, k$^{h}$]), and unaspirated elsewhere; but we still understand an occurrence of the respective phonemic segment even if someone uses the aspirate in noninitial position, as for example "[sp$^{h}$ɛ́k]," interpretable as speck.
16. Brinton, "The Earliest Form of Human Speech, as Revealed by American Tongues" [read to the American Philosophical Society in 1888], in *Essays* (see n. 8), 390–409, at 397–98.
17. Ibid., 393.

18. Franz Boas, "On Alternating Sounds," *American Anthropologist,* o.s., 2, no. 1 (1889): 47–53. For its significance to Boas's whole oeuvre, see also George W. Stocking Jr., *Race, Culture, and Evolution: Essays in the History of Anthropology* (New York: Free Press, 1968), 157–60. For its significance to linguistics, see Rulon Wells, "Phonemics in the Nineteenth Century, 1876–1900," in *Studies in the History of Linguistics,* ed. Hymes (see n. 3), 434–53, esp. 445–50.
19. It is no wonder that in Morris Swadesh's obituary of Boas's greatest linguistic student, Edward Sapir (1884–1939), the anecdote is repeated—from Sapir himself—that for every generalization the younger scholar, trained in Germanics, offered at their first meeting, Boas offered a critical refutation by citing counterevidence from his own fieldwork-based research in Indigenous American languages. Morris Swadesh, "Edward Sapir," *Language* 15, no. 2 (1939): 132–35.
20. Brinton, *Essays,* 359. *Polysynthesis:* The various word forms carrying lexical senses are composed of complex, multiply tiered derivations that combine non-self-standing elements—"morphemes"—of numerous sense categories coding multiple kinds of meaning relations. Sapir (*Language: An Introduction to the Study of Speech* [1921; repr. New York: Harcourt, 1949], 228) likened such polysynthetic lexical stems of Algonquian languages—those known to Du Ponceau (see n. 7)—to "tiny imagist poems" for his lay Anglophone readership. *Incorporation:* Predicating words, e.g., verbs, include—"incorporate"—morphemes for one or more of the semantic subject, object, recipient, benefactee, location, etc., of whatever action or state is denoted. In current terms, such languages are "head [syntactic constituent] marking" in type, rather than Indo-European languages like Sanskrit, Greek, and Latin, Russian, German, etc., which are in large measure "dependent [constituent] marking" ones. See Johanna Nichols, "Head-Marking and Dependent-Marking Grammar," *Language* 62, no. 1 (1986): 56–119, for an elaboration of the distinction. Some languages are rigidly consistent in this word structure, so that other kinds of phrases as well as verb-headed ones have precisely parallel structure coded in "incorporating" word forms.
21. Brinton, *Essays,* 404. The claim of absence is untrue, as also the larger claim. Connected discourse that relates proposition-coding clause to proposition-coding clause in "holophrastic" languages is well structured by machinery that simultaneously codes referents being tracked once introduced as subjects, objects, etc. and the particular relationships—causal-effected, circumstantial, temporal, relative-clausal, etc.—between states or events represented in such "clause-words." These subtleties were not observed until well into the twentieth century, when linguists studied these languages through intensive fieldwork.
22. Boas, "Introduction," *Handbook of American Indian Languages* (Washington, DC: Government Printing Office, 1911), 26.
23. Brinton, *Essays,* 361–62.
24. Boas, "Introduction," 25–26, and *The Mind of Primitive Man,* 145–46, clearly responding to statements such as Powell's discussion of holophrasis ("perhaps there will be a verb to go up a hill, another to go up a valley") and of parts of speech ("meagerly differentiated") in the first edition of his *Introduction* (104), which well illustrates the perspective against which Boas wrote.
25. Note the continuity in this epistemological stance in the later American cultural anthropology influenced by anthropological linguistics (see n. 27), lucidly presented by

the late Ward Goodenough (1919–2013) in his *Description and Comparison in Cultural Anthropology* (Chicago: Aldine, 1970), focusing on the analysis of kinship terminological systems, at the time the very heart as well of the competing "social anthropological" trend in America centered at the University of Chicago, where it had taken hold under the influence of A. R. Radcliffe-Brown (1881–1955).

26. And let us note in passing how the scientifically generalizable and the culture-historically specific are the key dichotomously opposed terms of his epistemological paper of 1887, "The Study of Geography," in which he invokes Alexander von Humboldt's "Cosmography." It has been reprinted in Franz Boas, *Race, Language and Culture* (New York: Macmillan, 1940), 639–47, and it is now widely seen to have constituted a kind of manifesto for Boasian anthropology.

27. A whole movement in cultural anthropology, prominently centered at Yale from the late 1940s through the 1960s, developed these notions under the banners of "ethnoscience," "cognitive anthropology," etc. See the pedagogic reader assembled by Stephen A. Tyler, *Cognitive Anthropology: Readings* (New York: Holt, Rinehart and Winston, 1969).

28. Boas, "Introduction," 67. Saussure's lectures were posthumously published in his name as *Cours de linguistique générale,* ed. Charles Bally and Albert Sechehaye (Paris: Payot, 1916).

29. See Edward Sapir, "The Unconscious Patterning of Behavior in Society" [1927], 544–59, and "The Psychological Reality of Phonemes" [1933], 46–60, in *Selected Writings of Edward Sapir in Language, Culture, and Personality,* ed. David G. Mandelbaum (Berkeley: University of California Press, 1949). Whorf (1897–1941) invented the term *cryptotype* (as opposed to the *phenotype*), in fact, to characterize the denotational purport of categories of grammar coded only by configurations of overt form and thus not easily associated with obvious ("lexicalized") individual stretches of form, from the smallest, a stem or affix, to whole continuous words or phrases. See John B. Carroll, ed., *Language, Thought, and Reality: Selected Writings of Benjamin Lee Whorf* (Cambridge: MIT Press, 1956), 79–83, 88–93.

30. Boas, "Introduction," 67.

31. Ibid., 71–72.

32. Ibid., 64–65. Boas is contrasting the grammatical pattern of many languages, for example, most in the Algonquian family, which requires that a possessor be expressed for any denotable body part, hence "someone's foot," with the abstraction of denoting merely "a foot." His particular examples come from his own Kwakwa̱ka̱'wakw [Kwakiutl] research.

33. Boas, *The Mind of Primitive Man,* 152.

34. Boas, "Introduction," 67; Boas, *The Mind of Primitive Man,* 198. Boas is groping here for a langue / parole distinction. Whorf's ultimate formulation of this problem in his Sapir Gedenkschrift paper of 1941, "The Relation of Language to Habitual Thought and Behavior" (repr. in *Language, Thought, and Reality* [see n. 29], 134–59), deals precisely with this dialectic relationship of cultural practice and the discursive terms for conceptualizing and representing it. See Michael Silverstein, "Whorfianism and the Linguistic Imagination of Nationality," in *Regimes of Language: Ideologies, Polities, and Identities,* ed. Paul V. Kroskrity (Santa Fe: School of American Research Press, 2000), 85–138, esp. 85–109.

35. Boas, *The Mind of Primitive Man,* 154.

36. Ibid., 242.

37. Ibid., 243.

# Chapter 7 Why White People Love Franz Boas; or, The Grammar of Indigenous Dispossession

*Audra Simpson*

> *Our* Indian relations, from the foundation of the Republic to the present moment, have been administered with reference to the ultimate advantage of the government itself.
> Lewis Henry Morgan, *The League of the Iroquois,* 1851

> In the composition of *our* people, the indigenous element has never played an important rôle, except for very short periods.
> Franz Boas, *The Mind of Primitive Man,* 1911

## THE MIND OF CIVILIZED MAN

This essay considers the significance of Boas's treatise on race and culture, *The Mind of Primitive Man,* attending to the text through a reading of its articulation of social ideals and their theoretical and political implications. Such a reading helps us see that Boas's work of 1911 was far from the revolutionary or paradigm-shifting text it has been hailed as.[1] Instead, a set of conclusions emerge that require further conceptual and political attention, particularly regarding the dispossession of Indigenous peoples. Indeed, reading the text alongside the anthropological framework that Boas intended it to supplant—Lewis Henry

Morgan's social evolutionist ordering of the world's peoples—one sees that the nineteenth-century cultural hierarchy Morgan envisioned continued to inform subsequent theories of difference.

Rather than liberating Indigenous people from colonialism *The Mind of Primitive Man* erases indigeneity. It establishes a dualistic binary regarding the value of cultural and bodily differences and their presumed vitality and value as well as their suitability for state and settler absorption. Its political use, then, remains in keeping a particular political order intact. Crucial to uncovering the political supposition of absorption that serves in this book as an unquestioned virtue is Boas's presumption of the sturdiness of precise differences between peoples, differences defined through notions of decline and flourishing as well as demographic and statistical notions of bodily and cultural integrity. Such integrity becomes a form of evidence in Boas's book, creating a line of argumentation that leads one to think about who will live and who will die within a new political state: who will be worthy of salvage, sympathy, and, ultimately, incorporation—enfranchisement and equality.

The presumed inevitability of Indigenous decline and disappearance is present throughout Boas's thinking. This declensionist narrative—a story about Indigenous culture loss and demographic weakness necessitating Boas's salvage of those whose displacement he pretends is inevitable—seems rather remarkable, coming as it does from an ethnographer and linguist who spent considerable time with Native people, living and dead.[2] Such a view is thus far from a break with the past. Boas, like his anthropological predecessor Morgan, worked in concert with a settler state that sought to disappear Indian life and land in order to possess that land and absorb that difference into a normative sociopolitical order.[3]

## "OUR"

Boas and Morgan both enjoy a central place in American anthropology. Each is seen as a progenitor of the current discipline. Each deserves critical, genealogical, and political contemplation. Moreover, each laid the groundwork for an American variant of anthropology that lives within the present, either in a disavowed but nonetheless living form (Morgan) or in a celebrated form (Boas). No matter what the gravitational pull of each is, both are central figures in American anthropology, and both, as evidenced by the epigraphs to this essay taken from key works by them, are directly concerned not only with the study of culture but also with the lives of Native people—constructed by Morgan as "our Indian relations" and by Boas as "the indigenous element."

By the time of their scholarly recognition, both Morgan and Boas had published articles and monographs that catalogued or documented various forms of Indian life. Some of their works were considered groundbreaking in the study of Indigenous life and culture. Each had become an advocate, of a sort, for his ethnological and ethnographic subjects—thus, the possessive pronoun underscored in the epigraphs was also, in the mind of its writer, a form of advocacy. However, the discursive move from "peoples" to "element" in these quotations charts a larger political process that maintains structuring presuppositions of property, of ownership, and of inheritance (as culture, as difference). Both Morgan and Boas maintain the allegory and the structure of *possession* to make such claims and require that culture and difference be defined as something like, or equivalent to, property.[4]

It is this claim of ownership, not in *relation to* but *over* people in the first epigraph, and in distance but presumed *with* place, over people (as possessions) in the second epigraph, that helps us see the shared world of assumptions from which both remarks developed: both are claims of possession fundamentally in accord with the state these men and their anthropologies were in.

What do I mean by "state"? Quite literally, the conceptual and political state in which these enunciations were made, states that are connected to the writing and thinking that the two authors were engaged in. Anthropology is sometimes still hard-pressed to consider the political contexts of theorization and writing, but scholars have thought very explicitly about the political consequences of knowledge and, in particular, of writing.[5] *The Mind of Primitive Man* invites such interrogation. But its self-conscious efforts to demolish racist assumptions reside within a larger context that accounts for its possibility and its findings. So, what is the context for this book, especially in relation to Morgan's work? More specifically, what is the context for the ideation that Boas and Morgan put forth? Here I want to center the *dispossession* of Indigenous peoples in what is now the United States, Canada, and the Arctic as the critical context for these enunciations, as the context for the further science to which they contributed. Such dispossession makes possible not only the conditions for their science, but also for *settler states,* that is, states predicated upon the active and ongoing dispossession of Indian people from land and life. Anthropology has served to mark such difference within that political frame.

Patrick Wolfe has argued that the settler variant of colonialism is a "structure not an event," and this intervention, which has impacted thinking about the temporality and form of colonialism, has its place in the architecture of this argument. Yet anthropologists, who were part of this structure, exhibited a blind spot with regard to the critical context of their regional or local "investigations."

They elided settler state formation from their studies, instead focusing, especially in the Boasian moment, on what was being lost: "culture." Boas's ethnological move was to break into a locality and gesture toward meaning—to imagine that the forms of life he studied and witnessed were, indeed, different, driven by their own logic, that they should be understood in their own terms, and that they could not be judged (or ranked, as Morgan would have it) but ought to be explained by recourse to a preexisting cultural world.[6] Yet what was being lost was not culture but land—Indian land, and lots of it.

## MORGAN AND BOAS

We are reminded at every anniversary of Boas's—his death, his birth, his books (see, for example, the occasion that led to this book)—that he is significant. Part of that significance lies in the unstated and stated move away from Morgan's approach—the way in which "culture" could theoretically have life beyond an ethnological grid and then, normatively, should be understood in its own terms. Boas's significance is measured by his hands-on ethnographic work with the difference that he documents, and its departure from Morgan's evolutionary sequence of geographic and temporal difference, each people belonging to a temporal type, read through material objects, economics, political density, and so on.[7]

Boas, according to the reigning interpretation, reshaped an American version of the field.[8] He moved away from Morgan's evolutionary scale, and he stood up against scientific and racist orthodoxy in scholarly and popular texts. His linguistic science proliferated a reconstruction of the notion of culture itself, and he labored to institutionalize his model of anthropology through vanguard students who became notable scholars and public intellectuals. He took political stands in public and scholarly forums. His approach and his scholarship, in short, thoroughly reshaped anthropological theory and method, a development that manifested itself in the establishment of the first Department of Anthropology in the United States, at Columbia University.

Because of this significance, it may seem odd to think about Boas in terms of what predates him, of that which precipitates or perhaps anticipates him. We know from *The Mind of Primitive Man* that at the very least Boas took a range of presumptions—craniology as an indicator of intellectual capacity, for example—and revealed them to be unscientific, thus false. But are there deeper commonalities between Boas and Morgan? And can we use them not only to see how Indigenous peoples are perceived but also, to a certain extent, how they perceive themselves and push back against expectations?

Morgan's master ethnography, *The League of the Iroquois,* predates Boas's first collection of a people's tales, *Chinook Texts* (1894), by forty-three years. Just as Boas's book was the work of the Chinook storyteller Charles Cultee, Morgan relied upon the lineage and the knowledge of Ely S. Parker, a condoled Seneca Chief ("Donehogowa") who provided Morgan with much of the data for his book—so much that Morgan inscribed the book as "a product of their joint researches." This collaboration resulted in a procedural account of Iroquois history, material culture, and ceremony, one that encodes a revivalist tradition—Karihwí:io, the "Good Message" of Handsome Lake—as the paradigmatic version of ceremony and, by virtue of its iconic status, a form of traditional culture. Philip Deloria and Scott Michaelsen have assessed the relationship of Morgan and Parker. Deloria located Morgan's desire to understand the Iroquois within a white male masculinity that feared its own decline amid the waning influence of the industrial Northeast, the "closing" of the West, and thus the closing of opportunities to create oneself through bodily violence.[9] These concerns belong, in Wolfe's terms, to "the settler complex": the settler seeks to establish roots and to indigenize such roots where ancestries are lacking.[10]

For Morgan the manufacture of roots, of ownership, began in Aurora, New York, with his discovery of arrowheads that required explanation, explanation that would find answers through the practice of "playing Indian." Such play became impersonation and hobbyist practice, which in turn morphed into amateur science once Morgan and Ely Parker began to share information and Morgan gained access to the Seneca community of Tonawanda. Morgan became linked with the family of Parker—his sister, Carrie, and his brother Nicholson—who also provided Morgan with information on Iroquois history as well as material and symbolic culture.[11]

Morgan's early work with the Iroquois occurred within the maelstrom of unambiguous settler force exercised through the law. When he met Morgan, Parker was attempting to reverse the Buffalo Creek Treaty, which in 1838 had dispossessed the Tonawanda band of the Seneca in favor of the Ogden Land Company, laying the groundwork for the removal of the Tonawanda to the West. The Seneca pointed out that this treaty was signed illegally, without the consent of the Seneca, and was thus in violation of Iroquois diplomatic protocols. At the age of twenty, Parker was "raised up" as a condoled chief to fight against the treaty. Bilingual and coming from a chiefly line, he gave testimony in the US Senate and in the courts. His work with Morgan on *The League of the Iroquois* was partly motivated by this attempt to maintain Seneca sovereignty and prevent the removal of his people from their home.[12]

Much changed in anthropology between Morgan's *League* and Boas's *Chinook Texts,* and these changes are not only theoretical but also historical and structural: the US Civil War, the "settlement" and dispossession of Indigenous territory via law in the United States, the legislative apex of federal Indian law known as the Dawes Act of 1887, the Indian Act of Canada in 1876, the opening of the Bureau of Ethnology in 1879, the outlawing of the potlatch in 1884 in Canada, the popularization of scientific racism from the 1850s on, and the "closing" of the (American) frontier—in short, the geographic formalization of the settler status of the nation-state with its attendant race-based "immigration." These processes contextualize Morgan's and, later, Boas's inquiries. It is only *because* of these processes that their inquiries could take place.

One need look only to the present to find the ways in which these precepts have moved through time. My ethnographic engagements and commitments are to the Mohawks of Kahnawà:ke. These cross-border Indigenous nationals refuse the techniques of settler governance (the "gift" of citizenship, for example) and articulate their forms of self-governance and nationhood within a biopolitical state of care that has geopolitical designs on Iroquois territory. The ongoing dispossession of Indians from land and life in Canada cannot be excised from a discussion of Morgan's legacy. As the people I work with traverse the international boundary line between the United States and Canada, they deal with two settler states predicated upon their consent, upon their disappearance, upon access to their territory and to the stark, structural, and historical process that Wolfe has described as "elimination."[13]

Wolfe distinguishes the settler colonial goal of Native elimination from genocide, in which the goal is the erasure of a people, by highlighting the settler's territorial imperative.[14] All Indians have to do is be Indians to ensure that settlers will attempt to eliminate them, for to be Indian is to be defined materially, in relation to a stretch of territory, and thus to be in the way. In Wolfe's critical formulation, settler colonialism seeks to destroy in order to replace and does so in a bid for territory—setter colonialism's "irreducible element."[15] This is its grammar, its organizing principle. "The Native" then, must be eliminated, for Native people are always in the way. Their land is what is desired, not their labor, not their souls.

The effect of this state project on the people I work with at Kahnawà:ke is not only a radically depleted land base. With territories historically throughout the Mohawk Valley and a recognized influence upon the formation of all eastern North American colonial and national spheres, Iroquois, or Haudenosaunee, communities now live on fourteen reservations in the United States and Canada—a radical reduction of their historic territory. The people I work with live on a fraction of their own original seigniorial grant. My work assesses the challenges of formulating tribal membership on such a radically depleted land base, amid a scene of dispossession, within a reservation that is located on traditional territory but whose people simultaneously traverse two settler states to work and live in accordance with their sovereign imperatives in their land base.

Like all Indians in what is now the United States and Canada, Mohawks were reframed as populations to be managed rather than nations to be treated with. Contemporary Mohawk citizens thus work to articulate their sovereignty and nationhood against techniques of dispossession, which include racialized forms of recognition that issue from the geopolitical project of settler sovereignty. State-articulated classifications of reservation membership limit the numbers of people that are recognized as Indian via regimes of gendered and raced management. Such regimes also limit the land that Indians can lawfully possess. Even such legal possession is not substantive, as it is simply the "right to reside" on land "held for your use and benefit."

This biopolitical regime of recognition arose at the same time that an anthropological regime of knowledge cemented itself in museums and in the annual reports published by the Bureau of American Ethnology. In the representations disseminated by these reports, Mohawks are *known* in a particular way: as people organized into clans, as "Romans of the Forest," as this continent's first Democracy, not to mention the many other highly laudatory assemblages of cultural difference that have circulated in anthropological and popular discourse on Indians. These marks of laudatory difference are predicated upon an ethnological trope that is common to both Morgan and Boas: the wonder of complexity that delights the observer who greets those presumed to be fundamentally *savage* and finds instead the surprisingly civil.

Morgan and his followers in Iroquois studies have bequeathed to his successors, including Boas, such concepts and forms. This is a vexed legacy, a strange laurel, like a backhanded compliment but on a much larger scale and with far more serious consequences. The people I work with, who are unambiguously Iroquois and who know themselves as such, fail gloriously at being classical Iroquois. Generally, I would argue that the entire "gens" of Iroquois are anthropological classics no more. And perhaps they never were. The classic texts made them appear so through categorizing, storytelling, and through the phantasm of expectation that governed their apprehension. Such frames became distilled into the procedural: what could be seen—law; kin; apparent, unambiguous, and graspable "culture." Or what would become culture.

Morgan's love of hierarchy, the evolutionary infrastructure of his work, established expectations that most Indians would fail, particularly within his evolutionary stages of Upper Savagery and Barbarism. Morgan anticipated that his Iroquois subjects could climb above their present conditions and, with the help of his advocacy, enter the colonizer's imaginary as whitened citizens of the modern West. Citizenship would adjudicate the tensions he saw between the noble savage and the actually barbaric.[16] But those who were most enmeshed with colonial economies were impossible to fit into such neatly arranged categories of identity. These include the Kahnawà:ke Mohawks of the nineteenth century and also of today.

## ORDER AND INSIGNIFICANCE

What are the stakes of Morgan's concept of Indigenous perfection, and what has this done to the politics and possibilities of Native lives as they are lived today? These questions emerge from the aforementioned settler colonial project to eliminate indigeneity, as usefully defined by Wolfe, but also from the efforts to continue to dispossess and to impose settler sovereignty over land and lives. This project has been the focus of less analysis, but so much is missed without it.

The logic of this project as it bears upon Indigenous culture (the lived and difficult kind, the imperfect, uncodable kind) is revealed in Mark Rifkin's *When Did Indians Become Straight?* In this book Rifkin has offered a crucial intervention that demonstrates the biopolitical techniques of settler society to render Indigenous romance, governance, and philosophical systems knowable and governable.[17] These systems were imaged and textualized into a heteronormative social order that, in effect, made Indians straight. The system relies on a model-driven social science that is blind to a people's true family relationships, circuits of affection, and modes of governance.

In making a *science* of relationships through a system and study of "kinship," much was effaced: philosophical order, political order, and the practice and representation of sovereignty. In *The League of the Iroquois,* Morgan, with the help of Ely Parker, rendered the "clan" as the basis of Iroquois political order. Through this reduction of Indigenous life to a discernable unit of analysis, the clan, meaning and political possibility—sovereignty, romance, gender formation—are served up for governmental management by the state. Such processes were imaged through the seemingly neutral, depoliticized anthropological study of family structure.[18] Indigenous kinship was rendered, in Rifkin's terms, "either as a block to national citizenship to be eradicated or as a curiosity to be preserved so as to indicate the nation's positive inclusion of aboriginal residues."[19] The Iroquois "enjoy" a prominent position in this history because they were Morgan's template.[20]

Rifkin's central intervention is to track the translations of Native social and political life within North America as something other than what they were, political orders as well as forms of love and affection. Such a process requires a critique of heteronormativity, which not only privileges the "domestic sphere" of the household but also the "domestic space" of settler nationalism.[21] By destabilizing social science's natural order of social and familial definitions, Rifkin demonstrates how Native peoples have been structured out of their own social and romantic orders into a literary and ultimately liberal imaginary of heteronormative domesticity and governmentality. Indians became known as clans, gens, and other apparent orders rather than subjects of sovereign political orders, domesticities, sexualities, and political trajectories. They became, in a word, "governable."

This transition to another political order via citizenship carries more than a burden of signs. It carries a cost to sociability and meaning. If one is enfolded within a new regime of citizenship, other forms of intragroup recognition are soon undermined—in this case, an intragroup recognition that goes beyond the "clan" and its presumably totemic functions. By the time of *The Mind of Primitive Man,* this process simply did not concern Boas. Indigenous specificity, Indigenous sovereignty had become nonissues for him (unlike *race*). The purpose of his book was to demolish, case by case, any scientific basis for the presumption of racial inferiority, preparing those proven to be up to the task for entry into mainstream society. This was Boas's version of Morgan's settler assimilationism. Just as they had been enfolded into Canadian and American governance and into the settler imaginary through the study of kinship, Indians would now be enfolded into the concept of race (though not, at first, into citizenship), a new form of nonrecognition and imminent disappearance. The idea of Indigenous disappearance was statistically untrue; the erasure of a sovereign history within the broader category of race was shockingly dismissive.

*The Mind of Primitive Man* was a scientific restoration of the capacity of the formerly degraded and an extended argument for the integrity of all cultures. Boas's conceptual architecture would produce a nascent liberal defense of the value of difference that, once defined in particular ways, could then be protected.[22] His concern was for the discernment of culture, including "primitive" culture: "From our point of view, the striking features of primitive culture are the great number of associations of entirely heterogenous groups of phenomena, such as natural phenomena and individual emotion, social groupings and religious concepts, decorative art and symbolic interpretation. These tend to disappear with the approach to our present civilization, although a careful analysis reveals the persistence of many, and the tendency of each automatic action to establish its own associations according to the mental relations in which it regularly occurs."[23] This definition of culture (of a sort) presents itself as dispassionate analysis, an objective effort to understand many groups of people (difference), "solved on the basis of scientific knowledge, not according to emotional clamor."[24]

But what of a "culture" that is not sturdy enough to withstand the assault of "civilization"? Boas argued that such cultures, though perhaps less sturdy and vigorous, should not be considered as belonging to "an earlier stage of development." This is a differently articulated, temporally equivalent form of life. A new language does not avail itself to Boas (that comes later), and he has to deploy the binary of "primitive" and "civilized" as he restores the former to a form of recuperated integrity. Freed from Morgan's temporal grid of hierarchical value, this new approach to culture became a salvage project, the effects of which shape policy and law today.

Elizabeth Povinelli, Michael Asch, and others involved in Native rights cases query the intersections of such cultural definitions with specific policies and forms of political restriction.[25] I will simply note the pitfalls of "pure" culture as a constraint upon Indigenous people today. Such definitions feed directly into settler regimes of exclusion in maddeningly lawful ways, calling into question the very lawfulness of the law itself. What jumps to mind are federal recognition requirements in the United States, land title cases in Australia, aboriginal rights cases in Canada, particularly the 1996 *Van der Peet* decision.[26]

Throughout *The Mind of Primitive Man,* despite his critique of popular and scholarly science on differences between the races, Boas accords little space to Indigenous people. In the critical chapter "Race in America," he assigns them only four sentences. Such limited attention is glaring given his numerous ethnological publications on the Northwest Coast, his work in museums across the continent, his articles on Inuit peoples, his time spent measuring animate and inanimate bodies, collecting material and discursive culture, training and collaborating with field-workers such as George Hunt and with students such as the Yankton Sioux linguist and novelist Ella Deloria, with whom he began working shortly after 1911. These were Indigenous people who clearly were in possession of the culture and the politics of their communities.[27] How, then, does Boas assign to indigeneity the space of not only diminishment but also infinitesimal insignificance?

Consider this narration, which acquiesces to the settler notion of the *inevitable,* incontrovertible disappearance of Native people: "When British immigrants first flocked to the Atlantic coast of North America, they found a continent inhabited by Indians. The population of the country was thin, and vanished comparatively rapidly before the influx of the more numerous Europeans."[28] Boas goes on to write that Indians, since that time, "have never become sufficiently numerous in any populous part of the United States to be considered as an important element in *our* population."[29] Indians are here seen as a possessed group, weak and vitiated and above all statistically insignificant to "our" population—that is, Boas's readers, sympathetic or unsympathetic but presumably white, requiring persuasion of just this sort. Native people were insignificant to this readership, if not yet completely disappeared.

By considering the racial and biological discourse that creates this structure of disappearance, Boas develops new considerations about difference. He distinguishes culture as an attribute of the biopolitical and raced thinking of the day, pushing back against the dominant, popular thinking of the day on difference: "Without any doubt, Indian blood flows in the veins of quite a number of our people, but the proportion is so insignificant that it may well be disregarded."[30] *Our.* Such sentiments are expressed during the moment when Iroquois people on the Canadian side of the international boundary line were crossing the border to work steel, when they were living according to traditional governance on reservations on both sides of the border, when they were participating in pan-Indian rights associations on the American side of the border such as the Society of American Indians (founded in 1911, the year *The Mind of Primitive Man* appeared). These are people who in 1914 would declare war on Germany before the United States did so and would, as members of sovereign nations, refuse citizenship from both Canada and the United States. In 1924 Iroquois leaders were incarcerated when their longhouse government was forcibly dismantled by Canada, and, because of Canada's violation of existing treaties, they subsequently sought recognition as a nation-state at the League of Nations.[31] These actions, animated from prior and existing forms of sovereignty, are evidence that the Iroquois of that time were firmly, assertively their *own* people.

By contextualizing *The Mind of Primitive Man* within the history of the Iroquois, the logic of these engagements with settler force, these interruptions of the settler narrative of Indigenous disappearance, these refusals of the possessive logic of "our people" is clearly registered. Given Boas's residency in New York and extensive familiarity with the developing ethnography of the Northeast, how could such actions not become part of his critical imaginary? Consider this permissive moment within the text and recall the previous point about blood: "Much more important has been the *introduction* of the negro, whose numbers have increased many fold, so that they form now about one-eighth of *our* whole nation."[32]

Boas specifies this notion of "introduction" several pages later with a reference to the "tearing-away from the African soil and the consequent complete loss of the old standards of life, which were replaced by the dependency of slavery and by all it entailed."[33] Still, his talk of "introduction" in place of bondage or enslavement parallels his inability to discuss contemporary Indigenous politics. His softening of the historical injustice of slavery, his effacement of the individual and collective will in violent bondage in his construction of the origins of the "race problem," is imbricated in Indigenous dispossession. The elimination of Indigenous peoples from their lands enabled enslaved black bodies to be imported for white aggrandizement. This triangle of capital accumulation is not clear to him. In a book purporting to be about race, this is a staggering oversight.

To develop a more robust intersectional analysis at the confluence of racial enslavement and Indigenous dispossession would require a deeper consideration of Boas's legacy—one that would take into account his dismissal of the claims and political concerns of contemporary Indigenous peoples and the conceptual limits of Boas himself. In many ways this book promises to dismantle or destroy the theories of the day but in doing so reinvigorates key concepts in the maintenance of an ongoing settlement project. Such ideas reach beyond bodily differentiation into a heuristic of incontrovertible disappearance—a heuristic that carries Morgan's project through Boas into our times more fully than we recognize.

Ultimately such oversights are about more than irony. This is oversight with fangs. How could Boas spend so much time and energy with living Indigenous people and assign them a role of such insignificance? Analytically and politically, we might want to consider the costs of this conceptual architecture to social scientific inquiry more broadly, particularly since those Boas worked with did not disappear but persisted within deeply challenging times. The question is not about the conditions for protecting salvaged cultural forms within a multicultural regime of valued differences, but about the costs of that imaginary and governmental form. What are the costs of that liberal framing of difference as well as the routing of sympathy?

The costs have been an anthropological story of effacement and disappearance: a normative and empirical oversight that is both empirically false (as Native people did not disappear) and, in its easy reductionism, either in the form of "clans" (Morgan) or "blood" (Boas), theoretically abusive. This reductionism would serve the intellectual and political project of settler governance well indeed. Paradoxically, even though Boas sought in *The Mind of Primitive Man* to demolish scientific bias and the operable premises of scientific racism, Native people occur within the text only in their insignificance, their political life ignored along with their deep history and rightful possession of their territories. This essay has demonstrated that Boas's oversight is preconditioned on an inability to see or read Indigenous sovereignty and politics in any form other than the reduced, the primitive, or the ethnographically classic, a reading that disappears Indigenous political form, is blind to it, easily hitches it to other things, or dismisses it altogether. The settler governance of Boas's time and of ours loves this sort of social science because it keeps things—and people—in a possessive form and, presumably, thus in place.

## Notes

This essay was written for "Indigenous Visions," a conference convened at Yale in 2011 by Ned Blackhawk and Isaiah Wilner to mark the anniversary of *The Mind of Primitive Man.* The conversations there were excellent, as was the engagement of the audience at the Canadian Anthropology Society meetings in Victoria in 2013. I am grateful to the editors for their comments on an earlier version of this chapter as well as the close readings of Cassie Fennell, Brian Goldstone, Rocío Mañaga, Sean Mitchell, and Sarah Muir, who offered wonderful, strengthening suggestions. Mark Rifkin read this work and helped immensely.

The epigraphs are from Lewis Henry Morgan, *The League of the Iroquois* (1851; repr. Secaucus, NJ: Carol Publishing Group, 1996), 458, and Franz Boas, *The Mind of Primitive Man* (New York: Macmillan, 1911), 252 (emphasis added).

1. See Isaiah Lorado Wilner, "A Global Potlatch: Identifying the Indigenous Influence on Western Thought," *American Indian Culture and Research Journal* 37, no. 2 (2013): 87–114. Wilner locates a profound and heretofore unknown Indigenous influence on Boas's culture concept, which Boas expressed to a broad public in *The Mind of Primitive Man.* In Wilner's reading, the Kwakwa̱ka̱'wakw moved Boas from a static notion of culture toward a dynamic notion of culture during their potlatches at Fort Rupert in 1894–95, leading to a study of individuals rather than groups and of diversity rather than difference. I offer here a different interpretation of *The Mind of Primitive Man.*
2. Boas excavated, or some would say, robbed, dead Indigenous bodies for the purposes of his research. This, he claimed, was a "repulsive task" but "someone had to do it." Douglas Cole, *Captured Heritage: The Scramble for Northwest Coast Artifacts* (Seattle: University of Washington Press, 1985), 308. See also Laura Peers, "On the Treatment of Dead Enemies: Indigenous Human Remains in Britain in the Early Twenty-First Century," in *Social Bodies,* ed. Helen Lambert and Maryon McDonald (New York: Berghahn Books, 2009), 77–99.
3. This is not to say that *all* white people love Franz Boas, whose identity as a German Jewish expatriate has yielded rich ideological fodder for anti-Semitic and white supremacist groups circulating literature on the dangers of "amalgamation"—a world skillfully revealed by Lee D. Baker in "The Cult of Franz Boas and His 'Conspiracy' to Destroy the White Race," *Anthropology and the Racial Politics of Culture* (Durham: Duke University Press, 2010), 156–219. What I pursue here is not that political fringe but the contemporary mainstream of whiteness, the liberal variant that continues to uphold an ideational and governmental settler project that is ultimately whitening and ultimately

"settling," even where it reaches for multiculturalism. See also Nell Irvin Painter, *The History of White People* (New York: W. W. Norton, 2010), 228–44.

4. Yael Ben-zvi makes this crucial argument regarding the disappearance of indigeneity in her analysis of Lewis Henry Morgan's project, "Where Did Red Go? Lewis Henry Morgan's Evolutionary Inheritance and U.S. Racial Imagination," *CR: The New Centennial Review* 7, no. 2 (2007): 201–29. "Red" disappeared through a mechanism of evolutionism that enabled "inheritance," an imagined patrimony of the United States that simultaneously contributed to the black–white binary noted by W. E. B. Du Bois. I am demonstrating in my reading that Boas, who is supposed to have innovated upon and extended beyond Morgan, actually performs the same absorption. For a general, descriptive account of the importance of inheritance in both Morgan's and Boas's kinship projects, see Staffan Müller-Wille, "Race and Kinship in Anthropology: Morgan and Boas," *A Cultural History of Heredity III: Nineteenth and Early Twentieth Centuries*, preprint 294 (Berlin: Max Planck Institute for the History of Science, 2005), 255–63.
5. Edward Said's *Orientalism* (London: Vintage, 1979) is a paradigmatic example of this. Explicit reflection on the politics of anthropological knowledge may be found in Talal Asad, ed., *Anthropology and the Colonial Encounter* (London: Ithaca Press, 1973). Responsive reflection on anthropological theory and ethnography and the implications of both may be found in George Marcus and James Clifford, eds., *Writing Culture: The Poetics and Politics of Ethnography* (Berkeley: University of California Press, 1986), and a more recuperative history of ideas appears in George E. Marcus, ed., *Anthropology as Cultural Critique: An Experimental Moment in the Human Sciences* (1986; 2d ed., Chicago: University of Chicago Press, 1999).
6. A significant moment is "On Alternating Sounds," *American Anthropologist* 2, no. 1 (1889): 47–54, in which Boas ruminated on perception, apperception, and savagery (just who is a savage?).
7. On Boas's fieldwork with the Inuit of Baffin Island and Pacific Northwest peoples, see Douglas Cole, *Franz Boas: The Early Years, 1858–1906* (Seattle: University of Washington Press, 1999). On Boas's collaborative, or perhaps less collaborative, ways of acquiring data from the Kwakwa̱ka̱'wakw, see Paige Raibmon, *Authentic Indians: Episodes of Encounter from the Late-Nineteenth-Century Northwest Coast* (Durham: Duke University Press, 2005).
8. Boas's biographer Douglas Cole contextualized his standpoint within the secular (and assimilationist) Jewish experience in Germany. Boas underwent a rigorous classical humanist Gymnasium education that culminated in arduous examinations and a university life of philosophical speculation, club life, and dueling. His intellectual virtuosity served him well in the United States, where he wrote, "It is quite easy to be one of the first among anthropologists here." By 1906, Cole writes, Boas ranked first among his colleagues in folklore, ethnology, linguistics, and physical anthropology. Cole, *Franz Boas*, 284.
9. Philip J. Deloria, *Playing Indian* (New Haven: Yale University Press, 1998); Scott Michaelsen, "Ely S. Parker and Amerindian Voices in Ethnography," *American Literary History* 8, no. 4 (1996): 615–38; Patrick Wolfe, "The Settler Complex," *American Indian Culture and Research Journal* 37, no. 2 (2013): 1–22.
10. On archeological practice providing material for preferred histories on dispossessed land, see Nadia Abu El-Haj, *Facts on the Ground: Archaeological Practice and Territorial Self-Fashioning in Israeli Society* (Chicago: University of Chicago Press, 2001), 99–129.

11. On Ely Parker, see the work of his nephew, the archaeologist Arthur C. Parker, *The Life of General Ely S. Parker, Last Grand Sachem of the Iroquois and General Grant's Military Secretary* (Buffalo: Buffalo Historical Society, 1919). See also William H. Armstrong, *Warrior in Two Camps: Ely S. Parker, Union General and Seneca Chief* (Syracuse: Syracuse University Press, 1978); C. Joseph Genetin-Pilawa, "Ely S. Parker and the Contentious Peace Policy," *Western Historical Quarterly* 41, no. 2 (2010): 196–217; C. Joseph Genetin-Pilawa, *Crooked Paths to Allotment: The Fight over Federal Indian Policy after the Civil War* (Chapel Hill: University of North Carolina Press, 2012); Audra Simpson, *Mohawk Interruptus: Political Life Across the Borders of Settler States* (Durham: Duke University Press, 2014).
12. See Genetin-Pilawa, *Crooked Paths to Allotment,* esp. 42–45, for a nuanced account of this legal and political landscape in what is now New York State. There were also settler–Tonawanda solidarities. Some settlers believed the Seneca should not be removed since they also farmed the land.
13. Patrick Wolfe, "Settler Colonialism and the Elimination of the Native," *Journal of Genocide Research* 8, no. 4 (2006): 387–409.
14. Ibid.; on genocide, see also Ben Kiernan, *Blood and Soil: A World History of Genocide and Extermination from Sparta to Darfur* (New Haven: Yale University Press, 2007).
15. Wolfe, "Settler Colonialism and the Elimination of the Native," 388.
16. Morgan ranked the Iroquois as Barbarians on his ethnological scale of difference.
17. Mark Rifkin, *When Did Indians Become Straight? Kinship, the History of Sexuality, and Native Sovereignty* (New York: Oxford University Press, 2011).
18. See David M. Schneider, *American Kinship: A Cultural Account* (Chicago: University of Chicago Press, 1980); Kath Weston, *Families We Choose: Lesbians, Gays, Kinship* (New York: Columbia University Press, 1991); Elizabeth A. Povinelli, The *Empire of Love: Toward a Theory of Intimacy, Genealogy, and Carnality* (Durham: Duke University Press, 2006).
19. Rifkin, *When Did Indians Become Straight?* 11. Rifkin reads Dakota romance, family, and allotment logics through the writings of Ella Deloria. A related example is the settler panic over affection, sexuality, and governmental form that issued from that complex but ultimately graspable form "Hawaiian kinship" in light of missionary efforts to control and enfold Kanaka Maoli life on their islands. Noenoe K. Silva, *Aloha Betrayed: Native Hawaiian Resistance to American Colonialism* (Durham: Duke University Press, 2004); J. Kēhaulani Kauanui, *Hawaiian Blood: Colonialism and the Politics of Sovereignty and Indigeneity* (Durham: Duke University Press, 2008); Sally Engle Merry, *Colonizing Hawai'i: The Cultural Power of Law* (Princeton: Princeton University Press, 2000).
20. See Meyer Fortes, *Kinship and the Social Order: The Legacy of Lewis Henry Morgan* (Chicago: Aldine, 1969), for a crucial rehabilitation of Morgan's use within British structural functionalism, a regime of analysis focused upon institutions of order such as kinship.
21. Rifkin, *When Did Indians Become Straight?* 38.
22. On social and racial differentiation in US settler policy and governance, see Jodi Melamed, *Represent and Destroy: Rationalizing Violence in the New Racial Capitalism* (Minneapolis: University of Minnesota Press, 2011).
23. Boas, *The Mind of Primitive Man,* 238.
24. Ibid., 252.

25. Elizabeth A. Povinelli, *The Cunning of Recognition: Indigenous Alterities and the Making of Australian Multiculturalism* (Durham: Duke University Press, 2002); Michael Asch, "The Judicial Conceptualization of Culture after *Delgamuukw* and *Van der Peet,*" *Review of Constitutional Studies* 5, no. 2 (2000): 119–37.
26. See Glen S. Coulthard, "Subjects of Empire: Indigenous Peoples and the 'Politics of Recognition' in Canada," *Contemporary Political Theory* 6 (2007): 437–60.
27. María Eugenia Cotera, *Native Speakers: Ella Deloria, Zora Neale Hurston, Jovita González, and the Poetics of Culture* (Austin: University of Texas Press, 2008).
28. Boas, *The Mind of Primitive Man,* 252.
29. Ibid., 253 (emphasis added).
30. Ibid.
31. See Simpson, *Mohawk Interruptus,* 136, for a cross-border summary of this political moment.
32. Boas, *The Mind of Primitive Man,* 253 (emphasis added).
33. Ibid., 272.

# Part Three **Routes of Race: The Transnational Networks of Ethnicity**

# Chapter 8 Utter Confusion and Contradiction: Franz Boas and the Problem of Human Complexion

*Martha Hodes*

When Franz Boas set out to measure and describe the skin color of Native Americans, he left behind a sheaf of documents both cryptic and intriguing. In the late nineteenth century, Boas joined other men of science who keenly hoped to establish a rational method of labeling and organizing variations in human complexion. For Boas, it was imperative to include Native Americans, especially given the prevailing notion that, in collision with white civilization, they were soon to become extinct. Thus did Boas undertake a massive endeavor of calculation and quantification of Indian bodies, with the intention of displaying the results in the anthropology exhibitions at the World's Columbian Exposition of 1893. The part of the project related to schematizing skin color, however, turned out to be much more perplexing than he had imagined. Whereas other men of science at the turn of the twentieth century persisted in this inevitably futile venture, Boas's findings gave him pause.

Boas never wrote substantially about the data he gathered on Indian complexion, and he never articulated a direct link between its undeniably disorderly outcome and his ideas about race. Yet when Boas published his key work, *The Mind of Primitive Man,* in 1911, he had clearly taken important, if tentative, steps toward disrupting the scientific drive toward racial classification.

By reading Boas's raw data sheets from the early 1890s in tandem with his writings on an array of topics, we can speculate on the significance of this little-studied aspect of his progressive assertions about race in *The Mind of Primitive Man*. Indeed, it appears that Boas grasped the denunciations of skin-color measurement articulated by some of his Native subjects themselves.[1]

## ARCHIVES OF COMPLEXION

Historical sources that offer information about human complexion must be approached not as transcriptions of any reality but as a way to illuminate the workings, meanings, and consequences of the ever-fickle endeavor of racial classification, an endeavor that draws its very strength from the powerful fiction of race. No historical record is ever a transparent window onto the past, yet scholars have often treated written sources (like census listings) and visual sources (like photographs) as definitive evidence of a person's identification, incorporating those labels into the stories we tell about the lives of our historical actors. In writing histories of race—which are fundamentally histories of racial classification and racism—the more productive endeavor would be to spotlight and call out the unreliability of racial documentation in our historical records.[2]

Boas's data sheets on Native American skin color must be considered in the context of a wide range of archival documents that inventory human complexion. Among these are advertisements for runaway slaves, designating the missing with racial categories like Negro and mulatto, augmented by adjectives (intended to aid in recapture) like brownish, tawny, red, yellowish, and white. Similarly, forms filled out by slave masters when the city of Washington, DC, abolished slavery in 1862 required a description of each freedperson; the terms there range from dark black to chestnut, copper-colored, bright yellow, pale yellow, very light, and nearly white. State enlistment rolls for African American soldiers in the Civil War likewise carry notations such as ebony, brown, medium, coffee, yellow, and light.[3]

Such invocations were not confined to people of African descent. Advertisements for runaway indentured servants, presumably of exclusive British or European descent, included terms like white, dark, swarthy, brown, fresh, and fair, while enlistment rolls for white Civil War soldiers encompassed such notations as sandy, florid, ruddy, muddy, sallow, and swarthy, and passport applications from the late nineteenth century labeled white people as fair, florid, brown, rosy, and sunburnt.[4] Similar inventories can be found in legal testimony, medical records, and prison records as well as in personal recollections.

Mamie Garvin Fields, born in South Carolina in 1888, described relatives and neighbors as being very dark, very fair, chocolate-brown, and olive; she remembered " 'white' colored girls" and "light 'black' people" and families who were "a basketful of different skin colors."[5]

Approaching the archives of complexion as historical documents entails, first, interrogating their purposes: Who wanted to know, and why? Who retained the power to name and fix the record of a person's complexion? What inquiry invoked the description? Was a slavemaster hoping to capture his runaway property? Was a grandparent wishing to preserve a particular version of family history? Was an anthropologist hoping to discern natural distinctions among people of different continents? Equally important, we must interrogate the historical meanings and significance of particular terminology. A description of a woman's skin as pale, for example, can signify delicacy and therefore a privileged class-status; a description of a man's complexion as dark may be bound up with ideas of criminality. Narratives of skin color can also be tied to perceptions and descriptions of a person's features, or "phenotype," and to the historically contextual meanings assigned to those perceptions and descriptions. This could include the contours of the nose or lips, the texture of hair, even the appearance of a person's fingernails. Narratives of skin color are ultimately contingent upon racial systems, along with knowledge about past generations, including national origin, ancestry, enslavement and freedom, self-presentation, local status and treatment, and legal designations. When we write about human skin color, then, it is not the descriptions themselves that matter, but rather the purposes and consequences of the quest to classify and describe human beings.[6]

Descriptions of complexion—found in the archives of slavery, war, travel, law, medicine, science, memoir—tend to rely simultaneously on three kinds of inventories: categories, such as white, Negro, and mulatto; colors, such as white, brown, and red; and descriptions, such as dark and light. (Note that the terms "white" and "black" can appear in all three inventories, though with different meanings in different contexts.) To employ the first, inventories of categories, is necessarily to simplify, by relying upon schematized, if often ill-defined, labels. To draw upon the second and third, inventories of colors and descriptions, is more complicated. Both lend greater specificity and at once greater ambiguity to records of human complexion: greater specificity because the terminology is more evocative than labeling a person simply as a member of a category like Negro or white; greater ambiguity because each word or phrase, intended to conjure a tone or a hue, is necessarily subjective and comparative.

Confusion lies at the heart of any historical interpretation of such inventories. Yet it is not simply that the historical record offers an unsystematic miscellany of terms. It is also that perceptions of human complexion, notations of human complexion, and ideas about human complexion were confusing at the time in which they were recorded and within the lives in which they were lived. In attempting to measure American Native complexions in the 1890s, Boas seems to have discovered—I necessarily employ speculative language since he did not write directly on these matters—just how meaningless this particular undertaking of physical anthropology was. Haltingly, but against the grain of dominant ideas in the late nineteenth century, Boas moved in the direction of grasping the absurdity of a profusion of categories, colors, and descriptions in the service of science. My investigation into Boas's entanglements with Native American skin color during this period is also, in the end, an argument about the problem of skin color in historical sources, an argument that Boas made both implicitly and explicitly in *The Mind of Primitive Man.*

## FRANZ BOAS AT THE WORLD'S FAIR OF 1893

In the early 1890s, the Harvard anthropologist Frederic Ward Putnam asked Franz Boas to take charge of the physical anthropology exhibitions at the World's Columbian Exposition of 1893 in Chicago. "I then had a lucky inspiration," Boas wrote, "and suggested whether he would not like to have a number of charts made to represent the bodily forms of the Indians," an "important piece of work which I have for so long wanted done." Boas's mentor Rudolf Virchow had conducted a survey of schoolchildren's complexions in the 1870s and 1880s, and in 1885 Boas had watched him measure a group of American Indians in Berlin. Now Boas was optimistic that his own venture would be "useful to science." Because he aimed both to define a racial "type" and to prove variation within that type, he required a large number of subjects, and he would never again produce such a quantity of anthropometric data as he did for the Chicago world's fair.[7] With the aid of some sixty assistants, including college students, teachers, missionaries, and government officials, Boas gathered the measurements of some seventeen thousand American Natives from two hundred tribes across the United States and Canada.[8]

Boas's assistants recorded an assortment of physical traits for each man and woman they measured, encompassing the body, head, and face. Inquiry number 31, the ten words on the data sheets that are the focus of my exploration here, reads as follows: "Color of skin: covered parts; uncovered parts;

palms of hands."[9] This inquiry must be placed in a variety of contexts. First, because the organizers of the world's fair proclaimed their theme to be progress, with a focus on science, ideas about race mattered a great deal, and unsurprisingly the fair reflected and furthered the racial politics of the 1890s. In the Anthropology Building viewers famously gazed upon statues of a Harvard man and a Radcliffe woman (also called Adam and Eve) intended to represent ideal types of humankind, while on the commercial Midway a major attraction consisted of real live Native Americans, Africans, and Chinese people on display in presumably authentic settings.[10] Second, Boas's collection of measurements can be situated within the anthropological tradition of gathering material artifacts that preceded the method of participant observation. Here, however, it was not artifacts that were being hoarded but data. In several presentations to the Congress of Anthropology, a meeting of scholars held in conjunction with the fair in 1893, Boas included "an exhaustive summary of the known physical characteristics of the American Indians."[11] Third, Boas was likely familiar with the judgments of the French anthropologist Paul Topinard, who pointed out the problem of describing Native American complexions as "red." That term, Topinard explained, had been employed largely because of dye and paint and was therefore inaccurate; his array of alternatives included dark olive, copper, cinnamon, rhubarb-yellow, and mahogany red.[12]

In a larger frame of reference, Boas was working in the context of the often-obsessive attempt to schematize skin color, itself part of the late nineteenth-century postemancipation pursuit to isolate whiteness from the supposed contamination of nonwhite ancestry (or "colored blood"). As Nell Irvin Painter reminds us, the purpose of racial classification is "to rank people and keep them in place," and Boas's project coincided with a historical moment in which white Americans were becoming increasingly obsessed with the fractional ancestry of both African Americans and Native Americans. The federal census of 1890 was the first to enumerate four fractionally defined classifications of African Americans—black, mulatto, quadroon, and octoroon—designated for the unstated purposes of Jim Crow segregation and exclusion. In turn, census takers in 1900 asked for fractions of Native American "blood," with the unstated intent of absorbing Indians into whiteness, necessary for the appropriation of Native lands; here, census takers were instructed to fill in a column that designated zero, one-half, one-quarter, or one-eighth "white blood."[13]

That particular governmental enumeration was intertwined, too, with ideas about supposedly vanishing Indians. The superintendent of the 1890 census had proclaimed the American frontier "closed" on the basis of the extent of white invasion and settlement, and the "vanishing Indian" was a central concern of the discipline of anthropology in the late nineteenth century. ("The notion of dynamic Aboriginal culture," writes one scholar of anthropology, "was beyond the imagination of those who controlled dominant images of Aboriginal people.") Wedding these two concerns—the drive for fractional ancestry and the notion of a static and vanishing Indian population—anthropologists now focused on so-called full-blooded Indians, hoping to study them before extinction in the face of Anglo-Saxon "civilization."[14]

Boas shared that hope, employing the language of full-blood, half-blood, three-quarter blood, and mixed race. In this view, the demise of American Natives was being hastened by so-called mixture: not only were particular tribes increasingly reproducing with one another due to migration and displacement, but Native women were also producing children fathered by white men. Boas was interested in what this meant for the Native American "type." As he wrote in 1887, "The ethnological character of these Indians is disappearing rapidly through their permanent contact with the whites; and within a few years it will be too late to collect that vast material that may readily be gathered at the present time." A few years later he worried that the "disappearance of tribes, their intermixture with each other, and with whites" was "so rapid that little time remains." Thus Boas wished to gather data not only about disappearing Native cultures but also about disappearing Native bodies.[15]

Like all anthropometric enterprises, Boas's attempts to measure and describe human complexion could be both dehumanizing and invasive. First, the entire undertaking, of which skin-color measurement was but one aspect, was an intrusive one, including measurements of stature, shoulder height, arm length, arm span, sitting height, shoulder width, head length, head width, face width, face height, nose height, and nose width. "Some of the measurements, too, were not pleasant to the subject," wrote one worker, describing the viselike and sharp-tipped contraptions clamped to heads and faces. (Visitors to the fair could amuse themselves by volunteering to be measured with some of these instruments.) The questionnaire also asked for descriptions of traits like eye color, hair color and texture, men's beards, and the shape of the earlobe.[16]

Prior to his world's fair project Boas had acknowledged, at least obliquely, the prying nature of bodily inspections. "I did not consider it advisable to make anthropometrical measurements in the villages of the natives," he wrote in 1889, "as I feared to rouse their distrust, and had nowhere time to become well acquainted with them." Elsewhere Boas explained, "Only a short series of measurements of each individual was taken, such as could be made by the removal of only a small portion of the clothing." With or without Boas's sensitivity, these efforts had the effect of fragmenting the bodies of the men and women who were the subjects—or objects—of study, breaking them down into segmented components.[17] Too, the men and women with whom Boas worked likely had no say in how they were to be described, since the imprecision of self-description was to be avoided. There is, in fact, evidence of resistance. Working with the eastern Cherokees for the world's fair project, one worker noted that "serious questions arose about the purpose of our work." Some of the subjects made disparaging comments during the process, and some refused to take part, one man announcing, "I see no sense in the thing" and "It is most ridiculous." Although this man was eventually convinced to participate, one sixteen-year-old girl, at least, never gave in.[18]

To measure skin color, Boas and his assistants worked from a chart labeled with gradations of skin tones numbered from 1 to 24, obviously intended to yield precise results. By matching a person's skin to a particular level on the scale, one could presumably improve upon general racial categories like Indian, avoid the subjectivity of the names of colors, and move beyond vague descriptors like dark and light. Though one worker mentioned "a book of colors (for determining tint of skin approximately)," we do not know which scale Boas and his assistants put to use.[19]

Boas might have used the "international color scale" devised by the German geographer Otto Radde. "I recorded the colour of the skin according to Radde's standard colours," Boas noted in an 1895 report about a different project, yet the world's fair data sheets contain numerals only, whereas Radde's scheme also contained letters.[20] Or Boas might have used the scale invented by the French anthropologist Paul Broca, reproduced in an 1874 publication of the British Association for the Advancement of Science, one of the sponsors of Boas's work in British Columbia; *Notes and Queries on Anthropology, for the Use of Travellers and Residents in Uncivilized Lands* included a section devoted to skin, hair, and eye color (with the byline of the British ethnologist John Beddoe), offering tables devised by Broca, with colored blocks numbered from 21 to 52 (the numerals 1 to 20 were reserved for eye color). The eugenicist Charles Davenport later described the Broca scale as "a set of tinted standards, each bearing a name or number, to which any skin color can be referred."[21] Or perhaps Boas employed the von Luschan scale, a set of thirty-six samples of colored glass, invented by the Austrian anthropologist Felix von Luschan. Alternatively, Boas may have used another, similar device or fashioned his own method altogether. No matter Boas's apparatus, it is clear from the world's fair data sheets that the chart resembled modern-day samples of paint colors.[22]

Many of Boas's assistants wrote down what was expected of them, a single numeral for each of the three questions related to complexion: one for "covered parts," one for "uncovered parts," and one for "palms of hands." Yet quite a few left this question blank, a compelling omission in the face of the quest for exactitude. Indeed, others simply could not make sense of the scale. Some observers recorded one number, followed by the next highest number in parentheses, say, "23 (24)." (As Beddoe wrote of Broca's color scale, "Where the skin did not very nearly match any one of the types, I set down the two or even three between which I conceived the true colour to lie.") Others recorded a single number, then qualified it with an adjective: "darker than 17" or "lighter than 17." Some notations told plainly how difficult it was to select an answer at all, as in "23 probably—but painted bright yellow" or "In house all the time hence 23" followed by a question mark. The commentary of still others pointed to the inadequacy of the 24-point scale: "13 too dark" or "20 too light"; or, even more revealing, "a color between 17 & 13 but considerably lighter." Yet others recorded a single number qualified with a description of their own: "19 browner," "8 with tinge of red," or "chocolate about the shade of 4." Sometimes the observers dispensed with the numbers altogether and simply crafted their own phrases: "light rosy" or, in a comparative vein, "darker than others."[23]

The data sheets that record a single numeral for each question give the impression of the greatest accuracy. Tellingly, however, these records were less precise than those that recognized the arbitrariness and subjectivity of the entire system. In fact, all kinds of questions arise from the data sheets. Were the scales employed by each worker consistent? (Davenport pointed out that Broca's colors differed from one printing to another and that exposure to light could alter the printed blocks.) What time of day was each person observed? If outdoors, was it sunny or overcast? If indoors, was there a light source? How quickly were the assistants working, and how tired or bored did that make them? It is virtually doubtless that these kinds of questions occurred to Boas, and we can surmise that as he read through the numbers and notations he came to understand the failure of skin-color measurement, moving him, if tentatively, toward the conviction that schematizing human complexion was absurd.[24]

## NARRATIVES OF AMBIGUITY

The responses to query number 31 on Boas's data sheets can best be understood as narratives of ambiguity whose meaning could not have escaped him. Anthropologists working in the late nineteenth century, both before and after Boas's world's fair work, composed similar narratives about human

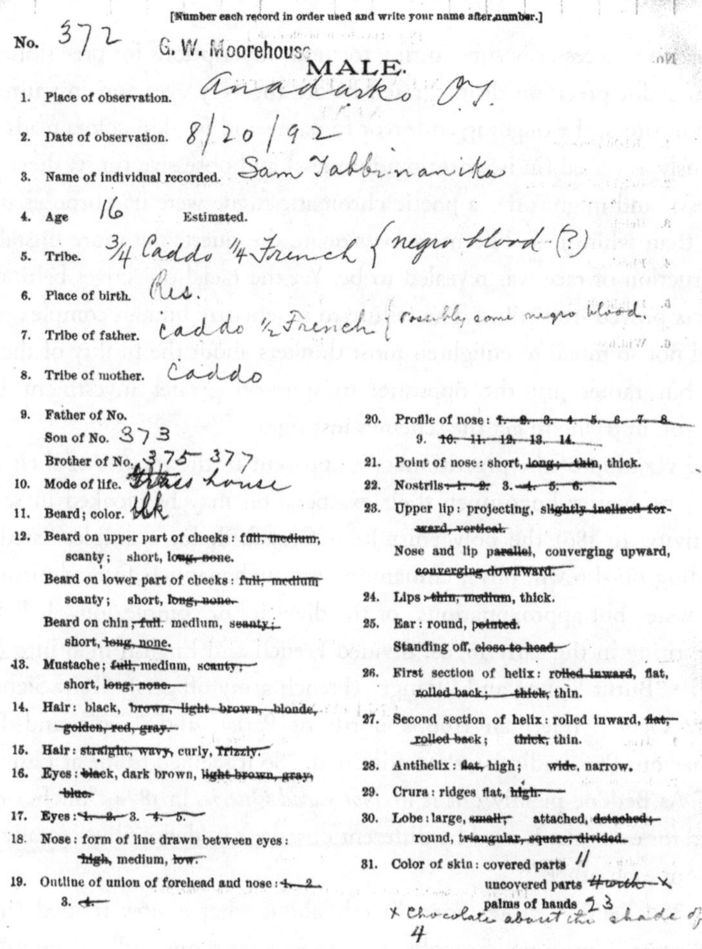

[Number each record in order used and write your name after number.]

No. 372 G. W. Moorehouse

MALE.

1. Place of observation. Anadarko O.T.
2. Date of observation. 8/20/92
3. Name of individual recorded. Sam Tabbinanika
4. Age 16 Estimated.
5. Tribe. 3/4 Caddo 1/4 French {negro blood-(?)
6. Place of birth. Res.
7. Tribe of father. Caddo 1/2 French {possibly some negro blood.
8. Tribe of mother. Caddo
9. Father of No.
   Son of No. 373
   Brother of No. 375 377
10. Mode of life. Grass house
11. Beard; color. blk
12. Beard on upper part of cheeks: ~~full, medium,~~ scanty; short, ~~long, none.~~
    Beard on lower part of cheeks: ~~full, medium~~ scanty; short, ~~long, none.~~
    Beard on chin; ~~full.~~ medium, ~~scanty;~~ short, ~~long, none.~~
13. Mustache; ~~full,~~ medium, ~~scanty;~~ short, ~~long, none.~~
14. Hair: black, ~~brown, light brown, blonde, golden, red, gray.~~
15. Hair: ~~straight, wavy,~~ curly, ~~frizzly.~~
16. Eyes: ~~black,~~ dark brown, ~~light brown, gray, blue.~~
17. Eyes: ~~1. 2.~~ 3. ~~4. 5.~~
18. Nose: form of line drawn between eyes: ~~high,~~ medium, ~~low.~~
19. Outline of union of forehead and nose: ~~1. 2.~~ 3. ~~4.~~
20. Profile of nose: ~~1. 2. 3. 4. 5. 6. 7. 8.~~ 9. ~~10. 11. 12. 13. 14.~~
21. Point of nose: short, ~~long, thin,~~ thick.
22. Nostrils: ~~1. 2.~~ 3. ~~4. 5. 6.~~
23. Upper lip: projecting, ~~slightly inclined forward, vertical.~~
    Nose and lip ~~parallel,~~ converging upward, ~~converging downward.~~
24. Lips: ~~thin, medium,~~ thick.
25. Ear: round, ~~pointed.~~
    Standing off, ~~close to head.~~
26. First section of helix: ~~rolled inward,~~ flat, ~~rolled back; thick,~~ thin.
27. Second section of helix: rolled inward, ~~flat, rolled back;~~ ~~thick,~~ thin.
28. Antihelix: ~~flat,~~ high; ~~wide,~~ narrow.
29. Crura: ridges flat, ~~high.~~
30. Lobe: large, ~~small;~~ attached, ~~detached;~~ round, ~~triangular, square, divided.~~
31. Color of skin: covered parts 11
    uncovered parts ~~4 with~~ ×
    palms of hands 23
    × Chocolate about the shade of 4

This anthropometric data sheet is one of more than four thousand preserved in the Franz Boas papers. The subject, Sam Tabbinanika, a boy about sixteen years old in 1892, was born on a reservation and lived in the town of Anadarko, in Oklahoma Territory. One of Boas's assistants, G. W. Moorehouse, identified Tabbinanika as three-quarters Caddo Indian and one-quarter French, adding a query about his father's possible African ancestry. Boas designed many of his questions as multiple choice (with minor differences for female subjects). For skin color, he employed a numerical scale, but the response at bottom right—"chocolate about the shade of 4"—indicates the failure of rigid schematization. "Recorded at Anadarko, Fort Sill, and Grantham Springs, Indian Territory (Oklahoma). Data for Kiowa, Comanche, Apache, etc.," 1892, pt. 3, Franz Boas Field Notebooks and Anthropometric Data, Collection V, Box 2, Anthropometric Data Sheets, Franz Boas Papers, American Philosophical Society.

complexion, necessarily substituting tortuous descriptions for precision. But as the quest for precision disintegrated before the very eyes and instruments of the inquisitors, the ongoing endeavor to name and fix skin colors reads simultaneously as casual (in its sheer randomness) and obsessive (in its sheer relentlessness), and might offer a poetic chromatic fugue were its purposes nothing more than whimsical. The more passionate the quest, the more unstable the construction of race was revealed to be. Yet the racial objectives behind these projects proved irresistible. The failure to schematize human complexion thus served not so much to enlighten most thinkers about the futility of the enterprise but rather just the opposite: to spur on greater investment in that endeavor, in trying to get the schemes just right.[25]

The vexation of the practitioners is apparent in the reports of their experiments, no matter how much their exasperation may be cloaked in scientific objectivity. In 1861 the polygenist John Crawfurd, for example, listed terms including nut-brown, olive, cinnamon, and mahogany, before admitting that these were "but approximations" of the diversity of complexions. J. F. Campbell, writing in the early 1870s, divided French and English men into categories like "Burnt Sienna and Orange" (French army officers), "Raw Sienna and Yellow Ochre" (German troops north of Paris), and "Sepia and Brown" (pugnacious Paris radicals), then admitted, "So it seemed to me at Easter time, 1871." As Beddoe plainly put it in *Notes and Queries* in 1874, "Such a term as 'olive,' for example, is used by different observers to denote hues totally different from each other."[26]

In 1890 Beddoe wrote more directly about what is now termed "interobserver error." Someone "brought up among a xanthous [yellow] population," he wrote, would "apply the name black to dark shades of brown, and one belonging to a melanochroic [dark] district will call the chestnuts 'blonde' and the yellows 'red.' " William Z. Ripley included a chapter entitled "Blonds and Brunets" in his work *The Races of Europe* (1899), in which he divided the world populations into black, brownish, yellow, and white. Although his use of the suffix "-ish" gives away his own appreciation for the impossibility of accuracy, Ripley further defined the "brownish group" as ranging from "deep chocolate through coffee-colour down to olive and light or reddish brown," thereby clarifying one approximation, "brownish," with another, "reddish."[27]

An illuminating example that preceded Boas in the United States can be found in the work of Benjamin Apthorp Gould, whose reflections on his failed attempts at rigor are particularly frank. Gould, the president of the American Association for the Advancement of Science, directed statistical investigations of Union Army soldiers in 1864, measuring the men's bodies, heads, and faces, and recording hair, eye, and skin color, among other endeavors. Gould hoped to discover what he called a type, asserting that "typical characteristics" must not merely be identified but also that their typicality "must be rendered probable" in order for the system to attain perfection. Gould employed a small regiment of assistants who collected and tabulated the data, resulting five years later in an ungainly six-hundred-page compilation.[28]

In the realm of skin color, Gould gathered information for 668,000 men with a printed form that offered a choice among fair, ruddy, medium, and dark, although the published tables appear instead with the headings dark, light, and medium, likely indicating that more general terms seemed less subject to mutable perceptions and definitions. Moreover, some of the information about complexion came not from Gould's investigators but from the Union Army's mustering officers, who, Gould cautioned, offered only "a rough description." Gould imagined that these observers considered their entries "satisfactory" as long as they were "not in clear contradiction to the truth." Elsewhere in Gould's report, now assessing the muscles of black soldiers, the inspectors were to give "an estimate of the proportion of black blood" with the suggested categories "Full Black, Mulatto, Quadroon, Octoroon," but only "if this can be discriminated." Elsewhere still, Gould wrote about "three or more distinct races of negroes," noting "every degree and mode of admixture with one another and with the Indians and white races." Ultimately dividing African American men into "Full Blacks" and "Mixed Races," Gould defined the former as "all in whom no admixture of white or red ancestry was perceptible," making clear that classification depended upon whether the observer could tell just by looking.[29]

In the end, Gould's language roamed freely among inventories of categories, colors, and descriptions, interrupted occasionally by pseudoscientific terms like Caucasian. Although he hoped his work on human complexion would contribute to the field of anthropology, the volume's prefatory remarks rightly insisted upon "diffidence and distrust." "Deductions from these tables must be drawn with caution," Gould acknowledged in his synopsis of the data on complexion. "The descriptions were evidently entered very loosely in most cases." Gould's work on human complexion reads as a narrative of both ambiguity and exasperation, even as he strove mightily to write within the parameters of objective observation. Boas would echo these ambiguities thirty years later, on his world's fair data sheets, though not yet with a direct follow-up admission of their uselessness.[30]

Although Boas never wrote analytically about his own foray into the measurement of American Native skin color, other parts of his writings from the late nineteenth century yield scattered reflections pertaining to that undertaking. Writings that preceded his world's fair work offer early clues. Boas's 1881 dissertation at the University of Kiel, entitled "Contributions to the Understanding of the Color of Water," considered the subjectivity of perception, a topic to which Boas would return in decades following. As George Stocking noticed, Boas's letters to his fiancée during his Canadian travels in the early 1880s "reveal a frequent interest in the color of sea water and more generally in problems of perception" (though Stocking's assertion that these were "matters of incidental interest" deserves rethinking). Boas's writings at the end of the nineteenth century do not present a chronological progression of thought moving increasingly toward enlightened ideas about race; instead, they offer fragments that tack back and forth between dissatisfaction with anthropological methods and embracing—or resorting to—those same methods.[31]

After the completion of his dissertation Boas expressed grave reservations about the entire endeavor of classification. These doubts are evident in his early disagreement with other anthropologists over the categorization of material objects. Boas wanted artifacts arranged according to the tribes that used them rather than according to the object's function, and in words that could apply just as well to the measurement of human complexion, he wrote, "The object of study is the individual, not abstractions from the individual under observation." By the same token, some of Boas's reflections on the phenomenon of color concern not human complexion but language and perception: "If I am shown a bluish white first and a yellowish white a little later," he wrote in a well-known 1889 essay on language, "the probability is that, on being asked, I shall declare both to be of the same color."[32]

To be sure, even as Boas struggled with the subjectivity of the language invoked to describe human bodies, he continued to fall back on inventories of categories, colors, and descriptions, employing problematic words and phrases like light-complexioned, brownish, reddish, very light, and almost white. Too, in the mid-1890s Boas defended anthropometry as a means to "establish types," yet he also admitted that trouble came in "defining the type." In one of the few instances in which he specifically mentioned the world's fair data on skin color, Boas echoed Beddoe's recognition of interobserver error. For queries requiring descriptions, Boas noted, "the personal equation proved so great that the observations did not yield any comparable results." At the same time, Boas expressed reservations about any category that had to be described rather than measured, pointing out how difficult it was "to compare descriptive features on account of the large personal equation of the observers," a point that could well have been informed by the unsystematic variety of notations made by his workers under inquiry number 31 on the world's fair data sheets. Taking this a step farther, Boas included the problem of variation "even of the same observer at different times." A few years later, in 1899, Boas again grappled with Indian anthropometry, now offering a reflection on judging the size of ears (as large, medium, or small) and the fullness of lips (as thick, medium, or thin) that could also apply to human complexion. "It will easily be seen that different observers would use the same terms with still less accuracy," he noted, contending that descriptions "are of value only in extreme cases." Indeed, the accompanying chart included the phrase "judged as" when recording sizes of ears and lips. That same year, in an essay entitled "Some Recent Criticisms of Physical Anthropology," Boas asserted the necessity of measurement when "local varieties of mankind were very much alike—so much so that a verbal description failed to make their characteristics sufficiently clear," since calculation was superior to "vague verbal description."[33]

How could Boas write about "vague verbal description" without thinking of inquiry number 31 on his stacks of world's fair data sheets? With that experience in the back of his mind, or perhaps at the forefront, he voiced reservations about the anthropological construct of "types." Physical anthropology, he asserted in "Some Recent Criticisms," "cannot possibly lead to a classification of mankind as detailed as does the classification based on language." Although these fragmentary pronouncements conflict with one another in various ways, it is virtually certain that Boas was immediately aware of the problem with question number 31: he had intended all three queries (about covered skin, uncovered skin, and the palms of the hands) to be answered with a numerical measurement, but the answers had devolved into a collection of meandering and unsystematic labels, indicating that measurement and description alike proved inadequate in the quest to record human complexion. It is unclear whether the exhibitions in Chicago included the data on skin color within its many maps and diagrams; my guess is that they did not. If that was the case, then we can match that fact with an explanation that Boas gave in unpublished reflections on the world's fair project. Discussing the phenomenon of interobserver error, Boas wrote that the results would have proven more reliable had there been only a single person gathering all the data; because that had not been the case, he made sure to check the work of each observer against that of a second observer, as a way to filter out unreliable information. This made it possible, he wrote, "to avoid serious errors and to exclude material, which for one reason or another, appeared doubtful." This points to the possibility that comparing the responses of two workers who had measured the same subject for inquiry number 31 made the data's uselessness abundantly apparent to Boas.[34]

In his writings at the turn of the century Boas challenged the endeavor of racial measurement, description, and classification even as he continued to employ language that pointed the way toward absurdity. These kinds of contradictions can be found, too, in another pioneer of racial thinking. In 1906 W. E. B. Du Bois convened a conference at Atlanta University titled "The Health and Physique of the Negro American," at which Boas presented a paper. Boas was the commencement speaker during the same visit, and the two men corresponded about wishing to further physical anthropological studies of African Americans. In the conference report Du Bois dispensed with the problem of skin color, writing, "The human species so shade and mingle with each other" that it was "impossible to draw a color line between black and other races," a heterodox declaration at a moment in which white Americans endowed an artificial black–white color line with tremendous power. At the same time, though, parsing the complexions of three hundred subjects, Du Bois invoked all three kinds of inventories—categories (such as mulatto), colors (such as brown and yellow), and descriptions (for example, cream-tinted)—and resorted as well to the vocabulary of blood-fractions (octoroon; five-eighths Negro). Then, in language more direct than Boas's, Du Bois freely admitted that the divisions were "by no means clear in my own mind."[35]

On the one hand, Du Bois's categorizations, followed by his admission of their ambiguity, reads no differently from that of anthropologists obsessed with color schemes. On the other hand, Du Bois was laboring specifically in response to the studies of white scientists who hoped to prove black inferiority, and that context turned Du Bois's evidence into what one scholar has called an assemblage of "daring taxonomic categories," offering, as it did, an array of complexions for people of African descent. Du Bois would later turn his narratives of ambiguity into a powerful indictment. Yes, race was a social construct, he asserted in *Dusk of Dawn* more than thirty years later; still, he could easily recognize blackness: "The black man," Du Bois explained, "is a person who must ride 'Jim Crow' in Georgia." By the early twentieth century Boas was firmly making the point, now in plainer language, that the Jim Crow quest for racially pure human beings was worthless. It was, Boas asserted in 1907, "exceedingly difficult, if not impossible, to find what might be called a pure type," and the search for such "pure races" should therefore "be given up."[36]

### *THE MIND OF PRIMITIVE MAN* AND BEYOND

As Boas continued to think through the challenges inherent in the relationship between physical anthropology and the construct of race, he further reflected on the topics of language, color, complexion, measurement, and description in his influential work *The Mind of Primitive Man*. Unsurprisingly, his statements in 1911 do not smooth out the contradictions or untangle the inconsistencies that characterized his previous work, for in these pages Boas did not reject the endeavor of racial classification. Instead, he persisted in writing about "distinctions between races" and "members of distinct races," even naming "color of the skin" as first among the "great differences" found within "the physical characteristics of the races of man." Accordingly, it would be a mistake to dismiss the parts of *The Mind of Primitive Man* that echoed dominant language and ideas about race, for the tenacity of those ideas—and their coexistence with Boas's bolder, more innovative conclusions—is precisely the point: Boas simultaneously challenged and was trapped by those ideas.[37]

In *The Mind of Primitive Man* Boas continued to reflect on the problem of language related to color-descriptions, pointing out that different languages reflected different perceptions and therefore different clusters of colors. For example, "the groupings of yellow, green, and blue" were not uniform across languages, he wrote. "Often yellow and the yellowish-greens are combined in one group; green and blue, in another." This meant that each language could be "arbitrary in its classifications," a conclusion that could well harken back to the responses to inquiry number 31 on the world's fair data sheets. Boas also offered the qualification that descriptions of human complexion were "only abstractions of what we think we have noticed most commonly in each type," in this instance calling attention to Norwegians of "light or dark" complexions, to the "degree of blackness" in Negroes, and to the "innumerable transitions" among "all the races."[38]

Boas grappled as well in *The Mind of Primitive Man* with the dominant turn-of-the-century American conviction of racial purity that was so deeply bound up with whites' efforts to maintain racial hierarchy in the aftermath of racial slavery. In the book's final chapter Boas wrote directly about "the policy of many of our Southern States that try to prevent all racial intermixture," naming the "alleged reason" as "protecting the white race against the infusion of negro blood." Because most such "unions" occurred between white men and black women, Boas wrote, "no such infusion of negro blood into the white race through the maternal line occurs, so that the process is actually one of lightening the negro race without corresponding admixture in the white race." While at least obliquely challenging prohibitions against black–white unions, Boas also here endorsed the fiction that only white women could contaminate the supposed purity of white America by having sex across racial lines, thereby excusing white men for their sexual exploitation of black women.[39]

In the face of these alternatingly insightful and faltering reflections, *The Mind of Primitive Man* foreshadowed present-day criticisms of racial classification in two arresting ways. First, Boas wrote that "the varieties constituting each race overlap" in complexion, for example, and that "the differences between different types of man are, on the whole, small as compared to the range of variation in each type." As the Harvard biologist Richard Lewontin writes, the greatest genetic variation (he puts the figure at 85 percent) is found "among individuals within local national or linguistic populations," so much that "there is no objective way to assign the various human populations to clear-cut races." Lewontin adds that what differences exist "are in the process of breaking down" owing to the enormous increase in migration, a point Boas had anticipated just after the world's fair in 1893, writing that because a tribe may have reproduced with other tribes for centuries, "its original type may have disappeared entirely." Second, in an unpublished discussion of the world's fair data, Boas averred that it was better to "designate types" by "geographical area" than by tribal names.[40] Pursuing this point in *The Mind of Primitive Man,* he anticipated the present-day formulation that best substitutes for the concept of race: that of continental origin. In writing about "difference in type between the European races and the races of other continents," Boas's work—even as he remained inside the construct of race—foreshadowed that of the biological anthropologist Alan Goodman, who maintains that "geographic location is the best single explanation for human genetic variation."[41]

In blatant contradiction to his own invocation of racial categories, colors, and descriptions in the pages of the very same book, Boas wrote in *The Mind of Primitive Man* that attempts at racial classification demonstrated "clearly a condition of utter confusion and contradiction." These exact words he recited, too, in his *Handbook of American Indian Languages,* published the same year, in which he entitled one subheading, "Artificial Character of All Classifications of Mankind." *The Mind of Primitive Man* is in some ways itself an example of that very confusion and contradiction. On the one hand, Boas repeated contemporary racist ideas, once describing the projection of the alveolar arch characteristic of "the black races" as "a type slightly nearer the animal than the European type." On the other hand, he anticipated ideas about the artificiality of race that have been slow to take hold even in the twenty-first century.[42]

Circling back to the world's fair of 1893, we can see that Boas's project was caught in the historical particulars of late nineteenth-century science (to which he contributed) and yet was at once instrumental in helping him to develop convictions about the futility of racial classification. In *The Mind of Primitive Man,* as in his later writings, Boas, like Du Bois, turned the narratives of ambiguity inherent in the endeavor of measuring and describing human skin color into a powerful indictment. Lecturing in 1916, the black scholar and philosopher

Alain Locke ruminated on a "pure science of race," naming Boas as one who had dismissed that possibility: "After a very long attempt to pursue the subject upon a very rigid scientific basis," Locke wrote, Boas found that such an endeavor "could never successfully hope to compete with what men really believe human society to be."[43]

In the mid-1920s Boas defined a "race" as "a group of people descended from a common ancestry," a formulation again remarkably akin to the present-day idea of "continental origin." Ten years later Boas stepped back even farther, writing, "We talk all the time glibly of races and nobody can give us a definite answer to the question [of] what constitutes a race." Surely Boas had not forgotten about his 1890s data on Native American skin color and the ensuing narratives of ambiguity so starkly apparent in the responses to inquiry number 31. Whereas other anthropologists and investigators expressed doubts about the measurement of skin color, both before and after Boas, few apart from the pioneering Du Bois drew the kinds of conclusions about race that we find in *The Mind of Primitive Man* and beyond.[44]

Why did Franz Boas not make public the failures of his world's fair efforts to measure and describe human complexion? Had he offered an analysis of his foiled attempts, had he explained why he ultimately set aside these data, would that have made a difference in the discipline of anthropology in the age of Jim Crow? Perhaps in some small way it would have, yet the obsession with objectivity and rigor in determining human complexion was grounded in powerful convictions about racial hierarchies. Indeed, the search for instruments that could measure human skin color with precision continued on. Charles Davenport, for one, tried a "color top," with which, he wrote in 1925, "it is now possible to describe in exact quantitative terms the skin color of the different races of mankind and hybrids between them." Well apart from scientific quests related to racism, physical anthropologists have continued to measure human skin color, even developing an instrument called the Evans Electroselenium Reflectometer, which was praised in the 1980s for improving upon the still-popular von Luschan color scale.[45] As well, Boas's measurements of Native Americans were rediscovered by scientists in the 1990s and analyzed anew. To be sure, these scholars did not comment on the skin-color data, though some reiterated the construct of the vanishing Indian and invoked the language of fractional ancestry.[46]

It is possible that Boas's silence on the results of query number 31 in the world's fair project speaks to his understanding of the data not only as irreparably flawed but also as dangerous. For the very randomness inherent in the crusade to schematize human skin color served not to enlighten turn-of-the-century anthropologists about the artificial nature of race, but rather to sustain and strengthen the authority of science and the power of racial ideologies. As I have written elsewhere, although we tend to equate "the exposure of unstable racial categories with an assault on the very construct of race itself," that instability constitutes part of the power that resides within the endeavor of racial classification.[47]

In the twenty-first century we can invoke the "utter confusion and contradiction" of Boas's 1893 world's fair data on Native skin color as a means to discredit the endeavor of racial classification. At the time, however, that confusion was just as likely to stand as a manifestation *of* racism: to take its place easily among the innumerable lyrical phrasings of those so deeply preoccupied with how to measure, describe, and talk about the complexions of people already divided and ranked: the black, brown, red, yellow, and white; the dark and the light; the tawny and ruddy; the chocolate, cinnamon, and coffee; the copper, olive, sienna, and sepia; the "quite," the "very," and the approximate "-ish." For all his invocations of traditional and dominant inventories of complexion, for all his long and stubborn searches into racial types, and for all his repetitions of plainly racist propositions, Boas also pointed in another direction: toward the idea that a profusion of labels produced by the persistent striving for scientific objectivity in the quest to map human complexions could serve to shore up racism. This exploration of Boas's venture into the naming and fixing of human skin color is also, in the end, an argument about the problem of how to approach the many and varied archives of complexion in our historical sources. Franz Boas, I venture to say, understood this.

## Notes

I thank Bruce Dorsey, and I thank audiences to whom I have presented previous incarnations of this work: in the United States, at Yale University, where I especially thank Isaiah Wilner, and at the California Institute of Technology; in Germany, at the University of Cologne, the University of Leipzig, Martin Luther University at Halle-Wittenberg, and the University of Erfurt; and in Portugal, at the University of Coimbra.

1. On Boas and race, see Nell Irvin Painter, *The History of White People* (New York: W. W. Norton, 2010), 228–44; Lee D. Baker, "Columbia University's Franz Boas: He Led the Undoing of Scientific Racism," *Journal of Blacks in Higher Education* 22 (1998–99): 89–96; Vernon J. Williams Jr., *The Social Sciences and Theories of Race* (Urbana: University of Illinois Press, 2006), 16–47; Herbert S. Lewis, "The Passion of Franz Boas," *American Anthropologist* 103, no. 2 (2001): 447–67; Vernon J. Williams Jr., *Rethinking Race: Franz Boas and His Contemporaries* (Lexington: University Press of Kentucky, 1996), 4–36; George W. Stocking Jr., "Anthropology as *Kulturkampf*: Science and

Politics in the Career of Franz Boas," in *The Ethnographer's Magic and Other Essays in the History of Anthropology* (Madison: University of Wisconsin Press, 1992), 92–113.

2. On race as a social construction, see the foundational Barbara J. Fields, "Ideology and Race in American History," in *Region, Race, and Reconstruction: Essays in Honor of C. Vann Woodward,* ed. J. Morgan Kousser and James M. McPherson (New York: Oxford University Press, 1982), 143–77.
3. Billy G. Smith and Richard Wojtowicz, *Blacks Who Stole Themselves: Advertisements for Runaways in the* Pennsylvania Gazette, *1728–1790* (Philadelphia: University of Pennsylvania Press, 1989), 84, 135, 73, 20, 114; Emancipation Papers Resulting from the Act of April 16, 1862, M433, Records of the United States District Court for the District of Columbia Relating to Slaves, Record Group 21, National Archives, Washington, DC (hereafter NA); Descriptive Lists of Recruits for Massachusetts Volunteers, 1863–64, Middlesex County and Suffolk County, 477X, Massachusetts State Archives, Boston.
4. Smith and Wojtowicz, *Blacks Who Stole Themselves,* 161–72; Descriptive Lists of Recruits for Massachusetts Volunteers; Passport Applications, Jan.–Feb. 1864, M1372, roll 121, vol. 258; Jan.–March 1874, M1372, roll 200, vol. 431; Jan.–Feb. 1884, M1372, roll 261, vol. 575; Jan. 1894, M1372, roll 414, vol. 768, General Records of the Department of State, Passport Division, Record Group 59, NA.
5. Martha Hodes, *White Women, Black Men: Illicit Sex in the Nineteenth-Century South* (New Haven: Yale University Press, 1997), 96–122 (legal testimony); New England Hospital for Women and Children, Records of the New England Hospital, 1866–1902, vols. 1–3, Rare Books B MS b19, Countway Library of Medicine, Harvard University; Descriptive Registers, Prison Population Records, Eastern State Penitentiary, 1829–1903, and Western State Penitentiary, 1826–73, Records of the Department of Justice, Record Group 15, Pennsylvania State Archives, Harrisburg, PA; Mamie Garvin Fields with Karen Fields, *Lemon Swamp and Other Places: A Carolina Memoir* (New York: Free Press, 1983), 37, 46, 91, 143, 13, 20, 64.
6. Joan C. Stevenson, *Dictionary of Concepts in Physical Anthropology* (New York: Greenwood, 1991), 291–95 (phenotype); Werner Sollors, *Neither Black nor White yet Both: Thematic Explorations of Interracial Literature* (1997; repr. Cambridge: Harvard University Press, 1999), 142–61 (fingernails). And see Edward E. Telles, *Race in Another America: The Significance of Skin Color in Brazil* (Princeton: Princeton University Press, 2004), 95–106.
7. Franz Boas to parents, Worcester, MA, Apr. 3, 1891, and Franz Boas to parents, New York, NY, May 12, 1891, translated typescripts, Box 6, Franz Boas Professional Papers, Mss. B.B61p, American Philosophical Society (hereafter APS). On Virchow, see Benoit Massin, "From Virchow to Fischer: Physical Anthropology and 'Modern Race Theories' in Wilhelmine Germany," in *Volksgeist as Method and Ethic: Essays on Boasian Ethnography and the German Anthropological Tradition,* ed. George W. Stocking Jr. (Madison: University of Wisconsin Press, 1996), 82–94. On "type," see Richard L. Jantz, "The Anthropometric Legacy of Franz Boas," *Economics and Human Biology* 1, no. 2 (2003): 278; Yu Xie, "Franz Boas and Statistics," *Annals of Scholarship* 5 (1988): 276–77.
8. On the world's fair project, see Franz Boas, "The Anthropology of the North American Indian," in *Memoirs of the International Congress of Anthropology,* ed. C. Staniland Wake (Chicago: Schulte, 1894), 37–49; Franz Boas, "Toward the Anthropology of North American Indians," in *Proceedings of the Berlin Society for Anthropology, Ethnology, and*

*Prehistory* (1895), trans. Richard L. Bland, with introduction and notes by Ann G. Simonds, *Journal of Northwest Anthropology* 39, no. 2 (2005): 90–132; Franz Boas, "The Varieties of the American Race in North America" [1926?], p. 5, typescript with manuscript edits, MS 1308, "Numbered Manuscripts 1850s–1980s," National Anthropological Archives, Smithsonian Institution. And see Douglas Cole, *Franz Boas: The Early Years, 1858–1906* (Seattle: University of Washington Press, 1999), 152–66; Jantz, "Anthropometric Legacy," 278–79; Ann G. Simonds, "Physical Anthropological Studies by Franz Boas: Introduction and Notes," *Journal of Northwest Anthropology* 39, no. 2 (2005): 87–90.

9. This essay works with the information in Franz Boas Field Notebooks and Anthropometric Data, Boxes 1–2, Mss. B.B61.5, APS: "Winnebago Reservation, Minn. Data for Winnebago. 1892"; "Tahlequah, Oklahoma, and other locations. Data for Cherokee. 1892"; "Lincoln College, Philadelphia. Data for Oglalla [sic], Cheyenne, Omaha, etc. 1892"; "Santee, Yankton, etc. Data for Santee, Yankton & Teton. 1892"; "Ontario. Data for Mississagua, Chippewa, Oneida, Munsee, Ottawa, etc. 1892"; "Crow Agency, N.D. Data for Crow. 1892"; "Cheyenne River Agency, S. D. Data for Dakota, etc. 1891"; "White Earth Agency, Leech Lake and Pine Point, Minn. Data for Chippewa, etc. 1892"; "Anadarko, Fort Sill, and Grantham Springs, Indian Territory (Oklahoma). Data for Kiowa, Comanche, Apache, etc. 1892"; "Omaha Government School, Nebraska. Data for Omaha. ca. 1891–92"; "Stonewall and Tishimingo, Indian Territory (Oklahoma). Data for Chickasaw. 1891"; "Saskatchewan and Manitoba. Data for Ojibwa, Cree, Saulteux, etc. 1891"; "Kamloops, Lytton, and other locations in British Columbia, Spokane, Washington. Data for Thompson, etc. 1892." Each set contains between 80 and 170 sheets.

10. John J. Flinn, comp., *Official Guide to the World's Columbian Exposition* (Chicago: Columbian Guide Company, 1893), 52–59; M. P. Handy, ed., *World's Columbian Exposition 1893 Official Catalogue, Part XII: Anthropological Building, Midway Plaisance and Isolated Exhibits, Department M.: Ethnology* (Chicago: W. B. Conkey, 1893), 3; [William H. Dall], "The Columbian Exposition—IX: Anthropology," *Nation*, Sept. 28, 1893, 224–26; Franz Boas, "Ethnology at the Exposition," *Cosmopolitan* 15 (Sept. 1893): 607–9. And see Ida B. Wells, Frederick Douglass, et al., *The Reason Why the Colored American Is Not in the World's Columbian Exposition* (1893), ed. Robert W. Rydell (Chicago: University of Chicago Press, 1999); Robert W. Rydell, *All the World's a Fair: Visions of Empire at American International Expositions, 1876–1916* (Chicago: University of Chicago Press, 1984), 38–71.

11. W. H. Holmes, "The World's Fair Congress of Anthropology," *American Anthropologist* 6, no. 4 (1893): 424 (quotation); Susan Hegeman, "Franz Boas and Professional Anthropology: On Mapping the Borders of the 'Modern,'" *Victorian Studies* 41, no. 3 (1998): 455–83; Ira Jacknis, "The Ethnographic Object and the Object of Ethnology in the Early Career of Franz Boas," in *Volksgeist as Method and Ethic*, ed. Stocking, 185–214.

12. Paul Topinard, *Anthropology* (London: Chapman and Hall, 1890), 345. See also, for example, Nancy Shoemaker, "How Indians Got to Be Red," *American Historical Review* 102, no. 3 (1997): 625–44.

13. Nell Irvin Painter, "'Social Equality,' Miscegenation, Labor, and Power," in *The Evolution of Southern Culture*, ed. Numan V. Bartley (Athens: University of Georgia Press, 1988), 48; Martha Hodes, "Fractions and Fictions in the United States Census of 1890,"

in *Haunted by Empire: Geographies of Intimacy in North American History,* ed. Ann Laura Stoler (Durham: Duke University Press, 2006), 240–70. And see Patrick Wolfe, "Land, Labor, and Difference: Elementary Structures of Race," *American Historical Review* 106, no. 3 (2001): 866–905.

14. Frederick J. Turner, "The Significance of the Frontier in American History," *Annual Report of the American Historical Association for the Year 1893* (Washington, DC: Government Printing Office, 1894), 199; Paige Raibmon, *Authentic Indians: Episodes of Encounter from the Late-Nineteenth-Century Northwest Coast* (Durham: Duke University Press, 2005), 46. On "vanishing Indians," see, for example, Steven Conn, *History's Shadow: Native Americans and Historical Consciousness in the Nineteenth Century* (Chicago: University of Chicago Press, 2004), 154–97; Philip J. Deloria, *Playing Indian* (New Haven: Yale University Press, 1998), 71–94.

15. Franz Boas, "The Coast Tribes of British Columbia," *Science* 9 (Mar. 25, 1887): 289; Franz Boas, "Physical Characteristics of the Indians of the North Pacific Coast," *American Anthropologist* 4, no. 1 (1891): 32. See also Franz Boas, "The Half-Blood Indian: An Anthropometric Study," *Popular Science Monthly* 45 (Oct. 1894): 761–70; Boas, "Mixed Races," *Science* 17 (Mar. 27, 1891): 179.

16. Frederick Starr, "Measuring Cherokees," *Christian Union* 46 (Oct. 1, 1892): 586 (not pleasant); Boas, "Ethnology at the Exposition," 609 (visitors); see also Franz Boas, "Remarks on the Theory of Anthropometry," *Publications of the American Statistical Association* 3, no. 24 (1893): 569–75. On measuring bodies, see Lucile E. Hoyme, "Physical Anthropology and Its Instruments: An Historical Study," *Southwestern Journal of Anthropology* 9, no. 4 (1953): 408–30.

17. Franz Boas, "First General Report on the Indians of British Columbia," *Report of the Meeting of the British Association for the Advancement of Science* 59 (1889): 808; Boas, "Physical Characteristics of the Indians of the North Pacific Coast," 25.

18. Starr, "Measuring Cherokees," 587. The eastern Cherokee data sheets are not in the Boas papers with which I worked.

19. Starr, "Measuring Cherokees," 586. R. L. Jantz writes, "We have been unsuccessful in locating a reference to a measurement authority on which Boas relied"; see "Franz Boas and Native American Biological Variability," *Human Biology* 67, no. 3 (1995): 348.

20. Franz Boas, "Fifth Report on the Indians of British Columbia," *Report of the Meeting of the British Association for the Advancement of Science* 65 (1895): 546; see also Franz Boas, "Anthropometrical Observations on the Mission Indians of Southern California," *Proceedings of the American Association for the Advancement of Science* 44 (1895) [Salem: American Association for the Advancement of Science, 1896], 269 (describing complexion as "33*l* or 33*m* of Radde's standard colors"). On Radde's chart, see Rolf G. Kuehni and Andreas Schwarz, *Color Ordered: A Survey of Color Order Systems from Antiquity to the Present* (New York: Oxford University Press, 2008), 72, 86; the original is Otto Radde, *Radde's Internationale Farbenskala: 42 Gammen mit circa 900 Tönen* (Hamburg: Verlag der Stenochromatischen Anstalt von Otto Radde, 1877).

21. [John] Beddoe, "Colour," in British Association for the Advancement of Science, *Notes and Queries on Anthropology, for the Use of Travellers and Residents in Uncivilized Lands* (London: Edward Stanford, 1874), illustrations between pp. 8 and 9; the original is Paul Broca, *Instructions Générales Pour Les Recherches Anthropologiques à Fair Sur le Vivant*

(Société d'Anthropologie de Paris/G. Masson, 1879), 100–102, with 54 (not 52) color samples reproduced on unnumbered end pages. For Davenport's description, see Charles Davenport, "The Skin Colors of the Races of Mankind," 1925, typescript with manuscript edits, p. 5, Box 28, Charles B. Davenport Papers, Mss. B.D27, APS. Concerned that Broca's color blocks altered over time, Francis Galton searched in Rome for the material used to make mosaics, which he believed offered unalterable "specimens of standard colours for the description of tints of skin"; see F. Galton, "Notes on Permanent Colour Types in Mosaic," *Journal of the Anthropological Institute of Great Britain and Ireland* 16 (1887): 145.

22. Davenport, "Skin Colors," 1–2. See also John David Smith, "W. E. B. Du Bois, Felix von Luschan, and Racial Reform at the Fin de Siècle," *Amerikastudien / American Studies* 47, no. 1 (2002): 23–38. Boas and von Luschan both studied with Virchow, and von Luschan became "obsessed with measuring and recording skin color differentiations," though he was "unclear and ambiguous" on their significance (26). Louis R. Sullivan claimed that Boas used the von Luschan color scale; see "Anthropometry of the Siouan Tribes," *Anthropological Papers of the American Museum of Natural History* 23, pt. 3 (1925): 91. For the ceramic tiles reproduced in color, see Ruth Moore, *Evolution* (New York: Time-Life Books, 1964), 164–65.
23. For Boas's data sheets, see n. 9, above. [John] Beddoe, "Observations on the Natural Colour of the Skin in Certain Oriental Races," *Journal of the Anthropological Institute of Great Britain and Ireland* 19 (1890): 258.
24. Davenport, "Skin Colors," 1.
25. See Hodes, "Fractions and Fictions," 258.
26. John Crawfurd, "On the Classification of the Races of Man," *Transactions of the Ethnological Society of London* 1 (1861): 365; J. F. Campbell, "Kimmerians and Atlanteans," *Journal of the Anthropological Institute of Great Britain and Ireland* 1 (1872): clviii, clix; Beddoe, "Colour," in *Notes and Queries,* 8.
27. John Beddoe, "On Anthropological Colour Phenomena in Belgium and Elsewhere," *Journal of the Anthropological Institute of Great Britain and Ireland* 10 (1881): 375; William Z. Ripley, *The Races of Europe: A Sociological Study* (New York: D. Appleton, 1899), 60–61. And see Stanley J. Ulijaszek and John A. Lourie, "Intra- and Inter-Observer Error in Anthropometric Measurement," in *Anthropometry: The Individual and the Population,* ed. S. J. Ulijaszek and C. G. N. Mascie-Taylor (Cambridge: Cambridge University Press, 1994), 30–55.
28. Benjamin Apthorp Gould, *Investigations in the Military and Anthropological Statistics of American Soldiers* (New York: U.S. Sanitary Commission / Hurd and Houghton, 1869), 360, 240–49, x; on complexion, see 185–207.
29. Ibid., 185, 226, 203, 206, 227, 297, 298. The term "perceptible" indicates awareness of arbitrariness; Gould commented no further, even as he agonized over imprecisions of bodily measurement.
30. Ibid., 310, 626.
31. Boas's lack of analysis is explained in part by the precomputer era; see R. L. Jantz et al., "Variation Among North Amerindians: Analysis of Boas's Anthropometric Data," *Human Biology* 64, no. 3 (1992): 436; Cole, *Franz Boas,* 270. On the dissertation, see Cole, *Franz Boas,* 52–54. See also George W. Stocking Jr., "From Physics to Ethnology,"

in *Race, Culture, and Evolution: Essays in the History of Anthropology* (Chicago: University of Chicago Press, 1968), 142–43, 145.

32. Franz Boas, "The Occurrence of Similar Inventions in Areas Widely Apart," *Science*, n.s., 9, no. 224 (1887): 485; Franz Boas, "On Alternating Sounds," *American Anthropologist* 2, no. 1 (1889): 48. Stocking writes that the latter essay "foreshadows much of Boas's later criticism of late nineteenth-century racial thought"; see Stocking, "From Physics to Ethnology," 159.
33. See, for example, Franz Boas, "The Indians of British Columbia," *Journal of the American Geographical Society of New York* 28, no. 3 (1896): 229, 230 (words and phrases); Franz Boas, "The Correlation of Anatomical or Physiological Measurements," *American Anthropologist* 7, no. 3 (1894): 313 (types); Boas, "Toward the Anthropology of North American Indians," 91 (equation); Boas, "Fifth Report on the Indians of British Columbia," 545–46 (compare); Franz Boas, "Anthropometry of Shoshonean Tribes," *American Anthropologist* 1, no. 4 (1899): 758, 757 (ears); Franz Boas, "Some Recent Criticisms of Physical Anthropology," *American Anthropologist* 1, no. 1 (1899): 102–3 (varieties). An anthropologist who worked with Boas's Siouxian data in the 1920s concluded that the skin-color data were "especially unsatisfactory"; see Sullivan, "Anthropometry of the Siouan Tribes," 91.
34. Boas, "Some Recent Criticisms," 106; Boas, "Varieties of the American Race," 7.
35. W. E. B. Du Bois, ed., *The Health and Physique of the Negro American: Report of a Social Study Made under the Direction of Atlanta University* (Atlanta: Atlanta University Press, 1906), 16, 30–33, 31. On the conference, see Rosemary Lévy Zumwalt and William Shedrick Willis, "Franz Boas and W. E. B. Du Bois at Atlanta University, 1906," *Transactions of the American Philosophical Society* 98, pt. 2 (2008): 41–77.
36. Maria Farland, "W. E. B. Du Bois, Anthropometric Science, and the Limits of Racial Uplift," *American Quarterly* 58, no. 4 (2006): 1025; W. E. B. Du Bois, *Dusk of Dawn: An Essay Toward an Autobiography of a Race Concept* (1940; repr. New York: Schocken Books, 1968), 153; Franz Boas, *Anthropology: A Lecture Delivered at Columbia University in the Series on Science, Philosophy and Art, December 18, 1907* (New York: Columbia University Press, 1908), 13–14.
37. Franz Boas, *The Mind of Primitive Man* (1911; repr. New York: Macmillan, 1921), 30, 39, 18–19.
38. Ibid., 144, 147, 31, 32, 33.
39. Ibid., 276–77. Hodes, *White Women, Black Men*, 176–208, esp. 199–200.
40. Boas, *The Mind of Primitive Man*, 34, 94; R. C. Lewontin, "Confusions About Human Races," in "Is Race 'Real'?: A Web Forum Organized by the Social Science Research Council," June 7, 2006, raceandgenomics.ssrc.org/Lewontin/; Boas, "Anthropology of the North American Indian," 38; Boas, "Varieties of the American Race," 3–4. See also Shirley M. Tilghman, "The Meaning of Race in the Post-Genome Era," James Baldwin Lecture, Princeton University, Mar. 9, 2010, princeton.edu/president/speeches/20100309/.
41. Boas, *The Mind of Primitive Man*, 3; Alan Goodman, "Two Questions About Race," in "Is Race 'Real'?," June 7, 2006, raceandgenomics.ssrc.org/Goodman/.
42. Boas, *The Mind of Primitive Man*, 127; Franz Boas, "Introduction," *Handbook of American Indian Languages*, pt. 1 (Washington, DC: Government Printing Office, 1911), 7, 14; Boas, *The Mind of Primitive Man*, 21.

43. Alain LeRoy Locke, *Race Contacts and Interracial Relations: Lectures on the Theory and Practice of Race,* ed. Jeffrey C. Stewart (Washington, DC: Howard University Press, 1992), 7, 8.
44. Franz Boas, "What Is a Race?" *Nation,* Jan. 28, 1925, 90; Franz Boas, "History and Science in Anthropology: A Reply," *American Anthropologist* 38, no. 1 (1936): 140.
45. Davenport, "Skin Colors," 5; Guy L. Tasa et al., "Reflectometer Reports on Human Pigmentation," *Current Anthropology* 26, no. 4 (1985): 511–12; and see J. S. Weiner, "A Spectrophotometer for Measurement of Skin Colour," *Man* 51, no. 253 (1951): 152–53. The anthropologist Nina G. Jablonski, who rejects the concept of race, summarizes methods of skin-color measurement in *Skin: A Natural History* (Berkeley: University of California Press, 2006), 73–74.
46. Jantz, "Anthropometric Legacy." For late twentieth-century uses of Boas's data, see *Human Biology* 67, no. 3 (1995), special issue.
47. Martha Hodes, "The Mercurial Nature and Abiding Power of Race: A Transnational Family Story," *American Historical Review* 108, no. 1 (2003): 85.

# Chapter 9 The Death of William Jones: Indian, Anthropologist, Murder Victim

*Kiara M. Vigil*

On March 21, 1910, the Supreme Court of the Philippines issued a surprising ruling in *The United States v. The Ilongots Palidat et al.*, a criminal case prosecuted by the US government against three Indigenous men from the island of Luzon. The three men had been found guilty of murdering William Jones, an American anthropologist working in the so-called headhunting country of the northernmost Philippines during the previous year. According to the law of the Philippines, however, the defendants were unable to conceive of "the value of human life," and therefore the death penalty "should not be imposed" upon them.[1]

This case was about life and death, but it was also about the identities of the main actors. The defendants were members of the Ilongot tribe, and the victim, William Jones, was an American Indian. Furthermore, as the trial had revealed, the events leading up to Jones's death—a series of mixed messages and missteps culminating in his decision to take an Ilongot chieftain captive—reflected a critical shift in an imperial discourse that shaped Jones's ideas about his Indigenous identity and Western civilization. Many of these ideas Jones had derived from his schooling in the United States, including his work with Franz Boas.

Jones was an Indian as much as an anthropologist, but his indigeneity did not make him any less fit to stand in as a representative for the United States in the eyes of the American press and the foreign court that examined the facts of his death. Once situated within the tense political atmosphere of a new satellite of American empire, a colony struggling with internal battles related to nationalism, Jones's identity could be reshaped to fit a vision of the United States as the global carrier of a modern civilization. Yet if the Philippines Americanized Jones, the reverse was true at home, where his pursuit of anthropological adventure originated from his experience of colonization. In the United States, despite Jones's success by the standards of the elite who had educated him, he was always viewed as an American Indian and thus of inferior racial fiber.

Who was William Jones and why did he die? This essay illuminates the identity of an Indigenous intellectual as it intersected with imperial discourses, first in the United States and later in the Philippines. Through an examination of Jones's death, I consider how Gilded Age ideas of race and civilization functioned as a discourse to frame Jones in one way and his Ilongot assailants in another, ultimately producing the tragic misunderstanding between them. Yet the same discourse could also operate for an Indian abroad as a site of power and possibility. By transforming himself into an agent of empire, Jones managed (for a time) to resituate himself in the Philippines, exchanging his identity as a colonial specimen for the persona of a Native conqueror and collector. He also left behind a record of this reinvention, for Jones's attempt at performance politics produced an ethnographic archive: a diary, field notes, letters home, and a set of objects and photographs that, when read together, supply evidence of Native self-fashioning along an emergent imperial frontier. If we make use of this archive, we can embed the story of Native North America within a wider narrative, a multivocal orchestration that pays witness to the interactions of the globe's many Indigenous peoples.[2] This historical moment allowed for and even necessitated shifts in Jones's identity, from that of a Meskwaki man to that of an anthropologist, an American, and finally, much to his surprise, a murder victim.

## THE LAST DAY

I begin with the moments preceding Jones's murder. The penultimate chapter of a posthumous biography of Jones written by a friend and former college classmate, Henry Milner Rideout, is titled "The Last Day." Rideout and Jones had met at Phillips Academy in Andover, Massachusetts, before they were undergraduates at Harvard. Their boyhood friendship must have informed Rideout's characterization of Jones as a noble savage among the benighted. Rideout claimed that in the Philippines Jones "made not even the simplest movement rashly," for he knew how "bloody, childish, and bestial were the folk among whom he ate and slept."[3]

When Rideout contended that Jones ought to have outsmarted the people he was studying—"his Indian caution more than matched the wiles of these head-hunters, his sleep was infinitely lighter than theirs, his footfall more wary"—he indulged in the urge to remember his friend through a prism of nostalgia for the salvific qualities of the noble savage. Jones, Rideout suggested, was a better type of Indigenous person than the ones he intended to study, a view that mirrored Jones's sense of himself.[4] From within the jungle, Jones took pride in his wilderness instincts, writing in his diary, "I came upon a family resting in the shade of a booth, and was on them before they knew anything."[5] This stealth, Jones implied, stemmed from his upbringing in Indian Territory. Yet his diary also reveals that he felt considerable foreboding, even worrying about the possibility of an untimely death. On August 28, 1908, he wrote, "The Alikod people had an interesting story to tell me last night. They told me that when I was in Panipagan a plan was set to kill me; that I was to be made to pass a place where a tree would be felled upon me; that the tree was felled but missed me; that the man who was commissioned to carry this out was Kandag . . ."[6]

The ominous atmosphere crested on the evening of Saturday, March 27, 1909, as Jones waited near the Ilongot village of Panipagan for a delivery of bamboo rafts known as *balsas* that he required to transport himself and his "ethnologic freight" down the Cagayan River from the village of Dumobatu to the Christian town of Echague, more than three hundred kilometers north of Manila. As the hours passed, Jones grew frustrated, then restless, at last turning in for the night. The next morning, after writing what would turn out to be his final journal entry, he set off for Panipagan with his servant, Romano Dumaliang, and their boatman, a Dumobatu man named Gonaut. About noon the men reached the Pung-gu, a series of rapids where the Cagayan ran through a narrow gorge. They were soon on their way to Panipagan, where Jones would make the mistake of his life.[7]

Jones had grown quite impatient as he waited for the balsas for a second day, so impatient that he joked, according to a report published soon after his death by the *Chicago Tribune,* that he ought to keep an Ilongot chief with him until he received his rafts.[8] The story that later came out in court, during Romano's testimony, was more direct. While speaking to three of Chief Tacadan's aides, Jones delivered an ultimatum: Either the two villages under the chief's control would have six rafts delivered to Jones or Jones would hold Tacadan hostage.[9]

Expecting his rafts, Jones paused to take a midday meal with some Ilongot villagers, who warned him that he was acting rashly. They counseled another approach: temperance, delay. Jones, however, was exasperated. Still without hope of receiving his rafts, he "laid his hand on the old man's shoulder," attempting to guide Tacadan toward the boat.[10] This was the action that provoked an attack by Palidat, Magueng, and Gacad, the three Indigenous men who would later appear manacled in court before W. C. Bryant, the governor of Nueva Vizcaya Province.[11]

At first the attackers assaulted Jones with a bolo, a sword similar to a machete. Jones felt a gash open across his forehead. Seeing Jones reach for his revolver, the men sliced into his right arm. Jones fell from this second wound to be stabbed repeatedly in the chest and abdomen. These were the fatal injuries. On March 28, 1909, a Sunday, Jones died of internal bleeding. On April 1, 1909, he was buried in the Municipal Cemetery in Echague, where two Americans, their names now unknown, read a eulogy over his grave. The three men who were seen attacking Jones admitted to the crime, offering in atonement the payment of one *carabao,* a water buffalo. This would not satisfy the US government. The men were apprehended by Hilario Logan, a lieutenant in the Philippines Constabulary, and brought to the municipality of Bayombong in the province of Nueva Vizcaya to stand trial for murder.[12]

## THE EDUCATION OF WILLIAM JONES

Born in Indian Territory in 1871, Jones spent his first years in what later became the state of Oklahoma. Like many Indian boys of his generation he pursued his American education in a boarding school, the Hampton Normal and Agricultural Institute in Hampton, Virginia. Hampton had been created as a land grant school with a special racial purpose, the education and uplift of black men, but it would also set an ideological pattern for the assimilation of American Indians. In 1878 Hampton established a formal education program for American Indians, and Jones was among a select group of promising Indian boys who arrived from the reservations, in his case in 1889. Between his scientific and industrial courses, the ordinary fare of Gilded Age racial uplift, he also embarked on a classical studies curriculum.[13]

Jones's intelligence must have been evident early, for just three years later he entered the prestigious Phillips Academy.[14] There he met his friend Rideout. After graduating from Andover in 1896, Jones worked with his father to recruit Indian students from across Indian Territory to attend the Carlisle

Indian Industrial School in Pennsylvania, founded by Richard Pratt, a Civil War lieutenant who sought to assimilate Native youth to American life, remaking them into proper citizens.[15] Jones's path diverged that fall, however, when he enrolled at Harvard.

As an undergraduate Jones began to study medicine in the hope of returning to the reservation as a physician, much like other Native intellectuals in this period, such as Charles Eastman, Carlos Montezuma, and Susan La Flesche Picotte.[16] But in Cambridge Jones met Frederic Ward Putnam, Harvard's professor of anthropology and the director of the Peabody Museum. Largely owing to Putnam's influence, Jones shifted his focus in 1897 from medicine to anthropology. Furthering this new interest, the Boston Folk-Lore Society sponsored Jones for a summer research trip to Tama, Iowa, where he would conduct research among the Meskwaki Indians.[17] Then known as the Fox, the Meskwaki had stretched across the Great Lakes region, including lands in Canada, but they had been forced to resettle further south, in Iowa, Kansas, Nebraska, and Oklahoma, including the Sauk and Fox Reservation in Stroud, Oklahoma, where Jones's grandparents lived.[18]

Jones was raised by his maternal grandmother because his mother had died not long after he was born. In a letter from Harvard, Jones wrote about these years with reverence for her teachings about the natural world, including her ecological view of time:

> My dear old grandmother used to tell me that I was born in the springtime, when the bluebirds were coming from the south and were looking about in the dead trees for holes to build their nests in. Grass was just coming up, and with it the flowers. She used to tell me how she would carry me about, and a whole lot more things which I sometimes live over, though more often they seem but a tale. Then the summer went by, and the winter followed, and the next spring they laid my mother to rest. This is the way she recorded time, and that is the way it has always come to me.[19]

Jones's childhood memories of this time formed the basis of his identity. For, as Rideout emphasized, "William Jones lived, saw, spoke, and thought as an Indian."[20] His interests in medicine, folklore, and linguistics received their first stimulus as he watched his grandmother, a medicine woman, search for ingredients, mix remedies, and relate the stories connected with her activities to her grandson.[21] Jones's research trip was partly a return to these childhood roots—a return that formed the basis of a departure.

In 1900, when Jones finished his undergraduate studies at Harvard, he entered Columbia University to study anthropology with Putnam's protégé Franz Boas.[22] At Columbia Jones achieved a rare distinction when he became the first

American Indian to complete a doctoral degree in anthropology—the first in the country, in fact.[23] One might think pursuing a doctoral degree in a subject that defined Indians as the objects of study, not as the scientists who conducted it, would have forced Jones to contend with an assimilationist discourse that framed him as a success story at best or, at worst, a curiosity. Rideout, however, believed that Jones's colleagues valued him as a scholar and personality. He made "warm and lasting friendships," Rideout wrote, with the men who "did the most thorough work" but "at the close of the day could brush off the class-room chalk or the Museum dust, and cheerfully rejoin the outer world."[24]

The study of global culture linked whiteness to civilization, yet here Jones was, an Ivy League Indian earning an advanced degree at Columbia. His summers in Tama, Iowa, conducting fieldwork among the Meskwaki must have heightened his sense of himself as an outsider, observing his people from a relatively privileged position. Among his peers Jones held a different kind of outsider status, given that his early research focused on his own people, a people whose ways and words were now thought to be "vanishing" and were therefore enthusiastically sought out by anthropologists.[25] Until Jones arrived, there had been no comprehensive study of Meskwaki material culture. Today, his *Ethnography of the Fox Indians,* Bulletin 125 of the Bureau of American Ethnology at the Smithsonian Institution, remains a foundational text on the topic.[26]

From 1902 to 1905 Jones shifted his research focus to the Sioux and Ojibwa. The primary patron of this work was Boas, who drew upon his connections at the American Museum of Natural History and the Bureau of American Ethnology to fund Jones's fieldwork in the Great Lakes region.[27] Boas viewed Jones as one of the most promising linguists of his time, and Jones fulfilled that promise quickly, publishing in the journal of the American Ethnological Society. In 1904 his dissertation, "Some Principles of Algonquian Word Formation," was published by the *American Anthropologist.*[28] Part of the dissertation was later included in Boas's *Handbook of American Indian Languages,* which set a template for the study of Indigenous languages according to their own grammatical principles.[29] Two years after receiving his degree, despite advancing considerably in his work on Ojibwa, Jones set aside his linguistics research to accept an offer from a fellow Putnam protégé, George Dorsey, to do fieldwork for the Field Museum of Natural History in Chicago.[30]

Given Jones's recognized promise, his talent for linguistics, the support he enjoyed from Putnam, Boas, Harvard, Columbia, and the Carnegie, his rapid progress in the study of Algonquian culture, and the enthusiastic reception of his scholarship, his decision to abandon his career in America seems a mystery—until one considers Jones's personal experience of race. Notwithstanding some

The portrait of William Jones that appeared with his obituary in the May 1909 issue of the *Southern Workman.* The unsigned article was written by his graduate school mentor, Franz Boas. Courtesy of Hampton University Archives.

part-time work as a curator and the backing of the Carnegie, Jones's position in anthropology remained marginal. As an Indian, he could have little hope of receiving permanent employment at either a university or the bureau.[31] Jones seems to have discussed his frustrations with Rideout, who later wrote that Jones had been "carefully led" to the door of anthropology, "only to find it locked." Jones felt "the whole situation was exceedingly absurd."[32]

For a man who had lived his life as a success story, an "example" to his race, Chicago represented a chance to enjoy another kind of life, one Jones richly deserved: that of a permanent and valued member of an everyday scientific community. Before he left for the Philippines, Jones delighted in the contemplation afforded by his Hyde Park museum regimen. "The part of the city I am in is like an inland country town with lots of open air and space; and so I never go down town into the dust, cinders, rush and noise," he wrote a friend.

"The Museum, you know, is on the Lake. There are green plots, with trees often. For example, a maple comes up to my window."[33]

The Field Museum was growing rapidly, assembling collections from around the world, and Jones arrived there just as the American military occupied parts of Asia and Latin America, presenting anthropologists with an opportunity for their own conquests. Offered the choice of three expeditions, one to Africa, one to the South Sea Islands, and one to the Philippines, Jones selected the last option, which he considered the thorniest.[34] Five years after the close of what is now called the Philippine War of Independence (1899–1902), American teachers, scientists, and bureaucrats were being sent in large numbers to join military officials who were attempting to pacify the country, ultimately contributing to a civil war.[35] In this era of imperial expansion, politicians and intellectuals drew parallels between American Indians and other "dependent" peoples along the American empire's expanding frontiers.

When he took his assignment, Jones joined a private–public network of museums, government departments, and freelance colonists who were taking up the imperial quest without government aid or accreditation. There was freedom in this field, room for action and enterprise. In his diary Jones noted his hope to move beyond the Philippines to other portions of the Pacific and beyond, even India. Emboldened by the promise of a new adventure and by an escape from his ethnic confines, a child of the conquered now began to envision himself as a conqueror, or at least as one able to participate, to a degree, in conquest. In letters to friends Jones mused that he would be spending time "with the pygmy black man called the Negrito . . . wild in the sense that he lives in out of the way places, and not that he is ferocious."[36] Assuming the stance of an empathetic imperialist who understood his wayward charges even before he met them, this Indian took up the white man's burden.[37]

Although set on the idea that he could advance his career by working abroad, Jones was not supported in his choice by his mentor. Shortly before he departed for Chicago, he spent some time with Boas and his wife, Marie, in upstate New York, where Boas may have asked Jones to consider altering his plans. If so, Boas's plea may have been partially successful, for Jones packed his Algonquian research among his belongings destined for the Philippines.[38] In August 1907 Jones boarded a passenger ship, the *Aki Maru* of Seattle, which set sail for the islands.[39]

## HUNTING LIKE AT HOME

On October 6, 1907, Jones sent a letter from Manila to northern Luzon, where his friend, museum colleague, and fellow Boas student Fay-Cooper Cole was conducting his own research. The letter, recounting Jones's plans to document the "primitives" of the Philippines, bore the hallmarks of a chillingly familiar narrative. As a newly minted agent of American empire Jones drew a parallel between his "discovery" of "naked natives" in the Philippines and the earlier, strained intimacy of colonial contact between the American military and Indians.[40] "It is the same old thing we have become familiar with in our country," he wrote. "Army officers have been stationed for years among some of our most interesting Indians, and yet know nothing about them."[41]

What is striking here is Jones's statement that the American military lacked proper knowledge about the people it aimed to conquer and control. As the discoverer of that knowledge, Jones repositioned himself as a new kind of imperial agent. He could tame and balance the drive of empire, humanizing its prospects, owing to his success as a "civilized" Indian. By refashioning himself as an Indigenous expert, Jones positioned himself in his letters home as a different sort of Native and a different sort of imperialist: an Indian who knew more about the Natives than the soldiers did. In truth, Jones's romanticized description of himself as a man of expertise masked an ignorance of local history and geography that he shared with the military that prepared his path.[42] This was not Indian Country, and Jones did not know it.

Not long after he arrived in Manila Jones began preparing for his research expedition. It was only then, it seems, that he formalized his plans to reach the northern end of Luzon. Given the lack of roads there, he would have to travel by sea to Aparri at the mouth of the Cagayan River, in Isabela Province. From there Jones would follow the river southward among the hills, searching for subjects yet unknown and collecting their material possessions. He would have to make several stops along the way, at Ilagan and Dumobatu, reporting his progress to his colleagues at the Field Museum and thus chronicling his journey and adding to the archive of observations.

Before Jones reached Ilongot country he planned to stay for some time in the "small Cristiano town" of Echague, situated along the Cagayan River. This region of Luzon would later become known as the rice bowl because of its fertile soils spanning the Cagayan Valley. In Echague, a place of sedentary agriculture—"civilization"—Jones would gather supplies, hire a servant, and obtain a dog for his travels, while also studying the geography of the "wilds" he planned to navigate. Writing to Dorsey, his supervisor, in November 1907, Jones noted that he found himself perched temporarily among bamboo shacks lined up to suggest the places where streets should be, squalid Chinese shops, and Native stores—"the end of things, in a way."[43] Echague, he wrote, was "the fringe of our white man's world."[44]

For the first time, if from a great distance, Jones belonged to the "we." He could be a white man now, so long as there were no other white men around—at least according to the terms Jones used to define whiteness. "There is one other white man in town, but he, too, is gone," Jones wrote, "or rather, I should say, one other American, for there are several Spaniards."[45] To define himself as a white man Jones emphasized his status as an American, a Protestant American, in contrast to the Catholic remnants of the Spanish empire that remained. As an Andover alum, a Harvard man, an assimilated Indian, Jones ranked himself above the mongrelized decadence of Latinized Southeast Asia; he was ethnically mixed, perhaps, but boasting a moral whiteness achieved through contrast, even if he had taken up the habit of a midday siesta. Having claimed for himself the position of a white man, Jones began his venture into darkness. In April 1908, accompanied by his Native servant Lorenzo, a German shepherd named Dona, and two bull carts laden with books, paper, and articles for barter, Jones made his way out of Echague to study the Ilongots. He carried a Luger pistol.[46]

As an Indigenous anthropologist Jones actually occupied a middle category according to white academia, a position that no doubt influenced his scholarly observations. Having established himself as an observer of the Ilongot, Jones quickly realized that he was not the only one doing the seeing. "I know now what a tiger feels like at a show, where he is fetched out upon an arena, with crowds of faces looking down upon him from everywhere," he wrote upon his arrival in Majatungut. "Eyes were riveted on me from the moment I entered until I don't know when. They were still looking when I fell asleep on my cot."[47] It is difficult to know whether this feeling of being part of a show emerged from Jones's status as a foreigner, an American, an anthropologist, or an Indian—or perhaps all together. Quite likely the Ilongots were curious to know not only who Jones was but also, above all, what he wanted. He was as much "other" to them as they were to him. In any case, the evidence Jones provides of double looking shows he was not ignorant of the thoughts of those he studied.

The Ilongot people seem to have brought Jones face-to-face with Indigenous ideas about their political world. On April 16, 1908, while still in Dumobatu, along the river in the Cagayan Valley, Jones began to write about his subjects in a new way, portraying them within the contours of civilization. The group of villagers he now lived with, Jones wrote on May 7, maintained a system of housing units constituting "one political group of Ilongots."[48] Given their deliberate political organization, they were not "uncivilized," as the Filipino court's penal code would have it. Jones went on to recognize that his subjects had created four distinct units based on four geographical positions, with Dumobatu representing one unit, and Panipagan, Kagadyangan, and Tamsi representing the other three. These "four groups," Jones wrote, "make up one division . . . my present subjects for study. They are friends, and of one culture. Beyond them toward the south and west are other Ilongots who are their enemies."[49] Jones's ability to parse these distinctions among various Ilongot communities and his recognition of their claiming and naming of specific places suggest that he had found a teacher in the community.

As Jones came to understand from within the political contours of Ilongot culture, he also came to face the ideological paradox that emerged from his identity as an American Indian. To accomplish his work as an anthropologist he would need to know the Ilongot, to spend time among them and to create friendly relations with them, meaning that they would come to know him too. Yet this globalizing interaction of indigeneities would also draw him nearer his Native origins, potentially undermining his provisional status as a white (American) man. Despite his romantic notion of himself as an Indigenous imperialist, Jones found this status being undermined. The better he performed his work, the more Native he became.

Jones managed this performance in his writings, emphasizing his feeling of otherness among the Natives and his inability to extract information about his surroundings. In a letter sent later that summer to a friend, one Mr. Smith, Jones wrote that he could be found, theoretically, not far from a dot marking Echague, but that would be only an approximation: "The region is unknown, and the present mapping of it is based largely on pipe dreams."[50] Jones's reference to the unknowable, the unmapped, made a specific claim, one that was, in fact, untrue. Jones did know where he was because the Ilongot had told him. To admit as much would acknowledge a connection, drawing Jones closer to his Native status than he might have preferred. But the negotiation between growing closer to one's Native subject in order to empathetically embody a nonwhite status and maintaining an objective—that is, outsider and white—scientific position is also the dilemma of ethnography.

Another option for Jones was to map what he had called unmappable: to draw upon his Meskwaki upbringing, his education, and his work in the United States not to define himself as a white American, in contrast to the Spanish settlers of Echague, but to invent a third ideological space, framing a global indigeneity that he shared with the Ilongot. In his letters home Jones consistently used "the native name of the place" to describe his location. He strove through the mastery and enumeration of detail to portray his intimacy with Indigenous life, detailing the "dwelling places" of the Ilongot, composed of thatched roofs made of long grass or palm leaves.[51] These evocative descriptions portrayed Jones as an insider: he lived *inside* an Ilongot hut, he saw *inside* their political system, he took their secret paths.

Yet, having drawn himself toward his hosts, Jones would often rebel, underlining their differences from him in racist language, the terms of progress and civilization he had learned in school. "Think of the lousiest Indians you've ever seen, and you will have a partial notion of how lousy my friends are," Jones wrote to Smith in July 1898. "Society is pretty simple, and government is largely according to custom."[52]

If the references to wild places and unclean people revealed an attempt to draw a border—to define oneself as a bearer of civilization—they were also a case of the anthropologist who protests too much. Like any adventurer, Jones liked to live on the "wild" side. If he had not wanted that adventure, he would not have taken the job. And he was not the only one who enjoyed the novelty of his performance. On one occasion Jones recorded his ambivalence—his sense of being at home with the Ilongot and his sense of not wanting to feel that way—even as he hinted at another story taking place, one filled with actors whom he normally obscured. Jones wrote in his diary that he had announced his plan to leave Dumobatu to travel upstream, but his hosts vehemently rejected the idea. "These wild people," Jones wrote, "have told me that I must not go; but if I do, to be sure to return as soon as possible."[53]

"The call of the wild," as Jack London had termed it five years earlier in his novel of the Klondike gold rush, is a fundamentally modern experience.[54] There is no wilderness apart from what is imagined to be empty by the person who claims to conquer it. Yet for Jones that call arrived in the form of a yearning for *return,* for psychic unity with an Indigenous status long denied him. Writing to his friend Marlborough in 1908, Jones mused about life as a wanderer and adventurer, defining himself as wild and also Indian:

> My work makes me lead the life of a gypsy, but it suits my heart nevertheless. I was born out of doors, and the only sheltered life I have had was when you and I came to know each other. Now it looks as if I shall keep on under the open sky, and at the end lie down out of doors, which, of course, is as it should be. I don't know how long I shall remain on this side of the spinning ball. My stay is indefinite. The plan was for me to journey also to other islands away from this Archipelago, go to India, and the good old Lord only knows where else.[55]

As much as Jones embraced the opportunity to play imperialist, a part of him understood the limits of his thinking. References to being "out of doors" intimate that he could not escape his origins, nor did he wish to. The longing to map a new frontier, a replacement for the settled West, represented to him an expression of Indigenous identity.

In Jones's writings the Philippines aligned with nostalgic visions of the American West as a place of wilderness and promise, a virgin land valued for rugged hills and vast plains rather than the Native people who lived on them. In one striking entry in his journal Jones drew an explicit parallel between the wilds of Asia and America. "It is not so much the society of the Ilongot that has enchanted me, but rather the free life in these wild, rugged hills and silent gloomy jungles," he wrote. "The way is up and down mountains, along and over bogs and boulders, through dense thickets and tall razor-bladed grass, up and down streams up the ankle or to the waist. Deer and wild hogs are abundant. Where the country is open I can get a little hunting like at home."[56]

The romantic voice of this journal entry suggests that Jones was at last beginning to align his anthropologist's vision of a people and a place with his Indigenous identity. The final sentence draws on experiences and memories of his earlier life, before Hampton and Harvard, Columbia and Chicago, among the Meskwaki in Oklahoma. Jones likely did not realize that by explicitly comparing the countryside of the Philippines to his former hunting places as an Indian youth he also emptied that landscape of its owners. In such moments he reimagined the Philippines as a colonized space, thus indulging in the ideology that underpinned American empire.

In one of his last letters sent from the Philippines, written on February 25, 1909, Jones had offered Marlborough a critical assessment of his linguistics research—one that Boas would not have agreed with—which must be read as a defense of his decision to go abroad. "You know I was no intellectual light, no winner of scholastic prizes," Jones claimed. "Therefore, I'm doing no miracles, nor clouding the air with dust and sand."[57] He then recounted his journey to East Asia, providing a summary of his travels so far that suggested he was growing entranced by his adventurous line of work: "Then a couple of years ago I went to the Field Museum of Natural History in Chicago, to come on the chase out here. I had a pleasing journey through Japan and down the China coast, lingering here and there, and became infected with the something that makes those who have been there to desire to return, despite its filth, plagues, and all the other horrors."[58] Jones offered Marlborough no details about how he "became infected" or what "the something" was that could be powerful enough to make men like him want to return to such places, or what their "horrors" were. Even so, the letter reveals a moment of redefinition. By extending "the chase" beyond the United States, Jones placed himself among the scientists, missionaries, soldiers, and settlers who had "pacified" the Indians of the American West, including his own grandparents. Perhaps, if Jones had not performed so well in his role as an Indigenous imperialist, he might have seen a better way to procure the rafts he needed to ensure the proper transport of his treasure.

Jones, who had gone out to collect, was enfolded within his own archive when the assistant curator of ethnology at the Field Museum, S. Chapman Simms, returned to the Philippines nearly a year after the murder to retrieve Jones's field notes and his accumulation of nearly five thousand Philippines specimens—"enough to insure Chicago the greatest ethnological collection in the world from this archipelago."[59] In addition to bolstering the museum's reputation, Simms's trip provided "an authentic account of the murder of his comrade, Dr. William Jones." He offered it to the *Chicago Tribune,* which soon published the story "in the interest of science."[60] The newspaper reported that "at the time of his assassination" Jones had penetrated farther into the interior of Luzon "than any other known white man."[61]

## MEMBERS OF AN UNCIVILIZED TRIBE

The court records documenting Jones's trial show that the United States, acting as plaintiff, called for justice in the name of an American. As a Native anthropologist, Jones occupied a unique position between two colonies, one beyond the United States, the other within it: the Philippines and Indian Country. But Jones's Indigenous identity mattered little to the American prosecutors, who sought to hold the Ilongot who had killed him accountable for their actions—and, by doing so, to remind the court that the colonizers and the colonized existed on opposite ends of a racial hierarchy.

If the trial of Jones's accused assailants revealed fissures in the ideology of American imperialism, its resolution would rely upon those contradictions. On April 25, 1909, Hilario Logan, a second lieutenant of the Constabulary, submitted a formal statement to the Court of the Justice of the Peace accusing Palidat, Magueng, and Gacad of murdering William Jones. On the same day all three men submitted a guilty plea to W. C. Bryant, the governor of Nueva Vizcaya Province. Following their plea and the testimony of Romano Dumaliang, Jones's servant and the sole witness for the prosecution, the men were sentenced to death by the Court of the First Instance, a lower court of the Province of Nueva Vizcaya, on May 27, 1909.[62]

Rather than call the defendants to take the stand on their own behalf, their attorney, one Mr. Kanlas, merely presented their confessions to the court. He stated that all three men had admitted to killing Jones but that they had done so in defense of Tacadan. Many months later, Kanlas could hope, the final verdict of the Supreme Court of the Philippines might grant clemency to the accused by relying on Article 11 of the penal code, under which the defendants would be defined as savages incapable of conceiving of the value of human life; they would thereby elude a death sentence and be sentenced instead to a life of hard labor.[63]

As for the defendants, their honest declaration that they had assaulted Jones bore a message of its own, one that went unrecorded by the imperialist press. It captured the resistance of the Ilongot to the imposition of an empire, Spanish or American, especially the desire of US administrators to bolster their power by intervening in the affairs of their colonized subjects, whether by trial, force, or scientific study. The Ilongot defendants accepted responsibility for their actions, but they did not apologize.

Following the initial death sentence issued by the Court of the First Instance in Nueva Vizcaya Province, the convicts were taken to a prison, where they hoped for a different outcome from the Supreme Court of the Philippines. In his decision, Isidro Paredes, the judge at large for an intermediate court, acting in the Mountain Judicial District, found that the three Ilongot men, though "members of an uncivilized tribe," had "committed the fatal act from what was to them a high sense of duty and obligation, that of the protection of their chief, and not from cruelty and malice."[64] The killing had been committed against a man who was "endeavoring to abduct the[ir] chief." These mitigating circumstances, Paredes wrote, "should be considered in imposing the penalty."[65] It was this statement that would later convince the higher court to bring Article 11 of the penal code into play. On March 21, 1910, Judge Moreland of the Supreme Court of the Philippines characterized the defendants as "ignorant of law and order" and "impregnated with superstitions of a degrading character," thus defining them as members of an uncivilized tribe—precisely the way Jones had sought to see them all along.[66]

The American prosecutors' attempt to fit Jones into the racial narrative of American imperialism had failed. To the Supreme Court of the Philippines, race, politics, and cultural contexts were imbricated with one another. In the Boasian sense, they were mutually interacting variables that all had to be taken into account if one hoped to understand the social situation. The decision only tightened the ideological knot, however, for those in court must have wondered how the United States could maintain control over its colonial subjects when the "uncivilized" among them proved so unmanageable as to escape the death penalty, even when proved guilty of murder.[67]

The victors were not the Ilongot defendants, now sentenced to a life of labor, but the bilingual colonial leaders of the Philippines, who had redefined themselves by carrying out an anti-American and anti-Ilongot judicial doctrine. Fluent in Spanish and English, these adjudicators viewed themselves as the guardians of a delicately balanced civilization, one whose habits and morals they were anxious to protect by contrasting them with the culture of the Ilongot.[68] Moreland's ruling, if lenient compared to the death penalty, nonetheless erased the Ilongots' right to be judged according to their sovereign system of justice. Regardless of how the defendants understood their agency when they chose to accost Jones, they could not escape the policies set forth by the court or the watchful eye of their colonial rulers.

Until, that is, they did just that. Soon after the Supreme Court issued its decision, the *Chicago Tribune* released a shocking report. Immediately after the sentencing, the men who were to have spent their life in prison—Palidat, Magueng, and Gacad—had managed to escape. Apparently this was the result of the "negligence" and "neglect" of Mariano Tugab, Antonio Cruz, and Cecilio Cutaran, three men employed by the Constabulary who were later charged with violating Act No. 619, relative to order and discipline in the Philippines Constabulary. Having Palidat, Magueng, and Gacad "in their charge," the three officers were instructed to take them to Bilibid Prison in Manila. Somewhere along the way, however, the captives escaped. In the eyes of the court, Tugab, Cruz, and Cutaran had "voluntarily disobeyed the express orders received from their officer as to the vigilance, custody, and escorting of the said sentenced prisoners." They were sentenced to a year in prison and forced to reimburse the court for the money spent to prosecute them.[69]

Does the reckless behavior of these Filipino officers of the Constabulary reveal a weakness in America's imperial armor, something the *Chicago Tribune* might not have wished to report? Perhaps, in a moment of solidarity, the "civilized" and "savage" subjects of US imperial power came together to resist the imposition of a judicial ruling that favored the rights of their oppressors. Or perhaps the initial offer of a *carabao* as payment for Jones's life seemed fair enough given the circumstances. In any case, Jones's accused assailants avoided imprisonment. It is said that one of them was captured and returned to jail, but the other two never returned to Manila. They had "probably died" in a spirit of "condolence," sneered the *Chicago Tribune.* Either way, these Native men had thwarted the colonial elite and outrun the grasp of America's imperial power, though their story did become part of the archive Jones left behind.

## IMAGES FROM ECHAGUE

Before their trial and escape the defendants were photographed by an American officer named E. Murray Bruner, who was stationed in Echague. Since there appear to be no other photographs of the defendants, we cannot know with certainty that the men in these images are the people Bruner thought they were, much less Jones's actual assailants. He called them the "Ilongot warriors" accused of murdering Jones. We do know that the subjects are three Native men arrested at Echague. The images therefore offer a glimpse of the atmosphere surrounding the trial.

In one image two of the prisoners sit almost casually on the steps of a house in Echague.[70] Chained together at the ankle, each with his hands bound, they look directly toward the photographer. The Ilongot man on the left seems almost relaxed, sitting slightly slouched, his lips pursed. He holds the viewer's gaze with ease, exuding a sense of pride. The other man, leaning toward his fellow, appears to be caught in midsentence: perhaps he is asking his friend a question or perhaps he is speaking directly to Bruner. Might he be wondering, What do you want a photograph of us for? Or perhaps he is fearful, asking for reassurance.

In a second image the same two men are framed within the context of local Filipinos, themselves colonized subjects of the United States, who appear to be acting as a military police force.[71] There is also one unnamed American official present, his role unknown. Although several Filipinos look upon the prisoners along with the colonial official, both Ilongot men stare directly toward the photographer. Their glares push back against the power of the camera as an imperial apparatus. What, they may wonder, does the photographer see? If so, they are watching not so much to make a statement—to declare their defiance—as to inquire.

In a third image the same men stand in profile, still bound and under the control of armed guards.[72] This reads almost as a documentary moment, capturing the prisoners in transport, either to or from the courthouse. Curiously, and perhaps prefiguring the escape, one of the armed guards in the background looks toward the photographer, his expression one of surprise as much as suspicion. Both of the accused stand erect, one quite comfortably. It seems as if they are asking, Are we the uncivilized ones, or is it you who keep us shackled who are the less civilized among us?

Read together, these three images of the Ilongot prisoners suggest they may have killed Jones as an act of solidarity and resistance. Jones's achievements as an Indigenous anthropologist reveal a complex portrait of a man who resisted being trapped by an American civilization that marginalized the role of an Indian practicing anthropology. While living abroad in the Philippines, Jones at times used anthropology to seek out moments of solidarity among those he was studying. So perhaps the distance between the murder victim and his assailants was not so great as the court or the press would have them be. Ultimately Jones's legacy, even as a temporary agent of imperial America, is the

Ilongot prisoners charged with the murder of William Jones (opposite, top). These photographs were taken by E. Murray Bruner, who was a member of the Philippine Constabulary, First Company Isabella, between 1906 and 1910. Opposite, bottom, the prisoners with an American official. Above, the prisoners in transport. E. Murray Bruner Philippine Image Collection, Southeast Asian Images and Texts, University of Wisconsin–Madison.

archive of materials generated by his colonial journey, which now helps to illustrate how entangled the work of an Indigenous anthropologist became with regard to the Natives of the Philippines.

## Notes

A special thanks to Armand Esai and Lauren Hancock at the Field Museum in Chicago and the archivists at Hampton University and the University of Wisconsin–Madison for their help in acquiring the images for this essay and to Collis Davis for his research and work on William Jones. I am grateful for the scholarly advice I have received from J. Kēhaulani Kauanui at different stages of this project, and I am always grateful for research support made possible by Amherst College and my colleagues in American Studies. Finally, a huge thank you to the editors of this collection for their tireless efforts in making this piece the best it could be.

1. *United States v. Ilongots Palidat et al.*, Mar. 1910 decision, G.R. no. L-5620 Mar. 21, 1910, Philippine Supreme Court Decisions Online, Chan Robles Virtual Law Library, accessed Mar. 12, 2013, www.chanrobles.com/index1.htm. For court records pertaining to previous rulings by the provincial court, see copies of the criminal complaint and case documents in Box 4, Folder 33, R. F. Cummings Expedition to the Philippines, 1906–1911, Field Museum of Natural History Archives, Chicago, Illinois (hereafter FM).
2. James Clifford, "On Ethnographic Authority," *Representations* 1, no. 2 (1983): 119, 139.
3. Henry Milner Rideout, *William Jones: Indian, Cowboy, American Scholar, and Anthropologist in the Field* (New York: Frederick A. Stokes, 1912), 191.
4. Ibid., 194; "Luzon Explorer Safe in Chicago: Dr. S. Chapman Simms Returns with Stories of Sleepless Nights, Facing Peril," *Chicago Daily Tribune*, Feb. 6, 1910, 5.
5. Rideout, *William Jones*, 194.
6. Ibid., 193.
7. Ibid., 202.
8. "Luzon Explorer Safe in Chicago: Dr. S. Chapman Simms Returns with Stories of Sleepless Nights, Facing Peril," *Chicago Daily Tribune*, Feb. 6, 1910, 5.
9. Ibid., 204.
10. Ibid., 205.
11. *The United States v. The Ilongots Palidat et al.*, Apr. 25, 1909. Box 4, Folder 33, R. F. Cummings Expedition to the Philippines, 1906–1911, FM.
12. *United States of America vs. Antonio Cruz, Mariano Tugab, and Cecilio Cutaran*, Nov. 8, 1909, Box 4, Folder 33, R. F. Cummings Expedition to the Philippines, 1906–1911, FM.
13. Donal F. Lindsey, *Indians at Hampton Institute, 1877–1923* (Urbana: University of Illinois Press, 1995), 18, 165.
14. Rideout, *William Jones*, 24–35.
15. On this "Americanization" project, see Hayes Peter Mauro, *The Art of Americanization at the Carlisle Indian School* (Albuquerque: University of New Mexico Press, 2011).
16. Kiara M. Vigil, *Indigenous Intellectuals: Sovereignty, Citizenship, and the American Imagination, 1880–1930* (New York: Cambridge University Press, 2015).
17. Rideout, *William Jones*, 44–45.
18. Barbara Stoner, "Why Was William Jones Killed?" *Field Museum of Natural History Bulletin* 42, no. 8 (1971): 10–13; Sophilia Keahna, "Meskwaki Anthology: William Jones," April 1998, accessed Aug. 22, 2017 at http://meskwakipowwow.com/Meskwaki%20History/MeskinteractiveCD1/Pages/Culture/Anthology/Keahna%20William%20Jones.htm.
19. Ibid., 9.
20. Ibid., 11.
21. Ibid., 12.
22. Gerald Vizenor, *The People Named the Chippewa: Narrative Histories* (Minneapolis: University of Minnesota Press, 1984), 155; Chip Colwell-Chanthaphonh, *Inheriting the Past: The Making of Arthur C. Parker and Indigenous Archaeology* (Tucson: University of Arizona Press, 2009), 59.
23. Rosalyn R. LaPier and David R. M. Beck, *City Indian: Native American Activism in Chicago, 1893–1934* (Lincoln: University of Nebraska Press, 2015), 52–55.

24. Rideout, *William Jones,* 106.
25. Brian W. Dippie, *The Vanishing American: White Attitudes and U.S. Indian Policy* (Lawrence: University Press of Kansas, 1991); Robert F. Berkhofer, *The White Man's Indian: Images of the American Indian from Columbus to the Present* (New York: Knopf, 1978).
26. James W. VanStone, "Mesquakie (Fox) Material Culture: The William Jones and Frederick Starr Collections," in *Fieldiana. Anthropology,* n.s., 30 (1998): i–iv, 1–89; William Jones, *Ethnography of the Fox Indians,* ed. Margaret Welpley Fisher, Bureau of American Ethnology Bulletin 125 (Washington: Government Printing Office, 1939).
27. Douglas Cole, *Franz Boas: The Early Years, 1858–1906* (Seattle: University of Washington Press, 1999).
28. William Jones, "Some Principles of Algonquian Word-Formation," *American Anthropologist,* n.s., 6, no. 3 (1904): 369–411.
29. Franz Boas, *Handbook of American Indian Languages,* pt. 2, Bureau of American Ethnology Bulletin 40 (Washington: Government Printing Office, 1922).
30. David L. Browman and Stephen Williams, *Anthropology at Harvard: A Biographical History, 1790–1940,* Peabody Museum Monographs 11 (Cambridge: Harvard University Press, 2013), 262.
31. Ibid.
32. Rideout, *William Jones,* 121.
33. Ibid, 127.
34. Ibid.
35. See Paul A. Kramer, *The Blood of Government: Race, Empire, the United States, and the Philippines* (Chapel Hill: University of North Carolina Press, 2006), 178.
36. Rideout, *William Jones,* 128.
37. Winthrop D. Jordan, *The White Man's Burden: Historical Origins of Racism in the United States* (Oxford: Oxford University Press, 1974), 205–6; Kramer, *The Blood of Government,* 7, 11–12, 121, 158.
38. William Jones to Franz Boas, June 18, 1906; William Jones to Marie Boas, July 1, 1906; Franz Boas to William Jones, Sept. 18, 1906; William Jones to Franz Boas, July 28, 1907, Franz Boas Papers, American Philosophical Society, Philadelphia, Pennsylvania.
39. Rideout, *William Jones,* 129.
40. See Ann Laura Stoler, ed., *Haunted by Empire: Geographies of Intimacy in North American History* (Durham: Duke University Press, 2006), and *Carnal Knowledge and Imperial Power: Race and the Intimate in Colonial Rule* (Berkeley: University of California Press, 2002).
41. William Jones, diary entry, Manila, Oct. 6, 1907, quoted in Rideout, *William Jones,* 130.
42. Renato Rosaldo, *Ilongot Headhunting, 1883–1974: A Study in Society and History* (Stanford: Stanford University Press, 1980), 8–9.
43. William Jones, diary entry, Echague, Nov. 1907, quoted in Rideout, *William Jones,* 135.
44. Ibid.
45. Ibid.
46. William Jones, diary entry, Cagayan, Apr. 10, 1907, quoted ibid., 139–40. Lorenzo was later replaced by the more capable Romano Dumaliang, who would witness Jones's murder.
47. William Jones, diary entry, Saturday Apr. 11, 1907, quoted ibid., 140–41.

48. William Jones to George Dorsey, May 7, 1908, quoted ibid., 147.
49. Ibid.
50. Ibid., 154.
51. William Jones to Smith, July 12, 1908, quoted ibid., 155.
52. Ibid.
53. William Jones, diary entry, May 25, 1908, quoted ibid., 152.
54. Jack London, *The Call of the Wild* (New York: Macmillan, 1903).
55. William Jones to Marlborough, Feb. 25, 1909, Department of Anthropology Archives, FM; see also Rideout, *William Jones,* 195–97.
56. William Jones to Marlborough, Feb. 25, 1909, quoted in Rideout, *William Jones,* 198–99.
57. Ibid.
58. Ibid.
59. "Luzon Explorer Safe in Chicago," 5.
60. Ibid.
61. Ibid.
62. For copies of court records documenting the Jones murder trial, see the criminal complaint: *The United States v. The Ilongots Palidat et al.*, Apr. 25, 1909, and the criminal case: *United States of America vs. Antonio Cruz, Mariano Tugab, and Cecilio Cutaran,* Nov. 8 1909, Box 4, Folder 33, R. F. Cummings Expedition to the Philippines 1906–1911, FM. See also Collis Davis, *Headhunting William Jones* (Manilla, PH: Okara Video, 2016), DVD.
63. *The United States v. The Ilongots Palidat et al.*, Apr. 25, 1909, Box 4, Folder 33, R. F. Cummings Expedition to the Philippines, 1906–1911, FM.
64. *United States v. Ilongots Palidat et al.*, Mar. 1910 decision, G.R. no. L-5620 Mar. 21, 1910, Philippine Supreme Court Decisions Online, Chan Robles Virtual Law Library, accessed Mar. 12, 2013.
65. Ibid.
66. Ibid.
67. Kramer, *The Blood of Government,* 13, 212; Stoler, *Haunted by Empire,* 94–97; Julian Go and Anne L. Foster, eds., *The American Colonial State in the Philippines: Global Perspectives* (Durham: Duke University Press, 2003), 182–216.
68. Rosaldo, *Ilongot Headhunting,* 2–9; Kramer, *The Blood of Government,* 119, 139.
69. *United States of America vs. Antonio Cruz, Mariano Tugab, and Cecilio Cutaran,* Nov. 8 1909, Box 4, Folder 33, R. F. Cummings Expedition to the Philippines, 1906–1911, FM.
70. E. Murray Bruner, "Ilongot Prisoners Implicated in Murder of Dr. Jones" [ca. 1909], E. Murray Bruner Philippine Image Collection, Center for Southeast Asian Studies, University of Wisconsin–Madison (hereafter UWM).
71. E. Murray Bruner, "Ilongot Warriors with American" [ca. 1909], E. Murray Bruner Philippine Image Collection, Center for Southeast Asian Studies, UWM.
72. E. Murray Bruner, "Bruner's House, Echague, P.I." [ca. 1909], E. Murray Bruner Philippine Image Collection, Center for Southeast Asian Studies, UWM. A description on the back of the photograph reads, "Dr. William Jones's killers in the custody of Filipino troops."

# Chapter 10 Woman on the Verge of a Cultural Breakdown: Zora Neale Hurston in Haiti and the Racial Privilege of Boasian Relativism

*Eve Dunbar*

Facts go down mighty hard with some folks, confirming my conviction that there is nothing so precious that men know as what they *want* to believe.
Letter from Zora Neale Hurston to Ruth Benedict

*Being broke made all the difference.* Without money of one's own in a capitalist society, there is no such thing as independence.
Alice Walker, "Zora Neale Hurston: A Cautionary Tale and a Partisan View"

In her ethnography of Haiti, *Tell My Horse* (1938), Zora Neale Hurston conjures zombies at the margins of American modernity. "Here in the shadow of the Empire State Building, death and the graveyard are final," Hurston writes from the vantage of New York City. "It is such a positive end that we use it as a measure of nothingness and eternity. We have the quick and the dead. But in Haiti there is the quick, the dead, and then there are Zombies."[1]

At first glance Hurston's categories of life and death in the United States appear fixed when read against the mutability of those same human conditions in Haiti. That fixedness might, in turn, seem to be an affirmation of national and racial hierarchies that posit the United States as a site of a rational and thus stable modernity. Yet Hurston's revelation of Haitian zombies resists such stable nationalistic differences. Because unlike the reanimated corpses that will shuffle through the American imaginary throughout the twentieth and twenty-first centuries. Hurston's zombies tell an untold story about race, gender, and anthropology. In Hurston's work we can begin to understand that the horror of zombie existence lies not in the fear that the *un*-dead might mindlessly devour the living, but in the reality that the act of documenting zombies speaks volumes about the horrors of the discipline into which Hurston was trained to write. When one looks upon Hurston's snapshot of Felicia Felix-Mentor, the first "zombie" ever captured on film, we are forced to face her proposition. Hurston is asking her readers to think deeply about the limits of "looking" at a black culture through the lens of American anthropology.

Before we look closely at Hurston's zombie, let's turn our eyes to another set of images, which will help to explain Hurston's obsession with the walking undead. Sandwiched between an article detailing the participation of African Americans in the War of 1812 and photographs of black women with perfectly coifed press 'n' curls, the December 1978 issue of the NAACP's *Crisis* magazine offers an unexpected glimpse of Zora Neale Hurston. She reveals herself in the issue's closing article, an announcement detailing the University of Florida's establishment of a Zora Neale Hurston Fellowship. Just eighteen years after Hurston's death, the article reports that the Hurston fellowship has been established to support an African American student in anthropology at the university. Coinciding with the beginning of Hurston's literary revival within the academy, the fellowship pinpoints a nascent commemoration within the black community of Hurston's contribution to the field of anthropology.[2]

The revival of Hurston's contributions to African American literature, American literature, and feminist studies proved so successful that by 1990 the scholar Hazel Carby would conclude that Hurston had been remade into a profitable industry by forces within the academy.[3] Notwithstanding Carby's explicit critique of the implicit racism behind the Hurston industry, the mainstream field of anthropology would take at least another decade to begin to acknowledge Hurston as a key originator of the postmodern methods utilized by many in the discipline. Hurston trained under Franz Boas when she was a student at Barnard College in the late 1920s; she even briefly enrolled as a graduate student in Columbia's Department of Anthropology. Although she never earned her doctoral degree, she would go on to publish two book-length ethnographies, *Mules and Men* (1935) and *Tell My Horse,* and write a variety of nonfiction pieces centered on the study of black diasporic cultures ranging from the American South to British Honduras and the Caribbean. So it may seem odd that two decades after the establishment in 1978 of a fellowship in

Zora Neale Hurston at drum, 1937. Library of Congress LC-USZ62–109672.

anthropology named in her honor, the American Anthropological Association (AAA) would still need educating on Hurston's disciplinary influence.

The historic tendency of the discipline to write out its marginalized members is confirmed throughout Louise Lamphere's 2001 presidential address to the AAA, in which she implored the association's members to consider "the contributions of selected women and minorities" connected to the most iconic figures of the discipline.[4] On the eve of the association's centennial, Lamphere recounted to her colleagues that "these women and minorities either struggled to gain a place at the center or remained marginal relative to their colleagues and mentors during their lifetimes."[5] Hurston is among the people Lamphere attempted to reintroduce to the AAA. Her vision of an anthropology from the "margins" suggests that one hundred years into its formal history, the field of American anthropology still had a few kinks to work out around issues of race, ethnicity, and gender. Moreover, it confirms that as late as the dawn of the twenty-first century the majority of anthropology's professional members would still be unable to recognize someone like Hurston as an important predecessor—someone who introduced key methodological and textual innovations to their field.

In this essay I argue that in spite of her training by Boas and her work as an intellectual arm of his theoretical and methodological machine, designed to push the discipline in new directions, Hurston's marginality to the discipline was no mere accident. I suggest that when recounting the history of how American anthropology positively challenged and changed foundational notions about racial difference and diversity in the United States, one must also account for the erasure of Hurston's centrality to narratives of modern anthropology's methodological innovations around diversity. Through the use of archival materials and Hurston's own scholarly production, I flesh out a story that rests squarely within the tension created by Hurston's sense of the discipline's desire to write her out. Hurston's failed attempts to circumvent her removal through an adherence to old disciplinary standards finally inspired her revolutionary critique of those very disciplinary standards within her work.

I'll focus on Hurston's Caribbean ethnography, *Tell My Horse,* paying special attention to a few textual examples in which she attempts to distinguish herself from laypersons treating Haiti in order to textually frame herself as a trained ethnographer. I focus on these framing moments to explore how Hurston makes use of what Judith Butler describes as *subversive repetition,* or the manipulation of disciplinary mores and practices around knowledge production that entails the simultaneous employment of and critique of these practices and mores in an attempt to subvert them.[6] Finally, I'll argue that what looks like adherence to the established tenets of the discipline's methods is always undergirded by a critical self-reflexivity indicative of Hurston's own sense of the profession and what would make for best practices in representing her work as a black ethnographer working within the black diaspora.

At the crux of my analysis rests a critique of capital and disciplinary gatekeeping that effectively produced a form of financial exclusion that contributed to Hurston's fall into poverty. Although Carby called Hurston studies an industry, Hurston herself never benefited from long-term financial stability through her creative and academic work. Much has been made of her status as a darling of the Harlem Renaissance, but Hurston never made more than $953.75 in royalties from any one of her books.[7] These funds would have been a windfall in the life of someone who lacked steady employment in her vocation of choice, but they weren't consistent. Hurston's professional narrative and the body of knowledge she helped to produce without ever fully reaping the economic rewards remind us that there are limits to diversification—institutional, social, and scholarly—when that diversification does not entail an institutional commitment to deep structural change in the areas of race, class, and gender.

## LETTERS IN INEQUITY: RUTH BENEDICT AND ZORA NEALE HURSTON IN THE ARCHIVE

There are a few missives between Ruth Benedict and Zora Neale Hurston among the Benedict papers housed in Vassar College's Special Collections. The papers of Benedict, one of Vassar's most well-known graduates, are a rich trove for any student interested in understanding the role she played in the early development of modern American anthropology, especially as it was practiced and taught at Columbia University from the 1920s to the 1940s. The archive contains more than Benedict's papers. As Boas's intellectual beneficiary, Benedict also retained many of Boas's teaching notes upon his retirement. The few letters between Hurston and Benedict, and those *about* Hurston written by Benedict and sent to others, reveal some things about the relationship between the two women and each woman's relationship to Boas and the field of anthropology. But more than merely revealing a set of relationships, the archive tells the story of the different professional paths open to different women in the early part of the twentieth century. Specifically, the archive reveals the limited paths to the profession available to a single, black woman during the early part of the twentieth century.

Hurston would spend a lifetime as the "junior scholar" to Benedict. Although the women were close in age—Benedict was born in 1887 and Hurston in 1891—Benedict was well established in the field of anthropology by the time their exchange began in 1932. She was teaching and serving as the administrative chair of Columbia's Department of Anthropology. Hurston, on the other hand, who had graduated from Barnard in 1928, spent the years after college collecting folklore in the American South and publishing the results in well-known folklore journals, writing and publishing short fiction, getting married and divorced, doing a little teaching, and staging theatrical reviews of some of the folk materials she collected. The latter effort is what brought Hurston and Benedict into correspondence.

The association captured in the archive begins through the mediation of a woman named Mary B. Chaffee. In a letter written to Benedict in February

1932, Chaffee identifies herself as Benedict's former student: "In the summer of 1928, when I sat under you—very close under: I was always in the front row—in your class in Anthropology. If you remember me at all it is probably as the oldest woman you ever had as a pupil."[8] Chaffee, hailing from a class of women for whom education serves the primary purpose of self-edification rather than professional development, goes on to tell Benedict that she happened to run into Hurston at a musical performance that Hurston organized for Rollins College in Winter Park, Florida. Chaffee praises Hurston's musical arrangement and keen attention to "negro" cultural difference in her recounting of the Florida event to Benedict. She goes on to suggest that the quality of Hurston's work and their shared experience with Boas and Benedict is what brought them into correspondence. Chaffee's letter not only illustrates the small intellectual circle within which women who shared elite educational experiences circulated but also gives some insight into Benedict's stature as an influential teacher and scholar in her day. While much of the letter serves as an occasion for Chaffee to plead Hurston's case, it is also a space for her to prove that she is part of an educated liberal class that knows, values, and is able to access the quality of cultural authenticity and difference. At some level Chaffee's letter rests on her implicit understanding of the sort of social cachet that can be garnered by a white, upper-middle-class woman trained to have the properly Boasian cosmopolitan palate.

The exchange is not without its benefit to Hurston. After demonstrating her social sensitivity, Chaffee tells Benedict that the real purpose of her letter is to help Hurston. A selection from the letter, excerpted below, illuminates a set of professional and personal realities that Hurston faced as a black woman:

> [Hurston] asked me to write about something, which really has brought me to the point of writing this letter which accompanies the program. At first I demurred about doing so, but later consented, believing that I could help her, busy woman as she is. In addition to her work among her people she is doing housework to repay a debt, and she has recently lost a sister.
>
> Miss Hurston asked me to ask you how much she owes to the Scientific Society that published her work. *She wants more copies of the book, realizes that she cannot have them without paying her dues.* If she knows the amount, she will try to raise the money and send it on.[9]

Chaffee's request to Benedict for an accounting of Hurston's dues highlights the very ways in which Hurston was forced by financial difficulty to have a nonproprietary relationship to her research. According to Chaffee, Hurston is in debt to her professional society, and she is also paying off a debt to some unnamed source, which requires her to supplement her professional work with domestic labor in order to eke out a living. These conflicting realities, the desire to set one's professional agenda and the need to work as a domestic servant, are what best characterize Hurston's experience in the scholarly and artistic-professional world of anthropology. She is neither a lady of leisure, like Chaffee, nor a stable professional ethnographer and folklorist like Benedict. Her identity as a working-class black woman is directly at odds with her ability to formulate a stable identity as a professional folklorist.

The intersectional reality of Hurston's professional and financial insecurity may be elucidated through comparison with Benedict's situation. Both Hurston and Benedict came from fairly humble beginnings: Hurston was raised by her widowed father, who was a preacher in the now-famous town of Eatonville, Florida; Benedict was raised by her widowed mother, a schoolteacher, with some help from her religious grandparents, farmers in upstate New York. Benedict was not wealthy by any stretch of the imagination. In fact, she was able to attend Vassar College only because of the sponsorship of a family friend. But black wealth has historically been paltry when compared to white wealth. Unlike Hurston, Benedict enjoyed access to formal educational credentialing, whiteness, and marital status, all of which afforded her the luxury to financially absorb the sexism of the period.

This is not to suggest that Benedict's life was without its inequity. Records at Columbia University show that Benedict received no salary between 1925 and 1928 while working there as a lecturing faculty member.[10] Her colleague and biographer, Margaret Mead, contends that while Boas came to treat Benedict as his "second self," entrusting his teaching to her and discussing with her a variety of professional issues, he didn't seek to formalize her relationship to Columbia's Department of Anthropology until she separated from her husband, Stanley Benedict, in 1930.[11] Upon her separation Boas secured Benedict an assistant professorship at the university, guaranteeing her a steady income and professional stature. As Virginia Young notes, this income was coupled with an inheritance from her husband's estate upon his death in 1936.[12] Although Benedict was far from a model of heteronormative, white femininity—she would partner with women throughout her adult life—she did receive long-term financial security from her early performance of sexual normativity and white womanhood.[13] Obviously the ill effects of sexism conspired to devalue Benedict's labor, especially while she was with her husband, yet she was able to leverage her whiteness, womanhood, and educational credentialing in ways that ensured her access to lifelong professional standing and financial security.

Such financial security and white-collar work would have been nearly unattainable for the majority of black men and women in the early decades of the twentieth century. Even a college-educated black woman who had been married remained limited in her earning potential and employment options owing to well-established racist labor practices in the United States. The historian Jacqueline Jones reminds us that for black Americans the increasing modernization and industrial progress of the early twentieth century replicated and reinforced "centuries-old traditions of labor exploitation."[14] Such exploitation was made possible by the Jim Crowing of jobs, which created a race-based labor system that marked some jobs as white and others as black.[15] Black jobs did not promise upward mobility, and well into the twentieth century black people had very little access to white work: "The structure of the paid labor force consistently thwarted black talent and ambition."[16]

One can see such work stratification in Hurston's life. For instance, in 1925 Hurston noted in her "Record of Freshman Interest" form at Barnard that she planned to pay for her living expenses while enrolled in college by working as "either a manicurist, social work, or waitress. Perhaps sell a manuscript or two."[17] While Benedict had her education at Vassar paid for by family friends, even making a postgraduation tour of Europe on the dime of a college friend's parents, Hurston knew that the expenses of living would be hers alone to bear.[18] Hurston saw the options in front of her as either service-oriented or artistic. Although she imagined that art might be a way out of more menial forms of labor, the triple bind resulting from the intersection of race, class, and gender defined her life in ways that higher education and artistry could not counteract. Though Piper Huguley-Riggins focuses on Hurston's autobiographical crafting of herself as a model of female professional possibility in post-World War II American society, for Hurston, if not for the Hurston industry, this sense of possibility was always tightly circumscribed. Hurston returned to domestic work throughout her lifetime because it was the only work *always* available to African American women.[19] She may have imagined and represented herself beyond the reach of Jim Crow, but it was a constant touchstone in her life.

In Chaffee's letter, then, we see Hurston attempting to use a white, female intermediary to guide Benedict, a senior female working in the role of professional gatekeeper, toward opening professional channels that remained closed to Hurston due to the realities of class, race, and gender. The intermediary proved useful. In February 1933, a year after Chaffee's posted letter, Benedict writes to Hurston inquiring as to whether she has received copies of the hoodoo essays that Chaffee requested on her behalf. Benedict also tells

Hurston that she need not worry about sending the dues for the Scientific Society until she absolutely has the money to pay them. Moreover, Benedict has secured over a hundred copies of Hurston's article, which will be available to her upon her return to New York City. The only thing Benedict requests from Hurston in return is Hurston's "unedited manuscript that was the result of [her] first trip," a folklore expedition in the American South, and "permission to edit it" so that it might be published in the society's journal.[20]

Hurston's correspondence suggests that she was keenly aware of the barter system—information in return for access to financial support and other research resources—into which she was stepping with Benedict. While Hurston asks Chaffee to write to Benedict because she herself is "too busy," Hurston does, in fact, find the time to post a letter to Benedict in April 1932, two months after Chaffee's letter. Hurston begins her letter by offering Benedict access to photographs and motion picture footage of conjuring ceremonies taken by one Faustin Wirkus, whose relationship to Haiti I'll explore a bit later in this essay. Hurston tells Benedict that Wirkus "has no formal preparation for the [collecting] work. But he is an excellent photographer and an intelligent man" who is interested in taking more documentary images.[21] This offer of access to images and information allows Hurston to launch into a funding request to start a comparative research project between conjuring practices in the West Indies and the United States. Hurston assures Benedict that it should cost only five hundred dollars for transportation plus six months' living expenses to do the research, and she wonders whether "the Dept. or any private individual could be induced to put up a little money for me to go to the Bahamas for a few months."[22]

While Hurston is well past her graduation from Barnard, throughout the early and mid-1930s she continues to maintain a research agenda and a relationship to Columbia faculty like Boas and Benedict. In fact, Hurston responds to Benedict's February 1932 request for her unedited manuscript by reminding Benedict that such publications are in direct violation of her contract with Charlotte Osgood Mason, who has been her funding source since 1927. Hurston writes in the February 1933 letter to Benedict, "You see I am down [in Florida] on very small income. Nothing from Mrs. Mason any more because I gave the conjure material to the Folklore Society. I don't care. I am getting on any way. But it was touch and go for the first month or two after her sudden cutting me off."[23] Hurston is still unable to pay the fees for the reprints that Chaffee referenced in her 1932 letter to Benedict, but she wants to let Benedict know that she is good for the money once she is able to get funds from her local supporters in Florida, who have taken up a subscription on her behalf.

I have described the exchange between Benedict and Hurston as one in which Hurston attempted to engage in a kind of barter, exchanging information for access to the professional resources collected at Columbia, where Benedict sits at the helm.[24] Yet this exchange, like most involving minority members of elite institutions, is not without its own form of exploitation. While Benedict was clearly engaged in supporting Hurston's research agenda, there is evidence that Benedict did not consider Hurston a member of the profession. I will focus on three particular moments captured in Benedict's correspondence in order to flesh out the story of Hurston's erasure: a letter from Benedict regarding Hurston's Guggenheim fellowship application; an early book review of *Mules and Men* that Benedict completes for Lippincott publishing house; and a postcard Hurston sends Benedict regarding the publication of *Mules and Men*. I am in no way suggesting that Benedict consciously ended Hurston's career within the profession. Rather, I suggest that in these ephemera we can begin to see the limits of interpersonal relationships when one of the parties is a black woman within an overwhelmingly white profession. Even when one is dealing on a regular basis with one of the most important female gatekeepers—a status earned by being a proxy for the ultimate gatekeeper, Franz Boas—the profession discounts the very work that one attempts to complete within the confines of a Jim Crowed labor system that has little space for a noncredentialed black woman.[25]

The first document is a letter from Benedict to a Guggenheim representative, a Dr. Moe, dated November 15, 1933. Before I turn to this letter, readers should remember that Hurston has spent the majority of the time between 1932 and the end of 1933 in direct and indirect negotiations with Benedict regarding funding while she was in "the field," that is, living in Florida. Not only does Hurston continuously ask Benedict to overlook a debt owed to the professional society, she also asks her to find departmental funds or a private donor to support her collecting trips. Hurston tells Benedict that she is also doing her part to secure funding via the Guggenheim Foundation. In the handwritten postscript to the April 1932 letter Hurston writes, "I am applying for a Guggenheim. If I can get it, I shall do my 'foreign' work in the West Indies. Bahamas, St. Martinique and perhaps a month or two in Hayti."[26]

A little more than a year after receiving the note from Hurston, on November 15, 1933, Benedict writes to a Guggenheim representative as follows: "I am shocked to find Zora Hurston's application in my desk. It had been slipped into the wrong file and overlooked. As you will see from my report on the application I don't think she is Guggenheim material, and I hope some of her patrons will provide the money for this trip and that she'll write up her experiences when she returns in collaboration with some anthropologist."[27] It would be pure speculation to comment upon the exact cause of the "shock" Benedict experiences upon finding Hurston's application in her desk. Is it produced because she misplaced her comments and is sending them in late; is it because she is surprised that she might be asked to review Hurston due to a potential conflict of interest; is it because she doesn't imagine Hurston's application could have moved so far through the review process as to arrive on her desk? What is clear is that Benedict does not believe Hurston worthy of institutional funding. Part of Hurston's lack of worthiness must be tied to the fact that Benedict doesn't perceive Hurston to be an actual anthropologist, as evidenced by her suggestion to the Guggenheim representative that Hurston might write up her experiences in the field in collaboration with an anthropologist.

The second document to which I turn is an early review of Hurston's *Mules and Men* written by Benedict to the publisher J. B. Lippincott, which illustrates the limited role within the profession that Benedict imagined for Hurston. In the short paragraph about the book, Benedict manages to shift Hurston's role within the field away from that of an ethnographer by stating that "no white man could have [access to black culture] without Miss Hurston's expert reporting." Hurston grants white readers access to black culture by fitting them "*with a cap of invisibility and lets [them] listen* to the shrewd, off-guard talk and jesting and storytelling of the Negroes of the Florida Everglades."[28] Benedict's sly transitioning of Hurston from ethnographer to reporter shifts the work Hurston should be recognized as completing from that of cultural analysis to that of transcription. I say this because the act of transcribing suggests a verbatim accounting of events, which itself belies the innovative work of ethnographic narrative that Hurston perfects in *Mules and Men.* Moreover, the frame of transcription suggests that Hurston's only role is to produce a text for the use of white voyeurs or, at best, white anthropologists. In either case, and in Benedict's estimation, Hurston hasn't produced a text that highlights her own capacity to analyze and make sense of black culture; rather, she has collected material that a "white man" could not have accessed, but that he (or *she,* Benedict) might later mine to produce true cultural analysis.

The final document is an undated postcard to Benedict in which Hurston exclaims in her handwritten script, "Yes, Lippincott is publishing the folk-tales and making an elaborate edition of it."[29] She goes on to tell Benedict that the publishing house has asked that she write the text for a nonscientific audience—it will lack documentation but have what Hurston describes as "inter-story dialogue." Hurston makes no concession that publishing ethnographic texts for the general public might be perceived as evidence of her professional failure; to the contrary, Hurston urges Benedict to also consider writing a book on American Indians for Lippincott. She boldly suggests to Benedict that an "Indian book of tales and ceremonies from a spectator or participant with plenty of *color* would be a great success."[30] This postscript, located in the top right corner of the postcard, is significant for a variety of reasons. One might detect an element of sly criticism leveled against professionals like Benedict, who write on themes and in ways that fail to engage a general-interest audience. It's impossible to say if that was Hurston's intention, but it is clear that Hurston has a sense of what American audiences might be inclined to consume. She knows there is money to be made from educating and making knowledge palatable to a wider audience than the small circle of professional social scientists.[31]

Once published, *Mules and Men* was well-received by audiences, illustrating that Hurston's sense of her work as an ethnographic innovation was correct, at least in the eyes of those who read it. Yet Hurston's career path gets no more clear or easy after the book's publication. In early 1935, just a few months before *Mules and Men* is published, Hurston briefly enrolls in the Columbia anthropology doctoral program. This experience is short-lived because her graduate funding source, the Rosenwald Fellowship, does not honor its original agreement to fund her through two years of study. According to Hurston in a letter to Benedict, the Rosenwald grant officers have told her they suspect Hurston to be a transient figure in the graduate program. "Now a little more than a month ago I had a letter from Dr. Embree saying that he had two letters from Dr. Boas," Hurston writes Benedict, "and the arrangement here at Columbia did not seem permanent enough to warrant the two year grant."[32] Hurston quickly drops out of Columbia's graduate program, thereby cutting short her chances of forging a truly formal relationship to the department and the profession.[33] In the next phase of her career one can begin to see what happens when a writer of Hurston's caliber and training moves beyond challenging the conventions of the field in order to perform the formal relationship so casually denied her.

## IF I WERE A NEGRO: THE PROBLEM OF DEEP RELATIVISM

Composed from material collected during her two years of Guggenheim-funded research in the Caribbean, Hurston's *Tell My Horse* received mixed reviews upon its publication in 1938. The *New York Times Book Review* favorably noted *Tell My Horse*'s publication, dubbing it an "unusual and intensely interesting book, richly packed with strange information."[34] Conversely, the *New Yorker*'s "Briefly Noted Fiction" section heralded the text by calling it "disorganized."[35] Between those two extremes, Elmer Davis argued in his *Saturday Review* essay that Hurston's ethnography was the antidote to previous treatments of the black Caribbean, which had depicted the area through either the lens of sensationalism or that of "mathematical" science.[36] Seven decades have not clarified the mixed reception. The text is considered Hurston's least culturally sensitive, most blatant work of US imperial gazing.[37] Ifeoma Nwankwo argues that Hurston's work, "while pioneering within the context of US black (women's) intellectual thought, also provides an example of the shades of the ethnocentrism that have continued to haunt transnational engagements between black people."[38] *Tell My Horse* poses an interpretative problem for Hurston scholars.

Yet, I would argue that what some critics over the decades have read as textual inadequacy might be the result of Hurston's commitment to the philosophical and methodological teachings central to a Boasian understanding of relativism. I would go further to argue that Hurston's own brand of self-reflexivity may have allowed her to conceive of the pitfalls that befall the black American writing about the black Caribbean. It's the tension between her adherence to methods and her critique and manipulation of those methods that makes *Tell My Horse* a text that invites mixed critical reception. Hurston's work might be read as a form of subversive repetition, allowing Hurston to work out her own race–gender status within a field that presumed a universalized subject in the form of the ethnographer. In other words, what *Tell My Horse* shows us isn't so much Hurston's failure to adhere to the conventions of the discipline, but her critique of the deep relativism that is inaccessible to the black ethnographer working on the black diaspora.

Benedict's work, once again, poses a foil for reconciling Hurston's seemingly paradoxical adherence to disciplinary expectations with her desire to critique. In an unpublished essay entitled "If I Were a Negro," Benedict works to hone her own skill at Boasian "deep relativism" by imagining herself the subject of racism in the United States.[39] What Benedict calls deep relativism is the practice of analyzing the subject of analysis thoughtfully and ethically in order to illustrate the moral transformation of thought made possible by Boasian relativity. "If I Were a Negro" is a short essay. Benedict imagines herself "suffering" under the social stigma of race: "I should have to steel myself against how the elevator man and the people riding in the elevator might treat me," she laments. She then moves back to her own racial self-identification by enumerating her advantages: "Being a white, I haven't been through the mill which grinds out repetitiously day after day this plea for human decency; it hasn't gotten so deep under my skin. I am on the top looking down and that is inevitably different from being on the bottom looking up. I can't forget. If I were a

Negro I couldn't. 'They' wouldn't let me."[40] In this essay Benedict not only practices deep relativism but also illustrates that the practice makes possible cultural empathy that could conceivably challenge inequality based on beliefs of racial difference and inferiority.

Yet what reads as an acute capacity to imagine and empathize with the culture of others owes much of its possibility to Benedict's access to aspects of white supremacy. In other words, Benedict can successfully imagine what life would be like for her if she were "a Negro" precisely because she is *not* black. The deep relativism that allows Benedict to imagine from above what it might mean to be "a Negro" is inaccessible to Hurston.

Unlike Benedict, Hurston doesn't have the luxury of imagining how difficult it might be to be a black person living in the Caribbean because she understands that her audience would probably have little capacity to distinguish the differences between her and other members of the black diaspora. It's this presumed inability of white readers to distinguish African Americans from members of the black Caribbean that encourages me to read Hurston's text through the lens of what Stephanie Batiste calls "imperial representation." Imperial representation describes performance practices in which African Americans identify as agents of US imperial power. One feature of the practice is the black American's use of tropes of domination when representing other members of the black diaspora. Accepting that African Americans perform imperial representations allows us to see black Americans as having "fluency in dominant cultural forms that glorify nation, celebrate modernity, and emphasize the difference of others."[41] Hurston's use of imperial representation takes the form of her employment of a dominant anthropological voice in *Tell My Horse.* While the black Caribbean at large would have been a research site that allowed Hurston to exercise a will to act as an American imperialist among nonwhite subjects, it also afforded her a people with whom she could share some racial affinity and pride. This dual relationship is experienced by many African Americans representing other members of the black diaspora.

Moreover, Haiti's long history of racial revolution and black sovereignty, paradoxically coupled with its occupation by the US military from 1915 to 1934, would have provided a fertile historical field for African American imperial representation. Haiti could offer Hurston both a mirror and a foil to conduct the sort of self-reflexive cultural analysis that would mark her brand of ethnographic production. As Mary Renda suggests, Hurston picked Haiti as her research site because the island's decades-long military occupation bolstered the American taste for "the exotic." In Haiti, Hurston found a locale where she could personally benefit from American paternalism while also

Felicia Felix-Mentor, as photographed in Haiti by Zora Neale Hurston, who sold her picture of the woman to Time Inc. "THIS IS THE ONLY ZOMBIE EVER PHOTOGRAPHED," proclaims the caption below Felix-Mentor's portrait in the December 12, 1937, issue of *Life* magazine.

challenging hegemonic forms of that paternalism.[42] The tension between benefiting from and critiquing US imperialism speaks to the dual relationship of Hurston to the methods of her profession.

A variety of rhetorical evocations of professional authority are weaved through Hurston's ethnography of the black Caribbean. She represents herself not only as a professional trained in the methods of ethnography but also as one of the only people, outside of Melville Herskovits, capable of representing the black Caribbean and voodoo culture.[43] One example of Hurston's unique authority is her explanation to the reader of why she has chosen to study La Gonave, an island that figures in Haitian folklore: she is intrigued by the folklore as it is juxtaposed against the island's infamous treatment by the lay anthropologist William Seabrook in his book *The Magic Island* (1929). As Hurston lounges in a hammock in Port-au-Prince, she watches La Gonave "disappear" at dawn and "reappear" at dusk, growing more interested in knowing the difference between Haitian folklore and Seabrook's white fantasy. Joined by her friend Frank Crumbie, who knows "people and Creole," Hurston heads to La Gonave because she knows "methods."[44] Through this rhetorical triangulation of Seabrook, Crumbie, and herself, Hurston is able to situate herself as a trained ethnographer against Crumbie's role as "translator" and Seabrook's role as cultural voyeur and sensationalist.

More than a source of intellectual authority, Hurston's treatment of La Gonave differentiates her authoritative narrative from that of Seabrook's, further authenticating her status as a legitimate cultural critic. Where Seabrook finds the "White King of La Gonave," Hurston finds mosquitoes and the destructive remnants of US imperialism. More particularly, if Seabrook finds on La Gonave Faustin Wirkus, an American Marine who becomes the community's "God-sent" ruler, Hurston finds a black man who has turned "black Marine" under the US military occupation of Haiti and its island dependency, La Gonave. Hurston's critique is most starkly readable when we set it beside Seabrook's narrative regarding Wirkus.[45]

Seabrook introduces Wirkus to the world through *The Magic Island* by describing him as the "hardboiled . . . white ruler" and "benevolent despot of an island inhabited by ten thousand blacks."[46] And in Seabrook's introduction to Wirkus's autobiographical text, *The White King of La Gonave* (1931), he also argues that readers will find Wirkus's story "fantastic" and compelling because "every boy ever born, if he is any good, wants, among other things, to be king of a tropical island."[47] Seabrook's treatment of Wirkus's role in La Gonave suggests a particular imperial relationship to land and people that marches in step with the representation of Haiti and Haitians during the island's occupation by the US military. Seabrook considers Wirkus's despotic ordering and regimentation of La Gonave's husbandry beneficial to the island's long-term prosperity.

Moreover, a centerpiece of Seabrook's description of Wirkus rests upon the latter's disciplining of a man named Alliance Laurent, who had been coveting the land and women of others. In Seabrook's account, Wirkus threatens Laurent with a punishment that will entail community shaming and his indenturing to Wirkus on behalf of the women of the island. Laurent promises to behave and to restore the usurped lands to their owners. Seabrook tells readers that Wirkus's reward for such acts of despotism—the organizing of land and animals and, most important, the policing of Haitian men—is a coronet symbolizing his status as "King." Wirkus becomes an intriguing character to Seabrook and other Americans because, according to Seabrook, he is willing to save La Gonave's citizens from themselves, while also soliciting a deep sense of gratitude and commitment from the islanders. It's a classic narrative example of what Gayatri Chakravorty Spivak calls "white men saving brown women from brown men."[48] The Seabrook and Wirkus narratives frame La Gonave's land and residents—and Haiti, by extension—as an imperial holding. The Haitian nation is depicted as needing social, political, and structural intervention by white, male agents of the United States.

In contrast, Hurston finds La Gonave a place of wonder and tranquility. "La Gonave is the mother of peace," she writes; more pointedly, Hurston tells her readers, "I found on this remote island a peace I have never known anywhere else on earth."[49] By introducing this island under the sign of peace, Hurston signals to her readers that the land and its people were never in need of being saved from their own violence. In fact, implicit in Hurston's representation of La Gonave is the reality that the violence associated with the island is not native to it but a product of actions by non-Haitians. For instance, in place of Seabrook's Laurent figure, Hurston finds the figure of the "black Marine." This man first captures Hurston's attention with his constant shouting of English curses. She learns that he's picked up this habit after serving "with the Marines" during the occupation, causing Hurston to "facetiously" dub him "a black Marine."[50] More disturbing than the black Marine's cursing, however, is his lust for violence. "I am a black Marine," he tells Hurston, "I speak like one always. Perhaps you would like me to kill something for you. I kill that dog for you."[51] Hurston doesn't allow him to kill the dog, but his offer to kill, like his offering of English curses, illustrates the long-lasting violence that still exists on the island as a legacy of the American military occupation.

Further fleshing out a vision of Haiti suffering under the violence of Seabrook's misrepresentation and the US occupation, Hurston tells the story of an island that has suffered the appropriation of important ceremonial objects. She follows the trail of Wirkus's work on the island from a description of the dock he builds to an interview with a man he has charged with collecting the sacred stones of the island. Unlike Seabrook, Hurston focuses on the fact that the islanders have been stripped of their cultural belongings: priceless stones held by families for generations and stolen by American officers during the occupation.[52] Again, what's most important to note in Hurston's representation of La Gonave is her rhetorical configuration of violence and theft with the legacy of American intervention on the island. This critique manifests itself over the course of the book through Hurston's development of a critical ethnographic authority consciously opposed to Seabrook's sensationalist salvation narrative, which renders La Gonave nothing more than a playground for US imperialism. The establishment of this critical ethnographic authority is key to understanding Hurston's relationship to the field.

Hurston's lack of access to deep relativism when writing about the black condition might have read to some of her contemporaries as an inability to master the professional techniques of cross-cultural analysis that Boas hoped would limit the cultural distortion imposed by casual observation.[53] In the oft-quoted opening to the chapter "Women of the Caribbean" in *Tell My Horse,* Hurston attempts to perform a cross-cultural analysis of womanhood, contrasting the United States and the Caribbean. Referencing the US context, Hurston contends that the "majority of men in the states are pretty much agreed that just for being born a girl-baby you ought to have laws and privileges and pay and perquisites. . . . The majority of the solid citizens strain their ears trying to find out what it is that their womenfolk want so they can strain around and try to get it for them, and that is a *very* good idea and the right way to look at things."[54] Conversely, Hurston writes that in the Caribbean an American woman will find the following: "a lot of darkish men who make vociferous love to you, but otherwise pay you no mind. If you try to talk sense, they look at you right pitifully. . . . It is not that they try to put you in your place, no. They consider that you never had any."[55] Hurston goes further to differentiate between the class and color (race) of the women she meets, distinctions she doesn't accord to the US context, observing that poor black women are "beasts of burden" in the Caribbean, expected to work as hard as men. I have argued elsewhere against ironic readings of this cross-cultural gender analysis, readings that assume Hurston's comparison is meant not to point out differences between the women of each cultural region but rather to highlight structural and social similarities between women of the Caribbean and women of the United States.[56]

Instead, I would encourage us to understand Hurston's assumption of the identity of an "American woman" as an attempt to project her universal anthropological voice upon an imperial context. If this gender analysis rings hollow, it is not the result of irony; rather, it is the result of the fissures that become recognizable when a female anthropologist of color attempts to employ the sort of deep relativism that is traditionally accessible to mainstream members of the profession. Benedict is encouraged to reach the deepest levels of cross-cultural knowledge by cultivating the empathy that allows her to imagine herself as someone she will never be, a Negro. Her imagined time as "a Negro" yields insights that are possible only when one is *not* an actual member of the culture one is examining. The rhetorical space that Hurston has to occupy in order to reflect on differences between (nonracialized) American women and their (racialized) Caribbean counterparts requires her to commit to the racial and class erasure of her own subject position as a black American woman from a rural, working-class background. This erasure produces the hollowness of which many contemporary Hurston scholars write.

This rhetorical self-erasure is further highlighted by Hurston's employment of the second person when narrating what the American woman will find when she approaches womanhood in the Caribbean. This shift in point of view—having neither the intimacy of the *I* nor the outright distance of the *she*—speaks to the direct relationship that Hurston is attempting to cultivate in her discussion of nationalized gender differences. Again, Batiste's notion of imperial representation provides a useful register for deciphering such passages and for seeing why they continue to confound contemporary scholars of Hurston. When we read Hurston on Haiti, we have to hold the tension created by her performance of professional authority alongside our understanding that this very performance necessitates a second gesture: the establishment of an imperial voice that compromises her own subjectivity.

## A ZOMBIE TO THE PROFESSION: ETHNOGRAPHIC STRATEGIES OF RESISTANCE

Hurston's brand of self-reflexivity makes her a keen critic of the very processes and techniques that she must utilize in order to produce work recognizable by her contemporaries in the discipline. But it's a losing enterprise, and Hurston seems to be aware of this fact. One need only look to her representation of the key novelty that drew so many contemporaneous readers to *Tell My Horse:* zombies.

Hurston tells her readers that she is the first professional to provide photodocumentary evidence confirming the existence of zombies.[57] Although Seabrook might be credited with introducing American audiences to the zombie trope in *The Magic Island,* Hurston contends that she should be credited for providing the concrete evidence proving the existence of zombies, which had "never happened before in the history of man."[58] Hyperbole aside, Hurston's ethnographic treatment of zombies runs deeper than sensationalism; her chapter on zombies provides her a trope with which to ruminate upon and offer implicit criticism of the impending professional erasure of the black female ethnographer working within the black diaspora. It's in her treatment of zombies that we can see Hurston's most masterful intervention in the metadiscourse of American anthropological methods.

Zombies are victims in *Tell My Horse.* For, as Hurston tell us, zombies are "set to toiling ceaselessly in the banana fields, working like a beast, unclothed like a beast, and like a brute crouching in some foul den in the few hours allowed for rest and food. From an educated, intelligent being to an unthinking, unknowing beast. Then there is the helplessness of the situation."[59] What unhinges Hurston in her analysis of zombies is not that they are menacing—they aren't, in fact—but that they are reduced to nothing more than workable flesh. To be a zombie is to be divorced from one's thoughts.

The victim status of zombies in Hurston's ethnography must be read against the backdrop of a long-standing social anxiety rooted in the violent history of the black slave trade and slavery in the Americas. As Sarah Juliet Luaro and Karen Embry propose, the "zombi" (zombie) of Haitian origin is the zombie of slavery. The Haitian "zombi," in addition to being "a body raised from the dead to labor in the fields," also has "a deep association of having played a role in the Haitian Revolution (thus, simultaneously resonant with the categories of slave and slave rebellion)."[60] Hurston suggests in *Tell My Horse* that a violent reaction is inevitable when the loved ones of a person-turned-zombie find a relative held captive and reduced to mindless toil or theft: the family inevitably gathers a crowd and threatens "violence to the persons alleged to be responsible for the crime."[61]

The zombie's status as victim is linked to its capacity to incite revolution. And the violence produced around zombie-ism in Hurston's text, though not explicitly announced, implicitly harkens back to the revolutionary origins of the Haitian nation-state, which was founded in revolutionary antislavery action and politics.[62] More specifically, Sibylle Fischer compellingly argues in *Modernity Disavowed* that the slave origins of modernity and revolution in the Americas were purposefully silenced, vanished, and disavowed by most Western scholars.[63] Posing too much of a threat to Western rationality and democratic notions of freedom, the reality of a successful black revolution was systematically erased from Western narratives of modernity. Hurston nods to this history, slyly, and in so doing opens up space for critical reflection on form and metaphor within her Caribbean text.

The figure of the zombie has multiple and competing functions in *Tell My Horse:* it is a metaphor and an object of study, a reminder of the gross atrocities of slavery and of victim-agents capable of mobilizing revolution against their captors. This multiplicity allows Hurston to work within the disciplinary expectations of the profession in the 1930s, which assumed a universal subjectivity for the ethnographer, while also maintaining her subjectivity as a black woman producing a body of knowledge around the black diaspora. So when Hurston takes the photograph of Felicia Felix-Mentor, she appears to be documenting a zombie for Western eyes. She frames Felix-Mentor—a wife and mother supposedly dead and buried twenty-nine years earlier but later turned zombie—within photography's documentary lens in an attempt to appease rationalism's lust for hard evidence and social-scientific "truth." Remember

Hurston's note that Boas demanded "facts" and threatened removal from the profession without them.

Hurston comes into contact with Felix-Mentor during a visit to a government hospital, where Felicia has been taken after being found roaming the streets without purpose. Even the location of the photographed encounter, a government hospital, lends an air of authenticity through the site's association with modern rationalism. And while Hurston's photograph of Felix-Mentor appears in the *Saturday Review* for October 1938, the reviewer seems less than convinced by Hurston's evidence. Noting that Hurston's photographs are "exceptionally good" and "honest," he nonetheless questions the authenticity of the ceremonies captured and the validity of the zombies. He goes so far as to liken Hurston's Felix-Mentor story to the American folktale of Paul Bunyan plowing the Grand Canyon.[64]

It would be unwise to argue over the authenticity of Hurston's zombies. Instead, it is Hurston's response to coming face-to-face with and photographing Felix-Mentor that moves us beyond authenticity to the power of metaphor embedded in her disciplinary critique. Hurston describes the encounter as follows:

> I took her [picture] first in the position that she assumed herself whenever left alone. That is, cringing against the wall with the cloth hiding her face and head. Then in other positions. Finally the doctor forcibly uncovered her and held her so that I could take her face. And the sight was dreadful. That blank face with the dead eyes. . . . There was nothing that you could say to her or get from her except by looking at her, and the sight of this wreckage was too much to endure for long.[65]

Distressed by Felix-Mentor's mute visage and her inability to perform reflexive thought, Hurston and her colleague move to another space within the hospital to discuss the science behind zombie making. Again, the location of the encounter proves important. In the hospital, Hurston and the doctor begin to hypothesize that poison (drugging) lies at the root of the zombie phenomenon. They focus on the possibility that zombies might be living humans under the influence of traditional drugs or medicines—ingredients of "a secret brought from Africa and handed down from generation to generation"—which render a person not dead but not fully alive either, neurologically damaged. Hurston's inclusion of this conversation might suggest that she is actually in search of a rational explanation for zombies.[66] But she and her companion ultimately conclude that there is no way to know the truth, scientific or otherwise, because of the covertness of Haitian secret societies. One might be inclined to conclude that Hurston has taken the leap of faith into the unknown required by most religions, but I would like to return our focus to the lens and what Hurston sees when looking through it at Felix-Mentor.

Rather than a leap of faith or an affirmation of zombies' authenticity, Hurston's interface with Felix-Mentor always returns to the horror of lacking a voice and the capacity to consciously decide one's own fate. Hurston calls Felix-Mentor "wreckage" not simply because she is afraid of the living dead but because Felix-Mentor can't communicate about or speculate on the conditions of her existence. If we consider that Felix-Mentor functions as a metaphor in *Tell My Horse,* we can begin to link it to the larger methodological and critical interventions that Hurston's research makes. In particular, Hurston's treatment of the horror of zombies suggests that any being unable to practice self-reflexivity—anyone discouraged from critically assessing and articulating his or her own subject position in relation to the world around him or her—is living an unendurable life of wreckage.

Returning to Hurston's relationship to the profession as illustrated by the letters she exchanged with Benedict surrounding the funding and lack of funding for her research helps to contextualize Hurston's resistance to being reduced to a body sent into the field to collect on behalf of her intellectual masters.[67] Which is what Benedict suggests she should do when writing to the Guggenheim representative. Because Hurston worked to create a body of knowledge, her research is peppered with veiled critiques regarding what it might mean to toil in the profession for one's own benefit. In other words, she asks what it might mean to be a knowledge maker and reap the benefits that would allow her to make a living from her work and receive institutional acknowledgment as a researcher. She appears less concerned in proving the authenticity of zombies than in disavowing the erasure of a black revolutionary consciousness—her own and Haiti's.

In a 2013 issue of *Cultural Anthropology,* one of the premier academic journals in the field, Tami Navarro, Bianca Williams, and Attiya Ahmad document the state of race and gender in anthropology. While many are quick to herald disciplines such as anthropology for making great strides in diminishing racism and sexism within the academic profession, Navarro, Williams, and Ahmad contend that difficulties for female faculty of color have "not only continued, but have intensified in recent years."[68] These female anthropologists of color use their narratives of professional experiences on the job market and in the classroom, negotiating varying forms of "invisible labor" within predominantly white institutions, to illuminate the continued work necessary to make anthropology (and the academy at large) a more inclusive place for women of color. Unlike Hurston, Navarro, Williams, and Ahmad have earned doctorates and hold faculty positions within higher education institutions; yet their articles speak to the continued difficulty faced by women of color within anthropology. Hurston was at the cutting edge of a profession that sought to create a mode of inquiry sensitive to and capable of recognizing the value of and traditions inherent in black culture, but she failed to be integrated into the work of the academy owing to its need to professionalize and, most likely, to lingering notions of Victorian racial theory and long-term issues of sexism.

I would like to suggest that one might pinpoint the exact moment at which Hurston shuttled out of the profession of anthropology. It came much earlier than her failure to credential herself in Columbia's doctoral program and well before the publication of *Tell My Horse.* I believe it came as early as December 1933. In a letter to Benedict, Hurston gleefully recounts that she has placed her first novel, *Jonah's Gourd Vine* (1934), with J. B. Lippincott. Being a published author need not mark Hurston as unfit for the profession; even Benedict wrote and published poetry and short stories throughout her career as a social scientist, though she did so under a pseudonym.[69] Rather, it is the monetary advance for Hurston's work of fiction that marks her gateway out of the profession. Hurston tells Benedict in a letter that she plans to use the advance from her publishers to pay the dues she owes to the anthropological society—the same dues about which Mary Chaffee contacted Benedict. It is in this letter that one can witness how one type of professional success cements another type of professional failure.

While Hurston was able to make a living as a professional writer—an artist—the funds needed to do the labor of an anthropologist—a scientist—were too great and unstable to provide the sort of support a black woman of the period could be expected to earn, even if this woman was breaking boundaries of form and introducing a new self-reflexivity to the profession of anthropology and the practice of ethnographic collecting. "Now that I am going to get some cash from my book as well as some from another source, you will see me in New York soon," Hurston promises Benedict.[70] But the sad reality of this letter is that it calls into question what "the field" meant to Hurston if the only way she imagined she would be able to return to New York City as an anthropologist was by taking on a bit of domestic work and selling her stories.

"Without money," Alice Walker once contended, "an illness, even a simple one, can undermine the will. Without money, getting into a hospital is problematic and getting out without money to pay for the treatment is nearly impossible. Without money, one becomes dependent on other people, who are likely to be—even in their kindness—erratic in their support and despotic in their expectations of return."[71] With Walker's words in mind, one wonders how Hurston managed to practice anthropology for as long as she did in the face of her raced and gendered financial realities. But one need only return to Chaffee's letter to realize that "the field" was a tenuous place for a black female anthropologist. Such an anthropologist could never be certain when she might have to take up domestic work—the guaranteed work of her race and gender—in order to do the work of her training, anthropology. Boasian ideas of cultural diversity created a space for a black female anthropologist like Zora Neale Hurston to train and develop; but structural racism, sexism, and US imperialism conspired to limit her ability to thrive within the field and the profession. When Hurston tells Benedict that "facts go down mighty hard with some folks, confirming my conviction that there is nothing so precious that men know as what they *want* to believe," we know that she is speaking from experience.[72]

## Notes

1. Zora Neale Hurston, *Tell My Horse: Voodoo and Life in Haiti and Jamaica* (1938; repr. New York: HarperCollins, 1990), 179.
2. For foundational criticism on the importance of Hurston's work, see Robert Hemenway, *Zora Neale Hurston: A Literary Biography* (Urbana: University of Illinois Press, 1980); Alice Walker, *In Search of Our Mothers' Gardens: Womanist Prose* (New York: Harcourt, 1983); and Cheryl Wall, *The Women of the Harlem Renaissance* (Bloomington: University of Indiana Press, 1995).
3. Hazel Carby, "The Politics of Fiction, Anthropology, and the Folk: Zora Neale Hurston," in *New Essays on Their Eyes Were Watching God*, ed. Michael Awkward (New York: Cambridge University Press, 1990), 72.
4. Louise Lamphere, "Unofficial Histories: A Vision of Anthropology from the Margins," *American Anthropologist* 106, no. 1 (2004): 126.
5. Ibid.
6. Judith Butler, *Gender Trouble: Feminism and the Subversion of Identity* (New York: Routledge, 1990), 44.
7. "Zora Neale Hurston Fellowship," *Crisis Magazine* 5, no. 10 (1978): 358.
8. Mary B. Chaffee to Ruth Benedict, Feb. 6, 1932, Box 30, Folder 3, Ruth Fulton Benedict Papers, 1905–1948, Catherine Pelton Durrell '25 Archives and Special Collections Library, Vassar College, Poughkeepsie, New York (hereafter RFB).
9. Ibid. (emphasis added).
10. Virginia Young, *Ruth Benedict: Beyond Relativity, Beyond Pattern* (Lincoln: University of Nebraska Press, 2005), 8.
11. Margaret Mead, *An Anthropologist at Work: Writings of Ruth Benedict* (Westport, CT: Greenwood Press, 1977), 347.
12. Young, *Ruth Benedict*, 8.
13. See Lois Banner, *Intertwined Lives: Margaret Mead, Ruth Benedict and Their Circle* (New York: Vintage Books, 2003), for more information on Benedict's life and writings on sex and sexuality.

14. Jacqueline Jones, *American Work: Four Centuries of Black and White Labor* (New York: W. W. Norton, 1998), 315.
15. Ibid., 338.
16. Ibid., 330.
17. Zora Neale Hurston, "Record of Freshman Interest," Dec. 16, 1925, published by the Barnard Center for Research on Women in *The Scholar and Feminist Online* 3, no. 2 (2005), accessed Aug. 1, 2013, http://sfonline.barnard.edu/hurston/bcarchives/ZNH_freshman.pdf.
18. Young, *Ruth Benedict*, 6.
19. Piper Huguley-Riggins, "Zora Neale Hurston: A Black White-Collar Working Woman," in *"The Inside Light": New Critical Essays on Zora Neale Hurston*, ed. Deborah Plant (Santa Barbara: Praeger, 2012), 4.
20. Ruth Benedict to Zora Neale Hurston, Feb. 11, 1933, Box 30, Folder 3, RFB.
21. Zora Neale Hurston to Ruth Benedict, Apr. 17, 1932, Box 30, Folder 3, RFB.
22. Ibid.
23. Ibid.
24. The transactional nature of their exchange isn't unique to these two women; it is, in fact, common within a system that subjugates junior scholars to senior scholar-mentors.
25. On Benedict's role as gatekeeper, see also Sally Cole, *Ruth Landes: A Life in Anthropology* (Lincoln: University of Nebraska Press, 2003). Cole notes that Landes, a white, Jewish-American woman, refused to play the role of professional "good girl," instead fighting "against gender stereotypes" and adopting "an uncompromising 'bad girl' confrontational style." This led to her marginalization. While Benedict continued to fund Landes's research until her death in 1948, she never helped Landes secure a permanent position in anthropology (55–58).
26. Zora Neale Hurston to Ruth Benedict, Apr. 17, 1932, Box 30, Folder 3, RFB.
27. Ruth Benedict to Dr. Moe, Nov. 15, 1933, Box 30, Folder 3, RFB.
28. Ruth Benedict to J. B. Lippincott, Oct. 4, 1933, and Oct. 15, 1933, Box 30, Folder 3, RFB (emphasis added).
29. Zora Neale Hurston to Ruth Benedict, undated, Box 30, Folder 3, RFB.
30. Ibid.
31. Hurston was not the first to think such a palatable publication on American Indians necessary. In 1922 Elsie Clews Parsons edited an illustrated collection of stories written by anthropologists entitled *American Indian Life: By Several of Its Students* (New York: Viking Press, 1922). The volume, resting someplace between a social science monograph and James Fenimore Cooper's fiction, was intended to bridge the gap in the public's knowledge of Native peoples. In his introduction A. L. Kroeber outlined the creative process of the collection, which allowed its anthropologist-writers an opportunity to forego "objectivity" and instead employ memory to speculate on how "Indians feel, why they act as they do in a given situation, what goes on inside of them" (13). The tension between professional objectivity and fictional speculation is keenly felt in Kroeber's introduction. It speaks to the tentative nature of such fictionalizing then by trained professionals—a tension sustainable only if one believes, however, that anthropological practices aren't always already infused with the subjectivity of the practitioner.
32. Zora Neale Hurston to Ruth Benedict, Mar. 6, 1935, Box 30, Folder 3, RFB.

33. A contemporary of Hurston's, Katherine Dunham, also received Rosenwald and Guggenheim fellowships for the study of black diasporic culture in the Caribbean. In fact, Dunham and Hurston traveled to and wrote about many of the same sites within months of each other. In 1936 Hurston wrote to Melville Herskovits expressing her belief that the Rosenwald Foundation rejected her fellowship application because Dunham had been awarded funds for a similar project only a year before. Like Hurston, Dunham would opt out of the academy, pursuing work within the performing arts on Broadway and in Hollywood. Unlike Hurston, Dunham would remain a relevant cultural producer throughout her career, which lasted until her death in 2006. See Joyce Aschenbrenner, "Katherine Dunham: Anthropologist, Artist, Humanist," in *African-American Pioneers in Anthropology,* ed. Ira Harrison and Faye Harrison (Urbana: University of Illinois Press, 1999), 137–53; Ramsay Burt, *Alien Bodies: Representations of Modernity, "Race" and Nation in Early Modern Dance* (New York: Routledge, 1998), 136–61; and Daphne Lamothe, *Inventing the New Negro: Narrative, Culture, and Ethnography* (Philadelphia: University of Pennsylvania Press, 2008), 115–40.
34. "Lore of Haiti," review of *Tell My Horse* by Zora Neale Hurston, *New York Times Book Review,* Oct. 23, 1938, 12.
35. "*Tell My Horse,*" *New Yorker,* Oct. 15, 1938, 95.
36. Elmer Davis, review of *Tell My Horse,* in *Zora Neale Hurston: Critical Perspectives Past and Present,* ed. Henry Louis Gates and Kwame Anthony Appiah (New York: Amistad, 1987), 25.
37. Eve Dunbar, *Black Regions of the Imagination: African Americans Between the Nation and the World* (Philadelphia: Temple University Press, 2013), 47–49.
38. Ifeoma Nwankwo, "Insider and Outsider, Black and American: Rethinking Zora Neale Hurston's Caribbean Ethnography," *Radical History Review* 87 (Fall 2003): 74.
39. Young, *Ruth Benedict,* 199.
40. Ruth Benedict, "If I Were a Negro," undated manuscript, Box 120, Folder 8, RFB.
41. Stephanie Leigh Batiste, *Darkening Mirrors: Imperial Representation in Depression-Era African American Performance* (Durham: Duke University Press, 2011), 4.
42. Mary Renda, *Taking Haiti: Military Occupation and the Culture of U.S. Imperialism, 1915–1940* (Chapel Hill: University of North Carolina Press, 2001), 293.
43. Hurston, *Tell My Horse,* 204.
44. Ibid., 134.
45. Seabrook, *The Magic Island* (New York: Literary Guild of America, 1929), 175.
46. Ibid.
47. William Seabrook, introduction to *The White King of La Gonave* by Faustin Wirkus and Taney Dudley (New York: Doubleday, Doran, 1931), xiii.
48. Gayatri Chakravorty Spivak, "Can the Subaltern Speak?" in *Marxism and the Interpretation of Culture,* ed. Cary Nelson and Lawrence Grossberg (Chicago: University of Illinois Press, 1988), 93.
49. Hurston, *Tell My Horse,* 135.
50. Ibid., 136.
51. Ibid., 137.
52. Ibid.
53. Hurston does practice cross-racial imaginative work in her final published novel, *Seraph on the Suwanee* (1948), which explores a love relationship between white Florida

"crackers." Although poorly received, the novel has yielded a growing body of literary criticism. See Alice Walker's foreword to Hemenway, *Zora Neale Hurston,* xvi.

54. Hurston, *Tell My Horse,* 57.
55. Ibid., 58.
56. Dunbar, *Black Regions of the Imagination,* 54.
57. Hurston, *Tell My Horse,* 182.
58. Zora Neale Hurston, *Dust Tracks on a Road: An Autobiography* (1942; repr. New York: HarperPerennial, 1991), 168–69.
59. Ibid., 181.
60. Sarah Juliet Lauro and Karen Embry, "A Zombie Manifesto: The Nonhuman Condition in the Era of Advanced Capitalism," *boundary 2* 35, no. 1 (2008): 87.
61. Hurston, *Tell My Horse,* 181.
62. Sibylle Fischer, *Modernity Disavowed: Haiti and the Cultures of Slavery in the Age of Revolution* (Durham: Duke University Press, 2004), 2.
63. Ibid., 10.
64. Harold Courlander, "Witchcraft in the Caribbean Islands," *Saturday Review of Literature,* Oct. 15, 1938, 7.
65. Hurston, *Tell My Horse,* 195.
66. Ibid., 196.
67. See also Eve Dunbar, "Becoming American Through Ethnographic Writing," chap. 1 of *Black Regions of the Imagination,* for the restrictions Charlotte Osgood Mason placed on Hurston's early research as well as Hurston's response to those restrictions.
68. Tami Navarro, Bianca Williams, and Attiya Ahmad, "Sitting at the Kitchen Table: Fieldnotes from Women of Color in Anthropology," *Cultural Anthropology* 28, no. 3 (2013): 443.
69. Mead, *An Anthropologist at Work,* 83–91.
70. Zora Neale Hurston to Ruth Benedict, Dec. 4, 1933, Box 30, Folder 3, RFB.
71. Alice Walker, "Zora Neale Hurston: A Cautionary Tale and a Partisan View," in *In Search of Our Mothers' Gardens: Womanist Prose* (San Diego: Harcourt Brace Jovanovich, 1983), 90.
72. Zora Neale Hurston to Ruth Benedict, June 19, 1935, Box 30, Folder 3, RFB.

# Chapter 11 "A New Indian Intelligentsia": Archie Phinney and the Search for a Radical Native American Modernity

*Benjamin Balthaser*

There is a scene in John Joseph Mathews's novel of Osage life, *Sundown* (1934), that captures all the contradictory potential of Native Americans' engagement with modernity. Challenge Windzer, the mixed-blood heir to his father's oil lease fortune, experiences his first feelings of power when flying a single-engine fighter on a training exercise near his military base: "He had a feeling of superiority, and he kept thinking of the millions of people below him as white men. When he became conscious that he was thinking of them as white men he smiled to himself."[1] The airplane, with its mix of deadly power and technical expertise, has long symbolized the aspirations and exclusions of modernity. We may think of Richard Wright's Bigger Thomas gazing up from the South Side of Chicago at an airplane he is not allowed to fly as the flip side of John Dos Passos's symbol of flight and wealth in *The Big Money*—each enraptured with the elegance of flight as a symbol of the modern world's mastery. That an Osage college dropout could master the airplane to fly above the heads of "white men" not only suggests Challenge's incorporation within the modern world, it also suggests that modernity itself may be channeled into a vehicle of power and liberation—and it may be channeled by Indigenous people.

For all the exhilaration Challenge feels, however, Mathews meant to pose his flight as an act of alienation. In *Sundown* Challenge denies his Native ancestry while serving in the armed forces, and his soaring aerial command is undermined by his aimless drinking and driving—eventually leading to a car crash—even as he inherits his father's fortune. The final image that Mathews offers of Osage modernity is not a car or an airplane but an oil well, polluting the prairie where Challenge used to imagine himself as an Osage warrior. By presenting modernity in technological forms—as airplanes, automobiles, oil wells—and implicating them in Challenge's downward spiral into alcoholic confusion, Mathews undoubtedly meant to criticize the proponents of the allotment policy of the United States, who argued for Indian assimilation within a nation that defined itself as the agent of techno-historical progress. Yet Challenge exceeds Mathew's grasp here, so that a twentieth-century novel begs for today's critics a different question: How might we envision Indians as agents of modernity?

Native Americans and modernity are often considered to be a contradiction in terms, opposite halves of an unbreachable binary. Modernity, after all, is often predicated on the eradication of the "primitive" presence of Indigenous people. The notion that "Indians have missed out on modernity," Philip Deloria writes, has justified their erasure from history and the logic for their conquest.[2] Yet Mathews, even as he associated allotment with the disastrous policies dictated by ideologies of rationality and supposed progress, also toyed with the possibility that modernity may serve as a road toward Native American sovereignty. The image of an enrolled Osage tribal member flying above and possibly terrifying "white men" is laden not only with metaphors of mastery but also with the threat of armed conflict and even revolt. One doesn't have to recall Malcolm X's satirical threat to join the army in order to "shoot crackers" any more than the real-life Houston riot of 1917 to consider that Challenge's enlistment in the air force and commandeering of an airplane opens a pathway to radical potentialities.

Partly through an analysis of Mathews's pioneering work, Deloria suggests that it has often been possible for Indians to envision forms of modernity that are not based on their exclusion from the modern world. Recovering the image of the Indian driver, Deloria discusses the ways that automobiles assisted in the formation of powwow culture, contributing to the shaping of a new Indian self-image at the beginning of the twentieth century, a time of increased confidence and self-possession that often confounded white observers.[3] By appending this addendum to the first modern novel of Native American life, Deloria offers a glimpse of Native engagements—or, as Deloria calls them, "flirtations"—with modernity.

The vexed question of Indigenous modernity, of Native American involvement in a world that defines itself by denying their presence, takes on an especially rich significance because of its close connection to the politics of sovereignty. As Mathews suggests, going "back to the blanket"—rejecting the claims of modernity as defined by the Western nation-state—is one way to think about Osage sovereignty. Yet the practice of Indigenous sovereignty in the twentieth century often involved far more than a "flirtation" with modernity. Sovereignty, as we now know it, is itself a modern concept, voiced by Indigenous people in response to changing circumstances. In his descriptions of the debate over Native American citizenship in 1924, Kevin Bruyneel offers another way to consider the conflict between Indian sovereignty and Indian citizenship, one that rejects the picture of modern Indians as subjects of Western assimilation. "The third space of sovereignty" that Bruyneel depicts is a multisite citizenship, inside and outside US political institutions, making use of methods of colonial incorporation to press for modes of Indigenous autonomy. Citing Zitkala-Sa's formation of the National Council of American Indians in response to Indigenous ideals of citizenship, Bruyneel makes the case that practices of Native self-determination often eclipsed the binary dictating that Indians would have to choose between being themselves and being active participants in a broader polity. As Bruyneel succinctly puts it, they have refused "the false choice of either destruction or denial."[4]

Defying through their practice those who envisioned their absence, Indian activists and intellectuals took all roads possible when pressing for sovereignty, even if those roads were to be traveled by automobile and airplane. While Bruyneel and Deloria write of democratic politics and consumer technology, missing is yet a third window into the possibilities for Native American engagement with modernity. I would suggest that the midcentury Nez Perce activist and anthropologist Archie Phinney offers a look at Native practices of modernity through the lens of Marxism and Soviet policy. Phinney posited that a modern Native sovereignty could arise and be realized via a dialectical engagement with the very forces by which Indians experienced their dispossession.

Just as C. L. R. James described modern slaves and proletarians as violently "conscripted" by modernity, Phinney came to argue that Indigenous people had no choice but to take the ideas imposed upon them by modernity and convert them to their own purposes.[5] He contended that Indians must claim for themselves and proudly inhabit their modern racial identity. What distinguished Phinney from other, even much later, pan-Indian intellectuals was his insistence that modernity is not simply a possession of industrial society.

Modernity, as Phinney saw it, is a historical inheritance, a form of belonging to which Indigenous people may lay claim and which they must refashion in their own image to survive. Phinney's question, then, is not whether Indians can choose to be modern. It is how they may enter into relations with an imperial nation-state as "alert, modern communities, struggling for their own interests."[6]

An enrolled member of the Nez Perce nation, Archie Mark Phinney was born in 1903 in Culdesac, Idaho, the son of a Nez Perce mother and a white settler who lived on the Nez Perce reservation. His Native name was Kaplatsilpilp. Phinney showed great academic promise in public high school and went on to become the first Native American to graduate from the University of Kansas. Enamored of anthropology—whatever its faults, it gave him an opportunity to consider Native Americans as historical actors—Phinney went on to study at Columbia University as a student of Franz Boas. With Boas's encouragement he completed *Nez Percé Texts,* a collection of oral tales skillfully narrated by Phinney's mother, which has helped to popularize an anthropo-literary genre, the trickster cycle of Coyote. Along the way, he also created the first published transcription of the Nez Perce alphabet.[7]

After four years at Columbia, at Boas's suggestion and armed with letters of introduction from Boas and the leftist writer Agnes Smedley, Phinney found a teaching and research post at the Leningrad Academy of Sciences. While pursuing a Russian doctorate in Leningrad between 1932 and 1937, he conducted a comparative study of US federal Indian policy and Soviet policy toward its national minorities, especially its Siberian hunting-and-gathering peoples. This study would powerfully influence Phinney's subsequent involvement in the Indian New Deal and his career as a founding theoretician of Indian activism.

While he studied abroad Phinney learned Russian and took numerous graduate seminars on Marxist theory and anthropology. He made several trips to Siberia to research the impact of postrevolutionary policy on the Soviet Union's national minorities, hoping to find in the Soviet system a model that the United States could emulate.[8] And he also traveled to the Caucasus, where he learned about Indigenous peoples and policies in Soviet Central Asia. Although Phinney never published a book on his experiences in the Soviet Union, a close reading of his published and unpublished manuscripts reveals that both Soviet policy itself and Phinney's singular ideas about his experiences in the Soviet Union shaped his later ideas about American Indian politics and racial identity.

After his return, as an agent of the Bureau of Indian Affairs (BIA) under John Collier, an appointee of Franklin D. Roosevelt, and, later, as a founder of the National Congress of American Indians (NCAI), the longest enduring and arguably most influential pan-Indian organization of the twentieth century, Phinney emerged as an important intellectual during the period of reform that ran from the New Deal to the outset of the Cold War. Although Phinney is not regarded as a founding theorist of twentieth-century Native American activism, his ideas on the need for a new racial identity and modern forms of political action provided the intellectual architecture of nearly all pan-Indian organizations from the end of World War II to the present.

What does it mean that one of the most influential pan-Indian organizations was founded by a man who described the Soviet Union as "the first attempt of men to intelligently direct their own history"?[9] And why was Marxism an important optic for seeing and theorizing the problem of Native American sovereignty? The answers to these questions broaden our understanding of what modernity can be and how Indigenous people, in this case a member of the Boasian Circle, have shaped it.

That a young, Columbia-educated Nez Perce man would find the Soviet Union a place of intellectual discovery and political development requires a certain amount of contextualization, given the historical memory of the Soviet Union in the United States. One has to remember that Phinney became a student of Boas during an era in which the Communist International as well as many Marxist intellectuals abandoned a pure class critique and formally recognized the importance of decolonization struggles around the world. Many intellectuals of color believed that the Communist International took the question of anticolonial liberation seriously, forming, in Hakim Adi's words, the "era's sole international white-led movement . . . formally dedicated to a revolutionary transformation of the global political *and* racial order."[10] Building upon the writings of V. I. Lenin and anticolonial intellectuals such as Sen Katayama and Claude McKay, the Comintern declared that liberation struggles for national minorities within states and subjects of colonial powers deserved support. The Soviet Union itself became both a refuge and a nexus for anticolonial intellectuals around the globe who imagined they had found an ally in their struggle for racial and national liberation.[11]

This is not to suggest that Phinney's writings are products of Communist doctrine, or that Phinney traveled to the Soviet Union to become a revolutionary, but that global Marxism provided a lens through which the colonial experience could be understood by those attempting to alter it between the 1920s and the 1940s. Indeed, from the scant evidence in Phinney's archive about his personal life and thought process while he lived in the Soviet Union, it is clear that Phinney held the Soviet project at some level of ironic distance, even writing to Boas upon his arrival that he still needed to put on his "proletarian goggles" if he was to make his way in Leningrad.[12] And scattered among his notes on Marxism is a cryptic critique of the so-called citizenship possessed by Indigenous people in the Soviet Union. Such policies, Phinney wrote, "move the native . . . from the plane of the pitiful to the plane of [the] tragic."[13]

Despite such barbed asides on Soviet policy toward Native peoples, it is clear that Phinney applied Marxian theories of capitalist development to the situation of the Nez Perce. Perhaps more important with regard to his future as a pan-Indian activist, he began to develop a dialectical conception of identity that repositioned Indigenous experience as the product of an ongoing interaction between oppositional social forces rather than static and essential categories. As Phinney began to perceive the Nez Perce as dispossessed of their "mode of production" by capitalist colonialism, his changing theoretical outlook on Soviet policy, based on the principles of cultural autonomy for Indigenous people and collective economic development, allowed him to conceive of a "new synthesis" for Indian identity—one that could move past the binary that distinguished only two kinds of Indians, the colonized primitive and the assimilated citizen.

By conceiving of an Indian identity transformed by the material processes of colonial domination, Phinney also adopted the position that only by recognizing this new form of identity could one oppose it. In the founding document of the National Congress of American Indians, he argued that Indians must embrace their identity as a "racial" rather than a "tribal" people in order to assert political power, and to do so because of (not despite) the presence of race, a category imposed on Indigenous people by colonialism. One can hear a Marxian echo in such a dialectical formulation. In much the same way that Marx argued that workers must embrace their proletarian status to liberate themselves, Phinney held that Indians had to embrace race, the very category of their domination, to come out the other side.

Phinney's most widely circulated essay after his death, "Numipu Among the White Settlers," was written as he corresponded with Boas during his stay in Leningrad. He included the essay in his application to work for the BIA, which likely explains its positive assessment of the stated goals of the Indian Reorganization Act. Beyond its nuanced and far-reaching arguments about Niimíipu (Nez Perce) life, the essay is exceptional in that Phinney writes about Indians as contemporary people rather than as "primitives," directly violating the principle that Indians are members of a "vanishing race," interesting as

Archie Phinney, left, in Kislovodsk, Soviet Union, mid-1930s. Image no. 9, Nez Perce National Historical Park, National Park Service.

vestiges of an ancient way of life but destined to disappear from the contemporary world. In laying out the contradictions faced by the Nez Perce and other postallotment, land-poor Indian tribes, Phinney posed the following questions: What is the relationship between the past and the future for the Niimíipu? What would it mean for the Niimíipu to continue to exist as a tribal community in a modern settler colony? What is the Nez Perce relationship to the modern world, culturally, politically, and economically? It is Phinney's engagement with a Marxian critique of capitalism in order to define the condition of modernity that gives his essay its power.

Citing conquest, land theft by whites, and the division of collective property into individual allotments mandated by the Dawes Act, Phinney was unsparing in his assessment of the current state of the tribe. The Niimíipu, he wrote, were "crushed materially and spiritually" and therefore "on the verge of complete extinction."[14] As Phinney saw it, the precarious situation and potential extinction of the Niimíipu had not arisen from a single cause—and Phinney was clear to point out that the Niimíipu had survived their defeat at the hands of the US military. Rather, the people's "moribund" condition resulted from a forty-year process by which "the Indians, having been lifted out of, or divested of, one culture," were then "thrust into another one," a foreign mode of life for which they had neither the understanding nor the material resources with which to flourish.[15]

Phinney attributed this cultural divestment to the dispossession of the Niimíipu from their means of production and subsistence—their land—a process Marx described as primary, or "primitive," accumulation. By linking European settlement to capitalism, Phinney contextualized the seizure of Native American land within a larger, global process by which transnational capital, backed by Western nation-states, managed to dominate noncapitalist modes of life and production:

> In the former communal economy, all activity was one continuous communal experience in which work (food quest and manufacture), ritual, and recreation were a single process. In subsistence production Indians had no conception of work as distinct from other cultural activity—there was not even a word for "labor" in their language. But with the abrupt transition from general collective participation to advanced capitalistic economy and individualism, they were confronted with a distinction between labor on an individualistic basis and their communal activity and recreation. This contradiction, fundamentally between collectivism and individualism, now disrupted the tribal order, because material benefits were offered to Numipu tribespeople individually, without the requirement of work. The individuality of the Indians was developed, but not in consequence of individual enterprise and effort; on the other hand, the communal spirit survived and is expressed today in the form of the aforementioned recreational activities.[16]

Because he believed the Niimíipu had lost control of their mode of production, Phinney was not optimistic about the possibilities of "communal spirit," the idea that the Niimíipu could continue their cultural practices in the absence of the social and economic organization from which they arose. "The haughty demeanor, the flashy regalia and vivid performance of Indians today satisfy both the white man's taste for spectacular pageantry and the performer's love for the spotlight," Phinney wrote of Niimíipu celebrations, and yet "it must not be assumed that elements of Indian culture are being revived. On the contrary, this represents the last stage in the degradation of Numipu culture."[17]

This is not to suggest that Phinney was a cultural purist; he was not. But he had a keen eye for the political impact of daily experience, and he perceived that ceremonies that had once expressed and advanced the totality of a Native worldview had been segmented, reified, reduced to the status of "culture." In a time when the "younger generation are closer to the habits of whites . . . than the old Indians," Phinney wrote, cultural revival could not provide a social solution to the crisis of the Niimíipu. Indeed, to Phinney, the emergence of what we now call "powwow culture" was a sign of Indian assimilation into the racial politics of consumer spectacle.

If Native people were to construct a new Indigenous perspective, they would have to confront the separation of culture from politics, power from belief. In Marxist terms, there could be no cultural solution without an economic solution—no superstructure without a base.[18] For this reason Phinney departed from the progressive materialism of his time, which dictated that the Niimíipu must assimilate their lives and work patterns to the settler-colonial economy. He never suggested, for example, as so many others did, that the Nez Perce should rely on job training, farming techniques, or educational opportunities provided by the white social order. Instead, Phinney asked what *kind* of social order the Niimíipu were being asked to join.

Of particular note in Phinney's critique of colonialism, a factor often absent in the debate over assimilation, is his Marxist orientation: his focus on the relations of production into which Indians would be assimilated. Phinney wrote that the "ultimate assimilation by the whites" of the Niimíipu would mean more than the loss of cultural heritage; in a material sense it would mean "assimilation on the lowest level of white proletarian existence."[19] If the Niimíipu renounced their BIA guardianship and their allotment leases, they would be conscripted into modernity as "proletarian" individuals, often worse off than they had been on their allotments and food rations. Leaving the reservation and joining the ranks of the working class would result in "a condition wherein [the Nez Perce] must face the adversities of exploitation and class antagonism," trading the communal struggle against settler colonialism for the individual struggle for bare survival.[20]

The ideal of sovereignty Phinney eventually articulated began from this Marxist understanding of the alienation of labor, filtered through an Indigenous conception of land and community as one's economic *and* spiritual base. This is why Phinney further critiqued the proponents of assimilation for suggesting that Indians should give up their one enviable asset, their unusual relationship to the federal government: "There are today in the United States more Negro and more white citizens than Indians who are existing under inhuman conditions of misery and poverty; these non-Indians receive no special attention because they are unemployed proletarians and impoverished tenants and farmers—i.e., active components of capitalist society who are supposed to work out their own salvations individually—to live or die by their own efforts."[21] Phinney added, with characteristic acerbity, that "the U.S. government feels compelled to rehabilitate [the Niimíipu]" and bring them up to "the level equal to that of the average rural white family," yet that "average rural white family" was itself in need of a strong dose of "rehabilitation."[22] In this passage Phinney subtly unraveled the colonial bind that opposed modernity to indigeneity, for how could an Indian be assimilated into a social order that itself was fissured along axial lines of race and class? The situation of the Niimíipu was modernity, with a past out of reach and a present that was unsustainable.

In Phinney's analysis, any solution to what he most feared—not merely the decline but the eventual extinction of the Niimíipu—had to proceed from a dialectical relationship between the past and the present, one that allowed the Niimíipu to shape a modern future without imposing upon themselves exterior forms of modernity that would further alienate the people from their identity, land, and labor. Modernity was not a goal but a given, less an end in itself than a precondition of Niimíipu experience. Phinney therefore asked what kind of modernity the Niimíipu wished to choose for themselves: Would they consent to a life as racialized proletarians or could they become "alert, modern communities, struggling for their own interests?"[23]

In "Numipu Among the White Settlers," Phinney's answer to the question of what a future Indigenous modernity might look like proceeded from Marx's answer to the conditions of capitalism. Phinney asserted that Indians should fuse their Native traditions of communal ownership and tribal identity with the first principles of Marxist economics, namely, "ownership of the means of production." Indians, he suggested, should "make Indian groups economically self-supporting on the basis of cooperative (tribal) organization and corporate (common) ownership of the means of production."[24] In this way Phinney adapted Marx's modernism to an Indigenous framework, proposing that Indigenous culture could be supported only by the construction of a new collective economic base. Rather than imagine that self-supporting Indigenous communities would separate themselves from a modern, industrialized social order, Phinney believed that collective economic self-sufficiency would "break down the barriers of isolation," allowing the Niimíipu to align themselves with the mass of "average rural white families" in pressing on toward "new and better conditions of life."[25]

Here Phinney's modernism emerged from his dialectical outlook, his sense that life must be oriented toward a vision of social transformation. To try to revive the past, Phinney remarked, would be to live a " 'reservation' existence of befeathered museum specimens propagated to add to the local color of the 'wild west,' "—to become the vanishing Indian whose image justified the dispossession of the Nez Perce.[26] Yet Phinney also realized that progress came at an existential price. Confronting the future also meant confronting the profound experience of loss, even of destitution, that resulted from centuries of disease and dispossession followed by colonial rule. Modernity, as Phinney saw it, would therefore be an unfinished project, beginning from the realization of a social tragedy—not unlike Theodor Adorno's later dictum that "there is no getting out of this."[27]

Just as his exposure to Marxist thought helped Phinney define the problem of modernity faced by Indigenous people, his exposure to Communist Indigenous policy inspired him to think about potential practical solutions. Phinney expressed skepticism about whether the Soviet Union's policies on national minorities could be adopted in the United States because of the differences in status and condition between Native peoples in the two countries, even if in many of his published and unpublished writings he openly praised Soviet policy.[28]

In an essay titled "Racial Minorities in the Soviet Union," published in the left-leaning social science journal *Pacific Affairs* in 1935, Phinney promoted the Soviet Union's policies on national minorities as an answer to centuries of Russian colonialism.[29] In this essay Phinney expanded on the theme of "Numipu," that Indigenous people are not only threatened by cultural and political domination but also dangerously exposed to, while at the same time excluded from, the modern world. Writing of the Siberian tribes, Phinney observed that their "isolation has already been annihilated" by "scores of radio stations and by the establishment of a system of air lines for mail and passenger service."[30] His choice of words is suggestive, especially as the essay describes the traditional ways of life then under threat owing to game extinction. The question the article poses is this: Exactly how are the Siberian tribes to experience and construct their engagement with modernity?

Describing a process by which Native cultures are celebrated, preserved, and modernized, Phinney's essay was optimistic about the "Latinized alphabets" created by Soviet institutes and the thousands of minority newspapers, dances, theaters, and other cultural productions in Native languages funded by the state.[31] Phinney also celebrated the modernization projects in the Siberian oblasts, in which Native forms of economic life were "collectivized" and "developed." He cited, for example, industrialization and conservation efforts in the fur, fishing, and timber industries.[32] Phinney did not see this collective modernization and cultural institutionalization by the Soviet state as Western imperialism. Rather, he described it as a dialectical process in which the "new life" would not proceed from the top down but would spark "a native spontaneity reanimating the traditional elements and forms of culture and bringing them into a new synthesis." Traditional culture would be preserved precisely through its interaction with the modern Western state.[33]

In a long, handwritten essay, "On Minority Languages in the Soviet Union," written in 1934 on the back of a draft of *Nez Percé Texts,* Phinney theorized that such Soviet policies could become a means for Indigenous people to enter the world that defined itself as modern without losing their Native identity.[34] In a move that reminds one of Frantz Fanon's theory of imperialism—colonialism produces the Native against which it defines itself—Phinney wrote that colonial modernizing projects not only wipe out Native cultures but also ossify and paralyze what remains. Tsarist Russia had done exactly that, Phinney wrote, by installing a comprador class of Native chiefs, traders, landlords, and bureaucrats who "arrested and vitiated [the] growth of native culture."[35] Thus the task as Phinney saw it was not merely to end Russian imperialism but also to find a dialectical way forward so that Indigenous life could respond to the new conditions in which it found itself.

Phinney's desire to engage with the modern world, and yet to do so on terms of equality, cultural integrity, and self-determination, prefigures Robert Warrior's call to live out a new form of humanism in "a new situation."[36] Rather than measuring the Soviet model in the formal terms of American democracy, Phinney thought of the Soviet policy on national minorities much in the manner that other writers of color did at the time. In his memoir *I Wonder as I Wander* Langston Hughes assessed the Soviet Union's record on matters of import to people of color. Explaining the significance of the opening of film schools, arts programs, and economic development, Hughes distinguished his standpoint from a European companion's distaste for the "primitive" conditions of Soviet Asia by remarking that Turkmenistan was not "a primitive land moving into the twentieth century" so much as a "*colored* land moving into the orbits hitherto reserved for whites."[37]

Yet the task of imagining how Native people could enter the world "reserved for whites" was freighted with unique difficulties, problems shared by Native people around the world. When Phinney tried to translate Marx's definition of just one term, "historical materialism," from English into Sahaptin, a relative of Nez Perce, it took him 151 words to relay Marx's concept. In English, he wrote, it took only 50.[38] As Phinney wrote in his essay on Native languages, European languages contained a ready-made infrastructure of abstract concepts suited to the West's historical-material development. By imposing Russian on all aspects of tribal life, tsarist Russia had denied Native people access to modernity in their own languages. "One of the most effective instruments of bending national minority life to the devastating economic interests of an outside ruling bourgeoisie was that of language," Phinney wrote. "The Russianizing process was an outright system of making minor nationalities good subjects for exploitation."[39] Yet to exclude the Siberian peoples from the tools used to exploit them—from the Russian grammar of modernity—would rob them of a key power source. Even at the conceptual level, Indigenous people lived in a double bind.

Phinney therefore refused to accept the primitivism / modernity binary, which posits the Native as a static foil to the industrial order, to be mourned, praised, even cherished like a museum specimen, but never to seek change. He championed a practical bilingualism, in which Indigenous languages would not only survive but even develop in a country where "native conversation, tradition, mythology, folk tales and songs are glorified." Russian would be taught, too, as a means for Native peoples to enter "the new living world" of science, technology, philosophy, political science, art, and literature.[40] If each language expresses a "whole way of life," then for those tasks that are necessary for modern development Phinney encouraged the use of a language with centuries of exposure to European modernity. The Native language, he wrote, would be retained for the social and cultural life of the tribe, at some point overtaking Russian—or, in the United States, English—in wider and wider aspects of tribal life. Phinney's dialectical approach to "de-Russification" served him as a kind of metaphor: only through action, an alert adoption of the language of imperial practice, could Native people resist the power imbalance of imperialism.

While the Soviet legacy is at best mixed in its record with Siberian tribes, we can read Phinney's interest in Russia's Indigenous programs not as a promotion of Soviet policy but as an attempt to pose difficult questions about US policy to American readers. When Hughes mused on the speed with which the Soviet Union ended its racial segregation policy in Central Asia, he was not suggesting Central Asia as a global model so much as highlighting the shortcomings of the United States. By articulating a theoretical "way out" for Indigenous people, imagining a life beyond the modernity binary, Phinney demanded that the United States answer the question, What would it mean to bring American Indians into a positive relationship with modern America?

One might think that John Collier's vision of the Indian New Deal would constitute a plausible answer to Phinney's question. Collier, himself inspired by socialist ideals, could be said to have provided an American version of what Phinney had admired in the Soviet policy of economic development and cultural pluralism for national minorities.[41] Phinney recognized the affinities and eagerly sought work with the BIA when he returned from the Soviet Union. "I am very anxious to get into this work," he wrote to Boas, after sending Collier an outline of ideas no doubt inspired by his Soviet education. "It has been my goal for many years, and now through your help I am at last being considered."[42] While it took him a few more years, he was eventually hired by the Collier administration, under new employment guidelines with respect to Native American staff at the BIA.

Yet it is clear that Phinney ultimately developed his own vision of Indian self-empowerment, one that expressed a greater skepticism of the settler state than his subsequent decision to work for the government would suggest. Sending a long and critical letter to Collier several years after his employment with the BIA ended, Phinney reflected on what he felt was the fatal flaw of the Indian Reorganization Act. It had failed to break out of the "rigid guardianship of the government." Objecting to the dominance of white anthropologists and missionaries at the American Indian Conference in 1939, Phinney formed a new caucus, one "limited to bona fide Indian leaders," that would be independent of Collier's BIA.[43] This caucus became the National Congress of American Indians.

A reading of Phinney's published and unpublished writings reveals that it was finally this pan-Indian organization through which Phinney felt Native Americans could express a modern sense of self and exert a political force upon the nation.[44] In an essay entitled "A New Indian Intelligentsia" Phinney sketched out his vision of the NCAI. It would serve, he thought, as a way to respond to the meaning of being Indian in the modern world. Interestingly, Phinney began the essay with a call for American Indians to radically transform their concept of their own identity:

> Apart from any considerations of racism or nationalism, there must be ascribed to American Indians not only a tribal status but a racial status. The concept of an Indian "race" derives largely from our modern propensity for classifying groups of people rather than individualizing them. Anciently, Indians identified themselves

> by local groups or bands, later by tribes and ethno-linguistic stocks, until now they have gained a distinct consciousness of that all-embracing classification—"Indians." . . . This trend is already apparent among Indian tribes as it is among other minorities throughout the world.[45]

Whether Phinney's ideas on race developed from his frustrations with the tribalism imposed by the BIA or from his experiences with global racial solidarity in the Soviet Union we have no way of knowing. But it is clear that Phinney reconfigured his dialectical approach to modernity after he left Russia, ultimately applying it to Indian selfhood. By inhabiting a racial identity, Phinney came to believe, Indians could inhabit a modern political identity.

Ever the dialectician, Phinney now saw that the imposed identity of race, like the imposed identity of the worker under capitalism, could serve as a means of forming collective strength. Equally important, a new, pan-Indian racial identification would create resistance to modern definitions that prevented Indians from organizing. Anticipating that tribal identity would often prevent Native peoples from developing wider alliances, Phinney stressed the necessity of a broader affinity. "Indian racial heritage is not a thing that depends for its survival upon a reservation atmosphere," he wrote. "Non-reservation Indians are probably the most capable and aggressive element of the Indian population in the United States."[46]

Phinney's last point seems telling. Rather than imagine, as Mathews did in his pointedly titled *Sundown,* that modernity would bring only tragedy to those Indians brave or foolish enough to face it, Phinney envisioned the shift from local and ethnic forms of belonging toward a broader racial identity as a move that would help Indians govern their own affairs. Phinney envisioned the NCAI as the vanguard of this new, pan-Indian community. It would be far more "aggressive and militant" than earlier Indian organizations—more "aggressive and militant" precisely because it acknowledged the modernity of the Indian condition.[47]

Phinney's aggressively global approach to imperialism and his ultimate turn toward racial affiliation did not mean that he embraced assimilation. The NCAI limited its involvement with white-led organizations, and its membership was restricted solely to Indians. Indeed, the NCAI was so suspicious of white authority that any Indian working for the BIA was not allowed to assume a position of leadership. At its foundation, the NCAI considered self-determination and sovereignty its primary political concerns. The organization sought to advance Indian interests at the national level, articulating a broadly Native point of view separate from tribal and land-based identities yet inextricably interwoven with local concerns. The founders of the NCAI understood that their interests coincided with those of other people of color, yet they saw Indian identity as a precise form of belonging emerging from distinct histories, treaty claims, and legal relationships with the federal government.[48] In other words, the NCAI, through Phinney's visionary construction, made use of racial formations to function politically in the modern world while retaining a sovereign Indian identity and purpose.

Rather than understand Phinney as an Indian activist who was uninterested in socialism, as two critics suggest, or as a "white man's Indian" who adopted European ideas unsuited for Native life, as another critic suggests, we might therefore see him as being more like other intellectuals of color of his day: concerned with colonialism, racial identity, and self-determination for his people in a global context.[49] Just as the recent upsurge of scholarship on black internationalism between the 1920s and 1950s has done much to shift black political consciousness away from Harlem and Paris to the so-called peripheries of empire, it seems appropriate to consider the ways in which at least some Indian activists and intellectuals addressed their concerns not only across divergent dislocations and diasporas but through the lens of the international socialist left. While critics are obviously uncomfortable with Phinney's embrace of the Soviet Union in the 1930s, I would suggest that we consider it in much the same vein as we consider African American intellectuals' fascination with the Soviet project: they saw in Russia a non-Western nation modernizing on its own terms.

That Phinney's view simplified the Soviet Union and overlooked its many shortcomings did not rob him of the creative or analytical power posed by an alternate modernity, one that provided a template for imagining a new way of experiencing a colonizing and colonized world. The Soviet Union's official positions against racism, against imperialism, and in support of anticolonial liberation appealed to many intellectuals of the interwar years as an answer to the intractable forms of dispossession and exploitation inherent in capitalism. Had Phinney lived long enough, he, like many other radical intellectuals of color, would have been dragged before the House Un-American Activities Committee, banned from federal employment, and possibly arrested under the Smith Act. That Phinney's contributions are rarely remembered today and are sanitized when they are remembered is one by-product of this intellectual purge, which has shaped those hostile and those sympathetic to Phinney's vision.

Warrior and Bruyneel both have argued that moving beyond an "authentic" vision of Native identity and a spatially fixed terrain of struggle can serve as a form of "intellectual sovereignty," a way of imagining a mobile and flexible form of political identity suited to modern challenges.[50] If Phinney saw that Indigenous rights were tied to the fate of other people of color, if he understood equally that imperialism and racism were inseparable constructs, then his decision to write about the Soviet Union placed him squarely "among other minorities throughout the world." Phinney thus proved through his own example that modernity and sovereignty are not opposites; rather, a radical and race-conscious modernity could be one way for American Indians to express their sovereignty. Phinney's radicalism about modernity makes him no less Native. It suggests that the concept of indigeneity, like the concept of modernity, must be changed to address the way it shapes and is shaped by the people through which it lives.

## Notes

I would like to thank the Nez Perce Historical Park for help in locating images of Archie Phinney, the librarians at the National Archives—Pacific Alaska Region, and the Indiana University New Frontiers Foundation for the funds that made travel possible.

1. John Joseph Mathews, *Sundown* (New York: Longmans, Green, 1934), 218.
2. Philip J. Deloria, *Indians in Unexpected Places* (Lawrence: University Press of Kansas, 2004), 6.
3. Ibid., 168–70.
4. Kevin Bruyneel, *The Third Space of Sovereignty: The Post-Colonial Politics of U.S.–Indigenous Relations* (Minneapolis: University of Minnesota Press, 2007), 219, 107–9.
5. David Scott, *Conscripts of Modernity: The Tragedy of Colonial Enlightenment* (Durham: Duke University Press, 2004).
6. Archie Phinney, "Numipu Among the White Settlers," *Wicazo Sa Review* 17, no. 2 (2002): 42.
7. Andrew Roy Potter, "Archie Phinney as Archetype," in "Climbing into the Ring: Indian Employees in the Office of Indian Affairs, 1934–1946" (MA thesis, Western Washington University, 1992), 45.
8. Archie Phinney to Superintendent O. H. Lipps, quoted in William Willard, "An American Indian Odyssey," conference paper presented at "Honoring the Heritage of the Plateau Peoples: Past, Present, and Future," Pullman, WA, 2004, 12–13; William Willard, "The Nez Perce Anthropologist," *Journal of Northwest Anthropology* 38, no. 1 (2004): 16–17.
9. Archie Phinney, "On Understanding Soviet Russia," address delivered before the Tesceminium Club, Lewiston, Idaho, 1943, Box 2, Archie Phinney Papers, RG 075, National Archives—Pacific Alaska Region (hereafter AP).
10. Hakim Adi, "The Negro Question: The Communist International and Black Liberation in the Interwar Years," in *From Toussaint to Tupac: The Black International Since the Age of Revolution,* ed. Michael O. West, William G. Martin, and Fanon Che Wilkins (Chapel Hill: University of North Carolina Press, 2009), 155; Robin D. G. Kelley, "'This Ain't Ethiopia, But It'll Do': African Americans and the Spanish Civil War," *Race Rebels: Culture, Politics, and the Black Working Class* (New York: Free Press, 1994), 123–58.

11. For a description of the intellectual and political impact of Soviet policy on anticolonial intellectuals, see Kate A. Baldwin, *Beyond the Color Line and the Iron Curtain: Reading Encounters Between Black and Red, 1922–1963* (Durham: Duke University Press, 2002), and William J. Maxwell, *Old Negro, New Left: African-American Writing and Communism Between the Wars* (New York: Columbia University Press, 1999).
12. Archie Phinney to Franz Boas, quoted in William Willard, "Remembering Archie Phinney, a Nez Perce Scholar," *Journal of Northwest Anthropology* 38, no. 2 (2004): 1.
13. This note may be found on the margins of some class notes that Phinney took in a course on Marxism at the Leningrad Academy of Sciences. Archie Phinney, untitled class notes, 1934, AP.
14. Phinney, "Numipu Among the White Settlers," 34.
15. Ibid.
16. Ibid., 33. For a recent historical study of these links, see Lorenzo Veracini, "Settler Colonialism: Career of a Concept," *Journal of Imperial and Commonwealth History* 41, no. 2 (2013): 313–33.
17. Phinney, "Numipu Among the White Settlers," 26.
18. Ibid., 28.
19. Ibid., 34.
20. Ibid., 32.
21. Ibid., 40.
22. Ibid., 42.
23. Ibid.
24. Ibid., 41.
25. Ibid.
26. Ibid., 42.
27. Theodor Adorno, *Negative Dialectics* (1973; repr. New York: Continuum, 2007), 362.
28. Archie Phinney to Franz Boas, Aug. 8, 1933, Box 70, Franz Boas Papers, American Philosophical Society (hereafter BP).
29. Archie Phinney, "Racial Minorities in the Soviet Union," *Pacific Affairs* 8, no. 3 (1935): 321.
30. Ibid., 324–25.
31. Ibid., 325.
32. Ibid.
33. Ibid., 327.
34. It is beyond the scope of this essay to open debates on Soviet policy; rather, the aim is to examine Phinney's use of his experiences in the Soviet Union to develop his ideas of modernity. For two nuanced, if divergent, analyses of the Soviet policy on national minorities, see Yuri Slezkine, *Arctic Mirrors: Russia and the Small Peoples of the North* (Ithaca: Cornell University Press, 1994), and Terry Martin, *The Affirmative Action Empire: Nations and Nationalism in the Soviet Union, 1923–1939* (Ithaca: Cornell University Press, 2001).
35. Archie Phinney, "On Minority Languages in the Soviet Union," written on the back of notes for *Nez Percé Texts,* 2, AP.
36. Robert A. Warrior, *Tribal Secrets: Recovering American Indian Intellectual Traditions* (Minneapolis: University of Minnesota Press, 1995), 111.
37. Langston Hughes, *I Wonder as I Wander: An Autobiographical Journey* (1956; repr. New York: Farrar, Straus, and Giroux, 1993), 116.

38. Phinney, "On Minority Languages in the Soviet Union," 5–6.
39. Ibid.
40. Ibid., 17.
41. See Kenneth R. Philp, *John Collier's Crusade for Indian Reform, 1920–1954* (Tucson: University of Arizona Press, 1977).
42. Archie Phinney to Franz Boas, Sept. 6, 1934, Box 70, BP.
43. Dolores E. Janiewski, "'Confusion of Mind': Colonial and Post-Colonial Discourses About Frontier Encounters," *Journal of American Studies* 32, no. 1 (1998): 101.
44. Archie Phinney, "Personal History and Experience Record," Office of Indian Affairs, quoted in Potter, "Climbing into the Ring," 49.
45. Archie Phinney, "The New Indian Intelligentsia," 1, AP.
46. Ibid., 2.
47. Thomas W. Cowger, *The National Congress of American Indians: The Founding Years* (Lincoln: University of Nebraska Press, 1999), 34–36.
48. Ibid., 35–39.
49. For a reading of Phinney as an anti-Communist, see David Price, "Archie Phinney, the FBI, and the FOIA," *Journal of Northwest Anthropology* 38, no. 2 (2004): 28–31, and Willard, "Remembering Archie Phinney," 1. For a reading of Phinney as an assimilated Indian, see Janiewski, "Confusion of Mind," 100. All three accounts understand Phinney on strictly binary terms: he must be a "pure Indian" or a Communist, an Indian nationalist or someone in favor of assimilation.
50. Warrior, *Tribal Secrets*, 124; Bruyneel, *The Third Space of Sovereignty*, xvii–xix, 217–29.

# Part Four **Boasiana: The Global Flow of the Culture Concept**

# Chapter 12 The River of Salvation Flows Through Africa: Edward Wilmot Blyden, Raphael Armattoe, and the Redemption of the Culture Concept

*Sean Hanretta*

The concept of culture, in the Boasian sense of the learned, variable, and mutable "structures" underlying "the behavior of the individuals composing a social group collectively and individually," has played an important role in the production of knowledge about many human societies. As a conceptual heuristic, Franz Boas's method facilitated the introduction not just of new facts but also new ideas and theories into the Western intellectual canon.[1] As contributors to this volume suggest, Boas's willingness to allow his own thinking to be influenced by that of his interlocutors, along with the willingness of those interlocutors to take Boas (and his students) on as targets of their own civilizing efforts, helped professional anthropology become one conduit in the global exchange of ideas.[2]

Yet Boasian cultural anthropology represented only one current in a broader turn toward culturalist thinking that contained many other varieties, several of which remained largely outside the scope of professional academia. This more general sense of culture consolidated in the mid-nineteenth century, but by the Second World War the crystallization of the nation-state system had revealed its limitations. Yet during that brief life this broader stream had significant intellectual and political implications for knowledge about West Africa. In this chapter I explore some ways of framing the intellectual and political implications of that broader stream by examining two moments in the history of the culture concept as applied to West Africa: first, a moment during the process of the concept's formation in the mid-nineteenth century; second, a moment in the 1950s that revealed the political limits of appeals to culture.

Whereas it was once necessary to assert Boas's importance to the development of the culture concept, his contribution to the transformation of ethnological thought away from racialist evolutionism through the application of German historicism to human differences is now generally accepted.[3] More complicated is the question of what it means to discuss the origin of the culture concept itself and the process of its emergence in Germany, England, the United States, and elsewhere. Insofar as any origin is conceived of as an event that brings about a rupture within a specific context even as that context simultaneously provides the local meaning and proximate significance for the event, identifying the "origin" of a concept can serve as a productive way to denaturalize present ideologies and open up new historical questions.[4] Suggesting that the origins of key elements of anthropological theory—in this case, of the culture concept itself—should be sought in "Indigenous theory" and, furthermore, attributing the entry of these theories into Western academic discourse to the "openness" of Boasian ethnographic practice has real consequences. It holds the potential to require a reimagining of the genealogy of anthropology itself. Such an approach, disrupting the progressive teleology running from German *Volksgeist* to the "postcolonial turn," can provide the theoretical framework for a new, robust global history of ideas. Not least, it forces a rethinking of the nature of the colonial encounter.[5]

The approach I propose here, however, highlights not origins but the instability of concepts that are tested and contested through practical use. Instead of imagining the conceptual or discursive space of an origin as a threshold between two regimes—epistemic, political, or otherwise—this mode of study explores the "vast accumulation of 'contradictions' . . . [that can occasionally] 'merge' into a real unity." This confluence constitutes a rupture in context, but one in which each individual contradiction determines the outcome "according to the specific modalities of . . . [its] action." In such a situation a phenomenon is what Louis Althusser called "over-determined in its principle."[6] My suggestion is thus that the history of the deployment of the culture concept in Africa reflected the contingent and shifting convergence of a vast range of global contradictions, including but not limited to those growing out of the internal development of various African intellectual projects. What I offer is not a history of this deployment—which would be beyond the scope of one essay—but a methodological exploration grouped around the salient figures of Edward Wilmot Blyden, widely considered as one of the founders of both Pan-Africanism and Afrocentrism, and Raphael Ernest Grail Armattoe, a largely forgotten biological researcher, poet, and minor politician from what is now Ghana.

Although they were very different kinds of intellectuals and were born eight decades apart, both Blyden and Armattoe operated within a conceptual space that came into existence in the middle part of the nineteenth century. The seventeenth, eighteenth, and early nineteenth centuries—the era of the peak of the transatlantic slave trade—had seen Africa integrated into the global economy and African cultural practices spread throughout an unprecedentedly wide geographic area. But Africa-based intellectuals were themselves rarely in a position during these centuries to frame European debates on civilization and social theory and, perhaps more significant, few Europeans had much interest in listening to them. The gradual decline of the transatlantic slave trade brought with it a new phase in Euro-African economic exchange, and the nineteenth century in many ways saw a kind of intellectual and political renaissance in Atlantic Africa as the tremendous chaos of the slaving era receded.

This shift opened up new discursive possibilities. The British anti-slave-trade naval blockade of the 1830s occasioned an explosion of English travel writing about West Africa and a new interest in the region among English-speaking merchants and missionaries. Further north, the French conquest of Algeria similarly afforded on-the-ground opportunities to fuse empirical investigations, universalist philosophy, and practices of racial differentiation.[7] The 1850s and 1860s came to be pivotal decades in the production of knowledge about Africa as new European-African relationships intersected with the emergence of history and anthropology as autonomous intellectual disciplines. To be sure, it was during these years that new forms of imperialism and the pseudoscientific version of racism began to crystallize, but one of the formative ironies of Western discourse on Africa is the degree to which such odious developments coincided with intellectual exchange.

Among the new questions Europeans began asking about Africa were ones about the place of Islam on the continent. The intersection of classic Orientalist fascination with the "East" and a newer interest in the "otherness" of African societies framed some major theorizing about culture and race. Travelers' accounts of Muslim Africa had a great influence on budding scientific specialists. Abd Salam Shabeeny's *An Account of Timbuctoo and Housa* came out in 1820 and gave substance to what had previously been scattered, quasi-legendary accounts of the region. René Caillié's *Journal d'un voyage à Temboctou et à Jenné dans l'Afrique Centrale* appeared in 1830, Nicolas Perron translated the Egyptian traveler Ibn Omar al-Tounsy's *Voyage au Darfur* and *Voyage au Ouaday* into French in 1845 and 1851, respectively, and Heinrich Barth's monumental *Reisen und Entdeckungen in Nord-und Zentralafrika* appeared in pieces and then fully in 1857–58. The translation of the writings of the famous fourteenth-century Muslim traveler Ibn Battuta into German and then English, followed by the discovery in Algeria of more versions of his manuscripts, brought older Arab knowledge of Africa into European studies by the late 1850s. In each of these accounts ideas about African history, about the role of Islam within it, and about the cultural meaning of racial differences were formed dialogically through interactions with Africans themselves.[8]

Theodor Waitz's foundational work, *Anthropologie der Naturvölker*, the first two volumes of which came out in 1859 and 1860, drew extensively on the new exploratory literature on Africa, including the accounts by Barth and al-Tounsy. Despite relying heavily on racial thinking, Waitz's text, more than any other, marked the appearance of the modern form of cultural anthropology with its claim that "the greatest actual differences in the development of psychical life are only the result of a *fluctuating* difference in culture."[9] In 1863 the translation into English of the first volume as *Introduction to Anthropology* placed an interpretive framework for organizing the flood of new data about Africa into the hands of British scholars and public figures, fitfully moving some of them away from the racialist anthropology of Samuel Morton and Louis Agassiz.[10] In doing so, it set the stage for the entry of African voices into the heart of European debates about culture and race. Ironically, the subsequent professionalizing of anthropology in the early twentieth century—in which the personal testimony of the trained field-worker came to be the gold standard for authenticating evidence—brought with it a devaluation of the very travelers' accounts that had opened up European thought to global intellectual currents in the nineteenth century. It is thus of no small import that culturalist thinking flourished during the second half of the 1800s, and it is to the nature of global intellectual developments in that period that we should look to understand the shifting parameters of Western thought.[11]

The moments of intellectual contact that took place during this fifty-year "window of opportunity" need to be theorized in a way that recognizes the fields of power in which encounters took place while also making room for contact's own causal force. Few today would embrace V.-Y. Mudimbe's idea of a closed "colonial library" that generated a stable image of Africa as the object of European contemplation. Nonetheless, too many studies of Western representations of Africa remain enthralled by the apparent coherence of European discourses on Africa, so that African discourses on Africa (or on Europe) remain in the position of providing only occasional, local emendations to or perturbations of a narrative that requires little beyond a familiarity with European intellectual history to sustain itself.[12] Blyden and Armattoe help illustrate how the idea of African culture(s) could coalesce and fray in those discursive spaces where theorizing was most open to eclectic influences.

In an effort to sketch a kind of global genealogy while avoiding an approach to intellectual history that makes individual prominent thinkers the main agents of change, my approach has been to take one figure who is typically seen as a nearly unique genius, Blyden, and place him back within a broader discursive context on race, religion, and culture to reveal the ways in which his ideas were prefigured, prompted, and amplified by those of others. At the same time, I take a marginal figure, Armattoe, who could easily be seen as a derivative intellectual operating as a kind of curiosity at the edges of various deeper currents of thought, and highlight the unique constellation of ideas and positions his lifework gathered together. Once resituated as vectors of intellectual exchange, these two thinkers suggest, on the one hand, that the culture concept arose out of a broad space of interaction between intellectual currents that were both global and particular, and, on the other, that the concept, once formalized, could be put to a wide range of political uses by those who sought to intervene in the pattern of those currents' interactions.

## THE RIVER OF SALVATION

Edward Wilmot Blyden was one of the towering intellectual figures of the nineteenth century, a touchstone for generations of Africanists, Afrocentrists, Pan-Africanists, and black Muslims. His influence on such figures as J. E. Casely Hayford, W. E. B. Du Bois, Marcus Garvey, Aimé Césaire, Léopold Sédar Senghor, Amílcar Cabral, Kwame Nkrumah, George Padmore, Elijah Muhammad, and Malcom X is well known, and Blyden has recently attracted the attention of postcolonialist scholars, for whom he appears as a precursor to Frantz Fanon.[13] Born in St. Thomas in 1832, Blyden moved to Liberia in 1851 out of frustration with the racial caste system that had blocked his educational aspirations in the United States. An extreme polymath, political idealist, Presbyterian pastor, and influential teacher, Blyden was famous by the 1870s for championing education as the way to transform Africa and as a harsh critic of missionization and Americo-Liberian domination in Liberia. But perhaps more than anything else, Blyden scandalized many with his writings on religion in West Africa. Celebrating West African Muslims for their sophistication,

Edward Wilmot Blyden posed for this photograph by Henry Maull during a visit to London sometime between 1866 and 1878, perhaps while en route to Egypt and Palestine in 1866 or perhaps during a longer stay in 1871. Blyden's trips to London were crucial to the circulation and cross-pollination of ideas about Islam in Africa. Library of Congress LC-USZ62–135638.

their self-possession, and their vigor, Blyden openly wondered why any African would convert to Christianity given the racism of many missionaries and the role of the Christian world in brutalizing the continent. Such ideas endeared him to generations of scholars and activists who sought to identify or fashion a global, cosmopolitan form of Africanness that could counter the insidious racism of the West.

That Blyden was simultaneously unique and globally resonant—what Harry Odamtten has called a "global African iconoclast"—has made him an emblem of countermodernization and a difficult thinker to categorize.[14] Certainly Blyden's great contribution to the critique of colonialism and of white supremacy was his construction of a counterhistory that valorized Africans as "Negroes" and celebrated their distinctive character. Much of that work took place in a "vindicationist" mode that would seem to be the opposite of Boas's deracialized sense of culture. Indeed, Blyden has often been interpreted as sharing a fundamentally Victorian sense of race that revealed his deep debt to his white Christian mentors and that today frequently leads scholars to compartmentalize him as a "race thinker" or activist.[15] To a certain extent this interpretation reflects the works that are typically read to illuminate his thought. While the locus classicus of Blyden's ideas about Islam in Africa is usually taken to be his *Christianity, Islam and the Negro Race,* a fuller understanding of his ideas and their sources can be gained from examining his most literary work, *From West Africa to Palestine,* written nearly a decade before his more celebrated essays, and his most philosophically ambitious work, *The Arabic Bible in the Soudan: A Plea for Transliteration,* a neglected pamphlet written near the end of his life in 1910. Together these writings reveal that Blyden's interest in African Islam was grounded in a sophisticated theory of human civilizational evolution and its relationship with both the environment and the working out through history of a deep, cosmological truth. By combining an attentiveness to the specifics of the African peoples he encountered with a theology that was grounded in Christianity but that, ultimately, exceeded the bounds of Christian orthodoxy, Blyden made major contributions to the concept of culture itself, contributions that would live on, albeit sometimes in repressed form, in the writings of those he influenced.

Blyden's sense of culture was part of the broader current of such thinking that would come to include Boas, even as Blyden's own ideas differed considerably from those that would shape anthropology in the twentieth century. But the fact that, nearly thirty years before Boas's own shift to a culturalist framework, Blyden argued that Islam was a better fit for Africans than Christianity on the grounds of cultural particularism and the historical impact of environment and society on collective thought highlights the importance of attending to the more subtle products of nineteenth-century global intellectual exchange. To see this, it is useful to place Blyden in a specific philosophical milieu. Teshale Tibebu has profitably identified the deep similarities between Blyden and G. W. F. Hegel, noting the ways in which an idealist historicism manifests itself both in Blyden's analyses and in his easily quotable rhetoric. Some of Blyden's most provocative claims, among them that "Islam is the form Christianity takes in Africa" or that slavery was Providence's indirect way of arranging for Africa's salvation, reveal a philosophy that imagines civilizational progress as taking place in precisely localized contexts even as the formal significance of events depended on the ways they instantiated the universal.

To be sure, Blyden has been criticized for associating Islam with a manifestation of universal truth at the expense of other African religions and for supporting the idea of colonization in general, even if he did criticize particular Americo-Liberians and most European colonialists. But lost in the fair complaint that he showed certain prejudices about "traditional" African culture is the fact that Blyden also insisted that "African Islam," a version of the religion that he imagined as humane and tolerant, constituted a unique human accomplishment. He never stopped asserting the particular genius of African cultural practices, insisting on the necessity of analyzing situation and form together and on the primacy of practice itself over abstract civilizational ideals.[16]

To understand Blyden's view of culture, we must start at the end, looking carefully at his most sophisticated formulation of his thoughts on African Islam, ideas he set down in *The Arabic Bible in the Soudan.* By the time Blyden wrote that pamphlet in 1910, he had long been accused of betraying Christianity and of having converted to Islam. But *The Arabic Bible* suggests his ideas went far beyond a mere advocacy for one faith or the other. Those who claim Blyden for Islam have suggested that his professed commitment to Christianity was a strategic posture, adopted to curry favor with his missionary supporters and funders or to protect him from the hostility of Liberia's Christian elites or British colonial officers in Sierra Leone. But a familiarity with Blyden's correspondence, published writing, and actions reveals that his sense of himself as a Christian remained strong and orientating. Nonetheless, Blyden's commitment to Christianity was somewhat situational—not the situationalism of a political pragmatist or opportunist but one derived from Christianity's own historical specificity.

Blyden's stated purpose in *The Arabic Bible* was to improve the translations produced by missionaries so as to make the Bible more intelligible and less offensive to West African Muslim scholars. But the way he pursued that objective revealed a much larger intellectual project. In this pamphlet Blyden posited the ideal unity of Islam and Christianity and suggested that they were similar endpoints of historically distinct developmental trajectories. Echoing some ideas about language expressed by Hegel's close associate Friedrich Hölderlin, ideas which themselves presaged the culturalist position, Blyden called for the various names of God that appeared in the Hebrew Bible to be "transliterated" into Arabic rather than "translated."[17] By this he meant that Arabic words whose roots were close cognates of the Hebrew names should be chosen rather than Arabic words that conveyed the theological meaning attributed to those names. Furthermore, Blyden made explicit his intellectual debt for this idea to the initiatives of his West African interlocutors:

> My attention was called to this subject some time ago by some Mohammedans, among whom in the interior of Liberia and Sierra Leone I had distributed Arabic Bibles. They seemed to admire the purity and simplicity of the Arabic employed in the translation . . . , the style of the Koran having been closely imitated by the translators.
>
> When asked, however, whether they had gained in religious knowledge by a perusal of the book, those more skilled in the language and theology of Islam replied that they had received a great deal of profitable information, but that they could not make use of the book in their schools, because in various parts of it language is employed in connection with the Supreme Being, ALLAH, in conflict with the teachings of the Koran.
>
> One of these learned men, a Mandingo from the interior, who has frequently honoured me with his visits, and is now a teacher in a Mohammedan village just across the river from Sierra Leone . . . , said the first thing that astonished and repelled him was the statement made in Gen. I., 26, 27, that God (*Allah*) made man in his own image and after his likeness, repeated in Gen. V., 1. To this he opposed Koran XLII., 9, which says: "There is nothing like God" (*Allah*).[18]

From this starting point Blyden moved to reconcile the two traditions by excavating their shared roots, roots that had been occluded, he believed, by an anxious Hellenizing of Christianity. "So far as I have been able to discover," he insisted, "there is no ground whatever in the original text of the Old Testament for the objections of the Muslim. There is no anthropomorphism in the Hebrew Bible, and there is none in the Koran. All the misunderstanding, it seems to me, has arisen partly from the mistake of *translating* instead of *transliterating* proper names." Translation, he argued, required a distorting movement from the Hebrew original, through Greek-influenced philosophical theism, and then back to Semitic Arabic. A proper understanding of the names used for "God" would reveal that attributing a monotheistic vision to the Hebrew Bible would be inaccurate, "implying that the Solidary, Supreme, Incomprehensible, Unknowable Power without form, name or place, is also subject to limitations. Neither can the word theology be properly applied to the Hebrew system." The concept of theology might be conceptually coherent within Greek philosophy, but "Yahwehology, Kuriology, Dominology is impossible." Transliteration of God's names would, by contrast, highlight the shared cultural origins of Arabic and Hebrew and allow Muslims to glimpse Christianity's authentic nature.[19]

On the surface this approach seems something like Max Müller's efforts to identify an underlying "natural religion" in all peoples; indeed, Blyden believed in the existence of such a religion, at least to some extent, noting, "There is no nation or tribe who has not access, by whatever medium—stone, tree, snake or crocodile—to the Divine ear and to the Divine guardianship." But the weight he attached to such a fact was conditioned by his historicism and his radically anti-Eurocentric inversion of Hegel's picture of world history. Nowhere else did Blyden make so explicit his own fusion of theology and history:

> Islam or Christianity for Africa is not the only alternative. . . . The ultimate fate of Africa does not depend exclusively upon Jerusalem, Rome or Mecca. It may be that from some height yet undiscerned, the river of Salvation may flow through Africa and may quench the thirst of other nations also. It will not be the first time that Africa has given religion to the outside world. Then will come the end, when all things shall be delivered up to Jehovah; when as Zechariah predicted, the Lord (Jehovah) shall be king over all the earth, in that one day there shall be one Jehovah and HIS NAME ONE. Zech. XIV, 9.[20]

It was by participating in this potentially world-historical development that African culture as a practical reality revealed its specific essence.

## SAME FAMILY, DIFFERENT CIRCUMSTANCES

As nuanced and idiosyncratic as they were, what is perhaps most striking about Blyden's thoughts about Africa and African Islam is how easily they grew out of attitudes circulating in the Atlantic world in the mid- and late 1800s. West African Muslims themselves played a decisive role in the emergence of these attitudes. The post-slave trade transformations taking place in Africa, Europe, and the Americas had created a new discursive space for Muslim scholars seeking to reach out and connect, promoting their own views about culture, civilization, race, and religion. Timing was crucial, for, not coincidentally, the early nineteenth century was a period of cataclysmic transformation in the institutions of Islam in West Africa, transformation whose consequences included the dispersal of a new generation of highly trained and confident Islamic scholars throughout the area between Lake Chad and the western tip of the continent. In other words, in the same moment that European travelers and analysts were newly encountering Africa, they were encountering a new type of Islamic African culture.[21] Muslim reformists impressed British travelers and ambassadors in northern Nigeria and the Gambia as well as French traders and officials in Senegal and the areas to its east, and both the form and content of those impressions proved consequential.

The most important site of exchange was Freetown, the British colonial capital in Sierra Leone. Established in 1787 as a semivoluntary settlement for the "Black Poor" of England, Freetown after 1808 became a resettlement point for Africans whom the British navy seized from slaving vessels. It was a deeply cosmopolitan site, occupied by people from all over West and West-Central Africa. From 1816 to the 1860s Protestant missionaries in Sierra Leone interacted with Muslims from throughout the region, gathering up information and manuscripts from them, translating texts from various languages into English, and sketching the outlines of a comparative theology of Islam and Christianity in an explicitly African context.

Most of these missionaries remained committed to a Eurocentric interpretation of African Islam, but they nonetheless became conduits for new voices. S. W. Koelle, the first Western scholar to do serious comparative work on the languages of Africa, was a Freetown missionary from 1847 to 1853, and he took advantage of the town's multilingual population to create his magnum opus, *Polyglotta Africana,* a comparative dictionary of four dozen West African languages.[22] Koelle helped publicize the existence of the Vai syllabary, an Indigenous script whose Muslim inventors became famous among scholars as an example of African civilizers and which Koelle came to know about through his friendship and interactions with local Muslims.[23] Yet Koelle's interest in Muslim culture did not translate into a defense of Islam. Instead, in 1865 he published an anti-Islamic tract, *Food for Reflection,* under the pseudo-Muslim name Abd Isā, that is, Servant of Jesus. A classic Christian apologetics, Koelle's book drew on the abolitionist rhetoric of the "Islamic slavery" of Africans to make a direct attack on those who saw Islam as having a *mission civilisatrice:*

> It is true, the Mohammedan nations in the interior of Africa, . . . invited by the weak and defenceless condition of the surrounding negro tribes, still occasionally make conquests, and after subduing a tribe of pagans, by almost extirpating its male population, and committing the most horrible atrocities, impose upon those that remain the creed of Islam; but, keeping in view the whole of the Mohammedan world, this fitful and far off activity reminds one only of those green branches sometimes seen on trees already and for long decayed at the core from age.[24]

Nonetheless, Koelle's work on the Vai syllabary contributed, gradually, to a reimagining of African Islam, at least partially because it was followed by further "discoveries" prompted by African Muslims. In 1858 Muhammad Sali brought manuscripts of Fula history to the head of the European intelligentsia in Freetown, Charles Reichardt.[25] In nearby Liberia the end of a series of conflicts in the Futa Jallon region northeast of Monrovia brought an increase in trade and visits by Muslim scholars to the capital. Arabic manuscripts arriving via these circuits were relayed from Monrovia to New York in 1862 and again in 1871. Coinciding with the increasing interest in North America's own previously unacknowledged Muslim population, specialists jumped on these documents, praising and publicizing them.[26]

In each of these acts the original initiative was taken by West African Muslims themselves, and while the content of these materials may have mattered less than their efforts to communicate with Europeans at the coast, Muslim scholars—whether advertently or inadvertently we may never know—found a receptive audience. The idea that Islam could offer an alternative to the flaws of European civilization had been toyed with in elite Western circles as early as Montesquieu's *Persian Letters* in 1721 and had even been forged into an explicit critique of Western racism by Olaudah Equiano in his famous *Narrative* of 1789.[27] The Napoleonic project in Egypt gave impetus to a post-Enlightenment fascination with Islam, much of which fitted the overall picture of the emergence of Orientalism with which we have become familiar. But the interplay of European ideas about race, religion, and the "Orient" generated complex descriptive accounts and programs. As did racial thinking more generally, this work interacted with the new social sciences. For instance, Pierre-Henri Stanislas d'Escayrac's *Le Désert et le Soudan* (1853) gave prominence to the idea that Islam had helped bring the civilization of the Mediterranean ecumene to Africa, where it developed a particularly tolerant form, less nationalistic and more humble than its Middle Eastern versions. For his part, Waitz judged that Islam was "more compatible" with African culture (and tropical cultures generally) than Christianity and had thus spread with greater ease and, in some cases at least, been more ameliorative.[28]

Blyden's interest in Islam grew out of these same dynamics. Indeed, Blyden did not arrive in Liberia espousing radical beliefs about race and Islam but rather developed them gradually, through reading the travel and scholarly literature on Africa and, above all, by interacting with the Indigenous Liberian population. Odamtten has revealed the extent to which Blyden's thought was shaped dialectically in opposition to that of the black Americo-Liberian elite. Although he initially shared the triumphalist vision of his fellow immigrants, his participation in a punitive expedition against the Grebo and Kru in 1856 brought him into contact with the people Monrovia's elite had targeted for colonial civilizational uplift. The horror and dissonance he experienced in being party to the destruction of these communities forced him to question his assumed moral and intellectual superiority and prompted him to study the history and customs of those living around him.[29]

Yet if this accounts for Blyden's sudden openness to learning about African cultures as such, it does not explain his precipitous turn to Islam. As late as

1864 Blyden showed little interest in Muslims. By 1866, however, he had taken a leave from his teaching duties at Liberia College and traveled to Egypt and the Levant to improve his Arabic and learn more about Islam. Accounting for this shift is not easy, but certain aspects of his experiences in Monrovia in the early 1860s, and especially the nature of his interactions with Muslims living in the area, are suggestive. For it was in this period, from 1863 to 1865, that Blyden became a prominent figure in Monrovia, first as a professor at Liberia College, then as secretary of state and as the preacher at the city's Presbyterian church. Perhaps this profile made him an attractive target of Muslim scholars seeking to establish commercial and intellectual relations with the American settlement, or perhaps his duties caused him to circulate more widely, making it easier for them to come into his presence. Certainly his growing abilities in Arabic facilitated such encounters greatly. Whatever caused Muslims to seek out Blyden personally, seek him out they did, with great consequence.

How Blyden first came to study Arabic remains unclear, but by 1866 he had clearly been exposed to the Qur'an and had at least rudimentary language skills and some awareness of Islamic theology. By May of that year he had determined to embark on a trip to the Middle East via Britain. The proximate cause of his departure was a conflict with his archrival, Joseph J. Roberts, the president of the college and former president of Liberia.[30] But his choice to travel east and devote his energies to Arabic was spurred by his relationships with African Muslims. Shortly before his departure he wrote,

> The other day, while on a visit to a native town, I met a couple of itinerant Mohammedan priests, with their books and papers. They could not speak a word of English. I wrote an Arabic passage from the Koran from memory. They read it, and raised their hands in astonishment that I should know anything of that language. They then showed me their papers, but I was not sufficiently acquainted with the language to read them. But I hope by perseverance to be able to learn that and several other native languages.[31]

Blyden's time in the Middle East solidified his desire to understand Islam and afforded him the opportunity to place his knowledge of African peoples and their history in a broader, theological framework. Famously, Blyden was deeply moved by the Great Pyramids of Egypt. A dramatic high point in his account of his journey, published as *From West Africa to Palestine* (1873), occurs when he descends into the ancient burial space itself:

> This, thought I, is the work of my African progenitors . . . : they had fame, and their descendants should strive, by nobler deeds, to "retake" it. Feelings came over me far different from those which I have felt when looking at the mighty works of

> European genius. I felt that I had a peculiar "heritage in the Great Pyramid"—built . . . by that branch of the descendants of Noah, the enterprising sons of Ham, from whom I am descended. The blood seemed to flow faster in my veins. I seemed to hear the echo of those illustrious Africans. I seemed to feel the impulse from those stirring characters who sent civilisation into Greece—the teachers of the fathers of poetry, history, and mathematics. . . . I felt lifted out of the commonplace grandeur of modern times; and, could my voice have reached every African in the world, I would have earnestly addressed him in the language of Hilary Teage—"Retake your fame!"[32]

This experience also drew Blyden's attention to the historical specificity of Liberia's civilizational project. "I felt that my perilous adventure [in the pyramid]," he wrote, "had given me the right of inscribing my name among the hundreds which I saw . . . on each side of the entrance, bearing dates as early as the sixteenth century. . . . I engraved, not far from a name dated 1685, the word LIBERIA, with my name and the date—July 11th, 1866—immediately under it. There is a tolerable degree of certainty, therefore, that the name at least of that little Republic will go down to posterity."[33]

Blyden's remarks at Giza have become the most eloquent evidence for an interpretation of his thought that is fundamentally Afrocentric and that privileges Blyden's thoughts on race over those on religion.[34] But a second realization took place some weeks later when he explored the holy sites of Jerusalem. There, he found opportunity to set in writing thoughts on race and religion that reflected his belief that environmental influence and cosmic revelation could together explain the relationship between cultural specificity and universality. He began with a biblical model of racial filiation that was built on the story of Ham, Shem, and Japheth, the sons of Noah. Long used by Christians to explain human diversity, the model was, by the mid-1800s, increasingly serving the interests of biological racists. Blyden, however, put it to different uses, first by injecting an evolutionary theme. He laid out a vision of racial history in which Africans were a young people, vital—"like the youthful and elastic Hebrews of old" or the contemporary "fresh and youthful Anglo-Saxon and Teutonic races"—and able to thrive in the New World and even delight "in the change of climate and circumstances." Echoing the theories of Carl Friedrich Philipp von Martius, Augustin Prichard, and other Humboldtians, he contrasted Africans to "American Indians, who were, without doubt, an old and worn-out people, could not survive the introduction of the new phases of life brought among them from Europe."

Historical evolution also helped resolve the apparent tension between claims about the youthfulness of the contemporary African race and the antiquity of its connections to the accomplishments of ancient Egypt. "We may conclude," Blyden wrote, "that as descendants of Ham had a share, as the most prominent actors on the scene, in the founding of cities and in the organisation of government, so members of the same family, developed under different circumstances, will have an important part in the closing of the great drama." But even then Blyden was beginning to blend physical evolution with the spiritual dialectics that would culminate in the theology of *The Arabic Bible.* Thinking back to his time in Egypt, Blyden averred that "what I felt [at the Pyramids] . . . was of the earth . . . drawn from worldly considerations . . . dwelt upon at length, because there have been such persevering efforts in modern times to ignore the participation of the African descendants of Ham in the great works of ancient civilisation. But *here* [in Jerusalem] the emotions I felt were such as are shared by every son of Adam who has been made to rejoice in the light of the gospel."[35]

It was this sense of human connection and shared destiny that accounted for Blyden's enthusiasm about the civilizational mixing that had produced African Islam. For despite his putative commitment to racial solidarity, Blyden valorized the "healthy amalgamation" of ideas and institutions rather than their containment within proprietary cultural zones.[36] But he had little optimism about the possibilities for genuine exchange with Europeans (or African Americans) so long as Africanness was synonymous for them with barbarism. It was the enthusiasm and pride with which African Muslims embraced their ostensibly alien faith that allowed Blyden to see in them both the spark of genius he had glimpsed at the pyramids and the hope for a future redemption of all humankind that had moved him in Jerusalem. Such were the fruits of the journey spurred by those fateful encounters with Liberia's Muslims.

But acknowledging the role of Africans in opening Blyden's eyes does not capture all the ways in which West African Muslims' thinking about their own cultures and the cultures of their neighbors came to be intertwined with European discourses and theories. A sliver of this can be seen in the broader Atlantic discussion of race and religion within which Blyden's work was received. As noted above, the antislavery efforts of the early 1800s, along with their complex and contradictory entanglements with the growing colonial lobby, spurred new interest in Africa and new theorizing about race and culture. The impact of this work on the popular understanding of African Islam was fitful and uneven. As late as 1821 Joseph Nightingale's *Religions and Religious Ceremonies of All Nations* still effectively conflated religion with race: Muslims were widely assumed to be either Arabs or "Moors," and black Africans were pagans.[37] But new descriptive and analytic works by merchants, administrators, and missionaries began to bring even the broader public around to an increasingly nuanced picture.

In England the circle that made the most of these ideas was the emerging Liberal movement. Many advocates of "free trade" in Africa were attracted to the idea of an expansive colonial project and had become frustrated with the missionaries who were influencing policy in the region. They made common cause with the staff of the early colonial outposts in West Africa. As early as 1850 Richard Graves MacDonnell, then governor of the Gambia, reported back to the House of Commons, "It is quite certain that the Mandingo Mahometan, in his clothing, his farming, his residence, and his education (for no Mandingo village is without its school), is a being infinitely superior to the naked liberated African treading bad mud-bricks for the British Government . . . or idling over unprofitable tasks. . . . I believe that the large sums expended . . . both by the British Government and the Wesleyan Society, benefited few."[38] The following year a caustic review of H. V. Huntley's *Seven Years' Service on the Slave Coast of Western Africa* appeared in the Benthamite *Westminster Review* and was partially reprinted and summarized by the American Colonization Society's *African Repository* and the Quaker *Friends Weekly Intelligencer.* The anonymous reviewer, who evidently had some experience in Gambia and Sierra Leone, lambasted the "amiable absurdity" of missionary and philanthropic efforts in the region. Insisting that only the expansion of free trade could bring about the end of slavery, the reviewer mocked the pretensions of Christians to improve women's lot in Africa and praised the educational achievements, political sophistication, and religious insights of Muslim Africans. The article stopped just short of implying that Islam was a better fit for Africans.[39] The *Westminster Review* and its American ideological counterpart, the *Colonization Herald,* were sharply critical of the missionary-led approach to antislavery, believing that missionaries wasted time and money and, perhaps more important, made life difficult for those true carriers of civilization, white merchants.[40] To be sure, these discussions still frequently invoked the specter of the Muslim slave dealer, but more often the Muslim merchant appeared as an attractive business partner for the development of a new phase of global commerce.

By 1865 the idea that Islam was not just good for Africa but better for Africa than Christianity was widespread, if not exactly popular. The idea drew nourishment from two separate traditions. On one side was the racism and romanticism of people like Richard Francis Burton, who saw an affinity between Islam's primitivism and that of Africans. On the other was the cultural relativism of Protestant reformers inspired by the "broad church" movement of theologians like Dean Arthur Stanley and the comparative theology of figures like Max Müller. This second group sought to explore elements of "true belief" in other faiths and to understand the historical circumstances of faith. They thus began to imagine an affinity between the Islamic version of monotheism and what they were coming to think of as "African culture." The most visible figure in this group to address African Islam was a school headmaster named R. Bosworth Smith. In 1872 Smith began to give lectures about Islam in Africa, drawing on the work of Waitz, Barth, and the Sierra Leone governor John Pope Hennessy; his audiences included Charles Darwin, William Gladstone, and Dean Stanley. Smith's ideas could have been borrowed from Blyden, but in fact the two men only came to meet later, through Dean Stanley's introduction in the 1870s. They quickly became friends, visiting one another and sharing a large correspondence, together and with Gladstone. Together, Blyden and Bosworth Smith amplified one another's impact on British intellectual life. Indeed, Smith's *Mohammed and Mohammedanism* (1874) provided the occasion for Blyden's most famous essay on Islam, his "Mohammedanism and the Negro Race" (1875).[41] Blyden was not, then, the sui generis inventor of such ideas, but one of their conduits and their most crucial node.

By the time Blyden composed *The Arabic Bible in the Soudan* he had experienced a series of upheavals that had torn him from the public life of Liberia and cast him ashore as an exile in Sierra Leone. By 1872 he was ensconced in Freetown, where he both partook in the cosmopolitan West African culture of Sierra Leone and continued his interactions with local Muslim scholars. The question of the impact this move had on his thought remains unresolved, though it certainly did nothing to reduce his animosity toward the Americo-Liberian elites of Monrovia or toward certain missionary groups. More positively, it might be imagined that the intellectual hothouse of nineteenth-century Sierra Leone contributed to a clarifying of his sense of the diversity of African cultures, while confirming his view that African peoples shared an underlying sensibility. In any case, it had been the predominant intellectual preoccupation of the luminaries of Freetown, Bible translation, that had set in motion the discussions that culminated in Blyden's provocative speculative theology. Blyden himself had encountered a group of American Protestant missionaries in Beirut who had been the leaders in the project to translate the Bible into Arabic and who had, since 1862, been sending Arabic Testaments to West Africa and requesting copies of Arabic manuscripts produced there. This work had been prompted by Protestant missionaries' own encounters with Islam and their dialectical hesitation between fascination for and fear of competition from the Levant's Muslims. Blyden's thoughts on translation and transliteration thus closed a circuit of intellectual exchange that began in West Africa, flowed through New York, Beirut, and London, and then returned to West Africa.

## THROUGH BLYDEN, THROUGH BOAS

The patterns of these circuits account for most of the differences between Blyden's approach to culture and those of other Western intellectuals, suggesting that what appear to be intellectual divergences have less to do with the development of scientific social theories or with the proclivities of individual scholars than with the particular circumstances by which various non-Western theories entered into Western discourse. So where Boas was secular, Blyden was deeply religious; where evolutionary movement for Boas came out of the confrontation of humans with one another and with their environment, for Blyden it came from the interaction of divine revelation with various social and physical settings.[42]

Part of what has allowed these differences to obscure the two thinkers' similarities has been the adoption of the anthropological definition of culture as a synecdoche for the family of culture concepts more broadly. Indeed, while Blyden himself often referred approvingly to the use of "culture" in a singular sense to designate human accomplishments of a certain order, his intellectual commitment was to an idea of "a system or code of life" such as a people's "environments have suggested—to be improved, not changed by larger knowledge."[43] Blyden understood a cultural "system" to include "the social, industrial, and economic arrangements" of a community as well as its members' ethical commitments and "inner feelings." African culture in particular was, for Blyden, defined by its attentiveness to the natural environment, a high degree of gender equality, a cooperative and egalitarian economy, and a refusal to distinguish the religious from the secular.[44]

In this, Blyden generated an analysis deeply compatible with the wide range of culturalist ideas coming out of Germany in the second half of the 1800s. Ranging, in terms of their emphasis on historicism, from Waitz's interest in the interplay of biology and environment, to Adolf Bastian's entelecho-evolutionary socio-psychological approach (itself an influence on Leo Frobenius, the European scholar with the closest connection to Pan-Africanism), to Boas's emphasis on diffusion and local modification, each of these approaches could be analyzed in terms of the circumstances of a generative encounter with specific interlocutors, in the manner in which Isaiah Wilner has resituated Boas and in which I have sought to resituate Blyden.[45] If Blyden came closest in this continuum to Bastian in his desire to move from specific historical conjunctures to more transcendental, universal insights (a tendency that perhaps accounts for the parallel careers of his ideas and those of Frobenius), this may suggest more about the particular conditions under which each dislodged his own prejudices than about their debts to a specifically European intellectual history.

The constant interplay of discursive context and personality allows us to understand why Blyden's work grew so influential among thinkers with very different agendas.[46] To be sure, the overall intellectual milieu in which Blyden worked remained hostile to any notion of the equality of African societies or peoples. Blyden's ideas provoked at least as much outrage and hostility as Boas, and above all Boas's students, faced some decades later.[47] But the range of responses was not restricted to affirmation or rejection. In the hands of missionaries who were committed to a civilizational struggle *against* Islam, Blyden's support of an "Africanized" version of that religion proved useful, even as they misunderstood or ignored the philosophical consequences.[48] More complex was Blyden's influence on the Orientalist and great colonial Africanist anthropologist Maurice Delafosse, who became acquainted with Blyden during a two-year stint in the 1890s as French vice-consul in Monrovia. Delafosse, who shared an intellectual lineage with both Frobenius and Boas, was a champion of African cultural interests, an antislavery campaigner, and later a participant in the political debates of the 1920s around Liberia, Marcus Garvey, and Pan-Africanism. By the 1910s he had become France's then-greatest scholar of Islam in West Africa, and he contributed greatly to the evolution of the culture concept in French anthropology. Delafosse adopted some of Blyden's specific views of Islam in West Africa, including the idea that it was a greater civilizing force there than Christianity, but, in a more solid cultural relativism, he also celebrated the value and complexity of African "traditional" religions, going so far as to suggest they had minimized the depth of the influence of Islamic thought in the region. He nonetheless kept the Liberian example as a template for the potentially negative influence of prejudicial European forces and drew on Blyden's own findings.[49]

Blyden also did much to spur broad interest in Liberia itself, and, for a time at least, some information about the specific context in which Blyden had developed his ideas traveled with those ideas themselves, helping to offset some of the more pernicious racialist appropriations of his thought. The 1870s were a kind of golden era for Liberia's place in the discourse on Africa, race, and religion. The publication of Henry M. Schieffelin's influential collection *The People of Africa* at the opening of the decade and of Benjamin J. K. Anderson's *Narrative of a Journey to Musardu* at its close, along with the escalating drama of Liberia's political turmoil, put the country itself on the global intellectual agenda.[50] The publication of Blyden's own influential essays on religion and blackness, the success of Bosworth Smith's lectures, and Gladstone's first premiership brought those three mutual admirers to the peak of their collective influence and gave ideas about African Islam a major platform.

A sign of how central Liberian Muslims were, briefly, to the scientific discourse on race was the interest shown in the matter by Tayler Lewis, a classicist at Union College and an influential intellectual who contributed to the development of a specifically American conservative theory of the state. Lewis was well versed in the Liberia question. He had been presented with a Qur'an from Liberia, he had read Theodore Dwight's "Condition and Character of Negroes in Africa" and Blyden's "Mohammedanism in West Africa" in the *Methodist Quarterly*, and he had read an Arabic letter from "Musardu" brought back by Anderson. Lewis opined that sophisticated Islamic scholars in Africa had fostered a "communal religious interest" and had thereby preserved "a measure of . . . social vitality." The areas where Islam was strongest could thus be made an "encouraging basis for missionary effort. . . . [For] the missionary might well prefer these Koran-taught Mandingo Negroes, as his field of labor, to the conscience-deadened inhabitants of Thibet, China, or Japan."[51]

But the anti-Islamic missionaries and the growing colonial lobby quickly closed ranks to remind the public of the putative link between Islam and slavery.[52] When, in 1865, the traveler, philosopher, and religious radical William Winwood Reade made a presentation to the Anthropological Society of London praising African Muslims (a paper that would later be cited by W. E. B. Du Bois), he provoked angry rebuttals even from the progressive Anglican bishop John Colenso and from David Livingstone himself, while Bosworth Smith suffered abuse for the rest of his career from many circles, including from Koelle, the Africa expert and linguist.[53] The American Missionary Association writer George P. Claflin offered a counter-reading of the Blyden model that revealed the missionary–colonial position's own contradictions. Implying that Islamophilic analysts had been swayed by Muslims' sense of their superiority to non-Muslims, Claflin nonetheless fretted about the impact these more sophisticated thinkers might have on their credulous neighbors. By "prejudicing the minds of the people against the Bible, whose claims are so unlike the mercenary character of its adherents," he argued, "Mohammedanism becomes an obstacle of no small magnitude to the progress of the Gospel, and it is steadily becoming greater. If Christians do not arise and possess the land, the followers of the false prophet will secure it for themselves."[54]

The majority of missionaries, then, saw in ideas like Blyden's a fundamental threat to the moral claims that underwrote their influence in the region and that motivated their efforts. They saw Europeans who spoke positively about Islam's role in Africa as instigators of a racial betrayal at best and, at worst, agents of a demonic plot. The significance of these debates was not lost on at least some African Muslim observers. In 1886 Smith claimed that "to this day" he was "prayed for in the mosques along the West Coast of Africa, as having attempted to do justice to Islam, as a civilising and elevating agency among pagan Negroes." While Blyden himself remains largely forgotten by most of the population today, the reformist-leaning National Repentance Muslims of Liberia still celebrate his birthday each year.[55] The complexity and diversity of more or less informed responses to figures like Blyden and Smith remind us, then, that it is not only in the moment of origin that encounter shapes the exchange of theories.

## RESTORING ETHICAL PRINCIPLES TO THE WORLD

If Blyden is a name recognized by historians and philosophers worldwide, the name of Raphael Ernest Grail Armattoe is nearly unknown, even in West Africa. Insofar as scholars and the public have taken an interest in Armattoe, it has been largely as a curiosity. A medical doctor by training, an anthropologist by acclaim, and a politician by coincidence, Armattoe has become the subject of a certain mythology, spurred and enabled by the superlative bare facts of his life. Born on August 12, 1913, in the section of German Togoland that is now part of Ghana, raised as a member of the Ewe-speaking community, and educated in Germany and Scotland, Armattoe opened a medical practice in the unlikely city of Derry in Northern Ireland. There he embarked on what would turn out to be a brilliant if brief career, befriending the physicist Erwin Schroedinger and corresponding with Du Bois. He was an accomplished biological researcher, one of the first black Africans to be nominated for the Nobel Peace Prize, an important early West African poet, and, tragically, an actor in the great drama of Africa's decolonization. All this by the time of his death at the age of forty.[56]

The connective tissue within Armattoe's variegated work and his idiosyncratic thought was a vindicationist model of African civilization coupled with an intellectual commitment to scientific anthropology and a political commitment to the self-determination of the Ewe-speaking people of West Africa. From the outset Armattoe drew much from the Boasian version of culture, but in his political work he would come to join the concept to a more biologically rigid understanding of group boundaries that could link practices, histories, and places together into a unit. In this, he was of his time ideologically if ahead of it in technique and in the range of his syntheses. Armattoe's most significant intellectual work took place during and was shaped by the Second World War, a war that would ultimately sound the death knell of the radical salience of culture concepts. As the nation-state system solidified in the wake of the anti-racist rhetoric of the post-1945 dispensation and with the rise of putatively anti-imperial powers, culture as an analytic tool gave way to national identity as a political tool, ironically folding the former's relativism into the bounded, homogenizing, static concept the latter has become in the neoliberal era. Insofar as colonial subjects themselves were instrumental in this outcome, one could frame a narrative in which the "non-West" played as crucial a role in the unraveling of anthropological culture as Wilner and others in this book suggest it played in its formation.[57] Armattoe was both a part of that process and its harbinger, clinging to an explicit articulation of the significance of biology to culture that would become its implicit, hidden unconscious.

Although his formal education was in medicine, Armattoe was self-taught in anthropology; in that field his major influences were Frobenius and, particularly, Boas. In 1942 he wrote Boas's obituary for *Man,* the journal of the Royal Anthropological Institute; he would publish in that journal for the rest of his life, and he became known as a commentator on anthropology from both its physical and anticolonial wings, writing, for example, a survey of Portuguese imperial anthropology for *Nature.* Even his medical research drew heavily on anthropology, focusing largely on the question of environmental influence on measurable indexes of health and mental ability. No less than Blyden or the Négritude poets, Armattoe fashioned the culture concept into a lens through which one could glimpse the universal, salvific importance of Africa. "I believe," he wrote in 1946, that "it is specifically the mission of African civilisation to restore ethical principles to world civilisation. Unless this attempt is made all civilisation must come to an end. The African by virtue of his detachment, his direct vision, and his innate kindness, is qualified to bring humanitarianism to the technical and materialistic concepts of the Western World."[58]

Like Blyden and Boas before him, Armattoe sought to explain the interaction of individual and collective values with the vagaries of the social and physical environment. Less precise or consistent in his terminology than the other two thinkers, Armattoe's theory of African history nonetheless made it clear that a colonial *mission civilisatrice* could not hope to compete with the transformations that grew organically out of the evolution of local cultures,

cultures in whose capacity he had great confidence. He urged his readers to learn the "lessons of the fall of the Congo kingdom," which had, he argued, uncritically adopted a Catholicism that was misaligned with its fundamental interests. This "must be a warning to all Africans to eschew the outward manifestations of an alien civilisation. A civilisation to endure must be grafted on the sound foundations of native institutions and must fulfill the legitimate aspirations of its people."[59]

From here it was a small step to the belief that political self-determination was the best practical instrument for the expression of such aspirations. This would be the intellectual underpinning of Armattoe's political work in the 1950s, but to take this next step he had to fuse his theory of culture and civilization with an explicitly Boasian understanding of race. This he had begun acquiring during the 1930s, under circumstances that remain unclear. By 1942, however, his obituary of Boas praised as "pregnant with revolutionary possibilities" Boas's conclusions about the mutability of "racial" differences.[60] In 1943 the British government commissioned Armattoe to study the comparative "vigor" of British and Irish youth as a way of assessing the impact of Britain's wartime rationing on morale and fitness for combat (Ireland having remained technically neutral and thus without systematic rationing). Armattoe's conclusion, that rationing was having few negative effects, was seized on by a jingoistic press, which brought him greater professional attention.[61]

His next major piece, "A Racial Survey of the British People," undertaken the following year and first presented, pointedly, at the Free German Institute of Science and Learning in London, drew on data taken from studies of public school attendees to trace changes in eye and hair color among the professional classes. In doing so, Armattoe adopted biological race as a heuristic category, only to demonstrate that no matter how far back one set one's baseline it was impossible to disentangle what appeared to be "race" from the systematic effects of environment: "We cannot distinguish, speaking scientifically, a distinct Irish or English race. What holds true for the British people, I am convinced will be found to apply all over Europe"—a conclusion whose importance, he noted, would not be lost on his audience of German refugees.[62] Armattoe thus brought together a sense of the historical contingency of human nature with an environmental theory of biological development.

Throughout his anthropological work Armattoe betrayed little interest in sociology, in the sense of the immediate structures of relations that might influence culture, or in the sociology of knowledge. He typically sought to explain biological differences through slower, gradual transformations rather than situational influences. His piece on wartime rationing, for instance, prompted critics to note that he had failed to take into account the ways students at upper-class schools could buy their way out of rationing, thus misleadingly mitigating the nutritional effects of the war on his sample.[63] Moreover, his sense of history was deeply idiosyncratic: In a "message" to his infant daughter which prefaced a pamphlet lionizing Schroedinger, Albert Schweitzer, and the painter Gaetano de Gennaro, Armattoe lamented, "Today there is, I am afraid, no great woman anywhere"; but he saw this as a temporary state brought about by the psychological consequences of industrialism and war, and he prophesied that a golden era of women's intellectual contributions would soon return, restoring intelligent women to prominence. Within such ideas one can glimpse the basic outlines of a Hegelianism that subsumes local social realities into the grand sweep of world-historical cultural change.[64]

From 1948 to 1951 Armattoe's academic work centered on the application of the tools of biological anthropology to the history of West Africa. In this work he collaborated with two key figures in the development of blood-group mapping, Elizabeth W. Ikin and Arthur E. Mourant, both of whom were associated with the eminent geneticist Ronald A. Fisher.[65] Their research, supported by a Viking Fund grant in 1948, culminated in a study of blood-group and Rhesus factor distributions among Ewe and Asante peoples in West Africa. This work coincided with a hardening of the meaning of biological groups in Armattoe's thinking; henceforth historical influences appeared more frequently in his work as the consequences of migration or genetic "infiltration" rather than of cultural development in a specific environment. It was during this same period that Armattoe was drawn into postcolonial politics.

Armattoe began to involve himself in international assemblies right after the war. It would be interesting to know more about how his years living in Northern Ireland shaped his political views, but no sources seem to shed direct light on the subject. But by whatever path, he arrived at a strong commitment to self-determination, the political analogue of his belief that civilizational progress had to reflect autochthonous roots. A participant in the famous Fifth Pan-African Congress held in Manchester in October 1945, Armattoe was not an official delegate but nonetheless was one of over a dozen African intellectuals and activists to give testimony at the congress about the state of the continent under colonial rule. As a Togolese by birth, he was the only attendee who could, even if only partially, represent the Francophone perspective. It was he who detailed to the congress the situation in the Congo, as part of a general overview he gave of western Africa. Calling the Congo's state tragic, Armattoe spoke out against colonial rule throughout the region, accusing Europeans of being "only concerned with economic exploitation, regardless of the condition of the people—the maximum profit with the minimum effort" and insisting that "most people in Africa feel that they want self-government." While he generally compared French rule in Africa favorably with that of the British, especially with regard to educational opportunities, Armattoe decried the division of Africans in the French colonies into the unequal categories of citizens and subjects and the lack of effort to extend to the population an appreciation for "political theory and freedom." Instead, he noted, "West Africans under French rule are trained with a view to becoming Frenchmen."[66]

In 1949 Armattoe appeared on a panel chaired by Franz Boas's son Ernst Boas as part of the Cultural and Scientific Conference for World Peace held that spring at the Waldorf Astoria Hotel in New York. Organized by an international network of scholars and activists to urge a de-escalation of Cold War tensions, the Waldorf conference was quickly hijacked by both Washington and Moscow, the former seeking to portray it as a Communist effort to infiltrate the United States, the latter using it to depict Stalinism in a humane light.[67] Though this controversy overshadowed the actual discussions that took place, Armattoe's involvement gave him an opportunity to link the question of peace to his interest in the forces that shaped the evolution of groups. In his speech to the conference Armattoe explored the role of group identity in fomenting violence. He spoke of "certain ideas which communities or groups of communities believe in" and which give them solidarity and coherence. Inequalities among these groups were poisonous and, he argued, "the main probable cause of war in the world today is the feeling of grievance due to alleged national or racial affront." Some sense of the context of Armattoe's speech can be glimpsed by looking at that of his fellow panelist, Boas's most politically active student, Gene Weltfish. One of the most influential promoters of Boasian ideas, Weltfish issued a stirring attack on colonial rule in Africa and on the racist underpinnings of geopolitics, and she drew direct connections between the growing independence movements in Africa and the civil rights struggles in the United States. The contrast with Armattoe's rather apolitical, temperate paper could not have been more dramatic.[68]

But it was Armattoe's equally moderate, if not conservative, political activity on behalf of the Ewe in West Africa that would bring him brief global attention and, perhaps, cost him his life. In this work Armattoe pulled together his interest in international politics and his biological research on blood groups and population movements, resulting in an approach to culture that cut in potentially dangerous directions. After the Second World War, Britain began moving to rid itself of some of its African colonies. The Gold Coast (Ghana),

R. E. G. Armattoe, third from right, at the Cultural and Scientific Conference for World Peace, which took place in 1949 at the Waldorf Astoria Hotel in New York City. Much of the American news media depicted the delegates and attendees—who included Albert Einstein, Dorothy Parker, and Langston Hughes—as "dupes and fellow travelers" carrying water for the Soviet Union. The composer Dmitri Shostakovich, a Soviet delegate, is seated third from left. Photograph by Leonard McCombe. Getty Images.

long one of the wealthiest and politically developed, with a high proportion of Western-educated elites, was the clear choice for bellwether. But there were internal difficulties to handle, including competing federalist and centralist visions of the new state as well as international problems raised by the adjacent, tiny British Togo mandate territory stripped from Germany after its defeat in 1918. These concerns collided in the question of the political dispensation of the Ewe-speaking peoples of the region, communities found in the southeastern Gold Coast as well as in southern British and French Togo.

A self-determination movement among the Ewe had been growing since the 1920s. Due to the oversight provided by the United Nations as part of the mandated territories system, the movement had gained greater traction than most such "ethnic" movements. From 1947 on, Ewe political groups were a major factor in negotiations between the Gold Coast and Britain over the form and timing of independence and in negotiations between Britain and

France over the location of the international frontier. Kwame Nkrumah, the emerging political leader of the Ghanaian independence movement, was determined to defend the Gold Coast's "territorial integrity" and would not accept any solution that detached the Ewe areas from the country. Furthermore, Nkrumah was equally determined to annex British Togo to the Gold Coast, for he had ambitious plans involving the damming of the Volta River in the area and also relished the tax revenues that could be generated by the cocoa grown there. The "Ewe question" was therefore truly vexing, entangling matters of great economic significance with a central diplomatic preoccupation of the 1950s and 1960s: the fate of colonial borders.[69]

Into this maelstrom Armattoe stepped with his now more rigid view of the links between culture, biology, and politics. By 1951 he had become a key member of the pro-self-determination Togoland Congress and emerged as a vocal public antagonist of his former friend Nkrumah. In November 1953 he gave a stirring speech to the United Nations, arguing against the annexation of Ewe lands by Ghana. Armattoe's UN speech made heavy rhetorical use of "culture" in two different ways, each of which illustrated the breakdown of his commitment to a Boasian model. Although the core of the Togoland movement—and the site of Armattoe's personal commitments—was the Ewe people, Armattoe spoke to the UN of "Togoland" and "Togolanders" and only mentioned Ewes when referring to several other ethnicities in the area. He referred to Togoland as a state, as if it were an already existing fact rather than a proposal, one possible outcome of the negotiations; he implied that there had been a Togoland in existence for an indeterminate amount of time and declared that it was "the most cultured indigenous State on the African Continent."

Culture now fused with blood and jingoistic pride. "Throughout the world," Armattoe insisted, "when scholars discuss African cultures they invariably have in mind Togoland, Ashanti and Benin," substantiating the claim with a history of "Togolander" iron smelting, art and music, advanced agriculture, and intellectualism in which most of the implied examples were actually Ewe. Using, in the space of a few sentences, culture in both absolute and relative senses, he went on to insist that other African states that were already moving toward independence were "admittedly inferior in indigenous and Western cultural experience." But if culture was an "experience" that could be acquired and that came in multiple varieties, Armattoe also sought to give Togoland's uniqueness (if not superiority) a biological component. "Recent blood group studies," he noted, "carried out by Dr. Mourant, Miss Ikin and the speaker have shown them as being remarkable among communities so far investigated in Africa." The "them" in this sentence was vague—perhaps intentionally so, for what it disguised was that the blood-group study had in fact taken the "Ewe" as its unit of analysis, not "Togoland." What that paper had in fact found was that, while most characteristics of the sampled populations accorded with of the composition of their neighbors, the Ewe people sampled were "remarkable among Africans for their high frequency of Rh negatives," a frequency that "approaches that found among Europeans."[70] The racial implications, left unstated, played into some of the continent's most divisive rhetoric.[71]

Throughout the UN speech Armattoe adopted the strategy of holding Europeans to the standards of their own rhetoric, telling his audience that if "they have any decency left, if they wish the Charter of the United Nations to mean what it says, if they want others to believe that they are better in keeping their pledges, if their protestations of sincerity are not a hollow mockery," then they would recognize Togoland's right to political recognition. Mobilizing the ambivalent use of collective categories, he defended the importance of other African cultural traditions while simultaneously arguing that the "Togolanders" could, through their unique civilizational greatness, modernize those other cultures. "The impact of the West on Africa," he warned, "whether by its religious precepts or technological processes, is bound to lead to much searching of heart in Africa." Recalling the argument he had made nearly a decade earlier in *The Golden Age of West African Civilization,* he insisted that "any attempt to breed by grafting or hot-house methods an alien civilization without due regard paid to the African traditional norms must inevitably lead to disaster." The solution? "The people of Togoland alone can bridge the gulf and act as interpreters and as cultural catalysts."

In making this claim, Armattoe gave "Ewe culture" more or less the same historical role in Africa that Blyden had given Islam. But with one crucial difference: Blyden had used "Islam" to designate a particular practical instantiation of a set of values, a historically specific manifestation of a transhistorical truth that could, by definition, be abstracted from the particular (Arab) culture that had produced it and given new—greater—meaning in another (African) culture. Armattoe instead championed the use of a single specific culture, upheld as inherently superior, to act on other peoples and modernize them. In essence, he displaced colonial white supremacy rather than deconstructing it as Blyden had done.[72]

Though it is not easy to assess the impact of Armattoe's UN speech, it made a strong impression on those present. The British assistant secretary of state for colonial affairs, W. A. C. Mathieson, described Armattoe as "a cosmopolitan

African who has lived most of his life in Europe [and] had some of the oratorical gifts of a revivalist preacher."[73] Mathieson, for one, believed that Armattoe's "venomous attacks" had "produced a substantial impression on the [Mandate] Committee" and that the "United Kingdom case was made the more difficult to promote through the skill with which Mr. Armattoe played on the emotions of the Committee." There is some reason to believe, then, that Armattoe's newfound international voice held the potential to derail the negotiations for the Gold Coast's independence, at least as the unified state of Ghana that Nkrumah envisioned. But such potential was not to be realized, for one month later Armattoe was dead in Germany, the victim, he and his wife both came to believe in the days before his passing, of poisoning at the hands of his political enemies.[74]

## CONCLUSIONS

Though inseparable from Ghana's specific political struggles, Armattoe's political tragedy symbolized the end of culture's role as a privileged tool of world-historical progress. The unequal relationships that would obtain among the global states of the postwar order gave birth to new conventions of sovereignty, conventions that demanded that culture play two distinct roles: Culture expressed the legitimacy of states as national entities, a status activated by the logic of sovereignty, even as it named one form of difference within states, a form whose logic articulated problems of toleration and justified strategies of governance. The distinction between these two levels—the national and the subnational—and the rules of sovereignty and tolerance largely followed from the interests of the "most sovereign" clusters of states. As a result, culture's ability to do the kind of subversively translational intellectual work it once performed was severely attenuated. Even if, in the twenty-first century, the logic of the nation-state has begun to recede in uneven, fitful ways—especially in those spaces that Siba Grovogui calls the "badlands" of neoliberalism, many of which are found in the areas Blyden and Armattoe knew best—the version of culture that flows through such areas is a radically transformed one, the entrepreneurial culture of what Jean and John Comaroff have labeled "Ethnicity, Inc."[75]

My suggestion, then, is that the history of the formation, deployment, and transformation of the culture concept in Africa cannot be formulated or understood if its intellectual structure is analyzed purely in terms of its academic genealogies or if its political valences are posited to be stable properties of its internal logic. The concept is better seen as a symptom of a particular moment in the reconfiguration of global discourses in which the voices of non-Western thinkers entered into theoretical conversations with interlocutors who encountered them within a specifically imperial space.[76] The collapsing of that space into the nation-state system of the post-1945 world order gave a new role to culture, one that was not easily separated from concepts of nationalism and self-determination. These in turn required, as a practical matter, a very different model of the interplay between history and group belonging than what Blyden or Boas had envisioned. The stakes of culture had been high—high enough to enable Blyden to give birth to Afrocentrism and one branch of the Western study of Islam in Africa and, in the opposite direction, to result in Weltfish's firing from Columbia in 1953 and her subsequent blacklisting—but the stakes of the nation-state system were even higher, too high for a somewhat politically naïve biological anthropologist like Armattoe to pay.

At least as illuminating, however, as Blyden's successes and Armattoe's failures are Blyden's own failures and the successes of those who spoke with the same vocabulary as Armattoe. For if Blyden's core assertions about Islam's role in Africa proved attractive to those with radically different goals for Africans—if the culturalist stream was not only unable to defeat either racialism or imperialism but indeed often flowed back into them—then the question Armattoe's case raises is the role of "Indigenous theory" in closing back down the spaces for even this limited transformative play. After all, the Richard Burtons of the nineteenth century had little interest in Blyden's complex Hegelian theology. When stripped of the idea that cultures were situated repositories of individual fragments that could someday be forged into a transcendent and universal ethics, African Islam became little more than a signpost on a map of ranked territories, a gradient between the Middle East and "true" Africa. Not only did such an idea shape and justify the forms colonial rule would take in each location, by the time of decolonization it also defined the limits of what many who valorized African "cultures" could fight for.

## Notes

Research supported by Stanford University. Philippa Robinson, Hilton Adolinama, numerous librarians and archivists, participants in the 2013 African Studies Association panel on Blyden, Chris Shannon, Bruce Hall, Alpha M. Bah, Kofi Anyidoho, Aishwary Kumar, Harry Odamtten, Timothy Nevin, and Eric Morier-Genoud all provided guidance, inspiration, and assistance. Jon Glassman, David Schoenbrun, Helen Tilley, Lindsay Ehrisman, and other participants in the Madison-Chicago-Northwestern workshop all asked penetrating questions, as did LaRay Denzer and Robert Launay. Ned Blackhawk and Isaiah Wilner provided heroic levels of editorial attention. Offered in memory of Kofi Awoonor, who shared an interest in R. E. G. Armattoe.

1. This version of Boas's definition of culture (which he frequently revised) is found in Franz Boas, *The Mind of Primitive Man,* rev. ed. (1911; repr. New York: Macmillan, 1938), 159. See also George W. Stocking Jr., "Franz Boas and the Culture Concept in Historical Perspective," *American Anthropologist* 68 (1966): 867–82. Boas's main impact on African studies was through his student Melville Herskovits. See Llewellyn Smith, Vincent Brown, and Christine Herbes-Sommers, producers, *Herskovits at the Heart of Blackness* (San Francisco: Vital Pictures, 2009), DVD.
2. For a discussion of these stakes, see Isaiah Lorado Wilner, "A Global Potlatch: Identifying the Indigenous Influence on Western Thought," *American Indian Culture and Research Journal* 37, no. 2 (2013): 87–114.
3. The literature on this movement is voluminous but see particularly Matti Bunzl, "Franz Boas and the Humboldtian Tradition: From *Volksgeist* and *Nationalcharakter* to an Anthropological Concept of Culture," in *Volksgeist as Method and Ethic: Essays on Boasian Ethnography and the German Anthropological Tradition,* ed. George W. Stocking Jr. (Madison: University of Wisconsin Press, 1996), 17–78, and Carl N. Degler, *Culture Versus Biology in the Thought of Franz Boas and Alfred L. Kroeber* (New York: Berg, 1989).
4. For a brief history of the historical theory of origins we could trace the trajectory between Karl Marx and Friedrich Engels, *The German Ideology: Part One,* 2d ed., ed. C. J. Arthur, trans. W. Lough (London: Lawrence and Wishart, 1970), 88–89, and Dominick LaCapra, *History and Criticism* (Ithaca: Cornell University Press, 1985). A theory of origin as leap can be glimpsed in Georg Lukács, "The Changing Function of Historical Materialism," in *History and Class Consciousness,* trans. Rodney Livingstone (1919; repr. London: Merlin, 1967), esp. 239–53, and in Walter Benjamin, *The Origin of German Tragic Drama,* trans. John Osborne (New York: Verso, 1998).
5. Wilner, "A Global Potlatch"; see also Neil L. Whitehead, "The Historical Anthropology of Text: The Interpretation of Ralegh's *Discoverie of Guiana,*" *Current Anthropology* 36, no. 1 (1995): 53–74.
6. Louis Althusser, *For Marx,* trans. Ben Brewster (London: Allen Lane, 1969), 99–101.
7. Philip D. Curtin, *The Image of Africa: British Ideas and Action, 1780–1850* (Madison: University of Wisconsin Press, 1964), esp. chaps. 9–17; Serge Daget, *La répression de la traite des Noirs au XIXe siècle: l'action des croisières françaises sur les côtes occidentales de l'Afrique, 1817–1850* (Paris: Karthala, 1997); Claude Wanquet, *La France et la première abolition de l'esclavage, 1794–1802: le cas des colonies orientales, Ile de France (Maurice) et la Réunion* (Paris: Karthala, 1998); and Alex Demeulenaere, *Le récit de voyage français en Afrique noire (1830–1931): essai de scénographie* (Berlin: Lit, 2009). See also Robin Hallett, "European Exploration as a Theme in African History," and the discussion of that paper in *The Exploration of Africa in the Eighteenth and Nineteenth Centuries,* seminar proceedings, University of Edinburgh, Dec. 3–4, 1971 (Edinburgh: Centre of African Studies, 1971), 1–16.
8. French anthropology in the nineteenth century absorbed and codified elements of such accounts into a racial theory of empire. Bruce S. Hall, *A History of Race in Muslim West Africa, 1600–1960* (New York: Cambridge University Press, 2011), chap. 3.
9. Theodor Waitz, *Introduction to Anthropology,* trans. J. Frederick Collingwood (1863; repr. New York: AMS Press, 1975), 285.

10. Joan T. Mark, "Anthropology as a Science," in Waitz, *Introduction to Anthropology,* iv–vi.
11. On the "closing" of the ethnographic window, see Andrew Zimmerman, *Anthropology and Antihumanism in Imperial Germany* (Chicago: University of Chicago Press, 2001), chap. 10.
12. V. Y. Mudimbe, *The Idea of Africa* (Bloomington: Indiana University Press, 1994). Compare Thomas Spear, "Neo-Traditionalism and the Limits of Invention in British Colonial Africa," *Journal of African History* 44, no. 1 (2003): 3–27; Carolyn Hamilton, *Terrific Majesty: The Powers of Shaka Zulu and the Limits of Historical Invention* (Cambridge: Harvard University Press, 1998); and Gaurav Desai, *Subject to Colonialism: African Self-Fashioning and the Colonial Library* (Durham: Duke University Press, 2001). See also Peter Geschiere's critique of Hamilton's project in "Shaka and the Limits of Colonial Invention," *African Studies Review* 44, no. 2 (2001): 167–76. My own sense of the stakes of this problem is indebted to Steven Feierman, "Colonizers, Scholars, and the Creation of Invisible Histories," in *Beyond the Cultural Turn: New Directions in the Study of Society and Culture,* ed. Victoria E. Bonnell and Lynn Hunt (Berkeley: University of California Press, 1999), 185.
13. See, for instance, Deborah Shapple Spillman, "Edward Blyden and the Politics of Language," unpublished paper, African Studies Association (Baltimore, MD, 2013). The definitive study of Blyden remains Hollis R. Lynch, *Edward Wilmot Blyden: Pan-Negro Patriot, 1832–1912* (New York: Oxford University Press, 1967). See also Hollis R. Lynch, ed., *Black Spokesman: Selected Published Writings of Edward Wilmot Blyden* (London: Cass, 1971); Hollis R. Lynch, ed., *Selected Letters of Edward Wilmot Blyden* (Millwood, NY: KTO Press, 1978); and Edith Holden, *Blyden of Liberia: An Account of the Life and Labors of Edward Wilmot Blyden, LL.D., as Recorded in Letters and in Print* (New York: Vantage Press, 1966).
14. Harry Nii Koney Odamtten, "A History of Ideas: West Africa, 'The Black Atlantic,' and Pan-Africanism" (PhD diss., Michigan State University, 2010), 238.
15. Such as the influential reading given by Kwame Anthony Appiah, *In My Father's House: Africa in the Philosophy of Culture* (New York: Oxford University Press, 1992), 21–22.
16. Teshale Tibebu, *Edward Wilmot Blyden and the Racial Nationalist Imagination* (Rochester: University of Rochester Press, 2012), 64–65. For a sense of how a similar system could be shared by two thinkers with such opposing senses of the empirical facts of history, see Andrew Buchwalter, "Is Hegel's Philosophy of History Eurocentric?" in *Hegel and History,* ed. Will Dudley (Albany: State University of New York Press, 2009), 87–110, which departs from postcolonial readings of Hegel.
17. Edward W. Blyden, *The Arabic Bible in the Soudan: A Plea for Transliteration* (London: C. M. Phillips, 1910). On Hölderlin, see Charlie Louth, *Hölderlin and the Dynamics of Translation* (Oxford: British Comparative Literature Association, 1998), and Walter Benjamin, "The Task of the Translator," in *Illuminations,* ed. Hannah Arendt, trans. Harry Zohn (1921; repr. New York: Harcourt, Brace and World, 1968), 69–82. In this, Blyden differed from those who favored the "enculturation of the gospel" and who took translation as their guiding metaphor. See, for instance, the revealing passages on Blyden in Lamin O. Sanneh, *Abolitionists Abroad: American Blacks and the Making of Modern West Africa* (1999; repr. Cambridge: Harvard University Press, 2001), 230–37.

18. Blyden, *Arabic Bible,* 5–6.
19. Ibid., 7–9.
20. Ibid., 19.
21. Inter alia, Murray Last, "Reform in West Africa: The Jihâd Movements of the Nineteenth Century," in *History of West Africa,* 2d. ed., ed. J. F. A. Ajayi and Michael Crowder (London: Longman, 1987), 2:1–47; and Usman Muhammad Bugaje, "The Tradition of *Tajdid* in Western Bilad Al-Sudan: A Study of the Genesis, Development and Patterns of Islamic Revivalism in the Region, 900–1900 AD" (PhD diss., University of Khartoum, 1991).
22. S. W. Koelle, *Polyglotta Africana* (1854; repr. Graz: Akademische Druck u. Verlagsanstelt, 1963).
23. Though not the first to write about the Vai syllabary, Koelle did the most to draw attention to it in his *Narrative of an Expedition into the Vy Country of West Africa, and the Discovery of a System of Syllabic Writing, Recently Invented by the Natives of the Vy Tribe* (London: Seeleys, 1849).
24. Abd Isã [Sigismund Wilhelm Koelle], *Food for Reflection: Being an Historical Comparison Between Mohammedanism and Christianity* (London: Church Missionary House, 1865), 37–38, 83–84. Koelle later reworked this material into a more extensive theoretical treatment, *Mohammed and Mohammedanism* (London: Rivingtons, 1889), in which he explicitly critiqued progressive theologians like Isaak Dorner; see esp., 450–51.
25. Church Missionary Society Archive (Marlborough, UK: Adam Matthew Publications, 1996), reel 91, and published as C. J. Reichardt, *Three Original Fulah Pieces: In Arabic Letters, in Latin Transcription, and in English Translation* (Berlin: C. and F. Unger, 1859).
26. Originally reported in New York's *Independent,* the existence of these manuscripts was celebrated widely. See, e.g., *The African Repository* 39, no. 1 (1863): 19–21; *Friends Review* 16, no. 24 (1863): 373–74.
27. Ian Duffield and Paul Edwards, "Equiano's Turks and Christians: An Eighteenth-Century African View of Islam," *Journal of African Studies* 2, no. 4 (1975): 433–44.
28. Pierre-Henri Stanislas d'Escayrac de Lauture, *Le Désert et le Soudan* (Paris: J. Dumaine, 1853), 204–5, 246–48, 262–63, 266–68, 400–402, 428–52; Waitz, *Introduction to Anthropology,* 325, 375, 388. Escayrac and Waitz both went so far as to endorse the idea that Islam improved the physical features of Africans (Escayrac, 248; Waitz, 66). For his part, Waitz specifically praised Escayrac as a source on Islam (377). Echoes of these ideas would continue all the way down to Boas and beyond: e.g., Boas, *The Mind of Primitive Man,* 13–15.
29. Odamtten, "Black Atlantic," 249–50.
30. Nathaniel R. Richardson, *Liberia's Past and Present* (London: Diplomatic Press, 1959), 82–92.
31. *African Repository* 42 (1866): 246, quoted in Holden, *Blyden of Liberia,* 141.
32. Edward W. Blyden, *From West Africa to Palestine* (Freetown: T. J. Sawyer, 1873), 104–5. Years later Blyden would poetically note the suggestive resemblance of the pyramids to the termite mounds of Africa; see Blyden, *African Life and Customs* (1908; repr. Baltimore: Black Classic Press, 1994), 30.
33. Blyden, *West Africa,* 112.

34. E.g., Jacob S. Dorman, "Lifted Out of the Commonplace Grandeur of Modern Times: Reappraising Edward Wilmot Blyden's Views of Islam and Afrocentrism in Light of His Scholarly Black Christian Orientalism," *Souls: A Critical Journal of Black Politics, Culture, and Society* 12, no. 4 (2010): 398–418.
35. Blyden, *West Africa,* 109–10, 157–58. Compare James Cowles Prichard, *Natural History of Man,* 4th ed. (London: H. Baillière, 1855), 497–500.
36. The phrase comes from his "Mohammedanism and the Negro Race," *Fraser's Magazine,* n.s., 12 (Nov. 1875): 606.
37. J[oseph] Nightingale, *The Religions and Religious Ceremonies of All Nations: Accurately, Impartially, and Fully Described,* 10th ed. (1821; repr. London: Sherwood, Gilbert, and Piper, 1835), 316–17.
38. House of Commons, *The Past and Present State of Her Majesty's Colonial Possessions: Transmitted with the Blue Books for the Year 1849,* Session 1850, 1232, pt. 2, 223.
39. "Sir H. Huntley's *Seven Years' Service on the Slave Coast, Western Africa,*" *Westminster and Foreign Quarterly Review* 56, no. 1 (1851): 5–16, 20–21. The article is unsigned (like most contributions to the *Westminster Review*), but possible authors include Richard R. Madden.
40. For a contemporary assessment of the *Review*'s anti-missionary inclinations, see "Christian Missions and the *Westminster Review,*" *London Quarterly* 7, no. 13 (1857): 209–61.
41. R. Bosworth Smith, *Mohammed and Mohammedanism: Lectures Delivered at the Royal Institution of Great Britain in February and March, 1874* (London: Smith, Elder, 1874), 55–64. On Smith's life, see Ellinor Flora Bosworth Smith Grogan, *Reginald Bosworth Smith: A Memoir* (London: James Nisbet, 1909), esp. 75–77, 134–57.
42. The most systematic analysis of Blyden's attitudes toward these concepts remains M. Yu. Frenkel, "Edward Blyden and the Concept of African Personality," *African Affairs* 73, no. 292 (1974): 277–89.
43. For instance, his praise of Jean Finot's observation that "there are no inferior and superior races, but only races living outside or within the influences of culture" or his own references to "Africans of culture." Blyden, *African Life and Customs,* 9, 48.
44. Ibid., 10, 16, 46–47.
45. Klaus-Peter Köpping, *Adolf Bastian and the Psychic Unity of Mankind: The Foundations of Anthropology in Nineteenth Century Germany* (Münster: Lit, 2005); Bunzl, "Boas and the Humboldtian Tradition"; Zimmerman, *Anthropology and Antihumanism,* esp. chaps. 2, 9; Wilner, "A Global Potlatch."
46. For a basic overview of Blyden's influence, see Thomas W. Livingston, *Education and Race: A Biography of Edward Wilmot Blyden* (San Francisco: Glendessary Press, 1975).
47. For a summary, see Dorothy Helly, "'Informed' Opinion on Tropical Africa in Great Britain, 1860–1890," *African Affairs* 68, no. 272 (1969): 195–217.
48. Holden, *Blyden,* 792.
49. Jean-Loup Amselle and Emanuelle Sibeud, eds., *Maurice Delafosse. Entre orientalisme et ethnographie: l'itinéraire d'un africaniste (1870–1926)* (Paris: Maisonneuve et Larose, 1998); Jean-Louis Triaud, "Islam in Africa Under French Colonial Rule," in *The History of Islam in Africa,* ed. Nehemia Levtzion and Randall L. Pouwels (Oxford: James Currey, 2000), 169–88; and Christopher Harrison, *France and Islam in West Africa, 1860–1960* (Cambridge: Cambridge University Press, 1988), 155–63. Maurice Delafosse,

*Les Libériens et les Baoulé: nègres dits civilisés et nègres dits sauvages* (Paris: Librairie africaine et coloniale, 1901); "L'État actuel de l'Islam dans l'Afrique Occidentale Française," *Revue du monde musulman* 11, no. 5 (1910): 32–53; *Haute-Sénégal-Niger* (Paris: Larose, 1912); and Robert A. Hill, ed., *The Marcus Garvey and Universal Negro Improvement Association Papers* (Berkeley: University of California Press, 1995), 9:220–24.

50. James Fairhead et al., eds., *African-American Exploration in West Africa* (Bloomington: Indiana University Press, 2003); Henry M. Schieffelin, ed., *The People of Africa: A Series of Papers on Their Character, Condition, and Future Prospects* (New York: A. D. F. Randolph, 1871).

51. Tayler Lewis, "The Koran: African Mohammedanism," *Independent* (New York), Apr. 6, 1871, 1. Theodore Dwight Jr. was a pioneer in writing about Muslim African Americans; see his "Condition and Character of Negroes in Africa," *Methodist Quarterly Review* 46 (Jan. 1864): 77–90. On Musardu, see Fairhead et al., *Exploration,* 227.

52. On the effects of their efforts, see E. Ann McDougall, "Discourse and Distortion: Critical Reflections on Studying the Saharan Slave Trade," *Outre-mers* 89, no. 336–37 (2002): 195–227.

53. Winwood Reade, "Efforts of Missionaries Among Savages," *Journal of the Anthropological Society of London* 3 (1865): clxiii–clxxxiii, and various responses, clxxxiv–ccxciv. Other critics included the missionary H. Burnard Owen of the Society for the Propagation of the Gospel in Foreign Parts, while Richard Burton was supportive. One anonymous critic of Reade who replied in the *Journal* may have been Koelle himself, or at least someone who shared many of Koelle's ideas. On Smith, see, e.g., *Church Missionary Intelligencer,* n.s., 10 (Aug. 1874): 225–47, and note on 320; Grogan, *Bosworth Smith,* 137–40; Koelle, *Mohammed,* 452–54.

54. Geo[rge] P. Claflin, "Mohammedan Influence in Western Africa," *African Repository* 45, no. 2 (1869): 54–55.

55. On Smith, see Grogan, *Smith,* 141. On Blyden's immediate impact on Muslims in Liberia, see his own account, "A Mandingo Scholar and the Arabic Class in Liberia College," *African Repository* 45, no. 2 (1869): 61. On his current place in Liberian consciousness, personal communication, Timothy Nevin, July 2013, and my interview with Alpha M. Ba, Monrovia, Aug. 17, 2013. On the National Repentance Muslims, see Thomas Jaye and Abiodun Alao, "Islamic Radicalisation and Violence in Liberia," in *Militancy and Violence in West Africa: Religion, Politics, and Radicalisation,* ed. James Gow, Funmi Olonisakin, and Ernst Dijxhoorn (London: Routledge, 2013), 125–60.

56. Most of what is reliably known about Armattoe's life is due to the efforts of Philippa Robinson. See Robinson, "R. E. G. Armattoe: The 'Irishman' from West Africa," *History Ireland* 14, no. 4 (2006): 12–13.

57. Key theoretical support for such a framework is provided by Siba Grovogui, *Beyond Eurocentrism and Anarchy: Memories of International Order and Institutions* (New York: Palgrave Macmillan, 2006), esp. chaps. 2, 3.

58. Raphael E. G. Armattoe, *The Golden Age of West African Civilization* (Londonderry: Lomeshie Research Centre, 1946), 19–20. He first formulated this idea in an analysis of Erwin Schroedinger: "But neither in religion and philosophy, nor in music and medicine, can Europe claim a spiritual supremacy over other continents. It is perhaps in science, particularly in the mathematical and physical sciences that modern Europe is

pre-eminent. It is, therefore, in science and the scientific spirit that we must seek the distinctive greatness of European civilisation." Raphael E. G. Armattoe, *Homage to Three Great Men: Schweitzer, Schroedinger, De Gonnaro* (Londonderry: Sentinel, 1945), 7.

59. Armattoe, *Golden Age*, 30.
60. R. E. G. Armattoe, "Obituary: Franz Boas: 21 December, 1942," *Man* 43, no. 72–74 (1943): 91.
61. R. E. G. Armattoe, "The Pattern of Youth: An Interim Report," *Nature*, Aug. 21, 1943, 217.
62. R. E. G. Armattoe, *A Racial Survey of the British People* (Londonderry: Sentinel, 1944), 1–7, quote on 5.
63. "Youth's Food and Physique," *Cavalcade*, Sept. 24, 1943, 13.
64. Armattoe, *Great Men*, 3. Compare his claim that "the universal admiration for military uniforms shown by European women is one of the fruitful but obscure causes of war in the world today." In many such passages it is difficult to tell how facetious Armattoe may have been.
65. Raphael Ernest Grail Armattoe, Arthur Ernest Mourant, and Elizabeth W. Ikin, "The ABO, Rh, and MN Blood Groups of the Ewe and Ashanti of the Gold Coast," *West African Medical Journal* 2 (1953): 89–93. On his coauthors, see Daniel J. Kevles, *In the Name of Eugenics: Genetics and the Uses of Human Heredity* (Berkeley: University of California Press, 1985), 202; Gary P. Misson, A. Clive Bishop, and Winifred M. Watkins, "Arthur Ernest Mourant," *Biographical Memoirs of the Fellows of the Royal Society* 45 (1999): 329–48.
66. George Padmore, ed., *History of the Pan-African Congress: Colonial and Coloured Unity, a Programme of Action*, 2d ed. (London: Hammersmith Bookshop, 1963), 35–36. For the more well-known participants, the best resource is Hakim Adi and Marika Sherwood, *Pan-African History: Political Figures from Africa and the Diaspora Since 1787* (London: Routledge, 2003).
67. Most of the local controversy was manufactured, both by the US State Department, which manipulated the visas of those invited to speak, and by the anticommunist provocateur Sidney Hook. Both Soviet and US media then amplified the idea that the conference was an act of political propaganda for their enemies.
68. For the speeches by Armattoe and Weltfish, see the transcripts in Daniel S. Gillmor, ed., *Speaking of Peace: An Edited Report of the Cultural and Scientific Conference for World Peace* (New York: National Council of the Arts, Sciences, and Professions, 1949), 53–54, 72–77.
69. "Gold Coast: The Ewe and Togoland Unification Problem," National Archives of the UK, FCO 141/5005. On the Ghana–Togo border, see Paul Nugent, *Smugglers, Secessionists and Loyal Citizens on the Ghana–Togo Frontier: The Life of the Borderlands Since 1914* (Oxford: James Currey, 2002).
70. "Statement by Dr. R. Armattoe, Representative of the Joint Togoland Congress, to the Fourth Committee at Its 367th Meeting on 17 November, 1953," *Official Records of the General Assembly, Eighth Session, Fourth Committee*; Armattoe, Mourant, and Ikin, "Blood Groups of the Ewe and Ashanti," 92. The study had also found high frequencies of the "d" and "Du" antigens, which, the authors speculated, may have reflected "North African influence."

71. Ideas about a non-African "race" that had diffused throughout the continent, bringing civilization and exercising natural leadership over "true" Africans, had a long and brutal history, underpinning colonial discrimination, white supremacy, and violent conflicts up through the Rwandan genocide and beyond.
72. "Statement by Dr. R. Armattoe."
73. "The Ewe Problem," Dec. 1953, Colonial Office: Togoland Administration, CO 554/1032, The National Archives, United Kingdom (hereafter TNA-UK). See also CO 537/7180: Togoland Administration, TNA-UK.
74. Robinson, "Irishman." While still in New York, Armattoe is said to have told acquaintances that he believed he had been poisoned and refused to be treated in the United States for fear his enemies could reach him there too easily. This is meant to explain his sudden return to Hamburg. But the fact that he stopped first to visit his daughter in Ireland and is reported to have taken ill en route to Germany suggests the story of his suspicion may be apocryphal.
75. Siba N. Grovogui, "The Secret Lives of the 'Sovereign': Rethinking Sovereignty as International Morality," in *The State of Sovereignty: Territories, Laws, Populations*, ed. Luise White and Douglas Howland (Bloomington: Indiana University Press, 2009), 271; John L. Comaroff and Jean Comaroff, *Ethnicity, Inc.* (Chicago: University of Chicago Press, 2009).
76. The category of "non-Western thinker" is one that, the argument advanced here suggests, became increasingly complicated over the course of the nineteenth century.

# Chapter 13 A Two-Headed Thinker: Rüdiger Bilden, Gilberto Freyre, and the Reinvention of Brazilian Identity

*Maria Lúcia Pallares-Burke*

> You put together two people who have not been put together before. Sometimes it is like that first attempt to harness a hydrogen balloon to a fire balloon: do you prefer crash and burn, or burn and crash? But sometimes it works, and something new is made, and the world is changed. Then, at some point, sooner or later, for this reason or that, one of them is taken away.
> Julian Barnes, *Levels of Life*

If the importance of ideas can be measured by the use made of them after they were originally formulated, then one can say that Franz Boas's ideas were so important that they contributed to the reinvention of a country's identity. Indeed, his ideas were put to creative use to study a part of the world about which he himself did not write, Brazil, in the work of two scholars, the Brazilian Gilberto Freyre and the German Rüdiger Bilden. They picked up the ball from Boas and ran with it in new directions, revolutionizing the way Brazilians thought of themselves: from being ashamed of their ethnic composition to being proud of it and conscious of its enriching power.

The two men met in New York, at Columbia University in 1921, and soon realized they were kindred spirits. Both were very ambitious young men to whom the United States appeared to offer ample opportunity to widen their

Rüdiger Bilden in Brazil during his research trip in 1926. Image no. POS 06448, Fundação Gilberto Freyre.

horizons. There, they thought, they would be distancing themselves from the negative attitudes current in their places of origin—that is, from the provincialism and backwardness of Recife, in the northeast of Brazil, in the case of Freyre; and from the oppressive nationalism and militarism that were rising in Germany, in the case of Bilden.

Freyre's life and career ensured that his early ambitions for knowledge and fame were richly fulfilled. He has been credited with the invention of Brazilian identity with the publication of his *Casa-Grande & Senzala* (translated into

Gilberto Freyre in New York, in 1920 or 1921, during his time as a student at Columbia University. Image no. POS 07201, Fundação Gilberto Freyre.

English as *The Masters and the Slaves*) in 1933 and described as Boas's most outstanding Latin American disciple, his only rival in this respect being the Mexican anthropologist Manuel Gamio. On the other hand, Bilden, a German scholar who was closer to Boas and once seemed to have a brilliant future, later dropped out of the academic world and disappeared into obscurity.

However, as I shall try to show in this chapter, the creative use of Boas's ideas to analyze Brazilian culture and society and to "discover" Brazil for the Brazilians was the work of both scholars. So, in what follows I will consider them together as a two-headed thinker.

## THE RISE OF AN IDEA

To begin with the older man, Rüdiger Bilden (1893–1980) was born in Eschweiler in the Rhineland, the son of a prominent citizen, and educated at the local Gymnasium before emigrating to the United States in 1914, just before the outbreak of the First World War.[1] He entered Columbia University in February 1917, at almost the same time that America entered the war against his native country. At Columbia he was an outstanding student who impressed his teachers and colleagues with his talent, culture, wide interests, linguistic knowledge, and "technique of scholarship," considered to be unusual.[2] Still more important, at the university he made the acquaintance of three intellectuals who would play important roles in his life, his career, and his intellectual development: the then-established but now-forgotten William R. Shepherd, Franz Boas, and the young Gilberto Freyre.

William R. Shepherd (1871–1934) was a professor at Columbia and one of the few American historians of the time who was interested in Latin America. Not only was Shepherd the first to teach a course on the history of Spanish America at Columbia in 1904, but he was also one of the founders of the pioneering *Hispanic American Historical Review,* which began publication in 1918. Acclaimed in the 1930s as "the pioneer who cleared the soil for the growth of the study of Latin American history," Shepherd was also known for his open-mindedness, fresh views, and understanding of diversity in cultures and modes of thought.[3] To Shepherd, scholarship was a tool for understanding and appreciating the Other, and for this reason he did not confine his actions to academic circles. Convinced that a considerable part of the recurring conflict between peoples and nations was due to prejudice, Shepherd pointed out the ignorance of one culture in relation to another in lectures, reviews, and articles written both for scholars and the general public.[4]

As early as the late 1890s, when the conflict between the United States and Spain was reaching the point of war, Shepherd did not hesitate to call himself a "yanqui-español" in public, in order to stress the fact that "beyond political and economic interests" there existed "intellectual fraternity" that no frontier should deter.[5] Aware that the Monroe Doctrine had become an instrument for the control of Latin America by the United States, and recognizing the justified anxiety of the Latin Americans confronted with "yanqui imperialism," he proposed in 1927 the creation of an Inter-American Commission of Inquiry and Conciliation, to which all American republics would submit disputes arising among them.[6]

A global point of view was what Shepherd presented, a way of eliminating the insularity, provincialism, and misunderstanding that came with having a narrow view of history. As Harry E. Barnes pointed out, "[If] it's becoming increasingly clear that . . . all types of modern history must, in a real sense, be world history and must adopt an international point of view," this fact is due to a "salutary departure" of which Shepherd was a pioneer. His lectures on the expansion of Europe, given for the first time at Columbia in 1918 but never published in their entirety, established the "basic historical significance of that worldwide contact of cultures" and stressed that the so-called historical peripheries were essential parts of what was mistakenly thought to be a purely European history. It was time, Shepherd argued, for the West to recognize that besides what the European "has done, or thinks he has done, for the 'little brown brother,' there is a lot that the 'little brown brother' has done for him." Interaction between Europeans and non-Europeans in a process of give and take was, according to him, a study that would contribute to the "consciousness of a common humanity."[7] Much earlier, in 1909, he had already spoken in terms of this interrelated process: "The history of the United States does not consist solely of the history of the Thirteen Colonies and what has proceeded from them. . . . The share of the Romance nations in shaping the history of America is ill understood and less appreciated."[8]

What led the young Bilden to seek him out, in 1916, when he needed advice on continuing his education, was the fact that Shepherd had studied in Germany, expressed sympathy for its culture, and, true to his anti-ethnocentrism, refused to join the trend of "patriotic enthusiasm" followed by many historians from 1914 until 1920, when partiality and bias against Germany became "de rigueur."[9] In the anti-German climate of the war period Shepherd was the right person for a young man to approach, for, although rejecting the militarism and nationalism of his country, Bilden was proud of his origins and culture and deeply distressed by the fate of his compatriots and the family he had left behind. From then on, even before he officially became Shepherd's graduate student in 1922, they had various conversations about important historical problems, especially those related to the "World War and the German situation." Bilden acknowledged that these discussions were crucial in helping him cope with the "catastrophic turn of events" at the end of the war, events like the Armistice, the Treaty of Versailles, and the occupation of the Rhine region by Senegalese troops.[10]

Shepherd's balanced, deep, and broad view of the international conflict, his reluctance to divide the world into heroes and villains, and his belief that the defeat of Germany would not solve a problem that it was not solely responsible for were in fact rare at the time.[11] No wonder, then, that these conversations, together with Shepherd's lectures, gave Bilden the "emotional relief" he so much needed. His lectures on "the Expansion of Europe," Bilden wrote, were "a revelation and a tremendous stimulus to me," and to them he owed the "broader interpretation" of his investigation on Brazil.[12] The two men remained in contact until Shepherd's unexpected death in Berlin in 1934, and in a very affectionate letter of 1925 Bilden confessed that Shepherd was the person to whom he was most indebted for his development, both as an individual and as an intellectual. With Shepherd's encouragement, Bilden chose Latin America as his field. From these studies emerged the idea of writing a doctoral dissertation on Brazil, one focusing on the place of slavery in the economic and social life of the country.

Brazilian history was a field that attracted very little scholarly interest "beyond its borders" before the Second World War. As Shepherd put it, "Of all the nations in the New World, the United States of Brazil stands alone as a country of great international importance which lacks a comprehensive and altogether adequate treatise of its past."[13]

If it was Shepherd who suggested that he study the history of Latin America and who supervised the dissertation, the way in which Bilden approached the subject came to owe more to the ideas and the example of Boas, whom he met at Columbia around 1921. The two German immigrants obviously had something important in common. Boas became a second mentor to Bilden and also a friend, always concerned about his never-ending financial difficulties and his need for support and encouragement. Bilden visited him frequently at his home in New Jersey and at least once accepted Boas's kind offer, made to him and his wife, to spend a part of the summer at his residence in Grantwood.[14] On the occasion of Boas's eightieth birthday, Bilden movingly expressed both his gratitude for having been his student and his "maximum wishes that he could see a change in Germany and the end of the present madness because," as he put it, "I know that nothing else would make you happier in the twilight of your life." As to his great debt to Boas, Bilden wrote, "The intellectual and cultural inheritance that I have received from you will always be the star to guide me in all my activities."[15]

In fact, Bilden could not have failed to see the similarity between Shepherd's and Boas's concerns. Boas's battle against ethnocentrism and racism, his concern with diversities and historical contexts, and his criticism of imperialism, together with his belief that science should be used "in the cause of man," resonated with many of Shepherd's ideas.[16]

In 1925, when Bilden was preparing for his first visit to Brazil (it turned out to be his only visit there), Boas asked him to do research in the state of Pernambuco in order to test an anthropological theory of the time according to which white families in the tropics faced a choice between racial mixture and extinction. He also asked for Bilden's help in addressing a second concern, the roots of "consciousness of race," considered either as the result of instinct or of "habits developed from childhood." After investigating these questions, Bilden replied from Brazil that in the case of two aristocratic families, the Cavalcanti Albuquerques and the Wanderleys (to the second of whom Freyre was related), there was no evidence of African blood, but that mixture with the Indigenous population had proved impossible to avoid. As to the question of consciousness of race, Bilden's information about Brazil—still deserving of "[much] more research"—strengthened Boas's strong suspicion that it was a question of habit and not instinct. Boas made use of this information in his book *Anthropology and Modern Life* (1928), citing Bilden as his source.[17]

The third important encounter for Bilden was with the young Gilberto Freyre. This time it was Bilden who was the mentor to a friend. Freyre was seven years younger than Bilden, and the older man advised him on books to read, on German writers and thinkers to study, including Nietzsche, Oswald Spengler, and Georg Simmel, for instance, languages to learn, habits of work to develop, topics to think about, and so on. Francis B. Simkins, a friend of the two men at Columbia and later a well-known historian of the Old South, regretting the difficult life of the most promising of the three friends, reminded Freyre of their great debt to him: "God knows, Rüdiger helped educate you and me, and we owe him something."[18]

Despite Bilden's ambitions, abilities, and hard work, he never completed his dissertation, published very little, and was unable to build a career, although he held a succession of temporary academic posts. When he died in 1980 at the age of eighty-seven, in poverty and away from his family, his name did not attract the attention even of specialists in his field. In short, by worldly criteria, Bilden, who had been so promising, ended up becoming what the Americans call a loser and what the English describe as someone who had a brilliant future behind him.

One of the problems was that Bilden was a perfectionist, concerned with what he called "accurate and scientific results" that could be produced only by a "complete and exhaustive investigation" of a kind that far exceeded the bounds of a doctorate and for which he needed funding on a scale that he never received.[19] Having arrived in the United States in 1914 and remaining there for the rest of his life, he found his ambitions and his fate marked, if not shaped, by the dramatic events through which he lived during the most turbulent period of the twentieth century: at the world level, the two world wars and the Great Depression, and at the American level, racial segregation, the

New Deal, the turbulent beginnings of the Civil Rights movement, McCarthyism, and so on. As an "enemy alien," Bilden could not but suffer from the climate of hostility and suspicion in the country during the two wars and even between the wars, a time when anti-German feeling was always ready to take hold of the United States.[20] As Bilden's friend Simkins testified, "Because of his Teutonic looks, his legal status as an enemy alien," and his praise of German institutions such as "the social welfare legislation which Bismarck had imposed," he was "suspected by the police and by the average American with whom he conversed."[21]

To reconstruct Bilden's thoughts on Brazil, since he published no books, it is necessary to rely on a few scattered documents, including his original project, an article he published in *The Nation* (1929), a conference paper on race relations in Latin America, given in 1931, and his letters to and from Boas, the anthropologist Melville Herskovits, the historian and activist Arthur Schomburg, the ethnomusicologist George Herzog, and Brazilians such as the diplomat-historian Manuel de Oliveira Lima, the anthropologists Edgar Roquette-Pinto and Arthur Ramos, and his lifelong friend Freyre.

To explore the paradoxical combination of the success of an idea and the failure of its author, we should start with the project entitled "Slavery as a Factor in Brazilian History." Summarized in twelve single-spaced pages of typescript sent to the Carnegie Institution, it was essentially a study of economic history, located in a wider context.[22] The central problem Bilden addressed was that of the productivity, or, more precisely, the lack of productivity, of the slave system. Examining it as a "method of production," both in agriculture and in industry, Bilden argued that the slave system was inefficient. It wasted both human energy and natural resources because the "proportion of the expenditure of energy to the gain of energy" was so low. Indeed, slavery was "the chief obstacle to the development of Brazil."

Such an innovative study of the economics of slavery—as was immediately acknowledged—would have been thought sufficient for a doctoral thesis by itself, but Bilden's project also included sections on slavery in the social, cultural, and political life of Brazil as well as a detailed account of the gradual abolition of the system. To Oliveira Lima, Bilden stressed that he did not "follow economic *determinismo*" and was attempting "to work out a conception of history which goes beyond the spiritual or economic conception."[23] This was part of the more daring cultural approach that would complement his more precise and accurate economic approach—the one that could lead to "concrete and accurate conclusions." Among the interesting and innovative ideas that Bilden floated in this project outline were that of "the humane treatment of slaves in Brazil," the plantation owner as a "feudal lord," the contribution of slavery to the "prevalence" of venereal disease in the country, the contrast between the British and the Portuguese colonial systems, and the influence of domestic slavery "on the mental, moral and cultural development of the children of the slave owners." Most important of all, it was this forgotten scholar who first emphasized in his project that the evils generally attributed to the racial composition and to the intermixture of the country should be blamed on slavery.

Important intellectuals who read Bilden's project and part of the unfinished work in the 1920s considered his ideas to be revolutionary and were certain that the whole history of Brazil would have to be rewritten once he published. "You have a new and valuable approach to Brazilian history" that will "have a revolutionary effect and will fall like a bomb on the Instituto Histórico Brasileiro, etc., exploding that nest of old cronies," wrote the diplomat-historian Hélio Lobo, then consul general for Brazil in New York.[24] No other historian, either Brazilian or foreign, had dealt properly with the economic factor in the development of Brazil, said Lobo, an opinion shared by Oliveira Lima. As Lima put it, "The question of slavery in my country will be at last thoroughly, competently and completely examined and exposed," and as a result, "the many vital problems of the social life of Brazil which have not yet been sufficiently treated, will be duly dealt with."[25] Impressed by the young scholar, who would become a close friend of his, Lima wrote, "If my library, where Mr. Bilden has been working for months, had not had any other use . . . I would nevertheless consider myself satisfied to have founded it."[26]

After reading part of Bilden's manuscript, the historian Vicente Licínio Cardoso reviewed it in the most favorable way.[27] Published in the widely circulated *O Estado de São Paulo,* the leading newspaper of the leading city in the country, the review of the pioneering study by Bilden could be read nationwide. As Cardoso put it, Bilden's "brave tenacity," "the seriousness of his studies," and the "solidity of his culture" would inaugurate a new phase of historical studies on Brazil: "The impact of blacks on our historical evolution was actually much greater than has been recognized until now by our historians," many of whom were dominated, in Cardoso's opinion, by a political "laziness . . . concerning the critical examination of historical facts."[28] In short, Bilden was praised for his brilliant account of the weight of the past in Brazil, showing that the legacy of slavery was still actively present as an obstacle to the development of the new republic.

Bilden's article on Brazil, "Brazil, Laboratory of Civilization," published in January 1929, raised even more expectations concerning the work in progress. We must remember that ideas about Brazil that today, ever since Freyre's *The*

*Masters and the Slaves,* seem to reflect common sense, were at that time far from conventional. Herskovits expressed his enthusiasm about the article, saying he was impatiently waiting for the "full results" of Bilden's work, which would represent a comprehensive attack on the so-called "scientific racismo" that gave an air of objective validity to prejudices and was so widespread at that time. Roquette-Pinto, who could be described as the Brazilian Franz Boas, did not hide his admiration for ideas aimed at a public in need of common sense.[29] As he put it, the "brilliant pages" of this "good friend of Brazil" added a historical foundation to his own idea that the mixed Brazilian was not a biological problem but an economic and social one. In other words, the mixed population should be educated, not replaced.[30]

Bilden's article was commissioned by *The Nation* to be published around the time Herbert Hoover, the president-elect, was visiting Latin America in 1928. What did Bilden mean by the phrase "laboratory of civilization"? The title certainly catches one's attention, though this metaphor cannot bear too much weight. Bilden was probably thinking of a chemical experiment in which one mixes different substances to see what they will produce. The result of the mixture in the Brazilian case was not yet clear, but the way that "fundamental problems of civilization" were being solved in the country could be of "vital importance . . . to the world at large."[31] As he wrote to Boas in 1926, Brazil was "an immense field work, and a very interesting one, for anthropologists and ethnologists, a field until now touched only very superficially by scientific research."[32]

The article developed some points announced earlier in Bilden's research project and had a very clear aim: to introduce to a violent, segregationist society an alternative vision of human relations. At the same time, it aimed at informing the American public that the United States had been committing "intellectual atrocities" against this part of the American hemisphere. Among these atrocities was the idea that Latin America in general and Brazil in particular were doomed to be inferior if their population was not whitened.[33] To Americans, as Walter Mignolo and many others have emphasized, even the whites in Latin America were "not white enough"—and were becoming "darker and darker in relation to the increasing discourse on White Supremacy that was implemented during the last decade of the nineteenth century in the US."[34] The results of the fusion of races, as a popular American travel writer put it, were not at all promising: "It looks less as if Brazil were solving the color question, than as if color were dissolving Brazil."[35]

Dismissing current American prejudices, which abounded "despite all protestations of Pan-American brotherhood and amity,"[36] Bilden argued that the alleged inferiority of these countries had a very complex cultural explanation and not an "invitingly simple" racial one.[37] Focusing on Brazil, which bore the "brunt of the stigma" for being the "most mixed" in Latin America, Bilden asserted, "The basic cause of the evil [in Brazil] is not race, but slavery"—a "conclusion," as he pointed out, that "the leading anthropologist of the country," "Dr. Roquette-Pinto," had also arrived at "by anthropological methods."[38]

In a Boasian manner, Bilden began by emphasizing that the country was "highly diversified in topography, climate, and human life."[39] He stressed the "historical factors" of Portuguese colonization, which explained the "mode of settlement . . . by means of the latifundium, imported slave labor and the creation of a half-breed class suited to the milieu and wedded to the Lusitanian cause." He emphasized the importance in Brazilian history of miscegenation, which was "officially encouraged," as well as "practiced individually from necessity and habit," thanks to "a propensity acquired by the Portuguese during the long centuries of Moorish conquest of Portugal." He emphasized the importance of historical circumstances like the "gradual abolition of slavery" and the establishment of the Republic in 1889 in "accelerating the social equalization and hence fusion of the diverse ethnic elements." As a result of all these historical antecedents, "race lines were drawn more loosely" in Brazil than elsewhere and were subject to "a gradual but steady softening" during the three centuries of the colonial regime, producing a "more humane" system of slavery than was to be found in other parts of the world.[40]

However, Bilden was far from denying the existence of antagonisms between the three main ethnic groups or of a certain degree of "discrimination and friction," which, though very far from the North American "cancerous growth in the social body," was not totally absent. Equalization and fusion were, as he pointed out, in progress, while "race lines still follow class lines," which means that "the lower the class, the darker the blood." As he put it, the "negroid elemento" in Brazil was still "handicapped," since "the abolition of slavery, while constructive, was not constructive to the point of freeing it from its dismal and insidious heritage. Only a number of generations can accomplish that end."[41] Up to that moment, what could be said about the Brazilian social experiment was that the country was modernizing itself "without war, revolution or other form of violence" and was still progressing "far on the road toward a harmonious blending of diverse and supposedly incompatible elements into a new tropical race."[42] So, in spite of all that remained to be achieved, if one considered the experiment in progress and the way in which the "more primitive groups . . . are surprisingly free to make characteristic and valuable contributions" to society, the proper question, concluded Bilden, was this: Should Brazil "be dubbed . . . a land of mongrels or rather be looked upon as a world laboratory of tropical civilization?"[43]

In spite of this promising essay and the great expectations of many, including himself, "Brazil, Laboratory of Civilization" proved to be the only published sample of the book that Bilden never finished. Two years later, in a paper given at a round table on "Latin American relations"—and widely circulated among friends and fellow scholars—Bilden offered an overview, in twelve pages, of race relations in the whole of Latin America, developing further the idea of another "intellectual atrocity" generally committed against this part of the continent: to consider it as composed of a set of homogenous countries.[44] Once again emphasizing diversity, thanks in particular to the different proportions of migrants from Europe in the populations of different states, Bilden concluded that "the ready attribution of a common Latin individuality to the Latin American countries . . . must be dismissed as smacking rather strongly of white men's presumption." Ignoring the non-European racial elements, which possess "widely varied cultural attainments," and stressing only "one set of factors—those of European origins" led to a total neglect of diversity in the making of Latin America. To avoid this danger, Bilden suggested interpreting Latin American history in the light of "the varying kind and degree of intermixture, juxtaposition, or antagonism of ethnic strains and corresponding cultural values . . . without any preconceived notions of the superiority of one race or culture over others."[45] This approach would mean distinguishing among four groups of countries, ranging from the predominantly European, such as Chile, to countries like Paraguay, where "the European element is at best a veneer."[46] In this case, Bilden's analysis followed not only Boas's ideas of intermixture and diversity but also the model of "culture areas" dominant in the German tradition of geography in which Boas had been trained.

Years later, just after Pearl Harbor, when awareness of the need to gain Latin America's support was growing faster, Bilden would return to this theme in a conference organized in May 1942 by the League for Industrial Democracy in New York. The discussions centered on racial equality as the key issue of the war. At that time, Bilden had already been barred, as a German, from participating in any "Latin American activities," such as the Pan-American Scientific Congress of May 1940, although, as he put it, "there is nothing that I desire more than to be of assistance in cementing the solidarity of North and South America" while fighting German propaganda.[47]

Hence, the invitation from Harry W. Laidler to participate in the league's conference on "the role of races in our future civilization" was a great opportunity for Bilden to address the injurious "racial myth" of the evils of intermixture as the greatest "obstacle to real friendship with the Latin Americans."[48] In fact, Bilden shared with Walter White, the executive secretary of the National Association for the Advancement of Colored People (NAACP), a concern about the link between race relations in the United States and its poor relations with its Latin American neighbors. Racism and segregation in America, they agreed, were obviously connected to the anti-American feelings in countries populated in great part by Indigenous people, Negroes, and mixed races. As long as the "good neighbor policy" did not wake up to this reality, all efforts to develop friendly relations with Latin American countries would fail.[49]

Along the lines of the previous papers, the topics of diversity and intermixture in Latin America and in Brazil were once again addressed by Bilden at the conference, together with the awkward question asked at the very start: "Unquestionably, most Latin Americans are ethnically mixed. But, in the last analysis, what people is not?"[50]

The foundation of a research institute for the comparative study of American areas with "similar racial, economic, social, and cultural history and problems," which was to include the West Indies, the Caribbean coast of Central and South America, the Guianas, and Brazil, was another of Bilden's efforts. Following Boas's idea of using "science in the cause of man," Bilden aimed at combining a study from the "purely scientific standpoint" with the improvement of human relations. Without the "sound foundation" that only an objective study could provide, argued Bilden, "cooperation between the American nations must always remain superficial and transitory."[51] Initially proposed in 1940 to the Division of Cultural Relations of the US State Department and to the Brazilian embassy, the project had the endorsement of various officials and intellectuals interested in Latin American relations, including White. As Bilden wrote to Boas, "a very auspicious beginning" had been made, but the main problem was the "financing of the project."[52] His efforts failed to turn the institute into reality in the early 1940s. However, with relentless determination, Bilden continued to fight for it until 1945–46.[53]

Over the course of Bilden's trajectory, it becomes clear that as the prospect of finishing his ambitious volumes on Brazilian slavery diminished, he devoted more and more attention to the cause of race relations in the United States, and this at a time when, as W. E. B. Du Bois put it, "the bravest of us are afraid to talk about race."[54] He was in contact with the NAACP and also with black artists and intellectuals of the Harlem Renaissance, sharing their aims of improving the social situation and self-esteem of African Americans. He knew and worked with leaders of the black intelligentsia, such as the sociologist

Charles Johnson, the artist Aaron Douglas, Schomburg, and White, and made a point of introducing his Brazilian friends to them.[55]

Bilden might, in fact, be considered an important member of the small group of Boas's disciples whose activities support the argument that interracial cooperation existed among the intellectuals and artists connected to the movement.[56] Also, his activities in Harlem are a useful reminder of what has almost been forgotten in the recent wave of assertions that Brazil is not a model to be followed, namely, that in the early twentieth century images of Brazil strengthened the determination to confront segregation in the United States and elsewhere.[57]

As a temporary lecturer at various educational institutions as well as in Negro societies, labor centers, and, at least once, in a church in Harlem and on a radio program in Richmond, Virginia, Bilden showed himself to be a true disciple of Boas, the Boas who was "always the activist!" and who gave the commencement address at Atlanta University in 1906 at the invitation of Du Bois, arguing that African Americans should learn about the history of Africa in order to take more pride in their race.[58]

Bilden's lectures were devoted not only to combating the "inferiority complex" many blacks had developed in a humiliating environment but also to attempting to bring race and racism to the forefront of American consciousness. As one of his program outlines stated, "The status of the Negro is the chief challenge to democracy in the Western Hemisphere. Understanding is the first step toward solution of the problems involved. . . . [A] knowledge of the forces which have made the race problem a danger to our entire civilization is necessary, not merely to members of the Negro race, but to all American citizens."[59] And in all of those lectures, Latin America and particularly Brazil were held up as examples of an alternative social organization, hence of proof that improvement was not a chimera.

Attesting to the novelty and practical relevance of Bilden's approach, the words of Charles Johnson, who welcomed his proposal to teach the history of race relations in Brazil at Fisk University, are revealing: "Certainly a series of lectures in this field would serve to lift the horizon of both white and Negro students who are inclined to be provincial in their considerations of race problems."[60]

## THE MAKING OF A CLASSIC

Gilberto Freyre (1900–1987) was born in Recife, in Pernambuco. His father was an academic, while his mother came from a family that owned sugarcane plantations that used to be worked by slaves until slavery was abolished in

Brazil in 1888. He was educated at the Baptist college in Recife and briefly converted to Protestantism, but then, since 1918 was not a good time to pursue his studies in Europe, which was his first choice, he went to Baylor University in Texas. In 1921 he moved to Columbia, where he began a master's thesis (supervised, as in Bilden's case, by Shepherd) titled "Social Life in Brazil in the Middle of the Nineteenth Century." He also attended lectures on sociology by Franklin Giddings, who impressed him, and lectures on anthropology by Boas, who impressed him even more. He wrote in 1922 that if American brains could be priced, that of Boas was worth $2.5 million, compared to Giddings's $2 million and Woodrow Wilson's $1 million.[61] From the 1930s on he regularly paid tribute to Boas, in his books and also in an obituary published in a Brazilian newspaper in early 1943.[62]

Still more important in Freyre's education, however, was his friendship with Bilden, formed during long "speculative conversations" in the latter's apartment in Greenwich Village. The African American poet and lawyer Sam Allen, who met Bilden at Fisk University in the late 1930s, still recalled in 2011 what a great conversationalist—but not of a "professorial kind"—he was, impressing all those around him by his "tremendous erudition," brilliance, openness, and broad interests: "It was an immense pleasure to be with him, to talk to him, to listen to him."[63] Freyre, at first, was no exception in voicing such appreciation of Bilden, although, as he became more famous, his references to his friend became much less frequent and less favorable.[64] He expressed his admiration for Bilden in public in an article in the *Diario de Pernambuco* in 1926, when his friend was visiting Brazil, describing him as a "brilliant historian" and noting the originality of Bilden's analysis of the history of slave civilization in terms of "a certain process of use of energy" or "method of production," since it disregarded the "rigid dividing line between the spiritual and the material." That is why, Freyre commented with enthusiasm, for Bilden, "to study slavery is to study the history of Brazil."[65]

Despite his early exposure to the ideas of Boas, the articles Freyre published in the 1920s as well as his private letters show that he generally accepted, if sometimes with misgivings, the conventional wisdom of his place and time concerning "scientific racism" and eugenics, especially the dangers of race mixture, and the need to "whiten" Brazil by encouraging immigration from Europe. If we examine his work well into the 1920s, long after he had studied with Boas, we can see that the powerful racist paradigm (in the Kuhnian sense) still informed much of his thinking and observation and that only very occasionally was he capable of glimpsing the importance of Boas's challenge to the notion that each race had an essential nature. As if walking along a zigzag path, he shifted from lamenting the loss of dignity of Brazilian aristocrats who had been consorting "with fat mulattas with fuzzy hair" to praising the physical and mental capacity of blacks, to showing sympathy for the Ku Klux Klan, to praising Boas, to praising the southern politician Benjamin Tillman's "sense of reality" for the violent way he fought for "white democracy," and so on.[66]

It was only at the beginning of the 1930s that Freyre came to be converted to the ideas of Boas about the need to analyze social problems in terms of culture rather than race. He owed this conversion partly to Bilden and partly to the writings of Roquette-Pinto, who, on one side, criticized the scientific pretensions of the "science of race" and, on another, drew attention to the positive contributions to Brazilian culture that "the more primitive groups" might be making.[67]

It was only from that time on that Freyre started to describe himself as a disciple of Boas, backdating this discipleship to the time that he had heard his "master" lecture at Columbia, strongly suggesting that Boas's ideas "came to him with the force of a revelation."[68] Freyre, whose concern with self-presentation became notorious as he grew older and more famous, put his literary gifts and brilliant prose to the task of creating myths about himself. As part of his self-presentation, he claimed to have been close to such famous writers and intellectuals as W. B. Yeats, whom he once heard lecture at Baylor, and H. L. Mencken, whom he met briefly, and Franz Boas, whose ideas were totally absent from his master's thesis and his articles of the 1920s and who had not noticed Freyre among the many students at his lectures at Columbia.[69] He later displayed a photograph of Boas in his study and liked to give the impression that his contact with him had been personal and intense.

The transformed Freyre can be seen in the book that made him famous, *Casa-Grande & Senzala.* In the preface to this book Freyre paid generous tribute to his "master," writing that it was the study of anthropology "under the supervision of Professor Boas" that "revealed to me the true value of the negro and the mulatto," teaching him as well "to consider the distinction between race and culture as fundamental." Freyre cited Boas on a number of occasions in the main body of the book, referring to *The Mind of Primitive Man,* for instance, to *Anthropology and Modern Life,* and to the famous article titled "Race" that Boas wrote for the *Encylopædia of the Social Sciences.* He also cited members of Boas's circle, such as Ruth Benedict, Robert Lowie, and Herskovits.

Like the following two volumes of the trilogy that narrated the social and cultural history of Brazil from 1500 to 1900, *The Mansions and the Shanties* and *Order and Progress, Casa-Grande* is a book that has appealed to different people for different reasons. It commanded attention when it was published for its racy prose, its pioneering "intimate history" of the family (including the sexual mores of upper-class males), and its "sensuous history" of sounds and smells. What appealed to some readers offended others, and the book was sometimes criticized for its informal style, for the inclusion of "pornography" (according to one Brazilian bishop), and for the expression of nostalgia for an old regime that was sometimes described as feudal and, more frequently, as patriarchal.

However, what has made *Casa-Grande* into a classic interpretation of Brazil, alongside the slightly later study by Sérgio Buarque de Holanda, *Roots of Brazil* (1936), and Caio Prado Júnior's *Formation of Contemporary Brazil* (1942), is its emphasis on miscegenation, viewed in a positive light. For some, like the writer Jorge Amado, Freyre's first book, like an "avalanche," "an explosion," or "a flash of lightning," transformed the literature and the cultural life of Brazil. It was with a similar metaphor that Lewis Hanke welcomed a book that challenged the widespread view that civilization and purity of race walked hand in hand. Deeply related to the "fundamental social and political problems of our times," as he put it, *Casa-Grande* defended a "doctrine . . . loaded with political dynamite" at a time when there prevailed in the world "the domination of one race or one culture which considers itself superior."[70]

Freyre argued that among the European colonizers the Portuguese were the most adaptable and that they owed their "plasticity" and their tendency to interbreed with the Indigenous populations of their empire to their history of interactions with the Muslim invaders of Iberia in the Middle Ages. The most famous single sentence in this long book is the following: "Every Brazilian, even the light-skinned fair one, carries about with him on his soul, when not on soul and body alike . . . the shadow, or at least the birthmark, of the aborigine or the Negro."[71] Reversing the traditional critique of miscegenation, Freyre presented it as something to be proud of and also as something especially Brazilian. In the early twentieth century Brazilian intellectuals had expressed anxiety about their country's lack of identity, precisely because it had been formed from the intermingling of three races. Freyre turned the problem into a solution: mixture was the essence of Brazilian identity.

This argument has of course been put forward by other writers about other countries besides Brazil, notably by a "real" student of Boas, the aforementioned Manuel Gamio, in his book *Forging a Nation* (1916), and by José Vasconcelos in *The Cosmic Race* (1925), both treating the case of Mexico, although the latter's book was more of a meditation on the philosophy of history than an empirical study of the kind that both Gamio and Freyre produced. In addition, the sociologist Fernando Ortiz, whose career and interests ran parallel to Freyre's in a number of ways, described his native Cuba in a positive manner as a mixture of races.[72]

In the case of Brazil, Freyre admitted that the rehabilitation of the Brazilian *mestiço* went back to two Brazilian anthropologists who preceded him, Alberto Torres, "the first among us to cite Professor Franz Boas and his researches on transplanted races," and Roquette-Pinto, a "forgotten pioneer" who was the first to distinguish the "sick *mestiço*" from the *mestiço* in general.[73] However, he surely owed still more to Bilden, who had kindly made available to Freyre his unpublished "first manuscript," where even syphilis was given an important role in the formation of Brazil—as he acknowledged in *Casa-Grande*—and who had already noted in a published article, as we have seen, important points that Freyre would develop: that miscegenation was particularly prevalent in Brazil, that the Portuguese were predisposed to this by their medieval history, and that a major consequence of the practice in Brazil was the softening of the system of slavery.[74]

No wonder, then, that after reading *Casa-Grande* Bilden wrote to its author, "I chuckled . . . when I saw how largely you have come around to my viewpoint, which twelve and fifteen years ago you criticized and called 'mechanistic.' Of course you have pre-empted to a certain extent my own subject and have made it somewhat harder for me to write my book."[75] Bilden had already written to Herskovits, when asked about "one Gilberto Freyre" who had sent him a book "entitled 'Casa-Grande & Senzala' ": "He is the only person who has seen my manuscripts." Bilden noted that Freyre's book "is very much akin to the book I am writing and in some important respects pre-empts the latter." He insisted, however, that "this should not in any way be interpreted as an accusation of plagiarism, conscious or unconscious. We have exchanged views so freely and often that we could not avoid influencing each other."[76]

Bilden's book, had it followed the outline summarized earlier, would have been a major innovative study of economic history in a broader context. As we have seen, the cultural influence of slavery upon Brazilian society as a whole was also of great interest to Bilden. He saw "idleness as the badge of freedom" and noted the influence of domestic slavery on "Brazilian morals and customs," on the seclusion of women, and so on. But Freyre's work, by contrast, was what the French call *histoire totale*. *Casa-Grande* did more than praise miscegenation, discuss its origins, and present it as typically Brazilian, as Bilden had done in his article on the "laboratory of civilization." Freyre ran further with the ball, applying the idea of cultural hybridity to what he often called the "interpenetration of cultures." Offering a long series of vivid, concrete examples, he argued that

Brazilian culture was a hybrid one, since the dominant European culture had borrowed heavily from the Indigenous cultures of the Indians and also, despite the reluctance of middle-class Brazilians of the 1930s to admit it, from the cultures of the African slaves; he even referred to slaves' "civilizing function." In Freyre's new interpretation of Brazil, therefore, the evils and vices attributed earlier to the black and mixed population could not be considered any longer as being innate to their race—the causes lay in the social and economic slave system. "Neither White nor Black acted for themselves as individuals, and much less as race," he wrote. It was the "spirit of the economic system that, like a powerful god, divided us into masters and slaves."[77]

Freyre made the point about the importance of "interpenetration" in one cultural domain after another. For example, he discussed the hybrid nature of Brazilian cuisine, which he took seriously as an anthropological or sociological phenomenon (as he did in everyday life). He adored the sweets (*doces*) of the Northeast and devoted a short book to their ethnography, history, and sociology, complete with recipes.[78] He was probably inspired to do this by the example of Boas, who, when carrying out fieldwork among the Kwakiutl (now known as the Kwakwa̱ka̱'wakw) on the Northwest Coast of America, asked his informant George Hunt to collect information about the preparation and consumption of food and then published over three hundred recipes provided by Hunt's wife.[79]

Freyre also discussed the hybridity of vernacular architecture, such as the *mucambos,* or cabins, in which poor people in Recife lived, which combined elements of African and Indigenous culture. In addition, he examined the hybridization of the Portuguese language, not only in vocabulary, by borrowing words from Tupi or Bantu, but also in accent, the harsh tones of peninsular Portuguese being softened, according to Freyre, in African mouths, while this softer way of speaking was passed on to the children of the plantation owners by their black nannies. Yet again, in 1938, on the occasion of the World Cup of soccer, or *futebol,* Freyre famously discussed the hybridity of what he called "mulatto football" in Brazil, not only in the sense of football played by mulattos but also of a style of football that was close to dance, modified by players whose legs were familiar with the samba as well as with *capoeira.*[80] If there is one element missing or nearly missing from this list it is music, an obvious example of cultural hybridity, especially in Brazil. In this respect Freyre's work differs from that of his friend Ortiz, who had much to write about music in Cuba. It might have made a difference if Freyre had followed Bilden's strong suggestion that he meet his ethnomusicologist friend Herzog, also a disciple of Boas.[81]

Freyre studied cultural hybridity from another angle in one of his lesser-known works, his recently translated *Ingleses no Brasil* (*The English in Brazil*, 1948).[82] In this collection of essays Freyre was concerned with the cultural impact of the "flood" of English artifacts, words, and ideas on the upper and middle classes of Rio de Janeiro and other major cities in the early nineteenth century, a time when English goods were in vogue. Putting some ideas of Thorstein Veblen to good use, Freyre examined the fashion for things English, from tea services to pianos, suggesting that they were viewed as symbols of civilization and used by consumers to fashion a new identity. Carried by the wave of British imperialism, these objects led to a quiet revolution in everyday life and in culture, in the broad anthropological sense of that term.

However, as often happens in situations where cultures interpenetrate, some Englishmen who had spent time in Brazil adopted some of the local customs, while Brazilians resisted anglicization by adapting the invading culture to their own traditions. In the case of furniture, for instance, angular English chairs, when copied by Brazilian craftsmen, lost their straight lines, "the English style of furniture rounding itself out in the Brazilian climate."[83] In similar fashion, in an essay published elsewhere, Freyre described Oscar Niemeyer as rounding out, and so tropicalizing, the straight lines of the architecture of Le Corbusier.[84]

Freyre described even the practice of interdisciplinarity, which he wholeheartedly approved of, as a kind of hybridity. When he came to write a textbook on sociology, he criticized what he called sociological purity and recommended that his readers be "polytheists," in other words, that they take an interest in anthropology, psychology, history, and literature. Again, he advocated what he variously called the "Brazilianization" and the "tropicalization" of sociology and other disciplines, thus avoiding European -isms such as Marxism, Freudianism, and Weberism. His essential point was that any sociology that was built on European and North American experience alone would be unable to provide valid generalizations about human society and culture.[85] In this sense he was already an advocate of what has become known as Southern Theory.

In a number of late works, slim volumes of essays for the most part, Freyre moved from history to the kind of theory he described as "tropicology." These works, never translated into English, include *Além do Apenas Moderno* (1973) and *Insurgências e Ressurgências* (1983). His reflections on the future in the first of these books center on time, on modernity, and on what he was one of the first to call the postmodern.[86] Drawing on the ideas of Jacques Ellul, Josef Pieper, and David Riesman, Freyre adapted them to the tropical environment, arguing that if northern time, rigid and mechanical, fitted well with industrial capitalism, it was southern or Iberian time, more relaxed and flexible, that fitted the coming age of leisure. The later book, looking at the recent past at a global level, suggested that one major trend was the interaction, or interpenetration, of traditions and modernities.[87]

Looking back on Freyre's work as a whole, one of the most striking features it displays is the recurrence of binary oppositions, together with a tendency to undermine them. Masters and slaves, mansions and shanties, northern Europe and southern Europe, East and West are opposed to each other. Freyre took the contrast between Dr. Jekyll and Mr. Hyde from the story by Robert Louis Stevenson and made it his own by using it again and again in different contexts, including an analysis of President Getúlio Vargas and his policies. One of the most famous of these oppositions, reiterated in Freyre's work, was that between the Apollonian and the Dionysian, an idea he took, with acknowledgment, from Boas's student Benedict (although he had read Nietzsche when he was young).[88]

However, these contrasts are rarely, if ever, simple. They are qualified, as one might expect from a thinker who was fascinated, if not obsessed, by the idea of hybridity, by a sharp awareness of the connections and interactions between the Big House and the slave quarters, for instance, or between the political culture of the Brazilian Empire and that of the Republic that followed it. Among Freyre's favorite words are "semi-," "quasi-," and "para-," employed in order to soften the oppositions from which he began. In short, one of the most important lessons readers of Freyre can learn from his work—appropriately enough, for a writer on race relations—is not to see the world in simple terms of black and white.

## PARTNERS

To sum up: Our two-headed thinker sometimes looked in different directions, but the two scholars shared some important ideas and could be described as partners in the interpretation of Brazil. Bilden, the outsider, was sometimes impatient with Brazilians, who did not work hard enough (one of the legacies of slavery), and before he visited Brazil he condemned what he called the paucity of Brazilian culture. He may be described as a disciple of Boas as well as a friend, even though he began by practicing economic history before turning to anthropology. Like Boas, he was an empiricist, though he did not reject theory.

Freyre, on the other hand, often celebrated the achievements of his country. He was an eclectic, an omnivorous reader, and an interdisciplinary scholar who excelled because of his sponge-like ability to soak up ideas, including theories, from many sources, adapt them to his interests ("tropicalization," once again), and make them his own. All the same, some ideas mattered more to him than others, and a number of those ideas came from Boas: the concern with the relative importance of race and culture, for instance; the interest in material culture (including cuisine); the love of museums, in Freyre's case the Museu Etnológico in Lisbon and the Museu Nina Rodrigues in Salvador; and the idea of what Freyre called significant details, in the spirit of the Boas who remarked, "To the ethnologist, the most trifling details of social life are important."[89]

To conclude, let us consider again the pioneering idea of "Brazil, a laboratory of civilization" put forward by Bilden and taken up and advanced by Freyre. There is no doubt that the idea of racial and cultural mixture and race harmony as the result of slavery in the past was very successful. Indeed, seen as Freyre's legacy to the country, it has long been incorporated in official or semi-official discourse on Brazil, even if it is also denounced from time to time as pure idealization.[90]

But what can be said of the fate of the other contributor to this successful idea?

In the short term, up to the early 1950s, Bilden's name was still connected to it. In Brazil, intellectuals such as Ramos, Roquette-Pinto, and Luis Washington Vita were quite clear about the pioneering efforts of Bilden to fight the prejudice against the so-called ugly races. Roquette even placed Bilden side by side with an important German scientist and correspondent of Charles Darwin, Fritz Müller, in the fight against race prejudice and the racial theories that supported it. Ramos and Vita refer to the ideas of Bilden on slavery and miscegenation as having been converted by Freyre to the leitmotif of his work on the "influence of the Negro in Brazil" and on slavery being the cause of the "evils of our social development." Abroad, we find both admirers and critics of the Brazilian solution to the race problem, praising or denouncing Bilden as a pioneer. To one critic, writing as late as the 1970s, Bilden was responsible for the "construction of a fantasy" that miscegenation is beautiful and racial harmony does exist "in the land of sun, samba and saudade."[91] Ironically, at that time Bilden was still alive but untraceable by his few surviving friends.

In the long term, the fate of this pioneering scholar reminds us of the "Matthew Effect," a phrase coined by Robert Merton to describe the process whereby important scientific discoveries are remembered by posterity as if they were the work of major figures alone, forgetting that "big steps in science are really built up out of a number of small contributions."[92] In the same way, one can say that important innovations in culture are not produced by one star alone but are, on the contrary, the result of the contribution of a constellation of individuals hardly ever recognized by posterity. Bilden's contribution to the study of race relations at the beginning of the twentieth century was innovative and not peripheral, but, as if confirming the Matthew Effect, it was obscured by the achievement of other members of the constellation to which he belonged and to which he greatly contributed.

The partners Bilden and Freyre had long and eventful lives, both of them dying at the age of eighty-seven. However, whereas Freyre was acclaimed worldwide for his achievements and described in an obituary as a "Universal Brazilian," many of Bilden's ambitions were frustrated, and his achievements and efforts were unacknowledged.[93] In 1953 he confessed to Freyre that he had "a little clerical job which keeps me from starving," that he was involved, with Dorothy Loos, in the translation of *Sobrados e Mucambos* for Macmillan, and that his "greatest desire" was to "get back into Brazilian work and, perhaps, return to Brazil." None of this came true, and the disconcerting fact is that Bilden disappeared without a trace in 1956 and died in obscurity twenty-four years later, in 1980.[94]

## Notes

1. For details and further references, see Maria Lúcia G. Pallares-Burke, *O Triunfo do Fracasso: Rüdiger Bilden, o Amigo Esquecido de Gilberto Freyre* (São Paulo: Editora Unesp, 2012).
2. Dixon Ryan Fox to Beardsley Ruml, July 17, 1924, Fellowships—Bilden, 1924–25, Laura Spelman Rockefeller Memorial Archives (hereafter LSRM), Rockefeller Archive Center, Sleepy Hollow, New York (hereafter RAC).
3. Helen Delpar, *Looking South: The Evolution of Latin Americanist Scholarship in the United States, 1850–1975* (Tuscaloosa: University of Alabama Press, 2008), 35; Pallares-Burke, *Triunfo do Fracasso,* 73–74.
4. Pallares-Burke, *Triunfo do Fracasso,* 66–67, 73–76.
5. "Mr. Shepherd," interview on the occasion of his visit to Buenos Aires in 1907, Buenos Aires, Sept. 8, 1907, *España: Revista Semanal de la Asociación Patriótica Española* 5, no. 201: 146–47, Box 5, William Robert Shepherd Papers (hereafter WRSP), Columbia University Rare Book and Manuscript Library.
6. William R. Shepherd, "The Reconciliation of Fact with Sentiment in Our Dealings with Latin America," *Annals of the American Academy of Political and Social Science* 132 (July 1927): 127–29.
7. Harry Elmer Barnes, *A History of Historical Writing* (New York: Dover Publishers, 1937), 307, 389; Harry Elmer Barnes, *The History of Western Civilization* (New York: Harcourt, Brace, 1935), 6; William R. Shepherd, "The Expansion of Europe I," *Political Science Quarterly* 34, no. 1 (1919): 51, 46.
8. William R. Shepherd, "The Contribution of the Romance Nations to the History of the Americas," in *Annual Report of the American Historical Association for the Year 1909* (Washington, DC: Government Printing Office, 1910), 221–27.

9. Harry E. Barnes et al., *Contemporary Social Theory* (1940; repr. New York: Russell and Russell, 1971), 567; Peter Novick, *That Noble Dream: The "Objectivity Question" and the American Historical Profession* (Cambridge: Cambridge University Press, 1992), 116–31.
10. Rüdiger Bilden to William R. Shepherd, Sept. 20, 1925 (letter with last page and signature missing), Box 2, WRSP; K. L. Nelson, "The 'Black Horror on the Rhine': Race as a Factor in Post-World War I Diplomacy," *Journal of Modern History* 42, no. 4 (1970): 606–27.
11. William R. Shepherd, "The German Colonies and Their Disposal," *The Nation*, Mar. 28, 1918, 340–41; William R. Shepherd, "The Expansion of Europe III," *Political Science Quarterly* 34, no. 3 (1919): 392–412.
12. Rüdiger Bilden to William R. Shepherd, Sept. 20, 1925, Box 2, WRSP.
13. Delpar, *Looking South*, 123; William R. Shepherd, "Brazil as a Field of Historical Study," *Hispanic American Historical Review* 13, no. 4 (1933): 427.
14. Rüdiger Bilden to Manuel de Oliveira Lima, May 23, 1927, July 20, 1927, July 28, 1927, Aug. 29, 1927, Oliveira Lima Family Papers (hereafter OLF), Catholic University of America, Washington, DC.
15. Rüdiger Bilden to Franz Boas, Sept. 5, 1938, Box 7, Franz Boas Papers (hereafter BP), American Philosophical Society.
16. Ruth Bunzel, introduction to Franz Boas, *Anthropology and Modern Life* (1929; repr. New York: Norton, 1962), 6.
17. Pallares-Burke, *Triunfo do Fracasso*, 164–65.
18. Francis B. Simkins to Gilberto Freyre, Nov. 23, 1949, Archives of the Fundação Gilberto Freyre (uncatalogued, hereafter FGF), Apipucos, Recife.
19. Rüdiger Bilden to John C. Merriam, president of the Carnegie Foundation, Jan. 24, 1924, OLF.
20. Daniel J. Leab, "Screen Images of the 'Other' in Wilhelmine Germany and the United States, 1890–1918," *Film History* 9, no. 1 (1997): 49–70; Arnold Krammer, *Undue Process: The Untold Story of America's German Alien Internees* (London: Rowman and Littlefield, 1997).
21. Francis B. Simkins, Autobiography [ca. 1948], unpublished manuscript, Francis Butler Simkins Collection (hereafter FBS), Greenwood Library Archives, Longwood University, Farmville, VA.
22. Rüdiger Bilden, "Slavery as a Factor in Brazilian History," enclosed with a letter to John C. Merriam, Jan. 24, 1924, OLF.
23. Rüdiger Bilden to Manuel de Oliveira Lima, Mar. 4, 1926, OLF.
24. Transcribed in a letter from Rüdiger Bilden to Francis B. Simkins, Feb. 6, 1924, FBS.
25. Manuel de Oliveira Lima to Rüdiger Bilden, June 15, 1924, Fellowships—Bilden, 1924–25, LSRM.
26. Manuel de Oliveira Lima, *Memórias (estas minhas reminiscências . . .)* (Rio de Janeiro: José Olympio, 1937), 64–65.
27. Vicente L. Cardoso was the editor of *À Margem da História da República* (1924), a collection of writings by intellectuals concerned with the future of the country who were born in the days of the Republic and had had the "great and sad surprise to feel that Brazil had gone backwards."

28. Vicente L. Cardoso, "O elemento Negro na História do Brasil," *O Estado de São Paulo,* May 13, 1927, 2.
29. Roquette had been corresponding with Boas since 1913, before meeting him personally at Columbia in 1924 (cf. Vanderlei S. de Souza, "Em Busca do Brasil: Edgar Roquette-Pinto e o Retrato antropológico brasileiro (1905–1935)" (PhD diss., Casa de Oswaldo Cruz—Fiocruz, Rio de Janeiro, 2011), 243–44.
30. Edgar Roquette-Pinto, "Fritz Muller e os Negros," *Diário Nacional,* São Paulo, May 31, 1929, reprinted in Edgar Roquette-Pinto, *Ensayos de antropologia brasiliana* (1933; repr. São Paulo, Companhia Editora Nacional, 1978), 29–31.
31. Rüdiger Bilden, "Brazil, Laboratory of Civilization," *The Nation,* Jan. 16, 1929, 73–74.
32. Rüdiger Bilden to Franz Boas, Dec. 6, 1926, Box 7, BP.
33. Bilden, "Brazil, Laboratory," 71.
34. Walter D. Mignolo, *The Idea of Latin America* (Malden, MA: Blackwell, 2005), 90.
35. Harry A. Franck, *Working North from Patagonia: Being the Narrative of a Journey, Earned on the Way, Through Southern and Eastern South America* (New York: The Century, 1921), 201.
36. Bilden, "Brazil, Laboratory," 71.
37. Rüdiger Bilden, "Brazil, Laboratory of Race and Civilization," manuscript enclosed with Rüdiger Bilden to Edgar Roquette-Pinto, Mar. 12, 1929, Personal Archives of Edgar Roquette-Pinto (hereafter ERP), Academia Brasileira de Letras. Notice that this, Bilden's original manuscript (later cut for publication), featured an additional word in its title: race.
38. Ibid. In the full version of the article, Bilden cited Roquette-Pinto's argument more than once. Roquette-Pinto, then the director of the Museu Nacional in Rio, published extracts of the excluded parts of Bilden's article in a newspaper article ("Fritz Müller e os negros," *Diário Nacional,* São Paulo, May 31, 1929) and years later reprinted them in his book *Ensaios de Antropologia Brasiliana* [1933]), 2d ed. (São Paulo: Companhia Editora Nacional, 1978).
39. Bilden, "Brazil, Laboratory," 71.
40. Ibid., 72.
41. Ibid., 72–73.
42. Ibid., 73–74.
43. Ibid., 74. In spite of his optimism, privately Bilden expressed his worries about the growing obstacles to the development of Brazil, the "worst danger, perhaps," being "the appearance of race discrimination in the North American sense," which could already be seen "in ascent." Soon after the First Brazilian Eugenics Congress in 1929, he wrote to Roquette-Pinto, "It will require the combined efforts of all enlightened critics" to combat "the vogue of semi-scientific sociological literature and the popular prestige of things North American," which he saw as a major contributor to the rise of racial discrimination. Rüdiger Bilden to Edgar Roquette-Pinto, Sept. 13, 1929, ERP.
44. Pallares-Burke, *Triunfo do Fracasso,* 200–203.
45. Rüdiger Bilden, "Race Relations in Latin America with Special Reference to the Development of Indigenous Culture," 3–4, Round Table on Latin American Relations, Institute of Public Affairs, July 1, 1931, Virginius Dabney Papers (hereafter VDP), Special Collections Library, University of Virginia.

46. Ibid., 11.
47. Rüdiger Bilden to Gilberto Freyre, May 30, 1940, FGF; Pallares-Burke, *Triunfo do Fracasso,* 305–13.
48. Rüdiger Bilden, "Racial Mixture in Latin America," in *The Role of Races in Our Future Civilization,* ed. Harry W. Laidler (New York: League for Industrial Democracy, 1942), 49. His fellow speakers included the authors and activists Pearl S. Buck and Walter White, the anthropologist Hortense Powdermaker, the Socialist Party leader Norman Thomas, the British Nobel Peace Prize laureate Norman Angell, the Chinese writer Lin Yutang, the minister of finance of New Zealand Walter Nash, and others.
49. Pallares-Burke, *Triunfo do Fracasso,* 281–84; Rüdiger Bilden to Walter White, Feb. 17, 1941, Good Neighbor Policy, *Papers of the NAACP* (Bethesda, MD: University Publications of America, 1982), microfilm reel 7.
50. Bilden, "Racial Mixture in Latin America," 49–54.
51. Rüdiger Bilden to Edgar Roquette-Pinto, Feb. 23, 1941 (including the "Memorandum for the Brazilian Embassy, concerning the Creation of a Research Institute for the Comparative Study of Brazilian Culture"), ERP; Bunzel, introduction to Boas, *Anthropology and Modern Life,* 6.
52. Rüdiger Bilden to Franz Boas, Dec. 15, 1940, Box 7, BP.
53. Pallares-Burke, *Triunfo do Fracasso,* 276–90, 322–24; Rüdiger Bilden to Virginius Dabney, Sept. 11, 1946, and Virginius Dabney to Rüdiger Bilden, Sept. 12, 1946, Box 6, VDP; Rüdiger Bilden, "Proposal for an Inter-American Regional Institute," University of Virginia, General Education Board Collection, Rockefeller Foundation Archives, RAC.
54. W. E. B. Du Bois to Melville J. Herskovits, Jan. 5, 1939, Box 7, File 11, Melville J. Herskovits Papers (hereafter MJH), Northwestern University Archives.
55. Pallares-Burke, *O Triunfo do Fracasso,* 251–53.
56. George Hutchinson, *The Harlem Renaissance in Black and White* (Cambridge: Harvard University Press, 1996).
57. Pallares-Burke, "Gilberto Freyre and Brazilian Self-Perception," in *Racism and Ethnic Relations in the Portuguese-Speaking World,* ed. Francisco Bethencourt and Adrian J. Pearce (Oxford: Oxford University Press, 2012), 113–32.
58. Bunzel, introduction to Boas, *Anthropology and Modern Life,* 6; Pallares-Burke, *Triunfo do Fracasso,* 244–54, 276–304, and passim. Bilden taught at the City College of New York (1934–37), Fisk University in Tennessee (1937–39), Hampton Institute in Virginia (1943), Tuskegee Institute in Alabama (1943), and the Rand School of Social Science in New York (1941–42).
59. Bilden used the psychoanalytical terms "inferiority complex" and "defense mechanism," at the time unusual, in the program of the series of lectures he gave at the Rand School of Social Science in 1941 and 1942 (which, at the invitation of the Negro Labor Committee, he repeated in 1942 at the Harlem Labor Center). See "The History of the Negro in the Western Hemisphere," Courses 1940–42, Rand School Papers, Tamiment Library and Robert F. Wagner Labor Archives, New York University. At least once, in 1941, Bilden had Walter White and Arthur Ramos as guest lecturers in his course.
60. Bilden quoted Johnson in an undated letter to Arthur Schomburg [ca. June 1936], Arthur A. Schomburg Papers (Bethesda, MD: University Publications of America, 1991), microfilm reel 5.

61. Gilberto Freyre, *Diário de Pernambuco,* 44 [Jan. 15, 1922], repr. in Gilberto Freyre, *Tempo de Aprendiz* (São Paulo: Ibrasa, 1979), 1:181–83.
62. Gilberto Freyre, "O velho Boas," *Jornal de Comercio,* Jan. 21, 1943.
63. Sam Allen, telephone conversation with the author, Dec. 17, 2011. Sam Allen was a student of James Weldon Johnson at Fisk and later studied law at Harvard.
64. Pallares-Burke, *Triunfo do Fracasso,* 350–55; Maria Lúcia G. Pallares-Burke, *Gilberto Freyre, um vitoriano dos Trópicos* (São Paulo: Editora Unesp, 2005), 403–6.
65. Pallares-Burke, *Gilberto Freyre, um vitoriano,* 441–46. Freyre made changes to the text in 1973 and in 1979, with a view to republication, deleting passages that praised Bilden, such as "brilliant historian" and "Bilden will give us the definitive study of slavery."
66. Ibid., 302–18.
67. Ibid., 332–45.
68. Bailey W. Diffie, Review of *The Masters and the Slaves [Casa-Grande & Senzala]: A Study in the Development of Brazilian Civilization* by Gilberto Freyre, *Hispanic American Historical Review* 26, no. 4 (1946): 497–99, 497.
69. Pallares-Burke, *Gilberto Freyre, um vitoriano,* 263–70, 298, 301, 309–18; Pallares-Burke, *Triunfo do Fracasso,* 351.
70. Jorge Amado, "Casa-Grande & Senzala e a Revolução Cultural," in *Gilberto Freyre—sua ciencia, sua filosofia, sua arte,* ed. Gilberto Amado et al. (Rio de Janeiro: José Olympio, 1962); Lewis Hanke, "Gilberto Freyre: Historiador social Brasileño," *Revista Hispánica Moderna* 5, no. 2 (1939): 118–19.
71. Gilberto Freyre, *The Masters and the Slaves,* abr. ed. (New York: Alfred Knopf, 1967), 255; Gilberto Freyre, *Casa-Grande & Senzala,* 29th ed. (Rio de Janeiro: Editora Record, 1994), 283.
72. Manuel Gamio, *Forjando patria (pro nacionalismo)* (México: Porrúa Hermanos, 1916); José Vasconcelos, *La Raza Cósmica: misión de la raza iberoamericana; notas de viajes a la América del Sur* (Paris: Agencia Mundial de Librería, 1925); Fernando Ortiz, *Cuban Counterpoint: Tobacco and Sugar,* trans. Harriet de Onís (1940; New York: A. A. Knopf, 1947).
73. Gilberto Freyre, *Perfil de Euclides e outros perfis* (1944; repr. Rio de Janeiro: Record, 1987), 40–41; Freyre, *Casa-Grande & Senzala,* 1st ed., preface, xlvii; Gilberto Freyre, *Sociologia,* 2d ed. (1945; repr. Rio de Janeiro: José Olympio, 1957), 101.
74. Freyre, *Casa-Grande,* 66, li.
75. Rüdiger Bilden to Gilberto Freyre, Mar. 29, 1936, FGF.
76. Melville J. Herskovits to Rüdiger Bilden, Jan. 4, 1935, and Rüdiger Bilden to Melville J. Herskovits, Jan. 11, 1935, Box 3, File 26, MJH.
77. Gilberto Freyre, *Casa-Grande & Senzala,* 307, 379.
78. Gilberto Freyre, *Açúcar: em torno da etnografia, da história e da sociologia do doce no nordeste canavieiro do Brasil* (Rio de Janeiro: José Olympio, 1939); Freyre, "Doces tradicionais de Brasil," *Correio da Manhã,* July 30, 1938.
79. Franz Boas, *Ethnology of the Kwakiutl, based on data collected by George Hunt,* pt. 1, Thirty-Fifth Annual Report of the Bureau of American Ethnology, 1913–1914 (Washington DC: Government Printing Office, 1921), 305–601.
80. Gilberto Freyre, "Football mulatto," *Diário de Pernambuco,* June 17, 1938, 4.
81. Rüdiger Bilden to Gilberto Freyre, Feb. 6 and 10, 1939, FGF; Rüdiger Bilden to George Herzog, Oct. 22, 1938, Nov. 10, 1938, and George Herzog to Rüdiger Bilden, Nov. 1, 1938, George Herzog Papers, Archives of Traditional Music, Indiana University.

82. Gilberto Freyre, *The English in Brazil* (Oxford: Boulevard Books, 2010).
83. Ibid., 202.
84. Gilberto Freyre, "A Brazilian's Critique of Brasília," *The Reporter,* Mar. 31, 1960.
85. Gilberto Freyre, *Sociologia: introdução ao estudo de seus princípios,* 2d ed. (1945; repr. Rio de Janeiro: José Olympio, 1957), 13–16, 30–31, 58, 64–65.
86. Gilberto Freyre, *Além do Apenas Moderno* (Rio de Janeiro: Topbooks, 2001), 67.
87. Gilberto Freyre, *Insurgências e Ressurgências Atuais: Argumentos de Sims e Nãos num mundo em transição* (Rio de Janeiro: Globo, 1983).
88. Freyre, *Casa-Grande & Senzala,* 289.
89. Franz Boas, "Race," in *Encyclopædia of the Social Sciences,* ed. Edwin Seligman (New York: Macmillan, 1930–35), 13:25–36. The formal name of the Museu Nina Rodrigues, known by the name of the institute in which it is located, is the Museu Antropológico Estácio de Lima.
90. Pallares-Burke, "Gilberto Freyre and Brazilian Self-Perception," 130–32.
91. Pallares-Burke, *Triunfo do Fracasso,* 367–71.
92. Robert K. Merton, "The Matthew Effect in Science: The Reward and Communication Systems of Science Are Considered," *Science* 159, no. 3810 (Jan. 5, 1968), 56–63.
93. Peter Burke and Maria L. G. Pallares-Burke, *Gilberto Freyre: Social Theory in the Tropics* (Oxford: Peter Lang, 2008).
94. Macmillan decided in the end that the book was more appropriate for a university publisher. The translation of *Sobrados e Mucambos,* published by Alfred Knopf, would finally appear ten years later. Pallares-Burke, *Triunfo do Fracasso,* 337–39, 343, 363, 378–81.

# Chapter 14 Seeing Like an Inca: Julio C. Tello, Indigenous Archaeology, and Pre-Columbian Trepanation in Peru

*Christopher Heaney*

## THE BOAS OF PERU

In 1942, when the North American anthropologist Alfred L. Kroeber likened the Peruvian archaeologist Julio César Tello to Franz Boas, the first professor of anthropology at Columbia University, he meant it as a compliment. Mostly.[1]

Kroeber had spent two months in Peru on the dime of the Committee on Inter-American Artistic and Intellectual Relations, a project funded by the US Office of Inter-American Affairs to wage war against the Axis powers in Latin America via cultural exchange and propaganda. Officially, Kroeber had been sent to spread goodwill within Peru's intellectual community and to observe the North American archaeological projects the committee had supported. Believing it was his last chance to work in Peru, the sixty-seven-year-old Kroeber hoped to advise "the men who will be on the firing-line of Peruvian archaeology during the next generation."[2]

Less officially, Kroeber approached his trip as a World War II campaign to gather intelligence on the Peruvian archaeological landscape and its actors, living and dead. "From the moment I saw the row of Peruvian valleys spread out like a map two miles below, I knew I was where I belonged," he wrote to the committee's coordinator. "When I return I want to prepare for you a confidential report on all archaeological personnel in Peru."[3]

The confidential report and the monograph it occasioned, *Peruvian Archeology in 1942*, were frank when it came to Tello, Peru's pre-Columbian patriarch. Kroeber had known the sixty-two-year-old Harvard-trained archaeologist since his first visit to Peru, in 1926, and believed him to be a "human dynamo." Through his "indomitable energy," Kroeber wrote, Tello had founded Peru's three greatest archaeological museums, filled them with hundreds of mummies, and knew "as much Peruvian archeology as the rest of us put together."[4]

Which was also Tello's problem. Kroeber believed that his Andean counterpart was *too* strong. Tello was like Heinrich Schliemann of Troy: "Endowed with extraordinary energy, with intuitional insight, with the gift of making startling finds and weaving them into constructive syntheses," he had used only evidence he deemed significant and had insufficiently published his proof.[5]

Kroeber's confidential estimate was even sharper:

> Disliked by most Peruvians, who consider him egotistic, domineering, greedy, jealous, ruthless, and (often) unscrupulous; but they unanimously respect and fear him. They would admire and hate anyone of his energy. Among American archaeologists, dislike prevails in half, tempered admiration in the others. He is not hard to deal with if one meets him without fear, but he overawes or overrides many people. He has himself and his work all identified; is at once a slave-driver and a father to his subordinates. His natural-history passion for archaeology is a consuming obsession. Not a scientist in his interpretations, he nevertheless has done more for Peruvian archaeology than anyone else, except possibly [the German Max] Uhle, its scientific founder. Tello is the grand old man in his field, and still going strong—the Boas of Peru; their personalities have much in common.[6]

Yet Tello and Boas—who had awarded Kroeber the first doctorate in anthropology ever earned at Columbia—differed in one crucial detail. In public and in private Kroeber began his reconnaissance of Tello with a label more racial than archaeological: "A mountain Indian, risen from the ranks."[7]

Why did Kroeber, the former friend of Ishi, the last Yahi, whose brain he had sent to the Smithsonian in 1916, think it relevant that Peru's greatest living collector and interpreter of the pre-Columbian dead was himself an Indigenous Peruvian?[8] What did it mean to label someone both Indian and archaeologist in the early twentieth century? And how did Tello himself address the challenge of being labeled?

Alongside Arthur C. Parker, the Seneca intellectual and first president of the Society of American Archaeology, Tello was once the most important

The Peruvian archaeologist Julio C. Tello, left, and the American anthropologist Alfred L. Kroeber in Peru, 1926. Image no. 94–12231, Smithsonian Institution Archives.

Indigenous archaeologist in the hemisphere.[9] In the 1940s he was the textbook example of that category, one of twenty-two historical figures profiled in *Builders of Latin America,* meant to educate North American high schoolers on the rich history of our "Good Neighbors."[10] Setting the tone for years to come, *Builders of Latin America* cheerily smoothed the rough edges of Tello's story: born in 1880 in a Quechua-speaking highland town, Tello traveled to Lima, Peru's capital, when he was thirteen and worked his way to a degree as a surgeon. In 1909 the Peruvian government gave him a fellowship to study anthropology at Harvard. Upon his return to the Andes he founded his three museums, excavated underground temples, and discovered 429 mummies in a sandy burial ground named Paracas. He was also a politician. While representing his largely Indigenous home region in the national Congress, he helped pass Peru's defining law on cultural patrimony and the protection of archaeological remains. By the time of his death in 1947, Tello had recharted the historical horizons of the Andes, asserted their local origins, and theorized complex societies in the Amazon.

Owing to his successes, Tello has figured prominently in twentieth-century histories of Andean anthropology, which debate his primacy over colleagues like Uhle, the *indigenista* Luis E. Valcárcel, the collector Rafael Larco Hoyle, and Americans like Kroeber and William Duncan Strong.[11] Tello is little studied by ethnohistorians, however, and his Indigenous identity and its relationship to his work are more celebrated than examined.[12] The default biography of Tello packages his heritage as a black box of Indian empathy, which sagely informed his scholarship and struggles against prejudice.[13] To avoid that sort of flattening, scholars sometimes label Tello an "indio-mestizo," reflecting the mixed heritage of his Spanish last name, or as a former "peasant," situating him in Peru's specific class context.[14] Archaeologists, however, have sometimes made Tello's Indigenous identity both question and answer to the field's historically fraught relationship to Native peoples. The editor of a recent translation of Tello's greatest essays into English—whose title proclaims Tello *America's First Indigenous Archaeologist*—wonders how North American archaeology might have developed had more Indigenous individuals like Tello "been brought in at [its] inception . . . to help direct its trajectory."[15]

Yet Indigenous individuals like Tello often *were* present at archaeology's inception, as informants and laborers, and their participation directed their more personal trajectories. In this chapter I suggest that before wondering how Tello's indigeneity affected his anthropology we must ask how anthropology affected Tello's sense of himself. Like Ishi, Tello came to anthropology at a moment when the physical categories that had informed the scientific racism of the nineteenth century were being complicated in favor of a more cultural bent. Tello, however, "became" Indian not by passing through the "two worlds" that Kroeber's wife, Theodora, cast for Ishi—one Native, the other "modern"—but by overlapping four worlds of experience, each already penetrated by anthropology and its categories of knowledge: First, a childhood in the *campesino* countryside, where his family members' indigeneity mattered less than its access to land, education, and the pre-Columbian skulls they collected for metropolitan elites; second, color-aware Lima, where Tello discovered that not only could he be read as an "indio" but his family's history with the pre-Columbian dead also gave him unique access to hemispheric anthropology; third, North America, where he would be read as a "mountain Indian" possessing an authority that whiter Peruvian colleagues lacked; and finally, a changed Peru, where his indigeneity took on a political edge, especially when deployed alongside his access to foreign anthropologists who believed him to be a Harvard-trained "American Indian" in the Andes.[16]

During this earliest stage of his career, ending in 1913, Tello honed his Indigenous consciousness through a particular research interest: pre-Columbian Peruvian trepanation, an early form of cranial surgery. Tello's attempt to place pre-Columbian Peru in the global history of medical knowledge demands that we understand his early career in terms of the nineteenth-century surgeons and physical anthropologists who employed Tello's family as collectors of crania. But when Tello discovered his family's importance to that history, he also learned that his North American contemporaries had mostly dismissed trepanation as superstitious and savage. Tello's early research argued instead that trepanation proved the existence of advanced medical knowledge in the Andes before the Spanish arrived, a fact that threatened anthropology's racialized hierarchies of civilization, barbarism, and savagery. Studying trepanation also allowed Tello, a surgeon himself, to both claim and create an inheritance of a rich tradition of sophisticated, Indigenous, preanthropological, and pre-Columbian knowledge of the human body.[17]

He was successful on all counts. Tello convinced the Smithsonian to accept, finally, pre-Columbian cranial surgery's importance to the global history of medicine and the study of humanity. But by turning those histories and hierarchies against themselves, he also created something new: an anthropology that was already Indigenous, relativist, and ready-made for political deployment. By working with pre-Columbian skulls less as objects than as subjects of Indigenous knowledge Tello learned how to "see like an Inca," assuming an intellectual authority and, with it, a set of historical burdens and ironies.

The fact that Julio C. Tello overcame multiple worlds of prejudice by using skulls, the materia prima of nineteenth-century scientific racism, is the final irony this chapter explores. Like Boas, Tello collected the Indigenous dead, and his collection was central to his early career.[18] Yet unlike Boas, whose turn to a cultural study of texts in a university setting forestalled an honest reckoning with the physical collections of Native remains held by America's museums, Tello never left the dead behind. Understanding this distinction reveals how North American anthropology's turn to culture also prefaced a tragic erasure of its obligations to the Indigenous dead. It reveals why Tello might be the "Boas of Peru" but also why Boas was never the Tello of America.

## TREPANATION BY GASLIGHT

One of the most sought-after specimens among late nineteenth-century collectors of human crania was a trepanned skull from Peru. Trepanation is the act of scraping, cutting, or drilling into the human skull to relieve maladies and injuries of the brain. As a word, "to trepan," from the Greek *trypanaon,* to "bore," was first recorded about 1400 CE in relation to a crown saw used in surgery.[19] Trepanation as a surgical practice, however, goes back much further, to the Neolithic era in France and, potentially at an embryonic level, to the epipalaeolithic era in Ukraine in 10,000–9000 BCE.[20] Although it may have begun as a means of freeing supernatural forces, humans came to use it surgically—to relieve pressure on the brain's surface caused by traumatic head wounds, skull fragments, and pooled blood; to cure epilepsy; and to address other conditions ascribed to the brain, from headaches to mental disorders. As such, it is sometimes referred to as humanity's oldest surgical operation and, because it is still practiced today as craniectomy, its longest lasting.[21]

The historical study of trepanation is far more recent, however, and flows from the confluence of Peru's unique medical antiquity with nineteenth-century skull collecting and surgery's interest in its origins.[22] Sometime before 1863 a landholder from Cusco, Peru, named Ramón Matto came to possess a curious skull that had been found in an "Inca cemetery" near a village called Yucay. Matto was a collector of antiquities, like many in Cusco, and he seemingly grasped the skull's import. Its frontal bone bore four perpendicular cuts, and the space between them had been punched out, leaving a quadrilateral opening of fifteen by seventeen millimeters. Matto gave the skull to Cusco's most accomplished collector, Ana María Centeno de Romainville, who made it a centerpiece in her palatial mansion, considered the best museum in Peru.[23] It was in Centeno de Romainville's collection when the North American archaeologist Ephraim George Squier passed through Cusco in 1863. Awestruck, Squier acquired it from her. It was "the most remarkable evidence of a knowledge of surgery among the aborigines yet discovered on this continent," he believed, and he hoped to prove that the operation was conducted when the patient was living.[24] Put another way, he wanted to start a referendum on ancient Peruvians' development: whether they practiced a relatively complex medical surgery or whether they opened the skulls of the dead for reasons of superstition or to take trophies, making them barbarous at best, in the accepted schema of nineteenth-century ethnology.[25]

When Squier introduced the skull to colleagues in North America and Europe, the response was decidedly mixed. At the New York Academy of Medicine in 1868 doctors debated whether the bones showed signs of healing—proof that the operation had occurred while the patient was alive. The physician August K. Gardner assured the audience that signs of reparation "were more easily discernible during the daytime than by gaslight."[26] Squier sent the skull on to France, where the famed surgeon and anthropologist Paul Broca

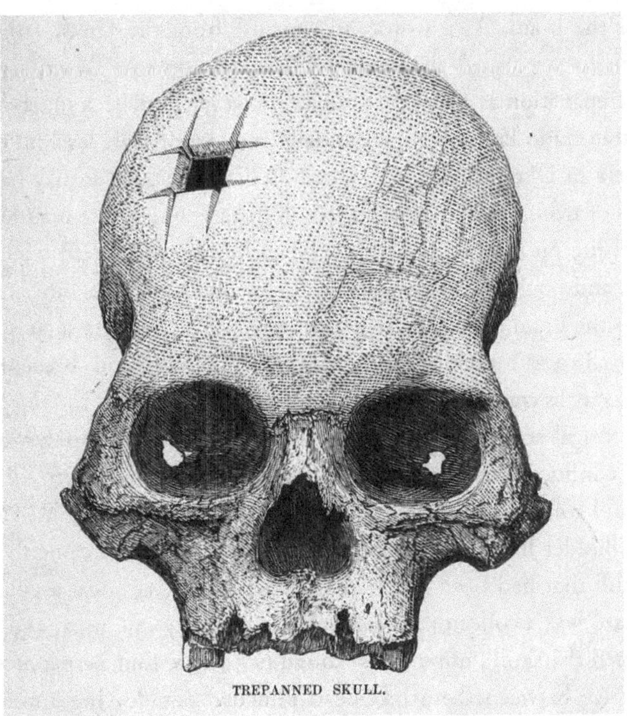


The Peruvian physician Ramón Matto collected this example of trepanation in the Sacred Valley near Cusco. It entered the collection of the Cusqueña antiquarian Ana María Centeno, ending up in the hands of Ephraim George Squier, who circulated the "Yucay" skull as history's first example of "ancient" trepanation. As printed in E. George Squier, *Peru: Incidents of Travel and Exploration in the Land of the Incas* (New York: Harper and Brothers, 1877), 457.

showed it to the Société d'Anthropologie de Paris in 1867. Broca believed it was proof of a surgical operation, and given the lack of evidence of a premortem fracture or fissure, it was also "astonishing" evidence that pre-Columbian surgeons diagnosed intracranial lesions and operated to evacuate blood pooling beneath the skull. "This idea, an entirely new one, is not without interest in American anthropology," he declared, with scholarly understatement.[27] The Yucay skull launched an entire subfield, the study of European Neolithic trepanation, as holes once believed to be injuries were reclassified as prehistoric surgery.[28]

North American ethnologists, however, having long debated Spanish claims of Inca civilization, were unconvinced that the Yucay skull demonstrated

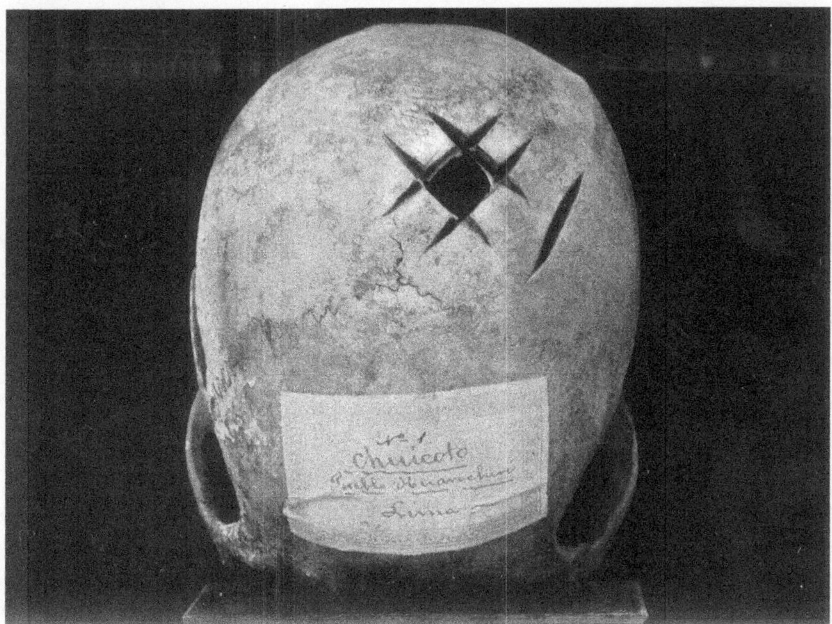

In the early 1900s a young Julio C. Tello discovered this image of a trepanned skull, collected in Huarochirí, and realized that it was one his father had collected for the Peruvian surgeon general Manuel Antonio Muñiz. It had then been sent to the United States, ending up at the Bureau of American Ethnology. Manuel A. Muñiz and W. J. McGee, "Primitive Trephining in Peru," *Sixteenth Annual Report of the Bureau of American Ethnology to the Secretary of the Smithsonian Institution 1984–'95* (Washington, DC: Government Printing Office, 1897), Plate I.

surgery.[29] The second skull to show definite signs of trepanation in the Americas was also from Peru, where it was collected by an American naval surgeon in 1884.[30] But when that skull reached the Smithsonian, the ethnologist Otis T. Mason saw it as an object of violence, not healing. "The work seems to have been done in the most bungling manner," Mason wrote in the *Proceedings of the U.S. National Museum,* hypothesizing that the skull, once harvested, had begotten further warfare. The removed bone fragments were likely "wrought into some useful thing, like the point of an arrow or spear," he guessed. "Instances are not wanting among peoples of low civilization where human bones have been considered to have great potency."[31]

Still, the matter was up for debate, in part because of the rarity of trepanned skulls. They were the holy grail for American collectors in Peru, almost unattainable. In 1888 an American collector named George Kiefer made a series of "perilous ascensions" to a highland region near Lima to build collections for the US Army Medical Museum in Washington. Of a collection of eighty-eight skulls he sold to the museum in June 1888, valuing each at about three dollars, none were trepanned, but that didn't stop him from hyping their possible connection to the famed operation. He pointed out that many of the skulls bore incisions that suggested "the kind of instrument they must have used in trephining as the marks are similar. I wish I was so fortunate as to find some of their surgical instruments as so far I have never seen any. I have found plenty of instruments to kill but none to cure."[32]

Satisfaction ultimately came from Kiefer's Peruvian colleagues, who had greeted the commotion caused by the Yucay skull with interest.[33] The question of trepanation recirculated in Peru in mostly elite circles, debated by surgeons caught between celebrating trepanation as ancient Peruvian medical skill and dismissing it as Indigenous superstition.[34] Some Peruvian intellectuals, like the physician Antonio Lorena, refused to believe that ancient Peruvians could have been more developed than the "primitive," "timid and unsure" peasants he knew near Cusco, let alone that they might have practiced a surgery that wasn't magical in nature. Lorena cast the holes as injuries caused by pre-Columbian weapons of war and necrotic syphilis—the product of "perpetual war" and Inca toleration of prostitution; barbarity, not medicine.[35]

A young surgeon named Manuel Antonio Muñiz countered Lorena's argument and built a collection that he hoped would settle the debate in North America as well. Born in 1861, Muñiz had studied hygiene, anthropometry, and the history of disease in Chile and Europe before returning to Peru in 1890 to retake his post as the army's surgeon general.[36] He was among the Latin American elites who used discourses of hygiene, disease, and crime to restrict Indigenous access to urban spaces and politics, but he also founded his authority on pre-Columbian Peru's apparent expertise in diagnosing and regulating disease.[37] Muñiz supported his argument by building what was likely the world's largest collection of pre-Columbian skulls at the time, "something over a thousand crania."[38] Of those thousand, a full nineteen were trepanned, the majority of which showed signs of postoperative healing. He organized the nineteen skulls in a way that he believed made the development of trepanation and its use as a therapeutic surgery inarguable and in 1893 took them to the International Congress of Anthropology at the World's Columbian Exposition in Chicago.

Muñiz's celebration of pre-Columbian Indigenous expertise at the world's fair was at first a success. While Boas groused that his northwestern skulls were being ignored, Muñiz took the stage to declare that "ancient Peruvians" were not only practicing surgery but were doing it as well as, if not better than, nineteenth-century Europeans.[39] Frederic Ward Putnam, the fair's anthropological director, was convinced of trepanation's value, and W. H. Holmes of the Bureau of American Ethnology called the collection "the richest ever made."[40] There were would-be buyers, but Muñiz refused to sell. He temporarily transferred the nineteen skulls to the bureau so that the ethnologist W. J. McGee might complete a report on the achievement, but he hoped to return the skulls to Peru.[41]

They never did return, as tragedy followed tragedy. In 1895 Muñiz had to flee Peru when his family ended up on the wrong side of a revolution and his house, along with his collection of nearly one thousand pre-Columbian skulls, burned to the ground.[42] He gave ownership of his trepanned skulls to the Smithsonian in exchange for a series of American scientific publications but was unable to use them for long.[43] He died suddenly in 1897, at the age of thirty-six, and there is no correspondence in the bureau's files to suggest that he saw McGee's proofs before his article was published later that year.

Muñiz would have been horrified if he had. After celebrating Muñiz's achievement to the media and largely endorsing the "native genius of the South American Indians," McGee made an incredible about-face.[44] The report he produced, "Primitive Trephining in Peru," was prefaced by Muñiz's grand claims of pre-Columbian scientific achievement, but McGee's text reversed that judgment. Having examined the skulls himself, he decided that they told a story of violence that began with the initial "desperate wounds" of weapons and warfare then continued through the "inexpert," "ignorant," and "skilless" efforts of "clumsy" quack healers. Their "primitive" stone implements may have torn delicate intracranial tissues, leaving patients dead on the table. "Thoughtless hacking, with no indication of diagnosis or intelligent adaptation of means to ends," McGee concluded. "Utter incompetence." He decided that trepanation was not medical after all but magical, demonstrating no "noteworthy intellectual development." It was a stunning subjugation of Muñiz's evidence to the universalist ethnology of the Smithsonian, reducing the "ancient Peruvians" to a "primitive," "uncivilized" status: trepanation as scalping's skeletal sibling.[45]

## COLLECTING ATAHUALPA IN HUAROCHIRÍ

Yet the very origins of Muñiz's collection derailed McGee's manipulations. A full eleven of Muñiz's nineteen trepanned skulls were collected in one place, Huarochirí, a highland region immediately east of Lima, and by one family—the

Tellos. Their youngest son discovered Muñiz's and McGee's successive erasures of his family's contributions and resurrected pre-Columbian surgery.

The son's name was Julio César Tello, and on an August 30, sometime in the late 1880s or early 1890s, when he was about ten years old, he watched as the men and women of Huarochirí acted out an annual drama: the Spanish execution of the Inca emperor Atahualpa. Tello remembered the experience for the rest of his life. There were many ways in which his highland community reinterpreted the precolonial and colonial past to serve their republican present, but this was perhaps the most direct. As the town's men and women danced and twirled, a villager dressed as Francisco Pizarro imprisoned a villager dressed as Atahualpa, and then—to the young boy's "horror"—removed the Inca's head.[46]

Given Tello's later efforts to transform pre-Columbian skulls from objects of violence to embodied historical subjects, it's hard not to examine this memory, often repeated by Tello and his students, as some sort of primal knot of Indigenous identity that his work sought to undo.[47] Tello encouraged that impression, later casting his childhood as authentically Indian, even Inca. It helped that he was from Huarochirí. Next to Cusco, the heart of the Inca empire, few other regions have been so important to the understanding of Peruvian history. Nestled in the shadow of the 18,865-foot-tall Pariacaca, the highest peak in that corner of the Andes, Huarochirí was and still is a relatively impoverished province of farmers and herders. Its steep slopes necessitate the upkeep of complex patrilineal descent groups, *ayllus,* that maintain canals and reservoirs through communal labor.[48] In the early seventeenth century Spanish church officials discovered that Huarochirí's isolation meant that its inhabitants had kept celebrating their precolonial ancestors as well as Pariacaca, the deity that was the mountain. The Spanish burned thousands of mummies in response, but they also documented what they destroyed, giving modern ethnohistorians some of their most revelatory documents of pre-Columbian and early colonial belief.[49]

Still, this was a place where local Indigenous culture survived to incorporate new traditions, like the death of Atahualpa. In 1876, four years before Tello was born, Peru's national census identified the region as 100 percent *indio.*[50] Through the 1920s Tello observed that ayllus kept track of members' work obligations by using *khipus,* a cord- and knot-based record-keeping system thousands of years old.[51] Most dramatically, the religious orders' bonfire of the mummies had assaulted their importance, but the dry countryside remained seeded with the remains of countless dead, crouched in fetal positions, knees bound to their chests. In the 1860s the Italian geographer Antonio Raimondi traveled the region and reported that its "Indians firmly believe that they can stop the rains by bringing down a mummy of the ancient [*indios*] that they refer to as *abuelitos,* or, the little grandparents."[52]

In later life Tello claimed that his family's belonging rested with the *indio* community discriminated against by the Peruvian state. His was an ancient family, Tello told the North American writer Blair Niles in 1935, one "whose ancestors, according to a tradition handed down through the years, were sons of a deity whose abode was the eternal snows of Paria Kaka." To another American, Tello described his grandmother as "an Indian, who still maintained with great veneration all of the idolatrous practices of the ancient ones." Her daughter, Tello's mother, could neither read nor write but was from a proud family of herders and weavers, and she clothed her children in the blankets, girdles, and mantles she made. Tello apparently remembered watching, terrified, as soldiers beat his father for failing to deliver an excessive tribute. "Julio Tello," Niles gushed to her readers, "is of untarnished Indian blood."[53]

This, of course, was the message Tello sent in 1935 to a North American audience. In Huarochirí in 1890, however, Tello might not have called himself Indian. Huarochirí's inhabitants were starting to "regard themselves as progressive *campesinos* (peasants) of Peruvian nationality, not as members of an Indigenous 'race,'" as the anthropologist Frank Salomon would later write.[54] Among those peasants, the Tellos were considered the local elite—"poor people," as one colleague put it, "but that sort of poor people who have lands, cattle, and besides, were the ones who gave the orders in Huarochirí."[55]

That status may have had deep colonial roots. Ethnohistorians have treated Huarochirí as a bellwether not only of religious transformation and survival in the Andes but also of the division of the peasantry by class. In the late sixteenth century Spanish authorities concentrated the scattered, vertically connected ayllus into villages governed by privileged Indigenous leaders, *kurakas.* Those kurakas protected peasants and their land from Spaniards but also siphoned off their wealth and labor for the Crown and their own families.[56]

Within that history Tello's family would have been among the fortunate. He claimed that his father and mother descended from the lower and upper moiety of leaders, Lurín Yauyo and Anan Yauyo, respectively.[57] Their family fortunes may have faltered during the republican era, when Lima's coastal elite waged war against Indigenous elites and the communal landholding rights they protected, but the Tellos had maintained their advantage, acquiring individual parcels of land while maintaining access to property belonging to the community.[58] Julio's father was an important man in Huarochirí, a *gobernador* who kept traditional ceremonies free of liquor and helped organize the town's irrigation system and school.[59] That school, mostly financed and run by the locals themselves, was no small matter within Huarochirí's ambitious, multiply literate society.[60] In 1890 Lima's elites amended Peru's Constitution to make Spanish literacy a requirement for the right to vote, and the Tellos used the school and the knowledge it delivered to build familial and patron–client relationships within their village and the capital.[61] Those ties to the capital were complex. Tello's aunt, María Tello, had been a *criada,* a "servant," in the home of Manuel Pardo, the first president from the Civilista party in Peru.[62] In Huarochirí such distinctions were far more valuable than one's Indianness, an object of greater scrutiny and prejudice the closer one got to sea level.

The apparent distance between the Tellos' Indigenous past and their Limeño future grew when Tello's father was asked to deliver a key aspect of Huarochirí's landscape to the capital: the ancient Peruvian dead. Sometime between 1890 and 1893, Julián Tello, Huarochirí's gobernador, apparently received an order from the surgeon Manuel Muñiz, via the prefect of the department of Lima, requesting that he collect a set of ancient skulls, preferably ones with unusual openings in their cranial vaults. Julián Tello and his elder sons did so, in some cases cutting or pulling fully intact heads from the shoulders of mummies stored in Huarochirí's caves and burial chambers.[63]

Their actions changed the landscape of Huarochirí's past and present. The relationship between Huarochirí's living and its pre-Columbian dead was more complex than simple respect for the abuelitos, sometimes also called the *gentiles.* Mummies and skulls were thanked and propitiated but also feared for their ability to cause sickness or agricultural collapse. Handling the dead was considered highly dangerous, and communities censured those who dared steal from the dead or disturb their graves, risking the livelihoods of everyone.[64]

But those known to have handled the dead anyway and survived the experience had power as well.[65] Young Julio Tello held at least one of the collected skulls in his hands, a cranium pulled from a semimummified body in a *chullpa,* or funerary tower, outside the nearby town of Chuicoto. It had a hole the shape of a diamond at its rear, its edges made with deep, manmade grooves. When Tello finished examining its lines, his father took the head, packed it up, and sent it to Lima.[66] It was an act whose message would have been as clear to the Tellos' neighbors as it was to the government: the Tellos' interest in the Peruvian state outweighed local fear of the dead, and loyalty to Atahualpas they no longer knew.

## A SHAMAN IN LIMA

The dead weren't through with the Tellos, however. A decade later Julio Tello reencountered the Chuicoto skull he had held in a different context. He realized that his family hadn't been collecting crania just for Lima but for the Americas as well. The skulls his family had separated from Huarochirí's mummified shoulders had grown new bodies, walked great distances, and now reached out, from across the hemisphere's past, to pull Tello into their future.

At the time, Tello was a medical student at the Universidad Mayor de San Marcos in Lima, the oldest continuously run university in the New World. He had always been clever, curious, sharp at mathematics, mischievous. At the encouragement of the aunt who had worked in the president's home, Tello was the only one of twelve siblings chosen to be educated in the capital. In 1893 the thirteen-year-old Tello traveled to Lima with his father, carrying his mother's gold and silver "antiquities" to pay his way. He started school among the elite children of the prestigious Colegio Labarthe—a choice suggestive of the Tellos' knowledge of the capital and its ruling class.[67] His father returned to Huarochirí and died soon after, forcing Tello to work out loyalties of his own. Wandering the streets in search of work to support his schooling, he ran into a classmate, the son of Ricardo Palma, the director of the National Library. Palma was impressed by the highland boy and gave him a place to sleep in the library. He paid Tello to fetch his mail each day, and when Tello needed money to support his entry to medical school, Palma gave him a job in the library itself.[68]

Tello might have been that character in the old Peruvian story who is made aware of his ethnic difference yet able to climb Lima's ladders of education and class.[69] In his later narration of his early years in the city, he emphasized his realization that he was not white, not elite, and not from Lima. He first lived in one of Lima's poorest barrios, where he rented a room from a family of *morenos,* "dark skins." One of his later students believed that his classmates had been disgusted by the food he brought with him, and they made fun of his clothing, "injuring him as cruelly as if they had beaten him, as others had done to his father." Tello, he continued, "sharply understood that this world was not his, that his world had been disfigured and demeaned to the point that it became a cruel joke."[70] In the face of prejudice, Tello had sold newspapers, run errands, and competed with the other urchins at the railroad station, hustling to carry bags: "I wandered the streets of Lima in those days when there was no compassion for *indios.*"[71]

But what if there was in fact power in his difference? One day, after starting his studies in surgery, Tello was reorganizing the National Library's anthropological works when his hands fell on the *Sixteenth Annual Report of the Bureau of American Ethnology*, published in the United States a few years before. Its first article was "Primitive Trephining in Peru," Muñiz's and McGee's investigation of whether ancient Peruvians were capable of cranial surgery. The subject matter resonated with Tello, who was training to become a surgeon himself, but the illustrated report's first photograph in particular attracted his notice: It depicted a skull whose label, in Spanish, clearly read "Chuicoto, Pueblo de Huarochirí." Tello knew this skull: it had been the skull he had once held that his father had collected and sent to Lima.[72] Tello now learned the rest of its transit, to the Chicago world's fair and on to the Bureau of American Ethnology.

It was like discovering a lost family album with empty pages free for his future. The skull and the article not only linked his own studies to the skill of surgeon predecessors who were, like him, Indigenous, they also showed him that he and his family had already been part of a hemispheric chain of anthropological research anchored to Peru. Just as Tello had followed his father to Lima, he could follow the skulls he had collected into the North American debates where knowledge of Huarochirí and its Indigenous heritage would be highly prized.[73] "Work and study like the *gringos*," one of his mentors, Sebastián Barranca, had advised him, warning him away from Peru's "lazy, envious, and traitorous" white elite.[74] By speaking not just to Lima but to North America, Tello could be a Peruvian, an Indian of elite Inca heritage, and a scientist, all without contradiction.

He would look back upon that moment as the beginning of his study of Peru's past—his past.[75] "The first time I had in my hands the skull of an Inca mummy to study, I felt a profound emotion," he later wrote. "That skull, honored by the centuries, connected with my heart and made me feel the message of the race whose blood ran through my veins. From that moment I became an anthropologist."[76]

Tello's transformation was rapid. Upon translating "Primitive Trephining in Peru," he learned that its American coauthor actually denied Muñiz's claim that the trepanned skulls showed pre-Columbian medical and scientific expertise. Tello set out to prove McGee wrong. He undertook his earliest research to show how Huarochirí was soaked in pre-Columbian and modern Indigenous medical knowledge. In print, he argued that the region was linked to the famed *kallawayas*, the traveling Indian healers of Bolivia.[77] He spent vacations at home and in surrounding provinces, collecting stories, plants, and, most important of all, a collection of between ten thousand and fifteen thousand crania and mummies—a number suggesting that it was the largest collection of human remains in the Americas at the time.[78]

Of those ten to fifteen thousand specimens, four hundred or more showed signs of trepanation. Collectively, they would become the essential instrument in Tello's attempt to elevate the intellectual status of his country's ancestors, but also his temporary escape route from Lima.[79] On May 4, 1906, Tello spoke to the Geographic Society of Lima on prehistoric trepanation among the Yauyos, the people who had inhabited Huarochirí before its conquest by the Incas. The hall was packed with male and female students and experts in Indigenous history. After establishing Huarochirí's importance as a locus of pre-Columbian knowledge and medical authority, Tello used a table covered with thirty trepanned skulls and a number of mummies to explain which surgical styles succeeded and which accelerated the individual's death. He declared that the operation was medical: "With trepanation, Peru achieves first place in prehistoric surgery throughout the world."[80] Encouraged by his advisors, Tello extended his studies to other areas of pre-Columbian medical knowledge, writing his thesis on the antiquity of syphilis in Peru. He argued that the Old World hadn't infected the New, that syphilis had been known in the Americas, diagnosed and depicted in ceramics by the ancient Peruvians, and that trepanation had developed, in part, to heal it.[81] His advisors helped him publish, and, once he had earned his title as surgeon in 1909, they convinced the government to award him a scholarship to continue his studies abroad.[82] Tello chose Harvard, which offered him free tuition.

Yet Tello's departure for North America was bittersweet. He had advanced his goal of studying his "ancestors" abroad, but his educational ambition distanced him from both Limeño society and his Huarochirí origins.[83] Although Tello remained close to his family for the rest of his life, he presented himself as altered when he returned home. On one visit, he tried, unsuccessfully, to convince his "indio" grandmother that a child's deformity was spinal bifida, not a spiritual punishment for its father's thieving ways.[84]

When he began collecting, his difference became even more pronounced. In Yauyos, near Huarochirí, a small town's gobernador had jailed Tello and two helpers, suspicious of their prying questions.[85] It may have been even worse in Huarochirí, where Tello collected the dead. Salomon has documented oral traditions that emphasize Tello's "aggressive emptying of burial caves . . . shocking to local sensibilities." In those stories, the collecting habits of Tello's family caught up with him: some modern Huarochiranos claim that he later died from illnesses inflicted by the mummies.[86]

The conflict was perhaps even harder in Lima. Rather than firmly marking Tello as a scientist, his collecting of skulls, an acceptable occupation for whites, had led him, as a person of Indigenous descent, into a territory charged with old stereotypes of Indian mysticism and savagery. A story later circulated that his neighbors in his poor barrio in Lima once reported him to the police as a *brujo*, a "shaman," bringing home the skulls of his victims, talking to them, cutting them to pieces, and burning them to forge a pact with the devil.[87]

By planning to leave for North America—daring to be both scientist and Indian—Tello had upset the balance yet further. When his mentor, Palma, toasted him at a banquet as one of his generation's leading lights, the wealthy young whites in attendance suspiciously eyed the upstart Indian, or *cholo*. Tello went home and wept.[88] He remembered the ensuing gossip painfully, righteously: "Have you all noticed what is happening to the *cholo* Tello? They say that he is now a doctor and plans to travel abroad! Don't you remember that he was one of so many *serranitos* who lived poorly and people said he was a 'witch' because at night he chatted with 'skulls' and 'bones of pagans'? Don't you all remember that the police took his skulls to see if he was 'crazy' or 'possessed,' like the newspapers said in Lima?"[89]

## SEEING LIKE AN INCA

In entering the world of North American anthropology, where racial boundaries were studiously sketched, Tello learned that he was not just a Peruvian of complex heritage but also an Indian of the Americas.[90] At first this was a challenge: how to present himself as a scholar with Indigenous knowledge and authority rather than a primitive informant and guardian of objects who lacked the ability to understand what he possessed. But by manipulating those categories Tello eventually enjoyed a success his fellow Peruvian scholars could only envy.

Tello's challenge was a rare one but it was not unique. He had been preceded in anthropology at Harvard by Arthur C. Parker, who had established his credentials by carrying out excavations for Harvard's Peabody Museum of Archaeology and Ethnology—despite confrontations with his fellow Seneca, who worried that he was profiting from their dead.[91] Conducting this kind of science was one way to define oneself as something other than its object. Neither Tello nor Parker would have wanted to be seen like Ishi, who would be hailed as America's last "wild" Indian when he walked out of the Sierra Nevadas in 1911. Kroeber would house Ishi in the Museum of Anthropology at the University of California until he died, whereupon doctors dissected him and Kroeber, distraught, sent his brain to the Smithsonian.[92]

Tello's opening bid to be recognized as a scholar and not as a specimen was not well received. Future colleagues dismissed his thesis on pre-Columbian syphilis as the presumptuous essay of an intellectual arriviste as much for its hard-to-substantiate claim that syphilis had killed the Inca emperor Huayna Capac as for the way Tello had interpreted his evidence.[93] Tello had claimed that every syphilitic cranium he recovered from the countryside was pre-Columbian despite the continuity of pre-Columbian burial practices through the early seventeenth century. Tello's thesis was "thoroughly unreliable, and should best be consecrated to oblivion," Aleš Hrdlička, the Smithsonian's physical anthropologist and gatekeeper of Indigenous antiquity, told his colleagues.[94]

Chastised, Tello tacked in the opposite direction, defending himself by referring to his Indigenous identity and the prejudice he had faced in Lima. "The labor to which I dedicated myself out of affection and care for my *raza* was without any pretension," he wrote to one standoffish scholar of pre-Columbian medicine and disease.[95] "As you will understand, when one works in an environment like that in which I've worked, and in which one doesn't have the sufficient preparation, one doesn't attempt to climb so high, without being a target of ridicule."[96] It was with that scholar that Tello then shared his interactions with his Indigenous grandmother over disease; he affirmed purported Andean sexual practices while asserting his own medical expertise over other "poor Indians."[97]

Offering himself as an informant still wasn't enough. Although Tello benefited from Harvard's classes in anthropology, he watched opportunities beyond Cambridge slip through his fingers, including the most famed archaeological discovery in Peruvian history. In the fall of 1910 Tello attempted to connect with Yale University's historian of Latin America, Hiram Bingham. He sent the explorer a copy of an article written by an archivist at Lima's National Library that detailed the possible locations of "lost" last sites of Inca resistance to the Spanish.[98] Bingham began planning what became the first Yale Peruvian Expedition. The following spring Tello asked Bingham via an intermediary whether he might be the expedition's "archaeological representative." Bingham, who became notorious for his territoriality in Peru and America, declined. In June 1911 Bingham departed for Peru, where Tello's lead helped him reach Machu Picchu, the "lost city of the Incas."[99]

Ultimately, it was only by playing upon his access to the Indigenous dead that Tello was able to reconcile his ambitions with his North American colleagues' expectations. In these last few years before Bingham's controversial work at Machu Picchu hardened Peruvian law on exporting archaeological collections, Tello acted as a dealer in skulls, bones, and artifacts. Soon after his arrival at Harvard, he attempted but failed to broker the sale of two large collections belonging to wealthy Limeños.[100] Tello facilitated the sale of another collection, and in the summer of 1910 he imported a thousand trepanned and diseased skulls from his own stock. Loath to part with the first great collection of his life, he hoped the Peruvian government might buy it for the National Museum.[101] But his grant from the Peruvian government was running out, and he began searching for other buyers in early 1911.[102] Hrdlička at the Smithsonian was supremely interested, having heard about the collection in Peru the previous year, but Tello ultimately sold it to a wealthy alumnus of Harvard, who gave it to the university's anatomical museum. Tello used the money to finish his master of arts degree in anthropology at Harvard and continue his education abroad.

Hrdlička was furious but also impressed. He accused Tello of venal motives, believing he had broken a promise to give the Smithsonian first option, and would whisper of his supposed duplicity for decades.[103] But Hrdlička's anger was second only to his jealousy at the collection Tello had built, sold, and—as Hrdlička soon discovered—transformed into the definitive proof of pre-Columbian trepanation.

When Tello and Hrdlička finally came face to face a year later at the Eighteenth International Congress of Americanists in London, the Peruvian was prepared. He had used his windfall to travel to Europe and study with anthropologists like Felix von Luschan in Berlin, thus arming himself with new framings and interpretive abilities that he brought to the conference, held in late May and early June of 1912. The congress proved the signal event of Tello's time away from Peru, the occasion of his international delivery of his first great paper, reinforced since its initial presentation in Lima years before: "Prehistoric Trephining Among the Yauyos."

Tello made explicit his challenge to McGee's reinterpretation of Muñiz's skulls—the skulls Tello's family had helped collect—by arguing that ancient Peruvian skull surgery was medical and civilized, not magical and savage. Projecting a series of slides taken from his former collection of four hundred trepanned skulls, Tello explained the range of surgical techniques, in which signs of healing in the bone suggested the technique's medical nature. He used his training as a surgeon, expertise McGee lacked, to argue that the trepanations had addressed a range of traumas and illnesses. Peruvians carried out so deadly an operation "due to an inherited empiricism, to the rational knowledge acquired by previous practice which had resulted in success," the healing of the patient. Two hundred and fifty of the skulls in his collection showed that trepanation patients had at least temporarily survived.[104]

The paper presaged a sea change in how institutions like the Smithsonian displayed the Indigenous dead. Hrdlička would argue with Tello for another two decades on the pre-Columbian existence of syphilis, but at the conference he declared that Tello had demonstrated Peruvian medical capability in trepanation: the young South American deserved credit for his "most careful study of his excellent collection."[105] Scholars throughout the Americas and Europe asked Tello for further details as well as for trepanned skulls of their own.[106] Hrdlička went a step further. He had already planned a trip to Peru for early 1913, hoping to assemble a collection of pre-Columbian human remains for the anthropology section of the Panama–California Exposition in San Diego in 1915.[107] He now refined his plans to include Huarochirí, openly admitting that he was trying to reproduce Tello's successes.[108] Hrdliçka ultimately collected over forty-five boxes filled with almost five thousand Peruvian skulls in 1913, but the jewels of the collection were the trepanations he gathered in Tello's homeland.[109] Those trepanned skulls were the culmination of the anthropological display in San Diego—not part of the rooms demonstrating race, but Room V, demonstrating what pre-Columbian human remains could tell anthropologists about the medical history of humanity.[110] No reference to Tello was made there or in the similar exhibit Hrdlička established at the Smithsonian, but the argument bore his influence. Pre-Columbian Indigenous knowledge of the body was not only medical but of global relevance. Science had evolved among these "early American surgeons," wrote the surgeon general of the US Navy, an impressed visitor to the fair. Peruvians had indeed been "quarrelsome," but their injuries were nevertheless "clinical material for experiment [for] the medicine-men of the tribe."[111]

This was Tello's first great academic victory, one to which his name would be permanently attached, but it was also something more radical: an Indigenous transformation of the territory claimed by anthropology the century before.[112] Tello influenced the thinking of the whites who attended his lecture and perused the collections his work inspired, teaching them to read old evidence in a new, more relative light in order to see healing and civilization where they once had seen only violence and savagery. Muñiz had made a similar presentation, but it had failed to definitively change the minds of North American anthropologists. Simply by taking the podium, Tello reset the debate, putting modern anthropology on a different footing. In that moment Tello was not just a Peruvian surgeon and a Harvard-trained anthropologist—subsequent correspondence shows that his audience also read him as specifically Indigenous: a highly skilled but also "authentic" scholar and practitioner who could analyze and rehearse the trepanning techniques the pre-Columbian surgeon would have used from a position of intellectual and cultural authority. Tello used all of these positions to his advantage. He may have even described his own attempt to reenact the operation using a pre-Columbian skull and *tumi,* an ancient bronze knife.[113] If he did so, in that moment he was no Pizarro offering Atahualpa's head to the Spanish king. Instead, he simultaneously adopted the role of the Inca's healer, who saw the skull as something to mend, and served in his own time as that healer's interpreter, uniting "Indigenous" and "global" knowledge even as he helped bring those very categories of belonging into existence.

## IDOLS WITH BAYONETS

If Tello achieved all he did without sacrificing his Indigenous identity—layering his worlds, not leaving them—then that lack of compromise confounded his colleagues, provoking a profusion of new classifications intended to resolve the "contradiction."[114] "Intelligent" and "more than half Indian," Hrdlička wrote privately.[115] A "Harvard doctor of philosophy and pure-blood Indian," wrote one traveler.[116] A "wise German within an Inca mold," wrote an Argentine.[117] Another participant wrote to assure Tello that she thought him clear of a conspiracy back in Lima: "I know the Indians of America and their high sense of honor."[118]

Nevertheless, from the late 1910s to the late 1920s, during the sometimes-*indigenista,* often-authoritarian presidency of Augusto B. Leguía, Tello flourished, bringing all his worlds in line. In August 1919 an American writer named William Belmont Parker spent several days following Tello around Lima and its environs. As might be expected, they visited a pre-Columbian field of burials; but Tello proved an able guide to Lima's living as well. Tello had returned to Peru in 1913, and in 1917 he had run for a position representing Huarochirí in the Cámara de Diputados of the Congress. His platform promoted literacy and fighting alcoholism among Indians and celebrated the character "heredado de nuestros antecesores indígenas," an ambiguous phrase that his Huarochirano constituents could hear either as "inherited from our Indigenous predecessors" or as "inherited from our Indigenous ancestors." His countrymen heard the message they needed. When opponents challenged his victory, over fifteen hundred of Tello's Huarochiranos marched to defend his win at the Supreme Court.[119] Tello continued his work as an archaeologist as well, and by the time Parker met him he had made himself indispensable to both communities.[120] Tello "is an Indian and also a Deputy, and therefore knows his way about," Parker wrote, following him through the maze of the presidential palace guarded by Indigenous soldiers, "descendants of the Incas, looking like idols with bayonets."[121] When Tello opened the country's first national Museum of Archaeology in 1924, he emphasized the importance of guarding "the sacred ashes of our fathers" and of understanding a country of "children of Indigenous mothers."[122]

He called himself El Indio Tello, flaunting his identity.[123] Although the Peruvian press made only oblique references to his ethnicity during his lifetime, *indio,* in Peru, was and still is a pejorative identifier, and when Tello returned to Peru in 1913, the director of the National Museum called him that to denigrate him.[124] He resigned from politics in 1929, apparently uncomfortable with the direction Leguía's politics had taken, and in 1930 was forced from the National Museum of Archaeology, dogged by rumors of corruption and the old hints that he had climbed beyond his station.[125] He labored for the rest of his life at a new museum, which he also founded, the Museo de Arqueología y Antropología, where he trained Indigenous artists and scholars and guarded and interpreted 429 mummies, several of them trepanned, that he had found in Peru's southern sands. Nevertheless, when he died of cancer in 1947, Huarochirí's favorite son was buried alongside presidents in the national cemetery and memorialized by the Peruvians and North Americans he had assisted.

His failure to be remembered in the United States since then is telling. If Tello was indeed a radius of the Boasian Circle—if not, as Kroeber thought, the "Boas of Peru"—it is a distinction that erases as much as it reveals. Like Boas's critique of racism, Tello's achievements obscured their antecedents, outshining the similar efforts of others, from E. G. Squier to Manuel Muñiz, to argue for a relativist understanding of all human civilizations—an approach that would undermine notions of savagery. Like Boas, Tello was his country's great anthropological critic and institution builder in the early twentieth century, both gadfly and gatekeeper of meaning. (They are alike if only for their mutual reception of Hrdlička's antagonism.)[126] The marginalization they experienced because of their backgrounds guided both to what might be called a go-between anthropology, a human science that thwarted racial classifications, making connections instead.[127] And, also like Boas, Tello pushed physical anthropology into more jagged terrain: discarding the primacy of a skull's measurements and shape to talk about how it was mutable, sensitive to environment, disease, and, in Peru's case, the edge of a surgeon's knife.[128]

Unlike Boas, however, Tello's critical use of evidence was not just intellectual but ethical as well, pointing out the uneasy contradictions of trading in the dead. It is no small irony that Tello built his challenge to the racial and intellectual prejudices of both Peru and North America by compiling the hemisphere's largest collection of Indigenous skulls, the sine qua non of nineteenth-century scientific racism—a collection he reproduced many times over on behalf of the Peruvian state and ultimately, as an enforcer of Peruvian archaeological law, prevented North Americans like Kroeber from reproducing. That knot of irony is slightly undone, however, when we understand that Tello made no move to deemphasize the centrality of human remains to his anthropological practice. Boas remained important in physical anthropology in the early twentieth century, but the turn of his interests, as well as that of the larger field, to the study of culture and non-Indian peoples forestalled reckoning with the Indigenous dead that North American institutions had assimilated as objects during the previous century. For Tello, however, the dead were subjects and bound to the present. His museums argued for an indigeneity that was transferrable through culture, knowledge, and respect for the dead—and not through racial purity. The holes that skulls bore mattered as much as the skulls themselves, and Tello's museums protected both.

Tello followed that logic beyond irony: the afterlife he made for the pre-Columbian dead overlapped with the afterlife he made for himself. Unlike Franz Boas, who has remained interred at a cemetery in Ossining, New York, since his death in 1942, Tello's time at Lima's most elite cemetery was only temporary. In 1948, a year after his death, he was disinterred according to his last wishes and buried a second time: not in Huarochirí, with his relatives, but in a "pre-Columbian" tomb built in the backyard of his last museum, not fifty yards from the trepanned skulls and quiet mummies in whose stories he had wrapped himself.

## Notes

This essay benefited greatly from advice given by many readers: Jorge Cañizares Esguerra, Seth Garfield, Pamela Henson, H. W. Brands, Circe Sturm, Ned Blackhawk, and Isaiah Wilner. Research was supported by the Smithsonian Institution Archives, the Philadelphia Area Council for the History of Science, the Fulbright-Hays Fellowship, and the Donald D. Harrington Endowment of the University of Texas at Austin. I particularly thank the tireless archivists of the Tello archives in Lima, at the Museo Nacional de Arqueología, Antropología e Historia del Peru, the Museo de Arqueología y Antropología de la Universidad Nacional Mayor de San Marcos, and the Instituto Riva-Agüero.

1. Alfred L. Kroeber, "Confidential Report by A. L. Kroeber on Archaeological Trip to Peru," Feb.–May, 1942, 13, Alfred L. Kroeber Correspondence, File 1, Henry Allen Moe Papers (hereafter HAMP), American Philosophical Society.
2. Alfred L. Kroeber to Henry Allen Moe, Dec. 2, 1941, Alfred L. Kroeber Correspondence, File 5, HAMP; Alfred L. Kroeber to Henry Allen Moe, Feb. 9, 1942, Alfred L. Kroeber Correspondence, File 9, HAMP.

3. Alfred L. Kroeber to Henry Allen Moe, Mar. 15, 1942, and Alfred L. Kroeber to Henry Allen Moe, Apr. 19, 1942, Alfred L. Kroeber Correspondence, File 9, HAMP. For other examples of contemporary American archaeological intelligence, see Quetzil Castañeda, "The Carnegie Mission and Vision of Science: Institutional Contexts of Maya Archaeology and Espionage," *Histories of Anthropology Annual* 1 (2005): 27–60; David Price, *Anthropological Intelligence: The Deployment and Neglect of American Anthropology in the Second World War* (Durham: Duke University Press, 2008), 203–16.
4. A. L. Kroeber, Confidential Report, 13, Alfred L. Kroeber Correspondence File 1, HAMP; Alfred L. Kroeber, *Peruvian Archeology in 1942* (New York: Viking Fund Publications in Anthropology, 1944), 5–6.
5. Kroeber, *Peruvian Archeology in 1942*, 93.
6. A. L. Kroeber, "Confidential Report," 13, HAMP.
7. Ibid.; Kroeber, *Peruvian Archeology in 1942*, 5.
8. For the story of Ishi and Kroeber, see Orin Starn, *Ishi's Brain: In Search of America's Last "Wild" Indian* (New York: Norton, 2004); Kroeber's handling of Ishi's remains may be found at 158–62.
9. For an excellent treatment of Parker and his identities, archaeological and Indigenous, see Chip Colwell-Chanthaphonh, *Inheriting the Past: The Making of Arthur C. Parker and Indigenous Archaeology* (Tucson: University of Arizona Press, 2009).
10. Tello was one of only five subjects still living and, with the Inca emperor Atahualpa, was one of only two of Indigenous descent. See Watt Stewart and Harold F. Peterson, *Builders of Latin America* (New York: Harper and Brothers, 1942), 269–78.
11. Thomas C. Patterson, "Political Economy and a Discourse Called 'Peruvian Archaeology,'" *Culture and History* 4 (1989): 35–84; César W. Astuhuamán and Richard E. Daggett, "Julio César Tello Rojas, una biografía," in *Paracas, Primera Parte. Obra Completa* (Lima: Clásicos Sanmarquinos, UNMSM, 2005), 1:17–52; Bruce G. Trigger, *A History of Archaeological Thought,* 2d ed. (Cambridge: Cambridge University Press, 2006), 276; Ricardo D. Salvatore, "Tres intelectuales peruanos: conexiones imperiales en la construcción de una cultura nacional," in *Ensayos en torno a la república de las letras en el Perú e Hispanoamérica (ss. XVI–XX),* ed. Carlos Aguirre and Carmen McEvoy (Lima: Instituto Francés de Estudios Andinos, Instituto Riva-Agüero, 2008), 353–84; Richard E. Daggett, "Julio C. Tello: An Account of His Rise to Prominence in Peruvian Archaeology," in *The Life and Writings of Julio C. Tello: America's First Indigenous Archaeologist,* ed. Richard L. Burger (Iowa City: University of Iowa Press, 2009), 7–54; Richard L. Burger, "The Intellectual Legacy of Julio C. Tello," in *The Life and Writings of Julio C. Tello,* 65–82; O. Gabriel Prieto Burmester, "Dos Forjadores de las Ciencias Sociales en el Perú: Sus Publicaciones y Confrontaciones," *Arqueología y Sociedad* 22 (2010): 1–34; Ann H. Peters and L. Alberto Ayarza, "Julio C. Tello y el desarrollo de estudios andinos en los Estados Unidos: intercambios e influencias 1915–1950," in *Historia de la Arqueología en el Perú del Siglo XX,* ed. César Astuhuamán and Henry Tantaleán (Lima: Instituto Francés de Estudios Andinos, Lima, 2013), 43–84.
12. A rare exception is Marisol de la Cadena, "From Race to Class: Insurgent Intellectuals *de provincia* in Peru, 1910–1970," in *Shining and Other Paths: War and Society in Peru, 1980–1995,* ed. Steve J. Stern (Durham: Duke University Press, 1998), 22–59.

13. Cf. Carlos Del Águila Chávez and Luis Lumbreras, *Julio C. Tello* (Lima: Centro Cultural de San Marcos, Museo de Arqueología y Antropología de la UNMSM, Instituto Cultural Peruano Norteamericano, 2007).
14. Prieto Burmester, "Dos Forjadores de las Ciencias Sociales en el Perú," 30; Patterson, "Political Economy and a Discourse Called 'Peruvian Archaeology,'" 37.
15. Richard L. Burger, introduction to *The Life and Writings of Julio C. Tello*, 2–3.
16. Cf. Theodora Kroeber, *Ishi in Two Worlds: A Biography of the Last Wild Indian in North America*, 3d ed. (1961; repr. Berkeley: University of California Press, 2011).
17. This essay thus rhymes with recent scholarship arguing for the cocreation of Indigenous and global knowledge. Helen Tilley, "Global Histories, Vernacular Science, and African Genealogies; or, Is the History of Science Ready for the World?" *Isis* 101, no. 1 (2010): 110–19; Sujit Sivasundaram, "Sciences and the Global: On Methods, Questions, and Theory," *Isis* 101, no. 1 (2010): 146–58.
18. For an introduction to Boas's skull-collecting career, see David Hurst Thomas, *Skull Wars: Kennewick Man, Archaeology, and the Battle for Native American Identity* (New York: Basic Books, 2000), 58–63.
19. Robert Arnott, Stanley Finger, and C. U. M. Smith, eds., preface to *Trepanation: History, Discovery, Theory* (Lisse, NL: Swets and Zeitlinger, 2003), x–xi. Trepanation is also known as trepanning and trephination. I use "trepanation," the most common term, but preserve the alternatives in my citation of primary sources.
20. Malcolm C. Lillie, "Cranial Surgery: The Epipalaeolithic to Neolithic Populations of Ukraine," ibid., 175.
21. For the nineteenth-century view of trepanation as the "trunk of the genetic tree of surgery," see Manuel Antonio Muñiz and W. J. McGee, "Primitive Trephining in Peru," *Sixteenth Annual Report of the Bureau of American Ethnology to the Secretary of the Smithsonian Institution 1894–95* (Washington: Government Printing Office, 1897), 72.
22. Cf. Toby A. Gordon and John L. Cameron, "Evolution of Modern Surgery," in *Evidence-Based Surgery*, ed. Toby A. Gordon and John L. Cameron (Hamilton, ON: B. C. Decker, 2000), 5–13; Francisco Alayza Escardó, *Historia de la Cirugía en el Perú* (Lima: Editorial Monterrico S.A., 1992); Ann Fabian, *The Skull Collectors: Race, Science, and America's Unburied Dead* (Chicago: University of Chicago Press, 2010).
23. David Matto, "La Trepanación en la época de los Incas," *La Crónica Médica* (Lima) 3, no. 29 (1886): 183–86. For Cusco's rich antiquarian culture, see Stefanie Gänger, "Disjunctive Circles: Modern Intellectual Culture in Cuzco and the Journeys of Incan Antiquities, c. 1877–1921," *Modern Intellectual History* 10, no. 2 (2013): 400–401.
24. E. George Squier, *Peru: Incidents of Travel and Exploration in the Land of the Incas* (New York: Harper and Brothers, 1877), 456–57, 577; Stanley Finger and Hiran R. Fernando, "E. George Squier and the Discovery of Cranial Trepanation: A Landmark in the History of Surgery and Ancient Medicine," *Journal of the History of Medicine and Allied Sciences* 56, no. 4 (2001): 353, provides an extensive discussion of Squier's involvement, pointing out that Samuel George Morton depicted a trepanned skull in *Crania Americana* in 1839, believing it to be a battlefield wound.
25. Squier believed Peruvian surgical expertise could demonstrate the originality of Inca civilization, free of European influence. Terry A. Barnhart, *Ephraim George Squier and the Development of American Anthropology* (Lincoln: University of Nebraska Press, 2005), 244–80.

26. Anonymous, "Committee Reports of December 6, 1865," *Bulletin of the New York Academy of Medicine* 2 (1862–66): 530.
27. Paul Broca, "Trepanning Among the Incas," *Journal of the Anthropological Institute of New York* 1, no. 1 (1871–72): 72. Squier's translation, with editorial introduction, of Paul Broca appears as [Ephraim George Squier], "Cas singulier de trepanation chez las Incas," *Bulletins de la Société d'Anthropologie de Paris* 2, no. 2 (1867): 403–8.
28. Francis Schiller, *Paul Broca: Founder of French Anthropology, Explorer of the Brain* (1979; repr., Oxford: Oxford University Press, 1992), 158. Stanley Finger and Hiran R. Fernando, "Ephraim George Squier's Peruvian Skull and the Discovery of Cranial Trepanation," in *Trepanation*, ed. Arnott, Finger, and Smith, 3.
29. Thomas, *Skull Wars*, 48.
30. William H. Jones to Spencer Fullerton Baird, Feb. 9, 1885, RU 305, ACC 15755, Smithsonian Institution Archives (hereafter SIA).
31. Otis T. Mason, "The Chaclacayo Trephined Skull," *Proceedings of the U.S. National Museum* 8 (1885): 410–12.
32. George Kiefer to J. S. Billings, June 30, 1888, United States Army Medical Museum Anatomical Section Records Relating to Specimens Transferred to the Smithsonian Institution, 2896–2973, National Anthropological Archives (hereafter NAA).
33. Broca's paper of 1867 on the Yucay skull was translated and published in Peru in 1886, when the surgeon David Matto, whose father had found the skull, lectured on it to the medical school of the Universidad de San Marcos in Lima. David Matto, "La Trepanación en la época de los Incas," *La Crónica Médica* 3, no. 26 (1886): 183–86.
34. For surgery as an elite Peruvian profession see Alayza Escardó, *Historia de la Cirugía en el Perú*.
35. Antonio Lorena, "La medicina y la Trepanación incásicas," *La Crónica Médica* (Lima) 6, no. 80 (1890): 226–28. Stefanie Gänger argues against the overdrawn modern perception that all nineteenth-century Peruvian elites perceived a breach between a gloriously developed Inca past and a brutish Indigenous present. Instead, like ethnologists at the Smithsonian, some Peruvian intellectuals believed in continuity between ancient Peruvians and "miserable" contemporary Indians—a continuity that degraded their opinions of the formers' development. Gänger, "Disjunctive Circles," 407. Cf. Rebecca Earle, *The Return of the Native: Indians and Myth-Making in Spanish America, 1810–1930* (Durham: Duke University Press, 2007), 20.
36. D.M., "Dr. Manuel Antonio Muñiz," *La Crónica Médica* 14, no. 204 (1897): 193–96.
37. Fiona Wilson, "Indian Citizenship and the Discourse of Hygiene/Disease in Nineteenth-Century Peru," *Bulletin of Latin American Research* 23, no. 2 (2004): 166; "Reglamentación de la Prostitución: Tesis leída y sostenida al optar el grado de Doctor por Manuel A. Muñiz," *La Crónica Médica* 4, no. 48 (1887): 457.
38. Muñiz and McGee, "Primitive Trephining in Peru," 5.
39. W. J. McGee to Francisco de P. [Suarez], June 14, 1894, Bureau of American Ethnology (hereafter BAE) Letterbook, May 8, 1894–Sept. 7, 1894, Box 17, BAE Papers, NAA. For Boas's grousing, see Thomas, *Skull Wars*, 60.
40. W. J. McGee to F. W. Putnam, Oct. 24, 1893, BAE Letterbook, June 21, 1893–Dec. 23, 1893, Box 17, BAE Papers, NAA; W. H. Holmes, "The World's Fair Congress of Anthropology," *American Anthropologist* 6, no. 4 (1893): 425.

41. W. J. McGee to Guy Hinsdale, Feb. 14, 1894, BAE Letterbook, Dec. 23, 1893–May 9, 1894, Box 17, BAE Papers, NAA.
42. Manuel Antonio Muñiz to W. J. McGee, June 12, 1895, Box 110, BAE Papers, NAA.
43. W. J. McGee to Manuel Antonio Muñiz, July 28, 1896, BAE Letterbook, May 6 1896–Jan. 16, 1897, Box 18, BAE Papers, NAA.
44. H. C. Hovey, "Peruvian Trepanning," *Scientific American Supplement,* Nov. 17, 1894, 15743–44; W. J. McGee, "Primitive Trephining. Illustrated by the Muñiz Peruvian Collection," 1, Box 54, BAE Papers, NAA.
45. McGee, "Primitive Trephining in Peru," 61, 63, 64, 66, 71–72.
46. This reading draws upon the nuanced interpretation of Huarochirí's historical literacy and production in Frank Salomon and George L. Urioste, eds. and trans., *The Huarochirí Manuscript: A Testament of Ancient and Colonial Andean Religion* (Austin: University of Texas Press, 1991); Frank Salomon, "Unethnic Ethnohistory: On Peruvian Peasant Historiography and Ideas of Autochthony," *Ethnohistory* 49, no. 3 (2002): 475–506; Frank Salomon, *The Cord Keepers: Khipus and Cultural Life in a Peruvian Village* (Durham: Duke University Press, 2004); Frank Salomon and Mercedes Niño-Murcia, *The Lettered Mountain: A Peruvian Village's Way with Writing* (Durham: Duke University Press, 2011). For the death of Atahualpa play, see Alberto Flores Galindo, *In Search of an Inca: Identity and Utopia in the Andes* (Cambridge: Cambridge University Press, 2010), 37–46, which suggests that villages that were more mestizo—of mixed Euro-Indigenous culture, if not descent—were more likely to end the drama with reconciliation between Pizarro and Atahualpa; that Tello remembered the drama in terms of Atahualpa's death is telling.
47. Blair Niles, *A Journey in Time: Peruvian Pageant* (Indianapolis: Bobbs-Merrill, 1937), 72. M. Toribio Mejía Xesspe, "Apuntes Biográficos sobre el Dr. Julio C. Tello," *Revista del Museo Nacional de Antropología y Arqueología* 2, no. 1 (1949): 36.
48. Salomon and Niño-Murcia, *The Lettered Mountain,* 18–22.
49. Pierre Duviols, *La lutte contre les réligions autochtones dans le Pérou colonial* (Lima: Institut Français d'Études Andines, 1971); Sabine MacCormack, *Religion in the Andes: Vision and Imagination in Early Colonial Peru* (Princeton: Princeton University Press, 1991); Kenneth Mills, *Idolatry and Its Enemies: Colonial Andean Religion and Extirpation, 1640–1750* (Princeton: Princeton University Press, 1997); Peter Gose, *Invaders as Ancestors: On the Intercultural Making and Unmaking of Spanish Colonialism in the Andes* (Toronto: University of Toronto Press, 2008), 153–60; Heidi V. Scott, *Contested Territory: Mapping Peru in the Sixteenth and Seventeenth Centuries* (Notre Dame: University of Notre Dame Press, 2009), chap. 4.
50. Salomon and Niño-Murcia, *The Lettered Mountain,* 23.
51. Salomon, *The Cord Keepers,* 49; Salomon and Niño-Murcia, *The Lettered Mountain,* 104–14.
52. Antonio Raimondi, "Itinerario de los viajes de Raimondi en el Perú de Lima a Morococha (1861)," *Boletín de la Sociedad Geográfica de Lima* 6, no. 1–3 (1896): 42. The original reads "judíos" instead of "indios," which might be an error of transcription, but it could also open up a dialogue with the fact that rural Andeans often call the dead *gentiles,* projecting upon them a pre-Christian, rather than pre-Columbian, identity. Salomon's research explores the continuing tension between ritual survival and "folk

archaeology" in Huarochirí; through the 1990s one ayllu in the village of Tupicochja propitiated two water deities that took the form of two skulls, possibly the remains of despoiled pre-Columbian mummy shrines. See Salomon, *The Cord Keepers,* 49; Salomon and Niño-Murcia, *The Lettered Mountain,* 104–14.

53. For Tello's description of his grandmother, see Julio C. Tello to Albert S. Ashmead, Nov. 20, 1909, Box 3, Julio C. Tello File 1, 1907–1909, Albert S. Ashmead Collection (hereafter ASAC), College of Physicians of Philadelphia. For the story of the Tello family's traditional clothes and the beating of Tello's father, see the eulogy given by Javier Pulgar Vidal in "Con honores de Ministro de Estado Fueron Sepultados ayer provisoriamente en cementerio general los restos del ilustre arqueólogo Doctor Julio C. Tello," *La Tribuna* (Lima), June 7, 1947. The quote appears in Niles, *A Journey in Time,* 72–73.
54. Salomon, *The Cord Keepers,* 11.
55. Salomon and Niño-Murcia, *The Lettered Mountain,* 245, translating Hernán Ponce Sánchez, *50 Anécdotas del Sabio Tello* (Lima: Editorial "La Universidad" Librería, 1957), 37.
56. Karen Spalding, *Huarochirí: Indian Society Under Inca and Spanish Rule* (Stanford: Stanford University Press, 1984).
57. Mejía Xesspe, "Apuntes Biográficos sobre el Dr. Julio C. Tello," 35; S. K. Lothrop, "Julio C. Tello, 1880–1947," *American Antiquity* 14, no. 1 (1948): 50.
58. Patterson, "Political Economy and a Discourse Called 'Peruvian Archaeology,'" 40. For shifting Indigenous elite fortunes in the republican era, see Spalding, *Huarochirí,* 303; Brooke Larson, *Trials of Nation Making: Liberalism, Race, and Ethnicity in the Andes, 1810–1910* (Cambridge: Cambridge University Press, 2004), 163; Salomon and Niño Murcia, *The Lettered Mountain,* 134.
59. Mejía Xesspe, "Apuntes Biográficos sobre el Dr. Julio C. Tello," 37.
60. Salomon and Niño-Murcia, *The Lettered City,* 83–84, 126.
61. Florencia Mallon, *Peasant and Nation: The Making of Postcolonial Mexico and Peru* (Berkeley: University of California Press, 1995), 275; Manuel Tello, "Huarochirí," *El Comercio* (Lima), Apr. 8, 1891. For Lima's interest in education in the countryside, see Larson, *Trials of Nation Making,* 159–61.
62. Mejía Xesspe, "Apuntes Biográficos sobre el Dr. Julio C. Tello," 38.
63. Niles, *A Journey in Time,* 74. For the mummified state of the skulls, see Crania 1, 2, 5, 14 in Muñiz and McGee, "Primitive Trephining in Peru," 29–31, 41.
64. Aleš Hrdlička, *My Journeys,* 703, Box 163, Folder MJ 3.26, Mar. 1913, Aleš Hrdlička Papers (hereafter AHP), NAA; Salomon, *The Cord Keepers,* 49, 60; Gose, *Invaders as Ancestors,* 317–19. For examples elsewhere in the Andes, see Thomas A. Abercrombie, *Pathways of Memory and Power: Ethnography and History Among an Andean People* (Madison: University of Wisconsin Press, 1998), 324–28, 495 n. 7; Christopher Heaney, *Cradle of Gold: The Story of Hiram Bingham, a Real-Life Indiana Jones, and the Search for Machu Picchu* (2010; repr. New York: Palgrave Macmillan, 2011), 55–56, 136, 139–40. Salomon offers the most convincing explanation of why the local dead are no longer ancestors but instead the "first and original owners," the true Indians who disappeared when they *all committed suicide* to protest Spanish rule. Modern Tupicochanos understand themselves as being redeemed from bondage by the "gentiles'" suicide and as inheriting their land, as nonbiological heirs. Salomon warns scholars not to pity this

apparent denial of Indigenous heritage. In the republican era, he argues, it is a way of maintaining modern, communal rights to the land without being an *indio,* a category devalued by elites and the state. Salomon, "Unethnic Ethnohistory," 479, 492–93.

65. In the late twentieth century Salomon would report being nervously asked to identify skulls as evidence of murders so they could be disposed of forensically. See Salomon, "Unethnic Ethnohistory," 478–79. Adolph Bandelier, excavating at Tiwanaku in the early twentieth century, observed that the Aymará Indians of the area "harbor a superstition that the bones of the dead may penetrate their bodies whenever disturbed and thus produce diseases and even death. But withal they do not hesitate to trample on these bones or to kick about and crush the skulls." Adolph Francis Bandelier, *The Ruins at Tiahuanaco* (Worcester, MA: American Antiquarian Society, 1911), 19, 25.
66. Muñiz and McGee, "Primitive Trephining in Peru," 26–27; Niles, *A Journey in Time,* 74.
67. Niles, *A Journey in Time,* 75; Rebeca Carrión Cachot, "Julio C. Tello y la Arqueología Peruana," *Revista del Museo Nacional de Antropología y Arqueología* 2, no. 1 (1949): 7; Mejía Xesspe, "Apuntes Biográficos sobre el Dr. Julio C. Tello," 38.
68. Teófilo Espejo Núñez, *Formación Universitaria de Julio C. Tello* (Lima: Editora Médica Peruana, 1959), 20.
69. For an example straddling the colonial and republican eras, see the surgeon José Manuel Valdes, the son of a *mulata* named María and an *indio* named Baltasar, who became independent Peru's Protomédico General, its highest-ranking medical examiner. Ann Twinam, *Public Lives, Private Secrets: Gender, Honor, Sexuality, and Illegitimacy in Colonial Spanish America* (Stanford: Stanford University Press, 1999), 331–34.
70. Again, as relayed by Pulgar V. on the occasion of Julio C. Tello's death. "Con honores de Ministro de Estado Fueron Sepultados ayer provisoriamente en cementerio general los restos del ilustre arqueólogo Doctor Julio C. Tello." See also Carrión Cachot, "Julio C. Tello y la Arqueología Peruana," 8.
71. Toribio Mejía Xesspe, "Prólogo," in Julio C. Tello, *Páginas Escogidas* (Lima: Universidad Nacional Mayor de San Marcos, 1967), vii.
72. In the earliest account of this episode, written in his lifetime, Niles sets it shortly after he began working for the National Library, in 1900. Niles, *A Journey in Time,* 76.
73. As Stefanie Gänger has observed, "The considerable international demand, traceable in the correspondence of Europe's and North America's scholars, museums and societies, was premised upon a peculiar kind of expertise attributed to Peruvian antiquaries: their presumed intimacy with indigeneity, and their capacity to mediate." Gänger, "Disjunctive Circles," 408.
74. Mejía Xesspe, "Apuntes Biográficos sobre el Dr. Julio C. Tello," 40.
75. Niles, *A Journey in Time,* 76.
76. Mejía, "Prólogo," viii. As translated by Burger, "The Intellectual Legacy of Julio C. Tello," 69.
77. Julio Tello, "La Calahuala," *La Prensa,* Sept. 25, 1905; Julio C. Tello, "Prehistoric Trephining among the Yauyos of Peru," in *The Life and Writings of Julio C. Tello,* ed. Burger, 113.
78. The Smithsonian's collection of human remains numbered no more than 5,340 in 1905, rising to 8,511 in 1909. Aleš Hrdlička, "Division of Physical Anthropology Annual Report 1904–1905," Box 32, RU 158, SIA.

79. Julio C. Tello to Albert S. Ashmead, Oct. 24, 1907, Box 3, Julio C. Tello File 1, 1907–1909, Albert S. Ashmead Collection (hereafter ASAC); Tello, "Prehistoric Trephining among the Yauyos of Peru," 112–13, 124; and Espejo Núñez, *Formación Universitaria de Julio C. Tello,* 28–29.
80. "La Craniectomía en el Perú Pre-Histórico," *El Comercio,* May 5, 1906.
81. Julio C. Tello, *La antigüedad de la Sífilis en el Perú* (Lima: Universidad Mayor de San Marcos, Sanmarti y Ca., 1909). This argument can be traced back to Muñiz, Lorena, and the prior generation of antiquarian physicians and students: Lorena, "La medicina y la Trepanación incásicas," 228; Espejo Núñez, *Formación Universitaria de Julio C. Tello,* 10.
82. Peters and Ayarza, "Julio C. Tello y el desarrollo de estudios andinos en los Estados Unidos," 43–50.
83. De la Cadena, "From Race to Class," 55. See also Marisol de la Cadena, *Indigenous Mestizos: The Politics of Race and Culture in Cuzco, Peru, 1919–1991* (2000; repr., Durham: Duke University Press, 2003).
84. Julio C. Tello to Albert S. Ashmead, Nov. 20, 1909, Box 3, Julio C. Tello File 1, 1907–1909, ASAC.
85. Mejía Xesspe, "Apuntes Biográficos sobre el Dr. Julio C. Tello," 40.
86. Salomon, "Unethnic Ethnohistory, 479; Salomon, *The Cord Keepers,* 134.
87. "La Anécdota de Hoy: Un Brujo," *La Noche* [Lima], Aug. 25, 1931. See also Espejo Núñez, *Formación Universitaria de Julio C. Tello,* 26.
88. "Julio C. Tello, Amauta Preclaro," *La Tribuna* (Lima), June 5, 1947.
89. Mejía Xesspe, "Prólogo," viii. De la Cadena, "From Race to Class," 22–25, deploys this anecdote to illustrate the prejudice Tello had to push through in the late 1910s–20s, noting that "Indianness, from within a serrano perspective, is not a function of the coastal–sierra dichotomy, but of relative location *within* the vertical environment of the Andean highlands."
90. He thus resembles the Puneño doctor Manuel Núñez Butrón, who later had a similar revelation while studying in Spain. Marcos Cueto, "'Indigenismo' and Rural Medicine in Peru: The Indian Sanitary Brigade and Manuel Núñez Butrón," *Bulletin of the History of Medicine* 65, no. 1 (1991): 30. For further discussion of challenges to translating ethnicity between Peru and the United States, see Marisol de la Cadena, "Are *Mestizos* Hybrids? The Conceptual Politics of Andean Identities," *Journal of Latin American Studies* 37, no. 2 (2005): 261.
91. Colwell-Chanthaponh, *Inheriting the Past,* 13.
92. Starn, *Ishi's Brain,* 158–62.
93. Albert S. Ashmead, "Utosic Syphilis and Some Other Things of Interest to Paleo-American Medicine, as Represented on the Huacos Potteries of Old Peru," *American Journal of Dermatology and Genito-Urinary Diseases* 14, no. 7 (1910): 329–43.
94. Aleš Hrdlička to William Curtis Farabee, Jan. 13, 1913, and William Curtis Farabee to Aleš Hrdlička, Jan. 19, 1911, Box 24, William Curtis Farabee File, AHP; Aleš Hrdlička to George F. Eaton, Jan. 26, 1915, Box 23, George F. Eaton File, AHP. For Hrdlička, race, and racism, see Michael L. Blakey, "Skull Doctors: Intrinsic Social and Political Bias in the History of American Physical Anthropology, with Special Reference to the Work of Aleš Hrdlička," *Critique of Anthropology* 7, no. 2: 7–35. For a complicating

view, see Robert Oppenheim, "Revisiting Hrdlička and Boas: Asymmetries of Race and Anti-Imperialism in Interwar Anthropology," *American Anthropologist* 112, no. 1 (2010): 92–103.

95. Julio C. Tello to Albert S. Ashmead, Oct. 1, 1909, Box 3, Julio C. Tello File 1, ASAC. By *raza* Tello may have been implying something very different from the "race" that Ashmead would have read. For its inexact translation, see Amy Kaminsky, "Gender, Race, Raza," *Feminist Studies* 20, no. 1 (1994): 7–31.

96. Julio C. Tello to Albert S. Ashmead, Oct. 28, 1909, Box 3, Julio C. Tello File 1, ASAC.

97. Julio C. Tello to Albert S. Ashmead, Nov. 20, 1909, Box 3, Julio C. Tello File 1, ASAC.

98. Heaney, *Cradle of Gold*, 66–67.

99. Christopher Heaney, *Las Tumbas de Machu Picchu: La Historia de Hiram Bingham y la Búsqueda de las Ultimas Ciudades de los Incas* (Lima: Fondo Editorial PUCP, 2012), 104–5. Tello was once again rejected by the Yale expedition back in Peru, in 1915, an event that precipitated Bingham's fall.

100. For the extensive correspondence between Tello and Ashmead in 1910 on the possible sale, see Julio C. Tello File 2 in Box 3, ASAC.

101. William Curtis Farabee to Julio C. Tello, Nov. 15, 1911, folio 191, Cuadernillo 2, Grupo 31: Correspondencia, Archivo Julio C. Tello (hereafter JCT), Archivos del Museo de Antropología e Arqueología, Centro Cultural, Universidad Nacional Mayor de San Marcos (hereafter AMA). Julio C. Tello to Albert S. Ashmead, June 6, 1910, June 10, 1910, July 10, 1910, Box 3, Julio C. Tello File 2, ASAC.

102. William Curtis Farabee to Aleš Hrdlička, Jan. 19, 1911, Box 24, William Curtis Farabee File, AHP.

103. Aleš Hrdlička to W. H. Holmes, June 30, 1910, Box 106, File G, AHP. For the sale of the collection—not a donation, as others have suggested—see the extensive correspondence between Farabee and Hrdlička, January and March of 1911, Box 24, William Curtis Farabee File, AHP. For Hrdlička's accusing Tello of double-dealing, see Aleš Hrdlička to T. Dale Stewart, Mar. 29, 1941, Box 61, T. Dale Stewart File, AHP, also cited in Samuel James Redman, "Human Remains and the Construction of Race and History, 1897–1945" (PhD diss., University of California, Berkeley, 2012), 141–42.

104. Tello, "Prehistoric Trephining among the Yauyos of Peru," 116, 124.

105. *International Congress of Americanists: Proceedings of the XVIII Session, London, 1912*, pt. 1 (London: Harrison and Sons, 1913), xxxix.

106. Oscar M. Rojas to Julio C. Tello, Apr. 14, 1914, folio 343, and Daniel J. Cranwell to Tello, Apr. 15, 1914, folio 344, Cuadernillo 2, Grupo 31, JCT.

107. For a full description of the exposition and Hrdlička's efforts on its behalf, see Redman, "Human Remains and the Construction of Race and History, 1897–1945," chap. 4.

108. Hrdlička, "Anthropological Work in Peru in 1913," *Smithsonian Miscellaneous Collections* 61, no. 18 (Washington: Smithsonian Institution, 1914): 4.

109. Aleš Hrdlička to W. H. Holmes, Mar. 28, 1913, Box 58, Folder C, AHP.

110. Aleš Hrdlička to W. H. Holmes, Jan. 29, 1912, Division of Physical Anthropology at the Panama–California Exposition, San Diego, 35–39, in Box 58, Folder A, AHP.

111. Joseph C. Thompson, "Savage Surgeons Fix Skulls," *San Diego Union*, Apr. 11, 1915. The article's title, likely written by the newspaper's editors, is belied by Thompson's more sensitive tone.

112. John W. Verano, "Trepanation in Prehistoric South America: Geographical and Temporal Trends over 2,000 Years," in *Trepanation*, ed. Arnott, Finger, and Smith, 223.
113. Julio B. Rodriguez, "Examen de Antropología," folios 83–84, AT–416–2001-MNAAHP, Archivo Julio C. Tello (AT), Museo Nacional de Arqueología, Antropología e Historia del Perú, Lima.
114. Cf. Elizabeth A. Povinelli, *The Cunning of Recognition: Indigenous Alterities and the Making of Australian Multiculturalism* (Durham: Duke University Press, 2002).
115. Hrdlička, *My Journeys*, 671, Box 163, Folder MJ 3.25—Peru, Jan.–Mar. 1913, AHP.
116. Edward Alsworth Ross, *South of Panama* (New York: Century, 1915), 70.
117. Quoted in Luis E. Valcárcel to Tello, folio 310, Cuadernillo 2, Grupo 31, JCT.
118. Adela Breton to Tello, Nov. 9, 1912, folio 249, Cuadernillo 2, Grupo 31, JCT.
119. Mejía Xesspe, "Apuntes Biográficos sobre el Dr. Julio C. Tello," 43.
120. Luis Guillermo Lumbreras, "Apuntes sobre Julio C. Tello, el Maestro," in *Julio C. Tello* (Lima: Centro Cultural de San Marcos, Museo de Arqueología y Antropología de la UNMSM, Instituto Cultural Peruano Norteamericano, 2007), 7, frames Tello's work as an archaeologist as part and parcel of the "social fight" that agitated Peru at the time. But he also must be understood as a partisan of then-President Augusto B. Leguía, who turned *indigenismo* to his own ends and was flushed from power for authoritarian excesses.
121. William Belmont Parker, *Casual Letters from South America* (New York: Hispanic Society of America, 1921), 96–97.
122. Julio C. Tello, "El Museo de Arqueología Peruana: Discurso Pronunciado en la Ceremonia de Inauguración del Museo el 13 de Diciembre de 1924," in *Presente y Futuro del Museo Nacional* (Lima: Instituto Cultural "Julio C. Tello," 1952), 23, 27.
123. Burger, "The Intellectual Legacy of Julio C. Tello," 69.
124. Tello called him *el español* in return. Luis E. Valcárcel (and José Matos Mar; José Destua; José Luis Renique), *Memorias* (Lima: IEP, 1981), 262.
125. Daggett, "Julio C. Tello," 30–32.
126. George W. Stocking Jr., *Race, Culture, and Evolution* (1968; repr. Chicago: University of Chicago Press, 1982), 288.
127. For Boas's social background, his marginality, his activism, and the relation of his experience of ethnicity to his thought, see Leonard B. Glick, "Types Distinct from Our Own: Franz Boas on Jewish Identity and Assimilation," *American Anthropologist* 84, no. 3 (1982): 545–65; George W. Stocking Jr., *The Ethnographer's Magic and Other Essays in the History of Anthropology* (Madison: University of Wisconsin Press, 1992), 92–113; Julia E. Liss, "Patterns of Strangeness: Franz Boas, Modernism, and the Origins of Anthropology," in *Prehistories of the Future: The Primitivist Project and the Culture of Modernism*, ed. Elazar Barkan and Ronald Bush (Stanford: Stanford University Press, 1995), 114–30 (I thank Isaiah Wilner for the preceding references). For go-betweens in the history of knowledge, see Simon Schaffer, Lissa Roberts, Kapil Raj, and James Delbourgo, eds., *The Brokered World: Go-Betweens and Global Intelligence, 1770–1820* (Sagamore Beach, MA: Science History Publications, 2009). I am unconvinced, however, by the editors' belief that there was a diminished role for Indigenous go-betweens in their era of study; and if it did diminish, it recharged in the late nineteenth century.

128. Between this essay's drafting and its publication, John W. Verano's *Holes in the Head: The Art and Archaeology of Trepanation in Ancient Peru* (Washington, DC: Dumbarton Oaks Research Library and Collection, 2016) became the new standard for scientific studies on trepanation's prevalence and success in Peru—a testament to its original Indigenous practitioners as well as to Tello's insistence on its medical foundation.

# Contributors

**Benjamin Balthaser** is Associate Professor of English at Indiana University South Bend.

**Ned Blackhawk** is Professor of History and American Studies at Yale University.

**Ryan Carr** is Adjunct Assistant Professor of English at Queens College, City University of New York.

**Eve Dunbar** is Associate Professor of English at Vassar College.

**Lewis R. Gordon** is Professor of Philosophy at the University of Connecticut–Storrs and Honorary Professor of the Humanities at Rhodes University in Grahamstown, South Africa.

**Sean Hanretta** is Associate Professor of History at Northwestern University.

**Christopher Heaney** is Assistant Professor of History at the Pennsylvania State University and the 2016–18 Barra Postdoctoral Fellow at the McNeil Center for Early American Studies at the University of Pennsylvania.

**Martha Hodes** is Professor of History at New York University.

**Harry Liebersohn** is Professor of History at the University of Illinois at Urbana–Champaign.

**Maria Lúcia Pallares-Burke** is Research Associate at the Centre of Latin American Studies, University of Cambridge. Previously she was Professor of History and Philosophy of Education at the University of São Paulo.

**Michael Silverstein** is Charles F. Grey Distinguished Service Professor of Anthropology, of Linguistics, and of Psychology and Director of the Center for the Study of Communication and Society at the University of Chicago.

**Audra Simpson** is Associate Professor of Anthropology at Columbia University.

**James Tully** is Distinguished Professor Emeritus of Political Science, Law, Indigenous Governance, and Philosophy at the University of Victoria.

**Kiara M. Vigil** is Assistant Professor of American Studies at Amherst College.

**Isaiah Lorado Wilner** is Postdoctoral Fellow in the Berlin Center for the History of Knowledge at the Max Planck Institute for the History of Science.

# Index

Note: Illustrations are indicated by **boldface**